STUDENT SOLUTIONS MANUAL

Abby Tanenbaum

INTRODUCTORY ALGEBRA for College Students

Third Edition

Robert Blitzer

Upper Saddle River, NJ 07458

Executive Editor: Karin E. Wagner
Supplements Editor: Elizabeth Covello
Editorial Assistant: Rudy Leon
Artist: Jim McLaughlin
Typist: Judy Martinez
Assistant Managing Editor, Math Media Production: John Matthews
Production Editor: Wendy A. Perez
Supplement Cover Management/Design: PM Workshop Inc.
Manufacturing Buyer: Alan Fischer

Upper Saddle River, NJ 07458

Printed in the United States of America

10 9 8 7 6 5 4 3

ISBN 0-13-034308-0

Prentice-Hall International (UK) Limited, London
Prentice-Hall of Australia Pty. Limited, Sydney
Prentice-Hall Canada, Inc., Toronto
Prentice-Hall Hispanoamericana, S.A., Mexico City
Prentice-Hall of India Private Limited, New Delhi
Pearson Education Asia Pte. Ltd., Singapore
Prentice-Hall of Japan, Inc., Tokyo
Editora Prentice-Hall do Brazil, Ltda., Rio de Janeiro

CONTENTS

CHAPTER 3 PROBLEM SOLVING

CHAPTER 4 LINEAR EQUATIONS AND INEQUALITIES IN TWO VARIABLES

CHAPTER 5 SYSTEMS OF LINEAR EQUATIONS AND INEQUALITIES

CHAPTER 6 EXPONENTS AND POLYNOMIALS

CHAPTER 7 FACTORING POLYNOMIALS

CHAPTER 8 RATIONAL EXPRESSIONS

CHAPTER 9 ROOTS AND RADICALS

CHAPTER 10 QUADRATIC EQUATIONS AND FUNCTIONS

Chapter 1

THE REAL NUMBER SYSTEM

1.1 Fractions

1.1 CHECK POINTS

CHECK POINT 1

a. $\frac{10}{15} = \frac{\cancel{5} \cdot 2}{\cancel{5} \cdot 3} = \frac{2}{3}$

b. $\frac{42}{24} = \frac{\cancel{6} \cdot 7}{\cancel{6} \cdot 4} = \frac{7}{4}$

c. Because 13 and 15 share no common factor (other than 1), $\frac{13}{15}$ is already reduced to lowest terms.

d. $\frac{9}{45} = \frac{\cancel{9} \cdot 1}{\cancel{9} \cdot 5} = \frac{1}{5}$

CHECK POINT 2

a. $\frac{4}{11} \cdot \frac{2}{3} = \frac{4 \cdot 2}{11 \cdot 3} = \frac{8}{33}$

b. $6 \cdot \frac{3}{5} = \frac{6}{1} \cdot \frac{3}{5} = \frac{18}{5}$

c. $\frac{3}{7} \cdot \frac{2}{3} = \frac{\cancel{3} \cdot 2}{7 \cdot \cancel{3}} = \frac{2}{7}$

CHECK POINT 3

a. $\frac{5}{4} \div \frac{3}{8} = \frac{5}{4} \cdot \frac{8}{3} = \frac{5 \cdot 8}{4 \cdot 3} = \frac{40}{12}$

$= \frac{\cancel{4} \cdot 10}{\cancel{4} \cdot 3} = \frac{10}{3}$

b. $\frac{2}{3} \div 3 = \frac{2}{3} \cdot \frac{1}{3} = \frac{2}{9}$

CHECK POINT 4

a. $\frac{2}{11} + \frac{3}{11} = \frac{2+3}{11} = \frac{5}{11}$

b. $\frac{5}{6} - \frac{1}{6} = \frac{5-1}{6} = \frac{4}{6} = \frac{\cancel{2} \cdot 2}{\cancel{2} \cdot 3} = \frac{2}{3}$

CHECK POINT 5

$\frac{2}{3} = \frac{2}{3} \cdot \frac{7}{7} = \frac{14}{21}$

CHECK POINT 6

a. $\frac{1}{2} + \frac{3}{5}$

The least common denominator for the denominators 2 and 5 is 10.

$$\frac{1}{2} + \frac{3}{5} = \frac{1}{2} \cdot \frac{5}{5} + \frac{3}{5} \cdot \frac{2}{2} = \frac{5}{10} + \frac{6}{10} = \frac{11}{10}$$

b. $\frac{4}{3} - \frac{3}{4}$

The least common denominator is 12.

$$\frac{4}{3} - \frac{3}{4} = \frac{4}{3} \cdot \frac{4}{4} - \frac{3}{4} \cdot \frac{3}{3} = \frac{16}{12} - \frac{9}{12} = \frac{7}{12}$$

c. $\frac{13}{18} - \frac{2}{9}$

The least common denominator is 18. The first fraction already has this denominator, so only the second one needs to be rewritten.

$$\frac{13}{18} - \frac{2}{9} = \frac{13}{18} - \frac{2}{9} \cdot \frac{2}{2} = \frac{13}{18} - \frac{4}{18} = \frac{9}{18} = \frac{\cancel{9} \cdot 1}{\cancel{9} \cdot 2} = \frac{1}{2}$$

CHECK POINT 7

First, add the fractions for all of the activities other than going to class. The least common denominator for all of these fractions is 24.

$$\begin{aligned}&\frac{1}{3}+\frac{7}{24}+\frac{1}{24}+\frac{1}{8}\\&=\frac{1}{3}\cdot\frac{8}{8}+\frac{7}{24}+\frac{1}{12}\cdot\frac{2}{2}+\frac{1}{8}\cdot\frac{3}{3}\\&=\frac{8}{24}+\frac{7}{24}+\frac{2}{24}+\frac{3}{24}\\&=\frac{20}{24}=\frac{\cancel{4}\cdot 5}{\cancel{4}\cdot 6}=\frac{5}{6}\end{aligned}$$

The fractions representing all activities must add up to 1, so the fraction of the student's time spent in class can be found by subtracting $\frac{5}{6}$ from 1.

$$1-\frac{5}{6}=\frac{6}{6}-\frac{5}{6}=\frac{1}{6}$$

Thus, the student spends $\frac{1}{6}$ of her time on weekdays attending class.

EXERCISE SET 1.1

1. $\frac{10}{16}=\frac{\cancel{2}\cdot 5}{\cancel{2}\cdot 8}=\frac{5}{8}$

3. $\frac{15}{18}=\frac{\cancel{3}\cdot 5}{\cancel{3}\cdot 6}=\frac{5}{6}$

5. $\frac{35}{50}=\frac{\cancel{5}\cdot 7}{\cancel{5}\cdot 10}=\frac{7}{10}$

7. $\frac{32}{80}=\frac{\cancel{16}\cdot 2}{\cancel{16}\cdot 5}=\frac{2}{5}$

9. $\frac{44}{50}=\frac{\cancel{2}\cdot 22}{\cancel{2}\cdot 25}=\frac{22}{25}$

11. $\frac{120}{86}=\frac{\cancel{2}\cdot 60}{\cancel{2}\cdot 43}=\frac{60}{43}$

13. $\frac{2}{5}\cdot\frac{1}{3}=\frac{2\cdot 1}{5\cdot 3}=\frac{2}{15}$

15. $\frac{3}{8}\cdot\frac{7}{11}=\frac{3\cdot 7}{8\cdot 11}=\frac{21}{88}$

17. $9\cdot\frac{4}{7}=\frac{9}{1}\cdot\frac{4}{7}=\frac{9\cdot 4}{1\cdot 7}=\frac{36}{7}$

19. $\frac{1}{10}\cdot\frac{5}{6}=\frac{1\cdot 5}{10\cdot 6}=\frac{5}{60}=\frac{5\cdot 1}{5\cdot 12}=\frac{1}{12}$

21. $\frac{5}{4}\cdot\frac{6}{7}=\frac{5\cdot 6}{4\cdot 7}=\frac{30}{28}=\frac{2\cdot 15}{2\cdot 14}=\frac{15}{14}$

23. $\frac{5}{4}\div\frac{4}{3}=\frac{5}{4}\cdot\frac{3}{4}=\frac{5\cdot 3}{4\cdot 4}=\frac{15}{16}$

25. $\frac{18}{5}\div 2=\frac{18}{5}\cdot\frac{1}{2}=\frac{18\cdot 1}{5\cdot 2}=\frac{18}{10}$
$=\frac{\cancel{2}\cdot 9}{\cancel{2}\cdot 5}=\frac{9}{5}$

27. $2\div\frac{18}{5}=\frac{2}{1}\cdot\frac{5}{18}=\frac{2\cdot 5}{1\cdot 18}=\frac{10}{18}$
$=\frac{\cancel{2}\cdot 5}{\cancel{2}\cdot 9}=\frac{5}{9}$

29. $\frac{3}{4}\div\frac{1}{4}=\frac{3}{4}\cdot\frac{4}{1}=\frac{3\cdot 4}{4\cdot 1}=\frac{12}{4}=3$

31. $\frac{7}{6}\div\frac{5}{3}=\frac{7}{6}\cdot\frac{3}{5}=\frac{7\cdot 3}{6\cdot 5}=\frac{21}{30}$
$=\frac{\cancel{3}\cdot 7}{\cancel{3}\cdot 10}=\frac{7}{10}$

33. $\frac{1}{14}\div\frac{1}{7}=\frac{1}{14}\cdot\frac{7}{1}=\frac{1\cdot 7}{14\cdot 1}=\frac{7}{14}$
$=\frac{\cancel{7}\cdot 1}{\cancel{7}\cdot 2}=\frac{1}{2}$

35. $\frac{2}{11}+\frac{4}{11}=\frac{2+4}{11}=\frac{6}{11}$

37. $\frac{7}{12}+\frac{1}{12}=\frac{8}{12}=\frac{\cancel{4}\cdot 2}{\cancel{4}\cdot 3}=\frac{2}{3}$

39. $\frac{5}{8}+\frac{5}{8}=\frac{10}{8}=\frac{\cancel{2}\cdot 5}{\cancel{2}\cdot 4}=\frac{5}{4}$

41. $\frac{7}{12}-\frac{5}{12}=\frac{2}{12}=\frac{1}{6}$

43. $\frac{16}{7}-\frac{2}{7}=\frac{14}{7}=2$

45. $\frac{1}{2}+\frac{1}{5}=\frac{1}{2}\cdot\frac{5}{5}+\frac{1}{5}\cdot\frac{2}{2}$
$=\frac{5}{10}+\frac{2}{10}$
$=\frac{5+2}{10}=\frac{7}{10}$

47. $\frac{3}{4}+\frac{3}{20}=\frac{3}{4}\cdot\frac{5}{5}+\frac{3}{20}$
$=\frac{15}{20}+\frac{3}{20}$
$=\frac{18}{20}=\frac{9}{10}$

49. $\frac{3}{8}+\frac{5}{12}=\frac{3}{8}\cdot\frac{3}{3}+\frac{5}{12}\cdot\frac{2}{2}$
$=\frac{9}{24}+\frac{10}{24}=\frac{19}{24}$

51. $\frac{11}{18}-\frac{2}{9}=\frac{11}{18}-\frac{2}{9}\cdot\frac{2}{2}=\frac{11}{18}-\frac{4}{18}=\frac{7}{18}$

53. $\frac{4}{3}-\frac{3}{4}=\frac{4}{3}\cdot\frac{4}{4}-\frac{3}{4}\cdot\frac{3}{3}$
$=\frac{16}{12}-\frac{9}{12}=\frac{7}{12}$

55. $\frac{7}{10}-\frac{3}{16}=\frac{7}{10}\cdot\frac{8}{8}-\frac{3}{16}\cdot\frac{5}{5}$
$=\frac{56}{80}-\frac{15}{80}=\frac{41}{80}$

57. $\frac{13}{4}+\frac{13}{9}=\frac{13}{4}\cdot\frac{9}{9}+\frac{13}{9}\cdot\frac{4}{4}$
$=\frac{117}{36}+\frac{52}{36}=\frac{169}{36}$

$\frac{13}{4}\times\frac{13}{9}=\frac{13}{4}\cdot\frac{13}{9}=\frac{169}{36}$

59. $\frac{512}{800}=\frac{\cancel{32}\cdot 16}{\cancel{32}\cdot 25}=\frac{16}{25}$

$\frac{16}{25}$ of the white adults thought that racism is a big problem.

61. $300-186=114$

114 black teenagers replied that racism is *not* a big problem.

$$\frac{114}{300}=\frac{\cancel{6}\cdot 19}{\cancel{6}\cdot 50}=\frac{19}{50}$$

$\frac{19}{50}$ of the black teenagers thought that racism is *not* a problem.

63. The word *of* indicates multiplication.

$$\frac{19}{20}\cdot 300=\frac{19}{20}\cdot\frac{300}{1}=\frac{5700}{20}=285$$

Of the 300 black teenagers surveyed, 285 planned to go to college.

65. $\frac{1}{2}\cdot\frac{3}{4}=\frac{3}{8}$

To make half a recipe, $\frac{3}{8}$ cup of sugar is needed.

67. $1-\frac{5}{12}-\frac{1}{4}=\frac{1}{1}\cdot\frac{12}{12}-\frac{5}{12}-\frac{1}{4}\cdot\frac{3}{3}$
$=\frac{12}{12}-\frac{5}{12}-\frac{3}{12}$
$=\frac{12-5-3}{12}=\frac{4}{12}=\frac{1}{3}$

$\frac{1}{3}$ of the business is owned by the third person.

69. 40 hours at \$12 an hour:

$$40\cdot \$12=\$480$$

"Time and a half":

$$\frac{3}{2}\cdot 12=\frac{3}{2}\cdot\frac{12}{1}=\frac{36}{2}=18$$

6 hours at \$18 an hour:

$$6\cdot \$18=\$108$$
$$\$480+\$108=\$588$$

The student's total pay before taxes was \$588.

For Exercises 71–75, answers may vary.

77. Statements a, b, and c are false. The methods illustrated are incorrect. The only true statement is d.

79. There are 4 measures:

The first measure contains two quarter-notes and two eighth-notes. Draw a vertical line after the fourth note, which corresponds to the end of the word *that.*
The second measure contains three quarter-notes. Draw a vertical line after the seventh note in the excerpt, which corresponds to the syllable *gled.*
The third measure contains one quarter-note and four eighth-notes. Draw a line after the twelfth note in the excerpt, which corresponds to the end of the word *yet.*
The fourth measure contains two quarter-notes and two eighth-notes. Draw a vertical line at the end of the excerpt.

81. $\frac{5}{24} + \frac{7}{30} = \frac{53}{120}$

83. $\frac{7}{24} - \frac{1}{15} = \frac{9}{40}$

1.2 The Real Numbers

1.2 CHECK POINTS

CHECK POINT 1

a. A debt of \$500 can be expressed by the negative integer -500.

b. The elevation of Death Valley, 282 feet below sea level, can be expressed by the negative integer -282.

CHECK POINT 2

(a) (b) (c)
-5 -4 -3 -2 -1 0 1 2 3 4 5 x

CHECK POINT 3

(b) (a)
-5 -4 -3 -2 -1 0 1 2 3 4 5 x

CHECK POINT 4

a.

$$\begin{array}{r} 0.375 \\ 8\overline{)3.000} \\ \underline{24} \\ 60 \\ \underline{56} \\ 40 \\ \underline{40} \\ 0 \end{array}$$

$$\frac{3}{8} = 0.375$$

b.

$$\begin{array}{r} 0.4545\ldots \\ 11\overline{)5.0000\ldots} \\ \underline{44} \\ 60 \\ \underline{55} \\ 50 \\ \underline{44} \\ 60 \\ \underline{55} \\ 50 \\ \vdots \end{array}$$

$$\frac{5}{11} = 0.\overline{45}$$

CHECK POINT 5

$$\left\{-9, -1.3, 0, 0.\overline{3}, \frac{\pi}{2}, \sqrt{9}, \sqrt{10}\right\}$$

a. Natural numbers: The only natural number in the set is $\sqrt{9} = 3$.

b. Whole numbers: $0, \sqrt{9}$

c. Integers: $-9, 0, \sqrt{9}$

d. Rational numbers: $-9, -1.3, 0, 0.\overline{3}, \sqrt{9}$

e. Irrational number: $\frac{\pi}{2}, \sqrt{10}$

f. Real numbers: $\left\{-9, -1.3, 0, 0.\overline{3}, \frac{\pi}{2}, \sqrt{9}, \sqrt{10}\right\}$ (all numbers in the given set)

CHECK POINT 6

a. $14 > 5$ because 14 is to the right of 5 on the number line.

b. $-5.4 < 2.3$ because -5.4 is to the left of 2.3 on the number line.

c. $-19 < -6$ because -19 is to the left of -6 on the number line.

d. To compare $\frac{1}{4}$ and $\frac{1}{2}$, use a common denominator: $\frac{1}{2} = \frac{2}{4}$. Since $\frac{1}{4}$ is to the left of $\frac{2}{4}$ on the number line, $\frac{1}{4} < \frac{1}{2}$.

CHECK POINT 7

a. $-2 \leq 3$ is true because $-2 < 3$ is true.

b. $-2 \geq -2$ is true because $-2 = -2$ is true.

c. $-4 \geq 1$ is false because neither $-4 > 1$ nor $-4 = 1$ is true.

CHECK POINT 8

a. $|-4| = 4$ because -4 is 4 units from 0.

b. $|6| = 6$ because 6 is 6 units from 0.

c. $|-\sqrt{2}| = \sqrt{2}$ because $-\sqrt{2}$ is $\sqrt{2}$ units from 0.

EXERCISE SET 1.2

1. -20

3. 8

5. -3000

7. -4 billion

9.

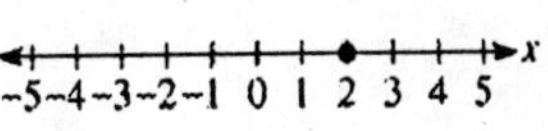

11.

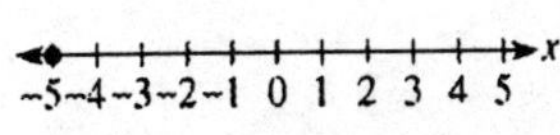

13.

15.

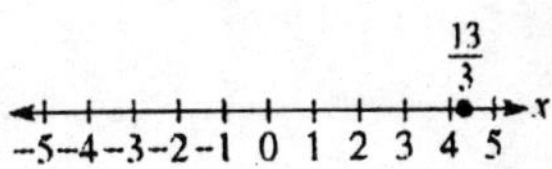

17.

19.

21.

$$\begin{array}{r} 0.75 \\ 4\overline{)3.00} \\ \underline{2\,8} \\ 20 \\ \underline{20} \\ 0 \end{array}$$

$$\frac{3}{4} = 0.75$$

23.

$$\begin{array}{r} 0.35 \\ 20\overline{)7.00} \\ \underline{6\,0} \\ 100 \\ \underline{100} \\ 0 \end{array}$$

$$\frac{7}{20} = 0.35$$

25.

$$\begin{array}{r} 0.875 \\ 8\overline{)7.000} \\ \underline{6\,4} \\ 60 \\ \underline{56} \\ 40 \\ \underline{40} \\ 0 \end{array}$$

$$\frac{7}{8} = 0.875$$

27.

$$\begin{array}{r} 0.818\ldots \\ 11\overline{)9.000\ldots} \\ \underline{8\,8} \\ 20 \\ \underline{11} \\ 90 \\ \underline{88} \\ 20 \\ \vdots \end{array}$$

$$\frac{9}{11} = 0.\overline{81}$$

29.

$$\begin{array}{r} 0.5 \\ 2\overline{)1.0} \\ \underline{1\,0} \\ 0 \end{array}$$

$$-\frac{1}{2} = -0.5$$

31.

$$\begin{array}{r} 0.833\ldots \\ 6\overline{)5.000\ldots} \\ \underline{4\,8} \\ 20 \\ \underline{18} \\ 20 \\ \underline{18} \\ 20 \\ \vdots \end{array}$$

$$\frac{5}{6} = 0.8\overline{3}$$

33. **a.** $\sqrt{100}$ $(= 10)$
b. $0, \sqrt{100}$
c. $-9, 0, \sqrt{100}$
d. $-9, -\frac{4}{5}, 0, 0.25, 9.2, \sqrt{100}$
e. $\sqrt{3}$
f. All numbers in the given set

35. **a.** $\sqrt{64}$ $(= 8)$
b. $0, \sqrt{64}$
c. $-11, 0, \sqrt{64}$
d. $-11, -\frac{5}{6}, 0, 0.75, \sqrt{64}$
e. $\sqrt{5}, \pi$
f. All numbers in the given set

37. The only whole number that is not a natural number is 0.

In Exercises 39–43, examples may vary.

39. One rational number that is not an integer is $\frac{1}{2}$.

41. One number that is an integer, a whole number, and a natural number is 5.

43. One number that is an irrational number and a real number is $\sqrt{2}$.

45. $\frac{1}{2} < 2$; $\frac{1}{2}$ is to the left of 2 on the number line, so $\frac{1}{2}$ is less than 2.

47. $3 > -\frac{5}{2}$; 3 is to the right of $-\frac{5}{2} = -2\frac{1}{2}$, so 3 is greater than $-\frac{5}{2}$.

49. $-4 > -6$; -4 is to the right of -6, so -4 is greater than -6.

51. $-2.5 < 1.5$; -2.5 is to the left of 1.5, so $-2.5 < 1.5$.

53. $-\frac{3}{4} > -\frac{5}{4}$; $-\frac{3}{4}$ is to the right of $-\frac{5}{4}$, so $-\frac{3}{4} > -\frac{5}{4}$.

55. $-4.5 < 3$; -4.5 is to the left of 3, so $-4.5 < 3$.

57. $\sqrt{2} < 1.5$; $\sqrt{2} \approx 1.414$, so $\sqrt{2}$ is to the left of 1.5 and $\sqrt{2} < 1.5$.

59. $0.\overline{3} > 0.3$; $0.\overline{3} = 0.333\ldots$, while $0.3 = 0.3000$, so $0.\overline{3}$ is to the right of 0.3 and $0.\overline{3} > 0.3$.

61. $-\pi > -3.5$; $-\pi \approx -3.14$, so -3.14 is to the right of -3.5 and $-3.14 > -3.5$.

63. $-5 \geq -13$ is true because $-5 > -13$ is true.

65. $-9 \geq -9$ is true because $-9 = -9$ is true.

67. $0 \geq -6$ is true because $0 > -6$ is true.

69. $-17 \geq 6$ is false because neither $-17 > 6$ nor $-17 = 6$ is true.

71. $|6| = 6$ because the distance between 6 and 0 on the number line is 6 units.

73. $|-7| = 7$ because the distance between -7 and 0 on the number line is 7 units.

75. $\left|\frac{2}{3}\right| = \frac{2}{3}$ because the distance between $\frac{2}{3}$ and 0 on the number line is $\frac{2}{3}$ unit.

77. $|-\sqrt{13}| = \sqrt{13}$ because the distance between $-\sqrt{13}$ and 0 on the number line is $\sqrt{13}$ units.

79. -3

81. The years for which

money collected < money spent

are 1996, and 1997. There was a budget deficit in these years.

For Exercises 83–93, answers may vary.

95. Statement c is true since some rational numbers are negative and also 0 is a rational number that is not positive.

97. Since $\sqrt{36} = 6$ and $\sqrt{49} = 7$, $-\sqrt{47}$ is between -7 and -6.

99. $\sqrt{3} \approx 1.732$

$\sqrt{3}$ should be graphed between 1 and 2.

101. $1 - \sqrt{2} \approx -0.414$

$1 - \sqrt{2}$ should be graphed between -1 and 0.

1.3 Ordered Pairs and Graphs

1.3 CHECK POINTS

CHECK POINT 1

$A(-2, 4)$: 2 units left, 4 units up (in quadrant II)
$B(4, -2)$: 4 units right, 2 units down (in quadrant IV)
$C(-3, 0)$: 3 units left, 0 units up or down (on the x-axis)
$D(0, -3)$: 0 units right or left, 3 units down (on the y-axis)

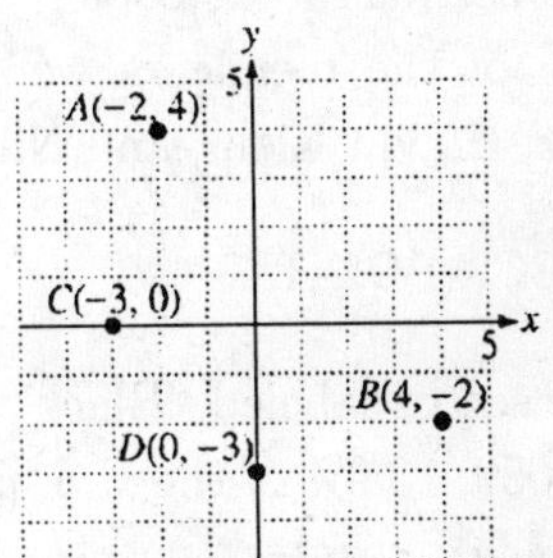

CHECK POINT 2

Point	Position	Coordinates
E	4 units left, 2 units down	$(-4,-2)$
F	2 units left, 0 units up or down	$(-2,0)$
G	6 units right, 0 units up or down	$(6,0)$

CHECK POINT 3

The coordinates of point B are $(8,200)$. This means that after 8 seconds, the watermelon is 200 feet above the ground.

CHECK POINT 4

The coordinates of point D are approximately $(8.8,0)$. This means that after 8.8 seconds, the watermelon is 0 feet above the ground. Equivalently, the watermelon splatters after 8.8 seconds.

CHECK POINT 5

According to the graph, the minimum average age at which U.S. women marry for the first time is 20 years old. This occurred in 1950, 1960, and 1970.

CHECK POINT 6

a. Approximately 14% of the teenagers named Levi's as one of the "coolest."

b. The brands rated "coolest" by more than 15% of the teenagers were Tommy Hilfiger, Calvin Klein, and Nike.

CHECK POINT 7

a. The sector labeled "Black" indicates that in 2050, 13.6% of the U.S. population will be black.

b. To estimate the number of Asian Americans in 2050, round 8.2% to 8% = 0.08, and multiply:

$$0.08(400{,}000{,}000) = 32{,}000{,}000.$$

In 2050, the population of Asian Americans is expected to be about 32,000,000.

EXERCISE SET 1.3

1. Quadrant I

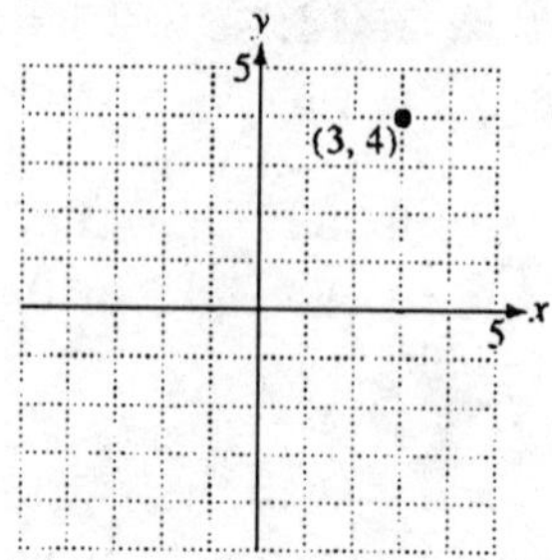

3. Quadrant II

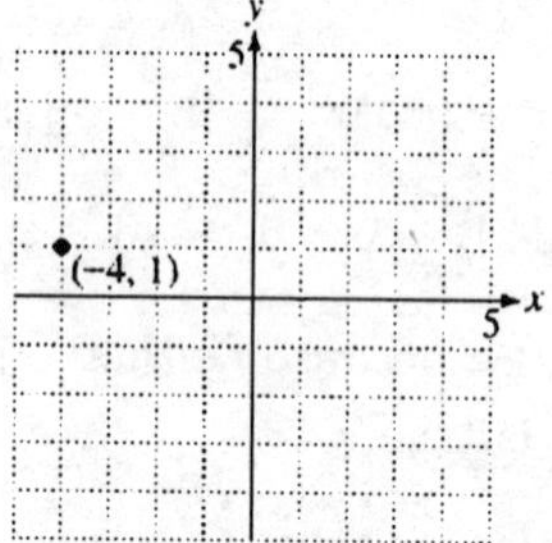

5. Quadrant III

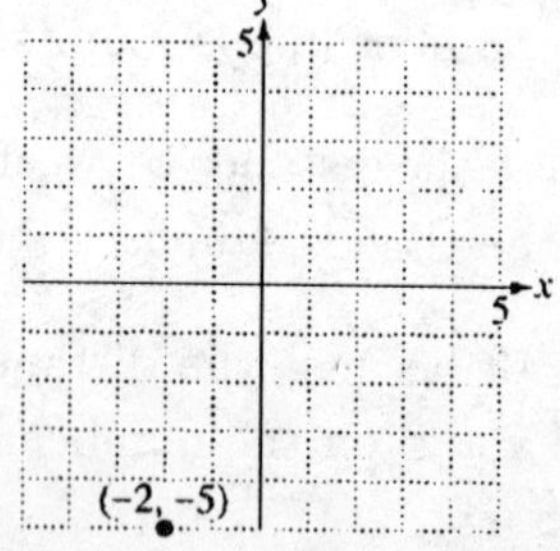

7. Quadrant IV

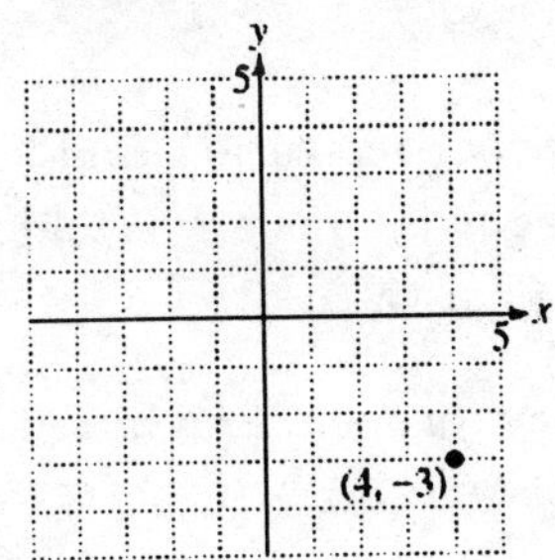

9.

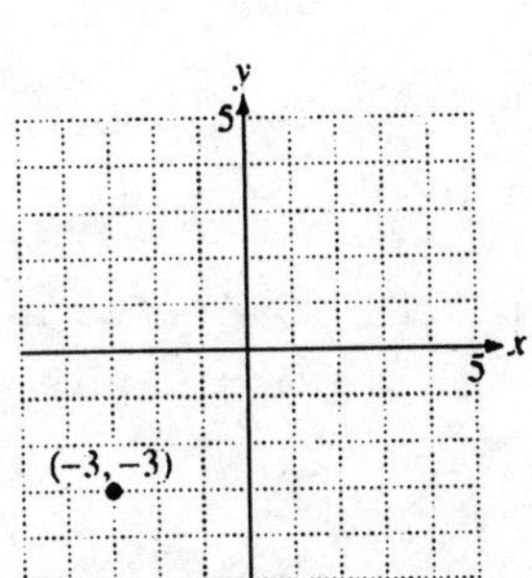

11.

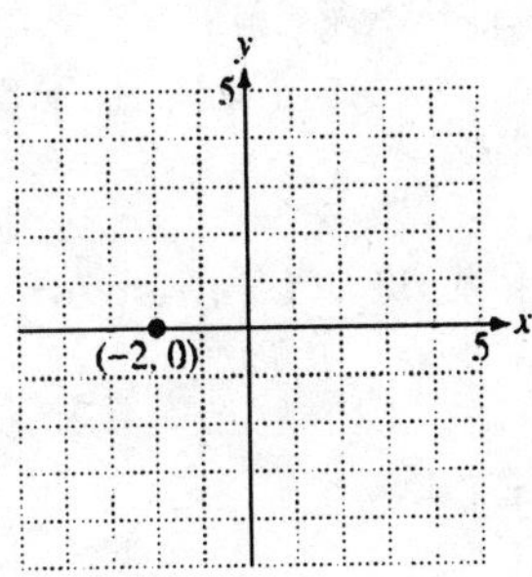

13.

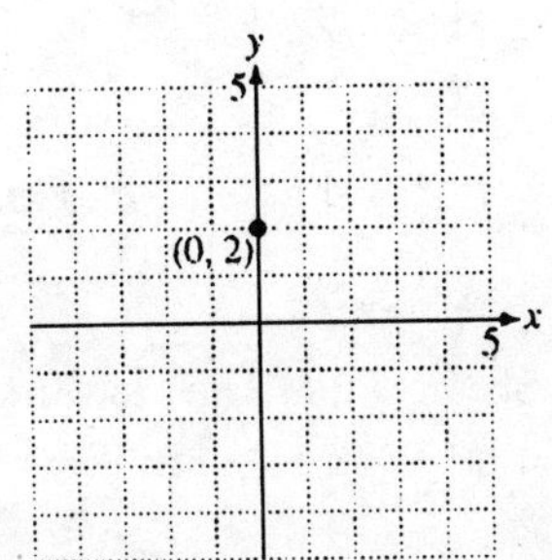

15.

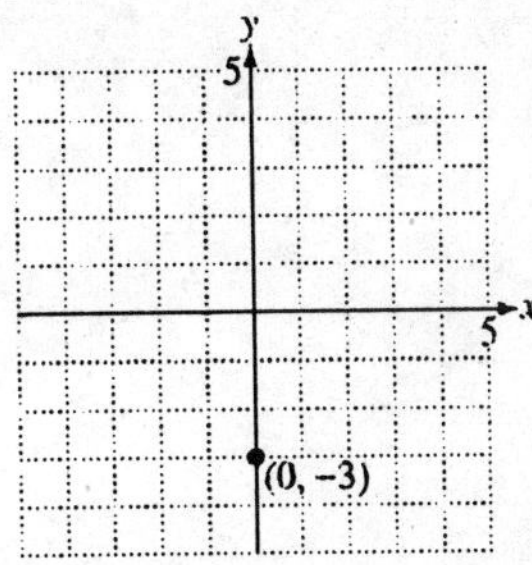

17.

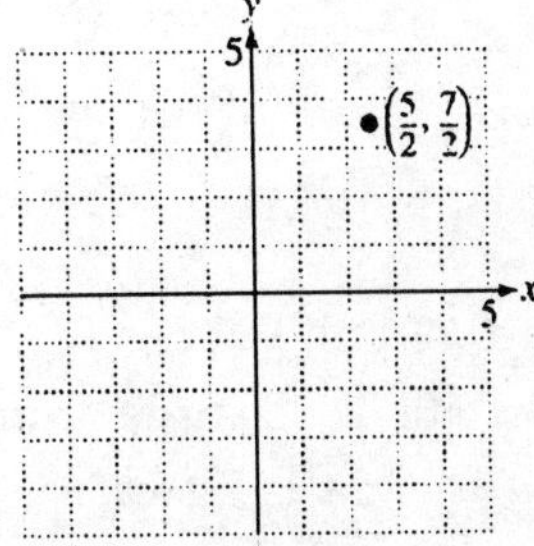

19.

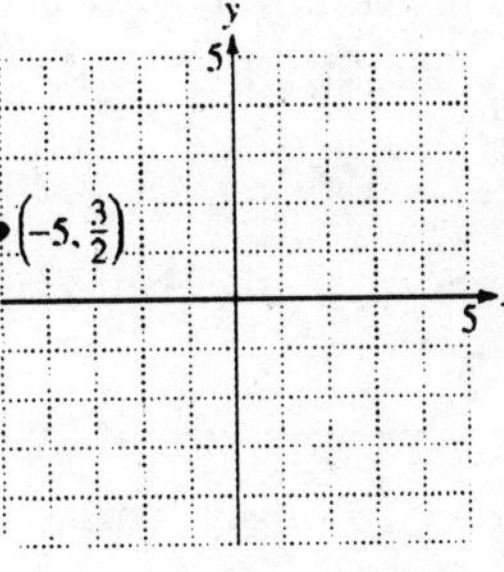

21.

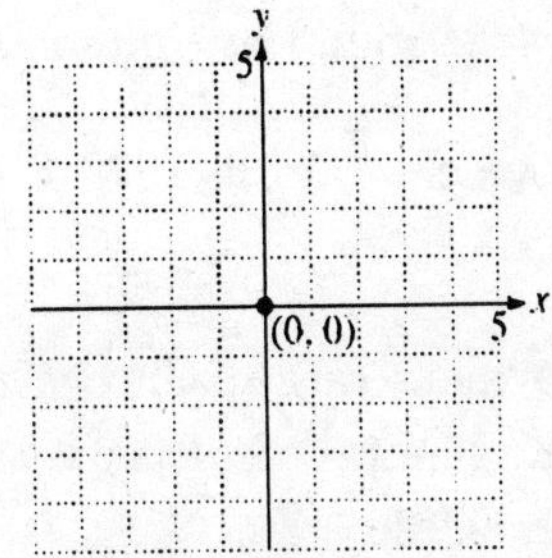

23.

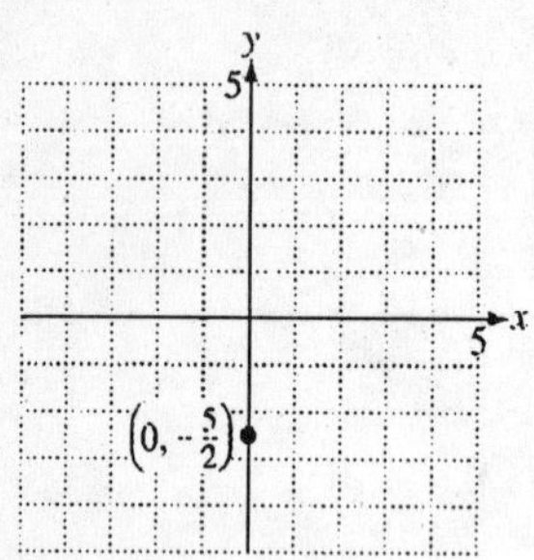

25. $A(5,2)$

27. $C(-6,5)$

29. $E(-2,-3)$

31. $G(5,-3)$

33. The coordinates of point A are $(2,7)$. When the football is 2 yards from the quarterback, its height is 7 feet.

35. The coordinates of point C are approximately $(3, 9.25)$.

37. The football's maximum height is 12 feet. It reaches this height when it is 15 yards from the quarterback.

39. The coordinates of point A are approximately $(1970, 61)$.
In 1970, there were approximately 61 million people under 16 in the United States.

41. The coordinates of point C are approximately $(1990, 60)$.
In 1990, there were approximately 60 million people under 16 in the United States.

43. The unemployment rate in 1970 was approximately 5%.

45. The unemployment rate reached a maximum in 1982. The rate in that year was approximately 9.9%.

47. Approximately 33% of vacations include shopping.

49. Shopping, outdoor recreation, and historical places and museums are included on more than 15% of vacations.

51. Life expectancy for men born in 1900 was approximately 48 years.

53. Women born in 1996 can expect to live approximately $(79 - 65 = 14)$ more years than men born in 1950.

55. Approximately \$470 was spent buying sports gear for scuba diving.

57. Approximately \$50 − \$30 = \$20 more is spent buying sports gear for table tennis than for croquet.

59. The number of Protestants was approximately 60% of 272 million, which is about 160 million or 160,000,000.

61. The number of hate-crime incidents motivated by race was approximately 60% of \$10,000 or \$6000.

For Exercises 63–71, answers may vary.

73. Statement c is false.

Review Exercises

75. $$\frac{3}{4}+\frac{2}{5}=\frac{3}{4}\cdot\frac{5}{5}+\frac{2}{5}\cdot\frac{4}{4}$$
$$=\frac{15}{20}+\frac{8}{20}=\frac{23}{20}$$

76. $-\frac{1}{4} < 0$; $-\frac{1}{4}$ is to the left of 0 on the number line.

77. $|-5.83| = 5.83$ because the distance between -5.83 and 0 on the number line is 5.83 units.

1.4 Basic Rules of Algebra

1.4 CHECK POINTS

CHECK POINT 1

$2.35x + 179.5$ when $x = 20$

$$\begin{aligned} 2.35x + 179.5 &= 2.35(20) + 179.5 \\ &= 47 + 179.5 \\ &= 226.5 \end{aligned}$$

This means that in 1980 (20 years after 1960), the population of the United States was 226.5 million.

CHECK POINT 2

$6x + 2x + 11$

a. Because terms are separated by addition, the expression contains 3 terms.

b. The coefficient of the first term, $6x$, is 6.

c. The constant term is 11.

d. The like terms are $6x$ and $2x$.

CHECK POINT 3

a. $x + 14 = 14 + x$

b. $7y = y7$

CHECK POINT 4

a. Change the order of the terms being added:

$$5x + 17 = 17 + 5x.$$

b. Change the order of the factors being multiplied:

$$5x + 17 = x5 + 17.$$

CHECK POINT 5

a. $$\begin{aligned} 8 + (12 + x) &= (8 + 12) + x \\ &= 20 + x \end{aligned}$$

b. $$\begin{aligned} 6(5x) &= (6 \cdot 5)x \\ &= 30x \end{aligned}$$

CHECK POINT 6

$$\begin{aligned} 8 + (x + 4) &= 8 + (4 + x) \\ &= (8 + 4) + x \\ &= 12 + x \end{aligned}$$

CHECK POINT 7

$$\begin{aligned} 5(x + 3) &= 5x + 5 \cdot 3 \\ &= 5x + 15 \end{aligned}$$

CHECK POINT 8

$$\begin{aligned} 6(4y + 7) &= 6 \cdot 4y + 6 \cdot 7 \\ &= 24y + 42 \end{aligned}$$

CHECK POINT 9

a. $$\begin{aligned} 7x + 3x &= (7 + 3)x \\ &= 10x \end{aligned}$$

b. $$\begin{aligned} 9a - 4a &= (9 - 4)a \\ &= 5a \end{aligned}$$

CHECK POINT 10

a. $$\begin{aligned} 8x + 7x + 10x + 3 &= (8x + 10x) + (7 + 3) \\ &= 18x + 10 \end{aligned}$$

b. $$\begin{aligned} 9x + 6y - 5x - 2y &= (9x - 5x) + (6y - 2y) \\ &= 4x + 4y \end{aligned}$$

CHECK POINT 11

$$\begin{aligned} 7(2x - 3) - 11x &= 7 \cdot 2x - 7 \cdot 3 - 11x \\ &= 14x - 21 - 11x \\ &= (14x - 11x) - 21 \\ &= 3x - 21 \end{aligned}$$

CHECK POINT 12

$7(4x+3y)+2(5x-y)$
$= 7\cdot 4x+7\cdot 3y+2\cdot 5x-2\cdot y$
$= 28x+21y+10x-2y$
$= (28x+10x)+(21y-2y)$
$= 38x+19y$

CHECK POINT 13

Using $0.6(220-a)$:
$0.6(220-40)$
$= 0.6(180)$
$= 108$

Using $132-0.6a$:
$132-0.6(40)$
$= 132-24$
$= 108$

Both forms of the algebraic expression indicate that the optimum heart rate for a 40-year-old runner is 108 beats per minute.

EXERCISE SET 1.4

1. $x+13;\ x=5$

$x+13=5+13=18$

3. $7x;\ x=10$

$7x=7(10)=70$

5. $5x+7;\ x=4$

$5x+7=5(4)+7$
$=20+7=27$

7. $4(x+3);\ x=2$

$4(x+3)=4(2+3)$
$=4(5)=20$

9. $\frac{5}{9}(F-32);\ F=77$

$\frac{5}{9}(F-32)=\frac{5}{9}(77-32)$
$=\frac{5}{9}(45)=25$

11. $3x+5$

a. 2 terms
b. 3
c. 5
d. No like terms

13. $x+2+5x$

a. 3 terms
b. 1
c. 2
d. x and $5x$ are like terms.

15. $4y+1+3$

a. 3 terms
b. 4
c. 1
d. No like terms

17. $y+4=4+y$

19. $5+3x=3x+5$

21. $4x+5y=5y+4x$

23. $5(x+3)=5(3+x)$

25. $9x=x\cdot 9$ or $x9$

27. $x+y6=x+6y$

29. $7x+23=x7+23$

31. $5(x+3)=(x+3)5$

33. $7+(5+x)=(7+5)+x=12+x$

35. $7(4x)=(7\cdot 4)x=28x$

37. $3(x+5)=3(x)+3(5)=3x+15$

39. $8(2x+3)=8(2x)+8(3)=16x+24$

41. $\frac{1}{3}(12+6r)=\frac{1}{3}(12)+\frac{1}{3}(6r)=4+2r$

43. $5(x+y)=5x+5y$

45. $3(x-2) = 3(x) - 3(2) = 3x - 6$

47. $2(4x-5) = 2(4x) - 2(5) = 8x - 10$

49. $\frac{1}{2}(5x-12) = \frac{1}{2}(5x) + \frac{1}{2}(-12) = \frac{5}{2}x - 6$

51. $(2x+7)4 = 2x(4) + 7(4) = 8x + 28$

53. $6(x+3+2y) = 6(x) + 6(3) + 6(2y)$
$= 6x + 18 + 12y$

55. $5(3x-2+4y) = 5(3x) - 5(2) + 5(4y)$
$= 15x - 10 + 20y$

57. $7x + 10x = (7+10)x = 17x$

59. $11a - 3a = (11-3)aa = 8a$

61. $3 + (x+11) = (3+11) + x = 14 + x$

63. $5y - 3 + 6y = (5y + 6y) - 3 = 11y - 3$

65. $2x + 5 + 7x - 4 = (2x + 7x) + (5 - 4)$
$= 9x + 1$

67. $11a + 12 - 3a - 2 = (11a - 3a) + (12 - 2)$
$= 8a + 10$

69. $5(3x+2) - 4 = 15x + 10 - 4 = 15x + 6$

71. $12 + 5(3x-2) = 12 + 15x - 10$
$= 15x + (12 - 10)$
$= 15x + 2$

73. $7(3a+2b) + 5(4a-2b)$
$= 21a + 14b + 20a - 10b$
$= 21a + 20a + 14b - 10b$
$= 41a + 4b$

75. $15x$; $x = 20$

$$15x = 15(20) = 300$$

This means that you can stay in the sun for 300 minutes (or 5 hours) without burning with a number 15 lotion.

77. $1527x + 31{,}290$; $x = 2000 - 1990 = 10$

$$\begin{aligned} 1527x + 31{,}290 &= 1527(10) + 31{,}290 \\ &= 15{,}270 + 31{,}290 \\ &= 46{,}560 \end{aligned}$$

This means that the average yearly earnings for elementary and secondary teachers in the United States in 2000 was \$46,560.

79. $$\begin{aligned} \frac{DA+D}{24} &= \frac{200(12)+200}{24} \\ &= \frac{2400+200}{24} \\ &= 108.\overline{3}\text{ mg} \end{aligned}$$

$$\begin{aligned} \frac{D(A+1)}{24} &= \frac{200(12+1)}{24} \\ &= \frac{200(13)}{24} = \frac{2600}{24} \\ &= 108.\overline{3}\text{ mg} \end{aligned}$$

The proper dose of a 12-year-old is approximately 108 milligrams.

For Exercises 81–91, answers may vary.

93. The only correct statement is c, which is an example of the distributive property.

95. $\frac{0.5x + 5000}{x}$

a. $x = 100$

$$\begin{aligned} \frac{0.5x+5000}{x} &= \frac{0.5(100)+5000}{100} \\ &= \frac{50+5000}{100} \\ &= \frac{5050}{100} = 50.5 \end{aligned}$$

The average cost per clock for 100 clocks is \$50.50.

$x = 1000$

$$\frac{0.5x + 5000}{x} = \frac{0.5(1000) + 5000}{1000} = \frac{500 + 5000}{1000} = \frac{5500}{1000} = 5.5$$

The average cost per clock for 1000 clocks is \$5.50.

$x = 10{,}000$

$$\frac{0.5x + 5000}{x} = \frac{0.5(10{,}000) + 5000}{10{,}000} = \frac{5000 + 5000}{10{,}000} = \frac{10{,}000}{10{,}000} = 1$$

The average cost per clock for 10,000 clocks is \$1.

b. $x = 2000$

$$\frac{0.5x + 5000}{x} = \frac{0.5(2000) + 5000}{2000} = \frac{1000 + 5000}{2000} = \frac{6000}{2000} = 3$$

The average cost per clock to manufacture 2000 clocks is \$3. Since the clocks cannot be sold for more than \$1.50, the business cannot make a profit so doesn't have a promising future.

Review Exercises

96.

$$\begin{array}{r} 0.44\ldots \\ 9\overline{)4.00\ldots} \\ \underline{3\,6} \\ 40 \\ \underline{36} \\ 40 \\ \vdots \end{array}$$

$\frac{4}{9} = 0.\overline{4}$

97.

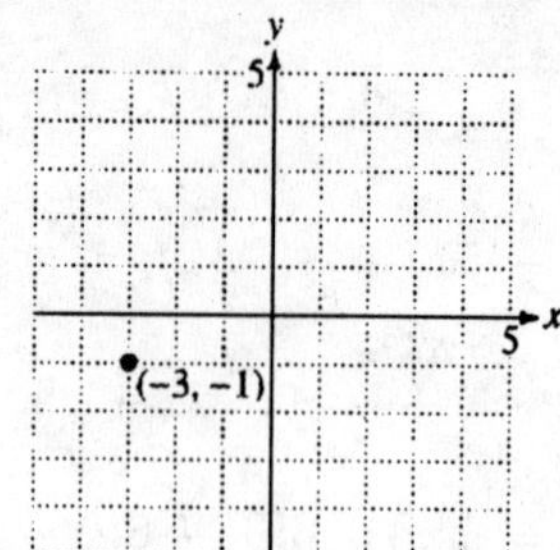

98. $\frac{3}{7} \div \frac{15}{7} = \frac{3}{7} \cdot \frac{7}{15} = \frac{21}{105} = \frac{1 \cdot \cancel{21}}{5 \cdot \cancel{21}} = \frac{1}{5}$

1.5 Addition of Real Numbers

1.5 CHECK POINTS

CHECK POINT 1

$4 + (-7)$

Step 1 Start at 4.

Step 2 Because -7 is a negative number, move 7 units to the left.

Step 3 Finish at -3, which represents the sum of 4 and -7. Thus, $4 + (-7) = -3$.

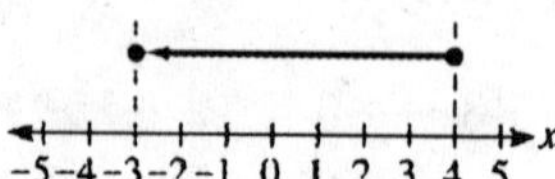

CHECK POINT 2

a. $-1 + (-3)$

Start at -1. Move 3 units to the left because -3 is negative. Finish at -4. Thus, $-1 + (-3) = -4$.

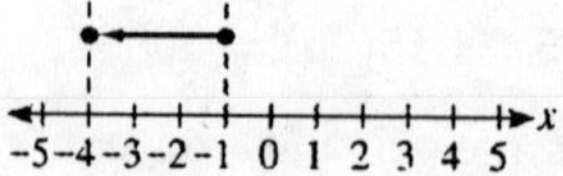

b. $-5+3$

Start -5. Move 3 units to the right because 3 is positive. Finish at -2. Thus, $-5+3=-2$.

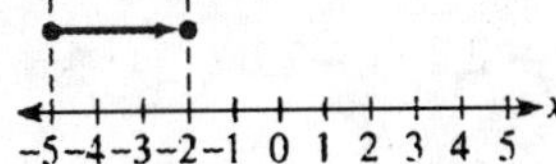

CHECK POINT 3

a. $-10+(-25)$

To add -10 and -25, first add their absolute values: $10+25=35$. The common sign is $-$, so this is the sign of the sum. Thus,

$$-10+(-25)=-35.$$

b. $-0.3+(-1.2)$

Add the absolute values: $0.3+1.2=1.5$. The common sign is $-$. Thus,

$$-0.3+(-1.2)=-1.5$$

c. $-\frac{2}{3}+\left(-\frac{1}{6}\right)$

Add the absolute values using 6 as the common denominator:

$$\frac{2}{3}+\frac{1}{6}=\frac{4}{6}+\frac{1}{6}=\frac{5}{6}.$$

The common sign is $-$. Thus,

$$-\frac{2}{3}+\left(-\frac{1}{6}\right)=-\frac{5}{6}.$$

CHECK POINT 4

a. $-15+2$

To add -15 and 2, first subtract the absolute values: $15-2=13$. Use the sign of the number with the greater absolute value. This is -15, so the sign of the sum will be negative. Thus,

$$-15+2=-13.$$

b. $-0.4+1.6$

Subtract the absolute values: $1.6-0.4=1.2$. Since 1.6 has the greater absolute value, the sign of the sum will be positive:

$$-0.4+1.6=1.2$$

c. $-\frac{2}{3}+\frac{1}{6}$

Subtract the absolute values using 6 as the common denominator:

$$\frac{2}{3}-\frac{1}{6}=\frac{4}{6}-\frac{1}{6}=\frac{3}{6}=\frac{1}{2}.$$

Since $\frac{2}{3}$ has the greater absolute value, the sign of the sum will be negative. Thus,

$$-\frac{2}{3}+\frac{1}{6}=-\frac{1}{2}.$$

CHECK POINT 5

a. $$\begin{aligned}-20x+3x&=(-20+3)x\\&=-17x\end{aligned}$$

b. $$\begin{aligned}&3y+(-10z)+(-10y)+16z\\&=3y+(-10y)+(-10z)+16z\\&=[3+(-10)]y+[(-10)+16)]z\\&=-7y+6z\end{aligned}$$

c. $$\begin{aligned}&4(10-8x)+4(4x-5)\\&=4\cdot 10+4(-8z)+4\cdot 3z+4(-5)\\&=40-32z+12z-20\\&=(40-20)+(-32+12)z\\&=20-20z\end{aligned}$$

CHECK POINT 6

Represent the amounts the water level rose by positive integers and the amounts it fell by negative numbers.

$$\begin{aligned}&2+(-4)+1+(-5)+3\\&=(2+1+3)+[(-4)+(-5)]\\&=6+(-9)\\&=-3\end{aligned}$$

The water level fell 3 feet at the end of 5 months.

EXERCISE SET 1.5

1. $3+(-7)=-4$

Start at 3. Move 7 units to the left because -7 is negative. Finish at -4.

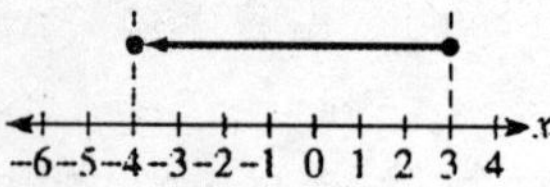

3. $-4+(-5)=-9$

Start at -4. Move 5 units to the left because -5 is negative. Finish at -9.

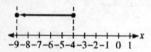

x
-9 -8 -7 -6 -5 -4 -3 -2 -1 0 1

5. $-8+2=-6$

Start at -8. Move 2 units to the right because 2 is positive. Finish at -6.

x
-9 -8 -7 -6 -5 -4 -3 -2 -1 0 1

7. $2+(-2)=0$

Start at 2. Move 2 units to the left because 2 is negative. Finish at 0.

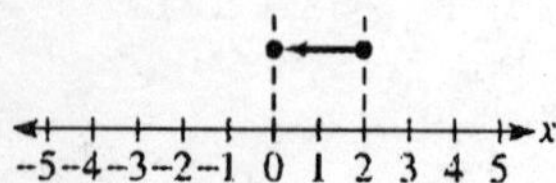

9. $-4+0=-4$

11. $9+(-9)=0$

13. $-9+(-9)=18$

15. $-7+(-5)=-12$

17. $-0.4+(-0.9)=-1.3$

19. $-\frac{7}{10}+\left(-\frac{3}{10}\right)=-\frac{10}{10}=-1$

21. $-9+4=-5$

23. $12+(-8)=4$

25. $6+(-9)=-3$

27. $-3.6+2.1=-1.5$

29. $-3.6+(-2.1)=-5.7$

31. $\frac{9}{10}+\left(-\frac{3}{5}\right)=\frac{9}{10}+\left(-\frac{6}{10}\right)=\frac{3}{10}$

33. $-\frac{5}{8}+\frac{3}{4}=-\frac{5}{8}+\frac{6}{8}=\frac{1}{8}$

35. $-\frac{3}{7}+\left(-\frac{4}{5}\right)=-\frac{15}{35}+\left(-\frac{28}{35}\right)=-\frac{43}{35}$

37. $4+(-7)+(-5)=[4+(-7)]+(-5)$
$=-3+(-5)=-8$

39. $85+(-15)+(-20)+12$
$=[85+(-15)]+(-20)+12$
$=70+(-20)+12$
$=[70+(-20]+12$
$=50+12=62$

41. $17+(-4)+2+3+(-10)$
$=13+2+3+(-10)$
$=15+3+(-10)$
$=18+(-10)=8$

43. $-45+\left(-\frac{3}{7}\right)+25+\left(-\frac{4}{7}\right)$
$=(-45+25)+\left[-\frac{3}{7}+\left(-\frac{4}{7}\right)\right]$
$=-20+\left(-\frac{7}{7}\right)$
$=-20+(-1)=-21$

45. $3.5+(-45)+(-8.4)+72$
$=[3.5+(-8.4)]+(-45+72)$
$=-4.9+27=22.1$

47. $-8x+5x=(-8+5)x=-3x$

49. $15y + (-2y) = [15 + (-12)]y = 3y$

51. $-7a + (-10a) = [-7 + (-10)a] = -17a$

53. $-4 + 7x + 5 + (-13x)$
$= -4 + 5 + 7x + (-13x)$
$= (-4 + 5) + [7 + (-13)]x$
$= 1 - 6x$

55. $7b + 2 + (-b) + (-6)$
$= 7b + (-b) + 2 + (-6)$
$= [7 + (-1)]b + [2 + (-6)]$
$= 6b - 4$ or $-4 + 6b$

57. $7x + (-5y) + (-9x) + 2y$
$= 7x + (-9x) + (-5y) + 2y$
$= [7 + (-9)]x + (-5 + 2)y$
$= -2x - 3y$

59. $4(5x - 3) + 6$
$= 4 \cdot 5x + 4(-3) + 6$
$= 20x - 12 + 6$
$= 20x - 6$

61. $8(3 - 4y) + 35y$
$= 8 \cdot 3 + 8(-4y) + 35y$
$= 24 - 32y + 35y$
$= 24 + (-32 + 35)y$
$= 24 + 3y$

63. $6(2 - 9a) + 7(3a + 5)$
$= 6 \cdot 2 + 6(-9a) + 7 \cdot 3a + 7 \cdot 5$
$= 12 - 54a + 21a + 35$
$= (12 + 35) + (-54 + 21a)$
$= 47 - 33a$

65. $-56 + 100 = 44$

The high temperature was 44°F.

67. $-1312 + 712 = -600$

The elevation of the person is 600 feet below sea level.

69. Temperature at 8:00 A.M. + rise 15°F by noon + fall 5°F by 4 P.M.
$= -7 + 15 - 5 = 3$
The temperature at 4:00 P.M. was 3°F.

71. Start at 27-yard line + 4-yard gain + 2-yard loss + 8-yard gain + 12-yard loss
$= 27 + 4 - 2 + 8 - 12 = 39 - 14 = 25$
The location of the football at the end of the fourth play is at the 25-yard line.

73. $1274 - 82 + 428 + 818 + 570 + 676 + 716 = 4400$

In the 2000 Olympics, 4400 women participated.

For Exercises 75–81, answers may vary.

83. Statement d is true. (Statement a is sometimes true, but is not considered true because it is not always true.)

85. $\_\_\_ + 11x + (-3y) + 3x = \_\_\_ + 14x + (-3y)$

$7(2x - 3y) = 14x - 2y$

Comparing these expressions gives

$\_\_\_ + (-3y) = -21y.$

Since $(-18y) + (-3y) = -21y$, the missing term is $-18y$.

87. Answers will vary according to the exercises chosen.

89. $3\sqrt{5} - 2\sqrt{7} - \sqrt{11} + 4\sqrt{3} \approx 5.0283$

Review Exercises

90. $-19 \geq -18$ is true because $-19 > -18$ is true.

91. a. $\sqrt{4}\ (= 2)$
b. $0, \sqrt{4}$
c. $-6, 0, \sqrt{4}$
d. $-6, 0, 0.\overline{7}, \sqrt{4}$
e. $-\pi, \sqrt{3}$
f. All numbers in given set

92. Quadrant IV

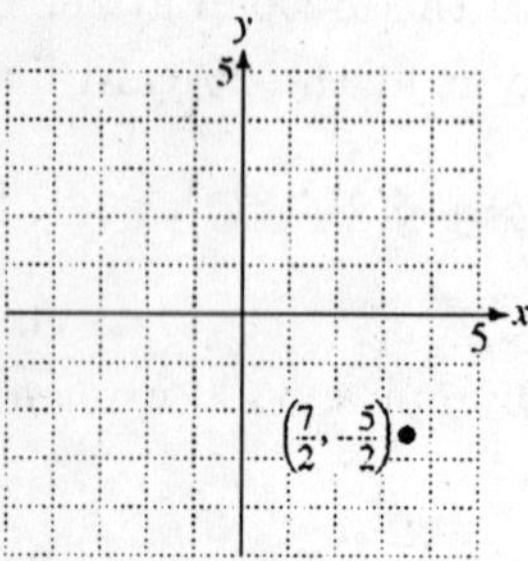

1.6 Subtraction of Real Numbers

1.6 CHECK POINTS

CHECK POINT 1

a. $3 - 11 = 3 + (-11) = -8$

b. $4 - (-5) = 4 + 5 = 9$

c. $-7 - (-2) = -7 + 2 = -5$

CHECK POINT 2

a. $$\begin{aligned} -3.4 - (-12.6) &= -3.4 + 12.6 \\ &= 9.2 \end{aligned}$$

b. $$\begin{aligned} -\frac{3}{5} - \frac{1}{3} &= -\frac{3}{5} + \left(-\frac{1}{3}\right) \\ &= -\frac{9}{15} + \left(-\frac{5}{15}\right) \\ &= -\frac{14}{15} \end{aligned}$$

c. $5\pi - (-2\pi) = 5\pi + 2\pi = 7\pi$

CHECK POINT 3

$$\begin{aligned} &10 - (-12) - 4 - (-3) - 6 \\ &= 10 + 12 + (-4) + 3 + (-6) \\ &= (10 + 12 + 3) + [(-4) + (-6)] \\ &= 25 + (-10) \\ &= 15 \end{aligned}$$

CHECK POINT 4

$$-6 + 4a - 7ab = -6 + 4a + (-7ab)$$

Because terms are separated by addition, the three terms are $-6, 4a$, and $-7ab$.

CHECK POINT 5

a. $$\begin{aligned} 4 + 2x - 9x &= 4 + 2x + (-9x) \\ &= 4 + [2 + (-9)]x \\ &= 4 + (-7x) \\ &= 4 - 7x \end{aligned}$$

b. $$\begin{aligned} &-3x - 10y - 6x + 14y \\ &= -3x + (-10y) + (-6x) + 14y \\ &= [(-3x) + (-6x)] + [(-10y) + 14y] \\ &= [-3 + (-6)]x + (-10 + 14) \\ &= -9x + 4y \end{aligned}$$

CHECK POINT 6

$$\begin{aligned} 8848 - (-10{,}915) &= 8848 + 10{,}915 \\ &= 19{,}763 \end{aligned}$$

The difference between the elevations is 19,763 meters.

EXERCISE SET 1.6

1. a. -12
b. $5 - 12 = 5 + (-12)$

3. a. 7
b. $5 - (-7) = 5 + 7$

5. $13 - 8 = 13 + (-8) = 5$

7. $8 - 15 = 8 + (-15) = -7$

9. $4-(-10)=4+10=14$

11. $-6-(-17)=-6+17=11$

13. $-12-(-3)=-12+3=-9$

15. $-11-17=-11+(-17)=-28$

17. $-25-(-25)=-25+25=0$

19. $13-13=13+(-13)=0$

21. $7-(-7)=7+7=14$

23. $0-8=0+(-8)=-8$

25. $0-(-3)=0+3=3$

27. $\frac{3}{7}-\frac{5}{7}=\frac{3}{7}+\left(-\frac{5}{7}\right)=-\frac{2}{7}$

29. $\frac{1}{5}-\left(-\frac{3}{5}\right)=\frac{1}{5}+\frac{3}{5}=\frac{4}{5}$

31. $-\frac{4}{5}-\frac{1}{5}=-\frac{4}{5}+\left(-\frac{1}{5}\right)=-\frac{5}{5}=-1$

33. $-\frac{4}{5}-\left(-\frac{1}{5}\right)=-\frac{4}{5}+\frac{1}{5}=-\frac{3}{5}$

35. $\frac{1}{2}-\left(-\frac{1}{4}\right)=\frac{1}{2}+\frac{1}{4}=\frac{2}{4}+\frac{1}{4}=\frac{3}{4}$

37. $\frac{1}{2}-\frac{1}{4}=\frac{1}{2}+\left(-\frac{1}{4}\right)=\frac{2}{4}+\left(-\frac{1}{4}\right)=\frac{1}{4}$

39. $9.8-2.2=9.8+(-2.2)=7.6$

41. $-3.1-(-1.1)=-3.1+1.1=-2$

43. $1.3-(-1.3)=1.3+1.3=2.6$

45. $-2.06-(-2.06)=-2.06+2.06=0$

47. $5\pi-2\pi=5\pi+(-2\pi)=3\pi$

49. $3\pi-(-10)=3\pi+10\pi=13\pi$

51.
$$\begin{aligned}13-2-(-8)&=13+(-2)+8\\&=(13+8)+(-2)\\&=21+(-2)\\&=19\end{aligned}$$

53.
$$\begin{aligned}9-8+3-7&=9+(-8)+3+(-7)\\&=(9+3)+[(-8)+(-7)]\\&=12+(-15)\\&=-3\end{aligned}$$

55.
$$\begin{aligned}&-6-2+3-10\\&=-6+(-2)+3+(-10)\\&=[(-6)+(-2)+(-10)]+3\\&=-18+3\\&=-15\end{aligned}$$

57.
$$\begin{aligned}&-10-(-5)+7-2\\&=-10+5+7+(-2)\\&=[(-10)+(-2)]+(5+7)\\&=-12+12=0\end{aligned}$$

59.
$$\begin{aligned}&-23-11-(-7)+(-25)\\&=(-23)+(-11)+7+(-25)\\&=[(-23)+(-11)+(-25)]+7\\&=-59+7\\&=-52\end{aligned}$$

61.
$$\begin{aligned}&-823-146-50-(-832)\\&=-823+(-146)+(-50)+832\\&=[(-823)+(-146)+(-50)]+832\\&=-1019+832\\&=-187\end{aligned}$$

63.
$$\begin{aligned}1-\frac{2}{3}-\left(-\frac{5}{6}\right)&=1+\left(-\frac{2}{3}\right)+\frac{5}{6}\\&=\left(1+\frac{5}{6}\right)+\left(-\frac{2}{3}\right)\\&=\left(\frac{6}{6}+\frac{5}{6}\right)+\left(-\frac{2}{3}\right)\\&=\frac{11}{6}+\left(-\frac{2}{3}\cdot\frac{2}{2}\right)\\&=\frac{11}{6}+\left(-\frac{4}{6}\right)=\frac{7}{6}\end{aligned}$$

65. $-0.16 - 5.2 - (-0.87)$
$= -0.16 + (-5.2) + 0.87$
$= [(-0.16) + (-5.2)] + 0.87$
$= -5.36 + 0.87$
$= -4.49$

67. $-\frac{3}{4} - \frac{1}{4} - \left(-\frac{5}{8}\right) = -\frac{3}{4} + \left(-\frac{1}{4}\right) + \frac{5}{8}$
$= -\frac{4}{4} + \frac{5}{8}$
$= -1 + \frac{5}{8}$
$= -\frac{8}{8} + \frac{5}{8} = -\frac{3}{8}$

69. $-3x - 8y = -3x + (-8y)$

The terms are $-3x$ and $-8y$.

71. $12x - 5xy - 4 = 12x + (-5xy) + (-4)$

The terms are $12x$, $-5xy$, and -4.

73. $3x - 9x = 3x + (-9x)$
$= [3 + (-9)]x$
$= -6x$

75. $4 + 7y - 17y = 4 + 7y + (-17y)$
$= 4 + [7 + (-17)]y$
$= 4 - 10y$

77. $2a + 5 - 9a = 2a + 5 + (-9a)$
$= 2a + (-9a) + 5$
$= [2 + (-9)]a + 5$
$= -7a + 5$ or $5 - 7a$

79. $4 - 6b - 8 - 3b$
$= 4 + (-6b) + (-8) + (-3b)$
$= 4 + (-8) + (-6b) + (-3b)$
$= 4 + (-8) + [-6 + (-3)]b$
$= -4 - 9b$

81. $13 - (-7x) + 4x - (-11)$
$= 13 + 7x + 4x + 11$
$= 13 + 11 + 7x + 4x$
$= 24 + 11x$

83. $-5x - 10y - 3x + 13y$
$= -5x + (-10y) + (-3x) + 13y$
$= -5x + (-3x) + (-10y) + 13y$
$= [-5 + (-3)]x + (-10 + 13)y$
$= -8x + 3y$ or $3y - 8x$

85. Elevation of Mount Kilimanjaro
− elevation of Qattara Depression
= 19,321 − (−436) = 19,757

The difference in elevation between the two geographic locations is 19,757 feet.

87. \$14 billion − \$6 billion = \$8 billion

The difference between veterinary costs for dogs and cats in 2000 was about \$8 billion.

89. $2 - (-19) = 2 + 19 = 21$

The difference between the average daily low temperatures for March and February is 21°F.

91. $-19 - (-22) = -19 + 22 = 3$

February's average low temperature is 3°F warmer than January's.

93. The maximum point on the graph is $(3, 0.05)$. This means that the drug's maximum concentration is 0.05 milligrams per 100 milliliters and this occurs 3 hours after the injection.

95. $0.045 - 0.03 = 0.045 + (-0.03) = 0.015$

The difference in concentrations between 4 hours and 1 hour after injection is 0.015.

97. The drug's concentration is increasing between 0 and 3 hours after the injection (from the time of the injection to three hours later).

99. $520 - (-112) = 520 + 112 = 632$

The difference in growth between systems and analysts and farmers is 632 thousand or 632,000 jobs.

For Exercises 101–105, answers will vary.

107. Consider dates B.C. as negative numbers and dates A.D. as positive numbers.

$$500 - (-212) = 500 + 212 = 712$$

Because there was no year 0, the number of elapsed years is $712 - 1 = 711$.

109. Student answers will vary according to the exercises chosen.

111. $4\sqrt{2} - (-3\sqrt{5}) - (-\sqrt{7}) + \sqrt{3}$
$= 4\sqrt{2} + 3\sqrt{5} + \sqrt{7} + \sqrt{3}$
≈ 16.7429

Review Exercises

113.

-4.5
-5 -4 -3 -2 -1 0 1 2 3 4 5 x

114. $10(a + 4) = 10(4 + a)$

115. Examples will vary. One integer that is not a natural number is -7.

1.7 Multiplication and Division of Real Numbers

1.7 CHECK POINTS

CHECK POINT 1

a. $8(-5)$

Multiply the absolute values: $8 \cdot 5 = 40$. Because the numbers have opposite signs, the product is negative. Thus,

$$8(-5) = -40.$$

b. $-\frac{1}{3} \cdot \frac{4}{7} = -\frac{1 \cdot 4}{3 \cdot 7} = -\frac{4}{21}$

c. $(-12)(-3)$

Multiply the absolute values: $12 \cdot 3 = 36$. Because the numbers have the same sign, the product is positive. Thus,

$$(-12)(-3) = 36.$$

d. $(-1.1)(-5) = 5.5$

e. $(-543)(0)$

The product of 0 and any number is 0. Thus,

$$(-543)(0) = 0.$$

CHECK POINT 2

a. $(-2)(3)(-1)(4)$

There is an even number of negative factors (two), so the product is positive.

$$(-2)(3)(-1)(4) = 24$$

b. $(-1)(-3)(2)(-1)(5)$

There is an odd number of negative factors (three), so the product is negative.

$$(-1)(-3)(2)(-1)(5) = -30$$

CHECK POINT 3

a. The multiplicative inverse of 7 is $\frac{1}{7}$ because $7 \cdot \frac{1}{7} = 1$.

b. The multiplicative inverse of $\frac{1}{8}$ is 8 because $\frac{1}{8} \cdot 8 = 1$.

c. The multiplicative inverse of -6 is $-\frac{1}{6}$ because $(-6)\left(-\frac{1}{6}\right) = 1$.

d. The multiplicative inverse of $-\frac{7}{13}$ is $-\frac{13}{7}$ because $\left(-\frac{7}{13}\right)\left(-\frac{13}{7}\right) = 1$.

CHECK POINT 4

a. $-28 \div 7 = -28 \cdot \frac{1}{7} = -4$

b. $\frac{-16}{-2} = -16 \cdot \left(-\frac{1}{2}\right) = 8$

CHECK POINT 5

a. $\frac{-32}{-4}$

Divide the absolute values: $\frac{32}{4} = 8$.
The quotient will be positive because the two numbers have the same sign.

$$\frac{-32}{-4} = 8$$

b. $-\frac{2}{3} \div \frac{5}{4}$

Divide the absolute values:

$$-\frac{2}{3} \div \frac{5}{4} = \frac{2}{3} \cdot \frac{4}{5} = \frac{8}{15}.$$

The quotient will be negative because the two numbers have opposite signs. Thus,

$$-\frac{2}{3} \div \frac{5}{4} = -\frac{8}{15}.$$

c. $\frac{21.9}{-3}$

Divide the absolute values: $\frac{21.9}{3} = 7.3$.
The quotient will be negative because the two numbers have opposite signs. Thus,

$$\frac{21.9}{-3} = -7.3.$$

d. $\frac{0}{-5}$

Any nonzero number divided into 0 is 0.

$$\frac{0}{-5} = 0$$

CHECK POINT 6

a. $-4(5x) = (-4 \cdot 5)x = -20x$

b. $9x + x = (9 + 1)x = 10x$

c. $13b - 14b = (13 - 14)b = -1b = -b$

d. $-7(3x - 4) = -7(3x) - 7(-4)$
$= -21x + 28$

e. $-(7y - 6) = -7y + 6$

Remove parentheses by changing the sign of every term inside parentheses.

CHECK POINT 7

$$\begin{aligned} &4(3y - 7) - (13y - 2) \\ &= 4 \cdot 3y - 4 \cdot 7 - (13y - 2) \\ &= 12y - 28 - 13y + 2 \\ &= (12y - 13y) + (-28 + 2) \\ &= -y - 26 \end{aligned}$$

CHECK POINT 8

$$\frac{30x + 300{,}000}{x}$$

a. $x = 1000$

$$\begin{aligned} \frac{30x + 300{,}000}{x} &= \frac{30(1000) + 300{,}000}{1000} \\ &= \frac{330{,}000}{1000} = 330 \end{aligned}$$

To manufacture 1000 pairs of running shoes per week, the average cost per pair is \$330.

b. $x = 10{,}000$

$$\begin{aligned} \frac{30x + 300{,}000}{10{,}000} &= \frac{30(10{,}000) + 300{,}000}{10{,}000} \\ &= \frac{300{,}000 + 300{,}000}{10{,}000} \\ &= \frac{600{,}000}{10{,}000} = 60 \end{aligned}$$

To manufacture 10,000 pairs of running shoes per week, the average cost per pair is \$60.

c. $x = 100{,}000$

$$\frac{30x + 300{,}000}{x} = \frac{30(100{,}000) + 300{,}000}{100{,}000} = \frac{3{,}000{,}000 + 300{,}000}{100{,}000} = \frac{3{,}300{,}000}{100{,}000} = 33$$

To manufacture 100,000 pairs of running shoes per week, the average cost per pair is $33.

EXERCISE SET 1.7

1. $6(-9) = -(6 \cdot 9) = -54$

3. $(-7)(-3) = +(7 \cdot 3) = 21$

5. $(-2)(6) = -12$

7. $(-13)(-1) = 13$

9. $0(-5) = 0$

11. $\frac{1}{2}(-14) = -7$

13. $\left(-\frac{3}{4}\right)(-20) = \frac{3 \cdot 20}{4 \cdot 1} = 15$

15. $-\frac{3}{5} \cdot \left(-\frac{4}{7}\right) = \frac{3 \cdot 4}{5 \cdot 7} = \frac{12}{35}$

17. $-\frac{7}{9} \cdot \frac{2}{3} = -\frac{7 \cdot 2}{9 \cdot 3} = -\frac{14}{27}$

19. $3(-1.2) = -3.6$

21. $-0.2(-0.6) = 0.12$

23. $(-5)(-2)(3) = 30$

25. $(-4)(-3)(-1)(6) = -72$

27. $-2(-3)(-4)(-1) = 24$

29. $(-3)(-3)(-3) = -27$

31. $5(-3)(-1)(2)(3) = 90$

33. $(-8)(-4)(0)(-17)(-6) = 0$

35. The multiplicative inverse of 4 is $\frac{1}{4}$.

37. The multiplicative inverse of $\frac{1}{5}$ is 5.

39. The multiplicative inverse of -10 is $-\frac{1}{10}$.

41. The multiplicative inverse of $-\frac{2}{5}$ is $-\frac{5}{2}$.

43. a. $-32 \div 4 = -32 \cdot \frac{1}{4}$

b. $-32 \cdot \frac{1}{4} = -8$

45. a. $\frac{-60}{-5} = -60 \cdot \left(-\frac{1}{5}\right)$

b. $-60 \cdot \left(-\frac{1}{5}\right) = 12$

47. $\frac{12}{-4} = 12 \cdot \left(-\frac{1}{4}\right) = -3$

49. $\frac{-21}{3} = -21 \cdot \frac{1}{3} = -7$

51. $\frac{-90}{-3} = -90 \cdot \left(-\frac{1}{3}\right) = 30$

53. $\frac{0}{-7} = 0$

55. $\frac{-7}{0}$ is undefined.

57. $-15 \div 3 = -15 \cdot \frac{1}{3} = -5$

59. $120 \div (-10) = 120 \cdot \left(-\frac{1}{10}\right) = -12$

61. $(-180) \div (-30) = -180 \cdot \left(-\frac{1}{30}\right) = 6$

63. $0 \div (-4) = 0$

65. $-4 \div 0$ is undefined.

67. $\frac{-12.9}{3} = -12.9 \cdot \frac{1}{3} = -4.3$

69. $-\frac{1}{2} \div \left(-\frac{3}{5}\right) = -\frac{1}{2} \cdot \left(-\frac{5}{3}\right) = \frac{5}{6}$

71. $-\frac{14}{9} \div \frac{7}{8} = -\frac{14}{9} \cdot \frac{8}{7} = -\frac{112}{63}$
$= \frac{\cancel{7} \cdot 16}{\cancel{7} \cdot 9} = -\frac{16}{9}$

73. $\frac{1}{3} \div \left(-\frac{1}{3}\right) = \frac{1}{3} \cdot (-3) = -1$

75. $6 \div \left(-\frac{2}{5}\right) = 6 \cdot \left(-\frac{5}{2}\right) = -\frac{30}{2} = -15$

77. $-5(2x) = (-5 \cdot 2)x = -10x$

79. $-4\left(-\frac{3}{4}y\right) = \left[-4 \cdot \left(-\frac{3}{4}\right)\right] y = 3y$

81. $8x + x = 8x + 1x = (8+1)x = 9x$

83. $-5x + x = -5x + 1x = (-5+1)x = -4x$

85. $6b - 7b = (6-7)b = -1b = -b$

87. $-y + 4y = -1y + 4y = (-1+4)y = 3y$

89. $-4(2x-3) = -4(2x) - 4(-3) = -8x + 12$

91. $-3(-2x+4) = -3(-2x) - 3(4)$
$= 6x - 12$

93. $-(2y-5) = -2y + 5$

95. $4(2y-3) - (7y+2)$
$= 4(2y) + 4(-3) - 7y - 2$
$= 8y - 12 + 7y - 2$
$= 8y - 7y - 12 - 2$
$= y - 14$

97. There were about 233 thousand or 233,000 liposuctions in the United States in 2000.

99. **a.** From the graph, a reasonable estimate is 11 words.

b. $\frac{5x+30}{x}$; $x = 5$

$$\frac{5x+30}{x} = \frac{5(5)+30}{5} = \frac{25+30}{5} = \frac{55}{5} = 11$$

According to the model, 11 Latin words will be remembered after 5 days. This is the same as the estimate from part (a).

101. **a.** $\frac{200x}{100-x}$; $x = 50$

$$\frac{200x}{100-x} = \frac{200(50)}{100-50} = \frac{10{,}000}{50} = 200$$

The cost for removing 50% of the contaminents is 200($10,000) = $2,000,000.

b. $\frac{200x}{100-x}$; $x = 80$

$$\frac{200x}{100-x} = \frac{200(80)}{100-80} = \frac{16{,}000}{20} = 800$$

The cost for removing 80% of the contaminants is 800($10,000) = $8,000,000.

c. As the percentage of contaminant removed increases, the cost of the cleanup rises very rapidly.

For Exercises 103–109, answers may vary.

111. Statement b is true.

113. $5x$

115. Student solutions will vary according to the exercises chosen.

117. $0.3(4.7x - 5.9) - 0.07(3.8x - 61)$
$= 0.3(4.7x) + 0.3(-5.9) - (0.07)(3.8x) - (0.07)(-61)$
$= 1.41x - 1.77 - 0.266x + 4.27$
$= [1.41x + (-0.266x)] + (-1.77 + 4.27)$
$= 1.144x + 2.5$

Review Exercises

119. $-6 + (-3) = -9$

120. $-6 - (-3) = -6 + 3 = -3$

121. $-6 \div (-3) = -6\left(-\frac{1}{3}\right) = 2$

1.8 Exponents, Order of Operations, and Mathematical Models

1.8 CHECK POINTS

CHECK POINT 1

a. $6^2 = 6 \cdot 6 = 36$

b. $(-4)^3 = (-4)(-4)(-4) = -64$

c. $(-1)^4 = (-1)(-1)(-1)(-1) = 1$

d. $-1^4 = -1 \cdot 1 \cdot 1 \cdot 1 = -1$

CHECK POINT 2

a. $16x^2 + 5x^2 = (16 + 5)x^2 = 21x^2$

b. $7x^3 + x^3 = 7x^3 + 1x^3 = (7 + 1)x^3 = 8x^3$

c. $10x^2 + 8x^3$ cannot be simplified because $10x^2$ and $8x^3$ are not like terms.

CHECK POINT 3

$$\begin{aligned} 20 + 4 \cdot 3 - 17 &= 20 + 12 - 17 \\ &= 32 - 17 \\ &= 15 \end{aligned}$$

CHECK POINT 4

$$\begin{aligned} 7^2 - 48 \div 4^2 \cdot 5 - 2 &= 49 - 48 \div 16 \cdot 5 - 2 \\ &= 49 - 3 \cdot 5 - 2 \\ &= 49 - 15 - 2 \\ &= 34 - 2 \\ &= 32 \end{aligned}$$

CHECK POINT 5

a. $(3 \cdot 2)^2 = 6^2 = 36$

b. $3 \cdot 2^2 = 3 \cdot 4 = 12$

CHECK POINT 6

$$\begin{aligned} (-8)^2 - (10 - 13)^2(-2) &= (-8)^2 - (-3)^2(-2) \\ &= 64 - 9(-2) \\ &= 64 - (-18) \\ &= 64 + 18 \\ &= 82 \end{aligned}$$

CHECK POINT 7

$$\begin{aligned} 4[3(6 - 11) + 5] &= 4[3(-5) + 5] \\ &= 4[-15 + 5] \\ &= 4[-10] \\ &= -40 \end{aligned}$$

CHECK POINT 8

$$\begin{aligned} &25 \div 5 + 3[4 + 2(7 - 9)^3] \\ &= 25 \div 5 + 3[4 + 2(-2)^3] \\ &= 25 \div 5 + 3[4 + 2(-8)] \\ &= 25 \div 5 + 3[4 + (-16)] \\ &= 25 \div 5 + 3[-12] \\ &= 25 \div 5 + (-36) \\ &= 5 + (-36) \\ &= -31 \end{aligned}$$

CHECK POINT 9

$$\begin{aligned} \frac{5(4 - 9) + 10 \cdot 3}{2^3 - 1} &= \frac{5(-5) + 10 \cdot 3}{8 - 1} \\ &= \frac{-25 + 30}{8 - 1} \\ &= \frac{5}{7} \end{aligned}$$

CHECK POINT 10

Evaluate $-x^2 - 4x$ for $x = -5$.

$$\begin{aligned} -x^2 - 4x &= -(-5)^2 - 4(-5) \\ &= -25 - 4(-5) \\ &= -25 + 20 \\ &= -5 \end{aligned}$$

CHECK POINT 11

$$\begin{aligned} &14x^2 + 5 - [7(x^2 - 2) + 4] \\ &= 14x^2 + 5 - [7x^2 - 14 + 4] \\ &= 14x^2 + 5 - [7x^2 - 10] \\ &= 14x^2 + 5 - 7x^2 + 10 \\ &= (14x^2 - 7x^2) + 5 + 10 \\ &= 7x^2 + 15 \end{aligned}$$

CHECK POINT 12

$N = 0.4x^2 - 36x + 1000$; $x = 40$

$$\begin{aligned} N &= 0.4x^2 - 36x + 1000 \\ &= 0.4(40)^2 - 36(40) + 1000 \\ &= 0.4(1600) - 1440 + 1000 \\ &= 640 - 1440 + 1000 \\ &= 200 \end{aligned}$$

For 40-year-old drivers, there are 200 accidents per 50 million miles driven.

CHECK POINT 13

$C = \frac{5}{9}(\text{F} - 32)$; F = 86

$$\begin{aligned} C &= \frac{5}{9}(F - 32) \\ &= \frac{5}{9}(86 - 32) \\ &= \frac{5}{9}(54) \\ &= 30 \end{aligned}$$

86°F is equivalent to 30°C.

EXERCISE SET 1.8

1. $9^2 = 9 \cdot 9 = 81$

3. $4^3 = 4 \cdot 4 \cdot 4 = 64$

5. $(-4)^2 = (-4)(-4) = 16$

7. $(-4)^3 = (-4)(-4)(-4) = -64$

9. $(-5)^4 = (-5)(-5)(-5)(-5) = 625$

11. $-5^4 = -5 \cdot 5 \cdot 5 \cdot 5 = -625$

13. $-10^2 = -10 \cdot 10 = -100$

15. $6x^2 + 11x^2 = (6 + 11)x^2 = 17x^2$

17. $9x^3 + 4x^3 = (9 + 4)x^3 = 13x^3$

19. $7x^4 + x^4 = 7x^4 + 1x^4 = (7 + 1)x^4 = 8x^4$

21. $$\begin{aligned} 16x^2 - 17x^2 &= 16x^2 + (-17x^2) \\ &= [16 + (-17)]x^2 \\ &= -1x^2 = -x^2 \end{aligned}$$

23. $$\begin{aligned} 17x^3 - 16x^3 &= 17x^3 + (-16x^3) \\ &= 1x^3 = x^3 \end{aligned}$$

25. $2x^2 + 2x^3$ cannot be simplified. The terms $2x^2$ and $2x^3$ are not like terms because they have different variable factors, namely, x^2 and x^3.

27. $$\begin{aligned} 6x^2 - 6x^2 &= 6x^2 + (-6x^2) = [6 + (-6)]x^2 \\ &= 0x^2 = 0 \end{aligned}$$

29. $7 + 6 \cdot 3 = 7 + 18 = 25$

31. $45 \div 5 \cdot 3 = 9 \cdot 3 = 27$

33. $6 \cdot 8 \div 4 = 48 \div 4 = 12$

35. $$\begin{aligned} 14 - 2 \cdot 6 + 3 &= 14 - 12 + 3 \\ &= 2 + 3 = 5 \end{aligned}$$

37. $$\begin{aligned} 8^2 - 16 \div 2^2 \cdot 4 - 3 &= 64 - 16 \div 4 \cdot 4 - 3 \\ &= 64 - 4 \cdot 4 - 3 \\ &= 64 - 16 - 3 \\ &= 48 - 3 = 45 \end{aligned}$$

39. $3(-2)^2 - 4(-3)^2 = 3 \cdot 4 - 4 \cdot 9$
$= 12 - 36$
$= 12 + (-36)$
$= -24$

41. $(4 \cdot 5)^2 - 4 \cdot 5^2 = 20^2 - 4 \cdot 25$
$= 400 - 100$
$= 300$

43. $(2-6)^2 - (3-7)^2 = (-4)^2 - (-4)^2$
$= 16 - 16 = 0$

45. $6(3-5)^3 - 2(1-3)^3 = 6(-2)^3 - 2(-2)^3$
$= 6(-8) - 2(-8)$
$= -48 + 16$
$= -32$

47. $[2(6-2)]^2 = (2 \cdot 4)^2 = 8^2 = 64$

49. $2[5 + 2(9-4)] = 2[5 + 2(5)]$
$= 2(5 + 10)$
$= 2 \cdot 15 = 30$

51. $[7 + 3(2^3 - 1)] \div 21 = [7 + 3(8-1)] \div 21$
$= (7 + 3 \cdot 7) \div 21$
$= (7 + 21) \div 21$
$= 28 \div 21$
$= \frac{28}{21} = \frac{\cancel{7} \cdot 4}{\cancel{7} \cdot 3} = \frac{4}{3}$

53. $\frac{10+8}{5^2 - 4^2} = \frac{18}{25-16} = \frac{18}{9} = 2$

55. $\frac{37 + 15 \div (-3)}{2^4} = \frac{37 + (-5)}{16}$
$= \frac{32}{16} = 2$

57. $\frac{(-11)(-4) + 2(-7)}{7 - (-3)} = \frac{44 + (-14)}{7+3}$
$= \frac{30}{10} = 3$

59. $4\,|10 - (8 - 20)| = 4\,|10 - (-12)|$
$= 4\,|22|$
$= 4 \cdot 22 = 88$

61. $8(-10) + |4(-5)| = -80 + |-20|$
$= -80 + 20$
$= -60$

63. $-2^2 + 4[16 + (3-5)]$
$= -4 + 4[16 + (-2)]$
$= -4 + 4(-8)$
$= -4 - 32 = -36$

65. $24 \div \frac{3^2}{8-5} - (-6) = 24 \div \frac{9}{3} - (-6)$
$= 24 \div 3 - (-6)$
$= 8 + 6 = 14$

67. $x^2 + 5x;\ x = 3$

$x^2 + 5x = 3^2 + 5 \cdot 3$
$= 9 + 5 \cdot 3$
$= 9 + 15 = 24$

69. $3x^2 - 8x;\ x = -2$
$3x^2 - 8x = 3(-2)^2 - 8(-2)$
$= 3 \cdot 4 - 8(-2)$
$= 12 + 16 = 28$

71. $-x^2 - 10x;\ x = -1$
$-x^2 - 10x = -(-1)^2 - 10(-1)$
$= -1 + 10 = 9$

73. $\frac{6y - 4y^2}{y^2 - 15};\ y = 5$

$\frac{6y - 4y^2}{y^2 - 15} = \frac{6(5) - 4(5^2)}{5^2 - 15}$
$= \frac{6(5) - 4(25)}{25 - 15}$
$= \frac{30 - 100}{25 - 15}$
$= \frac{-70}{10} = -7$

75. $3[5(x-2) + 1] = 3(5x - 10 + 1)$
$= 3(5x - 9)$
$= 15x - 27$

77. $3[6-(y+1)] = 3(6-y-1)$
$= 3(5-y)$
$= 15-3y$

79. $7-4[3-(4y-5)]$
$= 7-4(3-4y+5)$
$= 7-12+16y-20$
$= -25+16y \quad \text{or} \quad 16y-25$

81. $2(3x^2-5)-[4(2x^2-1)+3]$
$= 6x^2-10-(8x^2-4+3)$
$= 6x^2-10-(8x^2-1)$
$= 6x^2-10-8x^2-1$
$= -2x^2-9$

83. $W = 1.5x+7;\ x=4$

$$W = 1.5x+7 = 1.5(4)+7 = 13$$

On the average, a four-month-old infant girl weighs 13 pounds. This corresponds to the point $(4, 13)$ on the graph.

85. $R = 165-0.75A;\ A=40$

$$R = 165-0.75A = 165-0.75(40) = 165-30 = 135$$

The desirable heart rate during exercise for a 40-year-old man is 135 beats per minute. This corresponds to the point $(40, 135)$ on the graph.

87. Since $2000-1996=4$, the year 2000 corresponds to $x=4$.

$N = 0.4x^2+0.5;\ x=4$

$$N = 0.4x^2+0.5 = 0.4(4^2)+0.5 = 0.4(16)+0.5 = 6.4+0.5 = 6.9$$

According to the formula, 6.9 million people in the United States used cable TV modems in 2000. This is quite close to the 7 million shown by the bar graph.

89. Since $2000-1995=5$, the year 2005 corresponds to $x=5$.

$N = 1.2x^2+15.2x+181.4;\ x=5$

$$N = 1.2x^2+15.2x+181.4 = 1.2(5^2)+15.2(5)+181.4 = 1.2(25)+15.2(5)+181.4 = 30+76+181.4 = 287.4$$

According to the formula, the cost of Medicare in 2000 was \$287.4 billion. This is a very good estimate for the cost shown by the bar graph.

91. $C = \frac{5}{9}(F-32);\ F=68$

$$C = \frac{5}{9}(F-32) = \frac{5}{9}(68-32) = \frac{5}{9}(36) = \frac{5}{9}\cdot\frac{36}{1} = \frac{180}{9} = 20$$

$68°\text{F} = 20°\text{C}$

93. $C = \frac{5}{9}(F-32);\ F=-22$

$$C = \frac{5}{9}(F-32) = \frac{5}{9}(-22-32) = \frac{5}{9}(-54) = \frac{5}{9}\cdot\frac{54}{1} = -\frac{270}{9} = -30$$

$-22°\text{F} = -30°\text{C}$

For Exercises 95–99, answers may vary.

101. $\frac{1}{4} - 6(2+8) \div \left(-\frac{1}{3}\right)\left(-\frac{1}{9}\right)$

$= \frac{1}{4} - 6(10) \div \left(-\frac{1}{3}\right)\left(-\frac{1}{9}\right)$

$= \frac{1}{4} - 60 \div \left(-\frac{1}{3}\right)\left(-\frac{1}{9}\right)$

$= \frac{1}{4} - 60 \div (-3)\left(-\frac{1}{9}\right)$

$= \frac{1}{4} + 180\left(-\frac{1}{9}\right)$

$= \frac{1}{4} - 20$

$= \frac{1}{4} - \frac{80}{4} = -\frac{79}{4}$

103. $\left(2 \cdot 5 - \frac{1}{2} \cdot 10\right) \cdot 9 = (10-5) \cdot 9$

$= 5 \cdot 9 = 45$

105. Since $1999 - 1990 = 8$, the year 1999 corresponds to $x = 9$.

$N = -1.65x^2 + 51.8x + 111.44;\ x = 9$

$N = -1.65(9^2) + 51.8(9) + 111.44$
$= 443.99$

According to the formula, the cumulative number of AIDS deaths in 1999 was 443.99 thousand or 443,990.

Review Exercises

107. $-8 - 2 - (-5) + 11$

$= -8 + (-2) + 5 + 11$

$= [(-8) + (-2)] + (5 + 11)$

$= -10 + 16 = 6$

108. $-4(-1)(-3)(2) = -24$

109. Any rational number is a real number that is not an irrational number. One example is $-\frac{3}{4}$.

Chapter 1 Review Exercises

1. $\frac{15}{33} = \frac{\cancel{3} \cdot 5}{\cancel{3} \cdot 11} = \frac{5}{11}$

2. $\frac{40}{75} = \frac{\cancel{5} \cdot 8}{\cancel{5} \cdot 15} = \frac{8}{15}$

3. $\frac{3}{5} \cdot \frac{7}{10} = \frac{3 \cdot 7}{5 \cdot 10} = \frac{21}{50}$

4. $\frac{4}{5} \div \frac{3}{10} = \frac{4}{5} \cdot \frac{10}{3} = \frac{40}{15}$

$= \frac{\cancel{5} \cdot 8}{\cancel{5} \cdot 3} = \frac{8}{3}$

5. $\frac{2}{9} + \frac{4}{9} = \frac{2+4}{9} = \frac{6}{9} = \frac{2}{3}$

6. $\frac{5}{6} + \frac{7}{9} = \frac{5}{6} \cdot \frac{3}{3} + \frac{7}{9} \cdot \frac{2}{2}$

$= \frac{15}{18} + \frac{14}{18} = \frac{29}{18}$

7. $\frac{3}{4} - \frac{2}{15} = \frac{3}{4} \cdot \frac{15}{15} - \frac{2}{15} \cdot \frac{4}{4}$

$= \frac{45}{60} - \frac{8}{60} = \frac{37}{60}$

8. $1 - \frac{1}{4} - \frac{1}{3} = \frac{12}{12} - \frac{3}{12} - \frac{4}{12} = \frac{5}{12}$

At the end of the second day, $\frac{5}{12}$ of the tank is filled.

9.

−2.5

−5 −4 −3 −2 −1 0 1 2 3 4 5 x

10.

$4\frac{3}{4}$

−5 −4 −3 −2 −1 0 1 2 3 4 5 x

11.

$$\begin{array}{r} 0.625 \\ 8\overline{)5.000} \\ \underline{4\,8} \\ 20 \\ \underline{16} \\ 40 \\ \underline{40} \\ 0 \end{array}$$

$\frac{5}{8} = 0.625$

12.

$$\begin{array}{r} 0.2727\ldots \\ 11\overline{)3.0000\ldots} \\ \underline{2\,2} \\ 80 \\ \underline{77} \\ 30 \\ \underline{27} \\ 30 \\ \underline{22} \\ 8 \\ \vdots \end{array}$$

$\frac{3}{11} = 0.\overline{27}$

13. **a.** $\sqrt{81}\ (= 9)$
b. $0, \sqrt{81}$
c. $-17, 0, \sqrt{81}$
d. $-17, -\frac{9}{13}, 0, 0.75, \sqrt{81}$
e. $\sqrt{2}, \pi$
f. All numbers in given set.

In Exercises 14–16, examples may vary.

14. One integer that is not a natural number is -7.

15. One rational number that is not an integer is $\frac{3}{4}$.

16. One real number that is not a rational number is π.

17. $-93 < 17$; -93 is to the left of 17, so -93 is less than 17.

18. $-2 > -200$; -2 is to the right of -200, so -2 is greater than -200.

19. $0 > -\frac{1}{3}$; 0 is to the right of $-\frac{1}{3}$ so $0 > -\frac{1}{3}$.

20. $-\frac{1}{4} < -\frac{1}{5}$; $-\frac{1}{4} = -0.25$ is to the left of $-\frac{1}{5} = -0.2$, so $-\frac{1}{4} < -\frac{1}{5}$.

21. $-13 \geq -11$ is false because neither $-13 > -11$ nor $-13 = -11$ is true.

22. $-126 \leq -126$ is true because $-126 = -126$.

23. $|-58| = 58$ because the distance between -58 and 0 on the number line is 58.

24. $|2.75| = 2.75$ because the distance between 2.75 and 0 on the number line is 2.75.

25. Quadrant IV

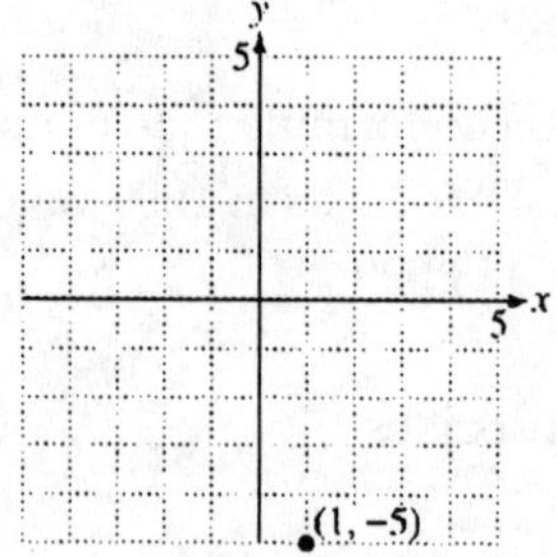

26. Quadrant IV

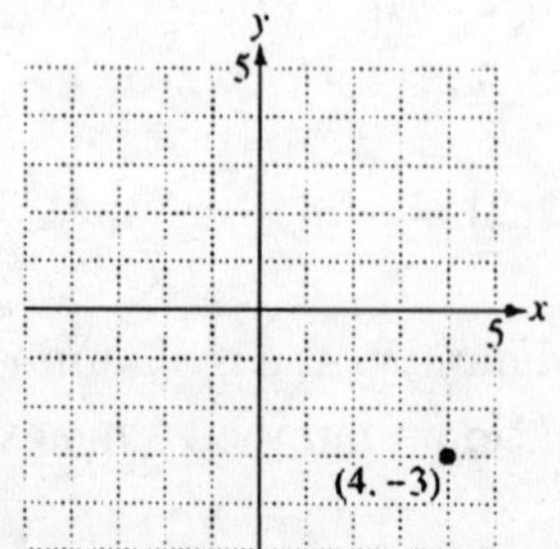

27. Quadrant I

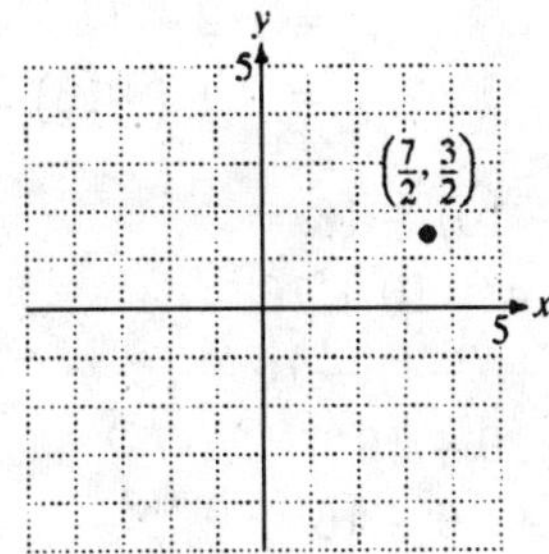

28. Quadrant II

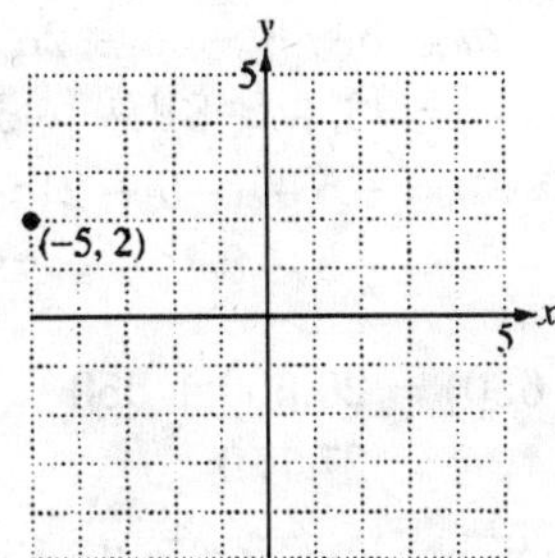

29. $A(5,6)$
$B(-2,0)$
$C(-5,2)$
$D(-4,-2)$
$E(0,-5)$
$F(3,-1)$

30. The number of murders per 100,000 people in 2000 was approximately 7.

31. The murder rate reached a maximum in 1980. There were approximately 10 murders per 100,000 people that year.

32. Approximately 90% of households in the United States have VCRs.

33. According to the graph, fewer than 40% of people in the United States use a camcorder or satellite dish.

34. 45% of 24 million = 0.45 (24 million)
= 10.8 million

There are about 10.8 million female runners in the United States.

35. $7x + 3$; $x = 10$

$$7x + 3 = 7(10) + 3 = 70 + 3 = 73$$

36. $5(x - 4)$; $x = 12$

$$5(x - 4) = 5(12 - 4) = 5 \cdot 8 = 40$$

37. $7 + 13y = 13y + 7$

38. $9(x + 7) = (x + 7)9$

39. $6 + (4 + y) = (6 + 4) + y = 10 + y$

40. $7(10x) = (7 \cdot 10)x = 70x$

41. $$\begin{aligned} 6(4x - 2 + 5y) &= 6(4x) + 6(-2) + 6(5y) \\ &= 24x - 12 + 30y \end{aligned}$$

42. $$\begin{aligned} 4a + 9 + 3a - 7 &= 4a + 3a + 9 - 7 \\ &= (4 + 3)a + (9 - 7) \\ &= 7a + 2 \end{aligned}$$

43. $$\begin{aligned} &6(3x + 4) + 5(2x - 1) \\ &= 6(3x) + 6(4) + 5(2x) + 5(-1) \\ &= 18x + 24 + 10x - 5 \\ &= 18x + 10x + 24 - 5 \\ &= (18 + 10)x + [24 + (-5)] \\ &= 28x + 19 \end{aligned}$$

44. $x - 0.25x$; $x = 2400$

$$\begin{aligned} x - 0.25x &= 2400 - 0.25(2400) \\ &= 2400 - 600 = 1800 \end{aligned}$$

This means that a computer with a regular price of \$2400 will have a sale price of \$1800.

45. $-6 + 8 = 2$

Start at −6. Move 8 units to the right because 8 is positive. Finish at 2.

46. $8 + (-11) = -3$

47. $-\frac{3}{4} + \frac{1}{5} = -\frac{3}{4} \cdot \frac{5}{5} + \frac{1}{5} \cdot \frac{4}{4}$
$= -\frac{15}{20} + \frac{4}{20} = -\frac{11}{20}$

48. $7 + (-5) + (-13) + 4$
$= [7 + (-5)] + (-13) + 4$
$= 2 + (-13) + 4$
$= [2 + (-13)] + 4$
$= -11 + 4 = -7$

49. $8x + (-6y) + (-12x) + 11y$
$= 8x + (-12x) + (-6y) + 11y$
$= [8 + (-12)]x + (-6 + 11)y$
$= -4x + 5y$ or $5y - 4x$

50. $10(4 - 3y) + 28y$
$= 10(4) + 10(-3y) + 28y$
$= 40 - 30y + 28y$
$= 40 + (-30 + 28)y$
$= 40 - 2y$

51. $-1312 + 512 = -800$

The person's elevation is 800 feet below sea level.

52. $25 - 3 + 2 + 1 - 4 + 2$
$= 25 + (-3) + 2 + 1 + (-4) + 2$
$= 23$

The reservoir's water level at the end of five months is 23 feet.

53. $9 - 13 = 9 + (-13)$

54. $-9 - (-13) = -9 + 13 = 4$

55. $-\frac{7}{10} - \frac{1}{2} = -\frac{7}{10} - \frac{1}{2} \cdot \frac{5}{5}$
$= -\frac{7}{10} - \frac{5}{10}$
$= -\frac{12}{10} = -\frac{6}{5}$

56. $-3.6 - (-2.1) = -3.6 + 2.1 = -1.5$

57. $-7 - (-5) + 11 - 16 = -7 + 5 + 11 + (-16)$
$= -2 + 11 + (-16)$
$= 9 + (-16) = -7$

58. $-25 - 4 - (-10) + 16$
$= -25 - 4 + 10 + 16$
$= (-25) + (-4) + 10 + 16$
$= -29 + 10 + 16$
$= (-29) + 10 + 16$
$= -19 + 16$
$= (-19) + 16 = -3$

59. $3 - 6a - 8 - 2a = 3 - 8 - 6a - 2a$
$= [3 + (-8)] + [-6a - 2a]$
$= -5 + (-6 - 2)a$
$= -5 - 8a$

60. $26{,}500 - (-650) = 26{,}500 + 650$
$= 27{,}150$

The difference in elevation is 27,150 feet.

61. $(-7)(-12) = 84$

62. $\frac{3}{5}\left(-\frac{5}{11}\right) = -\frac{3 \cdot \cancel{5}}{\cancel{5} \cdot 11} = -\frac{3}{11}$

63. $5(-3)(-2)(-4) = -120$

64. $\frac{45}{-5} = 45\left(-\frac{1}{5}\right) = -9$

65. $-17 \div 0$ is undefined.

66. $-\frac{4}{5} \div \left(-\frac{2}{5}\right) = -\frac{4}{5}\left(-\frac{5}{2}\right) = \frac{20}{10} = 2$

67. $-4\left(-\frac{3}{4}x\right) = \left[-4\left(-\frac{3}{4}\right)\right]x = 3x$

68. $-3(2x - 1) - (4 - 5x)$
$= -3(2x) + (-3)(-1) - 4 + 5x$
$= -6x + 3 - 4 + 5x$
$= -6x + 5x + 3 - 4$
$= (-6 + 5)x + [3 + (-4)]$
$= -1x - 1 = -x - 1$

69. $(-6)^2 = (-6)(-6) = 36$

70. $-6^2 = -6 \cdot 6 = -36$

71. $(-2)^5 = (-2)(-2)(-2)(-2)(-2) = -32$

72. $4x^3 + 2x^3 = (4+2)x^3 = 6x^3$

73. $4x^3 + 4x^2$ cannot be simplified. The terms $4x^3 + 4x^2$ are not like terms because they have different variable factors, x^3 and x^2.

74. $-40 \div 5 \cdot 2 = -8 \cdot 2 = -16$

75. $-6 + (-2) \cdot 5 = -6 + (-10) = -16$

76. $6 - 4(-3+2) = 6 - 4(-1) = 6 + 4 = 10$

77.
$$\begin{aligned} 28 \div (2 - 4^2) &= 28 \div (2 - 16) \\ &= 28 \div [2 + (-16)] \\ &= 28 \div (-14) = -2 \end{aligned}$$

78.
$$\begin{aligned} 36 - 24 \div 4 \cdot 3 - 1 &= 36 - 6 \cdot 3 - 1 \\ &= 36 - 18 - 1 \\ &= 18 - 1 = 17 \end{aligned}$$

79.
$$\begin{aligned} -8[-4 - 5(-3)] &= -8(-4 + 15) \\ &= -8(11) = -88 \end{aligned}$$

80.
$$\begin{aligned} \frac{6(-10+3)}{2(-15) - 9(-3)} &= \frac{6(-7)}{-30+27} \\ &= \frac{-42}{-3} = 14 \end{aligned}$$

81. $x^2 - 2x + 3;\ x = -1$

$$\begin{aligned} x^2 - 2x + 3 &= (-1)^2 - 2(-1) + 3 \\ &= 1 + 2 + 3 = 6 \end{aligned}$$

82. $-x^2 - 7x;\ x = -2$

$$\begin{aligned} -x^2 - 7x &= -(-2)^2 - 7(-2) \\ &= -4 + 14 = 10 \end{aligned}$$

83.
$$\begin{aligned} 4[7(a-1)+2] &= 4(7a - 7 + 2) \\ &= 4(7a - 5) \\ &= 4(7a) + 4(-5) \\ &= 28a - 20 \end{aligned}$$

84.
$$\begin{aligned} -6[4 - (y+2)] &= -6(4 - y - 2) \\ &= -6(2 - y) \\ &= -6(2) + (-6)(-y) \\ &= -12 + 6y \quad \text{or} \quad 6y - 12 \end{aligned}$$

85. Since 2004 − 1984 = 20, the year 2004 corresponds to $x = 20$.

$N = 0.07x + 4.1;\ x = 20$

$$\begin{aligned} N = 0.07x + 4.1 &= 0.07(20) + 4.1 \\ &= 1.4 + 4.1 \\ &= 5.5 \end{aligned}$$

According to the formula, 5.5 women will be enrolled in U.S. colleges in 2004. This is close to the enrollment shown in the line graph, which is about 5.3 million.

86. $N = 0.01x + 3.9;\ x = 20$

$$\begin{aligned} N = 0.01x + 3.9 &= 0.01(20) + 3.9 \\ &= 0.2 + 3.9 \\ &= 4.1 \end{aligned}$$

According to the formula, 4.1 million men will be enrolled in U.S. colleges in 2004. The line graph also shows about 4.1 million.

87. Since 1990 − 1980 = 10, the year 1990 corresponds to $x = 10$.

$N = 2x^2 + 22x + 320;\ x = 10$

$$\begin{aligned} N &= 2x^2 + 22x + 320 \\ &= 2(10^2) + 22(10) + 320 \\ &= 200 + 220 + 320 \\ &= 740 \end{aligned}$$

According to the formula, the U.S. prison population in 1990 was 740 thousand or 740,000. This is very close to the number shown in the line graph.

88. The prison population is growing at an increasing rate.

Chapter 1 Test

1. $1.4-(-2.6)=1.4+2.6=4$

2. $-9+3+(-11)+6=(-9+3)+(-11)+6$
$=-6+(-11)+6$
$=-17+6=-11$

3. $3(-17)=-51$

4. $\left(-\frac{3}{7}\right)\div\left(-\frac{15}{7}\right)=\left(-\frac{3}{7}\right)\left(-\frac{7}{15}\right)=\frac{21}{105}$
$=\frac{\cancel{21}\cdot 1}{\cancel{21}\cdot 5}=\frac{1}{5}$

5. $-50\div 10=-50\left(\frac{1}{10}\right)=-5$

6. $-6-(5-12)=-6-(-7)=-6+7=1$

7. $(-3)(-4)\div(7-10)$
$=(-3)(-4)\div[7+(-10)]$
$=(-3)(-4)\div(-3)$
$=12\div(-3)=-4$

8. $(6-8)^2(5-7)^3=(-2)^2(-2)^3$
$=4(-8)=-32$

9. $\frac{3(-2)-2(2)}{-2(8-3)}=\frac{-6-4}{-2(5)}$
$=\frac{-6+(-4)}{-2(5)}$
$=\frac{-10}{-10}=1$

10. $11x-(7x-4)=11x-7x+4$
$=11x+(-7x)+4$
$=[11+(-7)]x+4$
$=4x+4$

11. $5(3x-4y)-(2x-y)$
$=5(3x)+5(-4y)-2x+y$
$=15x-20y-2x+y$
$=15x-2x-20y+y$
$=13x-19y$

12. $6-2[3(x+1)-5]=6-2[3x+3-5]$
$=6-2(3x-2)$
$=6-6x+4$
$=10-6x$

13. Rational numbers can be written as the quotient of two integers.
$-7=-\frac{7}{1}, -\frac{4}{5}=\frac{-4}{5}, 0=\frac{0}{1}, 0.25=\frac{1}{4},$
$\sqrt{4}=2=\frac{2}{1}$, and $\frac{22}{7}=\frac{22}{7}$.
Therefore, $-7, -\frac{4}{5}, 0, 0.25, \sqrt{4}$, and, $\frac{22}{7}$ are the rational numbers of the set.

14. $-1>-100$; -1 is to the right of -100 on the number line, so -1 is greater than -100.

15. $|-12.8|=12.8$ because the distance between 12.8 and 0 on the number line is 12.8.

16. Quadrant II

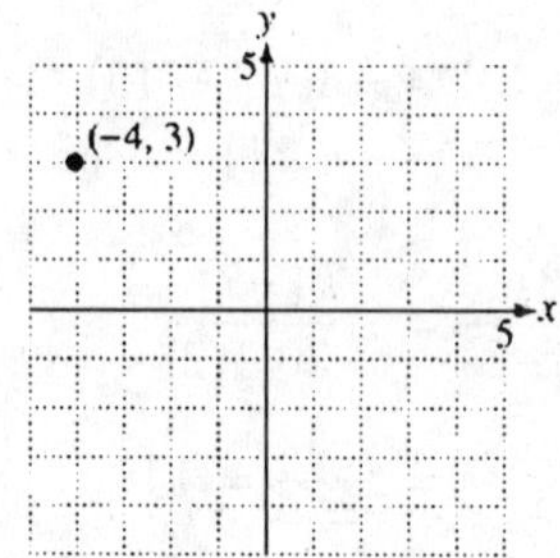

17. The coordinates of point A are $(-5,-2)$.

18. $5(x-7)$; $x=4$

$5(x-7)=5(4-7)=5(-3)=-15$

19. x^2-5x; $x=-10$

$x^2-5x=(-10)^2-5(-10)$
$=100+50=150$

20. $2(x+3)=2(3+x)$

21. $-6(4x)=(-6\cdot 4)x=-24x$

22. $7(5x - 1 + 2y) = 7(5x) + 7(-1) + 7(2y)$
$= 35x - 7 + 14y$

23. The coordinates of point A are $(30, 200)$. This means that 30 years after the elk were introduced into the habitat, the elk population was 200.

24. The point $(0, 50)$ indicates that 50 elk were introduced into the habitat.

25. According to the bar graph, approximately 9.7 million U.S. households will be investing online in 2003.

26. A good estimate is 37% of 17 = $0.37(17)$ $= 6.29 \approx 6.3$.

There are approximately 6.3 million acres of impaired lakes in the United States.

27. $T = 3(A - 20)^2 \div 50 + 10$; $A = 30$

$$\begin{aligned} T &= 3(A - 20)^2 \div 50 + 10 \\ &= 3(30 - 20)^2 \div 50 + 10 \\ &= 3(10^2) \div 50 + 10 \\ &= 300 \div 50 + 10 \\ &= 6 + 10 = 16 \end{aligned}$$

According to the formula, it takes a 30-year-old runner 16 seconds to run the 100-yard dash.

28. According to the line graph, the average mortgage loan in 1990 was about \$95 thousand or \$95,000.

29. Since $1990 - 1980 = 10$, the year 1990 corresponds to $x = 10$.

$N = 3.5x + 58$; $x = 10$

$$\begin{aligned} N = 3.5x + 58 &= 3.5(10) + 58 \\ &= 35 + 58 = 93 \end{aligned}$$

According to the formula, the average mortgage loan in 1990 was \$93 thousand or \$93,000.

30. $16{,}200 - (-830) = 17{,}030$

The difference in elevations is 17,030 feet.

Chapter 2

LINEAR EQUATIONS AND INEQUALITIES IN ONE VARIABLE

2.1 The Addition Property of Equality

2.1 CHECK POINTS

CHECK POINT 1

$5x - 3 = 17$

a. Substitute 3 for x.

$$\begin{aligned} 5x - 3 &= 17 \\ 5(3) - 3 &\stackrel{?}{=} 17 \\ 15 - 3 &\stackrel{?}{=} 17 \\ 12 &= 17 \text{ false} \end{aligned}$$

3 is not a solution to the given equation.

b. Substitute 4 for x.

$$\begin{aligned} 5x - 3 &= 17 \\ 5(4) - 3 &\stackrel{?}{=} 17 \\ 20 - 3 &\stackrel{?}{=} 17 \\ 17 &= 17 \text{ true} \end{aligned}$$

4 is a solution to the given equation.

CHECK POINT 2

$$\begin{aligned} x - 5 &= 12 \\ x - 5 + 5 &= 12 + 5 \\ x &= 17 \end{aligned}$$

Check

$$\begin{aligned} x - 5 &= 12 \\ 17 - 5 &= 12 \\ 12 &= 12 \text{ true} \end{aligned}$$

Because the check results in a true statement, the solution to the given equation is 17.

CHECK POINT 3

$$\begin{aligned} x + 2.8 &= 5.09 \\ x + 2.8 - 2.8 &= 5.09 - 2.8 \\ x &= 2.29 \end{aligned}$$

Check:

$$\begin{aligned} x + 2.8 &= 5.09 \\ 2.29 + 2.8 &\stackrel{?}{=} 5.09 \\ 5.09 &= 5.09 \text{ true} \end{aligned}$$

The solution is 2.29.

CHECK POINT 4

$$\begin{aligned} -\frac{1}{2} &= x - \frac{3}{4} \\ -\frac{1}{2} + \frac{3}{4} &= x - \frac{3}{4} + \frac{3}{4} \\ -\frac{2}{4} + \frac{3}{4} &= x \\ \frac{1}{4} &= x \end{aligned}$$

Check:

$$\begin{aligned} -\frac{1}{2} &= x - \frac{3}{4} \\ -\frac{1}{2} &\stackrel{?}{=} \frac{1}{4} - \frac{3}{4} \\ -\frac{1}{2} &\stackrel{?}{=} -\frac{2}{4} \\ -\frac{1}{2} &= -\frac{1}{2} \text{ true} \end{aligned}$$

The solution is $\frac{1}{4}$.

CHECK POINT 5

$$\begin{aligned} 8y + 7 - 7y - 10 &= 6 + 4 \\ y - 3 &= 10 \\ y - 3 + 3 &= 10 + 3 \\ y &= 13 \end{aligned}$$

Check:

$$\begin{aligned} 8y + 7 - 7y - 10 &= 6 + 4 \\ 8(13) + 7 - 7(13) - 10 &\stackrel{?}{=} 6 + 4 \\ 104 + 7 - 91 - 10 &\stackrel{?}{=} 6 + 4 \\ 111 - 101 &\stackrel{?}{=} 10 \\ 10 &= 10 \text{ true} \end{aligned}$$

The solution is 13.

CHECK POINT 6

$$\begin{aligned} 7x &= 12 + 6x \\ 7x - 6x &= 12 + 6x - 6x \\ x &= 12 \end{aligned}$$

Check:

$$\begin{aligned} 7x &= 12 + 6x \\ 7(12) &\stackrel{?}{=} 12 + 6(12) \\ 84 &\stackrel{?}{=} 12 + 72 \\ 84 &= 84 \text{ true} \end{aligned}$$

The solution is 12.

CHECK POINT 7

$$\begin{aligned} 3x - 6 &= 2x + 5 \\ 3x - 2x - 6 &= 2x - 2x + 5 \\ x - 6 &= 5 \\ x - 6 + 6 &= 5 + 6 \\ x &= 11 \end{aligned}$$

Check:

$$\begin{aligned} 3x - 6 &= 2x + 5 \\ 3(11) - 6 &\stackrel{?}{=} 2(11) + 5 \\ 33 - 6 &\stackrel{?}{=} 22 + 5 \\ 27 &= 27 \text{ true} \end{aligned}$$

The solution is 11.

CHECK POINT 8

Substitute 50 for A in the given formula, and find the corresponding value of V.

$$\begin{aligned} V + 900 &= 60A \\ V + 900 &= 60(50) \\ V + 900 &= 3000 \\ V + 900 - 900 &= 3000 - 900 \\ V &= 2100 \end{aligned}$$

According to the formula, the vocabulary of a 50-month-old child is 2100 words.

EXERCISE SET 2.1

1.

$$\begin{aligned} x - 7 &= 13 \\ x - 7 + 7 &= 13 + 7 \\ x + 0 &= 20 \\ x &= 20 \end{aligned}$$

Check:

$$\begin{aligned} x - 7 &\stackrel{?}{=} 13 \\ 20 - 7 &= 13 \\ 13 &= 13 \end{aligned}$$

The solution is 20.

3.

$$\begin{aligned} z + 5 &= -12 \\ z + 5 &= -12 - 5 \\ z &= -17 \end{aligned}$$

Check:

$$\begin{aligned} z + 5 &\stackrel{?}{=} -12 \\ -17 + 5 &\stackrel{?}{=} -12 \\ -12 &= -12 \end{aligned}$$

The solution is -17.

5.

$$\begin{aligned} -3 &= x + 14 \\ -3 &= x + 14 - 14 \\ -17 &= x \end{aligned}$$

Check:

$$\begin{aligned} -3 &\stackrel{?}{=} -17 + 14 \\ -3 &= -3 \end{aligned}$$

The solution is -17.

7. $-18 = y - 5$

$-18 + 5 = y - 5 + 5$

$-13 = y$

Check:

$-18 \stackrel{?}{=} -13 - 5$

$-18 = -18$

The solution is -13.

9. $7 + z = 13$

$z = 13 - 7$

$z = 6$

Check:

$7 + 6 \stackrel{?}{=} 13$

$13 = 13$

The solution is 6.

11. $-3 + y = -17$

$y = -17 + 3$

$y = -14$

Check:

$-3 - 14 \stackrel{?}{=} -17$

$-17 = -17$

The solution is -14.

13. $x + \frac{1}{3} = \frac{7}{3}$

$x = \frac{7}{3} - \frac{1}{3}$

$x = 2$

Check:

$2 + \frac{1}{3} \stackrel{?}{=} \frac{7}{3}$

$\frac{6}{3} + \frac{1}{3} = \frac{7}{3}$

$\frac{7}{3} = \frac{7}{3}$

The solution is 2.

15. $t + \frac{5}{6} = -\frac{7}{12}$

$t = -\frac{7}{12} - \frac{5}{6}$

$t = -\frac{7}{12} - \frac{10}{12} = -\frac{17}{12}$

Check:

$-\frac{17}{12} + \frac{5}{6} \stackrel{?}{=} -\frac{7}{12}$

$-\frac{17}{12} + \frac{10}{12} \stackrel{?}{=} -\frac{7}{12}$

$-\frac{7}{12} = -\frac{7}{12}$

The solution is $-\frac{17}{12}$.

17. $x - \frac{3}{4} = \frac{9}{2}$

$x - \frac{3}{4} + \frac{3}{4} = \frac{9}{2} + \frac{3}{4}$

$x = \frac{21}{4}$

Check:

$\frac{21}{4} - \frac{3}{4} \stackrel{?}{=} \frac{9}{2}$

$\frac{18}{4} \stackrel{?}{=} \frac{9}{2}$

$\frac{9}{2} = \frac{9}{2}$

The solution is $\frac{21}{4}$.

19. $-\frac{1}{5} + y = -\frac{3}{4}$

$y = -\frac{3}{4} + \frac{1}{5}$

$y = -\frac{15}{20} + \frac{4}{20} = -\frac{11}{20}$

Check:

$$-\frac{1}{5}-\frac{11}{20}\stackrel{?}{=}-\frac{3}{4}$$
$$-\frac{4}{20}-\frac{11}{20}\stackrel{?}{=}-\frac{3}{4}$$
$$-\frac{15}{20}\stackrel{?}{=}-\frac{3}{4}$$
$$-\frac{3}{4}=-\frac{3}{4}$$

The solution is $-\frac{11}{20}$.

21.
$$3.2+x=7.5$$
$$3.2+x-3.2=7.5-3.2$$
$$x=4.3$$

Check:

$$3.2+4.3\stackrel{?}{=}7.5$$
$$7.5=7.5$$

The solution is 4.3.

23.
$$x+\frac{3}{4}=-\frac{9}{2}$$
$$x+\frac{3}{4}-\frac{3}{4}=-\frac{9}{2}-\frac{3}{4}$$
$$x=-\frac{21}{4}$$

Check:

$$-\frac{21}{4}+\frac{3}{4}\stackrel{?}{=}-\frac{9}{2}$$
$$-\frac{18}{4}=-\frac{9}{2}$$
$$-\frac{9}{2}=-\frac{9}{2}$$

The solution is $-\frac{21}{4}$.

25.
$$5=-13+y$$
$$5+13=y$$
$$18=y$$

Check:

$$5\stackrel{?}{=}-13+18$$
$$5=5$$

The solution is 18.

27.
$$-\frac{3}{5}=-\frac{3}{2}+s$$
$$-\frac{3}{5}+\frac{3}{2}=s$$
$$-\frac{6}{10}+\frac{15}{10}=s$$
$$\frac{9}{10}=s$$

Check:

$$-\frac{3}{5}=-\frac{3}{2}+\frac{9}{10}$$
$$-\frac{6}{10}=-\frac{15}{10}+\frac{9}{10}$$
$$-\frac{6}{10}=-\frac{6}{10}$$

The solution is $\frac{9}{10}$.

29.
$$830+y=520$$
$$y=520-830$$
$$y=-310$$

Check:

$$830-310\stackrel{?}{=}520$$
$$520=520$$

The solution is -310.

31.
$$r+3.7=8$$
$$r=8-3.7$$
$$r=4.3$$

Check:

$$4.3+3.7\stackrel{?}{=}8$$
$$8=8$$

The solution is 4.3.

33.
$$-3.7+m=-3.7$$
$$m=-3.7+3.7$$
$$m=0$$

Check:

$$-3.7+0\stackrel{?}{=}-3.7$$
$$-3.7=-3.7$$

The solution is 0.

35. $6y + 3 - 5y = 14$

$$y + 3 = 14$$
$$y = 14 - 3$$
$$y = 11$$

Check:

$$6(11) + 3 - 5(11) \stackrel{?}{=} 14$$
$$66 + 3 - 55 \stackrel{?}{=} 14$$
$$14 = 14$$

The solution is 11.

37. $7 - 5x + 8 + 2x + 4x - 3 = 2 + 3 \cdot 5$

$$x + 12 = 2 + 15$$
$$x = 17 - 12$$
$$x = 5$$

Check:

$$7 - 5(5) + 8 + 2(5) + 4(5) - 3 \stackrel{?}{=} 2 + 3 \cdot 5$$
$$7 - 25 + 8 + 10 + 20 - 3 \stackrel{?}{=} 2 + 15$$
$$45 - 18 \stackrel{?}{=} 17$$
$$17 = 17$$

The solution is 5.

39. $7y + 4 = 6y - 9$

$$7y - 6y + 4 = -9$$
$$y = -9 - 4$$
$$y = -13$$

Check:

$$7(-13) + 4 \stackrel{?}{=} 6(-13) - 9$$
$$-91 + 4 \stackrel{?}{=} -78 - 9$$
$$-87 = -87$$

The solution is -13.

41. $18 - 7x = 12 - 6x$

$$18 = 12 + x$$
$$6 = x$$

Check:

$$18 - 7(6) \stackrel{?}{=} 12 - 6(6)$$
$$18 - 42 \stackrel{?}{=} 12 - 36$$
$$-24 = -24$$

The solution is 6.

43. Since $2005 - 1995 = 10$, the year 2005 corresponds to $x = 10$.

$D - 15x = 62$; $x = 10$

$$D - 15x = 62$$
$$D - 15(10) = 62$$
$$D - 150 = 62$$
$$D = 62 + 150$$
$$D = 212$$

According to the formula, about \$212 billion will be spend on prescription drugs in the United States in 2005.

45. $C + M = S$; $S = 1850$, $M = 150$

$$C + M = S$$
$$C + 150 = 1850$$
$$C = 1850 - 150$$
$$C = 1700$$

The cost of the computer is \$1700.

47. $d + 525{,}000 = 5000c$; $c = 210$

$$d + 525{,}000 = 5000c$$
$$d + 525{,}000 = 5000(210)$$
$$d + 525{,}000 = 1{,}050{,}000$$
$$d = 1{,}050{,}000 - 525{,}000$$
$$d = 525{,}000$$

According to the formula, 525,000 deaths per year from heart disease can be expected at this cholesterol level.

For Exercises 49–53, answers may vary.

55. $|x| + 4 = 10$

$$|x| = 10 - 4$$
$$|x| = 6$$

There are two numbers whose absolute value (distance from 0) is 6: -6 and 6. Therefore, the equation has two solutions, -6 and 6.

57.
$$6.9825 = 4.2296 + y$$
$$6.9825 - 4.2296 = y$$
$$2.7529 = y$$

The solution is 2.7529.

Review Exercises

58. Quadrant II

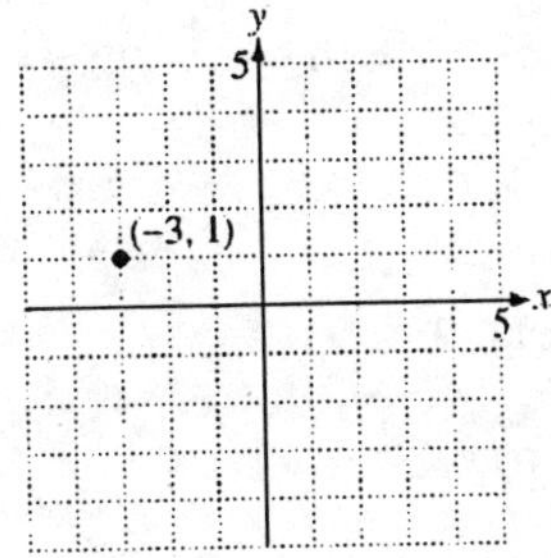

59. $-16 - 8 \div 4 \cdot (-2) = -16 - 2(-2)$
$= -16 + 4$
$= -12$

60. $3[7x - 2(5x - 1)] = 3(7x - 10x + 2)$
$= 3(-3x + 2)$
$= -9x + 6 \text{ or } 6 - 9x$

2.2 The Multiplication Property of Equality

2.2 CHECK POINTS

CHECK POINT 1

$$\frac{x}{3} = 12$$
$$3 \cdot \frac{x}{3} = 3 \cdot 12$$
$$1x = 36$$
$$x = 36$$

The solution is 36.

CHECK POINT 2

a. $4x = 84$
$$\frac{4x}{4} = \frac{84}{4}$$
$$x = 21$$

The solution is 21.

b. $-11y = 44$
$$\frac{-11y}{-11} = \frac{44}{-11}$$
$$y = -4$$

The solution is -4.

c. $-15.5 = 5z$
$$\frac{-15.5}{5} = \frac{5z}{5}$$
$$-3.1 = z$$

The solution is -3.1.

CHECK POINT 3

a. $\frac{2}{3}y = 16$
$$\frac{3}{2}\left(\frac{2}{3}y\right) = \frac{3}{2} \cdot 16$$
$$1y = 24$$
$$y = 24$$

The solution is 24.

b. $28 = -\frac{7}{4}x$
$$-\frac{4}{7}(28) = -\frac{4}{7}\left(-\frac{7}{4}x\right)$$
$$-16 = 1x$$
$$-16 = x$$

The solution is -16.

CHECK POINT 4

a.

$$\begin{aligned} -x &= 5 \\ -1x &= 5 \\ (-1)(-1x) &= (-1)(5) \\ 1x &= -5 \\ x &= -5 \end{aligned}$$

The solution is -5.

b.

$$\begin{aligned} -x &= -3 \\ -1x &= -3 \\ (-1)(-1x) &= (-1)(-3) \\ 1x &= 3 \\ x &= 3 \end{aligned}$$

The solution is 3.

CHECK POINT 5

$$\begin{aligned} 4x + 3 &= 27 \\ 4x + 3 - 3 &= 27 - 3 \\ 4x &= 24 \\ \frac{4x}{4} &= \frac{24}{4} \\ x &= 6 \end{aligned}$$

The solution is 6.

CHECK POINT 6

$$\begin{aligned} -4y - 15 &= 25 \\ -4y - 15 + 15 &= 25 + 15 \\ -4y &= 40 \\ \frac{-4y}{-4} &= \frac{40}{-4} \\ y &= -10 \end{aligned}$$

The solution is -10.

CHECK POINT 7

$$\begin{aligned} 2x - 15 &= -4x + 21 \\ 2x + 4x - 15 &= -4x + 4x + 21 \\ 6x - 15 &= 21 \\ 6x - 15 + 15 &= 21 + 15 \\ 6x &= 36 \\ \frac{6x}{6} &= \frac{36}{6} \\ x &= 6 \end{aligned}$$

The solution is 6.

CHECK POINT 8

$D = 0.2F - 1$

Substitute 19 for D and solve for F.

$$\begin{aligned} D &= 0.2F - 1 \\ 19 &= 0.2F - 1 \\ 19 + 1 &= 0.2F - 1 + 1 \\ 20 &= 0.2F \\ \frac{20}{0.2} &= \frac{0.2F}{0.2} \\ 100 &= F \end{aligned}$$

The daily fat intake is 100 grams.

EXERCISE SET 2.2

1.

$$\begin{aligned} \frac{x}{3} &= 4 \\ 3 \cdot \frac{x}{3} &= 3 \cdot 4 \\ 1x &= 12 \\ x &= 12 \end{aligned}$$

Check:

$$\begin{aligned} \frac{12}{3} &\stackrel{?}{=} 4 \\ 4 &= 4 \end{aligned}$$

The solution is 12.

3. $\frac{x}{-5} = 11$

$-5 \cdot \frac{x}{-5} = -5(11)$

$1x = -55$

$x = -55$

Check:

$\frac{-55}{-5} \stackrel{?}{=} 11$

$11 = 11$

The solution is -55.

5. $5y = 45$

$\frac{5y}{5} = \frac{45}{5}$

$y = 9$

Check:

$5(9) \stackrel{?}{=} 45$

$45 = 45$

The solution is 9.

7. $-7y = 56$

$\frac{-7y}{-7} = \frac{56}{-7}$

$y = -8$

Check:

$-7(-8) \stackrel{?}{=} 56$

$56 = 56$

The solution is -8.

9. $-24 = 8z$

$\frac{-24}{8} = \frac{8z}{8}$

$-3 = z$

Check:

$-24 \stackrel{?}{=} 8(-3)$

$-24 = -24$

The solution is -3.

11. $-15 = -3z$

$\frac{-15}{-3} = \frac{-3z}{-3}$

$5 = z$

Check:

$-15 \stackrel{?}{=} -3(5)$

$-15 = -15$

The solution is 5.

13. $-8x = 2$

$\frac{-8x}{-8} = \frac{2}{-8}$

$x = -\frac{2}{8} = -\frac{1}{4}$

Check:

$-8\left(-\frac{1}{4}\right) \stackrel{?}{=} 2$

$2 = 2$

The solution is $-\frac{1}{4}$.

15. $7y = 0$

$\frac{7y}{7} = \frac{0}{7}$

$y = 0$

Check:

$7(0) \stackrel{?}{=} 0$

$0 = 0$

The solution is 0.

17. $\frac{2}{3}y = 8$

$\frac{3}{2}\left(\frac{2}{3}y\right) = \frac{3}{2}(8)$

$1y = \frac{3}{2} \cdot \frac{8}{1} = \frac{24}{2}$

$y = 12$

Check:

$$\frac{2}{3}(12) \stackrel{?}{=} 8$$
$$\frac{2}{3} \cdot \frac{12}{1} \stackrel{?}{=} 8$$
$$\frac{24}{3} \stackrel{?}{=} 8$$
$$3 = 3$$

The solution is 12.

19.
$$21 = -\frac{7}{2}x$$
$$-\frac{2}{7}(21) = -\frac{2}{7}\left(-\frac{7}{2}x\right)$$
$$-\frac{42}{7} = 1x$$
$$-6 = x$$

Check:

$$21 \stackrel{?}{=} -\frac{7}{2}(-6)$$
$$21 \stackrel{?}{=} \frac{42}{2}$$
$$21 = 21$$

The solution is -6.

21.
$$-x = 7$$
$$-1x = 7$$
$$-1(-1x) = -1(7)$$
$$x = -7$$

Check:

$$-(-7) \stackrel{?}{=} 7$$
$$7 = 7$$

The solution is -7.

23. $-15 = -y$

$15 = y$

Check:

$$-15 = -15$$

The solution is 15.

25.
$$-\frac{x}{5} = -10$$
$$5\left(-\frac{x}{5}\right) = 5(-10)$$
$$-x = -50$$
$$x = 50$$

Check:

$$-\frac{50}{5} \stackrel{?}{=} -10$$
$$-10 = -10$$

The solution is 50.

27.
$$2x - 8x = 24$$
$$2x + (-8x) = 24$$
$$-6x = 24$$
$$\frac{-6x}{-6} = \frac{24}{-6}$$
$$x = -4$$

Check:

$$2(-4) - 8(-4) \stackrel{?}{=} 24$$
$$-8 - (-32) \stackrel{?}{=} 24$$
$$-8 + 32 \stackrel{?}{=} 24$$
$$24 = 24$$

The solution is -4.

29.
$$2x + 1 = 1$$
$$2x + 1 - 1 = 11 - 1$$
$$2x = 10$$
$$\frac{2x}{2} = \frac{10}{2}$$
$$x = 5$$

Check:

$$2(5) + 1 \stackrel{?}{=} 11$$
$$10 + 1 \stackrel{?}{=} 11$$
$$11 = 11$$

The solution is 5.

31.
$$\begin{aligned} 2x - 3 &= 9 \\ 2x - 3 + 3 &= 9 + 3 \\ 2x &= 12 \\ \frac{2x}{2} &= \frac{12}{2} \\ x &= 6 \end{aligned}$$

Check:

$$\begin{aligned} 2(6) - 3 &\stackrel{?}{=} 9 \\ 12 - 3 &\stackrel{?}{=} 9 \\ 9 &= 9 \end{aligned}$$

The solution is 6.

33.
$$\begin{aligned} -2y + 5 &= 7 \\ -2y + 5 - 5 &= 7 - 5 \\ -2y &= 2 \\ \frac{-2y}{-2} &= \frac{2}{-2} \\ y &= -1 \end{aligned}$$

Check:

$$\begin{aligned} -2(-1) + 5 &\stackrel{?}{=} 7 \\ 2 + 5 &\stackrel{?}{=} 7 \\ 7 &= 7 \end{aligned}$$

The solution is -1.

35.
$$\begin{aligned} -3y - 7 &= -1 \\ -3y - 7 + 7 &= -1 + 7 \\ -3y &= 6 \\ \frac{-3y}{-3} &= \frac{6}{-3} \\ y &= -2 \end{aligned}$$

Check:

$$\begin{aligned} -3(-2) - 7 &\stackrel{?}{=} -1 \\ 6 - 7 &\stackrel{?}{=} -1 \\ -1 &= -1 \end{aligned}$$

The solution is -2.

37.
$$\begin{aligned} 12 &= 4z + 3 \\ 12 - 3 &= 4z + 3 - 3 \\ 9 &= 4z \\ \frac{9}{4} &= \frac{4z}{4} \\ \frac{9}{4} &= z \end{aligned}$$

Check:

$$\begin{aligned} 12 &\stackrel{?}{=} 4\left(\frac{9}{4}\right) + 3 \\ 12 &\stackrel{?}{=} 9 + 3 \\ 12 &= 12 \end{aligned}$$

The solution is $\frac{9}{4}$.

39.
$$\begin{aligned} -x - 3 &= 3 \\ -x - 3 + 3 &= 3 + 3 \\ -x &= 6 \\ x &= -6 \end{aligned}$$

Check:

$$\begin{aligned} -(-6) - 3 &\stackrel{?}{=} 3 \\ 6 - 3 &\stackrel{?}{=} 3 \\ 3 &= 3 \end{aligned}$$

The solution is -6.

41.
$$\begin{aligned} 6y &= 2y - 12 \\ 6y + 12 &= 2y - 12 + 12 \\ 6y + 12 &= 2y \\ 6y + 12 - 6y &= 2y - 6y \\ 12 &= -4y \\ \frac{12}{-4} &= \frac{-4y}{-4} \\ -3 &= y \end{aligned}$$

Check:

$$\begin{aligned} 6(-3) &\stackrel{?}{=} 2(-3) - 12 \\ -18 &\stackrel{?}{=} -6 - 12 \\ -18 &= -18 \end{aligned}$$

The solution is -3.

43.
$$\begin{aligned} 3z &= -2z - 15 \\ 3z + 2z &= -2z - 15 + 2z \\ 5z &= -15 \\ \frac{5z}{5} &= \frac{-15}{5} \\ z &= -3 \end{aligned}$$

Check:

$$\begin{aligned} 3(-3) &\stackrel{?}{=} -2(-3) - 15 \\ -9 &\stackrel{?}{=} 6 - 15 \\ -9 &= -9 \end{aligned}$$

The solution is -3.

45.
$$\begin{aligned} -5x &= -2x - 12 \\ -5x + 2x &= -2x - 12 + 2x \\ -3x &= -12 \\ \frac{-3x}{-3} &= \frac{-12}{-3} \\ x &= 4 \end{aligned}$$

Check:

$$\begin{aligned} -5(4) &\stackrel{?}{=} -2(4) - 12 \\ -20 &\stackrel{?}{=} -8 - 12 \\ -20 &= -20 \end{aligned}$$

The solution is 4.

47.
$$\begin{aligned} 8y + 4 &= 2y - 5 \\ 8y + 4 - 2y &= 2y - 5 - 2y \\ 6y + 4 &= -5 \\ 6y + 4 - 4 &= -5 - 4 \\ 6y &= -9 \\ \frac{6y}{6} &= \frac{-9}{6} \\ y &= -\frac{3}{2} \end{aligned}$$

Check:

$$\begin{aligned} 8\left(-\frac{3}{2}\right) + 4 &\stackrel{?}{=} 2\left(-\frac{3}{2}\right) - 5 \\ -12 + 4 &\stackrel{?}{=} -3 - 5 \\ -8 &= -8 \end{aligned}$$

The solution is $-\frac{3}{2}$.

49.
$$\begin{aligned} 6z - 5 &= z + 5 \\ 6z - 5 - z &= z + 5 - z \\ 5z - 5 &= 5 \\ 5z - 5 + 5 &= 5 + 5 \\ 5z &= 10 \\ \frac{5z}{5} &= \frac{10}{5} \\ z &= 2 \end{aligned}$$

Check:

$$\begin{aligned} 6(2) - 5 &\stackrel{?}{=} 2 + 5 \\ 12 - 5 &\stackrel{?}{=} 2 + 5 \\ 7 &= 7 \end{aligned}$$

The solution is 2.

51.
$$\begin{aligned} 6x + 14 &= 2x - 2 \\ 6x - 2x + 14 &= -2 \\ 4x &= -2 - 14 \\ 4x &= -16 \\ x &= -4 \end{aligned}$$

Check:

$$\begin{aligned} 6(-4) + 14 &\stackrel{?}{=} 2(-4) - 2 \\ -24 + 14 &\stackrel{?}{=} -8 - 2 \\ -10 &= -10 \end{aligned}$$

The solution is -4.

53.
$$\begin{aligned} -3y - 1 &= 5 - 2y \\ -3y + 2y - 1 &= 5 \\ -y &= 5 + 1 \\ -y &= 6 \\ y &= -6 \end{aligned}$$

Check:

$$\begin{aligned} -3(-6) - 1 &\stackrel{?}{=} 5 - 2(-6) \\ 18 - 1 &\stackrel{?}{=} 5 + 12 \\ 17 &= 17 \end{aligned}$$

The solution is -6.

55. $M = \frac{n}{5}$; $M = 2$

$$\begin{aligned} M &= \frac{n}{5} \\ 2 &= \frac{n}{5} \\ 5(2) &= 5\left(\frac{n}{5}\right) \\ 10 &= n \end{aligned}$$

If you are 2 miles away from the lightening flash, it will take 10 seconds for the sound of thunder to reach you.

57. $M = \frac{A}{740}$; $M = 2.03$

$$\begin{aligned} M &= \frac{A}{740} \\ 2.03 &= \frac{A}{740} \\ 740(2.03) &= 740\left(\frac{A}{740}\right) \\ 1502.2 &= A \end{aligned}$$

The speed is 1502.2 miles per hour.

59. $P = -0.5d + 100$; $P = 70$

$$\begin{aligned} P &= -0.5d + 100 \\ 70 &= -0.5d + 100 \\ 70 - 100 &= -0.5d + 100 - 100 \\ -30 &= -0.5d \\ \frac{-30}{-0.5} &= \frac{-0.5d}{-0.5} \\ 60 &= d \end{aligned}$$

The parallel distance of separation is 60 yards.

For Exercises 61–63, answers may vary.

65. Statement d is true since the solution to $6x = 0$ is 0, which is not a natural number.

67. This would require either using a huge number of searchers, who may not be available, or covering a smaller area and possibly missing the area where the hikers are located.

69.

$$\begin{aligned} -72.8y - 14.6 &= -455.43 - 4.98y \\ -72.8y - 14.6 + 4.98y &= -455.43 - 4.98y \\ &\quad + 4.98y \\ -67.82y - 14.6 &= -455.43 \\ -67.82y - 14.6 + 14.6 &= -455.43 + 14.6 \\ -67.82y &= -440.83 \\ \frac{-67.82y}{-67.82} &= \frac{-440.83}{-67.82} \\ y &= 6.5 \end{aligned}$$

The solution is 6.5.

Review Exercises

70. $(-10)^2 = (-10)(-10) = 100$

71. $-10^2 = -10 \cdot 10 = -100$

72. $x^3 - 4x$; $x = -1$

$$x^3 - 4x = (-1)^3 - 4(-1) = -1 + 4 = 3$$

2.3 Solving Linear Equations

2.3 CHECK POINTS

CHECK POINT 1

$$\begin{aligned} -7x + 25 + 3x &= 16 - 2x - 3 \\ -4x + 25 &= 13 - 2x \\ -4x + 2x + 25 &= 13 - 2x + 2x \\ -2x + 25 &= 13 \\ -2x + 25 - 25 &= 13 - 25 \\ -2x &= -12 \\ \frac{-2x}{-2} &= \frac{-12}{-2} \\ x &= 6 \end{aligned}$$

Check:

$$\begin{aligned}
-7x+25+3x &= 16-2x-3\\
-7(6)+25+3(6) &\stackrel{?}{=} 16-2(6)-3\\
-42+25+18 &\stackrel{?}{=} 16-12-3\\
-17+18 &\stackrel{?}{=} 4-3\\
1 &= 1 \text{ true}
\end{aligned}$$

The solution is 6.

CHECK POINT 2

$$\begin{aligned}
8x &= 2(x+6)\\
8x &= 2x+12\\
8x-2x &= 2x+12-2x\\
6x &= 12\\
\frac{6x}{6} &= \frac{12}{6}\\
x &= 2
\end{aligned}$$

Check:

$$\begin{aligned}
8x &= 2(x+6)\\
8(2) &\stackrel{?}{=} 2(2+6)\\
16 &\stackrel{?}{=} 2(8)\\
16 &= 16 \text{ true}
\end{aligned}$$

The solution is 2.

CHECK POINT 3

$$\begin{aligned}
4(2x+1)-29 &= 3(2x-5)\\
8x+4-29 &= 6x-15\\
8x-25 &= 6x-15\\
8x-6x-25 &= 6x-15-6x\\
2x-25 &= -15\\
2x-25+25 &= -15+25\\
2x &= 10\\
\frac{2x}{2} &= \frac{10}{2}\\
x &= 5
\end{aligned}$$

Check:

$$\begin{aligned}
4(2x+1)-29 &= 3(2x-5)\\
4(2\cdot 5+1)-29 &\stackrel{?}{=} 3(2\cdot 5-5)\\
4(10+1)-29 &\stackrel{?}{=} 3(10-5)\\
4(11)-29 &\stackrel{?}{=} 3(5)\\
44-29 &= 15\\
15 &= 15
\end{aligned}$$

The solution is 5.

CHECK POINT 4

$$\frac{x}{4} = \frac{2x}{3} + \frac{5}{6}$$

Multiply both sides of the equation by the least common denominator, which is 12.

$$\begin{aligned}
12\cdot\frac{x}{4} &= 12\left(\frac{2x}{3}+\frac{5}{6}\right)\\
12\cdot\frac{x}{4} &= 12\cdot\frac{2x}{3}+12\cdot\frac{5}{6}\\
3x &= 8x+10\\
3x-8x &= 8x+10-8x\\
-5x &= 10\\
\frac{-5x}{-5} &= \frac{10}{-5}\\
x &= -2
\end{aligned}$$

Check:

$$\begin{aligned}
\frac{x}{4} &= \frac{2x}{3}+\frac{5}{6}\\
\frac{-2}{4} &\stackrel{?}{=} \frac{2(-2)}{3}+\frac{5}{6}\\
-\frac{1}{2} &\stackrel{?}{=} -\frac{4}{3}+\frac{5}{6}\\
-\frac{1}{2} &\stackrel{?}{=} -\frac{8}{6}+\frac{5}{6}\\
-\frac{1}{2} &\stackrel{?}{=} -\frac{3}{6}\\
-\frac{1}{2} &= -\frac{1}{2} \text{ true}
\end{aligned}$$

The solution is -2.

CHECK POINT 5

$$\begin{aligned}3x+7&=3(x+1)\\3x+7&=3x+3\\3x+7-3x&=3x+3-3x\\7&=3\end{aligned}$$

The original equation is equivalent to the false statement $7 = 3$, which is false for every value of x. The equation is inconsistent and has no solution.

CHECK POINT 6

$$\begin{aligned}3(x-1)+9&=8x+6-5x\\3x-3+9&=8x+6-5x\\3x+6&=3x+6\\3x+6-3x&=3x+6-3x\\6&=6\end{aligned}$$

The original equation is equivalent to the true statement $6 = 6$, which is true for every value of x. The equation is an identity and all real numbers are solutions.

CHECK POINT 7

$$\frac{W}{2}-3H=53$$

Substitute 3 for H since a man who is 5 feet, 3 inches tall is 3 inches over 5 feet.

$$\begin{aligned}\frac{W}{2}-3(3)&=53\\\frac{W}{2}-9&=53\\2\left(\frac{W}{2}-9\right)&=2\cdot 53\\W-18&=106\\W-18+18&=106+18\\W&=124\end{aligned}$$

The recommended weight for a man who is 5 feet, 3 inches tall is 124 pounds.

EXERCISE SET 2.3

For Exercises 1–45, students should check the proposed solutions. The checks will not be shown here.

1. $$\begin{aligned}5x+3x-4x&=10+2\\8x-4x&=12\\4x&=12\\\frac{4x}{4}&=\frac{12}{4}\\x&=3\end{aligned}$$

The solution is 3.

3. $$\begin{aligned}3x-7x+30&=10-2x\\-4x+30&=10-2x\\-4x+30&=10-2x-10\\-4x+20&=-2x\\-4x+20+4x&=-2x+4x\\20&=2x\\10&=x\end{aligned}$$

The solution is 10.

5. $$\begin{aligned}3x+6-x&=8+3x-6\\2x+6&=2+3x\\2x+6&=2+3x-2\\2x+4&=3x\\2x+4-2x&=3x-2x\\4&=x\end{aligned}$$

The solution is 4.

7. $$\begin{aligned}3(x-2)&=12\\3x-6&=12\\3x-6+6&=12+6\\3x&=18\\x&=6\end{aligned}$$

The solution is 6.

9.

$$\begin{aligned} 7(2x-1) &= 21 \\ 14x-7 &= 21 \\ 14x-7+7 &= 21+7 \\ 14x &= 28 \\ \frac{14x}{14} &= \frac{28}{14} \\ x &= 2 \end{aligned}$$

The solution is 2.

11.

$$\begin{aligned} 25 &= 5(3y+4) \\ 25 &= 15y+20 \\ 25-20 &= 15y+20-20 \\ 5 &= 15y \\ \frac{5}{15} &= \frac{15y}{15} \\ \frac{1}{3} &= y \end{aligned}$$

The solution is $\frac{1}{3}$.

13.

$$\begin{aligned} 2(4z+3)-8 &= 46 \\ 8z+6-8 &= 46 \\ 8z-2 &= 46 \\ 8z-2+2 &= 46+2 \\ 8z &= 48 \\ \frac{8z}{8} &= \frac{48}{8} \\ z &= 6 \end{aligned}$$

The solution is 6.

15.

$$\begin{aligned} 6x-(3x+10) &= 14 \\ 6x-3x-10 &= 14 \\ 3x-10 &= 14 \\ 3x-10+10 &= 14+10 \\ 3x &= 24 \\ \frac{3x}{3} &= \frac{24}{3} \\ x &= 8 \end{aligned}$$

The solution is 8.

17.

$$\begin{aligned} 14(y-2) &= 10(y+4) \\ 14y-28 &= 10y+40 \\ 14y-28-10y &= 10y+40-10y \\ 4y-28 &= 40 \\ 4y-28+28 &= 40+28 \\ 4y &= 68 \\ \frac{4y}{y} &= \frac{68}{4} \\ y &= 17 \end{aligned}$$

The solution is 17.

19.

$$\begin{aligned} 3(5-x) &= 4(2x+1) \\ 15-3x &= 8x+4 \\ 15-3x-8x &= 8x+4-8x \\ 15-11x &= 4 \\ 15-11x-15 &= 4-15 \\ -11x &= -11 \\ \frac{-11x}{-11} &= \frac{-11}{-11} \\ x &= 1 \end{aligned}$$

The solution is 1.

21.

$$\begin{aligned} 8(y+2) &= 2(3y+4) \\ 8y+16 &= 6y+8 \\ 8y+16-16 &= 6y+8-16 \\ 8y &= 6y-8 \\ 8y-6y &= 6y-8-6y \\ 2y &= -8 \\ y &= -4 \end{aligned}$$

The solution is -4.

23.

$$\begin{aligned} 3(x+1) &= 7(x-2)-3 \\ 3x+3 &= 7x-14-3 \\ 3x+3 &= 7x-17 \\ 3x+3-3 &= 7x-17-3 \\ 3x &= 7x-20 \\ 3x-7x &= 7x-20-7x \\ -4x &= -20 \\ \frac{-4x}{-4} &= \frac{-20}{-4} \\ x &= 5 \end{aligned}$$

The solution is 5.

25.
$$\begin{aligned}5(2x-8)-2&=5(x-3)+3\\10x-40-2&=5x-15+3\\10x-42&=5x-12\\10x-42+42&=5x-12+42\\10x&=5x+30\\10x&=5x+30-5x\\5x&=30\\\frac{5x}{5}&=\frac{30}{5}\\x&=6\end{aligned}$$

The solution is 6.

27.
$$\begin{aligned}6&=-4(1-x)+3(x+1)\\6&=-4+4x+3x+3\\6&=-1+7x\\6+1&=-1+7x+1\\7&=7x\\\frac{7}{7}&=\frac{7x}{7}\\1&=x\end{aligned}$$

The solution is 1.

29.
$$\begin{aligned}10(z+4)-4(z-2)&=3(z-1)+2(z-3)\\10z+40-4z+8&=3z-3+2z-6\\6z+48&=5z-9\\6z+48-48&=5z-9-48\\6z-5z&=5z-57-5z\\z&=-57\end{aligned}$$

The solution is -57.

31. $\frac{x}{5}-4=-6$

To clear the equation of fractions, multiply both sides by the least common denominator (LCD), which is 5.

$$\begin{aligned}5\left(\frac{x}{5}-4\right)&=5(-6)\\5\cdot\frac{x}{5}&=5\cdot4=-30\\x-20&=-30\\x-20+20&=-30+20\\x&=-10\end{aligned}$$

The solution is -10.

33. $\frac{2x}{3}-5=7$

LCD = 3

$$\begin{aligned}3\left(\frac{2x}{3}-5\right)&=3(7)\\3\cdot\frac{2x}{3}-3\cdot5&=21\\2x-15&=21\\2x-15+15&=21+15\\2x&=36\\\frac{2x}{2}&=\frac{36}{2}\\x&=18\end{aligned}$$

The solution is 18.

35. $\frac{2y}{3}-\frac{3}{4}=\frac{5}{12}$

LCD = 12

$$\begin{aligned}12\left(\frac{2y}{3}-\frac{3}{4}\right)&=12\left(\frac{5}{12}\right)\\12\left(\frac{2y}{3}\right)-12\left(\frac{3}{4}\right)&=5\\8y-9&=5\\8y-9+9&=5+9\\8y&=14\\\frac{8y}{8}&=\frac{14}{8}\\y&=\frac{14}{8}=\frac{7}{4}\end{aligned}$$

The solution is $\frac{7}{4}$.

37. $\frac{x}{3}+\frac{x}{2}=\frac{5}{6}$

LCD = 6

$$\begin{aligned}6\left(\frac{x}{3}+\frac{x}{2}\right)&=6\left(\frac{5}{6}\right)\\2x+3x&=5\\5x&=5\\\frac{5x}{5}&=\frac{5}{5}\\x&=1\end{aligned}$$

The solution is 1.

39. $20 - \frac{z}{3} = \frac{z}{2}$

LCD = 6

$$\begin{aligned} 6\left(20 - \frac{z}{3}\right) &= 6\left(\frac{z}{2}\right) \\ 120 - 2z &= 3z \\ 120 - 2z + 2z &= 3z + 2z \\ 120 &= 5z \\ \frac{120}{5} &= \frac{5z}{5} \\ 24 &= z \end{aligned}$$

The solution is 24.

41. $\frac{y}{3} + \frac{2}{5} = \frac{y}{5} - \frac{2}{5}$

LCD = 15

$$\begin{aligned} 15\left(\frac{y}{3} + \frac{2}{5}\right) &= 15\left(\frac{y}{5} + \frac{2}{5}\right) \\ 15\left(\frac{y}{3}\right) + 15\left(\frac{2}{5}\right) &= 15\left(\frac{y}{5}\right) + 15\left(-\frac{2}{5}\right) \\ 5y + 6 &= 3y - 6 \\ 5y + 6 - 3y &= 3y - 6 - 3y \\ 2y + 6 &= -6 \\ 2y + 6 - 6 &= -6 - 6 \\ 2y &= -12 \\ \frac{2y}{2} &= \frac{-12}{2} \\ y &= -6 \end{aligned}$$

The solution is -6.

43. $\frac{3x}{4} - 3 = \frac{x}{2} + 2$

LCD = 8

$$\begin{aligned} 8\left(\frac{3x}{4} - 3\right) &= 8\left(\frac{x}{2} + 2\right) \\ 8\left(\frac{3x}{4}\right) - 8 \cdot 3 &= 8\left(\frac{x}{2}\right) + 8 \cdot 2 \\ 6x - 24 &= 4x + 16 \\ 6x - 24 - 4x &= 4x + 16 - 4x \\ 2x - 24 &= 16 \\ 2x - 24 + 24 &= 16 + 24 \\ 2x &= 40 \\ \frac{2x}{x} &= \frac{40}{2} \\ x &= 20 \end{aligned}$$

The solution is 20.

45. $\frac{3x}{5} - x = \frac{x}{10} - \frac{5}{2}$

LCD = 10

$$\begin{aligned} 10\left(\frac{3x}{5} - x\right) &= 10\left(\frac{x}{10} - \frac{5}{2}\right) \\ 6x - 10x &= x - 25 \\ 6x - 10x - x &= x - 25 - x \\ -5x &= -25 \\ \frac{-5x}{-5} &= \frac{-25}{-5} \\ x &= 5 \end{aligned}$$

The solution is 5.

47.

$$\begin{aligned} 3x - 7 &= 3(x + 1) \\ 3x - 7 &= 3x + 3 \\ 3x - 7 - 3x &= 3x + 3 - 3x \\ -7 &= 3 \end{aligned}$$

The original equation is equivalent to the false statement $-7 = 3$, so the equation is inconsistent and has no solution.

49.
$$\begin{aligned}2(x+4) &= 4x+5-2x+3\\ 2x+8 &= 2x+8\\ 2x-8-2x &= 2x+8-2x\\ 8 &= 8\end{aligned}$$

The original equation is equivalent to the true statement $8 = 8$, so the equation is an identity and all real numbers are solutions.

51.
$$\begin{aligned}4x+1-5x &= 5-(x+4)\\ -x+1 &= 5-x-4\\ -x+1 &= 1-x\\ -x+1+x &= 1-x+x\\ 1 &= 1\end{aligned}$$

Since $1 = 1$ is a true statement, the original equation is an identity and all real numbers are solutions.

53.
$$\begin{aligned}4(x+2)+1 &= 7x-3(x-2)\\ 4x+8+1 &= 7x-3x+6\\ 4x+9 &= 4x+6\\ 4x+9-4x &= 4x+6-4x\\ 9 &= 6\end{aligned}$$

Since $9 = 6$ is a false statement, the original equation is inconsistent and has no solution.

55. $\frac{x}{3}+2=\frac{x}{3}$

Multiply by the LCD, which is 6.

$$\begin{aligned}6\left(\frac{x}{3}+2\right) &= 6\left(\frac{x}{3}\right)\\ 2x+12 &= 2x\\ 2x+12-2x &= 2x-2x\\ 12 &= 0\end{aligned}$$

Since $12 = 0$ is a false statement, the original equation has no solution.

57.
$$\begin{aligned}3-x &= 2x+3\\ 3-x-3 &= 2x+3-3\\ -x &= 2x\\ -x-2x &= 2x-2x\\ -3x &= 0\\ \frac{-3x}{-3} &= \frac{0}{-3}\\ x &= 0\end{aligned}$$

The solution is 0.

59. $F = 10(x-65)+50$; $F = 250$

$$\begin{aligned}F &= 10(x-65)+50\\ 250 &= 10(x-65)+50\\ 250-50 &= 10(x-65)+50-50\\ 200 &= 10x-650\\ 200+650 &= 10x-650+650\\ 850 &= 10x\\ \frac{850}{10} &= \frac{10x}{10}\\ 85 &= x\end{aligned}$$

A person receiving a \$250 fine was driving 85 miles per hour.

61. $\frac{c}{2}+80=2F$; $F = 70$

$$\begin{aligned}\frac{c}{2}+80 &= 2F\\ \frac{c}{2}+80 &= 2(70)\\ \frac{c}{2}+80 &= 140\\ \frac{c}{2}+80-80 &= 140-80\\ \frac{c}{2} &= 60\\ 2\left(\frac{c}{2}\right) &= 2(60)\\ c &= 120\end{aligned}$$

At 70°F, there are 120 cricket chirps per minute.

63. $p = 15 + \frac{5d}{11}$; $p = 201$

$$201 = 15 + \frac{5d}{11}$$
$$201 - 15 = 15 + \frac{5d}{11} - 15$$
$$186 = \frac{5d}{11}$$
$$11(186) = 11\left(\frac{5d}{11}\right)$$
$$2046 = 5d$$
$$\frac{2046}{5} = d$$
$$409.2 = d$$

He descended to a depth of 409.2 feet below the surface.

For Exercises 65–67, answers may vary.

69. Statement c is true. The solution to the linear equation is -3. When -3 is substituted into $y^2 + 2y - 3$, the result is 0.

71. $\frac{2x-3}{9} + \frac{x-3}{2} = \frac{x+5}{6} - 1$

LCD = 18

$$18\left(\frac{2x-3}{9} + \frac{x-3}{2}\right) = 18\left(\frac{x+5}{6} - 1\right)$$
$$18\left(\frac{2x-3}{9}\right) + 18\left(\frac{x-3}{2}\right) = 18\left(\frac{x+5}{6}\right) - 18 \cdot 1$$
$$2(2x-3) + 9(x-3) = 3(x+5) - 18$$
$$4x - 6 + 9x - 27 = 3x + 15 - 18$$
$$13x - 33 = 3x - 3$$
$$13x - 33 - 3x = 3x - 3 - 3x$$
$$10x - 33 = -3$$
$$10x - 33 + 33 = -3 + 33$$
$$10x = 30$$
$$\frac{10x}{10} = \frac{30}{10}$$
$$x = 3$$

Check:

$$\frac{2(3)-3}{9} + \frac{3-3}{2} \stackrel{?}{=} \frac{3+5}{6} - 1$$
$$\frac{6-3}{9} + \frac{0}{2} \stackrel{?}{=} \frac{8}{6} - 1$$
$$\frac{3}{9} + 0 \stackrel{?}{=} \frac{4}{3} - 1$$
$$\frac{1}{3} = \frac{1}{3}$$

The solution is 3.

73.
$$2.24y - 9.28 = 5.74y + 5.42$$
$$2.24y - 9.28 - 5.74y = 5.74y + 5.42 - 5.74y$$
$$-3.5y - 9.28 = 5.42$$
$$-3.5y - 9.28 + 9.28 = 5.42 + 9.28$$
$$-3.5y = 14.7$$
$$\frac{-3.5y}{-3.5} = \frac{14.7}{-3.5}$$
$$y = -4.2$$

The solution is -4.2.

Review Exercises

75. $-24 < -20$; -24 is to the left of -20 on the number line, so -24 is less than -20.

76. $-\frac{1}{3} < -\frac{1}{5}$; $-\frac{1}{3}$ is to the left of $-\frac{1}{5}$ on the number line, so $-\frac{1}{3}$ is less than $-\frac{1}{5}$. To compare these numbers, write them with a common denominator:

$$-\frac{1}{3} = -\frac{5}{15}, -\frac{1}{5} = -\frac{3}{15}.$$

77.
$$-9 - 11 + 7 - (-3)$$
$$= (-9) + (-11) + 7 + 3$$
$$= (7+3) + [(-9) + (-11)]$$
$$= 10 + (-20)$$
$$= -10$$

2.4 Formulas and Percents

2.4 CHECK POINTS

CHECK POINT 1

Solve $A = lw$ for l.

$$A = lw$$
$$\frac{A}{w} = \frac{lw}{w}$$
$$\frac{A}{w} = l \quad \text{or} \quad l = \frac{A}{w}$$

CHECK POINT 2

Solve $2l + 2w = P$ for l.

$$2l + 2w = P$$
$$2l + 2w - 2w = P - 2w$$
$$2l = P - 2w$$
$$\frac{2l}{l} = \frac{P - 2w}{2}$$
$$l = \frac{P - 2w}{2}$$

CHECK POINT 3

Solve $T = D + pm$ for m.

$$T = D + pm$$
$$T - D = D - D + pm$$
$$T - D = pm$$
$$\frac{T - D}{p} = \frac{pm}{p}$$
$$\frac{T - D}{p} = m \quad \text{or} \quad m = \frac{T - D}{p}$$

CHECK POINT 4

Solve $\frac{x}{3} - 4y = 5$ for x.

$$\frac{x}{3} - 4y = 5$$
$$3\left(\frac{x}{3} - 4y\right) = 3 \cdot 5$$
$$3 \cdot \frac{x}{3} - 3 \cdot 4y = 3 \cdot 5$$
$$x - 12 = 15$$
$$x - 12y + 12y = 15 + 12y$$
$$x = 15 + 12y$$

CHECK POINT 5

To express a decimal number as a percent, move the decimal point two places to the right and attach a percent sign.

$$0.023 = 2.3\%$$

CHECK POINT 6

To express a percent as a decimal number, move the decimal point two places to the left and remove the percent sign.

a. $67\% = 0.67$

b. $250\% = 2.5$

CHECK POINT 7

What is 9% of 50?
Use the percent formula $A = PB$ with $P = 9\% = 0.09$ and $B = 50$ to find the quantity A.

$$A = PB$$
$$A = 0.09 \cdot 50$$
$$A = 4.5$$

9% of 50 is 4.5.

CHECK POINT 8

9 is 60% of what?
Use the formula $A = PB$ with $A = 9$ and $P = 60\% = 0.6$ to find the quantity B.

$$A = PB$$
$$9 = 0.6 \cdot B$$
$$\frac{9}{0.6} = \frac{0.6B}{0.6}$$
$$15 = B$$

9 is 60% of 15.

CHECK POINT 9

18 is what percent of 50?
Use the percent formula $A = PB$ with $A = 18$ and $B = 50$ to find the quantity P.

$$A = PB$$
$$18 = P \cdot 50$$
$$\frac{18}{50} = \frac{P \cdot 50}{50}$$
$$0.36 = P$$

$0.36 = 36\%$, so 18 is 36% of 50.

CHECK POINT 10

The question is, "3.44 is what percent of 4.30?" Use the percent formula with $A = 3.44$ and $B = 4.30$ to find the quantity P.

$$A = PB$$
$$3.44 = P \cdot 4.30$$
$$\frac{3.44}{4.30} = \frac{P \cdot 3.40}{4.30}$$
$$0.8 = P$$

$0.8 = 80\%$, so 80% of the fuel cost is for taxes.

EXERCISE SET 2.4

1. $d = rt$ for r

$$\frac{d}{t} = \frac{rt}{t}$$
$$\frac{d}{t} = r \quad \text{or} \quad r = \frac{d}{t}$$

This is the distance formula:

distance = rate · time.

3. $I = Prt$ for P

$$\frac{I}{rt} = \frac{Prt}{rt}$$
$$\frac{I}{rt} = P \quad \text{or} \quad P = \frac{I}{rt}$$

This is the formula for simple interest:

interest = principal · rate · time.

5. $C = 2\pi r$ for r

$$\frac{C}{2\pi} = \frac{2\pi C}{2\pi}$$
$$\frac{C}{2\pi} = r \quad \text{or} \quad r = \frac{C}{2\pi}$$

This is the formula for finding the circumference of a circle if you know its radius.

7. $E = mc^2$

$$\frac{E}{c^2} = \frac{mc^2}{c^2}$$
$$\frac{E}{c^2} = m \quad \text{or} \quad m = \frac{E}{c^2}$$

This is Einstein's formula relating energy, mass, and the speed of light.

9. $y = mx + b$ for m

$$y - b = mx$$
$$\frac{y-b}{x} = \frac{mx}{x}$$
$$\frac{y-b}{x} = m \quad \text{or} \quad m = \frac{y-b}{x}$$

This is the slope-intercept formula for the equation of a line. (This formula will be discussed later in the textbook.)

11. $T = D + pm$ for p

$$T - D = D + pm - D$$
$$T - D = pm$$
$$\frac{T-D}{m} = \frac{pm}{m}$$
$$\frac{T-D}{m} = p \quad \text{or} \quad p = \frac{T-D}{m}$$

13. $A = \frac{1}{2}bh$ for b

$$2A = 2\left(\frac{1}{2}bh\right)$$
$$2A = bh$$
$$\frac{2A}{h} = \frac{bh}{h}$$
$$\frac{2A}{h} = b \quad \text{or} \quad b = \frac{2A}{h}$$

This is the formula for the area of a triangle:

$$\text{area} = \frac{1}{2}\cdot\text{base}\cdot\text{height}.$$

15. $M = \frac{n}{5}$ for n

$$5M = 5\left(\frac{n}{5}\right)$$
$$5M = n \quad \text{or} \quad n = 5M$$

17. $\frac{c}{2} + 80 = 2F$ for c

$$\frac{c}{2} + 80 - 80 = 2F - 80$$
$$\frac{c}{2} = 2F - 80$$
$$2\left(\frac{c}{2}\right) = 2(2F - 80)$$
$$c = 4F - 160$$

19. $A = \frac{1}{2}(a+b)$ for a

$$2A = 2\left[\frac{1}{2}(a+b)\right]$$
$$2A = a + b$$
$$2A - a = a + b - a$$
$$2A - b = a \quad \text{or} \quad a = 2A - b$$

This is the formula for finding the average of two numbers.

21. $S = P + Prt$ for r

$$S - P = P + Prt - P$$
$$S - P = Prt$$
$$\frac{S-P}{Pt} = \frac{Prt}{Pt}$$
$$\frac{S-P}{Pt} = r \quad \text{or} \quad r = \frac{S-P}{Pt}$$

23. $A = \frac{1}{2}h(a+b)$ for b

$$2A = 2\left[\frac{1}{2}h(a+b)\right]$$
$$2A = h(a+b)$$
$$2A = ha + hb$$
$$2A - ha = ha + hb - ha$$
$$2A - ha = hb$$
$$\frac{2A-ha}{h} = \frac{hb}{h}$$
$$\frac{2A-ha}{h} = b \text{ or } b = \frac{2A-ha}{h} \text{ or } \frac{2A}{h} - a$$

This is the formula for the area of a trapezoid.

25. $Ax + By = C$ for x

$$Ax + By - By = C - By$$
$$Ax = C - By$$
$$\frac{Ax}{A} = \frac{C-By}{A}$$
$$x = \frac{C-By}{A}$$

This is the standard form on the equation of a line. (This formula will be discussed later in the textbook.)

27. To change a decimal number to a percent, move the decimal point two places to the right and add a percent sign.

$$0.59 = 59\%$$

29. $0.003 = 0.3\%$

31. $2.87 = 287\%$

33. $100 = 10{,}000\%$

35. To change a percent to a decimal number, move the decimal point two places to the left and remove the percent sign.

$$72\% = 0.72$$

37. $43.6\% = 0.436$

39. $130\% = 1.3$

41. $2\% = 0.02$

43. $62.5\% = 0.625$

45. $A = PB;\ P = 3\% = 0.03, B = 200$

$$\begin{aligned} A &= PB \\ A &= 0.03 \cdot 200 \\ A &= 6 \end{aligned}$$

3% of 200 is 6.

47. $A = PB;\ P = 18\% = 0.18, B = 40$

$$\begin{aligned} A &= PB \\ A &= 0.18 \cdot 40 \\ A &= 7.2 \end{aligned}$$

18% of 40 is 7.2.

49. $A = PB;\ A = 3, P = 60\% = 0.6$

$$\begin{aligned} A &= PB \\ 3 &= 0.6 \cdot B \\ \frac{3}{0.6} &= \frac{0.6B}{0.6} \\ 5 &= B \end{aligned}$$

3 is 60% of 5.

51. $A = PB;\ A = 40.8, P = 24\% = 0.24$

$$\begin{aligned} A &= PB \\ 40.8 &= 0.24 \cdot B \\ \frac{40.8}{0.24} &= \frac{0.24B}{0.24} \\ 170 &= B \end{aligned}$$

24% of 170 is 40.8.

53. $A = PB;\ A = 3, B = 15$

$$\begin{aligned} A &= PB \\ 3 &= P \cdot 15 \\ \frac{3}{15} &= \frac{P \cdot 15}{15} \\ 0.2 &= P \end{aligned}$$

$0.2 = 20\%$
3 is 20% of 15.

55. $A = PB;\ A = 0.3, B = 2.5$

$$\begin{aligned} A &= PB \\ 0.3 &= P \cdot 2.5 \\ \frac{0.3}{2.5} &= \frac{P \cdot 2.5}{2.5} \\ 0.12 &= P \end{aligned}$$

$0.12 = 12\%$
0.3 is 12% of 2.5.

57. $A = \dfrac{x+y+z}{3}$

a. $A = \dfrac{x+y+z}{3}$ for z

$$\begin{aligned} 3A &= 3\left(\frac{x+y+z}{3}\right) \\ 3A &= x+y+z \\ 3A-x-y &= x+y+z-x-y \\ 3A-x-y &= z \end{aligned}$$

b. $z = 3A - x - y$; $A = 90, x = 86, y = 88$

$$\begin{aligned} z &= 3A - x - y \\ z &= 3(90) - 86 - 88 \\ z &= 96 \end{aligned}$$

You need to get 96% on the third exam to have an average of 90%.

59. $d = rt$

a. $d = rt$ for t

$$\begin{aligned} \frac{d}{r} &= \frac{rt}{r} \\ \frac{d}{r} &= t \end{aligned}$$

b. $t = \dfrac{d}{r}$; $d = 100, r = 40$

$$t = \frac{100}{40} = 2.5$$

You would travel for 2.5 (or $2\frac{1}{2}$) hours.

61. 23¢ is $\frac{23}{100}$ = 23% of a dollar, so 23% of the cost of prescription drugs goes to the pharmacy.

63. The total number of executions was 418 + 214 = 632. The percent of total executions that took place in Texas was

$$\frac{214}{632} \approx 0.34 = 34\%.$$

65. This question is equivalent to, "122 is 34% of what number?"

$A = PB$; $A = 122, P = 0.34$

$$\begin{aligned} A &= PB \\ 122 &= 0.34 \cdot B \\ \frac{122}{0.34} &= \frac{0.34 \cdot B}{0.34} \\ 359 &\approx B \end{aligned}$$

There were about 359 women in the poll.

67. $A = PB$; $A = 7500, B = 60{,}000$

$$\begin{aligned} A &= PB \\ 7500 &= P \cdot 60{,}000 \\ \frac{7500}{60{,}000} &= \frac{P \cdot 60{,}000}{60{,}000} \\ 0.125 &= P \end{aligned}$$

$0.125 = 12.5\%$

The charity has raised 12.5% of its goal.

69. $A = PB$; $P = 15\% = 0.15, B = 60$

$$\begin{aligned} A &= PB \\ A &= 0.15 \cdot 60 \\ A &= 9 \end{aligned}$$

The tip was \$9.

71. a. The sales tax is 6% of \$16,800.

$$0.06(16{,}800) = 1008$$

The sales tax due on the car is \$1008.

b. The total cost is the sum of the price of the car and the sales tax.

$$\$16{,}800 + \$1008 = \$17{,}808$$

The car's total cost is \$17,808.

73. a. The discount amount is 12% of \$860.

$$0.12(860) = 103.20$$

The discount amount is \$103.20.

b. The sale price is the regular price minus the discount amount.

$$\$860 - \$103.20 = \$756.80$$

The sale price is \$756.80.

For Exercises 75–77, answers may vary.

81. Statement d is true.

83. $v = -32t + 64;\ v = 16$

$$\begin{aligned} 16 &= -32t + 64 \\ -48 &= -32t \\ \frac{-48}{-32} &= \frac{-32t}{-32} \\ 1.5 &= t \end{aligned}$$

$h = -16t^2 + 64t;\ t = 1.5$

$$\begin{aligned} h &= -16(1.5^2) + 64(1.5) \\ h &= 60 \end{aligned}$$

When the velocity is 16 feet per second, the time is 1.5 seconds and the height is 60 feet.

Review Exercises

84.

$$\begin{aligned} 5x + 20 &= 8x - 16 \\ 5x + 20 - 8x &= 8x - 16 - 8x \\ -3x + 20 &= -16 \\ -3x + 20 - 20 &= -16 - 20 \\ -3x &= -36 \\ \frac{-3x}{-3} &= \frac{-36}{-3} \\ x &= 12 \end{aligned}$$

Check:

$$\begin{aligned} 5(12) + 20 &\stackrel{?}{=} 8(12) - 16 \\ 60 + 20 &= 96 - 16 \\ 80 &= 80 \end{aligned}$$

The solution is 12.

85.

$$\begin{aligned} 5(2y - 3) - 1 &= 4(6 + 2y) \\ 10y - 15 - 1 &= 24 + 8y \\ 10y - 16 &= 24 + 8y \\ 10y - 16 - 8y &= 24 + 8y - 8y \\ 2y - 16 &= 24 \\ 2y - 16 + 16 &= 24 + 16 \\ 2y &= 40 \\ \frac{2y}{2} &= \frac{40}{2} \\ y &= 20 \end{aligned}$$

Check:

$$\begin{aligned} 5(2 \cdot 20 - 3) - 1 &\stackrel{?}{=} 4(6 + 2 \cdot 20) \\ 5(40 - 3) - 1 &\stackrel{?}{=} 4(6 + 40) \\ 5(37) - 1 &\stackrel{?}{=} 4(46) \\ 185 - 1 &\stackrel{?}{=} 184 \\ 184 &= 184 \end{aligned}$$

86. $x - 0.3x = 1x - 0.3x = (1 - 0.3)x = 0.7x$

2.5 An Introduction to Problem Solving

2.5 CHECK POINTS

CHECK POINT 1

a. The algebraic expression for "four times a number, increased by 6" is $4x + 6$.

b. The algebraic expression for the quotient of a number decreased by 4 and 9" is $\frac{x-4}{9}$.

CHECK POINT 2

Step 1 Let $x =$ the number.

Step 2 There are no other unknown quantities.

Step 3 Write an equation that describes the situation.

$$6x - 4 = 68$$

Step 4 Solve the equation and answer the question.

$$\begin{aligned} 6x - 4 &= 68 \\ 6x - 4 + 4 &= 68 + 4 \\ 6x &= 72 \\ \frac{6x}{6} &= \frac{72}{6} \\ x &= 12 \end{aligned}$$

The number is 12.

Step 5 Check the proposed solution is the original wording of the problem. The proposed number is 12. Six times 12 is $6 \cdot 12$ or 72. Four subtracted from 72 is $72 - 4$ or 68, so the proposed solution checks.

CHECK POINT 3

Step 1 Let $x =$ the number (in millions) of *Saturday Night Fever* albums sold.

Step 2 Let $x + 5 =$ the number (in millions) of *Jagged Little Pill* albums sold.

Step 3 Combined, the two albums sold 27 million copies, so

$$x + (x + 5) = 27.$$

Step 4

$$\begin{aligned} x + x + 5 &= 27 \\ 2x + 5 &= 27 \\ 2x &= 22 \\ x &= 11 \\ x + 5 &= 16 \end{aligned}$$

Jagged Little Pill sold 16 million albums and *Saturday Night Fever* sold 11 million albums.

Step 5 The total number of albums sold was 16 million + 11 million = 27 million.

CHECK POINT 4

Let $\quad x =$ the page number of the page on the left.

Then $x + 1 =$ the page number of the page on the right.

$$\begin{aligned} x + (x + 1) &= 193 \\ 2x + 1 &= 193 \\ 2x &= 192 \\ x &= 96 \\ x + 1 &= 97 \end{aligned}$$

The page numbers are 96 and 97.

CHECK POINT 5

Let $x =$ the number of eighths of a mile.

$$\begin{aligned} 2 + 0.25x &= 10 \\ 0.25x &= 10 \\ \frac{0.25x}{0.25} &= \frac{8}{0.25} \\ x &= 32 \end{aligned}$$

You can go 32 eighths of a mile for \$10. Since $32 \cdot \frac{1}{8} = 4$, this is 4 miles.

CHECK POINT 6

Let $x =$ the width.
Then $3x =$ the length.

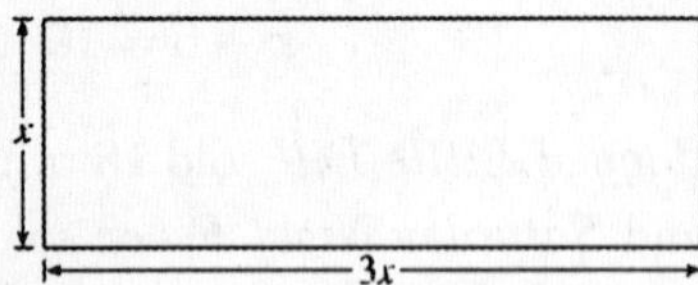

Use the formula for the perimeter of a rectangle to write the equation.

$$\begin{aligned} 2l + 2w &= P \\ 2(3x) + 2x &= 320 \\ 6x + 2x &= 320 \\ 8x &= 320 \\ \frac{8x}{8} &= \frac{320}{8} \\ x &= 40 \end{aligned}$$

Width $= x = 40$
Length $= 3x = 3(40) = 120$
The dimensions of the swimming pool are 120 feet by 40 feet.

CHECK POINT 7

Let $x =$ the price of the exercise machine before the reduction.

$$\begin{aligned} x - 0.4x &= 564 \\ 1x - 0.4x &= 564 \\ 0.6x &= 564 \\ \frac{0.6x}{0.6} &= \frac{564}{0.6} \\ x &= 940 \end{aligned}$$

The exercise machine's price before the reduction was $940.

EXERCISE SET 2.5

1. $x + 9$ **3.** $20 - x$ **5.** $8 - 5x$

7. $\frac{15}{x}$ **9.** $2x+20$ **11.** $7x-30$

13. $4(x + 12)$

15.
$$\begin{aligned} x + 40 &= 450 \\ x + 40 - 40 &= 450 - 40 \\ x &= 410 \end{aligned}$$

The number is 410.

17.
$$\begin{aligned} x - 13 &= 123 \\ x - 13 + 13 &= 123 + 13 \\ x &= 136 \end{aligned}$$

The number is 136.

19.
$$\begin{aligned} 7x &= 91 \\ \frac{7x}{7} &= \frac{91}{7} \\ x &= 13 \end{aligned}$$

The number is 13.

21.
$$\begin{aligned} \frac{x}{18} &= 6 \\ 18\left(\frac{x}{18}\right) &= 18(6) \\ x &= 108 \end{aligned}$$

The number is 108.

23.
$$\begin{aligned} 4 + 2x &= 36 \\ 2x &= 32 \\ x &= 16 \end{aligned}$$

The number is 16.

25.
$$\begin{aligned} 5x - 7 &= 123 \\ 5x &= 130 \\ x &= 26 \end{aligned}$$

The number is 26.

27. $x + 5 = 2x$
$x + 5 - x = 2x - x$
$5 = x$

The number is 5.

29. $2(x + 4) = 36$
$2x + 8 = 36$
$2x = 28$
$x = 14$

The number is 14.

31. $9x = 30 + 3x$
$6x = 30$
$x = 5$

The number is 5.

33. $\frac{3x}{5} + 4 = 34$
$\frac{3x}{5} = 30$
$3x = 150$
$x = 50$

The number is 50.

35. *Step 1* Let x = the cost to make *Waterworld* (in millions of dollars).

Step 2 $x + 40$ = the cost to make *Titantic.*

Step 3 The combined cost was \$360 million, so the equation is

$$x + (x + 40) = 360.$$

Step 4 $x + x + 40 = 360$
$2x + 40 = 360$
$2x = 320$
$x = 160$

It would cost \$160 million to make *Waterworld* and \$160 million + \$40 million = \$200 million to make *Titanic.*

37. *Step 1* Let x = the number of hours that the average motorist in Miami spends stuck in traffic in one year.

Step 2 $2x - 32$ = the number of hours that the average motorist in Los Angeles spends stuck in traffic in one year

Step 3 The total for the two cities is 139 hours, so the equation is

$$x + (2x - 32) = 139.$$

Step 4 $x + 2x - 32 = 139$
$3x - 32 = 139$
$3x - 32 + 32 = 139 + 32$
$3x = 171$
$\frac{3x}{3} = \frac{171}{3}$
$x = 57$

Step 5 In Miami, the average motorist spends 57 hours stuck in traffic. In Los Angeles, the average motorist spends $2(57) - 32 = 82$ hours stuck in traffic in one year.

In Exercises 39–41, the five-step problem in this section of the textbook and illustrated in the solutions for Exercises 35 and 37 should be used. This strategy is used in the following solutions, although the steps are not listed.

39. Let x = the smaller page number. Then $x + 1$ = the larger page number.

$$x + (x + 1) = 629$$
$$2x + 1 = 629$$
$$2x = 628$$
$$x = 314$$

The smaller page number is 314. The larger page number is $314 + 1 = 315$. The page numbers are 314 and 315.

41. Let $x =$ the losing score.
Then $x + 1 =$ the winning score.

$$\begin{aligned} x + (x+1) &= 39 \\ 2x + 1 &= 39 \\ 2x &= 38 \\ x &= 19 \end{aligned}$$

The losing score was 19. The winning score was 19 + 1 = 20. The sum of the scores was 19 + 20 = 39.

43. Two even integers differ by 2.
Let $x =$ the smaller integer.
Then $x + 2 =$ the larger integer.

$$\begin{aligned} x + (x+2) &= 66 \\ 2x + 2 &= 66 \\ 2x &= 34 \\ x &= 32 \end{aligned}$$

The smaller integer is 32. The larger integer is 32 + 2 = 34. Their sum is 32 + 34 = 66.

45. Let $x =$ the number of miles you can travel in one week for \$320.

$$\begin{aligned} 200 + 0.15x &= 320 \\ 200 + 0.15x - 200 &= 320 - 200 \\ 0.15x &= 120 \\ \frac{0.15x}{0.15} &= \frac{120}{0.15} \\ x &= 800 \end{aligned}$$

You can travel 800 miles in one week for \$320. This checks because \$200 + 0.15(\$800) = \$320.

47. Let $x =$ the number of months it will take for a baby girl to weigh 16 pounds.

$$\begin{aligned} 7 + 1.5x &= 16 \\ 7 + 1.5x - 7 &= 16 - 7 \\ 1.5x &= 9 \\ \frac{1.5x}{1.5} &= \frac{9}{1.5} \\ x &= 6 \end{aligned}$$

The average baby girl weighs 16 pounds after 6 months.

49. Let $x =$ the width of the field (in yards).
Then $4w =$ the width.
The perimeter of a rectangle is twice the length plus twice the width, so

$$2w + 2(4w) = 500.$$

Solve this equation.

$$\begin{aligned} 2w + 8w &= 500 \\ 10w &= 500 \\ w &= 50 \end{aligned}$$

The width is 50 yards and the length is 4(50) = 200 yards. This checks because 2(50) + 2(200) = 500.

51. Let $w =$ the width of a football field (in feet).
Then $w + 200 =$ the length.

$$\begin{aligned} 2w + 2(w + 200) &= 1040 \\ 2w + 2w + 400 &= 1040 \\ 4w + 400 &= 1040 \\ 4w &= 640 \\ w &= 160 \end{aligned}$$

The width 160 feet and the length is 160 + 200 = 360 feet. This checks because 2(160) + 2(200) = 720.

53. As shown in the diagram, let x = the height and $3x$ = the length. To construct the bookcase, 3 heights and 4 lengths are needed. Since 60 feet of lumber is available,

$$3x + 4(3x) = 60.$$

Solve this equation.

$$\begin{aligned} 3x + 12x &= 60 \\ 15x &= 60 \\ x &= 4 \end{aligned}$$

If $x = 4, 3x = 3 \cdot 4 = 12$.
The bookcase is 12 feet long and 4 feet high.

55. Let x = the price before the reduction.

$$\begin{aligned} x - 0.20x &= 320 \\ 1x - 0.20x &= 320 \\ 0.80x &= 320 \\ \frac{0.80x}{0.80} &= \frac{320}{0.80} \\ x &= 400 \end{aligned}$$

The price before the reduction was \$400.

57. Let x = the price before the reduction.

$$\begin{aligned} x - \frac{1}{4}x &= 21 \\ \frac{3}{4}x &= 21 \\ \frac{4}{3}\left(\frac{3}{4}x\right) &= \frac{4}{3}(21) \\ 1x &= 28 \\ x &= 28 \end{aligned}$$

The price before the reduction was \$28.

59. Let x = the price of the car without tax.

$$\begin{aligned} x + 0.06x &= 15{,}370 \\ 1x + 0.06x &= 15{,}370 \\ 1.06x &= 15{,}370 \\ \frac{1.06x}{1.06} &= \frac{15{,}370}{1.06} \\ x &= 14{,}500 \end{aligned}$$

The price of the car without sales tax was \$14,500.

61. Let x = the number of hours of labor.

$$\begin{aligned} 63 + 35x &= 448 \\ 63 + 35x - 63 &= 448 - 63 \\ 35x &= 385 \\ \frac{35x}{35} &= \frac{385}{35} \\ x &= 11 \end{aligned}$$

It took 11 hours of labor to repair the car.

For Exercises 63–65, answers may vary.

67. Statement a should be translated as $x - 10 = 160$.
Statement b should be translated as $5x + 4 = 6x - 1$.
Statement c should be translated as $7 = x + 3$.
Since none of these statements was translated correctly, the correct response is d.

69. Let x = the number of additional minutes (after the first).

$$\begin{aligned} 0.55 + 0.40x &= 6.95 \\ 0.55 + 0.40x - 0.55 &= 6.95 - 0.55 \\ 0.40x &= 6.40 \\ \frac{0.40x}{0.40} &= \frac{6.40}{0.40} \\ x &= 16 \end{aligned}$$

Since there were 16 additional minutes after the first, the length of the call was 17 minutes.

71. Let $x =$ weight of unpeeled banana.

Then $\frac{1}{8}x =$ weight of banana peel

and $\frac{7}{8}x =$ weight of peeled banana.

The information in the cartoon translates into the equation

$$x = \frac{7}{8}x + \frac{7}{8}.$$

To solve this equation, first eliminate fractions by multiplying both sides by the LCD, which is 8.

$$\begin{aligned} 8x &= 8\left(\frac{7}{8}x + \frac{7}{8}\right) \\ 8x &= 8\left(\frac{7}{8}x\right) + 8\left(\frac{7}{8}\right) \\ 8x &= 7x + 7 \\ 8x - 7x &= 7x + 7 - 7x \\ x &= 7 \end{aligned}$$

The unpeeled banana weighs 7 ounces.

Review Exercises

72.
$$\begin{aligned} \frac{4}{5}x &= -16 \\ \frac{5}{4}\left(\frac{4}{5}x\right) &= \frac{5}{4}(-16) \\ x &= -20 \end{aligned}$$

Check:

$$\begin{aligned} \frac{4}{5}(-20) &\stackrel{?}{=} -16 \\ \frac{4}{5} \cdot \frac{-20}{1} &\stackrel{?}{=} -16 \\ \frac{-80}{5} &\stackrel{?}{=} -16 \\ -16 &= -16 \end{aligned}$$

The solution is -20.

73.
$$\begin{aligned} 6(y-1) + 7 &= 9y - y + 1 \\ 6y - 6 + 7 &= 9y - y + 1 \\ 6y + 1 &= 8y + 1 \\ 6y + 1 - 1 &= 8y + 1 - 1 \\ 6y &= 8y \\ 6y - 8y &= 8y - 8y \\ -2y &= 0 \\ \frac{-2y}{-2} &= \frac{0}{-2} \\ y &= 0 \end{aligned}$$

Check:

$$\begin{aligned} 6(0-1) + 7 &\stackrel{?}{=} 9(0) - 0 + 1 \\ 6(-10 + 7 &\stackrel{?}{=} 0 - 0 + 1 \\ -6 + 7 &\stackrel{?}{=} 1 \\ 1 &= 1 \end{aligned}$$

The solution is 0.

74. $V = \frac{1}{3}lwh$ for w

$$\begin{aligned} V &= \frac{1}{3}lwh \\ 3V &= 3\left(\frac{1}{3}lwh\right) \\ 3V &= lwh \\ \frac{3V}{lh} &= \frac{lwh}{lh} \\ \frac{3V}{lh} &= w \quad \text{or} \quad w = \frac{3V}{lh} \end{aligned}$$

2.6 Solving Linear Inequalities

2.6 CHECK POINTS

CHECK POINT 1

a. $x < 4$

The solutions of $x < 4$ are all real numbers less than 4. Shade all points to the left of 4 and use an open dot at 4 to show that 4 is not a solution.

-5 -4 -3 -2 -1 0 1 2 3 4 5

b. $x \geq -2$

The solutions of $x \geq -2$ are all real numbers greater than or equal to -2. Shade all points to the right of -2 and the point -2 itself. Use a closed dot at -2 to show that -2 is a solution.

-5 -4 -3 -2 -1 0 1 2 3 4 5

c. $-4 \leq x < 1$

The solutions of $-4 \leq x < 1$ are all real numbers between -4 and 1, including -4 but not including 1. Use a closed dot at -4 and an open dot at 1.

-5 -4 -3 -2 -1 0 1 2 3 4 5

CHECK POINT 2

$$x + 6 < 9$$
$$x + 6 = 6 < 9 - 6$$
$$x < 3$$

The solution set is written is set-builder notation as $\{x|x < 3\}$.

-5 -4 -3 -2 -1 0 1 2 3 4 5

CHECK POINT 3

$$8x - 2 \geq 7x - 4$$
$$8 - 7x - 2 \geq 7x - 7x - 4$$
$$x - 2 \geq -4$$
$$x - 2 + 2 \geq -4 + 2$$
$$x \geq -2$$

Solution set: $\{x|x \geq -2\}$

-5 -4 -3 -2 -1 0 1 2 3 4 5

CHECK POINT 4

a. $\frac{1}{4}x < 2$

$$4 \cdot \frac{1}{4}x < 4 \cdot 2$$
$$x < 8$$

Solution set: $\{x|x < 8\}$

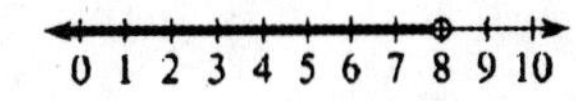

b. $-6x < 18$

$$\frac{-6x}{-6} > \frac{18}{-6}$$
$$x > -3$$

(Be sure to reverse the inequality symbol when dividing by a negative number.)
Solution set: $\{x|x > -3\}$

-5 -4 -3 -2 -1 0 1 2 3 4 5

CHECK POINT 5

$$5y - 3 \geq 17$$
$$5y - 3 + 3 \geq 17 + 3$$
$$5y \geq 20$$
$$\frac{5y}{5} \geq \frac{20}{5}$$
$$y \geq 4$$

Solution set: $\{y|y \geq 4\}$

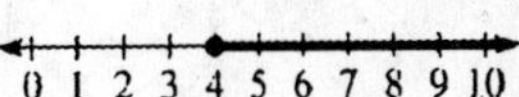

CHECK POINT 6

$$\begin{aligned} 6-3x &\le 5x-2 \\ 6-3x-5x &\le 5x-2-5x \\ 6-8x &\le -2 \\ 6-8x-6 &\le -2-6 \\ -8x &\le -8 \\ \frac{-8x}{-8} &\ge \frac{-8}{-8} \\ x &\ge 1 \end{aligned}$$

Solution set: $\{x|x \ge 1\}$

-5 -4 -3 -2 -1 0 1 2 3 4 5

CHECK POINT 7

$$\begin{aligned} 2(x-3)-1 &\le 3(x+2)-14 \\ 2x-6-1 &\le 3x+6-14 \\ 2x-7 &\le 3x-8 \\ 2x-3x-7 &\le 3x-3x-8 \\ -x-7 &\le -8 \\ -x-7+7 &\le -8+7 \\ -x &\le -1 \\ -1(-x) &\ge -1(-1) \\ x &\ge 1 \end{aligned}$$

Solution set: $\{x|x \ge 1\}$

-5 -4 -3 -2 -1 0 1 2 3 4 5

CHECK POINT 8

$$\begin{aligned} 4(x+2) &> 4x+15 \\ 4x+8 &> 4x+15 \\ 4x+8-4x &> 4x+15-4x \\ 8 &> 15 \end{aligned}$$

The original inequality is equivalent to the false statement $8 > 15$, which is false for every value of x. The inequality has no solution. The solution set is $\emptyset$, the empty set.

CHECK POINT 9

$$\begin{aligned} 3(x+1) &\ge 2x+1+x \\ 3x+3 &\ge 3x+1 \\ 3x+3-3x &\ge 3x+1-3x \\ 3 &\ge 1 \end{aligned}$$

The original inequality is equivalent to the true statement $3 \ge 1$, which is true for every value of x. The solution set is the set of all real numbers, written $\{x|x \text{ is a real number}\}$.

CHECK POINT 10

Let $x =$ your grade on the final examination.

$$\text{Average} = \frac{82+74+78+x+x}{5}$$

In order to get a B, your average must be at least 80, so

$$\frac{82+74+78+x+x}{5} \ge 80.$$

Solve this inequality.

$$\begin{aligned} \frac{234+2x}{5} &\ge 80 \\ 5\left(\frac{234+2x}{5}\right) &\ge 5(80) \\ 234+2x &\ge 400 \\ 234+2x-234 &\ge 400-234 \\ 2x &\ge 166 \\ \frac{2x}{2} &\ge \frac{166}{2} \\ x &\ge 83 \end{aligned}$$

You must get at least 83% on the final examination to earn a B in the course.

EXERCISE SET 2.6

1. $x > 6$

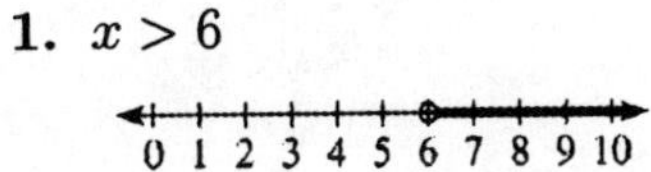

3. $x < -4$

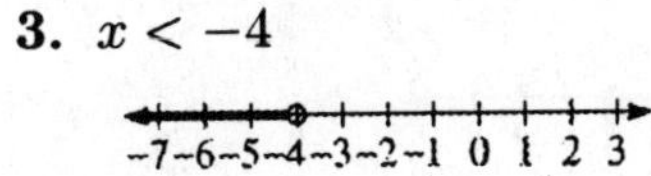

5. $x \geq -3$

-5 -4 -3 -2 -1 0 1 2 3 4 5

7. $x \leq 4$

-4 -3 -2 -1 0 1 2 3 4 5 6

9. $-2 < x \leq 5$

-3 -2 -1 0 1 2 3 4 5 6 7

11. $-1 < x < 4$

-3 -2 -1 0 1 2 3 4 5 6 7

13. $\{x|x > -2\}$

15. $\{x|x \geq 4\}$

17. $\{x|x \geq 3\}$

19.
$$\begin{aligned} x - 3 &> 2 \\ x - 3 + 3 &> 2 + 3 \\ x &> 5 \end{aligned}$$

$\{x|x > 5\}$

-1 0 1 2 3 4 5 6 7 8 9

21.
$$\begin{aligned} x + 4 &\leq 9 \\ x + 4 - 4 &\leq 9 - 4 \\ x &\leq 5 \end{aligned}$$

$\{x|x \leq 5\}$

-2 -1 0 1 2 3 4 5 6 7 8

23.
$$\begin{aligned} y - 3 &< 0 \\ y - 3 + 3 &< 0 + 3 \\ y &< 3 \end{aligned}$$

$\{y|y < 3\}$

-4 -3 -2 -1 0 1 2 3 4 5 6

25.
$$\begin{aligned} 3x + 4 &\leq 2x + 7 \\ 3x - 2x &\leq 7 - 4 \\ x &\leq 3 \end{aligned}$$

$\{x|x \leq 3\}$

-4 -3 -2 -1 0 1 2 3 4 5 6

27.
$$\begin{aligned} 5x - 9 &< 4x + 7 \\ 5x - 4x &< 7 + 9 \\ x &< 16 \end{aligned}$$

$\{x|x < 16\}$

12 13 14 15 16 17 18 19 20

29.
$$\begin{aligned} 7x - 7 &> 6x - 3 \\ 7x - 6x &> -3 + 7 \\ x &> 4 \end{aligned}$$

$\{x|x > 4\}$

-2 -1 0 1 2 3 4 5 6 7 8

31.
$$\begin{aligned} x - \frac{2}{3} &> \frac{1}{2} \\ x - \frac{2}{3} + \frac{2}{3} &> \frac{1}{2} + \frac{2}{3} \\ x &> \frac{3}{6} + \frac{4}{6} \\ x &> \frac{7}{6} \end{aligned}$$

$\{x|x > \frac{7}{6}\}$

$\frac{7}{6}$

-5 -4 -3 -2 -1 0 1 2 3 4 5

33.
$$y+\frac{7}{8}\le\frac{1}{2}$$
$$y+\frac{7}{8}-\frac{7}{8}\le\frac{1}{2}-\frac{7}{8}$$
$$y\le\frac{4}{8}-\frac{7}{8}$$
$$y\le-\frac{3}{8}$$

$\{y|y\le\frac{3}{8}\}$

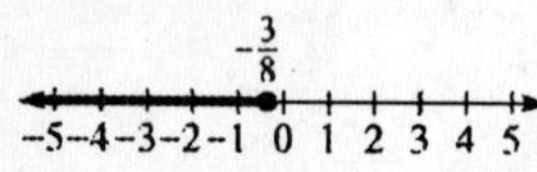

35.
$$-15y+13>13-16y$$
$$-15y+13+16y>13-16y+16y$$
$$y+13>13$$
$$y+13-13>13-13$$
$$y>0$$

$\{y|y>0\}$

37.
$$\frac{1}{2}x<4$$
$$2\left(\frac{1}{2}x\right)<2(4)$$
$$1x<8$$
$$x<8$$

$\{x|x<8\}$

39.
$$\frac{x}{3}>-2$$
$$3\left(\frac{x}{3}\right)>3(-2)$$
$$x>-6$$

$\{x|x>-6\}$

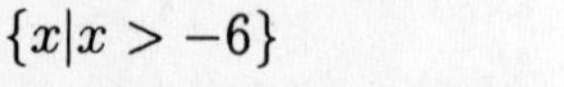

41. $4x<20$
$$\frac{4x}{x}<20$$
$$x<5$$

$\{x|x<5\}$

43. $3x\ge-21$
$$\frac{3x}{3}\ge\frac{-21}{3}$$
$$x\ge-7$$

$\{x|x\ge-7\}$

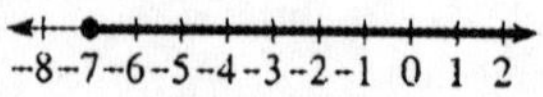

45. $-3x<15$
$$\frac{-3x}{-3}>\frac{15}{-3}$$

Notice that the direction of the inequality symbol was reversed when both sides were divided by a negative number.

$x>-5$

$\{x|x>-5\}$

47. $-3x\ge15$
$$\frac{-3x}{-3}\le\frac{15}{-3}$$
$$x\le-5$$

$\{x|x\le-5\}$

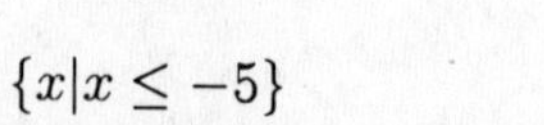

49. $-16x > -48$

$$\frac{-16x}{-16} < \frac{-48}{-16}$$

$$x < 3$$

$\{x|x < 3\}$

-4 -3 -2 -1 0 1 2 3 4 5 6

51. $-4y \le \frac{1}{2}$

$$2(-4y) \le 2\left(\frac{1}{2}\right)$$

$$-8y \le 1$$

$$\frac{-8y}{-8} \ge \frac{1}{-8}$$

$$y \ge -\frac{1}{8}$$

$\left\{y|y \ge -\frac{1}{8}\right\}$

$-\frac{1}{8}$

-5 -4 -3 -2 -1 0 1 2 3 4 5

53. $-x < 4$

$$-1(-x) > -1(4)$$

$$x > -4$$

$\{x|x > -4\}$

-9 -8 -7 -6 -5 -4 -3 -2 -1 0 1

55. $2x - 3 > 7$

$$2x - 3 + 3 > 7 + 3$$

$$2x > 10$$

$$\frac{2x}{2} > \frac{10}{2}$$

$$x > 5$$

$\{x|x > 5\}$

-1 0 1 2 3 4 5 6 7 8 9

57. $3x + 3 < 18$

$$3x + 3 - 3 < 18 - 3$$

$$3x < 15$$

$$\frac{3x}{3} < \frac{15}{3}$$

$$x < 5$$

$\{x|x < 5\}$

-1 0 1 2 3 4 5 6 7 8 9

59. $3 - 7x \le 17$

$$3 - 7x - 3 \le 17 - 3$$

$$-7x \le 14$$

$$\frac{-7x}{-7} \ge \frac{14}{-7}$$

$$x \ge -2$$

$\{x|x \ge -2\}$

-5 -4 -3 -2 -1 0 1 2 3 4 5

61. $-2x - 3 < 3$

$$-2x - 3 + 3 < 3 + 3$$

$$-2x < 6$$

$$\frac{-2x}{-2} > \frac{6}{-2}$$

$$x > -3$$

$\{x|x > -3\}$

-5 -4 -3 -2 -1 0 1 2 3 4 5

63. $5 - x \le 1$

$$5 - x - 5 \le 1 - 5$$

$$-x \le -4$$

$$-1(-x) \ge -1(-4)$$

$$x \ge 4$$

$\{x|x \ge 4\}$

-2 -1 0 1 2 3 4 5 6 7 8

65.
$$\begin{aligned} 2x-5 &> -x+6 \\ 2x-5+x &> -x+6+x \\ 3x-5 &> 6 \\ 3x-5+5 &> 6+5 \\ 3x &> 11 \\ \frac{3x}{3} &> \frac{11}{3} \\ x &> \frac{11}{3} \end{aligned}$$

$\{x|x > \frac{11}{3}\}$

$\frac{11}{3}$

-2 -1 0 1 2 3 4 5 6 7 8

67.
$$\begin{aligned} 2y-5 &< 5y-11 \\ 2y-5-5y &< 5y-11-5y \\ -3y-5 &< -11 \\ -3y-5+5 &< -11+5 \\ -3y &< -6 \\ \frac{-3y}{-3} &> \frac{-6}{-3} \\ y &> 2 \end{aligned}$$

$\{y|y > 2\}$

-2 -1 0 1 2 3 4 5 6 7 8

69.
$$\begin{aligned} 3(2y-1) &< 9 \\ 6y-3 &< 9 \\ 6y-3+3 &< 9+3 \\ 6y &< 12 \\ \frac{6y}{6} &< \frac{12}{6} \\ y &< 2 \end{aligned}$$

$\{y|y < 2\}$

-5 -4 -3 -2 -1 0 1 2 3 4 5

71.
$$\begin{aligned} 3(x+1)-5 &< 2x+1 \\ 3x+3-5 &< 2x+1 \\ 3x-2 &< 2x+1 \\ 3x-2-2x &< 2x+1-2x \\ x-2 &< 1 \\ x-2+2 &< 1+2 \\ x &< 3 \end{aligned}$$

$\{x|x < 3\}$

-5 -4 -3 -2 -1 0 1 2 3 4 5

73.
$$\begin{aligned} 8x+3 &> 3(2x+1)-x+5 \\ 8x+3 &> 6x+3-x+5 \\ 8x+3 &> 5x+8 \\ 8x+3-5x &> 5x+8-5x \\ 3x+3 &> 8 \\ 3x+3-3 &> 8-3 \\ 3x &> 5 \\ x &> \frac{5}{3} \end{aligned}$$

$\{x|x > \frac{5}{3}\}$

$\frac{5}{3}$

-2 -1 0 1 2 3 4 5 6 7 8

75.
$$\begin{aligned} \frac{x}{3}-2 &\geq 1 \\ \frac{x}{3}-2+2 &\geq 1+2 \\ \frac{x}{3} &\geq 3 \\ 3\left(\frac{x}{3}\right) &\geq 3(3) \\ x &\geq 9 \end{aligned}$$

$\{x|x \geq 9\}$

5 6 7 8 9 10 11 12

77.

$$1 - \frac{x}{2} > 4$$
$$1 - \frac{x}{2} - 1 > 4 - 1$$
$$-\frac{x}{2} > 3$$
$$2\left(-\frac{x}{2}\right) > 2(3)$$
$$-x > 6$$
$$-1(-x) < -1(6)$$
$$x < -6$$

$\{x|x < -6\}$

-9 -8 -7 -6 -5 -4 -3 -2 -1 0 1

79.

$$-4x - 4 < 4(x - 5)$$
$$-4x - 4 < 4x - 20$$
$$-4x - 4 + 4 < 4x - 20 + 4$$
$$-4x < 4x - 16$$
$$-4x - 4x < 4x - 16 - 4x$$
$$0 < -16$$

The original inequality is equivalent to the false statement $0 < -16$, so the inequality has no solution. The solution set is $\emptyset$ (the empty set).

81.

$$x + 3 < x + 7$$
$$x + 3 - x < x + 7 - x$$
$$3 < 7$$

The original inequality is equivalent to the true statement $3 < 7$, so the solution is the set of all real numbers, written $\{x|x \text{ is a real number}\}$.

83.

$$7x \le 7(x - 2)$$
$$7x \le 7x - 14$$
$$7x - 7x \le 7x - 14 - 7x$$
$$0 \le -14$$

Since $0 \le -14$ is a false statement, the original inequality has no solution. The solution set is $\emptyset$.

85.

$$2(x + 3) > 2x + 1$$
$$2x + 6 > 2x + 1$$
$$2x + 6 - 2x > 2x + 1 - 2x$$
$$6 > 1$$

Since $6 > 1$ is a true statement, the original inequality is true for all real numbers. The solution set is $\{x|x \text{ is a real number}\}$.

87.

$$5x - 4 \le 4(x - 1)$$
$$5x - 4 \le 4x - 4$$
$$5x - 4 + 4 \le 4x - 4 + 4$$
$$5x \le 4x$$
$$5x - 4x \le 4x - 4x$$
$$x \le 0$$

$\{x|x \le 0\}$

89. $x \ge 34.4\%$

The following cities have 34.4% or more of their population ages 25 and older with 16 or more years of education: Raleigh, NC; Seattle, WA; San Francisco, CA; and Austin, TX.

91. $x < 30.0\%$

The only city on the list with less than 30.0% of its population ages 25 and older with 16 or more years of education is San Diego, CA.

93. $30.0\% \le x \le 34.4\%$

The following cities have at least 30.0% but no more than 34.4% of their population ages 25 and older with 16 or more years of education: Washington, DC; Lexington-Fayette, KY; Minneapolis, MN; Boston, MA; and Arlington, TX.

95.

$$\begin{aligned} 3x - 4 &< 11 \\ 3x - 4 + 4 &< 11 + 4 \\ 3x &< 15 \\ \frac{3x}{3} &< \frac{15}{3} \\ x &< 5 \end{aligned}$$

The following disorders affect fewer than 5 million people in the United States: antisocial personality and schizophrenia.

97. $N = 550 - 9x$; $N < 370$

$$\begin{aligned} 550 - 9x &< 370 \\ 550 - 9x - 550 &< 370 - 550 \\ -9x &< -180 \\ \frac{-9x}{-9} &> \frac{-180}{-9} \\ x &> 20 \end{aligned}$$

Twenty years after 1988 is 2008. According to the model, there will be 370 billion cigarettes consumed in 2008 and less than 370 billion after 2008 (from 2009 onward).

99. a. Let $x =$ your grade on the final exam.

$$\begin{aligned} \frac{86 + 88 + x}{3} &\geq 90 \\ 3\left(\frac{86 + 88 + x}{3}\right) &\geq 3(90) \\ 86 + 88 + x &\geq 270 \\ 174 + x &\geq 270 \\ 174 + x - 174 &\geq 270 - 174 \\ x &\geq 96 \end{aligned}$$

You must get at least 96% on the final exam to earn an A in the course.

b.

$$\begin{aligned} \frac{86 + 88 + x}{3} &< 80 \\ 3\left(\frac{86 + 88 + x}{3}\right) &< 3(80) \\ 86 + 88 + x &< 240 \\ 174 + x &< 240 \\ 174 + x - 174 &< 240 - 174 \\ x &< 66 \end{aligned}$$

If you get less than 66% on the final exam, your grade will be below a B.

101. Let $x =$ number of miles driven.

$$\begin{aligned} 80 + 0.25x &\leq 400 \\ 80 + 0.25x - 80 &\leq 400 - 80 \\ 0.25x &\leq 320 \\ \frac{0.25x}{0.25} &\leq \frac{320}{0.25} \\ x &\leq 1280 \end{aligned}$$

You can drive up to 1280 miles.

103. Let $x =$ number of cement bags.

$$\begin{aligned} 245 + 95x &\leq 3000 \\ 245 + 95x - 245 &\leq 3000 - 245 \\ 95x &\leq 2755 \\ \frac{95x}{95} &\leq \frac{2755}{95} \\ x &\leq 29 \end{aligned}$$

Up to 29 pounds of cement can safely be listed on the elevator in one trip.

For Exercises 105–109, answers may vary.

111. Let $x =$ number of miles driven.

Weekly cost for Basic Rental: \$260
Weekly cost for Continental: $\$80 + 0.25x$

The cost for Basic Rental is a better deal if

$$80 + 0.25x > 260.$$

Solve this inequality.

$$\begin{aligned} 80 + 0.25x - 80 &> 260 - 80 \\ 0.25x &> 180 \\ \frac{0.25x}{0.25} &> \frac{180}{0.25} \\ x &> 720 \end{aligned}$$

Basic Car Rental is a better deal if you drive more than 720 miles in a week.

113.

$$\begin{aligned} 1.45 - 7.23x &> -1.442 \\ 1.45 - 7.23x - 1.45 &> -1.442 - 1.45 \\ -7.23x &> -2.892 \\ \frac{-7.23x}{-7.23} &< \frac{-2.892}{-7.23} \\ x &< 0.4 \end{aligned}$$

$\{x | x < 0.4\}$

Review Exercises

115. $A = PB$, $A = 8, P = 40\% = 0.4$

$$\begin{aligned} A &= PB \\ 8 &= 0.4B \\ \frac{8}{0.4} &= \frac{0.4B}{0.4} \\ 20 &= B \end{aligned}$$

8 is 40% of 20.

116. Let $w =$ the width of the rectangle.
Then $w + 5 =$ the length.

The perimeter is 34 inches.

$$2w + 2(w + 5) = 34.$$

Solve this equation.

$$\begin{aligned} 2w + 2w + 10 &= 34 \\ 4w + 10 &= 34 \\ 4w &= 24 \\ w &= 6 \end{aligned}$$

The width is 6 inches and the length is $6 + 5 = 11$ inches.

117.

$$\begin{aligned} 5x + 16 &= 3(x + 8) \\ 5x + 16 &= 3x + 24 \\ 5x + 16 - 3x &= 3x + 24 - 3x \\ 2x + 16 &= 24 \\ 2x + 16 - 16 &= 24 - 16 \\ 2x &= 8 \\ \frac{2x}{2} &= \frac{8}{2} \\ x &= 4 \end{aligned}$$

The solution is 4.

Chapter 2 Review Exercises

For Exercises 1–18 and 20–28, students should check all proposed solutions by substituting in the original equations. Checks will not be shown here.

1.

$$\begin{aligned} x - 10 &= 32 \\ x - 10 + 10 &= 32 + 10 \\ x &= 42 \end{aligned}$$

The solution is 42.

2.

$$\begin{aligned} -14 &= y + 6 \\ -14 - 6 &= y + 6 - 6 \\ -20 &= y \end{aligned}$$

The solution is -20.

3.

$$\begin{aligned} 7z - 3 &= 6z + 9 \\ 7z - 3 - 6z &= 6z + 9 - 6z \\ z - 3 &= 9 \\ z - 3 + 3 &= 9 + 3 \\ z &= 12 \end{aligned}$$

The solution is 12.

4.
$$\begin{aligned} 4(x+3) &= 3x-10 \\ 4x+12 &= 3x-10 \\ 4x+12-3x &= 3x-10-3x \\ x+12 &= -10 \\ x+12-12 &= -10-12 \\ x &= -22 \end{aligned}$$

The solution is -22.

5.
$$\begin{aligned} 6x-3x-9+1 &= -5x+7x-3 \\ 3x-8 &= 2x-3 \\ 3x-8-2x &= 2x-3-2x \\ x-8 &= -3 \\ x-8+8 &= -3+8 \\ x &= 5 \end{aligned}$$

The solution is 5.

6.
$$\begin{aligned} \frac{x}{7} &= 10 \\ 7\left(\frac{x}{7}\right) &= 7(10) \\ x &= 70 \end{aligned}$$

The solution is 70.

7.
$$\begin{aligned} \frac{y}{-8} &= 4 \\ -8\left(\frac{y}{-8}\right) &= -8(4) \\ y &= -32 \end{aligned}$$

The solution is -32.

8.
$$\begin{aligned} 7z &= 77 \\ \frac{7z}{7} &= \frac{77}{7} \\ z &= 11 \end{aligned}$$

The solution is 11.

9.
$$\begin{aligned} -36 &= -9y \\ \frac{-36}{-9} &= \frac{-9y}{-9} \\ 4 &= y \end{aligned}$$

The solution is 4.

10.
$$\begin{aligned} \frac{3}{5}x &= -9 \\ \frac{5}{3}\left(\frac{3}{5}x\right) &= \frac{5}{3}(-9) \\ 1x &= -15 \\ x &= -15 \end{aligned}$$

The solution is -15.

11.
$$\begin{aligned} 30 &= -\frac{5}{2}y \\ -\frac{2}{5} = &-\frac{2}{5}\left(-\frac{5}{2}y\right) \\ -12 &= y \end{aligned}$$

The solution is -12.

12.
$$\begin{aligned} -x &= 14 \\ -1(-x) &= -1(14) \\ x &= -14 \end{aligned}$$

The solution is -14.

13.
$$\begin{aligned} \frac{-x}{3} &= -1 \\ 3\left(\frac{-x}{3}\right) &= 3(-1) \\ -x &= -3 \\ -1(-x) &= -1(-3) \\ x &= 3 \end{aligned}$$

The solution is 3.

14.
$$\begin{aligned} 4x+9 &= 33 \\ 4x+9-9 &= 33-9 \\ 4x &= 24 \\ \frac{4x}{4} &= \frac{24}{4} \\ x &= 6 \end{aligned}$$

The solution is 6.

15.
$$\begin{aligned} -3y-2&=13\\ -3y-2+2&=13+2\\ -3y&=15\\ \frac{-3y}{-3}&=\frac{15}{-3}\\ y&=-5 \end{aligned}$$

The solution is -5.

16.
$$\begin{aligned} 5z+20&=3z\\ 5z+20-3z&=3z-3z\\ 2z+20&=0\\ 2z+20-20&=0-20\\ 2z&=-20\\ \frac{2z}{2}&=\frac{-20}{2}\\ z&=-10 \end{aligned}$$

The solution is -10.

17.
$$\begin{aligned} 5x-3=x+5&=x+5\\ 5x-3-x&=x+5-x\\ 4x-3&=5\\ 4x-3+3&=5+3\\ 4x&=8\\ \frac{4x}{4}&=\frac{8}{4}\\ x&=2 \end{aligned}$$

The solution is 2.

18.
$$\begin{aligned} 3-2x&=9-8x\\ 3-2x+8x&=9-8x+8x\\ 3+6x&=9\\ 3+6x-3&=9-3\\ 6x&=6\\ \frac{6x}{6}&=\frac{6}{6}\\ x&=1 \end{aligned}$$

The solution is 1.

19. $N=0.07x+4.1$; $N=6.2$

$$\begin{aligned} 6.2&=0.07x+4.1\\ 6.2-4.1&=0.07x+4.1-4.1\\ 2.1&=0.07x\\ \frac{2.1}{0.07}&=\frac{0.07x}{0.07}\\ 30&=x \end{aligned}$$

The enrollment for women is expected to reach 6.2 million 30 years after 1984, which is in the year $1984+30=2014$.

20.
$$\begin{aligned} 5x+9-7x+6&=x+18\\ -2x+15&=x+18\\ -2x+15-x&=x+18-x\\ -3x+15&=18\\ -3x+15-15&=18-15\\ -3x&=3\\ \frac{-3x}{-3}&=\frac{3}{-3}\\ x&=-1 \end{aligned}$$

The solution is -1.

21.
$$\begin{aligned} 3(x+4)&=5x-12\\ 3x+12&=5x-12\\ 3x+12-5x&=5x-12-5x\\ -2x+12&=-12\\ -2x+12-12&=-12-12\\ -2x&=-24\\ \frac{-2x}{-2}&=\frac{-24}{-2}\\ x&=12 \end{aligned}$$

The solution is 12.

22.
$$\begin{aligned} 1-2(6-y) &= 3y+2 \\ 1-12+2y &= 3y+2 \\ 2y-11 &= 3y+2 \\ 2y-11-3y &= 3y+2-3y \\ -y-11 &= 2 \\ -y-11+11 &= 2+11 \\ -y &= 13 \\ -1(-y) &= -1(13) \\ y &= -13 \end{aligned}$$

The solution is -13.

23.
$$\begin{aligned} 2(x-4)+3(x+5) &= 2x-2 \\ 2x-8+3x+15 &= 2x-2 \\ 5x+7 &= 2x-2 \\ 5x+7-2x &= 2x-2-2x \\ 3x+7 &= -2 \\ 3x+7-7 &= -2-7 \\ 3x &= -9 \\ \frac{3x}{3} &= \frac{-9}{3} \\ x &= -3 \end{aligned}$$

The solution is -3.

24.
$$\begin{aligned} -2(y-4)-(3y-2) &= -2-(6y-2) \\ -2y+8-3y+2 &= -2-6y-2 \\ -5y+10 &= -6y \\ -5y+10+6y &= -6y+6y \\ 10+y &= 0 \\ 10+y-10 &= 0-10 \\ y &= -10 \end{aligned}$$

The solution is -10.

25. $\frac{2x}{3} = \frac{x}{6} + 1$

To clear fractions, multiply both sides by the LCD, which is 6.

$$\begin{aligned} 6\left(\frac{2x}{3}\right) &= 6\left(\frac{x}{6}+1\right) \\ 6\left(\frac{2x}{3}\right) &= 6\left(\frac{x}{6}\right)+6(1) \\ 4x &= x+6 \\ 4x-x &= x+6-x \\ 3x &= 6 \\ \frac{3x}{3} &= \frac{6}{3} \\ x &= 2 \end{aligned}$$

The solution is 2.

26. $\frac{x}{2} - \frac{1}{10} = \frac{x}{5} + \frac{1}{2}$

Multiply both sides by LCD, which is 10.

$$\begin{aligned} 10\left(\frac{x}{2}-\frac{1}{10}\right) &= 10\left(\frac{x}{5}+\frac{1}{2}\right) \\ 10\left(\frac{x}{2}\right)-10\left(\frac{1}{10}\right) &= 10\left(\frac{x}{5}\right)+10\left(\frac{1}{2}\right) \\ 5x-1 &= 2x+5 \\ 5x-1-2x &= 2x+5-2x \\ 3x-1 &= 5 \\ 3x-1+1 &= 5+1 \\ 3x &= 6 \\ \frac{3x}{3} &= \frac{6}{3} \\ x &= 2 \end{aligned}$$

The solution is 2.

27.
$$\begin{aligned} 3(8x-1) &= 6(5+4x) \\ 24x-3 &= 30+24x \\ 24x-3-24x &= 30+24x-24x \\ -3 &= 30 \end{aligned}$$

Since $-3 = 30$ is a false statement, the original equation is inconsistent and has no solution.

28. $4(2x-3)+4=8x-8$

$$\begin{aligned} 8x-12+4&=8x-8\\ 8x-8&=8x-8\\ 8x-8-8x&=8x-8-8x\\ -8&=-8 \end{aligned}$$

Since $-8=-8$ is a true statement, the original equation is an identity and all real numbers are solutions.

29. $r=0.6(220-a)$; $r=120$

$$\begin{aligned} r&=0.6(220-a)\\ 120&=0.6(220-a)\\ 120&=132-0.6a\\ 120-132&=-0.6a\\ -12&=-0.6a\\ \frac{-12}{-0.6}&=\frac{-0.6a}{-0.6}\\ 20&=a \end{aligned}$$

If the optimal heart rate is 120 beats per minute, the person is 20 years old.

30. $I=Pr$ for r

$$\frac{I}{P}=\frac{Pr}{P}$$
$$\frac{I}{P}=r \quad\text{or}\quad r=\frac{I}{P}$$

31. $V=\frac{1}{3}Bh$ for h

$$3V=3\left(\frac{1}{3}Bh\right)$$
$$3V=Bh$$
$$\frac{3V}{B}=\frac{Bh}{B}$$
$$\frac{3V}{B}=h \quad\text{or}\quad h=\frac{3V}{B}$$

32. $P=2l+2w$ for w

$$P-2l=2l+2w-2l$$
$$P-2l=2w$$
$$\frac{P-2l}{2}=\frac{2w}{2}$$
$$\frac{P-2l}{2}=w \quad\text{or}\quad w=\frac{P-2l}{2}$$

33. $A=\frac{B+C}{2}$ for B

$$2A=2\left(\frac{B+C}{2}\right)$$
$$2A=B+C$$
$$2A-C=B+C-C$$
$$2A-C=B \quad\text{or}\quad B=2A-C$$

34. $T=D+pm$ for n

$$T-D=D+pm-D$$
$$T-D=pm$$
$$\frac{T-D}{p}=\frac{pm}{p}$$
$$\frac{T-D}{p}=m \quad\text{or}\quad n=\frac{T-D}{p}$$

35. $0.72=72\%$

36. $0.0035=0.35\%$

37. $65\%=0.65$

38. $150\%=1.5$

39. $3\%=0.03$

40. $A=PB$; $P=8\%=0.08$, $B=120$

$$A=PB$$
$$A=0.08\cdot 120$$
$$A=9.6$$

8% of 120 is 9.6.

41. $A = PB$; $A = 90$, $P = 45\% = 0.45$

$$\begin{aligned} A &= PB \\ 90 &= 0.45B \\ \frac{90}{0.45} &= \frac{0.45B}{0.45} \\ 200 &= B \end{aligned}$$

90 is 4% of 200.

42. $A = PB$; $A = 36, B = 75$

$$\begin{aligned} A &= PB \\ 36 &= P \cdot 75 \\ \frac{36}{75} &= \frac{P \cdot 75}{75} \\ 0.48 &= P \end{aligned}$$

36 is 48% of 75.

43. a. $r = \frac{h}{7}$

$$7r = 7\left(\frac{h}{7}\right)$$

$7r = h$ or $h = 7r$

b. $h = 7r$; $r = 9$
$h = 7(9) = 63$

The woman's height is 63 inches or 5 feet, 3 inches.

44. $A = PB$; $A = 1760, P = 22\% = 0.22$

$$\begin{aligned} A &= PB \\ 1760 &= 0.22B \\ \frac{1760}{0.22} &= \frac{0.22B}{0.22} \\ 8000 &= B \end{aligned}$$

8000 Americans suffer spinal cord injuries each year.

45. Let x = the unknown number.

$$\begin{aligned} 6x - 20 &= 4x \\ 6x - 20 - 4x &= 4x - 4x \\ 2x - 20 &= 0 \\ 2x - 20 + 20 &= 0 + 20 \\ 2x &= 20 \\ x &= 10 \end{aligned}$$

The number is 10. This solution checks because 6 times 10, which is 60, decreased by 20, is 40, which is 4 times the number.

46. Let x = the number of unhealthy air days in New York.
Then $3x + 48$ = the number of unhealthy air days in Los Angeles.

$$\begin{aligned} x + (3x + 48) &= 268 \\ 4x + 48 &= 268 \\ 4x &= 200 \\ x &= 55 \end{aligned}$$

New York has 55 unhealthy air days and Los Angles has $3(55) + 48 = 213$ unhealthy air days.
The solution checks since $55 + 213 = 268$.

47. Let x = the smaller page number.
Then $x + 1$ = the larger page number.

$$\begin{aligned} x + (x + 1) &= 93 \\ 2x + 1 &= 93 \\ 2x &= 92 \\ x &= 46 \end{aligned}$$

The page numbers are 46 and 47. This solution check because $46 + 47 = 93$.

48. Let $x =$ the number of Madonna's platinum records.
Then $x + 2 =$ the number of Barbra Streisand's platinum records.

$$\begin{aligned} x + (x+2) &= 96 \\ 2x + 2 &= 96 \\ 2x &= 94 \\ x &= 47 \end{aligned}$$

Madonna has 47 platinum records and Barbra Streisand has $47 + 2 = 49$ platinum records. This solution checks because $47 + 49 = 96$.

49. Let $x =$ the number of years after 2000.

$$\begin{aligned} 567 + 15x &= 702 \\ 567 + 15x - 567 &= 702 - 567 \\ 15x &= 135 \\ \frac{15x}{15} &= \frac{135}{15} \\ x &= 9 \end{aligned}$$

According to this model, the average weekly salary will reach $702 in 9 years after 2000, which is the year 2009.

50. Let $x =$ the number of checks written.

$$\begin{aligned} 6 + 0.05x &= 6.90 \\ 6 + 0.05x - 6 &= 6.90 - 6 \\ 0.05x &= 0.90 \\ \frac{0.05x}{0.05} &= \frac{0.90}{0.05} \\ x &= 18 \end{aligned}$$

You wrote 18 checks that month.

51. Let $w =$ the width of the field.
Then $3w =$ the length.

The perimeter of a rectangle is twice the length plus twice the width, so the equation is

$$2(3w) + 2w = 400.$$

Solve the equation.

$$\begin{aligned} 6w + 2w &= 400 \\ 8w &= 400 \\ w &= 50 \end{aligned}$$

The width is 50 yards and the length is $3(50) = 150$ yards.

52. Let $x =$ the original price of the table.

$$\begin{aligned} x - 0.25x &= 180 \\ 0.75x &= 180 \\ \frac{0.75x}{0.75} &= \frac{180}{0.75} \\ x &= 240 \end{aligned}$$

The table's price before the reduction was $240.

53. $x < -1$

-5 -4 -3 -2 -1 0 1 2 3 4 5

54. $-2 < x \leq 4$

-5 -4 -3 -2 -1 0 1 2 3 4 5

55. $\{x | x > 4\}$

56. $\{x | x \leq -3\}$

57.

$$\begin{aligned} 2x - 5 &< 3 \\ 2x - 5 + 5 &< 3 + 5 \\ 2x &< 8 \\ \frac{2x}{2} &< \frac{8}{2} \\ x &< 4 \end{aligned}$$

$\{x | x < 4\}$

0 1 2 3 4 5 6 7 8 9 10

58.

$$\begin{aligned} \frac{x}{2} &> -4 \\ 2\left(\frac{x}{2}\right) &> 2(-4) \\ x &> -8 \end{aligned}$$

$\{x | x > -8\}$

-9 -8 -7 -6 -5 -4 -3 -2 -1 0 1

59.
$$\begin{aligned} 3-5x &\le 18 \\ 3-5x-3 &\le 18-3 \\ -5x &\le 15 \\ \frac{-5x}{-5} &\ge \frac{15}{-5} \\ x &\ge -3 \end{aligned}$$

$\{x|x \ge -3\}$

-5 -4 -3 -2 -1 0 1 2 3 4 5

60.
$$\begin{aligned} 4x+6 &< 5x \\ 4x+6-5x &< 5x-5x \\ -x+6 &< 0 \\ -x+6-6 &< 0-6 \\ -x &< -6 \\ -1(-x) &> -1(-6) \\ x &> 6 \end{aligned}$$

$\{x|x > 6\}$

0 1 2 3 4 5 6 7 8 9 10

61.
$$\begin{aligned} 6x-10 &\ge 2(x+3) \\ 6x-10 &\ge 2x+6 \\ 6x-10-2x &\ge 2x+6-2x \\ 4x-10 &\ge 6 \\ 4x-10+10 &\ge 6+10 \\ 4x &\ge 16 \\ \frac{4x}{4} &\ge \frac{16}{4} \\ x &\ge 4 \end{aligned}$$

$\{x|x \ge 4\}$

0 1 2 3 4 5 6 7 8 9 10

62.
$$\begin{aligned} 4x+3(2x-7) &\le x-3 \\ 4x+6x-21 &\le x-3 \\ 10x-21 &\le x-3 \\ 10x-21-x &\le x-3-x \\ 9x-21 &\le -3 \\ 9x-21+21 &\le -3+21 \\ 9x &\le 18 \\ \frac{9x}{9} &\le \frac{18}{9} \\ x &\le 2 \end{aligned}$$

$\{x|x \le 2\}$

-5 -4 -3 -2 -1 0 1 2 3 4 5

63.
$$\begin{aligned} 2(2x+4) &> 4(x+2)-6 \\ 4x+8 &> 4x+8-6 \\ 4x+8 &> 4x+2 \\ 4x+8-4x &> 4x+2-4x \\ 8 &> 2 \end{aligned}$$

Since $8 > 2$ is a true statement, the original inequality is true for all real numbers, and the solution set is written $\{x|x \text{ is a real number}\}$.

64.
$$\begin{aligned} -2(x-4) &\le 3x+1-5x \\ -2x+8 &\le -2x+1 \\ -2x+8+2x &\le -2x+1+2x \\ 8 &\le 1 \end{aligned}$$

Since $8 \le 1$ is a false statement, the original inequality has no solution. The solution set is $\emptyset$.

65. Let x = the student's score on the third test.

$$\begin{aligned}\frac{42+74+x}{3} &\geq 60\\ 3\left(\frac{42+74+x}{3}\right) &\geq 3(60)\\ 42+74+x &\geq 180\\ 116+x &\geq 180\\ 116+x-116 &\geq 180-116\\ x &\geq 64\end{aligned}$$

The student must score at least 64 on the third test to pass the course.

66. $C = 10 + 5(x-1)$; $C \leq 500$

$$\begin{aligned}10+5(x-1) &\leq 500\\ 10+5x-5 &\leq 500\\ 5x+5 &\leq 500\\ 5x+5-5 &\leq 500-5\\ 5x &\leq 495\\ \frac{5x}{5} &\leq \frac{495}{5}\\ x &\leq 99\end{aligned}$$

You can talk no more than 99 minutes.

Chapter 2 Test

1.
$$\begin{aligned}4x-5 &= 13\\ 4x+5+5 &= 13+5\\ 4x &= 18\\ \frac{4x}{4} &= \frac{18}{4} = \frac{9}{2}\\ x &= \frac{9}{2}\end{aligned}$$

The solution is $\frac{9}{2}$.

2.
$$\begin{aligned}12x+4 &= 7x-21\\ 12x+4-7x &= 7x-21-7x\\ 5x+4 &= -21\\ 5x+4-4 &= -21-4\\ 5x &= -25\\ \frac{5x}{5} &= \frac{-25}{5}\\ x &= -5\end{aligned}$$

The solution is -5.

3.
$$\begin{aligned}8-5(x-2) &= x+26\\ 8-5x+10 &= x+26\\ 18-5x &= x+26\\ 18-5x-x &= x+26-x\\ 18-6x &= 26\\ 18-6x-10 &= 26-18\\ -6x &= 8\\ \frac{-6x}{-6} &= \frac{8}{-6}\\ x &= -\frac{8}{6} = -\frac{4}{3}\end{aligned}$$

The solution is $-\frac{4}{3}$.

4.
$$\begin{aligned}3(2y-4) &= 9-3(y+1)\\ 6y-12 &= 9-3y-3\\ 6y-12 &= 6-3y\\ 6y-12+3y &= 6-3y+3y\\ 9y-12 &= 6\\ 9y-12+12 &= 6+12\\ 9y &= 18\\ \frac{9y}{9} &= \frac{18}{9}\\ y &= 2\end{aligned}$$

The solution is 2.

5.
$$\begin{aligned}\frac{3}{4}x &= -15\\ \frac{4}{3}\left(\frac{3}{4}x\right) &= \frac{4}{3}(-15)\\ x &= -20\end{aligned}$$

The solution is -20.

6. $\frac{x}{10} + \frac{1}{3} = \frac{x}{5} + \frac{1}{2}$

Multiply both sides by the LCD, 30.

$$
\begin{aligned}
30\left(\frac{x}{10} + \frac{1}{3}\right) &= 30\left(\frac{x}{5} + \frac{1}{2}\right) \\
30\left(\frac{x}{10}\right) + 30\left(\frac{1}{3}\right) &= 30\left(\frac{x}{5}\right) + 30\left(\frac{1}{2}\right) \\
3x + 1- &= 6x + 15 \\
3x + 10 - 6x &= 6x + 15 - 6x \\
-3x + 10 &= 15 \\
-3x + 10 - 10 &= 15 - 10 \\
-3x &= 5 \\
\frac{-3x}{-3} &= \frac{5}{-3} \\
z &= -\frac{5}{3}
\end{aligned}
$$

The solution is $-\frac{5}{3}$.

7. $N = 2.4x + 180$; $N = 324$

$$
\begin{aligned}
2.4x + 180 &= 324 \\
2.4x + 180 - 180 &= 324 - 180 \\
2.4 &= 144 \\
\frac{2.4x}{2.4} &= \frac{144}{2.4} \\
x &= 60
\end{aligned}
$$

The U.S. population is expected to reach 324 million 60 years after 1960, which is in the year 2020.

8. $V = \pi r^2 h$ for h

$$
\begin{aligned}
\frac{V}{\pi r^2} &= \frac{\pi r^2 h}{\pi r^2} \\
\frac{V}{\pi r^2} &= h \quad \text{or} \quad h = \frac{V}{\pi r^2}
\end{aligned}
$$

9. $l = \frac{P - 2w}{2}$ for w

$$
\begin{aligned}
2l &= 2\left(\frac{P - 2w}{2}\right) \\
2l &= P - 2w \\
2l + 2w &= P - 2w + 2w \\
2l + 2w &= P \\
2l + 2w - 2l &= P - 2l \\
2w &= P - 2l \\
\frac{2w}{2} &= \frac{P - 2l}{2} \\
w &= \frac{P - 2l}{2}
\end{aligned}
$$

10. $A = PB$; $P = 6\% = 0.06$, $B = 140$

$$
\begin{aligned}
A &= PB \\
A &= 0.06(140) \\
A &= 8.4
\end{aligned}
$$

6% of 140 is 8.4.

11. $A = PB$; $A = 120, P = 80\% = 0.80$

$$
\begin{aligned}
A &= PB \\
120 &= 0.80B \\
\frac{120}{0.80} &= \frac{0.80B}{0.80} \\
150 &= B
\end{aligned}
$$

120 is 80% of 150.

12. $A = PB$; $A = 12, B = 240$

$$
\begin{aligned}
A &= PB \\
12 &= P \cdot 240 \\
\frac{12}{240} &= \frac{P \cdot 240}{240} \\
0.05 &= P
\end{aligned}
$$

12 is 5% of 240.

13. Let $x =$ the unknown number.

$$5x - 9 = 310$$
$$5x - 9 + 9 = 310 + 9$$
$$5x = 319$$
$$\frac{5x}{5} = \frac{319}{5}$$
$$x = \frac{319}{5} = 63.8$$

The number is 63.8.

14. Let $B =$ Buchanan's age.
Then $B + 4 =$ Reagan's age.

$$B + (B + 4) = 134$$
$$2B + 4 = 134$$
$$2B = 130$$
$$B = 65$$

Buchanan was 65 years old and Reagan was 65 + 4 = 69 years old.

15. Let $x =$ number of minutes of long-distance calls.

$$15 + 0.05x = 45$$
$$0.05x = 30$$
$$x = \frac{30}{0.05}$$
$$x = 600$$

You can talk long distance for 600 minutes.

16. Let $w =$ width of field (in yards).
Then $2w =$ length of field.

$$2(2w) + 2w = 450$$
$$4w + 2w = 450$$
$$6w = 450$$
$$w = 75$$

The width is 75 yards and the length is 2(75) = 150 yards.

17. Let $x =$ the book's original price.

$$x - 0.20x = 28$$
$$0.80x = 28$$
$$x = \frac{28}{0.80}$$
$$x = 35$$

The price of the book before the reduction was $35.

18. $x > -2$

-5 -4 -3 -2 -1 0 1 2 3 4 5

19. $-4 \leq x < 1$

-5 -4 -3 -2 -1 0 1 2 3 4 5

20. $\{x | x \leq -1\}$

21.

$$\frac{x}{2} < -3$$
$$2\left(\frac{x}{2}\right) < 2(-3)$$
$$x < -6$$
$$\{x | x < -6\}$$

-9 -8 -7 -6 -5 -4 -3 -2 -1 0 1

22.

$$6 - 9x \geq 33$$
$$6 - 9x - 6 \geq 33 - 6$$
$$-9x \geq 27$$
$$\frac{-9x}{-9} \leq \frac{27}{-9}$$
$$x \leq -3$$

$$\{x | x \leq -3\}$$

-9 -8 -7 -6 -5 -4 -3 -2 -1 0 1

23.
$$\begin{aligned} 4x - 2 &> 2(x+6) \\ 4x - 2 &> 2x + 12 \\ 4x - 2x &> 2x + 12 - 2x \\ 2x - 2 &> 12 \\ 2x &> 14 \\ x &> 7 \end{aligned}$$

$\{x|x > 7\}$

0 1 2 3 4 5 6 7 8 9 10

24. Let $x =$ the student's score on the fourth exam.

$$\frac{76+80+72+x}{4} \geq 80$$
$$4\left(\frac{76+80+72+x}{4}\right) \geq 4(80)$$
$$76+80+72+x \geq 320$$
$$228 + x \geq 320$$
$$x \geq 92$$

The student must score at least 92 on the fourth exam to have an average of at least 80.

25. Let $w =$ width of rectangle.

$$\begin{aligned} 2(20) + 2w &> 56 \\ 40 + 2w &> 56 \\ 2w &> 16 \\ w &> 8 \end{aligned}$$

The width must be greater than 8 inches.

Chapter 2 Cumulative Review Exercises (Chapters 1-2)

1. $-8 - (12 - 16) = -8 - (-4)$
$= -8 + 4 = -4$

2. $(-3)(-2) + (-2)(4) = 6 + (-8) = -2$

3. $(8 - 10)^3(7 - 11)^2 = (-2)^3(-4)^2$
$= -8(16)$
$= -128$

4. $2 - 5[x + 3(x + 7)] = 2 - 5(x + 3x + 21)$
$= 2 - 5(4x + 21)$
$= 2 - 20x - 105$
$= -103 - 20x$

5. The rational numbers are $-4, -\frac{1}{3}, 0,$ $\sqrt{4}$ $(= 2)$, and 1063.

6. Quadrant III

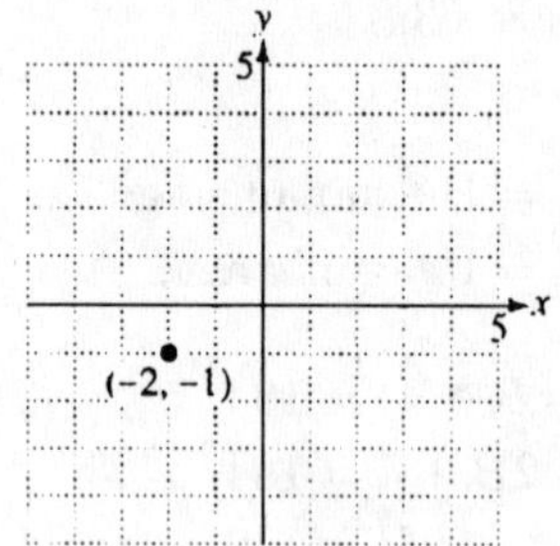

7. $-10{,}000 < -2$ since $-10{,}000$ is to the left of -2 on the number line.

8. $6(4x - 1 - 5y) = 6(4x) - 6(1) - 6(5y)$
$= 24x - 6 - 30y$

9. Unemployment was a minimum in 2000, with about 4% unemployed.

10. The unemployment rate reached a maximum during 1992 of about 7.8%.

11.
$$\begin{aligned} 5 - 6(x+2) &= x - 14 \\ 5 - 6x - 12 &= x - 14 \\ -7 - 6x &= x - 14 \\ -7 - 6x - x &= x - 14 - x \\ -7 - 7x &= -14 \\ -7 - 7x + 7 &= -14 + 7 \\ -7x &= -7 \\ \frac{-7x}{-7} &= \frac{-7}{-7} \\ x &= 1 \end{aligned}$$

The solution is 1.

12. $\frac{x}{5} - 2 = \frac{x}{3}$

Multiply both sides by the LCD, 15.

$$
\begin{aligned}
15\left(\frac{x}{5} - 2\right) &= 15\left(\frac{x}{3}\right)\\
15\left(\frac{x}{5}\right) - 15(2) &= 15\left(\frac{x}{3}\right)\\
3x - 30 &= 5x\\
3x - 30 - 3x &= 5x - 3x\\
-30 &= 2x\\
\frac{-30}{2} &= \frac{2x}{2}\\
-15 &= x
\end{aligned}
$$

The solution is -15.

13. $V = \frac{1}{3}Ah$ for A

$$
\begin{aligned}
V &= \frac{1}{3}Ah\\
3V &= 3\left(\frac{1}{3}Ah\right)\\
3V &= Ah\\
\frac{3V}{h} &= \frac{Ah}{h}\\
\frac{3V}{h} &= A \quad \text{or} \quad A = \frac{3V}{h}
\end{aligned}
$$

14. $A = PB$; $A = 48, P = 30\% = 0.30$

$$
\begin{aligned}
A &= PB\\
48 &= 0.30B\\
\frac{48}{0.30} &= \frac{0.48B}{0.30}\\
160 &= B
\end{aligned}
$$

48 is 30% of 160.

15. Let w = width of parking lot (in yards).

Then $2w - 10$ = length of parking lot.

$$
\begin{aligned}
2(2w - 10) + 2w &= 400\\
4w - 20 + 2w &= 400\\
6w - 20 &= 400\\
6w &= 420\\
w &= 70
\end{aligned}
$$

The width is 70 yards and the length is $2(70) - 10 = 130$ yards.

16. Let x = number of gallons of gasoline.

$$
\begin{aligned}
0.40x &= 30{,}000\\
\frac{0.40x}{0.40} &= \frac{30{,}000}{0.40}\\
x &= 75{,}000
\end{aligned}
$$

75,000 gallons of gasoline must be sold.

17. $-2 < x \leq 3$

-4 -3 -2 -1 0 1 2 3 4 5 6

18.

$$
\begin{aligned}
3 - 3x &> 12\\
3 - 3x - 3 &> 12 - 3\\
-3x &> 9\\
\frac{-3x}{-3} &< \frac{9}{-3}\\
x &< -3
\end{aligned}
$$

$\{x | x < -3\}$

-6 -5 -4 -3 -2 -1 0 1 2 3 4

19. $5 - 2(2 - x) \leq 2(2x + 5) + 1$

$$5 - 6 + 2x \leq 4x + 10 + 1$$
$$2x - 1 \leq 4x + 11$$
$$2x - 1 - 4x \leq 4x + 11 - 4x$$
$$-2x \leq 11$$
$$-2x - 1 \leq 11 + 1$$
$$-2x \leq 12$$
$$\frac{-2x}{-2} \geq \frac{12}{-2}$$
$$x \geq -6$$

$\{x|x \geq -6\}$

-9 -8 -7 -6 -5 -4 -3 -2 -1 0 1

20. Let x = value of medical supplies sold.

$$600 + 0.04x > 2500$$
$$600 + 0.04x - 600 > 2500 - 600$$
$$0.04x > 1900$$
$$\frac{0.04x}{0.04} > \frac{1900}{0.04}$$
$$x > 47{,}500$$

You must sell more than \$47,500 worth of medical supplies.

Chapter 3

PROBLEM SOLVING

3.1 Further Problem Solving

3.1 CHECK POINTS

CHECK POINT 1

$$I = Prt = \$3000 \cdot 0.05 \cdot 1 = \$150$$

The interest at the end of the first year is $150.

CHECK POINT 2

Let x = the amount invested at 9%.
Then $25{,}000 - x$ = the amount invested at 12%.

	Principal	× Rate	= Interest
9% Investment	x	0.09	$0.09x$
12% Investment	$25{,}000 - x$	0.12	$0.12(25{,}000 - x)$

$$\begin{aligned}
0.09x + 0.12(25{,}000 - x) &= 2550 \\
0.09x + 3000 - 0.12x &= 2550 \\
-0.03x + 3000 &= 1550 \\
-0.03x &= -450 \\
\frac{-0.03x}{-0.03} &= \frac{-450}{-0.03} \\
x &= 15{,}000
\end{aligned}$$

Because x represents the amount invested at 9%, $15,000 is invested at 9%. Because $25{,}000-x$ represents the amount invested at 12%, $25,000 – $15,000 = $10,000 is invested at 12%. **Check:** The interest earned on $15,000 at 9% is ($15,000)(0.09) = $1350. The interest earned on $10,000 at 12% is ($10,000)(0.12) = $1200. The total interest is $1350 + $1200 = $2550.

CHECK POINT 3

Amount of acid in the solution $= (0.45)(60) = 27$

There are 27 milliliters of acid in the solution.

CHECK POINT 4

Let $x =$ the number of liters of the 10% acid to be used in the mixture.

Then $50 - x =$ the number of liters of the 60% acid to be used in the mixture.

	Number of Liters	×	Percents of Acid	=	Amount of Acid
10% Acid Solution	x		0.10		$0.10x$
60% Acid Solution	$50 - x$		0.60		$0.60(50 - x)$
30% Acid Solution	50		0.30		$0.30(50)$

$$0.10x + 0.60(50 - x) = 0.30(50)$$
$$0.10x + 30 - 0.60x = 15$$
$$-0.50x + 30 = 15$$
$$-0.50x = -15$$
$$\frac{-0.50x}{-0.50} = \frac{-15}{-0.50}$$
$$x = 30$$

Because x represents the number of liters of the 10% solution, 30 liters of the 10% solution should be used in the mixture. Because $50 - x$ represents the number of liters of the 60% solution, $50 - 30 = 20$ liters of the 60% solution should be used.
This result should be checked in the original wording of the problem.

CHECK POINT 5

$$d = rt$$
$$27 = r \cdot 3$$
$$\frac{27}{3} = \frac{r \cdot 3}{3}$$
$$9 = r$$

Your average rate is 9 miles per hour.

CHECK POINT 6 Let $x =$ the number of hours it will take until the cars are 420 miles apart.

	Rate $\times$	Time $=$	Distance
Faster Car	55	x	$55x$
Slower Car	50	x	$50x$

$$55x + 50x = 420$$
$$105x = 420$$
$$\frac{105x}{105} = \frac{420}{105}$$
$$x = 4$$

The two cars will be 420 miles apart after 4 hours.
Check: After 4 hours, the faster car will have traveled $55 \cdot 4 = 220$ miles and the slower car will have traveled $50 \cdot 4 = 200$ miles. Since the cars are traveling in opposite directions, the distance between them will be 220 miles + 200 miles = 420 miles.

CHECK POINT 7

A good strategy for solving this problem is to look for a "catch." Because "a candle, a fireplace, and a woodburning stove" are grouped together, you may think that you must choose between these three possibilities. However, if you think about the problem some more, you realize that what you need to light first is the match!

EXERCISE SET 3.1

1. $I = Prt; P = 4000, r = 4\% = 0.04, t = 1$

$$I = Prt = (4000)(0.04)(1) = 160$$

The interest at the end of one year is $160.

3.

	Principal $\times$	Rate $=$	Interest
7% Investment	x	0.07	$0.07x$
8% Investment	$20{,}000 - x$	0.08	$0.08(20{,}000 - x)$

The interest for the two investments combined must be $1520, so the equation is

$$0.07x + 0.08(20,000 - x) = 1520.$$

Solve this equation.

$$\begin{aligned} 0.07x + 1600 - 0.08x &= 1520 \\ -0.01x + 1600 &= 1520 \\ -0.10x + 1600 - 1600 &= 1520 - 1600 \\ -0.01x &= -80 \\ \frac{-0.01x}{-0.01} &= \frac{-80}{-0.01} \\ x &= 8000 \end{aligned}$$

Because x represents the amount invested at 7%, \$8000 should be invested at 7%. Because 20,000$-x$ represents the amount invested at 8%, \$20,000$-$\$8000 = \$12,000 should be invested at 8%.

5.

	Principal	×	Rate	=	Interest
8% Loan	x		0.08		$0.08x$
18% Loan	$120{,}000 - x$		0.18		$0.18(120{,}000 - x)$

$$\begin{aligned} 0.08x + 0.18(120{,}000 - x) &= 10{,}000 \\ 0.08x + 21{,}600 - 0.18x &= 10{,}000 \\ -0.10x + 21{,}600 &= 10{,}000 \\ -0.10x + 21{,}600 - 21{,}600 &= 10{,}000 - 21{,}600 \\ -0.10x &= -11{,}600 \\ \frac{-0.10x}{-0.10} &= \frac{-11{,}600}{-0.10} \\ x &= 116{,}000 \end{aligned}$$

\$116,000 was loaned at 8% and \$120,000 – \$116,000 = \$4000 was loaned at 18%.

7. Let x = amount invested at 6%.
Then $6000 - x$ = amount invested at 9%.

The accounts earned the same amount of interest, so the equation is

$$0.06x = 0.09(6000 - x).$$

Solve this equation.

$$\begin{aligned} 0.06x &= 540 - 0.09x \\ 0.06x + 0.09x &= 540 \\ 0.15x &= 540 \\ \frac{0.15x}{0.15} &= \frac{540}{0.15} \\ x &= 3600 \end{aligned}$$

\$3600 was invested at 6% and \$6000 – \$3600 = \$2400 at 9%.

9. Let x = amount invested at 15%.
Then $50{,}000 - x$ = amount invested at 7%.

$$
\begin{aligned}
0.15x + 0.07(50{,}000 - x) &= 6000 \\
0.15x + 0.07(50{,}000) - 0.07 &= 6000 \\
0.15x + 3500 - 0.07x &= 6000 \\
0.08x + 3500 &= 6000 \\
0.08x + 3500 - 3500 &= 6000 - 3500 \\
0.08x &= 2500 \\
\frac{0.08x}{0.08} &= \frac{2500}{0.08} \\
x &= 31{,}250
\end{aligned}
$$

\$31,250 should be invested at 15% and \$50,000 − \$31,250 = \$18,750 should be invested at 7%.

11. $0.30(20) = 6$

There are 6 milliliters of acid in the solution.

13.

	Numbers of liters	×	Percent of Fungicide	=	Amount of Fungicide
5% Fungicide Solution	x		0.05		$0.05x$
10% Fungicide Solution	$50 - x$		0.1		$0.1(50 - x)$
8% Fungicide Solution	50		0.08		0.08(50)

$$
\begin{aligned}
0.05x + 0.1(50 - x) &= 0.08(50) \\
0.05x + 5 - 0.1x &= 4 \\
-0.05x + 5 &= 4 \\
-0.05x &= -1 \\
\frac{-0.05x}{-0.05} &= \frac{-1}{-0.05} \\
x &= 20
\end{aligned}
$$

20 liters of 5% fungicide solution and $50 - 20 = 30$ liters of 10% fungicide solution should be used.

15.

	Number of Ounces	×	Percent of Alcohol	=	Amount of Alcohol
15% Alcohol Solution	x		0.15		$0.15x$
20% Alcohol Solution	4		0.2		4(0.2)
17% Alcohol Solution	$x+4$		0.17		$0.17(x+4)$

$$\begin{aligned}
0.15x + 4(0.2) &= 0.17(x+4) \\
0.15x + 0.8 &= 0.17x + 0.68 \\
0.15x + 0.8 - 0.17x &= 0.17x + 0.68 - 0.17x \\
-0.02x + 0.8 &= 0.68 \\
-0.02x + 0.8 - 0.8 &= 0.68 - 0.8 \\
-0.02x &= -0.12 \\
-0.02x &= -0.12 \\
\frac{-0.02x}{-0.02} &= \frac{-0.12}{-0.02} \\
x &= 6
\end{aligned}$$

To make a 17% alcohol solution, 6 ounces of 15% alcohol should be used.

17. Let x = number of students at north campus before merger.
Then $1000 - x$ = number of students at south campus before merger.

$$\begin{aligned}
0.1x + 0.9(1000 - x) &= 0.42(1000) \\
0.1x + 900 - 0.9x &= 420 \\
-0.8x + 900 &= 420 \\
-0.8x &= -480 \\
\frac{-0.8x}{-0.8} &= \frac{-420}{-0.8} \\
x &= 600
\end{aligned}$$

There were 600 students at the north campus and $1000 - 600 = 400$ students at the south campus.

19.

	Rate ×	Time =	Distance
Slower Cyclist	10	x	$10x$
Faster Cyclist	12	x	$12x$

After x hours, the cyclists are 66 miles apart, so the equation is

$$10x + 12x = 66.$$

Solve this equation,

$$\begin{aligned} 22x &= 66 \\ x &= 3 \end{aligned}$$

They will be 66 miles apart after 3 hours.

21.

	Rate ×	Time =	Distance
Faster Truck	$x + 5$	5	$5(x + 5)$
Slower Truck	x	5	$5x$

$$\begin{aligned} 5(x + 5) + 5x &= 600 \\ 5x + 25 + 5x &= 600 \\ 10x + 25 &= 600 \\ 10x &= 575 \\ x &= 57.5 \end{aligned}$$

The rate of the slower truck is 57.5 miles per hour and the rate of the faster truck is $57.5 + 5 = 62.5$ miles per hour.

23.

	Rate ×	Time =	Distance
Car	55	x	$55x$
Bus	45	x	$45x$

The cars traveled a total of 240 miles, so the equation is

$$55x + 45x = 240.$$

Solve this equation.

$$\begin{aligned} 100x &= 240 \\ x &= 2.4 \end{aligned}$$

The car and bus meet after 2.4 hours (or 2 hours and 24 minutes).

25.

	Rate ×	Time =	Distance
First Part of Trip	50	x	$50x$
Second Part of Trip	40	$5 - x$	$40(5 - x)$

$$\begin{aligned} 50x + 40(5 - x) &= 220 \\ 50x + 200 - 40x &= 220 \\ 10x + 200 &= 220 \\ 10x &= 20 \\ x &= 2 \end{aligned}$$

The bus traveled for 2 hours at 50 miles per hour and for 3 hours at 40 miles per hour.

27. The missing information is the length of the original wire.

29. We don't need to know what the shop pays its employees.

Let $x =$ the number of hours the shop worked on the auto.

$$\begin{aligned} 40 + 35x &= 180 \\ 35x &= 140 \\ x &= 4 \end{aligned}$$

The shop spent 4 hours on the auto.

31.

1 quarter	1 quarter	1 quarter
2 dimes	1 dime	4 nickels
	2 nickels	

3 dimes	2 dimes
3 nickels	5 nickels

There are 5 ways to make the purchase.

33. A good strategy for solving this problem is to look for a pattern. (You could also make a systematic list.)

There are 10 numbers that have 7 as the ones digit: 7, 17, ..., 97.
There are 10 numbers that have 7 as the tens digit: $70, 71, \ldots, 79$. Therefore, 20 7's are needed.

35. The two planks put together are long enough to reach the middle of the pool.

37. A good strategy for solving this problem is to use the given information to eliminate possibilities.

Since the sum of the digits of 252 is 9, the sum of the digits in all three area codes must be 9. If the last digit is 1, the sum of the first two digits must be 8.

Consider the pairs of digits whose sum is 8 and use the given information to determine which of these will work.

$6 + 2 = 8$ No, because 6 and 2 appear in the other two area codes.

$5 + 3 = 8$ No because 5 appears in 252.

$4 + 4 = 8$ No because 5 because the first digit cannot be 4.

$7 + 1 = 8$ Yes, but first digit cannot be 1.

Therefore, the only possibility for the area code that ends in 1 is 711.

For Exercises 39–43, answers may vary.

45. Let $x =$ the amount invested at 8%.
Then $70{,}000 - x =$ the amount invested at 12%.

$$\begin{aligned} 0.08x + 0.12(70{,}000 - x) &= 0.09(70{,}000) \\ 0.08x + 8400 - 0.12x &= 6300 \\ -0.04x + 8400 &= 6300 \\ -0.04x &= -2100 \\ \frac{-0.04x}{-0.04} &= \frac{-2000}{-0.04} \\ x &= 52{,}500 \end{aligned}$$

You should invest \$52,500 at 8% and \$70,000 – \$52,500 = \$17,500 at 12%.

47. Let $x =$ number of pounds of \$2.50-per-pound candy.
Then $100 - x =$ number of pounds of \$3.50-per-pound candy.

$$\begin{aligned} 2.50x + 3.50(100 - x) &= 100(2.90) \\ 2.50x + 3.50 - 3.50x &= 290 \\ -x + 350 &= 290 \\ -x &= -60 \\ x &= 60 \end{aligned}$$

The mixture should contain 60 pounds of \$2.50 candy and 100 – 60 = 40 pounds of \$3.50 candy.

Review Exercises

49. $$\begin{aligned} 3^2 - 5[4 - 3(2 - 6)] &= 3^2 - 5[4 - 3(-4)] \\ &= 3^2 - 5(4 + 12) \\ &= 3^2 - 5(16) \\ &= 9 - 80 = -71 \end{aligned}$$

50. The integers are $-100, 0$, and $\sqrt{16} = 4$.

51.
$$\begin{aligned}3(x+3) &= 5(2x+6)\\ 3x+9 &= 10x+30\\ 3x+9-10x &= 10x+30-10x\\ -7x+9 &= 30\\ -7x+9-9 &= 30-9\\ -7x &= 21\\ \frac{-7x}{-7} &= \frac{21}{-7}\\ x &= -3\end{aligned}$$

The solution is -3.

3.2 Ratio and Proportion

3.2 CHECK POINTS

CHECK POINT 1

The graph shows that there were 160 divorced people for every thousand married people in 1995 and 180 divorced people for every thousand married people in 2000. Thus, the ratio for 1995 to 2000 is

$$\frac{160}{180} = \frac{\cancel{20}\cdot 8}{\cancel{20}\cdot 9} = \frac{8}{9} \text{ or } 8{:}9.$$

CHECK POINT 2

To solve each proportion, apply the cross products principle and then solve the resulting linear equation.

a.
$$\begin{aligned}\frac{10}{x} &= \frac{2}{3}\\ 10\cdot 3 &= 2x\\ 30 &= 2x\\ \frac{30}{2} &= \frac{2x}{2}\\ 15 &= x\end{aligned}$$

b.
$$\begin{aligned}\frac{-7}{9} &= \frac{21}{x}\\ -7x &= 9\cdot 21\\ -7x &= 189\\ \frac{-7x}{-7} &= \frac{189}{-7}\\ x &= -27\end{aligned}$$

CHECK POINT 3

Let $x =$ the tax on a house assesed at $112,500.

$$\frac{\text{Tax on \$45,000 house}}{\text{Assessed value (\$45,000)}} = \frac{\text{Tax on \$112,500 house}}{\text{Assessed value (\$112,500)}}$$

$$\begin{aligned}\frac{\$600}{\$45{,}000} &= \frac{x}{\$112{,}500}\\ \frac{600}{45{,}000} &= \frac{x}{112{,}500}\\ 45{,}000x &= (600)(112{,}500)\\ 45{,}000x &= 67{,}500{,}000\\ \frac{45{,}000x}{45{,}000} &= \frac{67{,}500{,}000}{45{,}000}\\ x &= 1500\end{aligned}$$

The tax on a house with an assessed value of $112,500 is $1500.

CHECK POINT 4

Let $x =$ the total number of deer in the refuge.

$$\frac{\text{Original number of tagged deer}}{\text{Total number of deer}} = \frac{\text{Number of tagged deer in sample}}{\text{Total number of deer in sample}}$$

$$\begin{aligned}\frac{120}{x} &= \frac{25}{150}\\ (120)(150) &= 25x\\ 18{,}000 &= 25x\\ \frac{18{,}000}{25} &= \frac{25x}{25}\\ 720 &= x\end{aligned}$$

There are approximately 720 deer in the refuge.

EXERCISE SET 3.2

1. 24 to 48

$$\frac{24}{48} = \frac{\cancel{24} \cdot 1}{\cancel{24} \cdot 2} = \frac{1}{2}$$

3. 48 to 20

$$\frac{48}{20} = \frac{\cancel{4} \cdot 12}{\cancel{4} \cdot 5} = \frac{12}{5}$$

5. 27:36

$$\frac{27}{36} = \frac{\cancel{9} \cdot 3}{\cancel{9} \cdot 4} = \frac{3}{4}$$

7. 20 men to 10 women

$$\frac{20}{10} = \frac{2}{1} \text{ or } 2{:}1$$

9. 10 women to 30 students

$$\frac{10}{30} = \frac{1}{3} \text{ or } 1{:}3$$

11. $\frac{24}{x} = \frac{12}{7}$

Apply the cross products principle and then solve the resulting equation.

$$12x = 24 \cdot 7$$
$$12x = 168$$
$$\frac{12x}{12} = \frac{168}{12}$$
$$x = 14$$

13. $\frac{x}{6} = \frac{18}{4}$

$$4x = 6 \cdot 18$$
$$4x = 108$$
$$\frac{4x}{4} = \frac{108}{4}$$
$$x = 27$$

15. $\frac{x}{3} = -\frac{3}{4}$

Rewrite the fraction on the right as $\frac{-3}{4}$ and then apply the cross products principle.

$$\frac{x}{3} = \frac{-3}{4}$$
$$4x = -9$$
$$x = -\frac{9}{4}$$

17. $\frac{-3}{8} = \frac{x}{40}$

$$8x = -120$$
$$\frac{8x}{8} = \frac{-120}{8}$$
$$x = -15$$

19. $\frac{x-2}{5} = \frac{3}{10}$

$$10(x-2) = 15$$
$$10x - 20 = 15$$
$$10x = 35$$
$$\frac{10x}{10} = \frac{35}{10}$$
$$x = \frac{7}{2}$$

21. $\frac{y+10}{10} = \frac{y-2}{4}$

$$4(y+10) = 10(y-2)$$
$$4y + 40 = 10y - 20$$
$$4y + 40 - 10y = 10y - 20 - 10y$$
$$-6y + 40 = -20$$
$$-6y + 40 - 40 = -20 - 40$$
$$-6y = -60$$
$$\frac{-6y}{-6} = \frac{-60}{-6}$$
$$y = 10$$

23. The ratio of the number of extinct languages in Brazil to that in the United States is

$$\frac{30}{22} = \frac{15}{11} \text{ or } 15{:}11.$$

25. Answers may vary.

27. Let $x =$ the tax on a property with an assessed value of \$162,500.

$$\frac{\text{Tax on \$65,000 property}}{\text{Assessed value (\$65,000)}} = \frac{\text{Tax on \$162,000 property}}{\text{Assessed value (\$162,500)}}$$

$$\frac{\$720}{\$65{,}000} = \frac{\$x}{\$162{,}500}$$

$$\frac{720}{65{,}000} = \frac{x}{\$162{,}500}$$

$$65{,}000x = (720)(162{,}500)$$

$$65{,}000x = 117{,}000{,}000$$

$$\frac{65{,}000x}{65{,}000} = \frac{117{,}000{,}000}{65{,}000}$$

$$x = 1800$$

The tax on a property assessed at \$162,500 is \$1800.

29. Let $x =$ the total number of fur seal pups in the rookery.

$$\frac{\text{Original number of tagged fur seal pups}}{\text{Total number of fur seal pups}} = \frac{\text{Number of tagged fur seal pups in sample}}{\text{Number of fur seal pups in sample}}$$

$$\frac{4963}{x} = \frac{218}{900}$$

$$218x = (4963)(900)$$

$$218x = 4{,}466{,}700$$

$$\frac{218x}{218} = \frac{4{,}466{,}700}{218}$$

$$x \approx 20{,}490$$

There were about 20,490 fur seal pups in the rookery.

31. Let $x =$ the monthly amount of child support for a father earning \$38,000 annually.

$$\frac{x}{\$38{,}000} = \frac{1}{40}$$

$$\frac{x}{\$38{,}000} = \frac{1}{40}$$

$$40x = 38{,}000$$

$$x = 950$$

A father earning \$38,000 annually should pay \$950 in monthly child support.

33. Let $x =$ the height of the critter.

$$\frac{\text{Foot length of person}}{\text{Height of person}} = \frac{\text{Foot length of critter}}{\text{Height of critter}}$$

$$\frac{10 \text{ inches}}{67 \text{ inches}} = \frac{23 \text{ inches}}{x}$$

$$\frac{10}{67} = \frac{23}{x}$$

$$10x = (67)(23)$$

$$10x = 1541$$

$$x = 154.1$$

The height of the critter is 154.1 inches.

35. To find the ratio 5 years after installation, substitute 5 for x.

$$\frac{C_{\text{Gas}}}{C_{\text{Solar}}} = \frac{12{,}000 + 700x}{30{,}000 + 150x} = \frac{12{,}000 + 700(5)}{30{,}000 + 150(5)}$$

$$= \frac{15{,}500}{30{,}750} = \frac{\cancel{250} \cdot 62}{\cancel{250} \cdot 123}$$

$$= \frac{62}{123} \text{ or } 62{:}123$$

To find the ratio 40 years after installation, substitute 40 for x.

$$\frac{C_{\text{Gas}}}{C_{\text{Solar}}} = \frac{12{,}000 + 700(40)}{30{,}000 + 150(40)} = \frac{40{,}000}{36{,}000}$$

$$= \frac{\cancel{4000} \cdot 10}{\cancel{4000} \cdot 9} = \frac{10}{9} \text{ or } 10{:}9$$

The ratio of the total cost of gas to solar heating increases over time. Over a short period of time, gas heating is more economical, but over many years, solar heating becomes more economical. In other words, solar heating pays off eventually, but it takes a long time.

For Exercises 37–41, answers may vary.

43. Statement b is true.

45. Let $x =$ age of friend if he were a dog.

$$\frac{7}{56} = \frac{x}{44}$$
$$56x = 308$$
$$x = 5.5$$

If the friend were a dog, he would be 5.5 years old.

47. Let $x =$ actual distance represented by 9.85 inches on a map.

$$\frac{2 \text{ inches}}{13.47 \text{ miles}} = \frac{9.85 \text{ inches}}{x \text{ miles}}$$
$$\frac{2}{13.47} = \frac{9.85}{x}$$
$$2x = (13.47)(9.85)$$
$$2x = 132.6795$$
$$x \approx 66.34$$

The person plans to travel 66.34 miles.

Review Exercises

48.
$$-6x + 2 \le 2(5 - x)$$
$$-6x + 2 \le 10 - 2x$$
$$-6x + 2 + 2x \le 10 - 2x + 2x$$
$$-4x + 2 \le 10$$
$$-4x + 2 - 2 \le 10 - 2$$
$$-4x \le 8$$
$$\frac{-4x}{-4} \ge \frac{8}{-4}$$
$$x \ge -2$$

$\{x | x \ge -2\}$

-5 -4 -3 -2 -1 0 1 2 3 4 5

49. $A = PB; A = 112, P = 40\% = 0.40$

$$A = PB$$
$$112 = 0.40 \cdot B$$
$$\frac{112}{0.40} = \frac{0.40B}{0.40}$$
$$280 = B$$

112 is 40% of 280.

50. $9 - 2[4(x - 3) + 7] = 9 - 2(4x - 12 + 7)$
$= 9 - 2(4x - 5)$
$= 9 - 8x + 10$
$= 19 - 8x$

3.3 Problem Solving in Geometry

3.3 CHECK POINTS

CHECK POINT 1

$$A = \frac{1}{2}bh$$
$$24 = \frac{1}{2}(4)h$$
$$24 = 2h$$
$$\frac{24}{2} = \frac{2h}{2}$$
$$12 = h$$

The height of the sail is 12 feet.

CHECK POINT 2

The radius is half the diameter, so $r = \frac{40}{2} = 20$ feet.

$A = \pi r^2$ $\qquad C = 2\pi r$
$A = \pi(20)^2$ $\qquad C = 2\pi(20)$
$A = 400\pi$ $\qquad C = 40\pi$

The area of the landing pad is 400π square feet and the circumference is 40π feet. Using 3.14 as an approximation for π, the area is approximately 1256 square feet and the circumference is approximately 126 feet.

CHECK POINT 3

The radius of the large pizza is $\frac{1}{2}\cdot 18$ inches $= 9$ inches, and the radius of the small pizza is $\frac{1}{2}\cdot 14$ inches $= 7$ inches. Find the area of the surface of each pizza.

Large pizza:

$$\begin{aligned} A = \pi r^2 &= \pi(9 \text{ in.})^2 \\ &= 81\pi \text{ in.}^2 \\ &\approx 254 \text{ in.}^2 \end{aligned}$$

Medium pizza:

$$\begin{aligned} A = \pi r^2 &= \pi(7 \text{ in.})^2 \\ &= 49 \text{ in.}^2 \\ &\approx 154 \text{ in.}^2 \end{aligned}$$

Now find the price per square inch for each pizza.

Price per square inch for large pizza

$$= \frac{\$20.00}{81\pi \text{ in.}^2} \approx \frac{\$20}{254 \text{ in.}^2} \approx \frac{\$0.08}{\text{in.}^2}$$

Price per square inch for medium pizza

$$= \frac{\$14.00}{49\pi \text{ in.}^2} \approx \frac{\$14.00}{154 \text{ in.}^2} \approx \frac{\$0.09}{\text{in.}^2}$$

The large pizza is the better buy.

CHECK POINT 4

Use the formula for the volume of a cylinder:

$$V = \pi r^2 h.$$

Smaller cylinder: $r = 3$ in., $h = 5$ in.

$$\begin{aligned} V_{\text{Smaller}} &= \pi(3)^2(5) \\ &= \pi(9)(5) \\ &= 45\pi \end{aligned}$$

The volume of the smaller cylinder is 45π in.^{3}.

Large cylinder: $r = 3$ in., $h = 2(5 \text{ in.}) = 10$ in.

$$\begin{aligned} V_{\text{Larger}} &= \pi(3)^2(10) \\ &= \pi(9)(10) \\ &= 90\pi \end{aligned}$$

The volume of the larger cylinder is 90π in.^{3}.

Write a ratio to compare the two volumes:

$$\frac{V_{\text{Larger}}}{V_{\text{Smaller}}} = \frac{90\pi}{45\pi} = \frac{2}{1}.$$

Thus, the volume of the larger cylinder is 2 times the volume of the smaller cylinder.

CHECK POINT 5

Use the formula for the volume of a sphere with $r = 4.5$ in.

$$\begin{aligned} V &= \frac{4}{3}\pi r^3 \\ V &= \frac{4}{3}\pi(4.5 \text{ in.})^3 \\ &= \frac{4}{3}\pi(91.125 \text{ in.}^3) \\ &\approx 382 \text{ in.}^3 \end{aligned}$$

Since the volume of the sphere is 382 cubic inches, 350 cubic inches of air will not fill it completely. About 32 more cubic inches of air are needed.

CHECK POINT 6

Let x = the measure of the second angle.

Then $3x$ = the measure of the first angle;

$x - 20$ = the measure of the third angle.

$$\begin{aligned} 3x + x + (x - 20) &= 180 \\ 5x - 20 &= 180 \\ 5x &= 200 \\ x &= 40 \end{aligned}$$

Measure of first angle $= 3x = 3 \cdot 40° = 120°$
Measure of second angle $= x = 40°$
Measure of third angle $= x - 2 = 20°$
The angles measure $120°, 40°$, and $20°$.
Check: The sum of the measure of the angles of this triangle is $120° + 40° + 20° = 180°$.

CHECK POINT 7

Let $x =$ the measure of the angle.
Then $90 - x =$ the measure of its complement.

$$x = 2(90 - x)$$
$$x = 180 - 2x$$
$$3x = 180$$
$$x = 60$$

The angle's measure is $60°$.
Check: The measure of the complement is $90° - 60° = 30°$. The angle's measure, $60°$, is twice $30°$.

EXERCISE SET 3.3

1. Use the formulas for the perimeter and area of a rectangle. The length is 6 m and the width is 3 m.

$$P = 2l + 2w$$
$$P = 2(6) + 2(3)$$
$$P = 12 + 6 = 18$$

The perimeter is 18 m.

$$A = lw$$
$$A = 6 \cdot 3 = 18$$

The area is 18 m^2.

3. Use the formula for the area of a triangle. The base is 14 in. and the height is 8 in. The lengths of the other two sides are not used in calculating the area.

$$A = \frac{1}{2}bh$$
$$A = \frac{1}{2}(14)(8) = 56$$

The area is 56 $in.^2$.

5. Use the formula for the area of a trapezoid. The bases are 16 m and 10 m and the height is 7 m. The lengths of the other two sides of the trapezoid are not used in calculating the area.

$$A = \frac{1}{2}h(a + b)$$
$$A = \frac{1}{2}(7)(16 + 10)$$
$$= \frac{1}{2} \cdot 7 \cdot 26 = 91$$

The area is 91 m^2.

7. $A = lw$; $A = 1250, w = 25$

$$A = lw$$
$$1250 = l \cdot 25$$
$$50 = l$$

The length of the swimming pool is 50 ft.

9. $A = \frac{1}{2}bh$; $A = 20, b = 5$

$$A = \frac{1}{2}bh$$
$$20 = \frac{1}{2} \cdot 5 \cdot h$$
$$20 = \frac{5}{2}h$$
$$\frac{2}{5}(20) = \frac{2}{5}\left(\frac{5}{2}h\right)$$
$$8 = h$$

The height of the triangle is 8 ft.

11. $P = 2l + 2w; P = 188, w = 44$

$$188 = 2l + 2(44)$$
$$188 = 2l + 88$$
$$100 = 2l$$
$$50 = l$$

The length of the rectangle is 50 cm.

13. Use the formulas for the area and circumference of a circle. The radius is 4 cm.

$$A = \pi r^2$$
$$A = \pi(4)^2$$
$$A = 16\pi \approx 50$$

The area is 16π cm^2 or approximately 50 cm^2.

$$C = 2\pi r$$
$$C = 2\pi(4)$$
$$C = 8\pi \approx 25$$

The circumference is 8π cm or approximately 25 cm.

15. Since the diameter is 12 yd, the radius is $\frac{12}{2} = 6$ yd.

$$A = \pi r^2$$
$$A = \pi(6)^2$$
$$A = 36\pi \approx 113$$

The area is 36π yd^2 or approximately 113 yd^2.

$$C = 2\pi r$$
$$C = 2\pi \cdot 6$$
$$C = 12\pi \approx 38$$

The circumference is 12π yd or approximately 38 yd.

17. $C = 2\pi r; C = 14\pi$

$$C = 2\pi r$$
$$14\pi = 2\pi r$$
$$\frac{14\pi}{2\pi} = \frac{2\pi r}{2\pi}$$
$$7 = r$$

The radius is 7 in. and the diameter is 2(7 in.) = 14 in.

19. Use the formula for the volume of a rectangular solid. The length and width are each 3 in. and the height is 4 in.

$$V = lwh$$
$$V = 3 \cdot 3 \cdot 4 = 36$$

The volume is 36 in.^{3}.

21. Use the formula for the volume of a cylinder. The radius is 5 cm and the height is 6 cm.

$$V = \pi r^2 h$$
$$V = \pi(5)^2 \cdot 6$$
$$V = 150\pi \approx 471$$

The volume is 150π cm^3 or approximately 471 cm^3.

23. Use the formula for the volume of a sphere. The diameter is 18 cm, so the radius is 9 cm.

$$V = \frac{4}{3}\pi r^3$$
$$V = \frac{4}{3}\pi(9)^3$$
$$V = 972\pi \approx 3052$$

The volume is 972π cm^3 or approximately 3052 cm^3.

25. Use the formula for the volume of a cone. The radius is 4 m and the height is 9 m.

$$V = \frac{1}{3}\pi r^2 h$$
$$V = \frac{1}{3}\pi(4)^2 \cdot 9$$
$$V = 48\pi \approx 151$$

The volume is 48π m^3 or approximately 151 m^3.

27. $V = \pi r^2 h$ for h

$$V = \pi r^2 h$$
$$\frac{V}{\pi r^2} = \frac{\pi r^2 h}{\pi r^2}$$
$$\frac{V}{\pi r^2} = h$$

29. Smaller cylinder: $r = 3$ in., $h = 4$ in.

$$V = \pi r^2 h$$
$$V = \pi(3)^2 \cdot 4$$
$$V = 36\pi$$

The volume of the smaller cylinder is 36π in.^{3}.
Larger cylinder: $r = 3(3 \text{ in.}) = 9$ in., $h = 4$ in.

$$V = \pi r^2 h$$
$$V = \pi(9)^2 \cdot 4$$
$$V = 324\pi$$

The volume of the larger cylinder is 324π. The ratio of the volumes of the two cylinders is

$$\frac{V_{\text{larger}}}{V_{\text{smaller}}} = \frac{324\pi}{36\pi} = \frac{9}{1}.$$

so the volume of the larger cylinder is 9 times the volume of the smaller cylinder.

31. The sum of the measures of the three angles of any triangle is 180°, so

$$x + x + (x + 30) = 180.$$

Solve this equation.

$$3x + 30 = 180$$
$$3x = 150$$
$$x = 50$$

If $x = 50, x + 30 = 80$, so the three angle measures are $50°, 50°$, and $80°$. This solution checks because $50° + 50° + 80° = 180°$.

33. $4x + (3x + 4) + (2x + 5) = 180$

$$9x + 9 = 180$$
$$9x = 171$$
$$x = 19$$

If $x = 19$, then $4x = 76, 3x + 4 = 61$, and $2x + 5 = 43$. Therefore, the angle measures are $76°, 61°$, and $43°$. This solution checks because $76° + 61° + 43° = 180°$.

35. Let $x =$ the measure of the smallest angle.
Then $2x =$ the measure of the second angle;
$x + 20 =$ the measure of the third angle.

$$x + 2x + (x + 20) = 180$$
$$4x + 20 = 180$$
$$4x = 160$$
$$x = 40$$

Measure of smallest angle $= x = 40°$
Measure of second angle $= 2x = 80°$
Measure of third angle $= x + 20 = 60°$

37. If the measure of an angle is 48°, the measure of its complement is $90° - 48° = 42°$.

39. If the measure of an angle is 89°, the measure of its complement is 1.

41. If the measure of an angle is 111°, the measure of its supplement is $180° - 111° = 69°$.

43. If the measure of an angle is 90°, the measure of its supplement is $180° - 90° = 90°$.

45. *Step 1* Let $x =$ the measure of the angle.

Step 2 Then $90 - x =$ the measure of its complement.

Step 3 The angle's measure is 60° more than that of its complement, so the equatioı is

$$x = (90 - x) + 60.$$

Step 4 Solve this equation.

$$\begin{aligned} x &= 90 - x + 60 \\ x &= 150 - x \\ 2x &= 150 \\ x &= 75 \end{aligned}$$

The measure of the angle is 75°.

Step 5 The complement of the angle is 90° − 75° = 15°, and 75° is 60° more than 15°.

47. Let $x =$ the measure of the angle.
Then $180 - x =$ the measure of its supplement.

$$\begin{aligned} x &= 3(180 - x) \\ x &= 540 - 3x \\ 4x &= 540 \\ x &= 135 \end{aligned}$$

The measure of the angle is 135°. The measure of its supplement is 180° − 135° = 45°, and 135° = 3(45°), so the proposed solution checks.

49. Let $x =$ the measure of the angle.
Then $180 - x =$ the measure of its supplement;
$90 - x =$ the measure of its complement.

$$\begin{aligned} 180 - x &= 3(90 - x) + 10 \\ 180 - x &= 270 - 3x + 10 \\ 180 - x &= 280 - 3x \\ 180 + 2x &= 280 \\ 2x &= 100 \\ x &= 50 \end{aligned}$$

The measure of the angle is 50°. The measure of its supplement is 130° and the measure of its complement is 40°. Since 130° = 3(40°)+10°, the proposed solution checks.

51. The area of the office is (20 ft)(16 ft) = 320 ft². Use a proportion to find how much of the yearly electric bill is deductible.

Let $x =$ the amount of the electric bill that is deductible.

$$\begin{aligned} \frac{320}{2200} &= \frac{x}{4800} \\ 2200x &= (320)(4800) \\ 2200x &= 1{,}536{,}000 \\ \frac{2200x}{2200} &= \frac{1{,}536{,}000}{2200} \\ x &\approx 698.18 \end{aligned}$$

\$698.18 of the yearly electric bill is deductible.

53. The radius of the large pizza is $\frac{1}{2} \cdot 14$ inches = 7 inches, and the radius of the medium pizza is $\frac{1}{2} \cdot 7$ inches = 3.5 inches.

Large pizza:

$$\begin{aligned} A = \pi r^2 &= \pi(7 \text{ in.})^2 \\ &= 49\pi \text{ in.}^2 \approx 154 \text{ in.}^2 \end{aligned}$$

Medium pizza:

$$\begin{aligned} A = \pi r^2 &= \pi(3.5 \text{ in.})^2 \\ &= 12.25 \text{ in.}^2 \approx 38.465 \text{ in.}^2 \end{aligned}$$

For each pizza, find the price per square inch by dividing the price by the area:

Price per square inch for large pizza

$$= \frac{\$12.00}{154 \text{ in.}^2} \approx \frac{\$0.08}{\text{in.}^2}$$

Price per square inch for medium pizza

$$= \frac{\$5.00}{38.465 \text{ in.}^2} \approx \frac{\$0.13}{\text{in.}^2}$$

The large pizza is the better buy.

55. The area of the larger circle is

$$A = \pi r^2 = \pi \cdot 50^2 = 2500\pi \text{ ft}^2.$$

The area of the smaller circle is

$$A = \pi r^2 = \pi \cdot 40^2 = 1600\pi \text{ ft}^2.$$

The area of the circular road is the difference between the area of the outer circle and the area of the smaller circle:

$$A = 2500\pi \text{ ft}^2 - 1600\pi \text{ ft}^2 = 900\pi \text{ ft}^2$$

The cost to pave the circular road is $\$0.08(900\pi) \approx \$2260.80$.

57. The perimeter of the bottom of two sides of the rectangular portion of the window is 3 ft + 6 ft + 6 ft = 15 ft. The radius of the semicircle is $\frac{1}{2} \cdot 3$ ft = 1.5 ft, so the circumference of the semicircular portion of the window is $\frac{1}{2} \cdot 2\pi r \approx 3.14(1.5) = 4.7$ ft. Therefore, approximately 15 ft + 4.7 ft = 19.7 ft of stripping would be needed to frame the window.

59. First, find the volume of water when the reservoir was full:

$$V = lwh$$
$$V = 50 \cdot 30 \cdot 20 = 30{,}000.$$

The volume was 30,000 yd^3. Now find the volume when the height of the water was 6 yards:

$$V = 50 \cdot 30 \cdot 6 = 9000.$$

The volume was 9000 yd^3. The amount of water used in the three-month period was

$$30{,}000 \text{ yd}^3 - 9000 \text{ yd}^3 = 21{,}000 \text{ yd}^3.$$

61. For the first can, the diameter is 6 in. so the radius is 3 in. Find the volume of this can.

$$V = \pi r^2 h$$
$$V = \pi(3)^2 \cdot 5$$
$$= 45\pi \approx 141.3$$

The volume is about 141.3 in.^{3}. For the second can, the diameter is 5 in., so the radius is 2.5 in. Find the volume of this can.

$$V = \pi r^2 h$$
$$V = \pi(2.5)^2 \cdot 6$$
$$= 37.5\pi \approx 117.75$$

The volume of the second can is 117.75 in.^{2}.
The first can (the one with a diameter of 6 in. and a height of 5 in.) contains more soup, so it is the better buy.

63. Find the volume of a cylinder with radius 3 feet and height 2 feet 4 inches or $2\frac{1}{3}$ feet or $\frac{7}{3}$ feet:

$$V = \pi r^2 h$$
$$V = \pi(3)^2 \left(\frac{7}{3}\right)$$
$$V = \pi \cdot 9 \cdot \frac{7}{3}$$
$$V = 21\pi \approx 65.94$$

The volume of the tank is about 65.94 ft^3, so it is a little over one cubic foot too small to hold 500 gallons of water. Yes, you should be able to win your case.

For Exercises 65–73, answers may vary.

75. Area of smaller deck $= (8 \text{ ft})(10 \text{ ft})$
$= 80 \text{ ft}^2$

Area of larger deck $= (12 \text{ ft})(15 \text{ ft})$
$= 180 \text{ ft}^2$

Find the ratio of the areas:

$$\frac{A_{\text{larger}}}{A_{\text{smaller}}} = \frac{180 \text{ ft}^2}{80 \text{ ft}^2} = \frac{2.25}{1} \text{ or } 2.25{:}1$$

The cost will increase 2.25 times.

77. Let $x =$ the radius of the original sphere.
Then $2x =$ the radius of the larger sphere.

Find the ratio of the volumes of the two spheres:

$$\frac{A_{\text{larger}}}{A_{\text{original}}} = \frac{\frac{4}{3}\pi(2x)^3}{\frac{4}{3}\pi x^3} = \frac{8x^3}{x^3} = \frac{8}{1} \text{ or } 8{:}1$$

If the radius of a sphere is doubled, the volume increases 8 times.

79. The angles marked $(2x)^\circ$ and $(2x+40)^\circ$ in the figure are supplementary, so

$$2x + (2x + 40) = 180.$$

Solve this equation.

$$\begin{aligned} 2x + 2x + 40 &= 180 \\ 4x + 40 &= 180 \\ 4x &= 140 \\ x &= 35 \end{aligned}$$

The angle of inclination is 35°.

Review Exercises

80.

$$\begin{aligned} P &= 2s + b \text{ for } s \\ P - b &= 2s \\ \frac{P-b}{2} &= \frac{2s}{2} \\ \frac{P-b}{2} &= s \quad \text{or} \quad s = \frac{P-b}{2} \end{aligned}$$

81. $\frac{x}{2} + 7 = 13 - \frac{x}{4}$

Multiply both sides by the LCD, which is 4.

$$\begin{aligned} 4\left(\frac{x}{2} + 7\right) &= 4\left(13 - \frac{x}{4}\right) \\ 2x + 28 &= 52 - x \\ 2x + 28 + x &= 52 - x + x \\ 3x + 28 &= 52 \\ 3x + 28 - 28 &= 52 - 28 \\ 3x &= 24 \\ \frac{3x}{3} &= \frac{24}{3} \\ x &= 8 \end{aligned}$$

82.

$$\begin{aligned} [3(12 \div 2^2 - 3)^2]^2 &= [3(12 \div 4 - 3)^2]^2 \\ &= [3(3-3)^2]^2 \\ &= (3 \cdot 0^2)^2 \\ &= 0^2 = 0 \end{aligned}$$

Chapter 3 Review Exercises

1.

	Principal	× Rate	=	Interest
8% Investment	x	0.08		$0.08x$
10% Investment	$10{,}000 - x$	0.10		$0.10(10{,}000 - x)$

The interest for the two investments combined must be \$940, so the equation is

$$0.08x + 0.10(10{,}000 - x) = 940.$$

Solve this equation.

$$\begin{aligned}
0.08x + 1000 - 0.10x &= 940 \\
-0.02x + 1000 &= 940 \\
-0.02x + 1000 - 1000 &= 940 - 1000 \\
-0.02x &= -60 \\
\frac{-0.02x}{-0.02} &= \frac{-60}{-0.02} \\
x &= 3000
\end{aligned}$$

\$3000 was invested at 8% and \$10,000 − \$3000 = \$7000 was invested at 10%.

2. Let x = amount invested at 10%.
Then $x + 6000$ = amount invested at 12%.

$$\begin{aligned}
0.10x + 0.12(x + 6000) &= 2480 \\
0.10x + 0.12x + 720 &= 2480 \\
0.22x + 720 &= 2480 \\
0.22x + 720 - 720 &= 2480 - 720 \\
0.22x &= 1760 \\
\frac{0.22x}{0.22} &= \frac{1760}{0.22} \\
x &= 8000
\end{aligned}$$

\$8000 was invested at 10% and \$8000 + \$6000 = \$14,000 was invested at 12%.

3.

	Number of Gallons	×	Percent of Salt	=	Amount of Salt
75% Saltwater Solution	x		0.75		0.75
50% Saltwater Solution	$10 - x$		0.50		$0.50(10 - x)$
60% Saltwater Solution	10		0.60		$0.60(10)$

$$\begin{aligned}
0.75x + 0.50(10 - x) &= 0.60(10)\\
0.75x + 5 - 0.50x &= 6\\
0.25x + 5 &= 6\\
0.25x &= 1\\
\frac{0.25x}{0.25} &= \frac{1}{0.25}\\
x &= 4
\end{aligned}$$

To obtain 10 gallons of a 60% saltwater solution, 4 gallons of a 75% saltwater solution and $10 - 4 = 6$ gallons of a 50% saltwater solution must be used.

4. In a mixture of two alloys, the percentage of copper will be between the percentage for each of the two alloys being combined. Since 70% is greater than both 30% and 50% rather than between these two percentages, it is not possible to obtain an alloy that is 70% copper.

5. Let $x =$ number of students at north campus before merger.
Then $150 - x =$ number of students at south campus before merger.

$$\begin{aligned}
0.05x + 0.80(150 - x) &= 0.05(150)\\
0.95x + 120 - 0.80x &= 75\\
-0.75x + 120 &= 75\\
-0.75x &= -45\\
\frac{-0.75x}{-0.75} &= \frac{-45}{-0.75}\\
x &= 60
\end{aligned}$$

Before the merger, there were 60 students in the department at the north campus and $150 - 60 = 90$ students at south campus.

6.

	Rate ×	Time =	Distance
Slower Train	60	x	$60x$
Faster Train	80	x	$80x$

$$60x + 80x = 420$$
$$140x = 420$$
$$\frac{140x}{140} = \frac{420}{140}$$
$$x = 3$$

They will be 400 miles apart after 3 hours.

7.

	Rate ×	Time =	Distance
Slower Bus	x	3	$3x$
Faster Bus	$x + 10$	3	$3(x + 10)$

$$3x + 3(x + 10) = 210$$
$$3x + 3x + 30 = 210$$
$$6x + 30 = 210$$
$$6x = 180$$
$$x = 30$$

The rate of the slower bus is 30 miles per hour and the rate of the faster bus is $30 + 10 = 40$ miles per hour.

8. A good strategy for solving this problem is to look for a pattern.

By examining the pattern of the terms, you can see that the next-to-last term is $99 - 99 = 0$. Since the product of 0 and any real number is 0, the expression is equal to 0.

9. The flight left Miami at 10 A.M. Eastern Standard Time (EST), which is the same as 7 A.M. Pacific Standard Time. The flight arrived in San Francisco at 1:30 P.M., which is $6\frac{1}{2}$ hours after 7 A.M. However, the flight stopped for 45 minutes or $\frac{3}{4}$ hour, so this amount of time should be subtracted from the flight time. The actual flight time was $6\frac{1}{2} - \frac{3}{4} = 5\frac{3}{4}$ hours.

10. Before After

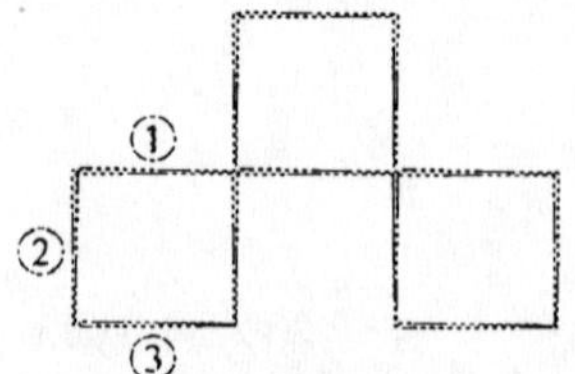

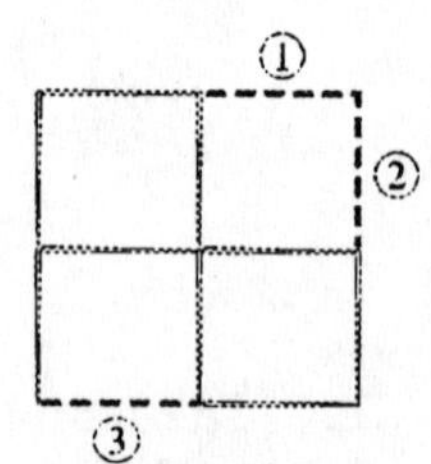

Move the three toothpicks labeled with numbers from their positions in the "Before" diagram to their positions in the "After diagram."

11. Student suggestions will vary.

12. Their are 10 women and a total of 25 students in the class. The ratio of the number of women to the number of students in the class is

$$\frac{10}{25} = \frac{2}{5} \quad \text{or} \quad 2{:}5.$$

13. The percentage of Americans who sleep 7 hours a night is 30% and the percentage who sleep 8 hours a night, so the ratio is

$$\frac{30\%}{28\%} = \frac{0.30}{0.28} = \frac{30}{28} = \frac{15}{14} \text{ or } 15{:}14.$$

14. The percentage of Americans who sleep less than 6 hours a night is 12% and the percentage who sleep more than 8 hours a night is 3%, so the ratio is

$$\frac{12\%}{3\%} = \frac{4}{1} \quad \text{or} \quad 4{:}1.$$

15. $\frac{3}{x} = \frac{15}{25}$

Apply the cross products principle and then solve the resulting equation.

$$15x = 3 \cdot 25$$
$$15x = 75$$
$$\frac{15x}{15} = \frac{75}{15}$$
$$x = 5$$

16. $\frac{-7}{5} = \frac{91}{x}$

$$-7x = 5 \cdot 9$$
$$-7x = 455$$
$$\frac{-7x}{-7} = \frac{455}{-7}$$
$$x = -65$$

17. $\frac{x+2}{2} = \frac{4}{5}$

$$5(x+2) = 3 \cdot 4$$
$$5x + 10 = 12$$
$$5x = 2$$
$$x = \frac{2}{5}$$

18. $\frac{5}{x+7} = \frac{3}{x+3}$

$$5(x+3) = 3(x+7)$$
$$5x + 15 = 3x + 21$$
$$5x + 15 - 3x = 3x + 21 - 3x$$
$$2x + 15 = 21$$
$$2x + 15 - 15 = 21 - 15$$
$$2x = 6$$
$$x = 3$$

19. Let x = number of teachers needed for 5400 students.

$$\frac{3}{50} = \frac{x}{5400}$$
$$50x = 3 \cdot 5400$$
$$50x = 16{,}200$$
$$\frac{50x}{50} = \frac{16{,}200}{50}$$
$$x = 324$$

For an enrollment of 5400 students, 324 teachers are needed.

20. Let x = number of trout in the lake.

$$\frac{\text{Original number of tagged trout}}{\text{Total number of trout}} = \frac{\text{Number of tagged trout in sample}}{\text{Number of trout in sample}}$$

$$\frac{112}{x} = \frac{32}{82}$$
$$32x = 112 \cdot 82$$
$$32x = 9184$$
$$\frac{32x}{32} = \frac{9184}{32}$$
$$x = 287$$

There are 287 trout in the lake.

21. Let x = monthly sales if \$96,000 is spent on advertising.

$$\frac{12{,}000 \text{ skates}}{\$60{,}000} = \frac{x \text{ skates}}{\$96{,}000}$$
$$\frac{12{,}000}{60{,}000} = \frac{x}{\$96{,}000}$$
$$\frac{1}{5} = \frac{x}{\$96{,}000}$$
$$5x = 96{,}000$$
$$x = 19{,}200$$

22. Find the area of a rectangle with length 6.5 ft and width 5 ft.

$$A = lw$$
$$A = (6.5)(5) = 32.5$$

The area is 32.5 ft^2.

23. Find the area of a triangle with base 20 cm and height 5 cm.

$$A = \frac{1}{2}bh$$
$$A = \frac{1}{2}(20)(5) = 50$$

The area is 50 cm^2.

24. Find the area of a trapezoid with bases 22 yd and 5 yd and height 10 yd.

$$A = \frac{1}{2}h(a+b)$$
$$A = \frac{1}{2}(10)(22+5)$$
$$= \frac{1}{2} \cdot 10 \cdot 27 = 135$$

The area is 135 yd^2.

25. Since the diameter is 20 m, the radius is $\frac{20}{2} = 10$ m.

$$C = 2\pi r$$
$$C = 2\pi(10)$$
$$C = 20\pi \approx 63$$

The circumference is 20π m or about 63 m.

$$A = \pi r^2$$
$$A = \pi(10)^2$$
$$A = 100 \approx 314$$

The area is 100π m^2 or about 314 m^2.

26. $A = \frac{1}{2}bh$; $A = 42, b = 14$

$$A = \frac{1}{2}bh$$
$$42 = \frac{1}{2} \cdot 14 \cdot h$$
$$42 = 7h$$
$$6 = h$$

The height of the sail is 6 ft.

27. Area of floor:

$$A = bh = (12 \text{ ft})(15 \text{ ft}) = 180 \text{ ft}^2$$

Area of base of stove:

$$A = bh = (3 \text{ ft})(4 \text{ ft}) = 12 \text{ ft}^2$$

Area of bottom of refrigerator:

$$A = bh = (3 \text{ ft})(14 \text{ ft}) = 12 \text{ ft}^2$$

The area to be covered with floor tile is

$$180 \text{ ft}^2 - 12 \text{ ft}^2 - 12 \text{ ft}^2 = 156 \text{ ft}^2.$$

28. First find the area of a trapezoid with bases 80 ft and 100 ft and height 60 ft.

$$A = \frac{1}{2}h(a+b)$$
$$A = \frac{1}{2}(60)(80+100)$$
$$A = 5400$$

The area of the yard is 5400 ft^2. The cost is

$$\$0.35(5400) = \$1890.$$

29. The radius of the medium pizza is $\frac{1}{2} \cdot 14$ inches $= 7$ inches, and the radius of each small pizza is $\frac{1}{2} \cdot 8$ inches $= 4$ inches.

Medium pizza:

$$A = \pi r^2 = \pi(7 \text{ in.})^2$$
$$= 49\pi \text{ in}^2. \approx 154 \text{ in.}^2$$

Small pizza:

$$A = \pi r^2 = \pi(4 \text{ in.})^2$$
$$= 16\pi \text{ in}^2. \approx 50.24 \text{ in.}^2$$

The area of one medium pizza is about 154 in.^{2} and the area of two small pizzas is about $2(50.24 \text{ in.}^2) = 100.48 \text{ in.}^2$. Since the price of one medium pizza is the same as the price of two small pizzas and the medium pizza has the greater area, the medium pizza is the better buy. (Because the prices are the same, it is not necessary to find the prices per square inch in this case.)

30. Find the volume of a rectangular solid with length 5 cm, width 3 cm, and height 4 cm.

$$A = lwh$$
$$A = 5 \cdot 3 \cdot 4 = 60$$

The volume is 60 cm^3.

31. Find the volume of a cylinder with radius 4 yd and height 8 yd.

$$V = \pi r^2 h$$
$$V = \pi(4)^2 \cdot 8$$
$$V = 128\pi \approx 402$$

The volume is 128π yd^3 ≈ 402 yd^3.

32. Find the volume of a sphere with radius 6 m.

$$V = \frac{4}{3}\pi r^3$$
$$V = \frac{4}{3}\pi(6)^3$$
$$V = \frac{4}{3} \cdot \pi \cdot 216$$
$$V = 288\pi \approx 904$$

The volume is 288π m^3 ≈ 904 m^3.

33. The volume of each box is

$$V = (8 \text{ m})(4 \text{ m})(3 \text{ m}) = 96 \text{ m}^3.$$

The space required for 50 containers is

$$50(96 \text{ m}^3) = 4800 \text{ m}^3.$$

34. Since the diameter of the fish tank is 6 ft, the radius is 3 ft.

$$V = \pi r^2$$
$$V = \pi(3)^2 \cdot 3$$
$$V = 27\pi \approx 84.78$$

The volume of the tank is about 84.78 ft^3.

$$\frac{84.78}{5} \approx 16.96$$

There is enough water in the tank for 16 fish. (There is not quite enough for 17 fish.)

35. The sum of the measures of the three angles of any triangle is 180°, so

$$x + 3x + 2x = 180.$$

Solve this equation.

$$6x = 180$$
$$x = 30$$

If $x = 30$, then $3x = 90$ and $2x = 60$, so the angle measures are $30°, 90°$, and $60°$.

36. Let x = the measure of the second angle.
Then $2x + 15$ = the measure of the first angle;
$x + 25$ = the measure of the third angle.

$$x + (2x + 15) + (x + 25) = 180$$
$$4x + 40 = 180$$
$$4x = 140$$
$$x = 35$$

If $x = 35$, then $2x+15 = 2(35)+15 = 85$, and $x+255 = 35+25 = 60$. The measures of the angles are $85°, 35°$, and $60°$.

37. If the measure of an angle is 57°, the measure of its complement is $90° - 57° = 33°$.

38. If the measure of an angle is 75°, the measure of its supplement is $180° - 75° = 105°$.

39. Let $x =$ the measure of the angle.
Then $90 - x =$ the measure of of its complement.

$$x = (90 - x) + 25$$
$$x = 115 - x$$
$$2x = 115$$
$$x = 57.5$$

The measure of the angle is 57.5°.

40. Let $x =$ the measure of the angle.
Then $180 - x =$ the measure of its supplement.

$$180 - x = 4x - 45$$
$$180 - 5x = -45$$
$$-5x = -225$$
$$x = 45$$

If $x = 45$, then $180 - x = 135$.
The measure of the angle is 45° and the measure of its supplement is 135°.

Chapter 3 Test

1. Let $x =$ amount invested at 9%.
Then $6000 - x =$ amount invested at 6%.

$$0.09x + 0.06(6000 - x) = 480$$
$$0.09x + 360 - 0.06x = 480$$
$$0.03x + 360 = 480$$
$$0.03x = 120$$
$$\frac{0.03x}{0.03} = \frac{120}{0.03}$$
$$x = 4000$$

\$4000 was invested at 9% at \$6000−\$4000 = \$2000 was invested at 6%.

2. Let $x =$ number of milliliters of 50% acid solution.
Then $100 - x =$ number of milliliters of 80% acid solution.

$$0.50x + 0.80(100 - x) = 0.68(100)$$
$$0.50x + 80 - 0.80x = 68$$
$$-0.30x + 80 = 68$$
$$-0.30x = -12$$
$$\frac{-0.30x}{-0.30} = \frac{-12}{-0.30}$$
$$x = 40$$

40 milliliters of 50% acid solution and $100 - 40 = 60$ milliliters of 80% acid solution must be used.

3.

	Rate	× Time	= Distance
Faster Car	45	x	$45x$
Slower Car	35	x	$35x$

$$45x + 35x = 400$$
$$80x = 400$$
$$x = 5$$

The two cars will meet after 5 hours.

4. $45 = 81 - 36$
$45 = 9^2 - 6^2$

5. All 12 months have 28 days. (Most have more, but the problem does say "exactly 28 days.")

6. The following combinations will work:

1 dime 1 nickel	1 dime 5 pennies	3 nickels
2 nickels 5 pennies	1 nickel 10 pennies	15 pennies

7. Answers may vary.

8. The next figure in the sequence is a square inside a square with a single tick at the bottom.

9. There are 35 students in the class. The ratio of the number of men to the number of students is

$$\frac{20}{35} = \frac{4}{7} \quad \text{or} \quad 4{:}7.$$

10. $\frac{-5}{8} = \frac{x}{12}$

$$8x = -60$$
$$x = \frac{60}{8} = -\frac{15}{2}$$

11. Let x = number of tule elk in the park.

$$\frac{200}{x} = \frac{5}{150}$$
$$5x = 30{,}000$$
$$x = 6000$$

There are 6000 tule elk in the park.

12. Let x = pressure on object 330 feet below the surface.

$$\frac{\text{25 pounds per square inch}}{\text{60 feet}} = \frac{x\text{ pounds per square inch}}{\text{330 feet}}$$
$$\frac{25}{60} = \frac{x}{330}$$
$$60x = 25 \cdot 330$$
$$60x = 8250$$
$$x = 137.5$$

The pressure 330 feet below the surface is 137.5 pounds per square inch.

13. Find the area of a triangle with base 47 m and height 22 m.

$$A = \frac{1}{2}bh$$
$$A = \frac{1}{2}(47)(22) = 517$$

The area is 517 m^2.

14. Find the area of a trapezoid with bases 40 in. and 30 in. and height 15 in.

$$A = \frac{1}{2}h(a+b)$$
$$A = \frac{1}{2}(15)(40+30)$$
$$A = \frac{1}{2} \cdot 15 \cdot 70 = 525 \text{ in.}^2$$

The area is 525 in.^2.

15. Find the volume of a rectangular solid with length 3 in., width 2 in., and height 3 in.

$$V = lwh$$
$$V = 3 \cdot 2 \cdot 3 = 18$$

The volume is 18 in.^3.

16. Find the volume of a cylinder with radius 5 cm and height 7 cm.

$$V = \pi r^2 h$$
$$V = \pi(5)^2 \cdot 7 = \pi \cdot 25 \cdot 7$$
$$V = 175\pi \approx 550$$

The volume is 175π cm^3 or about 550 cm^3.

17. The area of the floor is

$$A = (40 \text{ ft})(50 \text{ ft}) = 2000 \text{ ft}^2.$$

The area of each tile is

$$A = (2 \text{ ft})(2 \text{ ft}) = 4 \text{ ft}^2.$$

The number of tiles needed is

$$\frac{2000 \text{ ft}^2}{4 \text{ ft}^2} = 500.$$

Since there are 10 tiles in a package, the number of packages needed is $\frac{500}{10} = 50$. Since each package costs \$13, the cost for enough tiles to cover the floor is 50(\$13) = \$650.

18. $A = \frac{1}{2}bh$; $A = 56, b = 8$

$$\begin{aligned} A &= \frac{1}{2}bh \\ 56 &= \frac{1}{2} \cdot 8 \cdot h \\ 56 &= 4h \\ 14 &= h \end{aligned}$$

The height of the sail is 14 feet.

19. Let x = the measure of the second angle.
Then $3x$ = the measure of the first angle.
$x - 30$ = the measure of the third angle.

$$\begin{aligned} x + 3x + (x - 30) &= 180 \\ 5x - 30 &= 180 \\ 5x &= 210 \\ x &= 42 \end{aligned}$$

Measure of first angle $= 3x = 3(42°)$
$= 126°$
Measure of second angle $= x = 42°$
Measure of third angle $= x - 30 = 42° - 30°$
$= 12°$

20. Let x = the measure of the angle.
Then $90 - x$ = the measure of its complement.

$$\begin{aligned} x &= (90 - x) + 16 \\ x &= 106 - x \\ 2x &= 106 \\ x &= 53 \end{aligned}$$

The measure of the angle is 53°.

Chapter 3 Cumulative Review Exercises (Chapters 1-3)

1. $$\begin{aligned} &\frac{-9(3-6)}{(-12)(3) + (-3-5)(8-4)} \\ &= \frac{-9}{-36 + (-8)(4)} \\ &= \frac{27}{-36 - 32} \\ &= \frac{27}{-68} = -\frac{27}{68} \end{aligned}$$

2. $$\begin{aligned} 8 - 3[2(x-1) + 5] &= 8 - 3(2x - 2 + 5) \\ &= 8 - 3(2x + 3) \\ &= 8 - 6x - 9 \\ &= -1 - 6x \end{aligned}$$

3. The integers are $-3, 0$, and $\sqrt{9}$ (= 3).

4. Quadrant IV

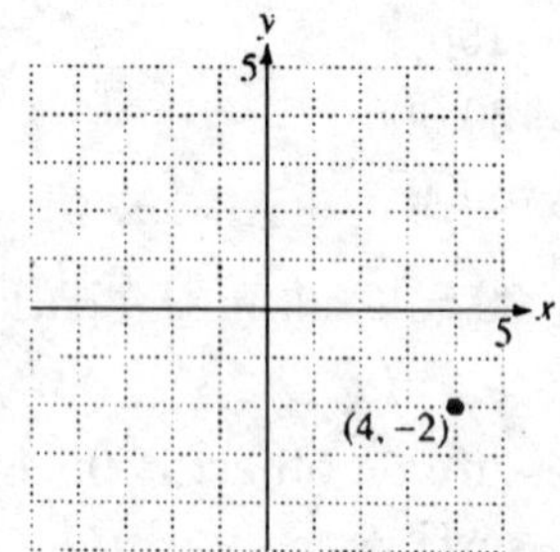

5. $-x^2 - 10x$; $x = -3$

$$\begin{aligned} -x^2 - 10x &= (-3)^2 - 10(-3) \\ &= 9 + 30 = 39 \end{aligned}$$

6. $-2000 < -3$; -2000 is to be left of -3 on the number line, so -2000 is less than -3.

7. $-4 + (-11) + 21 = -15 + 21 = 6$

The temperature at noon was 6°F.

8.
$$\begin{aligned}10(2x-1) &= 8(2x+1)+14\\ 20x-10 &= 16x+8+14\\ 20x-10 &= 16x+22\\ 20x-10-22 &= 16x+22-22\\ 20x-32 &= 16x\\ 20x-32+32 &= 16x+32\\ 20x &= 16x+32\\ 20x-16x &= 32\\ 4x &= 32\\ \frac{4x}{4} &= \frac{32}{4}\\ x &= 8\end{aligned}$$

The solution is 8.

9.
$$\begin{aligned}\frac{x}{5}+\frac{2x}{3} &= x+\frac{1}{15}\\ 15\left(\frac{x}{5}+\frac{2x}{3}\right) &= 15\left(x+\frac{1}{15}\right)\\ 3x+10x &= 15x+1\\ 13x &= 15x+1\\ 13x-5x &= 15x+1-15x\\ -2x &= 1\\ \frac{-2x}{-2} &= \frac{1}{-2}\\ x &= -\frac{1}{2}\end{aligned}$$

The solution is $-\frac{1}{2}$.

10.
$$\begin{aligned}A &= \frac{m+n}{2}\\ 2A &= 2\left(\frac{m+n}{2}\right)\\ 2A &= m+n\\ 2A-n &= m+n-n\\ 2A-n &= m \quad \text{or} \quad m = 2A-n\end{aligned}$$

11. $D = 4x+30;\ D = 150$

$$\begin{aligned}150 &= 4x+30\\ 120 &= 4x\\ 30 &= x\end{aligned}$$

According to the formula, the average debt will be \$150 thousand 30 years after 1985. Since $1985+30=2015$, this will happen in the year 2015.

12. $A = PB;\ A = 144,\ P = 60\% = 0.60$

$$\begin{aligned}A &= PB\\ 144 &= 0.60\cdot B\\ \frac{144}{0.60} &= \frac{0.60\cdot B}{B}\\ 240 &= B\end{aligned}$$

144 is 60% of 240.

13. Let w = the width of the rectangle.
Then $2w+14$ = the length.

$$\begin{aligned}2w+2(2w+14) &= 346\\ 2w+4w+28 &= 346\\ 6w+28 &= 346\\ 6w &= 318\\ w &= 53\end{aligned}$$

If $w = 53$, then $2w+14 = 2(53)+14 = 120$. The width is 53 meters and the length is 120 meters.

14. Let x = the person's weight before the weight loss.

$$\begin{aligned}x-0.10x &= 180\\ 0.90 &= 180\\ \frac{0.90x}{0.90} &= \frac{180}{0.90}\\ x &= 200\end{aligned}$$

The person's weight was 200 pounds.

15.
$$\begin{aligned}5x-5 &\le -5\\ 5x+5+5 &\le -5+5\\ 5x &\le 0\\ \frac{5x}{5} &\le \frac{0}{5}\\ x &\le 0\end{aligned}$$

-5 -4 -3 -2 -1 0 1 2 3 4 5

16.

$$-5x + 9 > -2x + 6$$
$$-5x + 9 + 2x > -2x + 6 + 2x$$
$$-3x + 9 > 6$$
$$-3x + 9 - 9 > 6 - 9$$
$$-3x > -3$$
$$\frac{-3x}{-3} < \frac{-3}{-3}$$
$$x < 1$$

-5 -4 -3 -2 -1 0 1 2 3 4 5

17.

	Rate ×	Time =	Distance
Slower Runner	6	x	$6x$
Faster Runner	8	x	$8x$

$$6x + 8x = 21$$
$$14x = 21$$
$$\frac{14x}{14} = \frac{21}{14}$$
$$x = \tfrac{3}{2} = 1\tfrac{1}{2}$$

They will be 21 miles apart in $1\frac{1}{2}$ hours.

18. $\frac{-5}{20} = \frac{x}{21}$

$$20x = (-5)(21)$$
$$20x = -105$$
$$\frac{20x}{20} = \frac{-105}{20}$$
$$x = -\frac{21}{4}$$

19. For each increased of 1 inch in foot length, the shoe size increases by 3. Therefore, the missing numbers (last three numbers in second row of table) are 14, 17, and 20.

20. The last column in the table shows that a man with foot length 14 inches wears size 20 shoes. Therefore, a size 23 shoe will be worn by a man with a foot length of 15 inches, and a size 26 shoe will be worn by a man with a foot length of 16 inches.

Chapter 4

LINEAR EQUATIONS AND INEQUALITIES IN TWO VARIABLES

4.1 Graphing Linear Equations

4.1 CHECK POINTS

CHECK POINT 1

$x - 3y = 9$

a. To determine whether $(3, -2)$ is a solution of the equation, substitute 3 for x and -2 for y.

$$\begin{aligned} x - 3y &= 9 \\ 3 - 3(-2) &\stackrel{?}{=} 9 \\ 3 - (-6) &\stackrel{?}{=} 9 \\ 9 &= 9 \text{ true} \end{aligned}$$

$(3, -2)$ is a solution.

b. To determine whether $(-2, 3)$ is a solution, substitute -2 for x and 3 for y.

$$\begin{aligned} x - 3y &= 9 \\ -2 - 3(3) &\stackrel{?}{=} 9 \\ -2 - 9 &\stackrel{?}{=} 9 \\ -11 &= 9 \text{ false} \end{aligned}$$

$(-2, 3)$ is a not solution.

CHECK POINT 2

$y = 3x + 2$

x	$y = 3x + 2$	(x, y)
-2	$y = 3(-2) + 2 = -4$	$(-2, -4)$
-1	$y = 3(-1) + 2 = -1$	$(-1, -1)$
0	$y = 3(0) + 2 = 2$	$(0, 2)$
1	$y = 3(1) + 2 = 5$	$(1, 5)$
2	$y = 3(2) + 2 = 8$	$(2, 8)$

Five solutions are $y = 3x+2$ are $(-2, -4)$, $(-1, -1)$, $(0, 2)$, $(1, 5)$, and $(2, 8)$.

CHECK POINT 3

$y = 2x$

x	$y = 2x$	(x, y)
-2	$y = 2(-2) = -4$	$(-2, -4)$
-1	$y = 2(-1) = -2$	$(-1, -2)$
0	$y = 2(0) = 0$	$(0, 0)$
1	$y = 2(1) = 2$	$(1, 2)$
2	$y = 2(2) = 4$	$(2, 4)$

Plot the five ordered pairs from the table and draw a line through the five points.

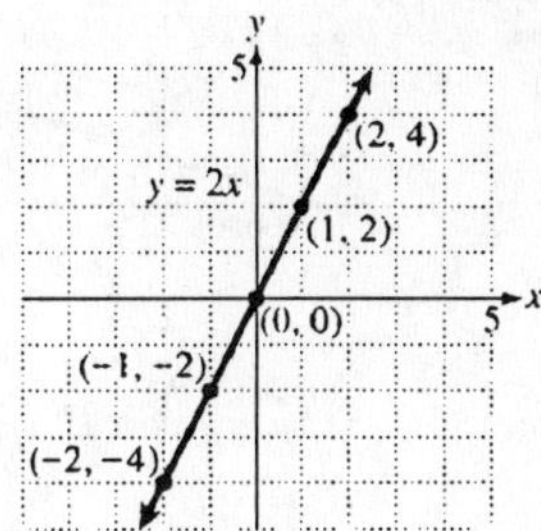

CHECK POINT 4

$y = 2x - 2$

x	$y = 2x - 2$	(x, y)
-2	$y = 2(-2) - 2 = -6$	$(-2, -6)$
-1	$y = 2(-1) - 2 = -4$	$(-1, -4)$
0	$y = 2(0) - 2 = -2$	$(0, -2)$
1	$y = 2(1) - 2 = 0$	$(1, 0)$
2	$y = 2(2) - 2 = 2$	$(2, 2)$

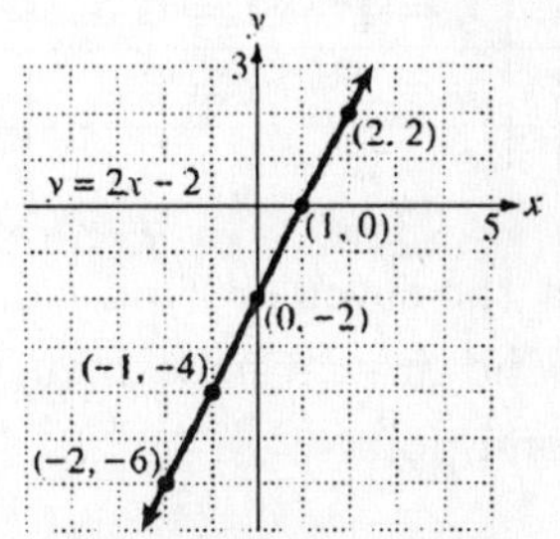

CHECK POINT 5

$$y = \frac{1}{3}x + 2$$

x	$y = \frac{1}{3}x + 2$	(x, y)
-6	$y = \frac{1}{3}(-6) + 2 = 0$	$(-6, 0)$
-3	$y = \frac{1}{3}(-3) + 2 = 1$	$(-3, 1)$
0	$y = \frac{1}{3}(0) + 2 = 2$	$(0, 2)$
3	$y = \frac{1}{3}(3) + 2 = 3$	$(3, 3)$
6	$y = \frac{1}{3}(6) + 2 = 4$	$(6, 4)$

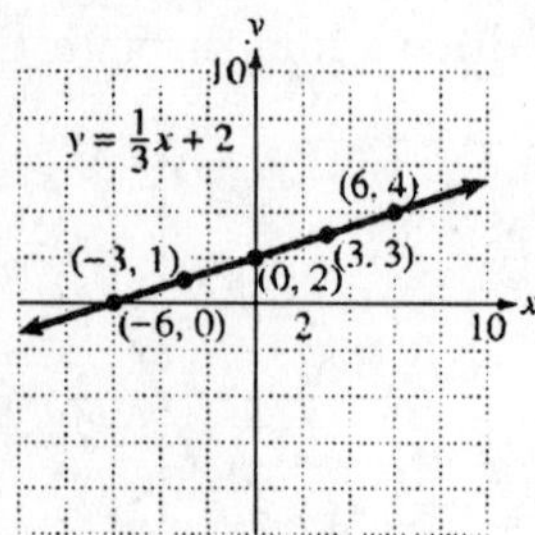

CHECK POINT 6

$y = x^2 - 1$

x	$y = x^2 - 1$	(x, y)
-3	$y = (-3)^2 - 1 = 8$	$(-3, 8)$
-2	$y = (-2)^2 - 1 = 3$	$(-2, 3)$
-1	$y = (-1)^2 - 1 = 0$	$(-1, 0)$
0	$y = 0^2 - 1 = -1$	$(0, -1)$
1	$y = 1^2 - 1 = 0$	$(1, 0)$
2	$y = 2^2 - 1 = 3$	$(2, 3)$
3	$y = 3^2 - 1 = 8$	$(3, 8)$

Plot the seven ordered pairs from the table and draw a smooth curve through the second points.

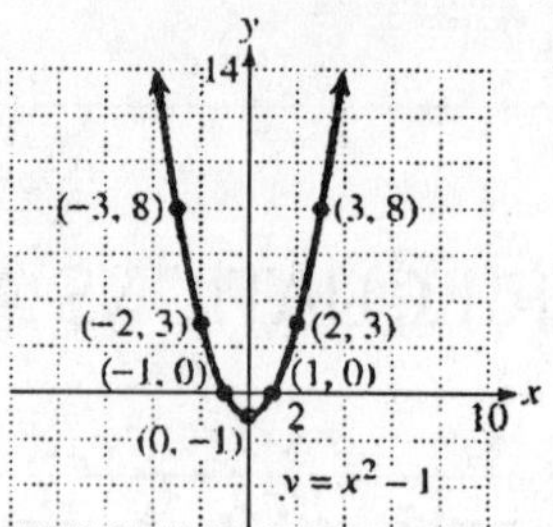

CHECK POINT 7

a. Without the coupon book:

x	$y = 2x$	(x, y)
0	$y = 2(0) = 0$	$(0, 0)$
2	$y = 2(2) = 4$	$(2, 4)$
4	$y = 2(4) = 8$	$(4, 8)$
6	$y = 2(6) = 12$	$(6, 12)$
8	$y = 2(8) = 16$	$(8, 16)$
10	$y = 2(10) = 20$	$(10, 20)$
12	$y = 2(12) = 24$	$(12, 24)$

With the coupon book:

x	$y = 10 + x$	(x, y)
0	$y = 10 + 0 = 10$	$(0, 10)$
2	$y = 10 + 2 = 12$	$(2, 12)$
4	$y = 10 + 4 = 14$	$(4, 14)$
6	$y = 10 + 6 = 16$	$(6, 16)$
8	$y = 10 + 8 = 18$	$(8, 18)$
10	$y = 10 + 10 = 20$	$(10, 20)$
12	$y = 10 + 22 = 22$	$(12, 22)$

b.

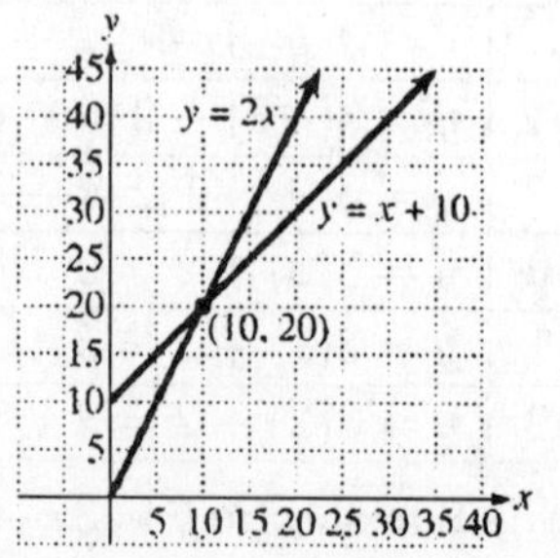

c. The intersection point is $(10, 20)$. This means that your cost for bridge tolls will be the same with or without the coupon book if you use the bridge 10 times a month, namely \$20.

EXERCISE SET 4.1

1. $y = 3x$

$(2, 3)$:

$3 \stackrel{?}{=} 3(2)$
$3 = 6$ false

$(2, 3)$ is not a solution.

$(3, 2)$:

$2 \stackrel{?}{=} 3(3)$
$2 = 9$ false

$(3, 2)$ is not a solution.

$(-4, -12)$:

$-12 \stackrel{?}{=} 3(-4)$
$-12 = -12$ true

$(-4, -12)$ is a solution.

3. $y = -4x$

$(-5, -20)$:

$-20 \stackrel{?}{=} -4(-5)$
$-20 = 20$ False

$(-5, -20)$ is not a solution.

$(0, 0)$:

$0 \stackrel{?}{=} -4(0)$
$0 = 0$ true

$(0, 0)$ is a solution.

$(9, -36)$:

$-36 \stackrel{?}{=} -4(9)$
$-36 = -36$ true

$(9, -36)$ is a solution.

5. $y = 2x + 6$

$(0, 6)$:

$6 \stackrel{?}{=} 2(0) + 6$
$6 = 6$ true

$(0, 6)$ is a solution.

$(-3, 0)$:

$0 \stackrel{?}{=} 2(-3) + 6$
$0 = 0$ true

$(-3, 0)$ is a solution.

$(2, -2)$:

$-2 \stackrel{?}{=} 2(2) + 6$
$-2 = 10$ false

$(2, -2)$ is not a solution.

7. $3x + 5y = 15$

$(-5, 6)$:

$3(-5) + 5(6) \stackrel{?}{=} 15$
$-15 + 30 \stackrel{?}{=} 15$
$15 = 15$ true

$(-5, 6)$ is a solution.

$(0, 5)$:

$3(0) + 5(5) \stackrel{?}{=} 15$
$0 + 25 \stackrel{?}{=} 15$
$25 = 15$ false

$(0, 5)$ is not a solution.

$(10, -3)$:

$3(10) + 5(-3) \stackrel{?}{=} 15$
$30 - 15 \stackrel{?}{=} 15$
$15 = 15$ true

$(10, -3)$ is a solution.

9. $x + 3y = 0$

$(0, 0)$:

$0 + 3(0) \stackrel{?}{=} 0$

$0 = 0$ true

$(0, 0)$ is a solution.

$\left(1, \frac{1}{3}\right)$:

$1 + 3\left(\frac{1}{3}\right) \stackrel{?}{=} 0$

$1 + 1 \stackrel{?}{=} 0$

$2 = 0$ false

$\left(1, \frac{1}{3}\right)$ is not a solution.

$\left(2, -\frac{2}{3}\right)$:

$2 + 2\left(-\frac{2}{3}\right) \stackrel{?}{=} 0$

$2 - 2 \stackrel{?}{=} 0$

$0 = 0$ true

$\left(2, -\frac{2}{3}\right)$ is a solution.

11. $x - 4 = 0$

$(4, 7)$:

$4 - 4 \stackrel{?}{=} 0$

$0 = 0$ true

$(4, 7)$ is a solution.

$(3, 4)$:

$3 - 4 \stackrel{?}{=} 0$

$-4 = 0$ false

$(3, 4)$ is not a solution.

$(0, -4)$:

$(0, -4) \stackrel{?}{=} 0$

$-4 = 0$ false

$(0, -4)$ is not a solution.

13. $y = 10x$

x	$y = 10x$	(x, y)
-2	$y = 10(-2) = -20$	$(-2, -20)$
-1	$y = 10(-1) = -10$	$(-1, -10)$
0	$y = 10(0) = 0$	$(0, 0)$
1	$y = 10(1) = 10$	$(1, 10)$
2	$y = 10(2) = 20$	$(2, 20)$

15. $y = -6x$

x	$y = -6x$	(x, y)
-2	$y = 6(-2) = 12$	$(-2, 12)$
-1	$y = -6(-1) = 6$	$(-1, 6)$
0	$y = -6(0) = 0$	$(0, 0)$
1	$y = -6(1) = -6$	$(1, 6)$
2	$y = -6(2) = -12$	$(2, -12)$

17. $y = 5x - 8$

x	$y = 5x - 8$	(x, y)
-2	$y = 5(-2) - 8 = -18$	$(-2, -18)$
-1	$y = 5(-1) - 8 = -13$	$(-1, -13)$
0	$y = 5(0) - 8 = -8$	$(0, -8)$
1	$y = 5(1) - 8 = -3$	$(1, -3)$
2	$y = 5(2) - 8 = 2$	$(2, 2)$

19. $y = -7x + 3$

x	$y = -7x + 3$	(x, y)
-2	$y = -7(-2) + 3 = 17$	$(-2, 17)$
-1	$y = -7(-1) + 3 = 10$	$(-1, 10)$
0	$y = -7(0) + 3 = 3$	$(0, 3)$
1	$y = -7(1) + 3 = -4$	$(1, -4)$
2	$y = -7(2) + 3 = -11$	$(2, -11)$

21. $y = x$

x	$y = x$	(x, y)
-2	$y = -2$	$(-2, -2)$
-1	$y = -1$	$(-1, -1)$
0	$y = 0$	$(0, 0)$
1	$y = 1$	$(1, 1)$
2	$y = 2$	$(2, 2)$

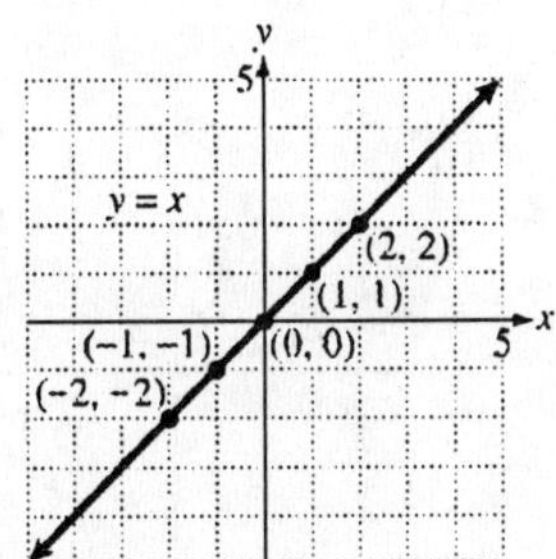

23. $y = x - 1$

x	$y = x - 1$	(x, y)
-2	$y = -2 - 1 = -3$	$(-2, -3)$
-1	$y = -1 - 1 = -2$	$(-1, -2)$
0	$y = 0 - 1 = -1$	$(0, -1)$
1	$y = 1 - 1 = 0$	$(1, 0)$
2	$y = 2 - 1 = 1$	$(2, 1)$

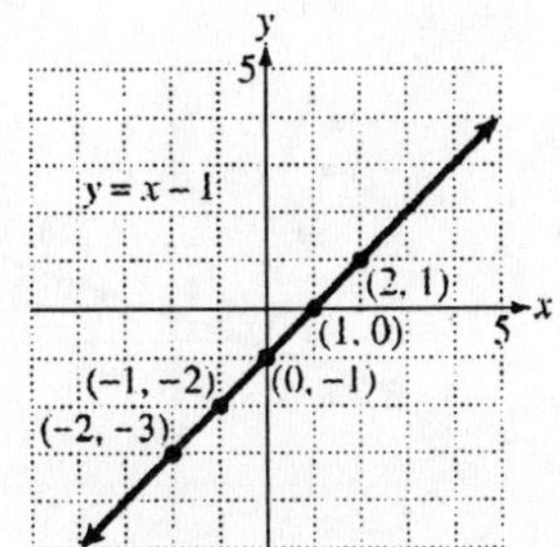

25. $y = 2x + 1$

x	$y = 2x + 1$	(x, y)
-2	$y = 2(-2) + 1 = -3$	$(-2, -3)$
-1	$y = 2(-1) + 1 = -1$	$(-1, -1)$
0	$y = 2(0) + 1 = 1$	$(0, 1)$
1	$y = 2(1) + 1 = 3$	$(1, 3)$
2	$y = 2(2) + 1 = 5$	$(2, 5)$

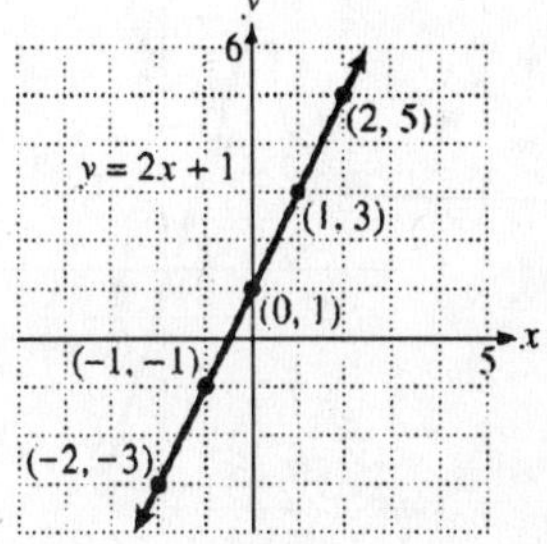

27. $y = -x + 2$

x	$y = -x + 2$	(x, y)
-2	$y = -(-2) + 2 = 4$	$(-2, 4)$
-1	$y = -(-1) + 2 = 3$	$(-1, 3)$
0	$y = -0 + 2 = 2$	$(0, 2)$
1	$y = -1 + 2 = 1$	$(1, 1)$
2	$y = -2 + 2 = 0$	$(2, 0)$

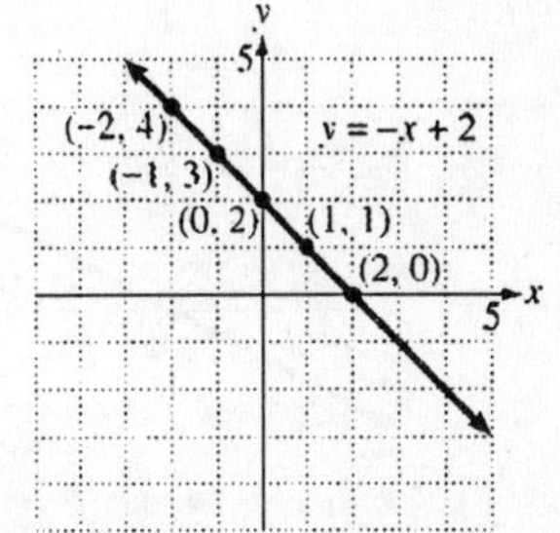

29. $y = -3x - 1$

x	$y = -3x - 1$	(x, y)
-2	$y = -3(-2) - 1 = 5$	$(-2, 5)$
-1	$y = -3(-1) - 1 = 2$	$(-1, 2)$
0	$y = -3(0) - 1 = -1$	$(0, -1)$
1	$y = -3(1) - 1 = -4$	$(1, -4)$
2	$y = -3(2) - 1 = -7$	$(2, -7)$

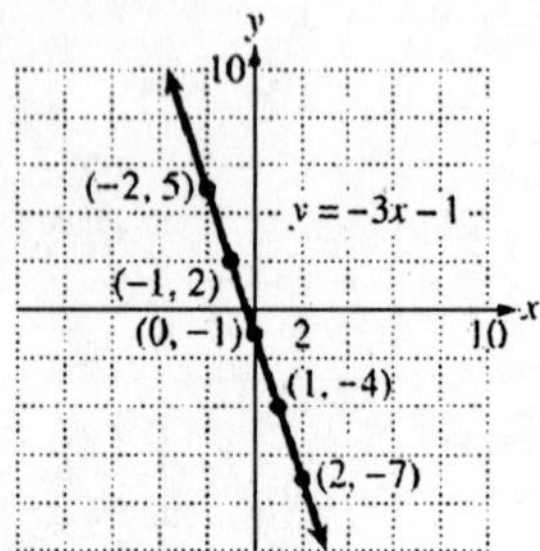

31. $x = \dfrac{1}{2}x$

x	$y = \frac{1}{2}x$	(x, y)
-4	$y = \frac{1}{2}(-4) = -2$	$(-4, -2)$
-2	$y = \frac{1}{2}(-2) = -1$	$(-2, -1)$
0	$y = \frac{1}{2}(0) = 0$	$(0, 0)$
2	$y = \frac{1}{2}(2) = 1$	$(2, 1)$
4	$y = \frac{1}{2}(4) = 2$	$(4, 2)$

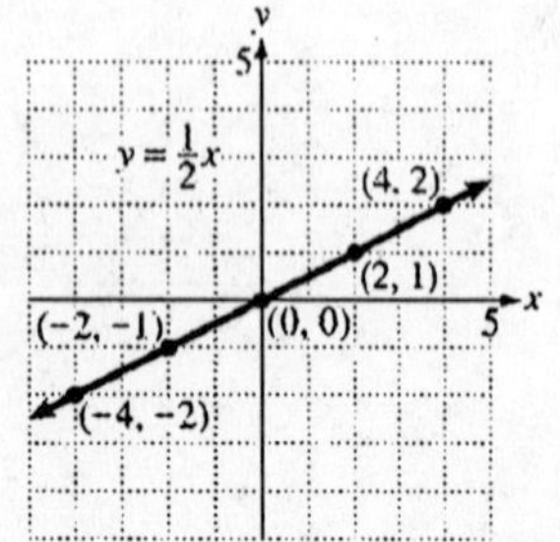

33. $y = -\dfrac{1}{4}x$

x	$y = -\frac{1}{4}x$	(x, y)
-8	$y = -\frac{1}{4}(-8) = 2$	$(-8, 2)$
-4	$y = -\frac{1}{4}(-4) = 1$	$(-4, 1)$
0	$y = -\frac{1}{4}(0) = 0$	$(0, 0)$
4	$y = -\frac{1}{4}(4) = -1$	$(4, -1)$
8	$y = -\frac{1}{4}(8) = -2$	$(8, -2)$

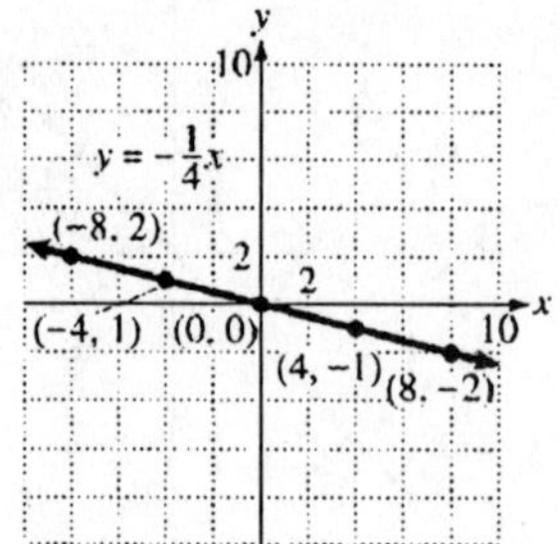

35. $y = \dfrac{1}{3}x + 1$

x	$y = \frac{1}{3}x + 1$	(x, y)
-6	$y = \frac{1}{3}(-6) + 1 = -1$	$(-6, -1)$
-3	$y = \frac{1}{3}(-3) + 1 = 0$	$(-3, 0)$
0	$y = \frac{1}{3}(0) + 1 = 1$	$(0, -1)$
3	$y = \frac{1}{3}(3) + 1 = 2$	$(3, 2)$
6	$y = \frac{1}{3}(6) + 1 = 3$	$(6, 3)$

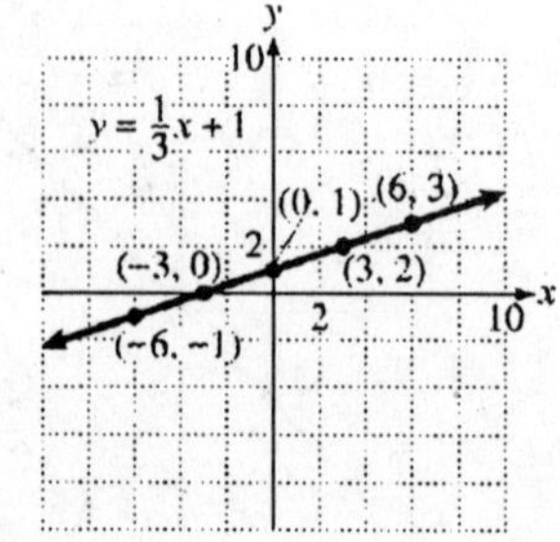

37. $y = -\dfrac{3}{2}x + 1$

x	$y = -\frac{3}{2}x + 1$	(x, y)
-4	$y = -\frac{3}{2}(-4) + 1 = 7$	$(-4, 7)$
-2	$y = -\frac{3}{2}(-2) + 1 = 4$	$(-2, 4)$
0	$y = -\frac{3}{2}(0) + 1 = 1$	$(0, 1)$
2	$y = -\frac{3}{2}(2) + 1 = -2$	$(2, -2)$
4	$y = -\frac{3}{2}(4) + 1 = -5$	$(4, -5)$

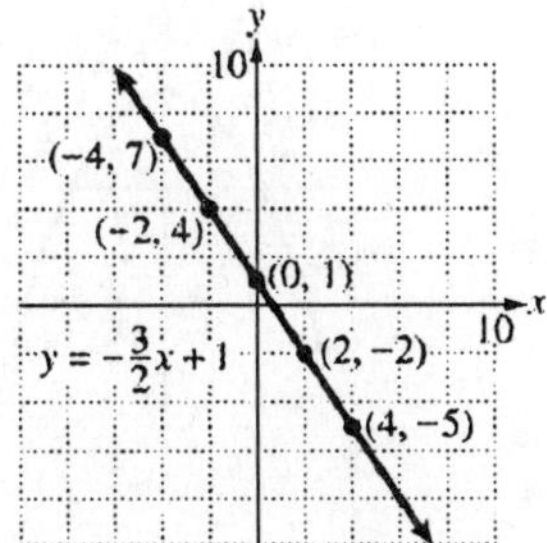

39. $y = -\dfrac{5}{2}x - 1$

x	$y = -\frac{5}{2}x - 1$	(x, y)
-4	$y = -\frac{5}{2}(-4) - 1 = 9$	$(-4, 9)$
-2	$y = -\frac{5}{2}(-2) - 1 = 4$	$(-2, 4)$
0	$y = -\frac{5}{2}(0) - 1 = -1$	$(0, -1)$
2	$y = -\frac{5}{2}(2) - 1 = -6$	$(2, -6)$
4	$y = -\frac{5}{2}(4) - 1 = -11$	$(4, -11)$

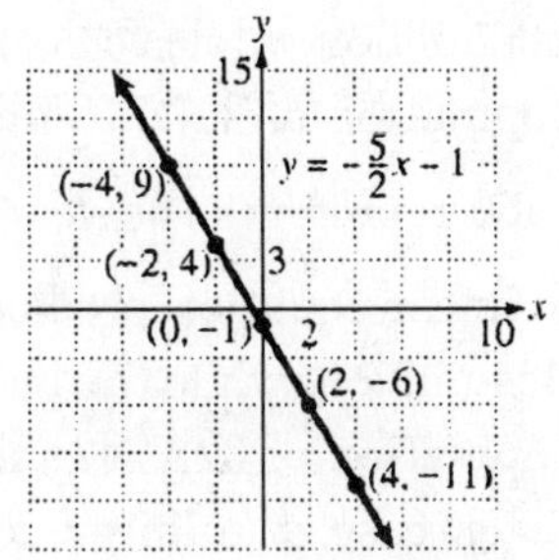

41. $y = x + \dfrac{1}{2}$

x	$y = x + \frac{1}{2}$	(x, y)
-4	$y = -4 + \frac{1}{2} = -3.5$	$(-4, -3.5)$
-2	$y = -2 + \frac{1}{2} = -1.5$	$(-2, -1.5)$
0	$y = 0 + \frac{1}{2} = 0.5$	$(0, 0.5)$
2	$y = 2 + \frac{1}{2} = 2.5$	$(2, 2.5)$
4	$y = 4 + \frac{1}{2} = 4.5$	$(4, 4.5)$

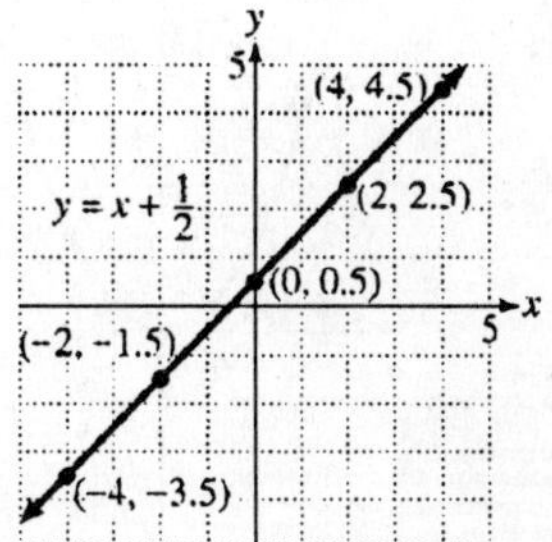

43. $y = 4$, or $y = 0x + 4$

x	$y = 0x + 4$	(x, y)
-6	$y = 0(-6) + 4 = 4$	$(-6, 4)$
-3	$y = 0(-3) + 4 = 4$	$(-3, 4)$
0	$y = 0(0) + 4 = 4$	$(0, 4)$
3	$y = 0(3) + 4 = 4$	$(3, 4)$
6	$y = 0(6) + 4 = 4$	$(6, 4)$

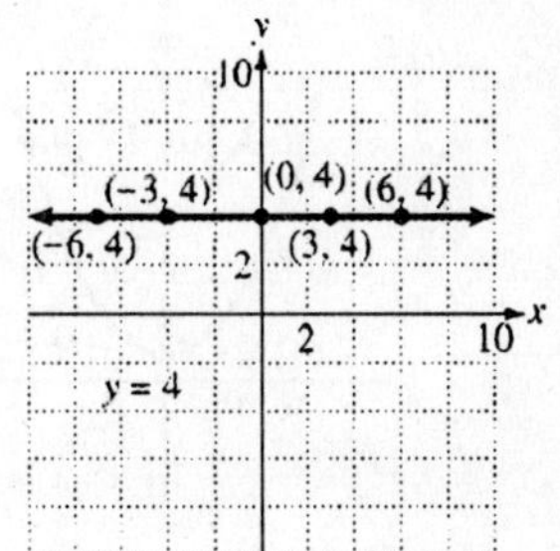

45. $y = x^2$

x	$y = x^2$	(x, y)
-3	$y = (-3)^2 = 9$	$(-3, 9)$
-2	$y = (-2)^2 = 4$	$(-2, 4)$
-1	$y = (-1)^2 = 1$	$(-1, 1)$
0	$y = 0^2 = 0$	$(0, 0)$
1	$y = 1^2 = 1$	$(1, 1)$
2	$y = 2^2 = 4$	$(2, 4)$
3	$y = 3^2 = 9$	$(3, 9)$

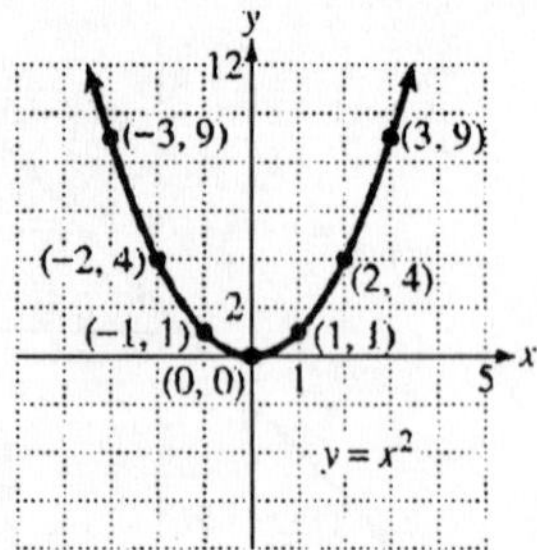

47. $y = x^2 + 1$

x	$y = x^2 + 1$	(x, y)
-3	$y = (-3)^2 + 1 = 10$	$(-3, 10)$
-2	$y = (-2)^2 + 1 = 5$	$(-2, 5)$
-1	$y = (-1)^2 + 1 = 2$	$(-1, 2)$
0	$y = 0^2 + 1 = 1$	$(0, 1)$
1	$y = 1^2 + 1 = 2$	$(1, 2)$
2	$y = 2^2 + 1 = 5$	$(2, 5)$
3	$y = 3^2 + 1 = 10$	$(3, 10)$

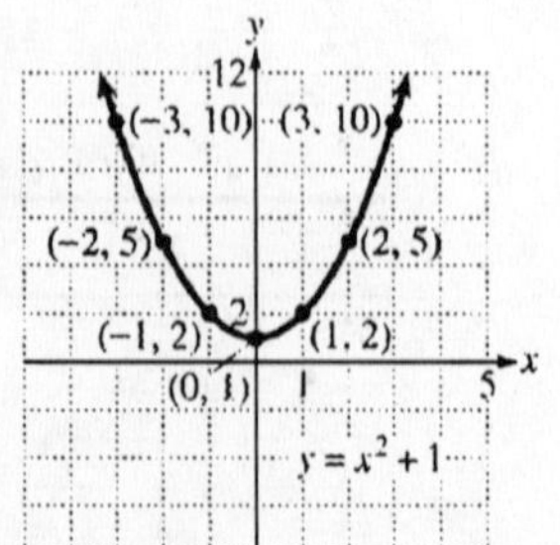

49. $y = 4 - x^2$

x	$y = 4 - x^2$	(x, y)
-3	$y = 4 - (-3)^2 = -5$	$(-3, -5)$
-2	$y = 4 - (-2)^2 = 0$	$(-2, 0)$
-1	$y = 4 - (-1)^2 = 3$	$(-1, 3)$
0	$y = 4 - 0^2 = 4$	$(0, 4)$
1	$y = 4 - 1^2 = 3$	$(1, 3)$
2	$y = 4 - 4^2 = 0$	$(2, 0)$
3	$y = 4 - 3^2 = -5$	$(3, -5)$

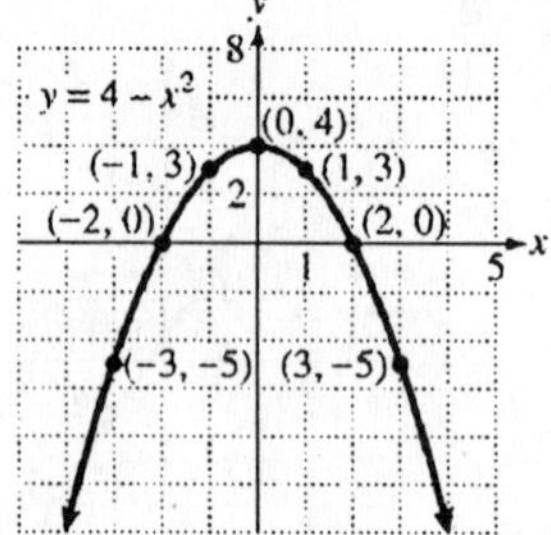

51. a.

x	$y = 2.4x + 180$	(x, y)
40	$y = 2.4(4) + 180 = 276$	$(40, 276)$
50	$y = 2.4(50) + 180 = 300$	$(50, 300)$
60	$y = 2.4(60) + 180 = 324$	$(60, 324)$

b. $x = 40$ represents the year 1960 + 40 = 2000.

The linear equation predicts a population of 276 million, while the bar graph projects a population of 274.634 million.

$x = 50$ represents the year 2010.

The linear equation predicts a population of 300 million, while the bar graph projects a population of 297.716 million.

$x = 60$ represents the year 2020.

The linear equation predicts a population of 324 million, while the bar graph projects a population of 322.742 million.
In each case, the linear equation models the projections shown in the bar graph quite well.

53. a.

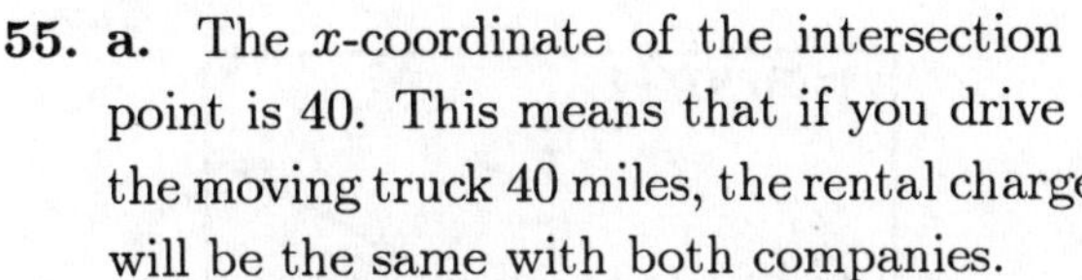

x	$y = 0.85x + 4.05$	(x, y)
11.6	$y = 0.85(11.6) + 4.05 = 13.91$	$(11.6, 13.91)$
8.3	$y = 0.85(8.3) + 4.05 = 11.105$	$(8.3, 11.105)$

b. The linear equation models the actual data quite well.

55. a. The x-coordinate of the intersection point is 40. This means that if you drive the moving truck 40 miles, the rental charge will be the same with both companies.

b. A reasonable estimate of the y-coordinate of the intersection point is 55.

c. $y = 40 + 0.35; x = 40$

$$y = 40 + 0.35(40)$$
$$y = 40 + 14 = 54$$

$$y = 36 + 0.45x; x = 40$$

$$y = 36 + 0.45(40)$$
$$y = 36 + 18 = 54$$

This value indicates that if you drive the moving truck 40 miles, the rental charge with either company will be \$54. This is almost the same as the estimate in part (b).

57. a.

x	$y = 50x + 30{,}000$	(x, y)
0	$y = 50(0) + 30{,}000 = 30{,}000$	$(0, 30{,}000)$
10	$y = 50(10) + 30{,}000 = 30{,}500$	$(10, 30{,}500)$
20	$y = 50(20) + 30{,}000 = 31{,}000$	$(20, 31{,}000)$
30	$y = 50(30) + 30{,}000 = 31{,}500$	$(30, 31{,}500)$
40	$y = 50(40) + 30{,}000 = 32{,}000$	$(40, 32{,}000)$

b.

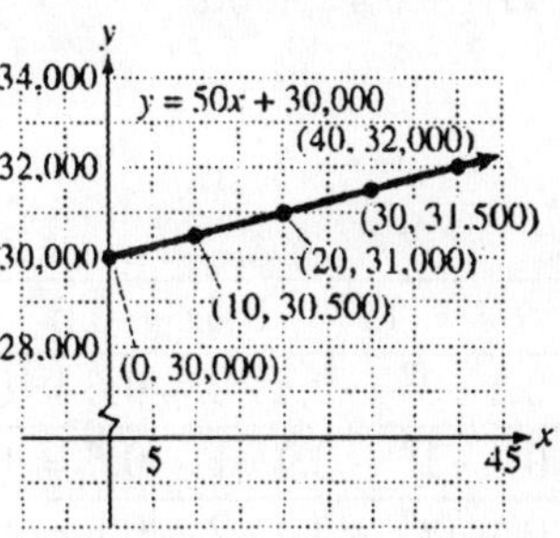

For Exercises 59–61, answers may vary.

63.

x	$y = \|x\|$	(x, y)
−3	$y = \|-3\| = 3$	$(-3, 3)$
−2	$y = \|-2\| = 2$	$(-2, 2)$
−1	$y = \|-1\| = 1$	$(-1, 1)$
0	$y = \|0\| = 0$	$(0, 0)$
1	$y = \|1\| = 1$	$(1, 1)$
2	$y = \|2\| = 2$	$(2, 2)$
3	$y = \|3\| = 3$	$(3, 3)$

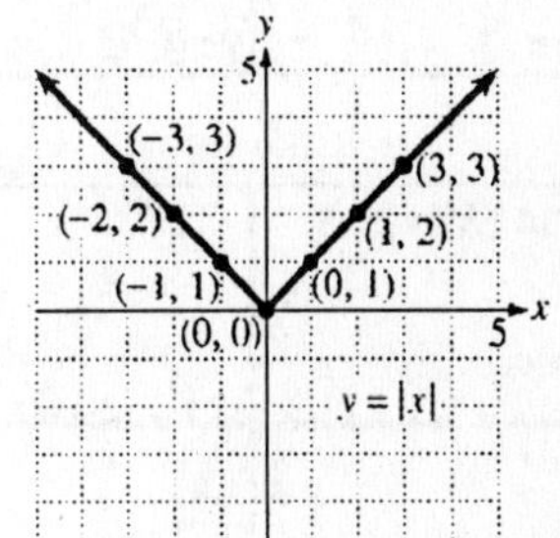

65. $y = 0.1x^2 - 0.4x + 0.6$

a.

x	$y = 0.1x^2 - 0.4x + 0.6$	(x, y)
0	$y = 0.1 \cdot 0^2 - 0.4 \cdot 0 + 0.6 = 0.6$	$(0, 0.6)$
1	$y = 0.1 \cdot 1^2 - 0.4 \cdot 1 + 0.6 = 0.3$	$(1, 0.3)$
2	$y = 0.1 \cdot 2^2 - 0.4 \cdot 2 + 0.6 = 0.2$	$(2, 0.2)$
3	$y = 0.1 \cdot 3^2 - 0.4 \cdot 3 + 0.6 = 0.3$	$(3, 0.3$
4	$y = 0.1 \cdot 4^2 - 0.4 \cdot 4 + 0.6 = 0.6$	$(4, 0.6)$
5	$y = 0.1 \cdot 5^2 - 0.4 \cdot 5 + 0.6 = 1.1$	$(5, 1.1)$

b. The air is considered unsafe when $y \geq 0.3$. This occurs when $x \leq 1$ or $x \geq 3$. Since $x = 1$ corresponds to 10 A.M. and $x = 3$ corresponds to noon. To avoid unsafe air, runners should exercise between 10 A.M. and noon.

67. $y = -3x + 2$

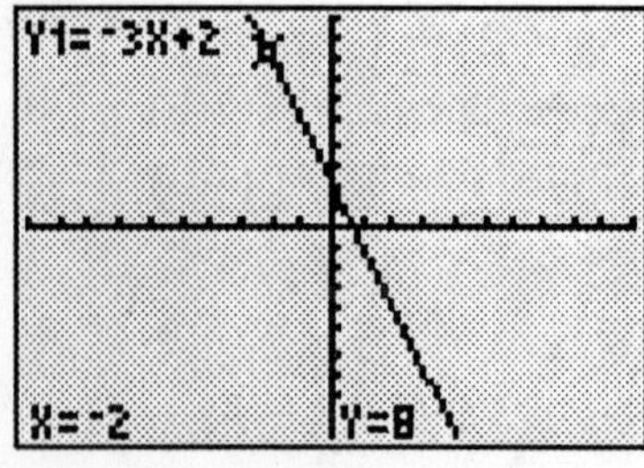

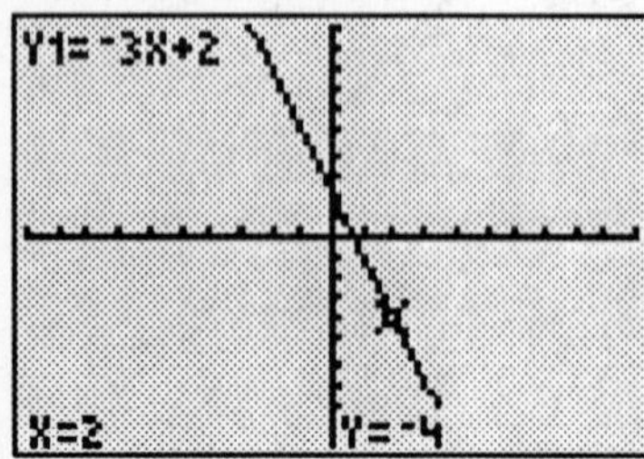

Two points on the graph are $(-2, 8)$ and $(2, -4)$.

69. $y = \frac{3}{4}x - 2$

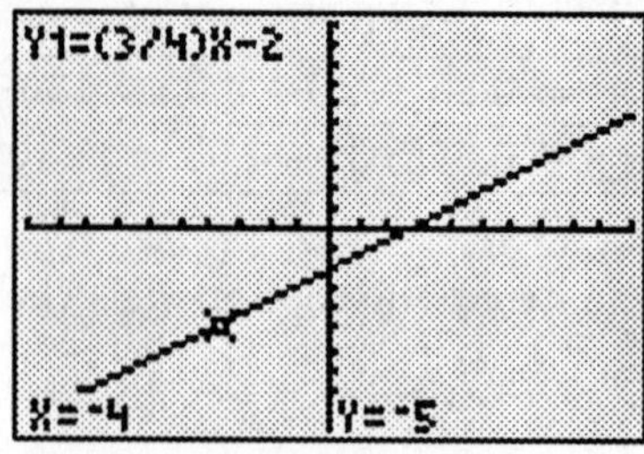

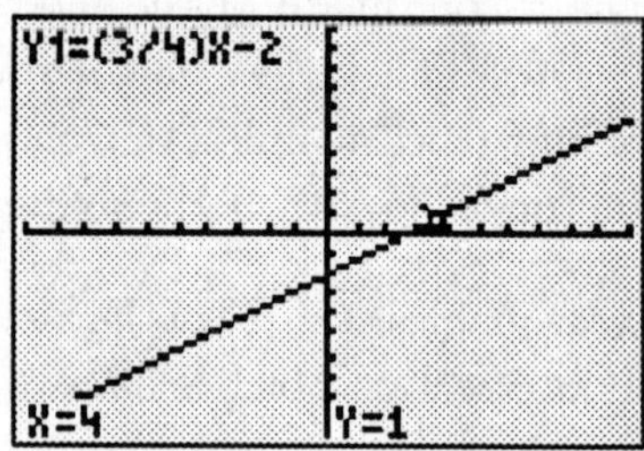

Two points on the graph are $(-4, -5)$ and $(4, 1)$.

71. $y = 2.4x + 180$

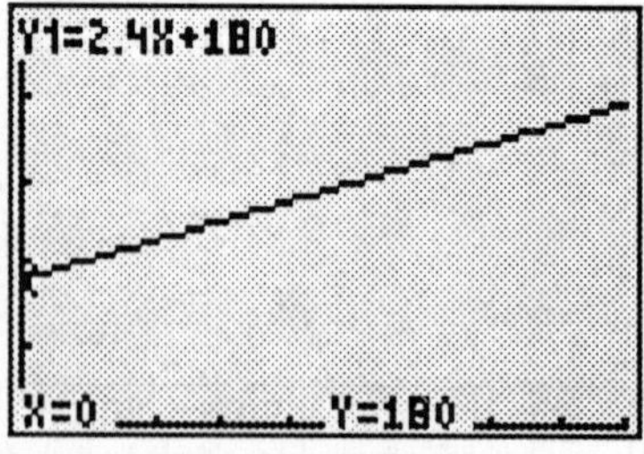

The shape of the graph indicates that the U.S. population is increasing at a steady rate.

Review Exercises

72.
$$\begin{aligned}
3x+5&=4(2x-3)+7\\
3x+5&=8x-12+7\\
3x+5&=8x-5\\
3x+5-8x&=8x-5-8x\\
-5x+5&=-5\\
-5x+5-5&=-5-5\\
-5x&=-10\\
\frac{-5x}{-5}&=\frac{-10}{-5}\\
x&=2
\end{aligned}$$

The solution is 2.

73. $3(1-2\cdot 5)-(-28)=3(1-10)+28$
$=3(-9)+28$
$=-27+28=-1$

74. $V=\frac{1}{3}Ah$ for h

$$V=\frac{1}{3}Ah$$
$$3V=3\left(\frac{1}{3}Ah\right)$$
$$3V=Ah$$
$$\frac{3V}{A}=\frac{Ah}{A}$$
$$\frac{3V}{A}=h \text{ or } h=\frac{3V}{A}$$

4.2 Graphing Linear Equations Using Intercepts

4.2 CHECK POINTS

CHECK POINT 1

a. The graph crosses the x-axis at $(-3,0)$, so the x-intercept is -3.
The graph crosses the y-axis at $(0,5)$, so the y-intercept is 5.

b. This horizontal line does not cross the x-axis, so there is no x-intercept. The graph crosses the y-axis $(0,4)$, so the y-intercept is 4.

c. The graph crosses the x- and y-axes at the same point, the origin. Because the graph crosses both axes at $(0,0)$, the x-intercept is 0 and the y-intercept is 0.

CHECK POINT 2

$4x-3y=12$

To find the x-intercept, let $y=0$ and solve for x.

$$\begin{aligned}
4x-4y&=12\\
4x-3\cdot 0&=12\\
4x&=12\\
x&=3
\end{aligned}$$

The x-intercept is 3.

CHECK POINT 3

$4x-3y=12$

To find the y-intercept, let $x=0$ and solve for y.

$$\begin{aligned}
4x-3y&=12\\
4\cdot 0-3y&=12\\
-3y&=12\\
y&=4
\end{aligned}$$

The y-intercept is -4.

CHECK POINT 4

$2x + 3y = 6$

Step 1 Find the x-intercept.

$$\begin{aligned} 2x + 3y &= 6 \\ 2x + 3 \cdot 0 &= 6 \\ 2x &= 6 \\ x &= 3 \end{aligned}$$

The x-intercept is 3.

Step 2 Find the y-intercept.

$$\begin{aligned} 2x + 3y &= 6 \\ 2 \cdot 0 + 3y &= 6 \\ 3y &= 6 \\ y &= 2 \end{aligned}$$

The y-intercept is 2.

Step 3 Find a checkpoint. Let $x = -3$ and find the corresponding value of y.

$$\begin{aligned} 2x + 3y &= 6 \\ 2(-3) + 3y &= 6 \\ -6 + 3y &= 6 \\ 3y &= 12 \\ y &= 4 \end{aligned}$$

This gives a third ordered pair, $(-3, 4)$. Plot the points $(3, 0), (0, 2)$, and $(-3, 4)$ and draw a line through them.

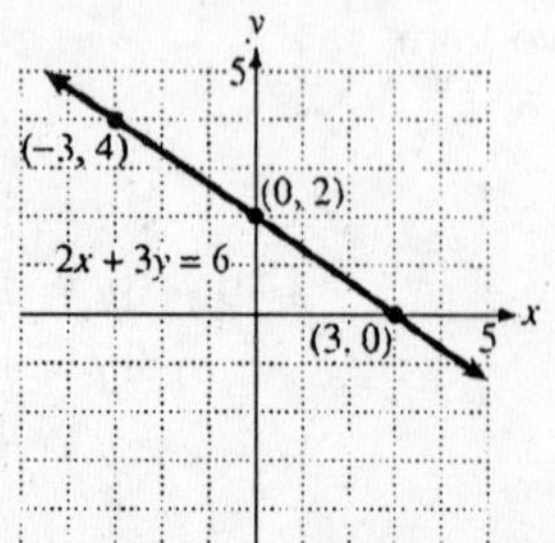

CHECK POINT 5

$x - 2y = 4$

Step 1 Find the x-intercept.

$$\begin{aligned} x - 2y &= 4 \\ x - 2 \cdot 0 &= 4 \\ x &= 4 \end{aligned}$$

The x-intercept is 4.

Step 2 Find the y-intercept.

$$\begin{aligned} x - 2y &= 4 \\ 0 - 2y &= 4 \\ -2y &= 4 \\ y &= -2 \end{aligned}$$

The y-intercept is -2.

Step 3 Find a checkpoint. Let $x = 2$ and find the corresponding value of y.

$$\begin{aligned} x - 2y &= 4 \\ 2 - 2y &= 4 \\ -2y &= 2 \\ y &= -1 \end{aligned}$$

A checkpoint is $(2, -1)$.
Draw a line through $(4, 0)$, $(0, -2)$, and $(2, -1)$.

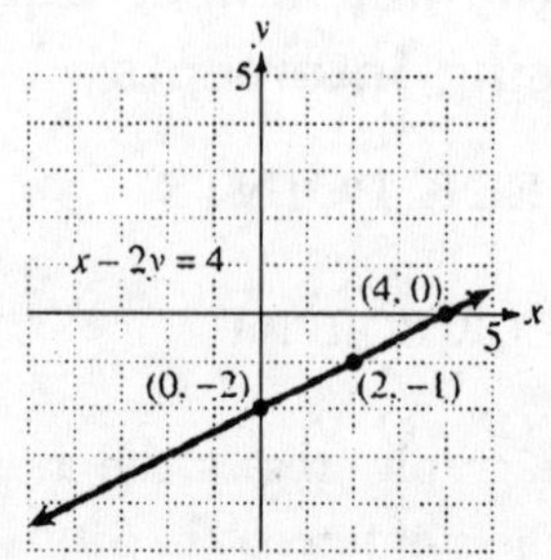

CHECK POINT 6

$x + 3y = 0$

Because the constant on the right is 0, the graph passes through the origin. The x- and y-intercepts are both 0. Two points other than $(0,0)$ should be found. Let $y = -1$ to find a second ordered-pair solution, and let $y = 1$ to find a third ordered-pair (checkpoint) solution.

$$\begin{aligned} x + 3y &= 0 \\ x + 3(-1) &= 0 \\ x + (-3) &= 0 \\ x &= 3 \end{aligned} \qquad \begin{aligned} x + 3y &= 0 \\ x + 3 \cdot 1 &= 0 \\ x + 3 &= 0 \\ x &= -3 \end{aligned}$$

Plot the points $(0,0)$, $(3,-1)$, and $(-3,1)$ and draw a line through them.

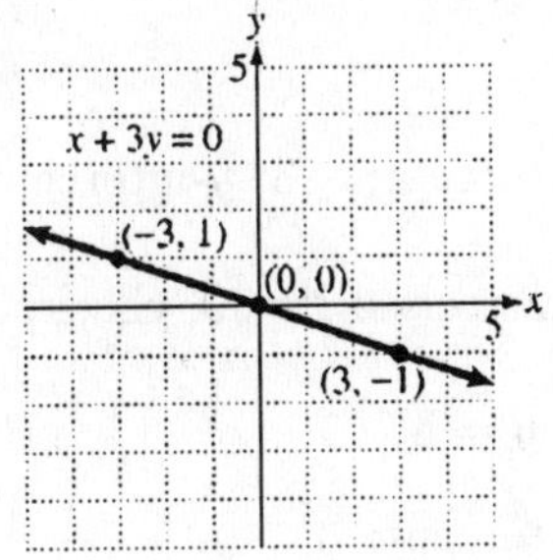

CHECK POINT 7

$y = 3$

All ordered pairs that are solutions of $y = 3$ have a value of y that is 3. Any value can be used for x. Three ordered pairs that are solutions are $(-3,3)$, $(0,3)$, and $(4,3)$.

Plot these three points and draw a line through them. The graph is a horizontal line.

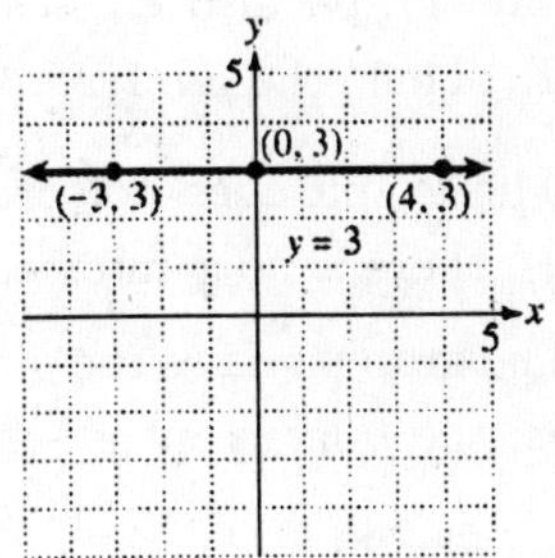

CHECK POINT 8

$x = -2$

All ordered pairs that are solutions have a value of x that is -2. Any value can be used for y. Three ordered pairs that are solutions are $(-2,-4)$, $(-2,0)$, and $(-2,3)$. The graph is a vertical line.

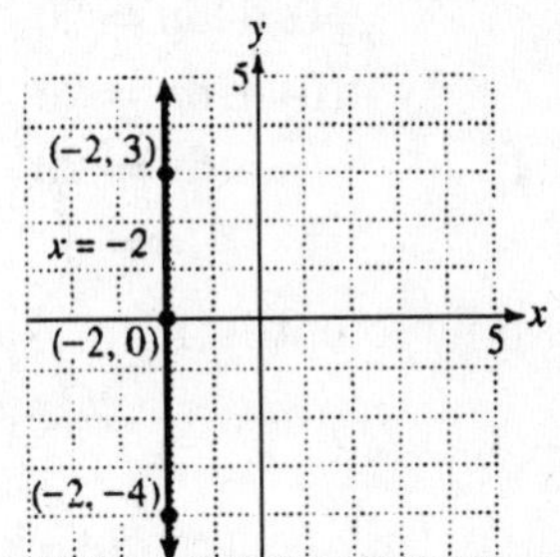

EXERCISE SET 4.2

1. **a.** The graph crosses the x-axis at $(3,0)$. Thus, the x-intercept is 3.

   b. The graph crosses the y-axis at $(0,4)$. Thus, the y-intercept is 4.

3. **a.** The graph crosses the x-axis at $(-2,0)$. Thus, the x-intercept is -2.

   b. The graph crosses the y-axis at $(0,-2)$. Thus, the y-intercept is -2.

5. **a.** The graph crosses the x-axis at $(0, 0)$ (the origin). Thus, the x-intercept is 0.

b. The graph also crosses the y-axis at $(0, 0)$. Thus, the y-intercept is 0.

7. **a.** The graph does not cross the x-axis. Thus, there is no x-intercept.

b. The graph crosses the y-axis at $(0, -2)$. Thus, the y-intercept is -2.

9. $4x + 5y = 20$

To find the x-intercept, let $y = 0$ and solve for x.

$$\begin{aligned} 4x + 5y &= 20 \\ 4x + 5(0) &= 20 \\ 4x &= 20 \\ x &= 5 \end{aligned}$$

The x-intercept is 5.

To find the y-intercept, let $x = 0$ and solve for y.

$$\begin{aligned} 4x + 5y &= 20 \\ 4(0) + 5y &= 20 \\ 5y &= 20 \\ y &= 4 \end{aligned}$$

The y-intercept is 4.

11. $7x - 3y = 42$

To find the x-intercept, let $y = 0$ and solve for x.

$$\begin{aligned} 7x - 3y &= 42 \\ 7x - 3(0) &= 42 \\ 7x &= 42 \\ x &= 6 \end{aligned}$$

The x-intercept is 6.
To find the y-intercept, let $x = 0$ and solve for y.

$$\begin{aligned} 7x - 3y &= 42 \\ 7(0) - 3y &= 42 \\ -3y &= 42 \\ y &= -14 \end{aligned}$$

The y-intercept is -14.

13. $-x + 4y = -8$

x-intercept:

$$\begin{aligned} -x + 4(0) &= -8 \\ -x &= -8 \\ x &= -8 \end{aligned}$$

y-intercept:

$$\begin{aligned} -0 + 4y &= -8 \\ 4y &= -8 \\ y &= -2 \end{aligned}$$

$x-$intercept: 8; y-intercept: -2

15. $3x - 5y = 0$

x-intercept:

$$\begin{aligned} 3x - 5(0) &= 0 \\ 3x &= 0 \\ x &= 0 \end{aligned}$$

y-intercept:

$$\begin{aligned} 3(0) - 5y &= 0 \\ -5y &= 0 \\ y &= 0 \end{aligned}$$

$x-$intercept: 0; y-intercept: 0

17. $2x = 3y - 6$

x-intercept:

$$\begin{aligned} 2x &= 3(0) - 6 \\ 2x &= -6 \\ x &= -3 \end{aligned}$$

y-intercept:

$$\begin{aligned} 2(0) &= 3y - 6 \\ 0 &= 3y - 6 \\ 6 &= 3y \\ 2 &= y \end{aligned}$$

x-intercept: -3; y-intercept: 2

In Exercises 19–39, checkpoints will vary.

19. $x + y = 3$

x-intercept: 3
y-intercept: 3
checkpoint: $(2, 1)$
Draw a line through $(3, 0)$, $(0, 3)$, and $(2, 1)$.

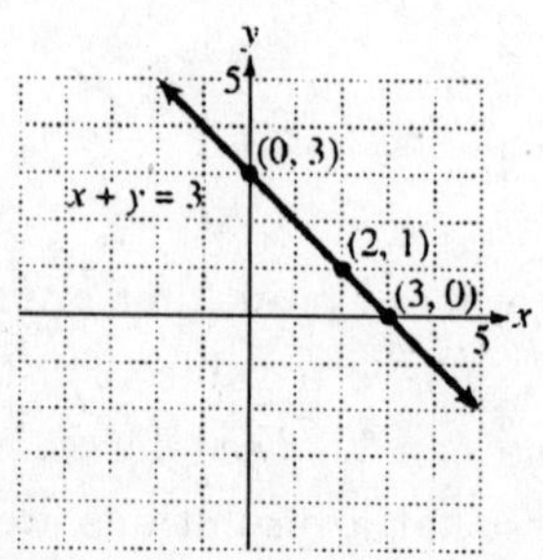

21. $3x + y = 6$

x-intercept: 2
y-intercept: 6
checkpoint: $(1, 3)$
Draw a line through $(2, 0), (0, 6)$, and $(1, 3)$.

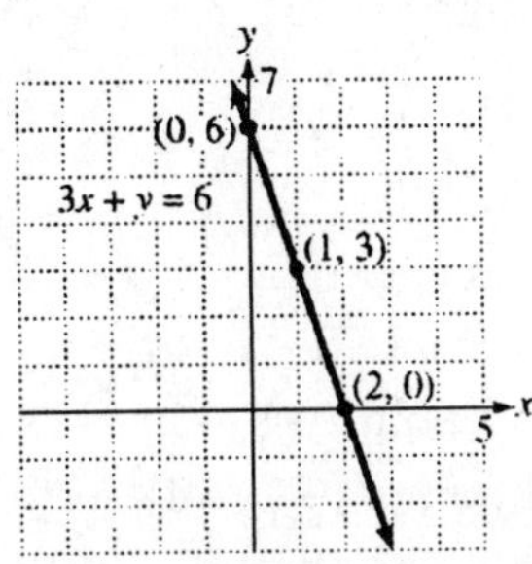

23. $9x - 6y = 18$

x-intercept: 2
y-intercept: -3
checkpoint: $(1, -\frac{3}{2})$
Draw a line through $(2, 0), (0, -3)$, and $(1, -\frac{3}{2})$.

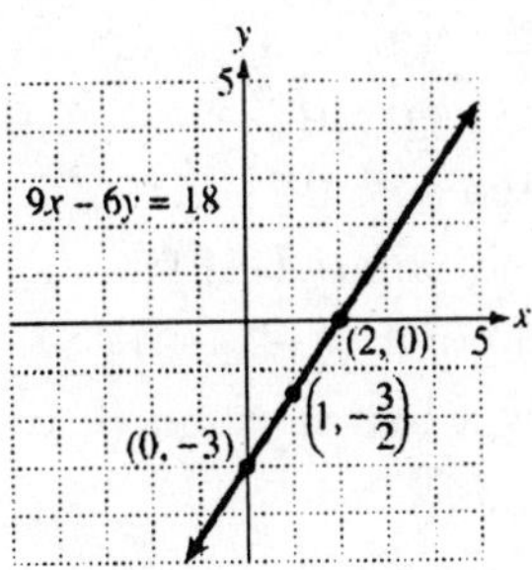

25. $-x + 4y = 8$

x-intercept: -8
y-intercept: 2
checkpoint: $(2, \frac{5}{2})$
Draw a line through $(-8, 0), (0, 2)$ and $(2, \frac{5}{2})$.

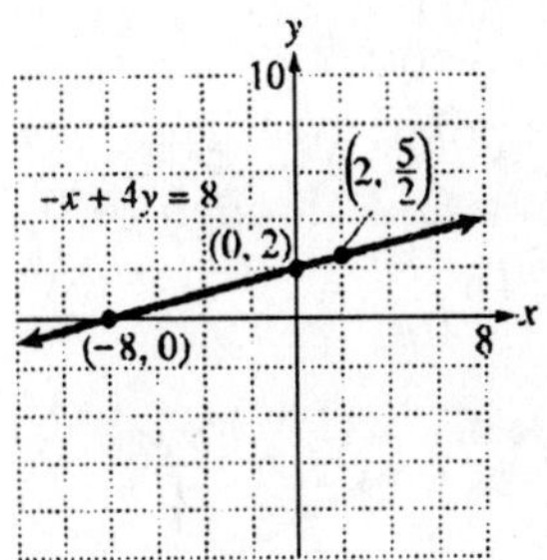

27. $2x - y = 6$

x-intercept: 3
y-intercept: -6
checkpoint: $(1, -4)$
Draw a line through $(3, 0), (0, -6)$, and $(1, -4)$.

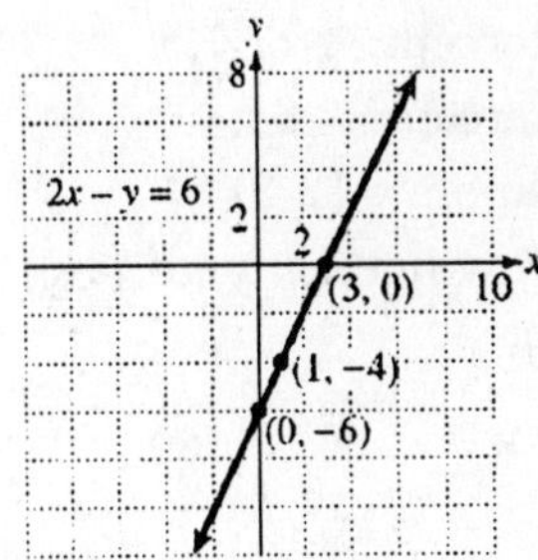

29. $5x = 3y - 15$

x-intercept: -3
y-intercept: 5
checkpoint: $(-6, -5)$
Draw a line through $(-3, 0), (0, 5)$, and $(-6, -5)$.

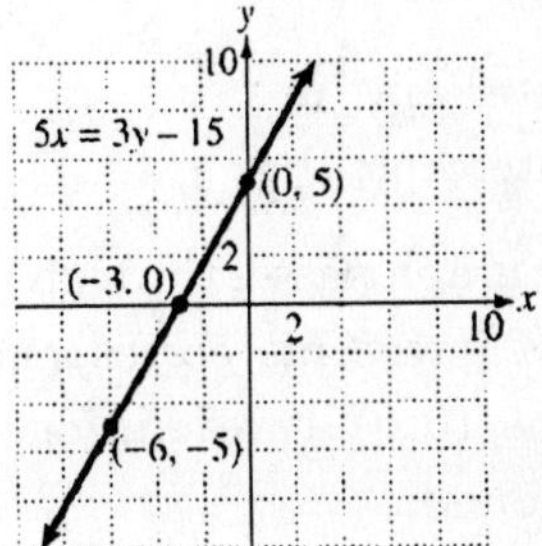

31. $50y = 100 - 25x$

x-intercept: 4
y-intercept: 2
checkpoint: $(-4, 4)$
Draw a line through $(4, 0), (0, 2)$ and $(-4, 4)$.

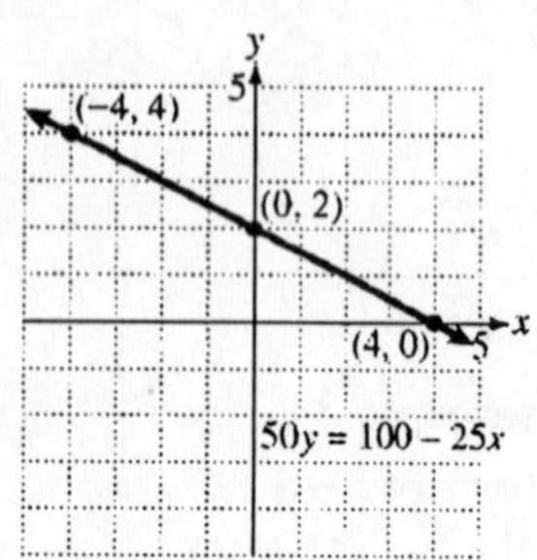

33. $8x - 2y = 12$

x-intercept: $\frac{3}{2}$ or 1.5
y-intercept: -6
checkpoint: $(2, 2)$
Draw a line through $(1.5, 0), (0, -6)$ and $(2, 2)$.

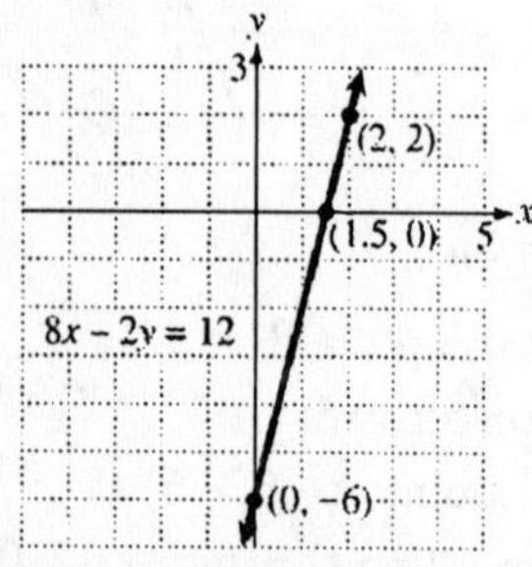

35. $x + y = 0$

x-intercept: 0
y-intercept: 0

The graph passes through the origin. Since both intercepts correspond to the same point, $(0, 0)$, two additional points should be found.
second point: $(-2, 2)$
checkpoint: $(4, -4)$

Draw a line through $(0, 0), (-2, 2)$ and $(4, -4)$.

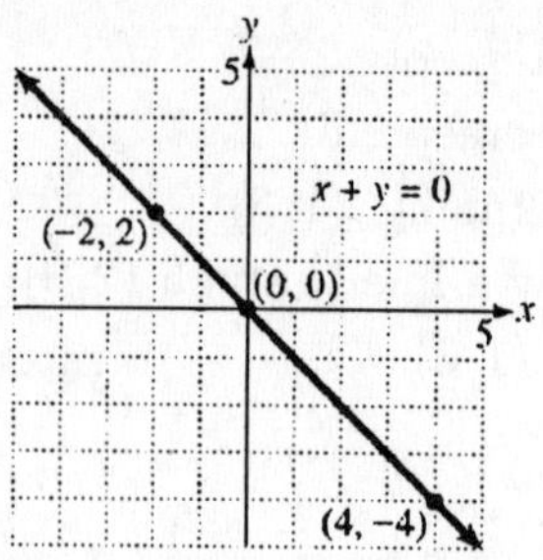

37. $2x + y = 0$
x-intercept: 0
y-intercept: 0
second point: $(1, -2)$
checkpoint: $(-2, -4)$
Draw a line through $(0, 0), (1, -2)$ and $(-2, 4)$.

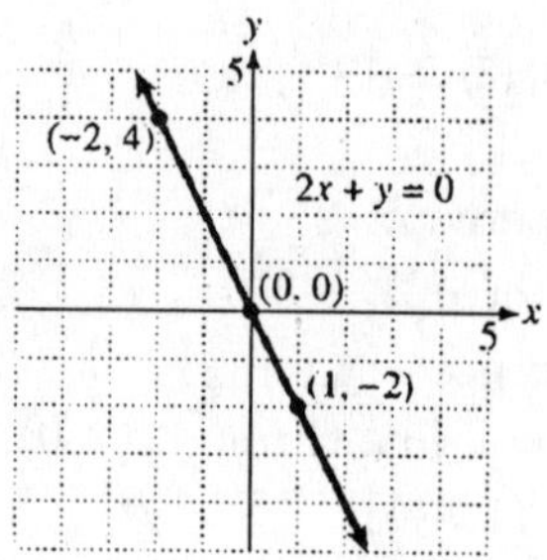

39. $y - 2x = 0$
x-intercept: 0
y-intercept: 0
second point: $(1, 2)$
checkpoint: $(-2, -4)$
Draw a line through $(0, 0), (1, 2)$, and $(-2, -4)$.

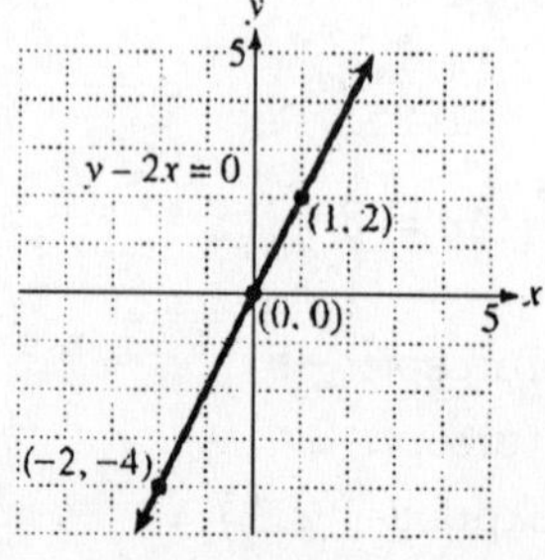

41. The equation for this horizontal line is $y = 3$.

43. The equation for this vertical line is $x = -3$.

45. The equation for this horizontal line, which is the x-axis, is $y = 0$.

47. $y = 4$

All ordered pairs that are solutions will have a value of y that is 4. Any value can be used for x. Three ordered pairs that are solutions are $(-2, 4), (0, 4)$, and $(3, 4)$. Plot these points and draw the line through them. The graph is a horizontal line.

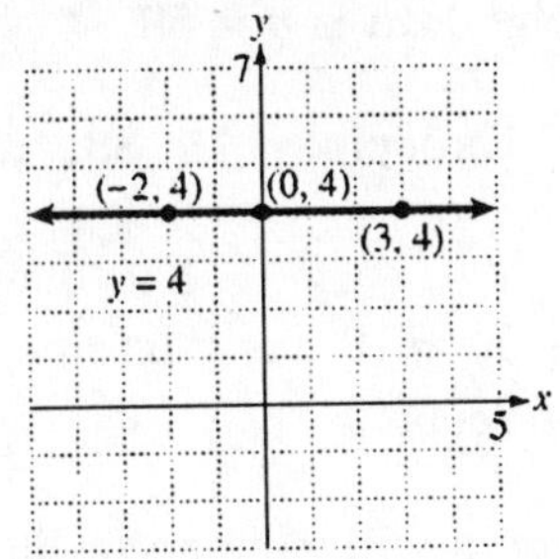

49. $y = -2$

Three ordered pairs are $(-3, -2), (0, -2)$, and $(4, -2)$. The graph is a horizontal line.

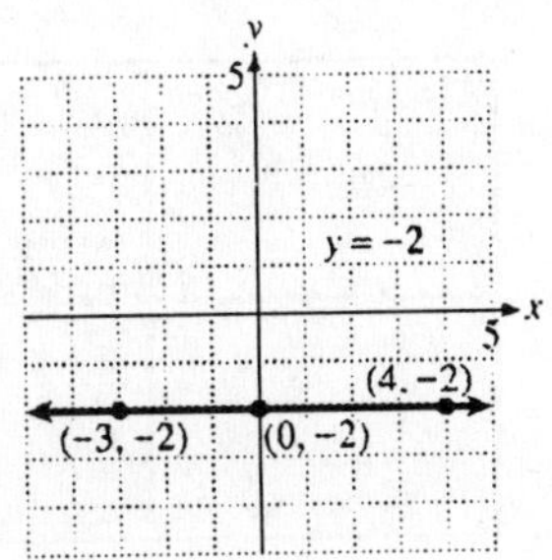

51. $x = 2$

All ordered pairs that are solutions will have a value of x that is 2. Any value can be used for y. Three ordered pairs that are solutions are $(2, -3), (2, 0)$, and $(2, 2)$. The graph is a vertical line.

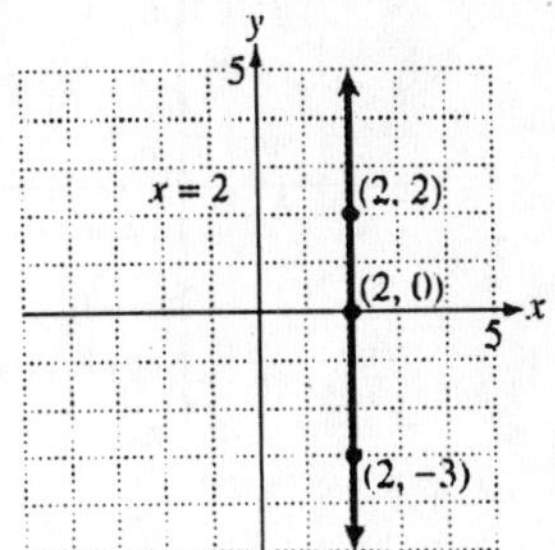

53. $x + 1 = 0$

$x = -1$

Three ordered pairs are $(-1, -3), (-1, 0)$, and $(-1, 3)$. The graph is a vertical line.

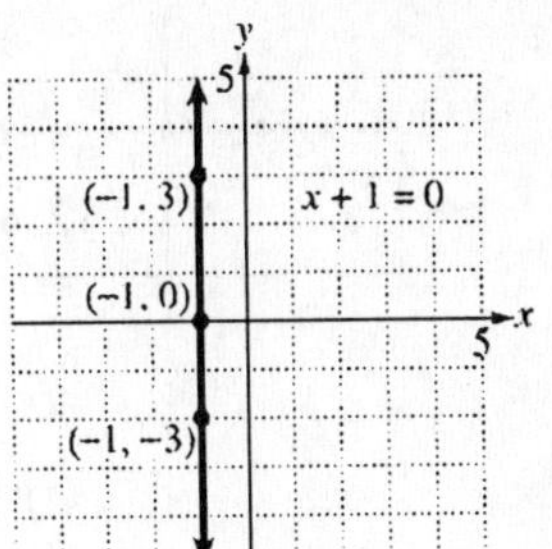

55. $y - 3.5 = 0$

$y = 3.5$

Three ordered pairs are $(-2, 3.5), (0, 3.5)$, and $(3.5, 3.5)$. The graph is a horizontal line.

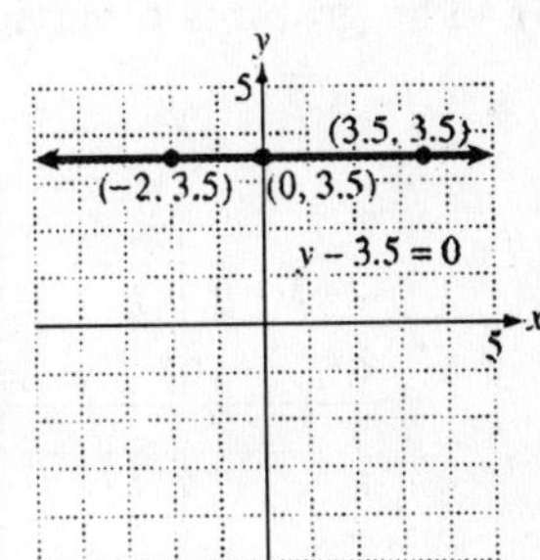

57. $x = 0$

Three ordered pairs are $(0, -2)$, $(0, 0)$, and $(0, 4)$. The graph is a vertical line, the y-axis.

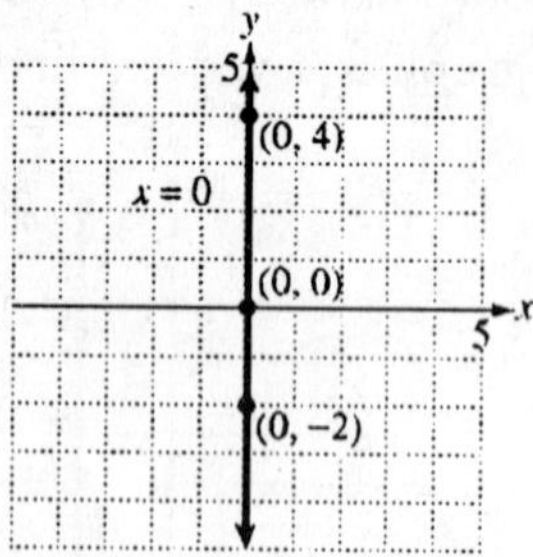

59. $3y = 9$

$y = 3$

Three ordered pairs are $(-3, 3)$, $(0, 3)$, and $(3, 3)$. The graph is a horizontal line.

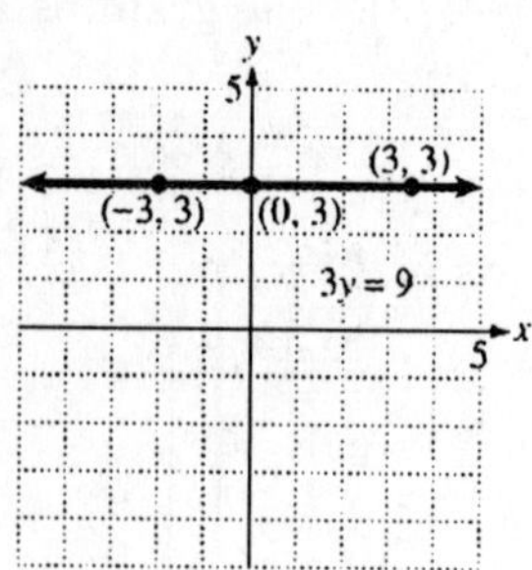

61. $12 - 3x = 0$

$-3x = -12$

$x = 4$

Three ordered pairs are $(4, -2)$, $(4, 1)$, and $(4, 3)$. The graph is a vertical line.

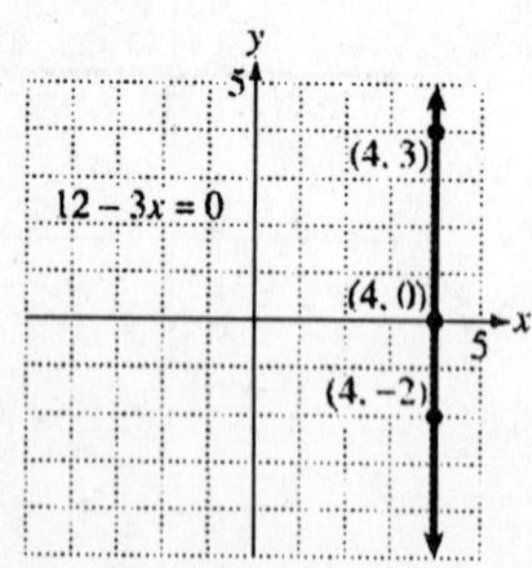

63. The vulture's height is decreasing from 3 seconds to 12 seconds.

65. The y-intercept is 45. This means that the vulture's height was 45 meters at the beginning of the observation.

67. Five x-intercepts of the graph are 12, 13, 14, 15, and 16. During these times (12–16 minutes), the vulture was on the ground.

69. Your temperature is decreasing from 8 A.M. to 11 A.M.

71. Your temperature is increasing from 11 A.M. to 1 P.M.

73. For all age groups, about 80% of people in the United States are satisfied with their lives, so an equation that reasonably models the data is $y = 80$.

For Exercises 75–83, answers may vary.

85. $2x + 5y = 10$ has x-intercept 5 and y-intercept 2.

87. Answers will vary according to the exercises chosen.

89.
$$\begin{aligned} 3x - y &= 9 \\ -y &= -3x + 9 \\ (-1)(-y) &= -1(3x + 9) \\ y &= 3x - 9 \end{aligned}$$

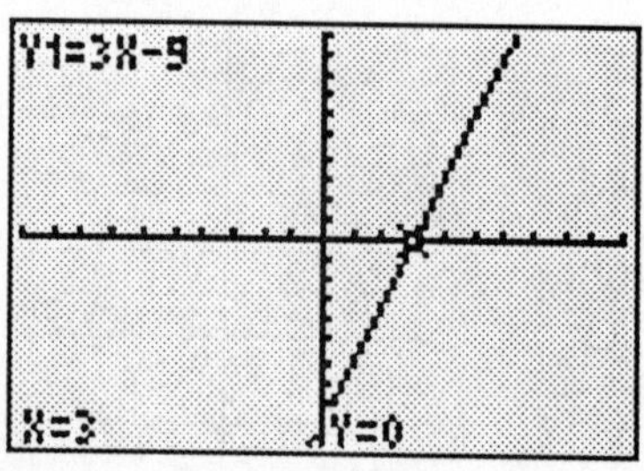

x-intercept: 3; y-intercept: -9

91. $4x - 2y = -40$

$$-2y = -4x - 40$$

$$\frac{-2y}{-2} = \frac{-4x - 40}{-2}$$

$$y = 2x + 20$$

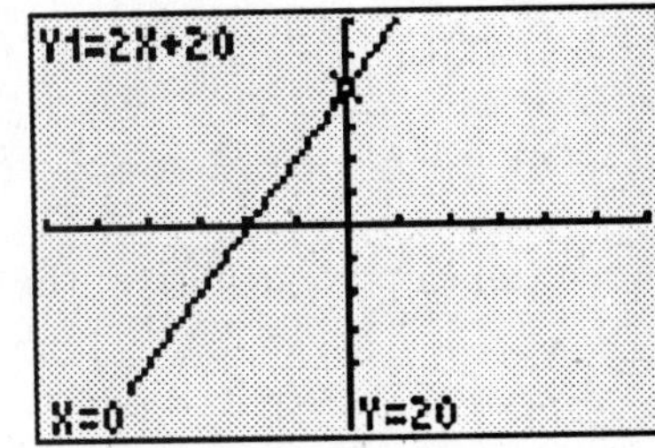

x-intercept: -10; y-intercept: 20

Review Exercises

92. $|-13.4| = 13.4$

93. $7x - (3x - 5) = 7x - 3x + 5 = 4x + 5$

94. $-2 \le x < 4$

-5 -4 -3 -2 -1 0 1 2 3 4 5

4.3 Slope

4.3 CHECK POINTS

CHECK POINT 1

a. $(-3, 4)$ and $(-4, -2)$

Let $(x_1, y_1) = (-3, 4)$ and $(x_2, y_2) = (-4, -2)$.

$$m = \frac{\text{Change in } y}{\text{Change in } x} = \frac{y_2 - y_1}{x_2 - x_1} = \frac{-2 - 4}{-4 - (-3)} = \frac{-6}{-1} = 6$$

The slope of the line through $(-3, 4)$ and $(-4, -2)$ is 6.

b. $(4, -2)$ and $(-1, 5)$

Let $(x_1, y_1) = (4, -2)$ and $(x_2, y_2) = (-1, 5)$.

$$m = \frac{\text{Change in } y}{\text{Change in } x} = \frac{y_2 - y_1}{x_2 - x_1} = \frac{5 - (-2)}{-1 - 4} = \frac{7}{-5} = -\frac{7}{5}$$

The slope of the line through $(4, -2)$ and $(-1, 5)$ is $-\frac{7}{5}$.

CHECK POINT 2

a. $(6, 5)$ and $(2, 5)$

Let $(x_1, y_1) = (6, 5)$ and $(x_2, y_2) = (2, 5)$.

$$m = \frac{y_2 - y_1}{x_2 - x_1} = \frac{5 - 5}{2 - 6} = \frac{0}{-4} = 0$$

The slope of the line through $(6, 5)$ and $(2, 5)$ is 0. (This is a horizontal line.)

b. $(1, 6)$ and $(1, 4)$

Let $(x_1, y_1) = (1, 6)$ and $(x_2, y_2) = (1, 4)$.

$$m = \frac{y_2 - y_1}{x_2 - x_1} = \frac{4 - 6}{1 - 1} = \frac{-2}{0}$$

Because division by 0 is undefined, the slope of the line through $(1, 6)$ and $(1, 4)$ is undefined. (This is a vertical line.)

CHECK POINT 3

Find the slope of each line.

Line through $(4, 2)$ and $(6, 6)$:

$$m = \frac{6 - 2}{6 - 4} = \frac{4}{2} = 2$$

Line through $(0, -2)$ and $(1, 0)$:

$$m = \frac{0-(-2)}{1-0} = \frac{2}{1} = 2$$

Both slopes are 2. Since their slopes are equal, the lines are parallel.

CHECK POINT 4

Let x represent a year and y the number of men living alone in that year. The two points shown on the line segment for women are $(1995, 10)$ and $(2010, 12)$. Use these points to compute the slope.

$$m = \frac{\text{Change in } y}{\text{Change in } x} = \frac{12-10}{2010-1995}$$
$$= \frac{2}{15} \approx \frac{0.13 \text{ million people}}{\text{year}}$$

The slope is $\frac{2}{15} \approx 0.13$. This indicates that the number of U.S. men living alone is projected to increase by 0.13 million each year.

EXERCISE SET 4.3

1. $(4, 7)$ and $(8, 10)$

Let $(x_1, y_1) = (4, 7)$ and $(x_2, y_2) = (8, 10)$.

$$m = \frac{\text{Change in } y}{\text{Change in } x} = \frac{y_2 - y_2}{x_2 - x_1}$$
$$= \frac{10-7}{8-4} = \frac{3}{4}$$

The slope is $\frac{3}{4}$. Since the slope is positive, the line rises.

3. $(-2, 1)$ and $(2, 2)$

$$m = \frac{2-1}{2-(-2)} = \frac{1}{4}$$

Since the slope is positive, the line rises.

5. $(4, -2)$ and $(3, -2)$

$$m = \frac{-2-(-2)}{3-4} = \frac{0}{-1} = 0$$

Since the slope is zero, the line is horizontal.

7. $(-2, 4)$ and $(-1, -1)$

$$m = \frac{-1-4}{-1-(-2)} = \frac{-5}{1} = -5$$

Since the slope is negative, the line falls.

9. $(5, 3)$ and $(5, -2)$

$$m = \frac{-2-3}{5-5} = \frac{-5}{0}$$

Since the slope is undefined, the line is vertical.

11. Line through $(-2, 2)$ and $(2, 4)$:

$$m = \frac{4-2}{2-(-2)} = \frac{2}{4} = \frac{1}{2}$$

13. Line through $(-3, 4)$ and $(3, 2)$:

$$m = \frac{2-4}{3-(-3)} = \frac{-2}{6} = -\frac{1}{3}$$

15. Line through $(-2, 1)$, $(0, 0)$, and $(2, -1)$
Use any two of these points to find the slope.

$$m = \frac{0-1}{0-(-2)} = \frac{-1}{2} = -\frac{1}{2}$$

17. Line through $(0, 2)$ and $(3, 0)$:

$$m = \frac{0-2}{3-0} = -\frac{2}{3}$$

19. Line through $(-2, 1)$ and $(4, 1)$:

$$m = \frac{1-1}{4-(-2)} = \frac{0}{6} = 0$$

(Since the line is horizontal, it is not necessary to do this computation. The slope of every horizontal line is 0.)

21. Line through $(-3,4)$ and $(-3,-2)$:

$$m = \frac{-2-4}{-3-(-3)} = \frac{-6}{0}; \text{ undefined}$$

(Since the line is vertical, it is not necessary to do this computation. The slope of every vertical line is undefined.)

23. Line through $(-2,0)$ and $(0,6)$:

$$m = \frac{6-0}{0-(-2)} = 3$$

Line through $(1,8)$ and $(0,5)$:

$$m = \frac{5-8}{0-1} = \frac{-3}{-1} = 3$$

Since their slopes are equal, the lines are parallel.

25. Line through $(0,3)$ and $(1,5)$:

$$m = \frac{5-3}{1-0} = \frac{2}{1} = 2$$

Line through $(-1,7)$ and $(1,10)$:

$$m = \frac{10-7}{1-(-1)} = \frac{3}{2}$$

Since their slopes are not equal, the lines are not parallel.

27. Line through $(1999, 1000)$ and $(2001, 1500)$:

$$m = \frac{1500-1000}{2001-1999} = \frac{500}{2} = 250$$

The amount spent online per U.S. online household was projected to increase by \$250 each year from 1999 to 2001.

29. Line through $(2001, 50)$ and $(2010, -286)$:

$$m = \frac{-286-50}{2010-2001} = \frac{-336}{9}$$

$$= -\frac{112}{3} \approx 37.33$$

The federal budget surplus will decrease at a projected rate of \$37.33 billion each year from 2001 to 2010.

31. The line segment represents the books sold in horizontal, so its slope is 0. This indicates that the number of books sold has not changed over the years shown on the graph.

33. Line through $(20{,}000, 8000)$ and $(40{,}000, 16{,}000)$:

$$m = \frac{16{,}000-8000}{40{,}000-20{,}000} = \frac{8000}{20{,}000} = 0.4$$

The cost is \$0.40 or 40¢ per mile.

35. $m = \dfrac{\text{Change in } y}{\text{Change in } x} = \dfrac{6}{18} = \dfrac{1}{3}$

The pitch of the roof is $\frac{1}{3}$.

37. The grade an access ramp is $\frac{1 \text{ foot}}{12 \text{ feet}} = \frac{1}{12} \approx 0.083 = 8.3\%$.

For Exercises 39–43, answers may vary.

45. Statement b is true.

47. Use the graph to observe where each line crosses the y-axis. In order of decreasing size, the y-intercepts are b_2, b_1, b_4, b_3.

49. $y = -3x + 6$

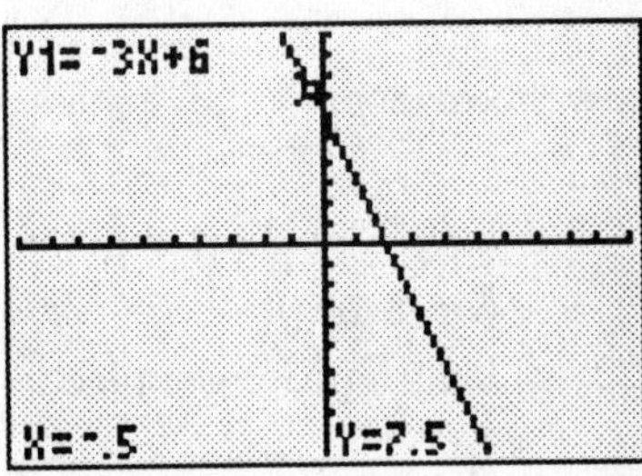

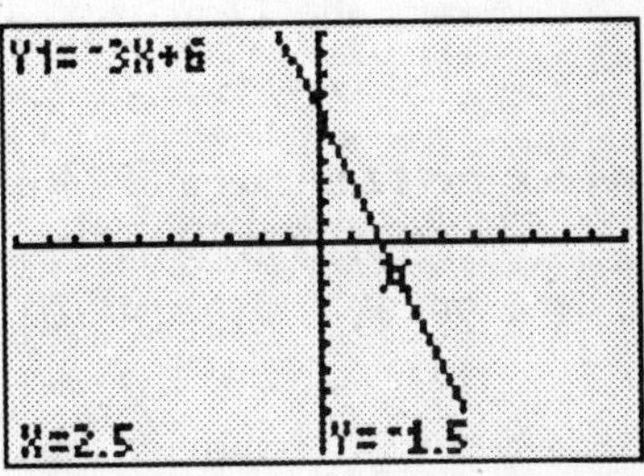

Two points on the graph are $(-0.5, 7.5)$ and $(2.5, -1.5)$.

$$m = \frac{7.5-(-1.5)}{-0.5-2.5} = \frac{9}{-3} = -3$$

51. $y = \frac{3}{4}x - 2$

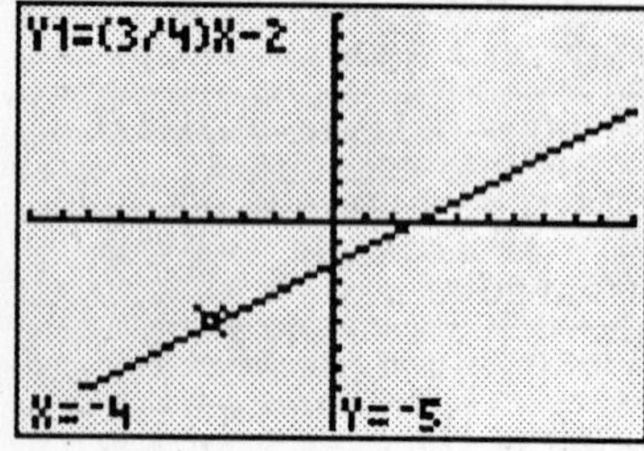

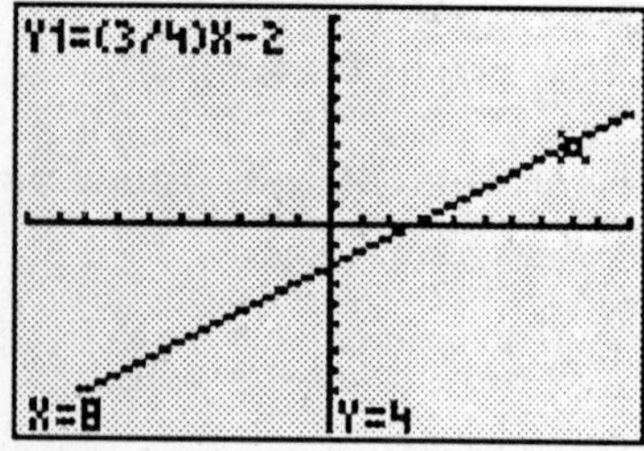

Two points on the graph are $(-4, -5)$ and $(8, 4)$.

$$m = \frac{4-(-5)}{8-(-4)} = \frac{9}{12} = \frac{3}{4}$$

Review Exercises

53. Let $x =$ length of shorter piece (in inches).
Then $2x =$ length of longer piece.

$$\begin{aligned} x + 2x &= 36 \\ 3x &= 36 \\ x &= 12 \end{aligned}$$

The pieces are 12 inches and 24 inches.

54. $$\begin{aligned} -10 + 16 \div 2(-4) &= -10 + 8(-4) \\ &= -10 - 32 \\ &= -10 + (-32) = -42 \end{aligned}$$

55. $$\begin{aligned} 2x - 3 &\le 5 \\ 2x &\le 8 \\ x &\le 4 \end{aligned}$$

$\{x | x \le 4\}$

−3 −2 −1 0 1 2 3 4 5 6 7

4.4 The Slope-Intercept Form of the Equation of a Line

4.4 CHECK POINTS

CHECK POINT 1

a. $y = 5x - 3$

Write $y = 5x - 3$ as $y = 5x + (-3)$. The slope is the x-coefficient, 5, and the y-intercept is the constant term, -3.

b. $y = \frac{2}{3}x + 4$

This equation is the form $y = mx+b$ with $m = \frac{2}{3}$ and $b = 4$. The slope is $\frac{2}{3}$ and the y-intercept is 4.

c. $7x + y = 6$

Put this equation in the form $y = mx+b$.

$$\begin{aligned} 7x + y &= 6 \\ 7x - 7x + y &= -7x + 6 \\ y &= -7x + 6 \end{aligned}$$

The slope is the x-coefficient, -7, and the y-coefficient is the constant term, 6.

CHECK POINT 2

$y = 3x - 2$

Write $y = 3x - 2$ in the form $y = mx + b$.

$$y = 3x + (-2)$$

The slope is 3 and the y-intercept is -2.

Step 1 Plot $(0, -2)$ on the y-axis.

Step 2 Write the slope as a fraction.

$$m = \frac{3}{1} = \frac{\text{Rise}}{\text{Run}}$$

Start at $(0, -2)$. Based on the slope, move 3 units up (the rise) and 1 unit to the *right* (the run) to reach the point $(1, 1)$.

Step 3 Draw a line through $(0, -2)$ and $(1, 1)$.

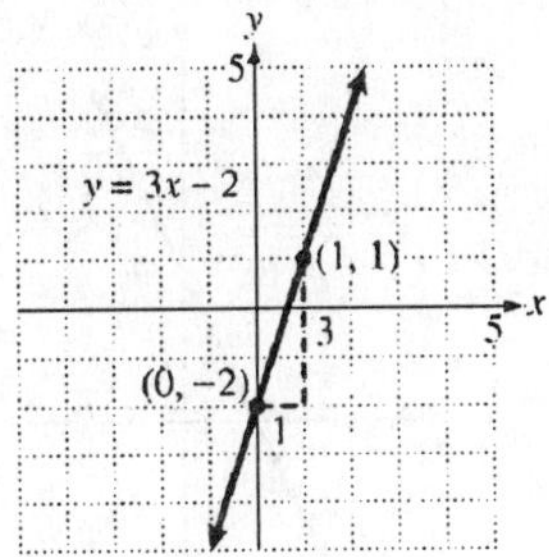

CHECK POINT 3

$y = \frac{3}{5}x + 1$

slope $= \frac{3}{5}$; y-intercept $= 1$

Plot $(0, 1)$. From the point, move 3 units *up* (the rise) and 5 units to the *right* (the run) to reach the point $(5, 4)$. Draw a line through $(0, 1)$ and $(5, 4)$.

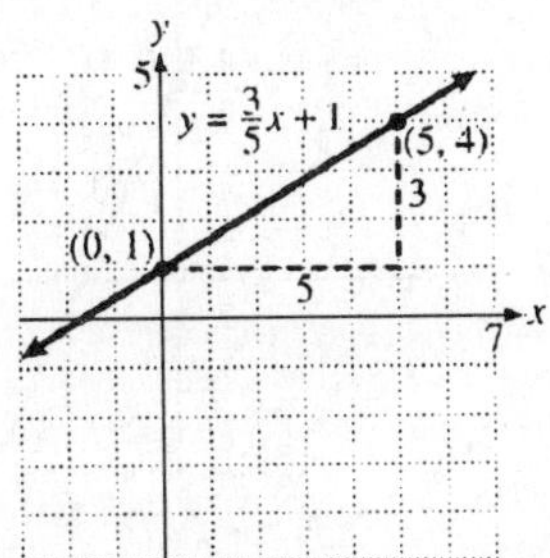

CHECK POINT 4

$3x + 4y = 0$

Put the equation in slope-intercept form by solving for y.

$$\begin{aligned} 3x + 4y &= 0 \\ 3x - 3x + 4y &= -3x + 0 \\ 4y &= -3x + 0 \\ \frac{4y}{4} &= \frac{-3x + 0}{4} \\ y &= \frac{-3x}{4} + \frac{0}{4} \\ y &= -\frac{3}{4}x + 0 \end{aligned}$$

slope $= -\frac{3}{4}$; y-intercept $= 0$

Use the y-intercept to plot $(0, 0)$.

$$m = -\frac{3}{4} = \frac{-3}{4} = \frac{\text{Rise}}{\text{Run}}$$

Because the rise is -3 and the run is 4, move 3 units *down* and 4 units to the *right* to reach the point $(4, -3)$. Draw a line through $(0, 0)$ and $(4, -3)$.

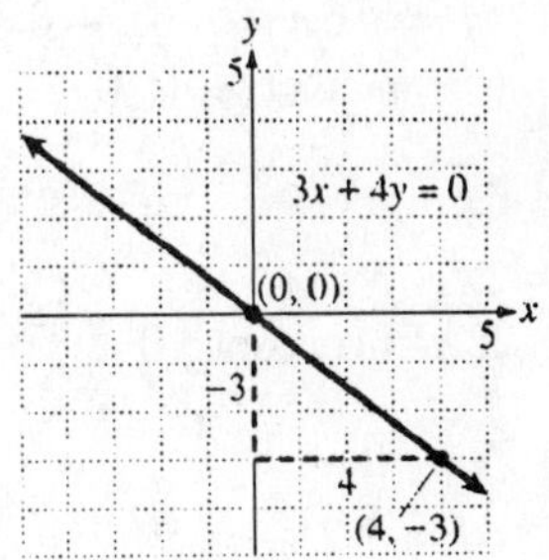

EXERCISE SET 4.4

1. $y = 3x + 2$

The slope is the x-coefficient, which is 3. The y-intercept is the constant term, which is 2.

3. $y = 3x - 5$
$y = 3x + (-5)$
$m = 3$; y-intercept $= -5$

5. $y = -\frac{1}{2}x + 5$

$m = -\frac{1}{2}$; $y -$ intercept $= 5$

7. $y = 7x$

$y = 7x + 0$

$m = 7$; y-intercept $= 0$

9. $y = 10$

$y = 0x + 10$

$m = 0$; y-intercept $= 10$

11. $y = 4 - x$

$y = -x + 4 = -1x + 4$

$m = -1$; y-intercept $= 4$

13. $-5x + y = 7$

$-5x + y + 5x = 5x + 7$

$y = 5x + 7$

$m = 5$; y-intercept $= 7$

15. $x + y = 6$

$y = -x + 6 = -1x + 6$

$m = -1$; y-intercept $= 6$

17. $6x + y = 0$

$y = -6x = -6x + 0$

$m = -6$; y-intercept: 0

19. $3y = 6x$

$y = 2x$

$m = 2$; y-intercept: 0

21. $2x + 7y = 0$

$7y = -2x$

$y = -\frac{2}{7}x$

$m = -\frac{2}{7}$; y-intercept: 0

23. $3x + 2y = 3$

$2y = -3x + 3$

$y = \frac{-3x + 3}{2}$

$y = -\frac{3}{2}x + \frac{3}{2}$

$m = -\frac{3}{2}$; y-intercept $= \frac{3}{2}$

25. $3x - 4y = 12$

$-4y = -3x + 12$

$\frac{-4y}{-4} = \frac{-3x + 12}{-4}$

$y = \frac{3}{4}x - 3$

$m = \frac{3}{4}$; y-intercept: -3

27. $y = 2x + 3$

Step 1 Plot $(0, 3)$ on the y-axis.

Step 2 $m = \frac{2}{1} = \frac{\text{Rise}}{\text{Run}}$

Start at $(0, 3)$. Using the slope, move 2 units *up* (the rise) and 1 unit to the *right* (the run) to reach the point $(1, 5)$.

Step 3 Draw a line through $(0, 3)$ and $(1, 5)$.

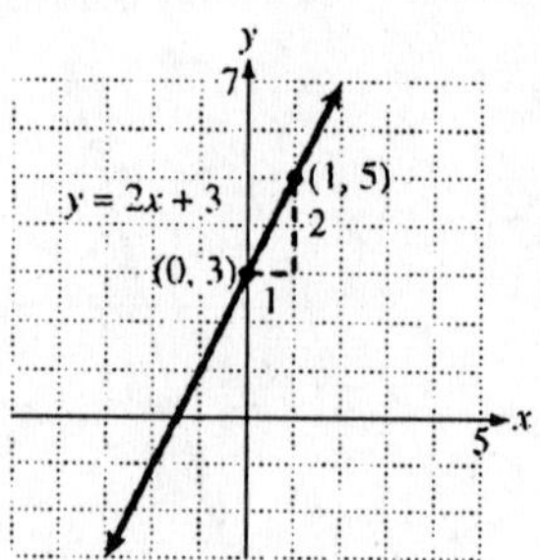

29. $y = -2x + 4$

Slope $= -2 = -\frac{2}{1}$; y-intercept $= 4$

Plot $(0, 4)$ on the y-axis. From this point, move 2 units *down* (because -2 is negative) and 1 unit to the *right* to reach the point $(1, 2)$. Draw a line through $(0, 4)$ and $(1, 2)$.

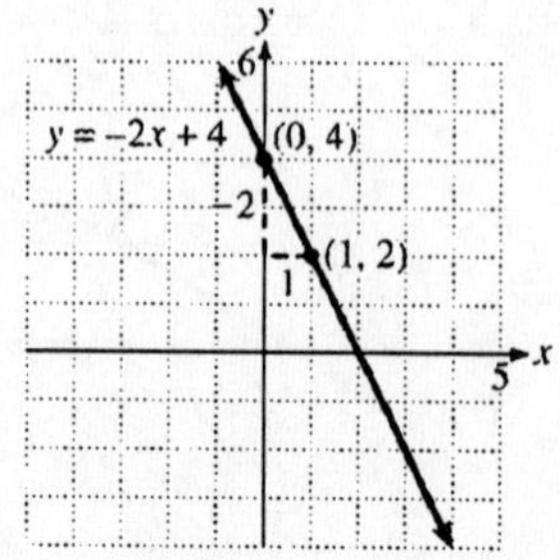

31. $y = \frac{1}{2}x + 3$

Slope $= \frac{1}{2}$; y-intercept $= 3$

Plot $(0, 3)$. From this point, move 1 unit *up* and 2 units to the *right* to reach the point $(2, 4)$. Draw a line through $(0, 3)$ and $(2, 4)$.

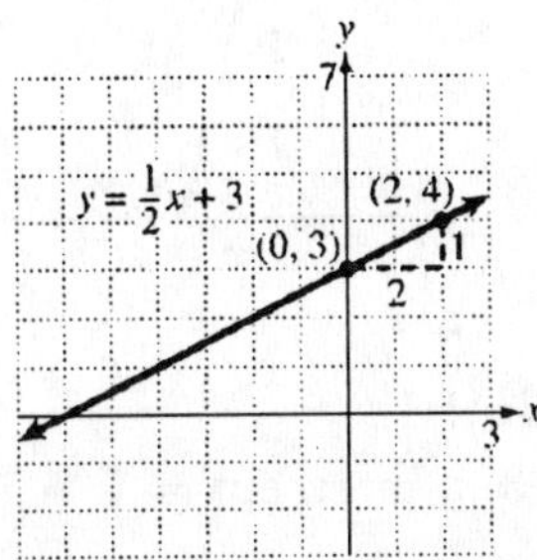

33. $y = \frac{2}{3}x - 4$

Slope $= \frac{2}{3}$; y-intercept $= -4$

Plot $(0, -4)$. From this point, move 3 units *up* and 3 units to the *right* to reach the point $(3, -2)$. Draw a line through $(0, -4)$ and $(3, -2)$.

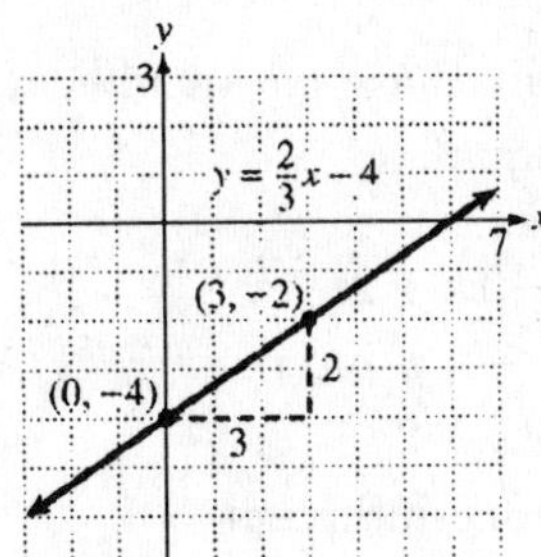

35. $y = -\frac{3}{4}x + 4$

Slope $= -\frac{3}{4} = \frac{-3}{4}$; y-intercept $= 4$

Plot $(0, 4)$. From this point, move 3 units *down* and 4 units to the *right* to reach the point $(4, 1)$.

Draw a line through $(0, 4)$ and $(4, 1)$.

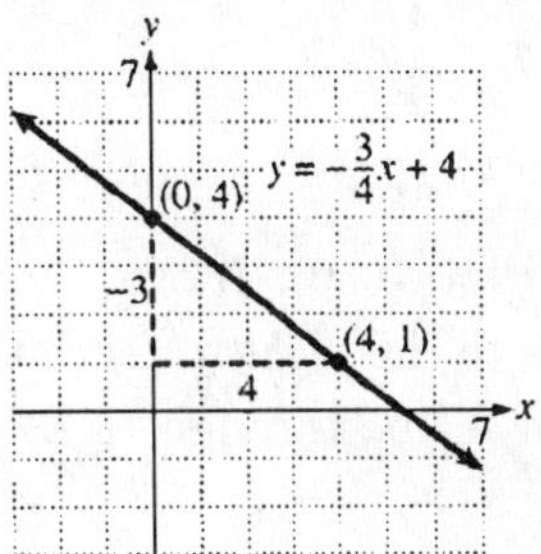

37. $y = -\frac{5}{3}x$

Slope $= -\frac{5}{3} = \frac{-5}{3}$; y-intercept $= 0$

Plot $(0, 0)$. From this point, move 5 units *down* and 3 units to the *right* to reach the point $(3, -5)$. Draw a line through $(0, 0)$ and $(3, -5)$.

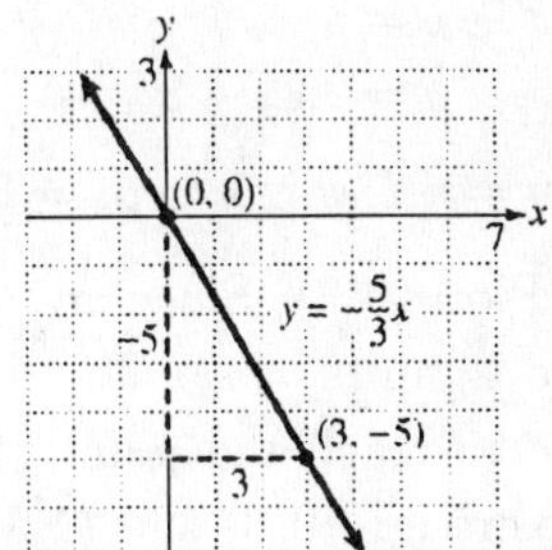

39. a. $3x + y = 0$

$y = -3x$

b. $m = -3$; y-intercept $= 0$

c. Plot $(0, 0)$. Since $m = -3 = -\frac{3}{1}$, move 3 units *down* and 1 units to the *right* to reach the point $(1, -3)$. Draw a line through $(0, 0)$ and $(1, -3)$.

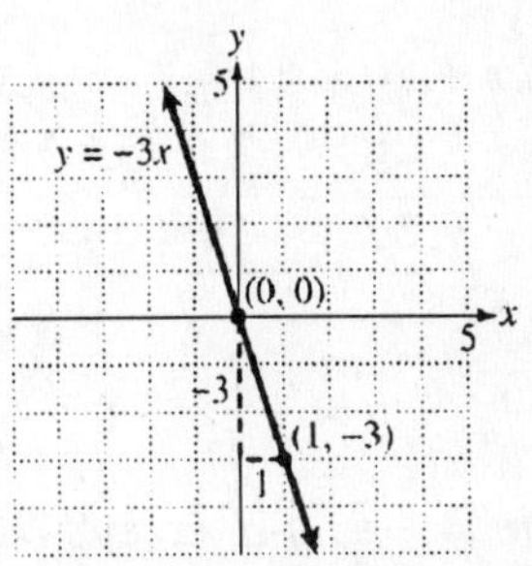

41. **a.** $3y = 4x$

$$y = \frac{4}{3}x$$

b. $m = \frac{4}{3}$; y-intercept $= 0$

c. Plot $(0, 0)$. Move 4 units *up* and 3 units to the *right* to reach the point $(3, 4)$. Draw a line through $(0, 0)$ and $(3, 4)$.

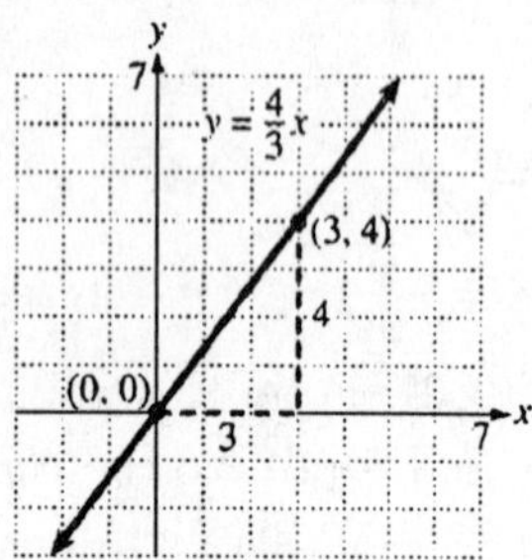

43. **a.** $2x + y = 3$

$$y = -2x + 3$$

b. $m = -2$; y-intercept $= 3$

c. Plot $(0, 3)$. Since $m = -2 = -\frac{2}{1}$, move 2 units *down* and 1 units to the *right* to reach the point $(1, 1)$. Draw a line through $(0, 3)$ and $(1, 1)$.

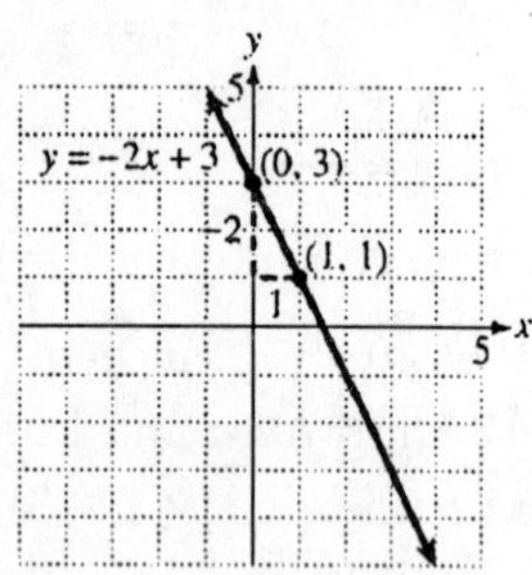

45. **a.** $7x + 2y = 14$

$$2y = -7x + 14$$

$$\frac{2y}{2} = \frac{-7x + 14}{2}$$

$$y = -\frac{7}{2}x + 7$$

b. $m = -\frac{7}{2}$; y-intercept $= 7$

c. Plot $(0, 7)$. Since $m = -\frac{7}{2} = -\frac{7}{2}$, move 7 units *down* and 2 units to the *right* to reach the point $(2, 0)$. Draw a line through $(0, 7)$ and $(2, 4)$.

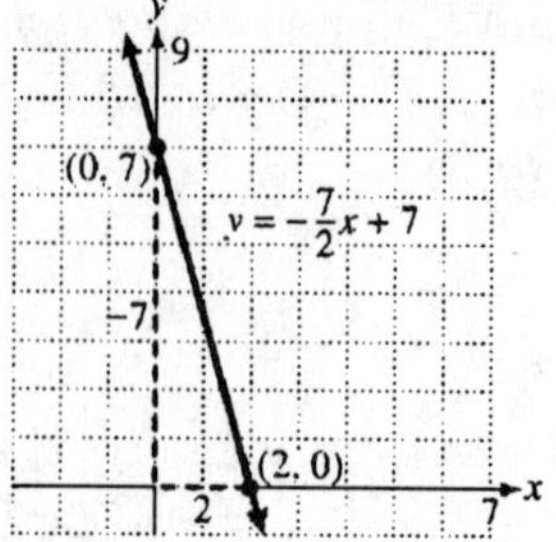

47. $y = 3x + 1$:

$m = 3$; y-intercept $= 1$

$y = 3x - 3$:

$m = 3, y$-intercept $= -3$

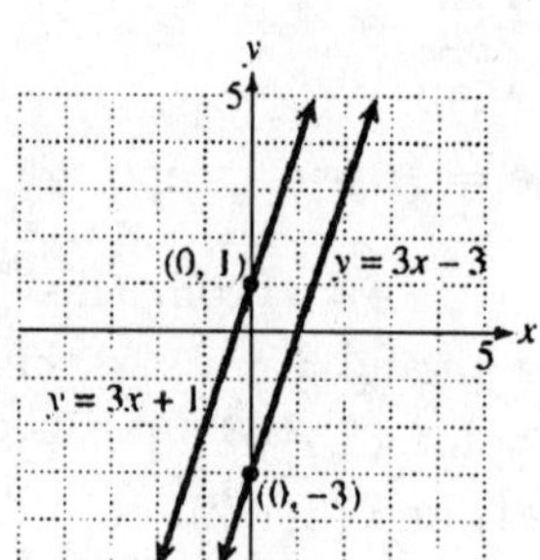

The lines are parallel because their slopes are equal.

49. $y = -3x + 2$:

$m = -3$; y-intercept $= 2$

$y = 3x + 2$:

$m = 3, y$-intercept $= 2$

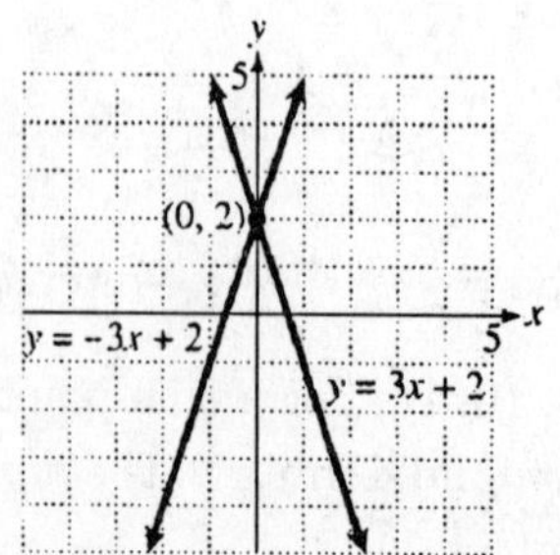

The lines are not parallel because their slopes are not equal.

51. $y = -0.4x + 38$

a. 1980: $x = 0$

$y = -0.4(0) + 38 = 38$

1981: $x = 1$

$y = -0.4(1) + 38 = 37.6$

1982: $x = 2$

$y = -0.4(2) + 38 = 37.2$

1983: $x = 3$

$y = -0.4(3) + 38 = 36.8$

1990: $x = 20$

$y = -0.4(10) + 38 = 34$

2000: $x = 20$

$y = -0.4(20) + 38 = 30$

According to the formula, 38% of U.S. men smoked in 1980, 37.6% in 1981, 37.2% in 1982, 36.8% in 1983, 34% in 1990, and 30% in 2000.

b. This slope of this model is -0.4. This indicates that the percentage of U.S. men smoking is decreasing by 0.4% each year.

c. The y-intercept is 38. This indicates that in 1980 (the initial year for the model), there were 38% if U.S. men smoking.

53. a. The y-intercept is 24. This indicates that in 1991, the cost of the average prescription was \$24.

b. Line through $(0, 24)$ and $(7, 38)$:

$$m = \frac{38 - 24}{7 - 0} = \frac{14}{7} = 2$$

This indicates that the cost was increasing by \$2 each year from 1991 to 2000.

c. $y = 2x + 24$

d. The year 2005 corresponds to $x = 14$.

$$y = 2(14) + 24 = 52$$

The model predicts that the average prescription will cost \$52 in 2005.

For Exercises 55–57, answers may vary.

59. Each multiple birth corresponds to 2 (if twins), 3 (if triplets), 4 (if quadruplets), or more births. Since this number varies, and most births are single births, the number of multiple births will not increase at the same rate as total births. Therefore, the slopes will not be equal and the lines will not be parallel.

Review Exercises

61. $\frac{x}{2} + 7 = 13 - \frac{x}{4}$

Multiply by the LCD, which is 4.

$$\begin{aligned} 4\left(\frac{x}{2} + 7\right) &= 4\left(13 - \frac{x}{4}\right) \\ 2x + 28 &= 52 - x \\ 3x + 28 &= 52 \\ 3x &= 24 \\ x &= 8 \end{aligned}$$

The solution is 8.

62. $$\begin{aligned} 3(12 \div 2^2 - 3)^2 &= 3(12 \div 4 - 3)^2 \\ &= 3(3 - 3)^2 \\ &= 3 \cdot 0^2 = 3 \cdot 0 = 0 \end{aligned}$$

63. $A = PB$; $A = 14$, $P = 25\% = 0.25$

$$\begin{aligned} A &= PB \\ 14 &= 0.25 \cdot B \\ \frac{14}{0.25} &= \frac{0.25B}{0.25} \\ 56 &= B \end{aligned}$$

14 is 25% of 56.

4.5 The Point-Slope Form of the Equation of a Line

4.5 CHECK POINTS

CHECK POINT 1

Line with slope 6 that passes through the point $(2, -5)$
Begin with the point-slope equation of a line with $m = 6$, $x_1 = 2$, and $y_1 = -5$.

$$\begin{aligned} y - y_1 &= m(x - x_1) \\ y - (-5) &= 6(x - 2) \\ y + 5 &= 6(x - 2) \end{aligned}$$

Now solve this equation for y and write an equivalent equation in slope-intercept form.

$$\begin{aligned} y + 5 &= 6x - 12 \\ y &= 6x - 17 \end{aligned}$$

CHECK POINT 2

Line passing through $(-2, -1)$ and $(-1, -6)$

a. First, find the slope of the line.

$$m = \frac{-6 - (-1)}{-1 - (-2)} = \frac{-5}{1} = -5$$

Either point can be used as (x_1, y_1). We will use $(x_1, y_1) = (-2, -1)$.

$$\begin{aligned} y - y_1 &= m(x - x_1) \\ y - (-1) &= -5[x - (-2)] \\ y + 1 &= -5(x + 2) \end{aligned}$$

Note: If $(-1, -6)$ is used as (x_1, y_1), the equation in point-slope form will be $y + 6 = -5(x + 1)$.

b. Now solve the point-slope equation for y and write an equivalent equation in slope-intercept form.

$$\begin{aligned} y + 1 &= -5(x + 2) \\ y + 1 &= -5x - 10 \\ y &= -5x - 11 \end{aligned}$$

Note: If $(-1, -6)$ is used as (x_1, y_1), the point-slope equation will be different, as shown above, but the slope-intercept equation will be the same.

CHECK POINT 3

Line through $(10, 203.3)$ and $(20, 226.5)$
First, find the slope.

$$m = \frac{226.5 - 203.3}{20 - 10} = \frac{23.2}{10} = 2.32$$

To find the slope-intercept of this line, begin with the point-slope form, using $(x_1, y_1) = (20, 226.5)$.

$$\begin{aligned} y - y_1 &= m(x - x_1) \\ y - 226.5 &= 2.32(x - 20) \\ y - 226.5 &= 2.32x - 46.4 \\ y &= 2.32x + 180.1 \end{aligned}$$

Now use this equation to predict the U.S. population in 2020. Because 2020 is 60 years after 1960, substitute 60 for x and compute the corresponding value of y.

$$y = 2.32(60) + 180.1 = 319.3$$

The equation predicts that the U.S. population in 2020 will be 319.3 million.

EXERCISE SET 4.5

1. Slope $= 2$, passing through $(3, 5)$
point-slope form: $y - 5 = 2(x - 3)$
$y - 5 = 2x - 6$
slope-intercept form: $y = 2x - 1$

3. Slope $= 6$, passing through $(-2, 5)$
point-slope form: $y - 5 = 6(x + 2)$
$y - 5 = 6x + 12$
slope-intercept form: $y = 6x + 17$

5. Slope $= -3$, passing through $(-2, -3)$
point-slope form: $y + 3 = -3(x + 2)$
$y + 3 = -3x - 6$
slope-intercept form; $y = -3x - 9$

7. Slope $= -4$, passing through $(-4, 0)$
$y - 0 = -4(x + 4)$
point-slope form: $y = -4(x + 4)$
slope-intercept form: $y = -4x - 16$

9. Slope $= -1$, passing through $\left(-\frac{1}{2}, -2\right)$

point-slope form: $y + 2 = -1\left(x + \dfrac{1}{2}\right)$

$y + 2 = -x - \dfrac{1}{2}$

slope-intercept form: $y = -x - \dfrac{5}{2}$

11. Slope $= \frac{1}{2}$, passes through the origin: $(0, 0)$

point-slope form: $y - 0 = \dfrac{1}{2}(x - 0)$

slope-intercept form: $y = \dfrac{1}{2}x$

13. Slope $= -\frac{2}{3}$, passing through $(6, -2)$

point-slope form: $y + 2 = -\dfrac{2}{3}(x - 6)$

$y + 2 = -\dfrac{2}{3}x + 4$

slope-intercept form: $y = -\dfrac{2}{3}x + 2$

15. Passing through $(1, 2)$ and $(5, 10)$

slope $= \dfrac{10 - 2}{5 - 1} = \dfrac{8}{4} = 2$

point-slope form: $y - 2 = 2(x - 1)$
or $y - 10 = 2(x - 5)$

$y - 2 = 2x - 2$
slope-intercept form: $y = 2x$

17. Passing through $(-3, 0)$ and $(0, 3)$

slope $= \dfrac{3 - 0}{0 + 3} = \dfrac{3}{3} = 1$

point-slope form: $y - 0 = 1(x + 3)$
or $y - 3 = 1(x - 0)$
slope-intercept form: $y = x + 3$

19. Passing through $(-3, -1)$ and $(2, 4)$

slope $= \dfrac{4 + 1}{2 + 3} = \dfrac{5}{5} = 1$

point-slope form: $y + 1 = 1(x + 3)$
or $y - 4 = 1(x - 2)$
slope-intercept form: $y = x + 2$

21. Passing through $(-3, -2)$ and $(3, 6)$

slope $= \dfrac{6 + 2}{3 + 3} = \dfrac{8}{6} = \dfrac{4}{3}$

point-slope form: $y + 2 = \dfrac{4}{3}(x + 3)$

or $y - 6 = \dfrac{4}{3}(x - 3)$

$y + 2 = \dfrac{4}{3}x + 4$

slope-intercept form: $y = \dfrac{4}{3}x + 2$

23. Passing through $(-3, -1)$ and $(4, -1)$

slope $= \dfrac{-1 + 1}{4 + 3} = \dfrac{0}{7} = 0$

point-slope form: $y + 1 = 0(x + 3)$
or $y + 1 = 0(x - 4)$
slope-intercept form: $y = -1$

25. Passing through $(2, 4)$ with x-intercept $= -2$

Use the points $(2, 4)$ and $(-2, 0)$.

slope $= \dfrac{0 - 4}{-2 - 2} = \dfrac{-4}{-4} = 1$

point-slope form: $y - 4 = 1(x - 2)$
slope-intercept form: $y = x + 2$

27. x-intercept $= -\frac{1}{2}$ and y-intercept $= 4$

Use the points $\left(-\frac{1}{2}, 0\right)$ and $(0, 4)$.

slope $= \dfrac{4 - 0}{0 + \frac{1}{2}} = \dfrac{4}{\frac{1}{2}} = 8$

point-slope form: $y - 0 = 8\left(x + \dfrac{1}{2}\right)$

or $y - 4 = 8(x - 0)$
slope-intercept form: $y = 8x + 4$

29. a. Line through $(2, 162)$ and $(8, 168)$:

$$m = \frac{168 - 162}{8 - 2} = \frac{6}{6} = 1$$

Using the point $(2,, 162)$ as (x_1, y_1), the point-slope equation is

$$y - y_1 = m(x - x_1)$$
$$y - 162 = 1(x - 2).$$

b. $y - 162 = x - 2$
$$y = x + 160$$

c. The year 2005 corresponds to $x = 15$.

$$y = 15 + 160 = 175$$

According to the equation, the average American adult will weigh 175 pounds in 2005.

31. Two points on the line are $(12, 3)$ and $(15, 1)$.

$$m = \frac{1-3}{15-12} = \frac{-2}{3} = -\frac{2}{3}$$

point-slope form using $(12, 3)$:

$$y - 3 = -\frac{2}{3}(x - 12)$$

Use this equation to find the point-slope equation.

$$y - 3 = -\frac{2}{3}x + 8$$
$$y = -\frac{2}{3}x + 11$$

If $x = 7$,

$$y = -\frac{2}{3}(7) + 11 = -\frac{14}{3} + 11 \approx 6.3.$$

The model predicts that a person with 7 years of education will score about 6.3 on the prejudice test.

33. a.

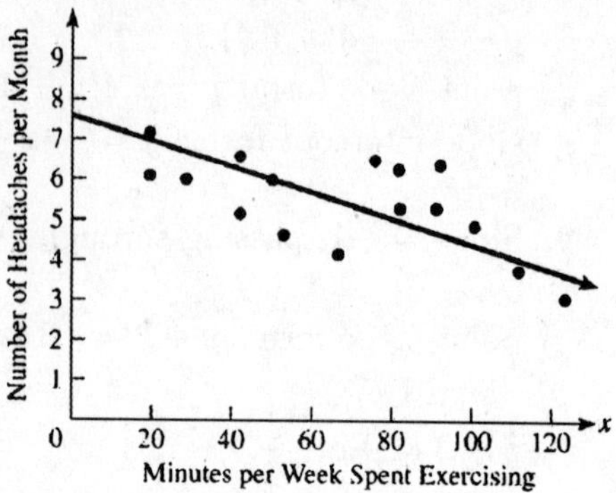

b. Two points on the line are $(50, 6)$ and $(80, 5)$.
The slope is

$$m = \frac{5-6}{80-50} = -\frac{1}{30}.$$

Using the point $(50, 6)$, the point-slope form is

$$y - 6 = -\frac{1}{30}(x - 50).$$

Use this equation to find the point-slope equation.

$$y - 6 = -\frac{1}{30}x + \frac{5}{3}$$
$$= -\frac{1}{30}x + \frac{23}{3}$$

or approximately

$$y = -0.03x + 7.67$$

c. If $x = 130$,

$$y = -0.03(130) + 7.67 = 3.77.$$

This model predicts that a person exercising 130 minutes a week will have 3.77 or about 4 headaches per week.

35. Answers may vary.

37. Statement c is true.
The line through $(2, -5)$ and $(2, 6)$ is vertical, so its slope is undefined.

39. Using the given information, write two ordered pairs in which $°M$ is the first coordinate and $°E$ is the second coordinate: $(25, 40)$ and $(125, 280)$. Find the slope-intercept equation of the line through these two points.

$$m = \frac{280 - 40}{125 - 25} = \frac{240}{100} = 2.4$$

Use the slope and the point $(25, 40)$ to find the point-slope equation of the line.

$$E - 40 = 2.4(M - 25)$$

Simplify this equation to find the slope-intercept equation.

$$E - 40 = 2.4M - 60$$
$$E = 2.4M - 20$$

41.

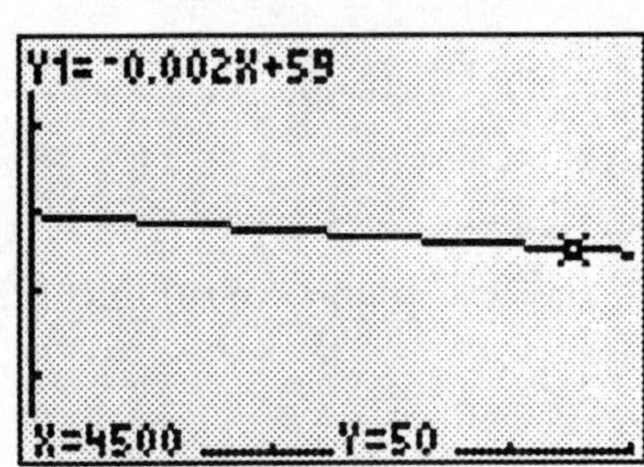

The graph shows that 4500 shirts can be sold at $50 each.

Review Exercises

43. Let $x =$ the number of sheets of paper.

$$4 + 2x \le 29$$
$$2x \le 25$$
$$x \le \tfrac{25}{2} \text{ or } 12\tfrac{1}{2}$$

Since the number of sheets of paper must be a whole number, at most 12 sheets of paper can put in the envelope.

44. The only natural numbers in the given set are 1 and $\sqrt{4}$ $(= 2)$.

45. $3x - 5y = 15$
x-intercept: 5
y-intercept: -3
checkpoint: $(-5, -6)$

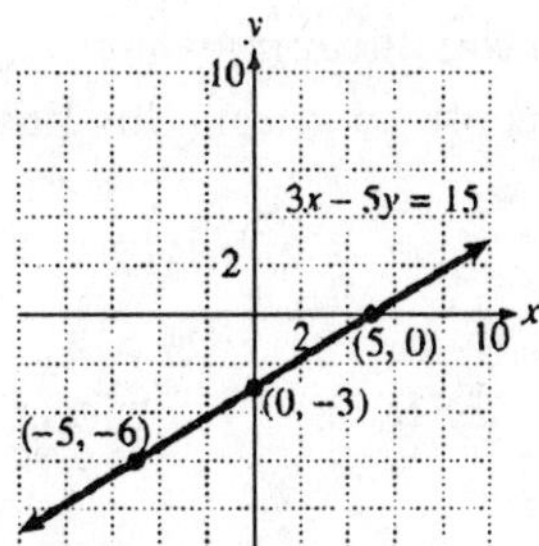

4.6 Linear Inequalities in Two Variables

CHECK POINT 1

$5x + 4y \le 20$

a. To determine whether $(0, 0)$ is a solution of the inequality, substitute 0 for x and 0 for y.

$$5x + 4y \le 20$$
$$5 \cdot 0 - 4 \cdot 0 \stackrel{?}{\le} 20$$
$$0 \le 20 \text{ true}$$

Because we obtained a true statement, $(0, 0)$ is a solution of the inequality.

b. To determine whether $(6, 2)$ is a solution of the inequality, substitute 6 for x and 2 for y.

$$5x + 4y \le 20$$
$$5 \cdot 6 + 4 \cdot 2 \stackrel{?}{\le} 20$$
$$30 + 8 \stackrel{?}{\le} 20$$
$$38 \le 20 \text{ false}$$

Because we obtained a false statement, $(6, 2)$ is not a solution of the inequality.

CHECK POINT 2

$2x - 4y < 8$

Step 1 Replace the inequality symbol by $=$ and graph the linear equation $2x-4y=8$. Use intercepts to graph this line.

x-intercept:	y-intercept:
$2x - 4y = 8$	$2x - 4y = 8$
$2x - 4 \cdot 0 = 8$	$2 \cdot 0 - 4y = 8$
$2x = 8$	$-4y = 8$
$x = 4$	$y = -2$

Draw a line through $(4, 0)$ and $(0, -2)$. Use a dashed line because the inequality symbol is $<$. (The dashed line shows that the line itself is not part of the graph.)

Step 2 Choose a test point that is not on the line. The origin, $(0, 0)$, is the easiest point to check.

$$2x - 4y < 8$$
$$\text{Is} \quad 2 \cdot 0 - 4 \cdot 0 < 8?$$
$$0 - 0 < 8$$
$$0 < 8 \text{ true}$$

Step 3 Because $0 < 8$ is a true statement, shade the half-plane containing $(0, 0)$.

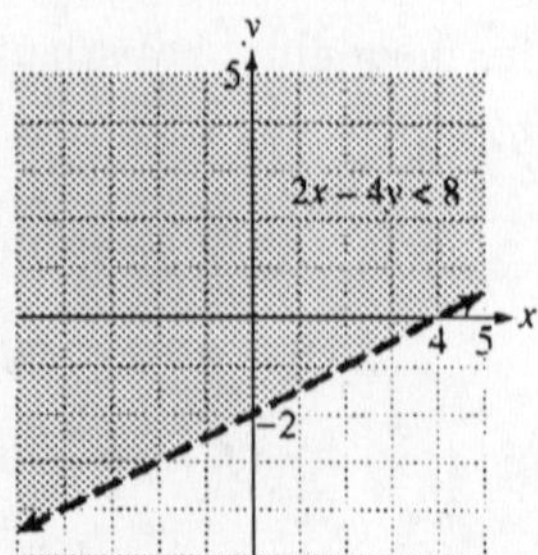

CHECK POINT 3

$y \geq \frac{1}{2}x$

Step 1 Graph the equation $y = \frac{1}{2}x$ using its slope, $\frac{1}{2}$, and y-intercept, 0. Use a solid line because the inequality symbol is $\geq$. (The solid line shows that the line itself is part of the graph.)

Step 2 We cannot use $(0, 0)$ as a test point because it lies on a line and not in a half-plane. Choose a point not on the line. Let's use $(2, 3)$, which lies in the half-plane above the line.

$$y \geq \frac{1}{2}x$$
$$\text{Is} \quad 3 \geq \frac{1}{2}(2) \text{ true?}$$
$$3 \geq 1 \text{ true}$$

Step 3 Because $3 \geq 1$ is a true statement, shade the half-plane containing $(2, 3)$.

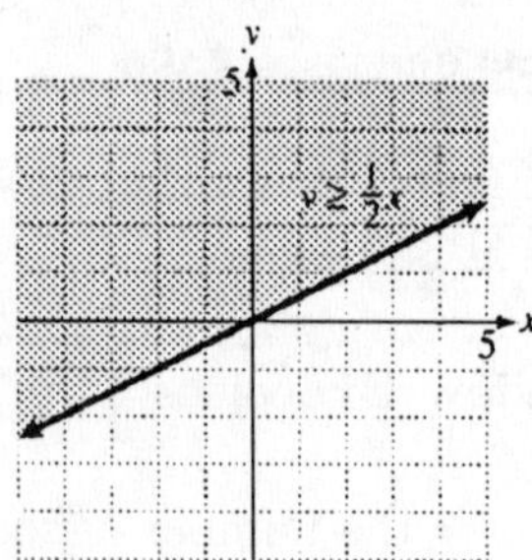

CHECK POINT 4

a. Point B has coordinates $(45, 4)$.

This means that if a region has an average annual temperature of 45°F and an average annual precipitation of 4 inches, there is a desert.

b. Substitute 45 for T and 4 for P in the given inequality.

$$3T - 35P > -140$$
$$3 \cdot 45 - 35 \cdot 4 \overset{?}{>} -140$$
$$135 - 140 \overset{?}{>} -140$$
$$-5 > -140 \text{ true}$$

EXERCISE SET 4.6

1. $x + y > 4$

$(2, 2)$: $2 + 2 > 4$; $4 > 4$ false
$(2, 2)$ is not a solution.
$(3, 2)$: $3 + 2 > 4$; $5 > 4$ true
$(3, 2)$ is a solution
$(-3, 8)$: $-3 + 8 > 4$; $5 > 4$ true
$(-3, 8)$ is a solution.

3. $2x + y \geq 5$

$(4, 0)$: $8 + 0 \geq 5$ true
$(4, 0)$ is a solution.
$(1, 3)$: $2 + 3 \geq 5$ true
$(1, 3)$ is a solution.
$(0, 0)$: $0 + 0 \geq 5$ false
$(0, 0)$ is not a solution.

5. $y \geq -2x + 4$

$(4, 0)$: $0 \geq -8 + 4 = -4$ true
$(4, 0)$ is a solution.
$(1, 3)$: $3 \geq -2 + 4 = 2$ true
$(1, 3)$ is a solution.
$(-2, -4)$: $-4 \geq 4 + 4 = 8$ false
$(-2, -4)$ is not a solution.

7. $y > -2x + 1$

$(2, 3)$: $3 > -4 + 1 = -3$ true
$(2, 3)$ is a solution.
$(0, 0)$: $0 > 0 + 1 = 1$ false
$(0, 0)$ is not a solution.
$(0, 5)$: $5 > 0 + 1 = 1$ true
$(0, 5)$ is not a solution.

9. $x + y \geq 4$

Step 1 Replace $\geq$ with $=$ and graph the linear equation $x + y = 4$. The x-intercept is 4 and the y-intercept is 4, so the line passes through $(4, 0)$ and $(0, 4)$. Draw a solid line because the inequality contains a $\geq$ symbol.

Step 2 Use $(0, 0)$ as a test point.

$$x + y \leq 4$$
$$\text{Is } 0 + 0 \leq 4\,?$$
$$0 \leq 4 \text{ true}$$

Step 3 The test point $(0, 0)$ is part of the solution set, so shade the half-plane containing $(0, 0)$.

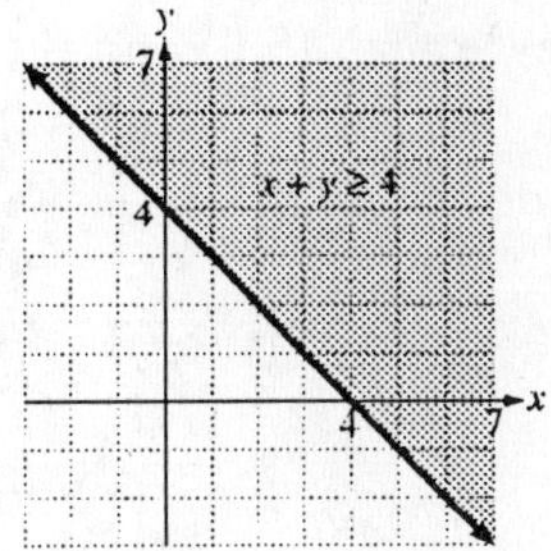

11. $x - y < 3$

Graph the equation $x - y = 3$, which passes through the points $(3, 0)$ and $(0, -3)$. Draw a dashed line because the inequality contains at $<$ symbol. Use $(0, 0)$ as a test point. Since $0 - 0 < 3$ is a true statement, shade the half-plane containing $(0, 0)$.

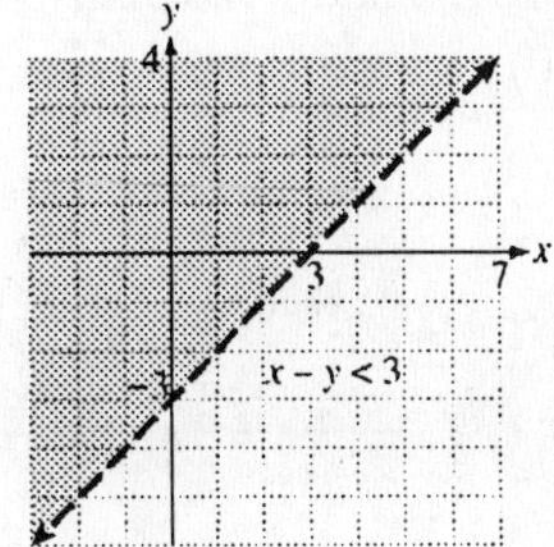

13. $2x + y > 4$

Graph the equation $2x+y = 4$ as a dashed line through $(2,0)$ and $(0,4)$. Use $(0,0)$ as a test point. Since $2(0) + 0 > 4$ is false, shade the half-plane *not* containing $(0,0)$.

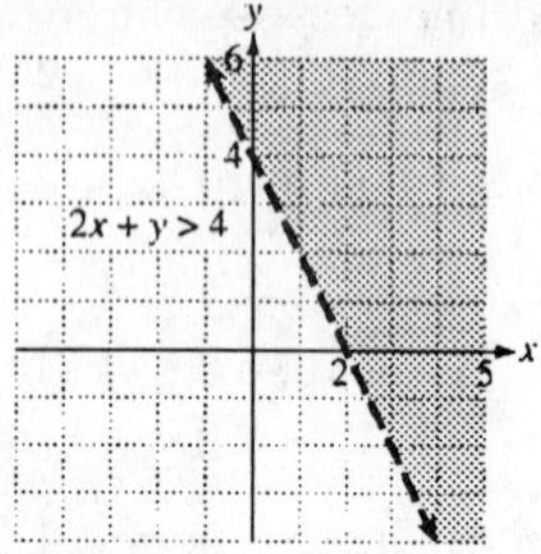

15. $x - 3y \le 6$

Graph the equation $x - 3y = 6$ as a solid line through $(6,0)$ and $(0,-2)$. Use $(0,0)$ as a test point. Since $0 - 3(0) \le 6$ is true, shade the half-plane containing $(0,0)$.

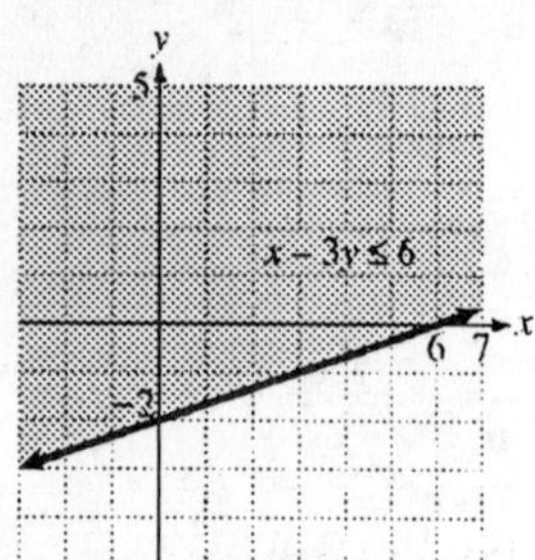

17. $3x - 2y \le 6$

Graph the equation $3x - 2y = 6$ as a solid line through $(2,0)$ and $(0,-3)$. Use $(0,0)$ as a test point. Since $3(0) - 2(0) \le 6$ is true, shade the half-plane containing $(0,0)$.

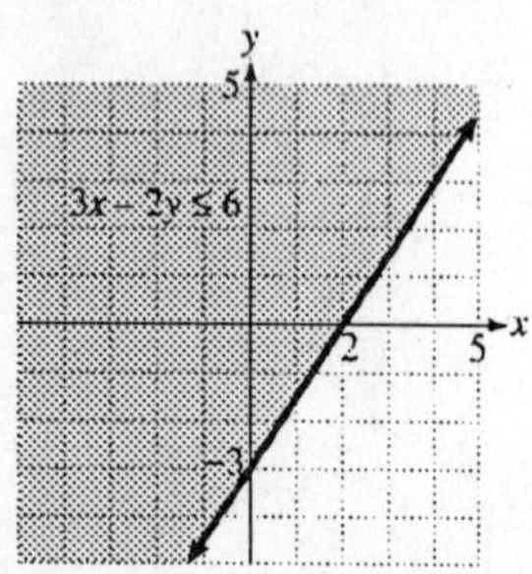

19. $4x + 3y > 12$

Graph $4x + 3y = 12$ as a dashed line through $(3,0)$ and $(0,4)$. Use $(0,0)$ as a test point. Since $4(0) + 3(0) > 12$ is false, shade the half-plane not containing $(0,0)$.

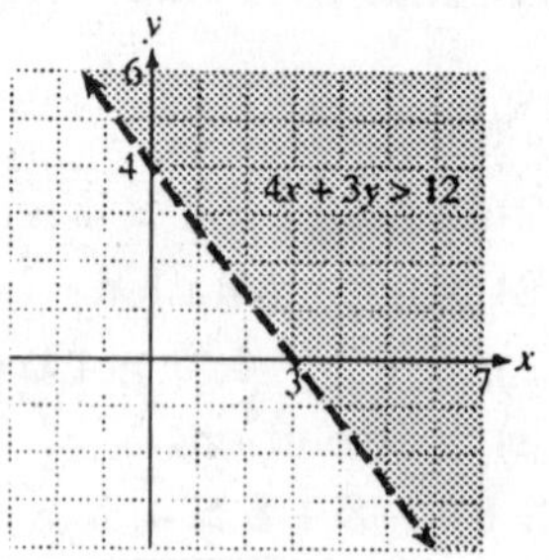

21. $5x - y < -10$

Graph the equation $5x - y = -10$ as a dashed line through $(-2,0)$ and $(0,10)$. Use $(0,0)$ as a test point. Since $5(0) - 0 < -10$ is false, shade the half-plane *not* containing $(0,0)$.

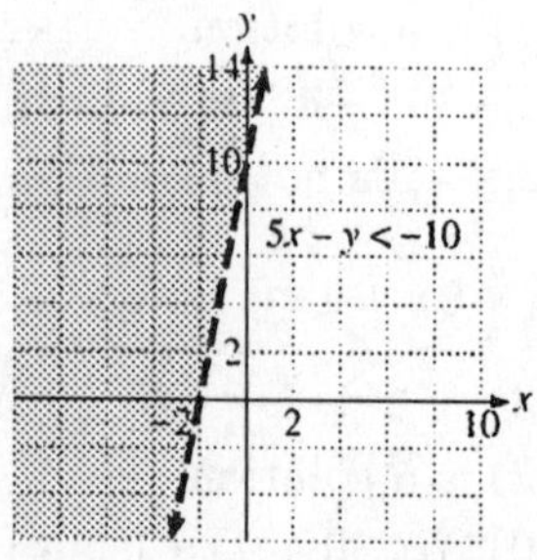

23. $y \le \dfrac{1}{3}x$

Graph the equation $y = \frac{1}{3}x$ as a solid line through $(0,0)$ and $(3,1)$. Because $(0,0)$ lies on the line, it cannot be used as a test point. Instead, use a point not on the line, such as $(0,6)$. Since $6 \le \frac{1}{2}(0)$ is false, shade the half-plane *not* containing $(0,6)$.

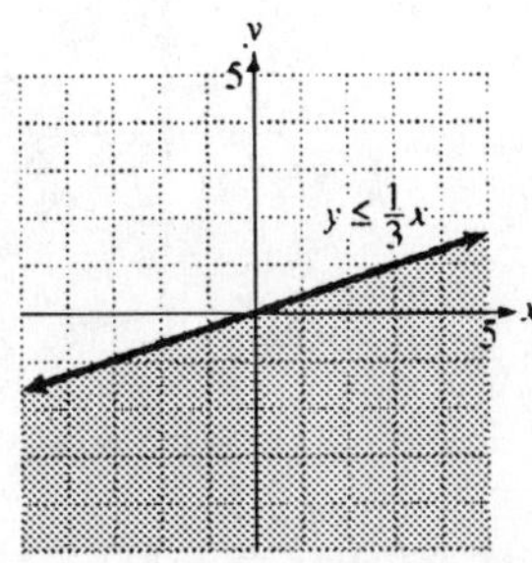

25. $y > 2x$

Graph the equation $y = 2x$ as a dashed line through the origin with slope 2. Use $(3,3)$ as a test point. Since $3 > 2(3)$ is false, shade the half-plane not containing $(3,3)$.

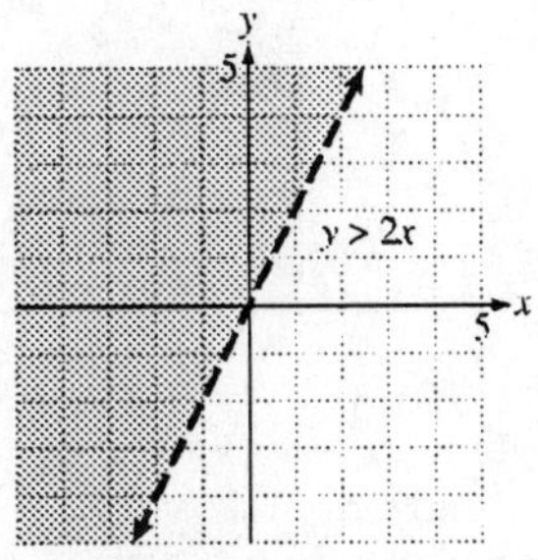

27. $y > 3x + 2$

Graph $y = 3x + 2$ as a dashed line using the slope and y-intercept. Use $(0,0)$ as a test point. Since $0 > 3(0) + 2$ is false, shade the half-plane *not* containing $(0,0)$.

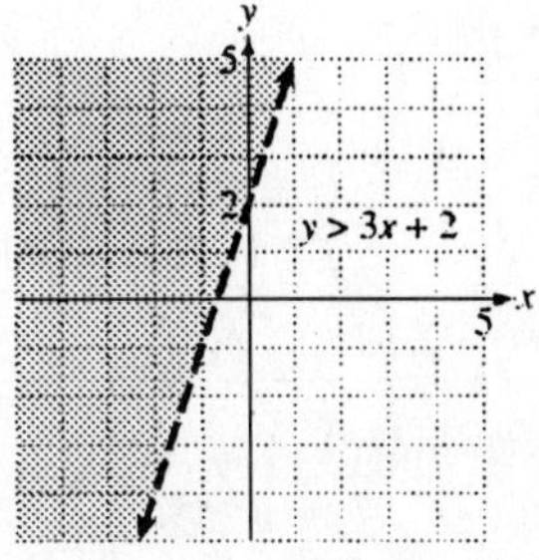

29. $y < \dfrac{3}{4}x - 3$

Graph $y = \frac{3}{4}x - 3$ as a dashed line using the slope and y-intercept. (Plot $(0,-3)$ and move 3 units up and 4 units to the right to the point $(4,0)$.) Use $(0,0)$ as a test point. Since $0 < \frac{3}{4}(0) - 3$ is false, shade the half-plane *not* containing $(0,0)$.

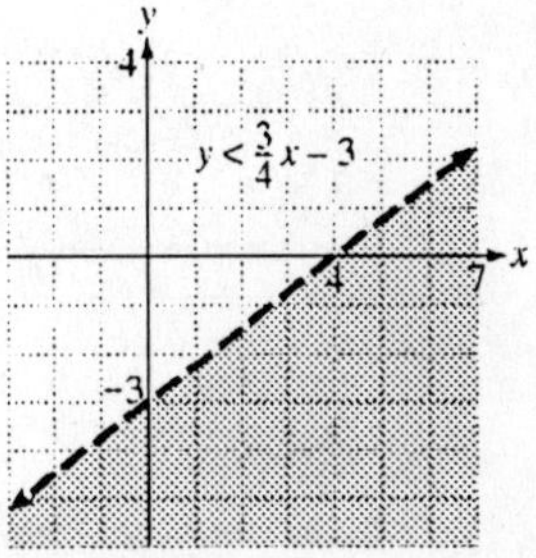

31. $x \leq 1$

Graph the vertical line $x = 1$ as a solid line. Use $(0,0)$ as a test point. Since $0 \leq 1$ is true, shade the half-plane containing $(0,0)$, which is the half-plane to the *left* of the line.

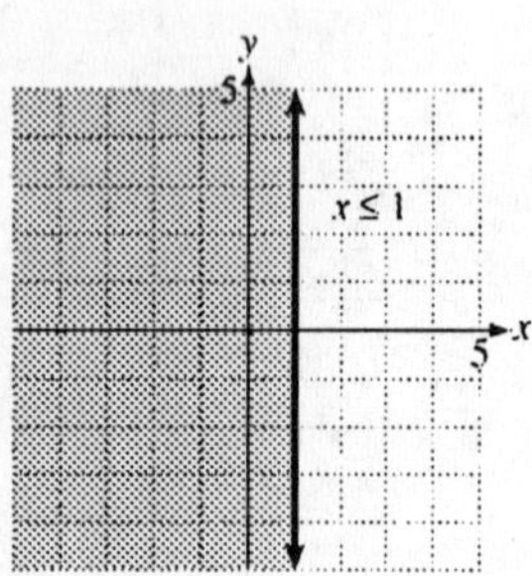

33. $y > 1$

Graph the horizontal line $y = 1$ as a dashed line. Use $(0,0)$ as a test point. Since $0 > 1$ is false, shade the half-plane *not* containing $(0,0)$, which is the half-plane *above* the line.

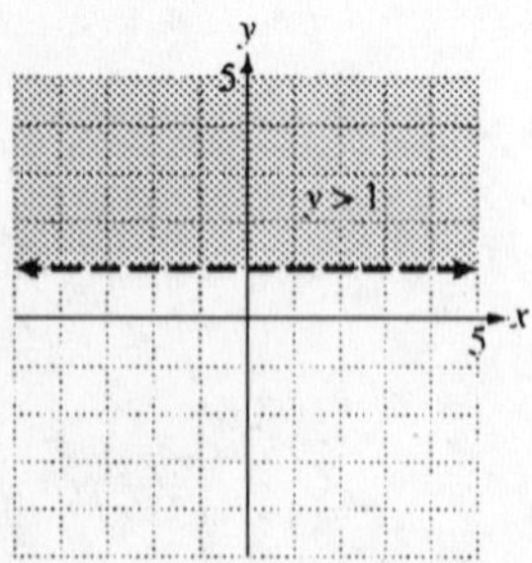

35. $x \geq 0$

Graph the vertical line $x = 0$ (the y-axis) as a solid line. Since $(0,0)$ is on the line, choose a different test point, such as $(3,3)$. Since $3 > 0$ is true, shade the half-plane containing $(3,3)$, which is the half-plane to the *right* of the y-axis.

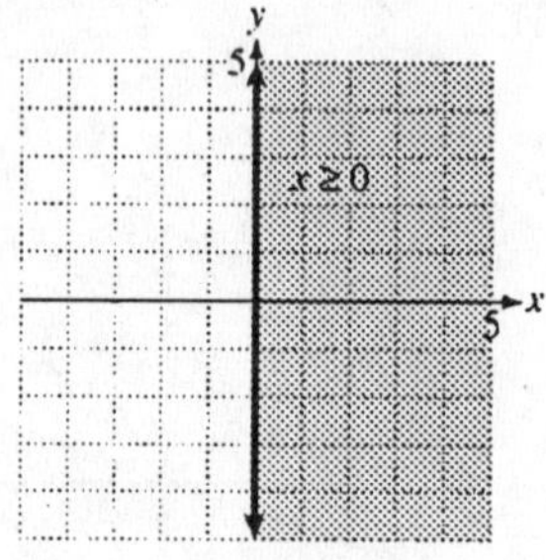

37. a. $20x + 10y \leq 80{,}000$

Graph the line $20x + 10y = 80{,}000$ as a solid line, using the x-intercept 4000 and the y-intercept 8000. Use $(1000, 1000)$ as a test point. Since $20(1000) + 10(1000) = 30{,}000 \leq 80{,}000$ is true, shade the half-plane containing $(1000, 1000)$. Draw the graph in quadrant I only.

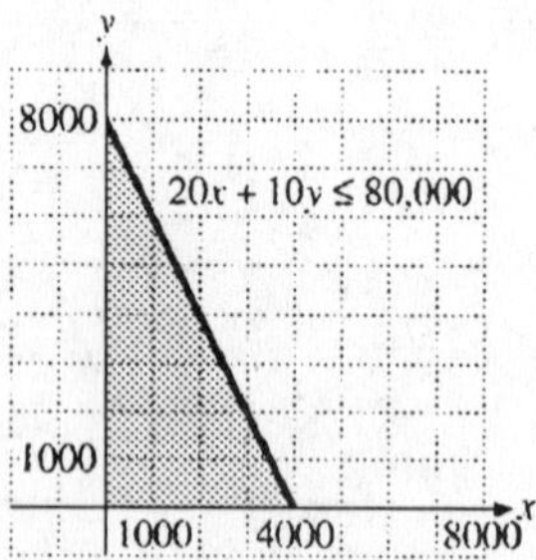

b. Answers will vary. One example is $(1000, 2000)$ since $20(1000) + 10(2000) = 20{,}000 + 20{,}000 = 40{,}000 < 80{,}000$. This indicates that the plane can carry 1000 bottles of water and 2000 medical kits.

39. a. $50x + 150y > 2000$

b. Graph $50x + 150y = 2000$ as a dashed line, using the x-intercept 40 and y-intercept $\frac{2000}{150} \approx 13.3$. Use $(10, 20)$ as a test point. Since $50(10) + 150(20) = 3500 > 2000$ is true, shade the half-plane containing $(10, 20)$. Draw the graph in quadrant I only.

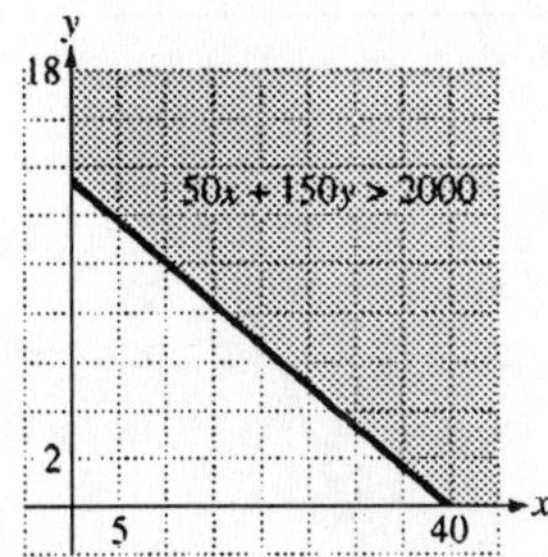

c. Answers will vary. One example is $(20, 15)$ since $50(20) + 150(150) = 3250 > 2000$. This indicates that the elevator cannot carry 20 children and 15 adults.

41. a. $\text{BMI} = \dfrac{703\,W}{H^2}$; $W = 200, H = 72$

$$\text{BMI} = \frac{703(200)}{72^2}$$
$$\text{BMI} = \frac{140{,}600}{5184}$$
$$\text{BMI} \approx 27.1$$

The men's BMI is 27.1.

b. Locate the point $(20, 27.1)$ on the graph for males. The point falls in the "Borderline" region, so the man is borderline overweight.

For Exercises 43–49, answers may vary.

51. The x- and y-intercepts of the line are both 3, so the equation of the line is $x + y = 3$ or $y = -x + 3$. The line is solid, so the inequality symbol must be either $\geq$ or $\leq$. Choose a test point in the shaded region, for example, $(4, 4)$. Since $4 + 4 > 3$, the inequality symbol must be $\geq$. Therefore, the inequality is $x + y \geq 3$ or $y \geq -x + 3$.

53. $y \leq 4x + 4$

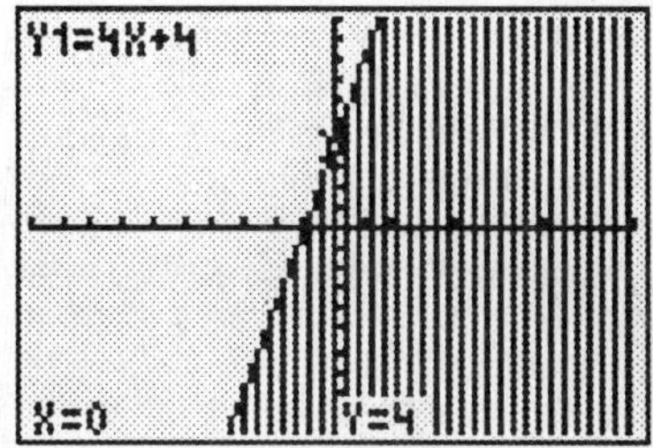

55. $y \geq \dfrac{1}{2}x + 4$

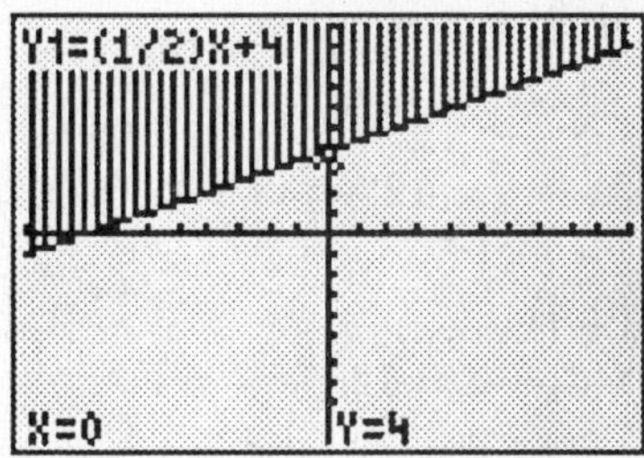

Review Exercises

57. $V = lwh$ for h

$$V = lwh$$
$$\frac{V}{lw} = \frac{lwh}{\ell w}$$
$$\frac{V}{lw} = h \text{ or } h = \frac{V}{lw}$$

58. $\dfrac{2}{3} \div \left(-\dfrac{5}{4}\right) = \dfrac{2}{3} \cdot \left(-\dfrac{4}{5}\right) = -\dfrac{8}{15}$

59. $x^2 - 4$; $x = -3$

$$x^2 - 4 = (-3)^2 - 4 = 9 - 4 = 5$$

Chapter 4 Review Exercises

1. $y = 3x + 6$

$(-3, 3)$:
$3 \stackrel{?}{=} 3(-3) + 6$
$3 \stackrel{?}{=} -6 + 9$
$3 = -3$ false

$(-3, 3)$ is a solution.

$(0, 6)$:
$6 = 3(0) + 6$
$6 = 6$ true

$(0, 6)$ is a solution.

$(1, 9)$:
$9 = 3(1) + 6$
$9 = 9$ true

$(1, 9)$ is a solution.

2. $3x - y = 12$

$(0, 4)$:
$3(0) - 4 \stackrel{?}{=} 12$
$-4 = 12$ false

$(4, 0)$ is not a solution.

$(4, 0)$:
$3(4) - 0 \stackrel{?}{=} 12$
$12 = 12$ true

$(4, 0)$ is a solution.

$(-1, 15)$:
$3(-1) - 15 \stackrel{?}{=} 12$
$-3 - 15 \stackrel{?}{=} 12$
$-18 = 12$ false

$(-1, 15)$ is not a solution.

3. $y = 2x - 3$

a.

x	$y = 2x - 3$	(x, y)
-2	$y = 2(-2) - 3 = -7$	$(-2, -7)$
-1	$y = 2(-1) - 3 = -5$	$(-1, -5)$
0	$y = 2(0) - 3 = -5$	$(0, -3)$
1	$y = 2(1) - 3 = -1$	$(1, -1)$
2	$y = 2(2) - 3 = 1$	$(2, 1)$

b.

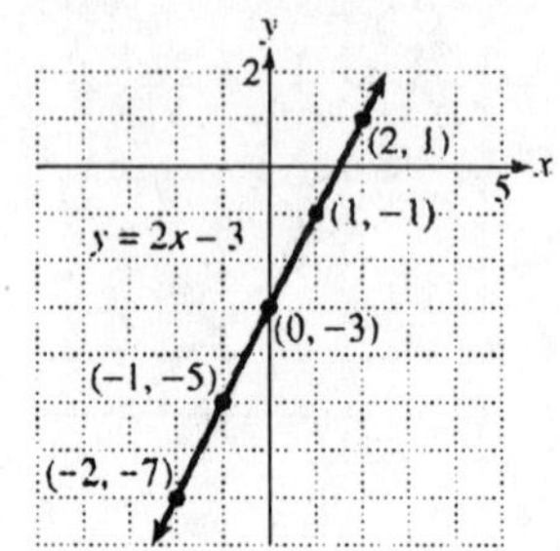

4. $y = \frac{1}{2}x + 1$

a.

x	$y = \frac{1}{2}x + 1$	(x, y)
-4	$y = \frac{1}{2}(-4) + 1 = -1$	$(-4, -1)$
-2	$y = \frac{1}{2}(-2) + 1 = 0$	$(-2, 0)$
0	$y = \frac{1}{2}(0) + 1 = 1$	$(0, 1)$
2	$y = \frac{1}{2}(2) + 1 = 2$	$(2, 2)$
4	$y = \frac{1}{2}(4) + 1 = 3$	$(4, 3)$

b.

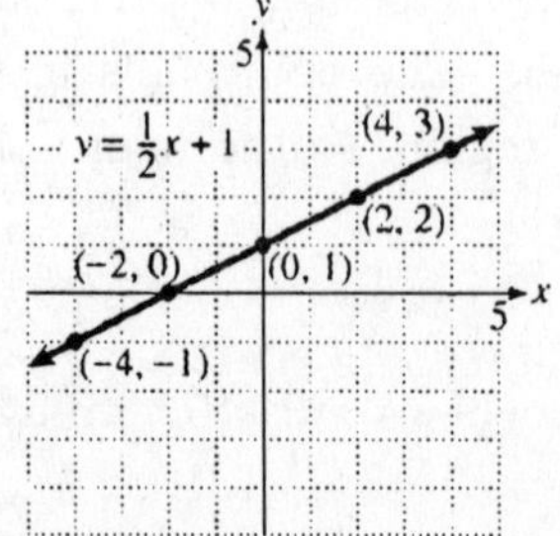

5. $y = x^2 - 3$

x	$y = x^2 - 3$	(x, y)
-3	$y = (-3)^2 - 3 = 6$	$(-3, 6)$
-2	$y = (-2)^2 - 3 = 1$	$(-2, 1)$
-1	$y = (-1)^2 - 3 = -2$	$(-1, -2)$
0	$y = 0^2 - 3 = -3$	$(0, -3)$
1	$y = 1^2 - 3 = -2$	$(1, -2)$
2	$y = 2^2 - 3 = 1$	$(2, 1)$
3	$y = 3^2 - 1 = 6$	$(3, 6)$

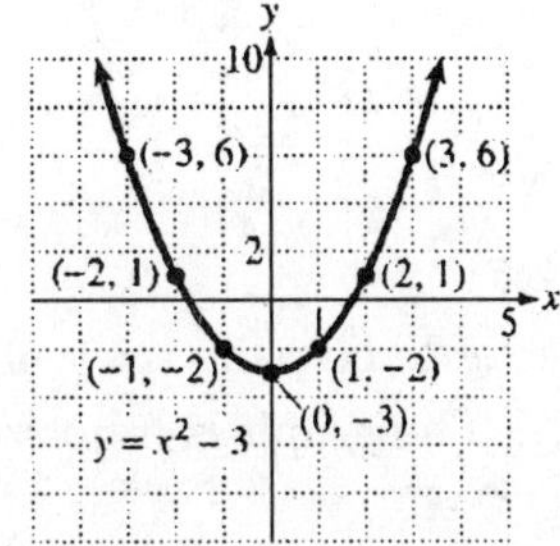

6. a.

x	$y = 5x - 41$	(x, y)
10	$y = 5(10) - 41 = 9$	$(10, 9)$
12	$y = 5(12) - 41 = 19$	$(12, 19)$
14	$y = 5(14) - 41 = 29$	$(14, 29)$
16	$y = 5(16) - 41 = 39$	$(16, 39)$

b. The equation models the data fairly well. The equation value vary from the data by 0.2% to 0.9%.

7. a. The graph crosses the x-axis at $(-2, 0)$, so the x-intercept is -2.

b. The graph crosses the y-axis at $(0, -4)$, so the y-intercept is -4.

8. a. The graph does not cross the x-axis, so there is no x-intercept.

b. The graph crosses the y-axis at $(0, 2)$, so the y-intercept is 2.

9. a. The graph crosses the x-axis at $(0, 0)$ (the origin), so the x-intercept is 0.

b. The graph also crosses the y-axis at $(0, 0)$, so the y-intercept is 0.

In Exercises 10–13, checkpoints will vary.

10. $2x + y = 4$

x-intercept:

$$2x + 0 = 4$$
$$2x = 4$$
$$x = 2$$

y-intercept:

$$2(0) + y = 4$$
$$y = 4$$

x-intercept: $(2, 0)$; y-intercept: $(0, 4)$
Find one other point as a checkpoint. For example, substitute 1 for x.

$$2(1) + y = 4$$
$$2 + y = 4$$
$$y = 2$$

checkpoint: $(1, 2)$
Draw a line through $(2, 0)$, $(0, 4)$, and $(1, 2)$.

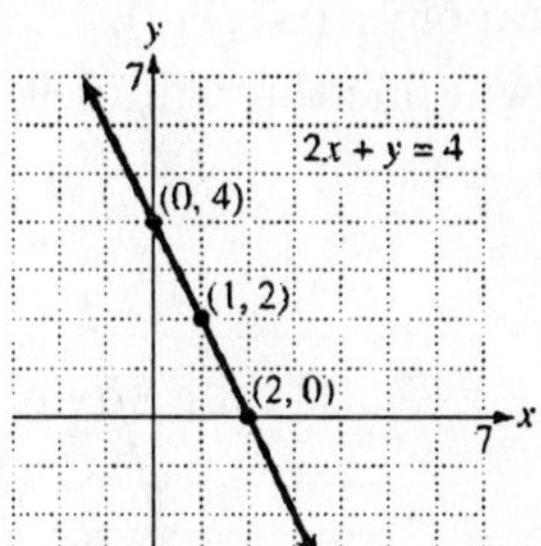

11. $3x - 2y = 12$

x-intercept: $(4, 0)$
y-intercept: $(0, -6)$
checkpoint: $(6, 3)$
Draw a line through $(4, 0)$, $(0, -6)$ and $(6, 3)$.

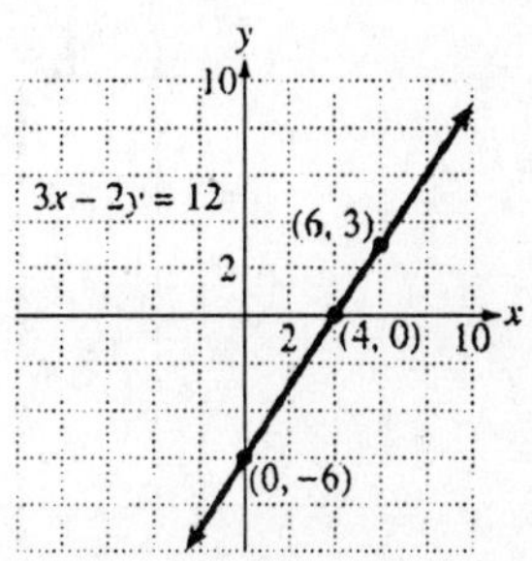

12. $3x = 6 - 2y$

x-intercept: $(2, 0)$
y-intercept: $(0, 3)$
checkpoint: $(4, -3)$
Draw a line through $(2, 0), (0, 3)$, and $(4, -3)$.

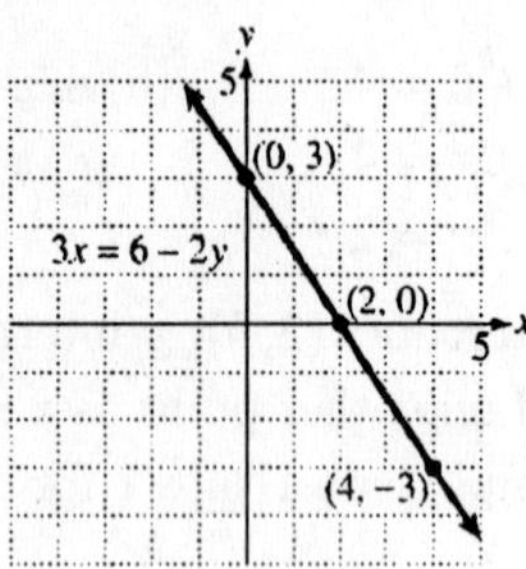

13. $3x - y = 0$

x-intercept: 0
y-intercept: 0
second point: $(1, 3)$
checkpoint: $(-1, -3)$
Draw a line through $(0, 0), (1, 3)$, and $(-1, -3)$.

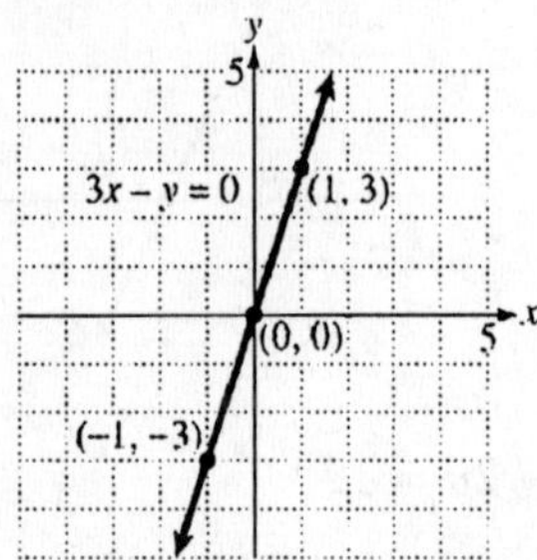

14. $x = 3$

Three ordered pairs are $(3, -2), (3, 0)$, and $(3, 2)$. The graph is a vertical line.

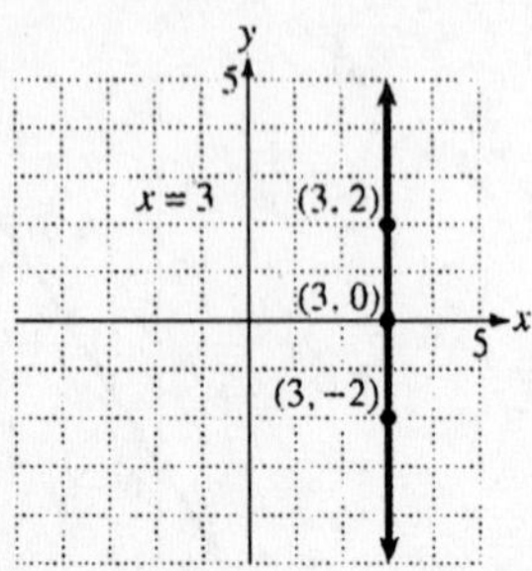

15. $y = -5$

Three ordered pairs are $(-2, -5), (0, -5)$, and $(2, 5)$. The graph is a horizontal line.

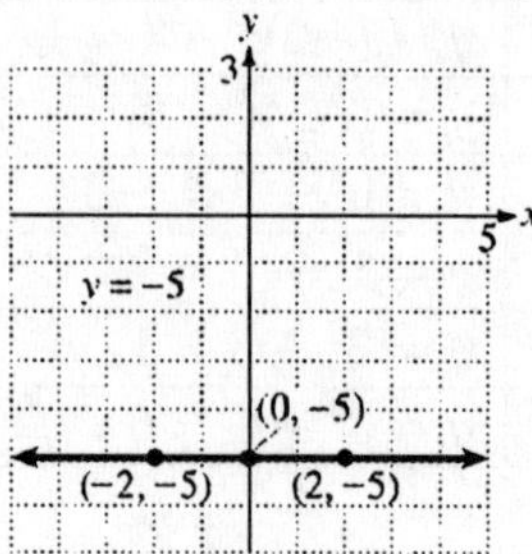

16. $y + 3 = 5$
$y = 2$

Three ordered pairs are $(-4, 2), (0, 2)$, and $(5, 2)$. The graph is a horizontal line.

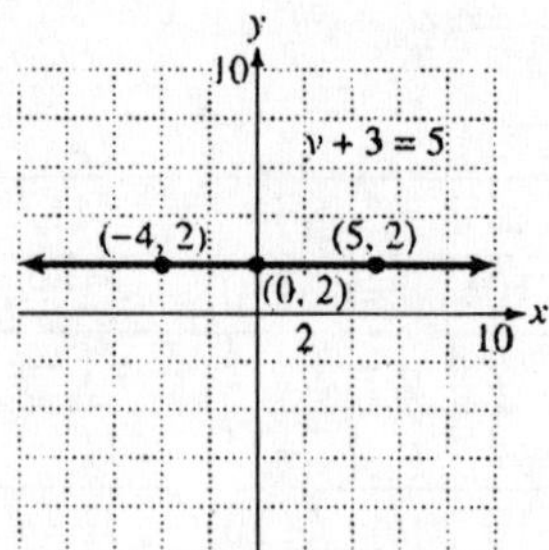

17. $2x = -8$
$x = -4$

Three ordered pairs are $(-4, -2), (-4, 0)$, and $(-4, 2)$. The graph is a vertical line.

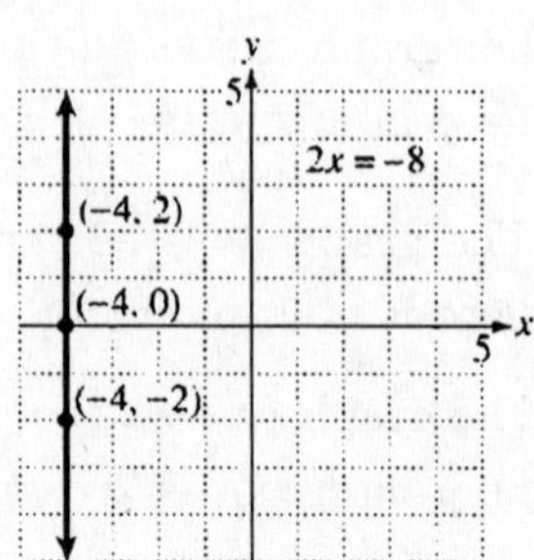

18. a. The minimum temperature occurred at 5 P.M. and was -4°F.

b. The maximum temperature occurred at 8 P.M. and was 16°F.

c. The x-intercepts are 4 and 6. This indicates that at 4 P.M. and 6 P.M., the temperature was 0°F.

d. The y-intercept is 12. This indicates that at noon the temperature was 12°F.

e. This indicates that the temperature stayed the same, at 12°F, from 9 P.M. until midnight.

19. $(3, 2)$ and $(5, 1)$

Let $(x_1, y_1) = (3, 2)$ and $(x_2, y_2) = (5, 1)$.

$$m = \frac{\text{Change in } y}{\text{Change in } x} = \frac{y_2 - y_1}{x_2 - x_2} = \frac{1-2}{5-3} = -\frac{1}{2}$$

The slope is $-\frac{1}{2}$. Since the slope is negative, the line falls.

20. $(-1, 2)$ and $(-3, -4)$

$$m = \frac{-4-2}{-3-(-1)} = \frac{-6}{-2} = 3$$

Since the slope is positive, the line rises.

21. $(-3, 4)$ and $(6, 4)$

$$m = \frac{4-4}{6-(-3)} = \frac{0}{9} = 0$$

Since the slope is 0, the line is horizontal.

22. $(5, 3)$ and $(5, -3)$

$$m = \frac{-3-3}{5-5} = \frac{-6}{0}; \text{ undefined}$$

Since the slope is undefined, the line is vertical.

23. Line through $(-3, -2)$ and $(2, 1)$:

$$m = \frac{1-(-2)}{2-(-3)} = \frac{3}{5}$$

24. Line through $(-2, 3)$ and $(-2, -3)$:

The line is vertical, so its slope is undefined.

25. Line through $(-4, -1)$ and $(2, -3)$:

$$m = \frac{-3-(-1)}{2-(-4)} = \frac{-2}{6} = -\frac{1}{3}$$

26. Line through $(-2, 2)$ and $(3, 2)$:

The line is horizontal, so its slope is 0.

27. Line through $(-1, -3)$ and $(2, -8)$:

$$m = \frac{-8-(-3)}{2-(-1)} = \frac{-5}{3} = -\frac{5}{3}$$

Line through $(8, -7)$ and $(9, 10)$:

$$m = \frac{10-(-7)}{9-8} = \frac{17}{1} = 17$$

Since their slopes are not equal, the lines are not parallel.

28. Line through $(5, 4)$ and $(9, 7)$:

$$m = \frac{7-4}{9-5} = \frac{3}{4}$$

Line through $(-6, 0)$ and $(-2, 3)$:

$$m = \frac{3-0}{-2-(-6)} = \frac{3}{4}$$

Since their slopes are equal, the lines are parallel.

29. a. Line through $(1974, 350)$ and $(2000, 1026)$:

$$m = \frac{1026-350}{2000-1974} = \frac{676}{26} = 26$$

The number of lawyers increased at a rate of 26 thousand each year from 1974 to 2000.

b. Line through $(1950, 200)$ and $(1974, 350)$:

$$m = \frac{350-200}{1974-1950} = \frac{150}{24} = 6.25$$

The number of lawyers increased at a rate of 6.25 thousand each year from 1950 to 1974.

30. $y = 5x - 7$

$y = 5x + (-7)$

The slope is the x-coefficient, which is 5. The y-intercept is the constant term, which is -7.

31. $y = 6 - 4x$

$y = -4x + 6$

$m = -4$; y-intercept $= 6$

32. $y = 3$

$m = 0$; y-intercept $= 3$

33. $2x + 3y = 6$

$$3y = -2x + 6$$

$$y = \frac{-2x + 6}{3}$$

$$y = -\frac{2}{3}x + 2$$

$m = -\frac{2}{3}$; y-intercept $= 2$

34. $y = 2x - 4$

slope $= 2 = \frac{2}{1}$; y-intercept $= -4$

Plot $(0, -4)$ on the y-axis. From this point, move 2 units *up* (because 2 is positive) and 1 unit to the *right* to reach the point $(1, -2)$. Draw a line through $(0, -4)$ and $(1, -2)$.

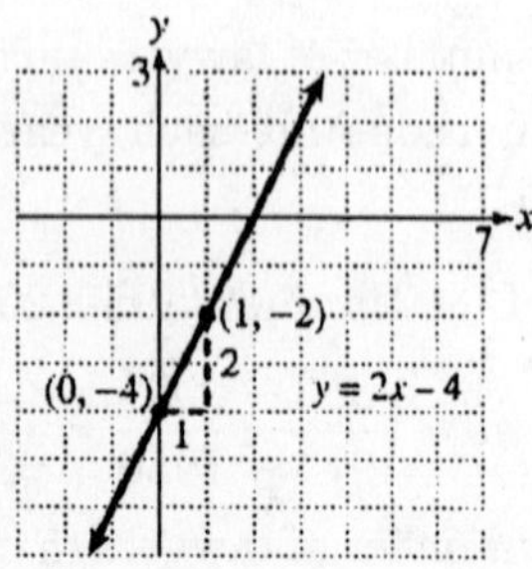

35. $y = \frac{1}{2}x - 1$

slope $= \frac{1}{2}$; y-intercept $= -1$

Plot $(0, -1)$. From the point, move 1 unit *up* and 2 units to the *right* to reach the point $(2, 0)$. Draw a line through $(0, -1)$ and $(2, 0)$.

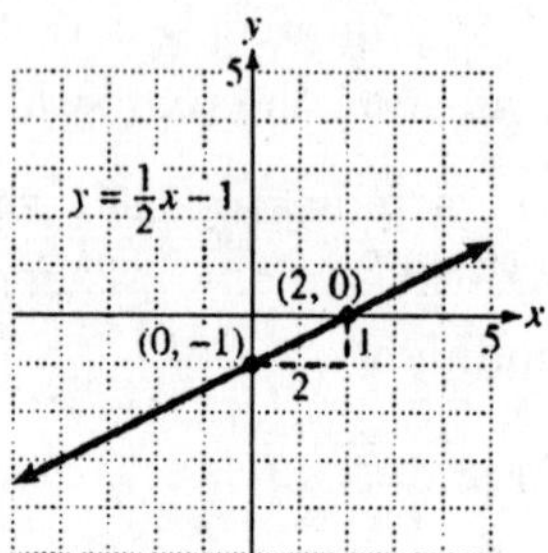

36. $y = -\frac{2}{3}x + 5$

slope $= -\frac{2}{3} = \frac{-2}{3}$; y-intercept $= 5$

Plot $(0, 5)$. Move 2 units *down* (because -2 is negative) and 3 units to the *right* to reach the point $(3, 3)$. Draw a line through $(0, 5)$ and $(3, 3)$.

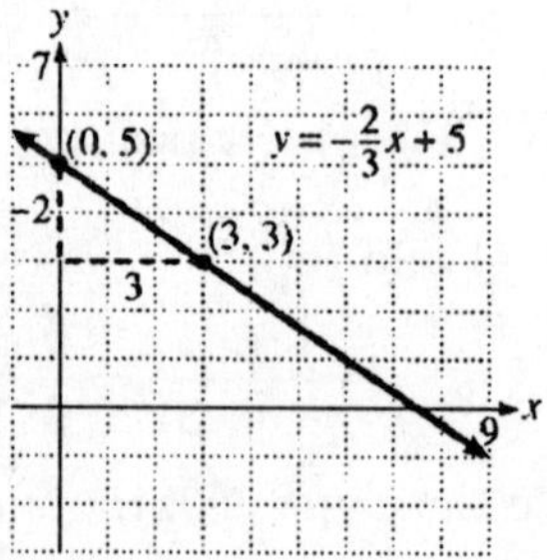

37. $y - 2x = 0$

$$y = 2x$$

slope $= 2 = \frac{2}{1}$; y-intercept $= 0$

Plot $(0, 0)$ (the origin). Move 2 units *up* and 1 unit to the *right* to reach the point $(1, 2)$.

Draw a line through $(0, 0)$ and $(1, 2)$.

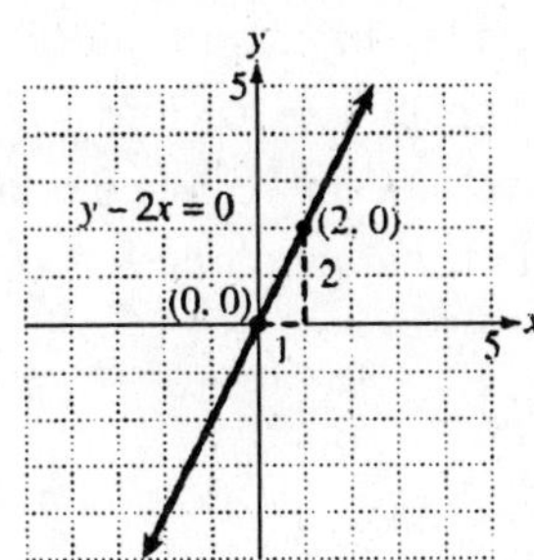

38. $\frac{1}{3}x + y = 2$

$$y = -\frac{1}{3}x + 2$$

slope $= -\frac{1}{3} = \frac{-1}{3}$; y-intercept $= 2$

Plot $(0, 2)$. Move 1 unit *down* and 3 units to the *right* to reach the point $(3, 1)$. Draw line through $(0, 2)$ and $(3, 1)$.

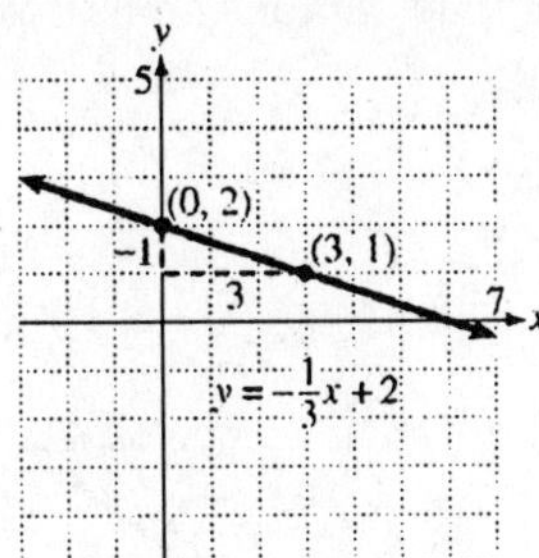

39. $y = -\frac{1}{2}x + 4$ $\qquad$ $y = -\frac{1}{2}x - 1$

slope $= -\frac{1}{2} = \frac{-1}{2}$ $\qquad$ slope $= -\frac{1}{2} = \frac{-1}{2}$

y-intercept $= 4$ $\qquad$ slope $= -1$

Graph each line using its slope and y-intercept.

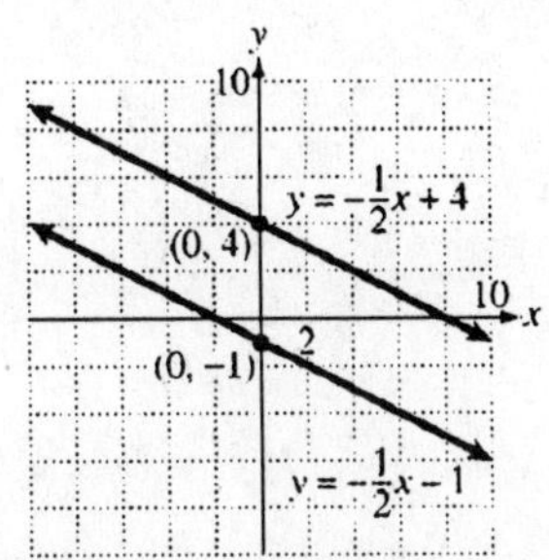

Yes, they are parallel since both lines have slope of $-\frac{1}{2}$.

40. **a.** The smallest y-intercept is 25. This indicates that in 1990 the average age of U.S. Hispanics was 25.

b. Line through $(0, 35)$ and $(10, 38)$:

$$m = \frac{38 - 35}{10 - 0} = \frac{3}{10} = 0.3$$

This means that the average age for U.S. whites increased at a rate of about 0.3 each year from 1990 to 2000.

c. $y = 0.3x + 35$

d. The year 2010 corresponds to $x = 20$. If $x = 20$,

$$y = 0.3(20) + 35 = 41.$$

According to the model, the average age for U.S. whites in 2010 will be 41 years old.

41. Slope $= 6$, passing through $(-4, 7)$
$y - 7 = 6[x - (-4)]$
point-slope form; $y - 7 = 6(x + 4)$
$y - 7 = 6x + 24$
slope-intercept form: $y = 6x + 31$

42. Passing through $(3, 4)$ and $(2, 1)$

$$m = \frac{1 - 4}{2 - 3} = \frac{-3}{-1} = 3$$

$$y - y_1 = m(x - x_1)$$

Using the point $(3, 4)$, the point-slope equation is

$$y - 4 = 3(x - 3).$$

Rewrite this equation in slope-intercept form.

$$y - 4 = 3x - 9$$
$$y = 3x - 5$$

43. Line through $(0,16)$ and $(30,12.1)$

a. $m = \dfrac{12.1-16}{30-0} = \dfrac{-3.9}{30} = -0.13$

Using the point $(0,16)$, the point slope-form is

$$y - 16 = -0.13(x-0)$$
$$\text{or}\quad y - 16 = -0.13x.$$

b. $y = -0.13x + 16$

c. The year 1970 corresponds to $x = 70$ and the year 1980 corresponds to $x = 80$. If $x = 70$,

$$y = -0.13(70) + 16 = 6.9.$$

If $x = 80$,

$$y = -0.13(80) + 16 = 5.6.$$

According to the equation, the average surfboard length was 6.9 feet in 1970 and 5.6 feet in 1980.

d. The year 2000 corresponds to $x = 100$. If $x = 100$,

$$y = -0.13(100) + 16 = 3.$$

According to the equation, the average surfboard length in 2000 was 3 feet. It does not seem realistic that surfboards would be this short.

44. $3x - 4y > 7$

$(0,0)$: $0 - 0 > 7$; $0 > 7$ false
$(0,0)$ is not a solution.
$(3,-6)$: $9 + 24 > 7$; $33 > 7$ true
$(3,-6)$ is a solution.
$(-2,-5)$: $-6 + 20 > 7$; $14 > 7$ true
$(-2,-5)$ is a solution.
$(-3,4)$: $-9 - 12 > 7$; $-21 > 7$ false
$(-3,4)$ is not a solution.

45. $x - 2y > 6$

Graph the equation $x - 2y = 6$ as a dashed line through $(6,0)$ and $(0,-3)$. Use $(0,0)$ as a test point. Since $0 - 2(0) > 6$ is false, shade the half-plane *not* containing $(0,0)$.

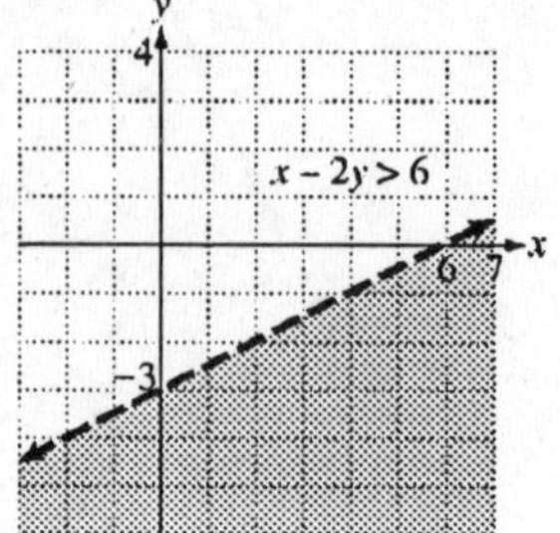

46. $4x - 6y \le 12$

Graph the equation $4x - 6y = 12$ as a solid line through $(3,0)$ and $(0,-2)$. Use $(0,0)$ as a test point. Since $4(0) - 6(0) \le 12$ is true, shade the half-plane containing $(0,0)$.

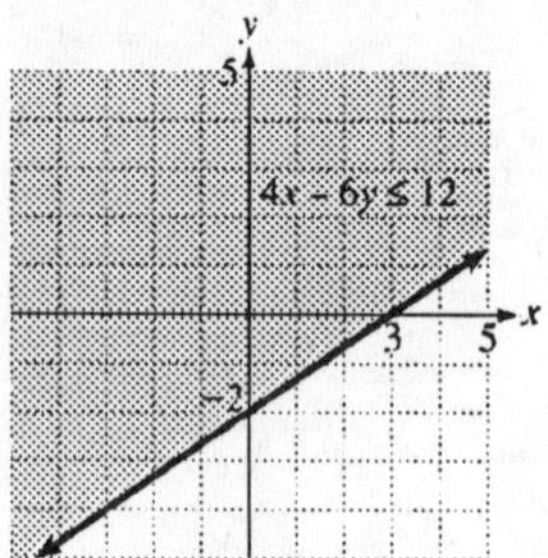

47. $y > 3x + 2$

Graph $y = 3x + 2$ as a dashed line using the slope and y-intercept. Use $(0,0)$ as a test point. Since $0 > 3(0) + 2$ is false, shade the half-plane *not* containing $(0,0)$.

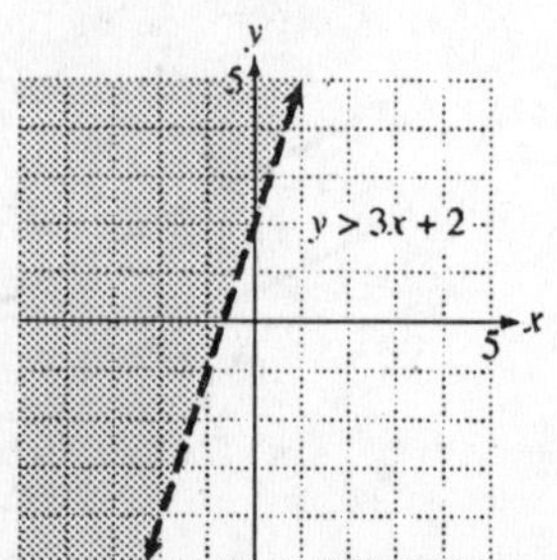

48. $y \leq \dfrac{1}{3}x - 1$

Graph $y = \frac{1}{3}x - 1$ as a solid line using slope and y-intercept. Use $(0, 0)$ as a test point. Since $0 \leq \frac{1}{3}(0) - 1$ is false, shade the half-plane *not* containing $(0, 0)$.

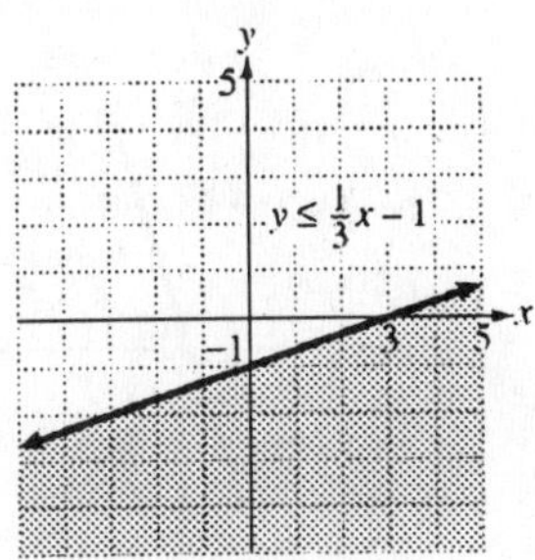

49. $y < \dfrac{1}{2}x$

Graph $y = -\frac{1}{2}x$ as a solid line using the slope and y-intercept. Since the line passes through the origin, a point other than $(0, 0)$ must be chosen as the test point, for example, $(4, 4)$. Since $4 \leq -\frac{1}{2}(4)$ is false, shade the half-plane not containing $(4, 4)$.

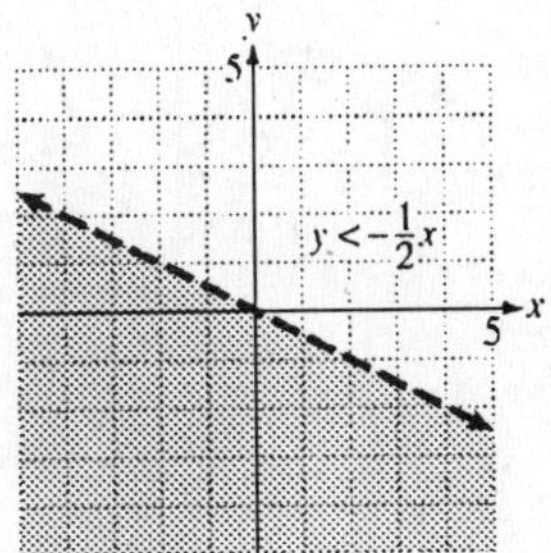

50. $x < 4$

Graph the vertical line $x = 4$ as a dashed line. Use $(0, 0)$ as a test point. Since $0 < 4$ is true, shade the half-plane containing $(0, 0)$, which is the half-plane to the *left* of the line.

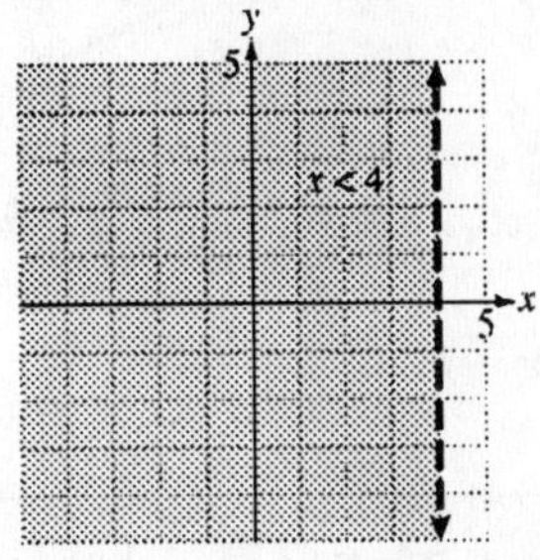

51. $y \geq -2$

Graph the horizontal line $y = -2$ as a solid line. Use $(0, 0)$ as a test point. Since $0 \geq -2$ is true, shade the half-plane containing $(0, 0)$, which is the half-plane *above* the line.

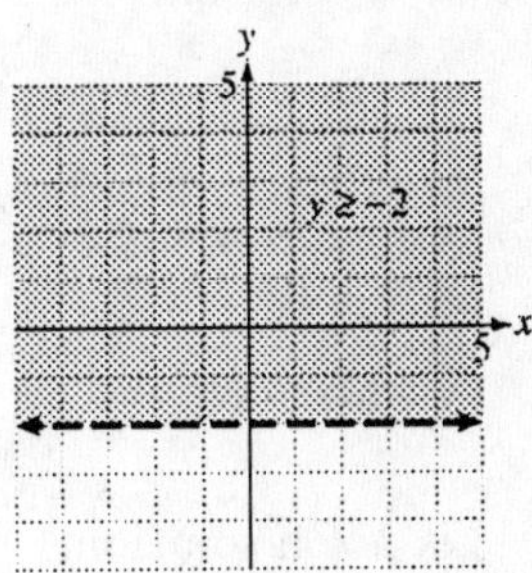

52. $x + 2y \leq 0$

Graph $x + 2y = 0$ as a solid line through $(0, 0)$ and $(2, -1)$. Since the line goes through the origin, choose another point as the test point, for example, $(1, 1)$.

Since $1+2(1) \le 0$ is false, shade the half-plane *not* containing $(0,0)$.

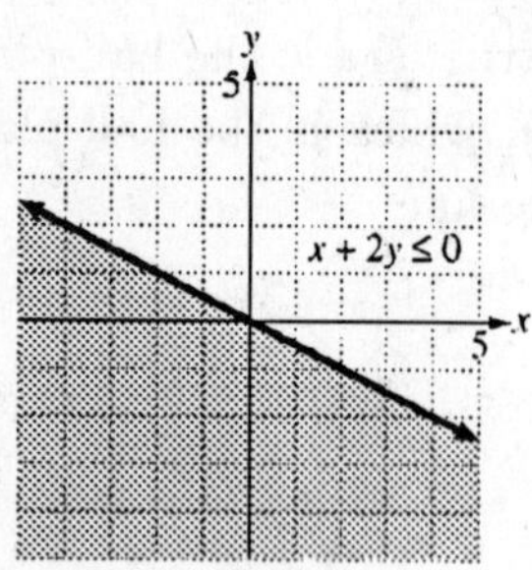

Chapter 4 Test

1. $4x - 2y = 10$

$(0,-5)$:
$4(0) - 2(-5) \stackrel{?}{=} 10$
$0 + 10 \stackrel{?}{=} 10$
$10 = 10$ true

$(0,-5)$ is a solution.

$(-2,1)$:
$4(-2) - 2(1) \stackrel{?}{=} 10$
$-8 - 2 \stackrel{?}{=} 10$
$-10 = 10$ false

$(-2,1)$ is not a solution.

$(4,3)$:
$4(4) - 2(3) \stackrel{?}{=} 10$
$16 - 6 \stackrel{?}{=} 10$
$10 = 10$ true

$(4,3)$ is a solution.

2. $y = 3x + 1$

x	$y = 3x + 1$	(x, y)
-2	$y = 3(-2) + 1 = -5$	$(-2,-5)$
-1	$y = 3(-1) + 1 = -2$	$(-1,-2)$
0	$y = 3(0) + 1 = 1$	$(0,1)$
1	$y = 3(1) + 1 = 4$	$(1,4)$
2	$y = 3(2) + 1 = 7$	$(2,7)$

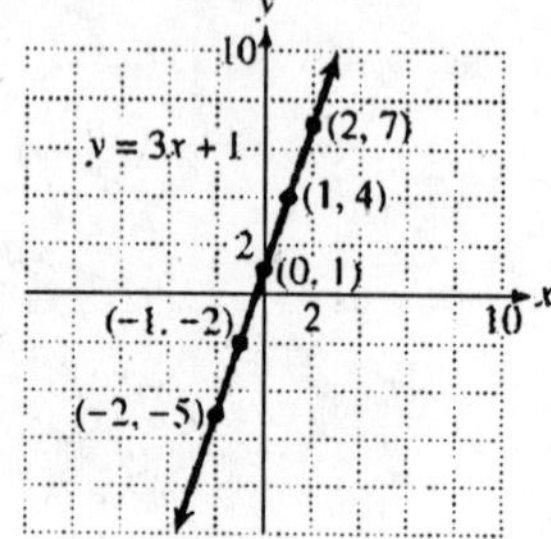

3. $y = x^2 - 1$

x	$y = x^2 - 1$	(x, y)
-3	$y = (-3)^2 - 1 = 8$	$(-3,8)$
-2	$y = (-2)^2 - 1 = 3$	$(-2,3)$
-1	$y = (-1)^2 - 1 = 0$	$(-1,0)$
0	$y = 0^2 - 1 = -1$	$(0,-1)$
1	$y = 1^2 - 1 = 0$	$(1,0)$
2	$y = 2^2 - 1 = 3$	$(2,3)$
3	$y = 3^2 - 1 = 8$	$(3,8)$

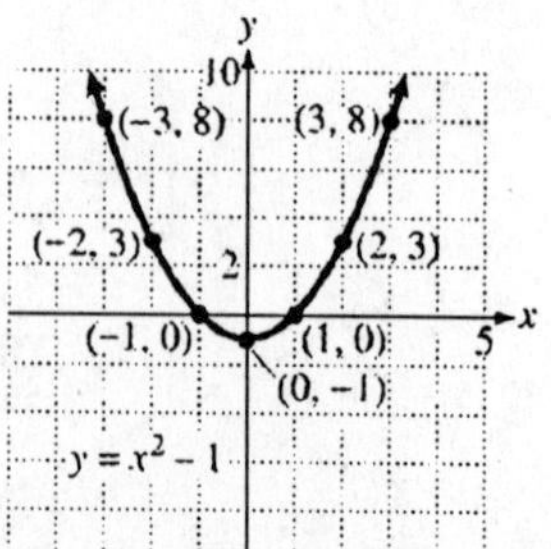

4. a. The graph crosses the x-axis at $(2,0)$, so the x-intercept is 2.

b. The graph crosses the y-axis at $(0,-3)$, so the y-intercept is -3.

5. $4x - 2y = -8$

x-intercept: $4x - 2(0) = -8$, $4x = -8$, $x = -2$

y-intercept: $4(0) - 2y = -8$, $-2y = -8$, $y = 4$

Find one other point as a checkpoint. For example, substitute -4 for x.

$$\begin{aligned} 4(-4) - 2y &= -8 \\ -16 - 2y &= -8 \\ -2y &= -8 \\ y &= -4 \end{aligned}$$

checkpoint: $(-4,-4)$
Draw a line through $(-2,0)$,$(0,4)$ and $(-4,-4)$.

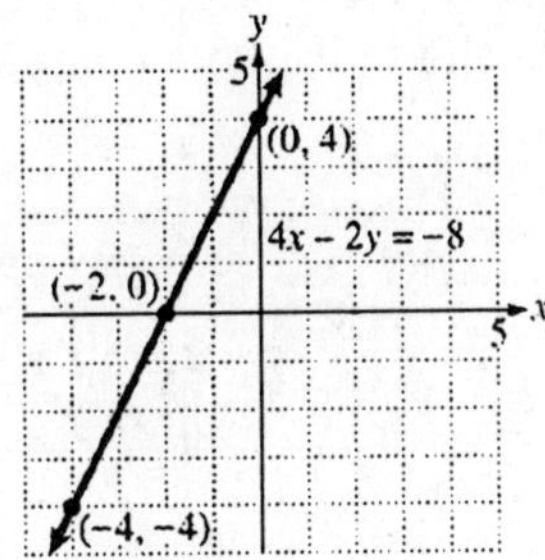

6. $y = 4$

Three ordered pairs are $(-2,4)$, $(0,4)$, and $(2,4)$. The graph is a horizontal line.

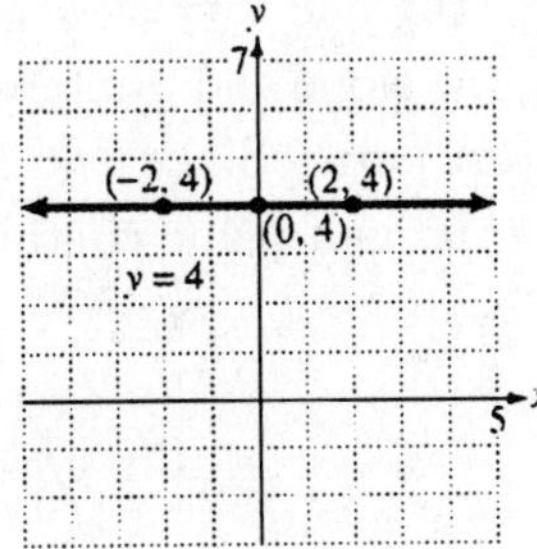

7. $(-3,4)$ and $(-5,-2)$

$$m = \frac{-2-4}{-5(-3)} = \frac{-6}{-2} = 3$$

The slope is 3. Since the slope is positive, the line rises.

8. $(6,-1)$ and $(6,3)$

$$m = \frac{3-(-1)}{6-6} = \frac{4}{0}; \text{ undefined}$$

Since the slope is undefined, the line is vertical.

9. Line through $(-1,-2)$ and $(1,1)$:

$$m = \frac{1-(-2)}{1-(-1)} = \frac{3}{2}$$

10. Line through $(2,4)$ and $(6,1)$:

$$m = \frac{1-4}{6-2} = \frac{-3}{4} = -\frac{3}{4}$$

Line through $(-3,1)$ and $(1,-2)$:

$$m = \frac{-2-1}{1-(-3)} = \frac{-3}{4} = -\frac{3}{4}$$

Since the slopes are equal, the lines are parallel.

11. $y = -x + 10$
$y = -1x + 10$

The slope is the coefficient of x, which is -1. The y-intercept is the constant term, which is 10.

12. $2x + y = 6$

$$y = -2x + 6$$

$m = -2$; y-intercept $= 6$

13. $y = \frac{2}{3}x - 1$

slope $= \frac{2}{3}$; y-intercept $= -1$

Plot $(0, -1)$. From this point, move 2 units *up* and 3 units to the *right* to reach the point $(3, 1)$. Draw a line through $(0, -1)$ and $(3, 1)$.

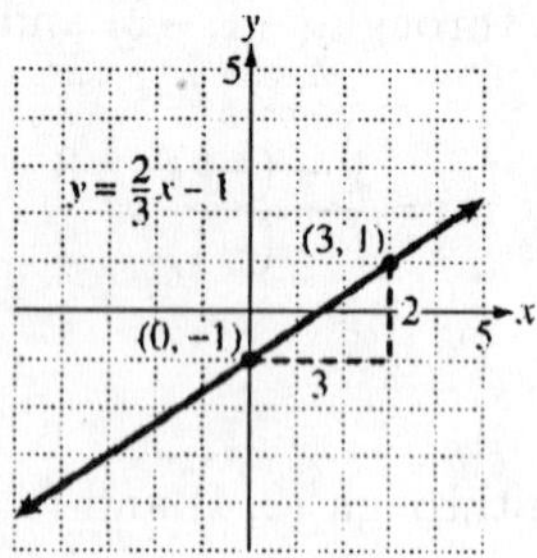

14. $y = -2x + 3$

slope $= -2 = \frac{-2}{1} = -2$; y-intercept $= 3$

Plot $(0, 3)$. Move 2 units *down* and 1 unit to the right to reach the point $(1, 1)$. Draw a line through $(0, 3)$ and $(1, 1)$.

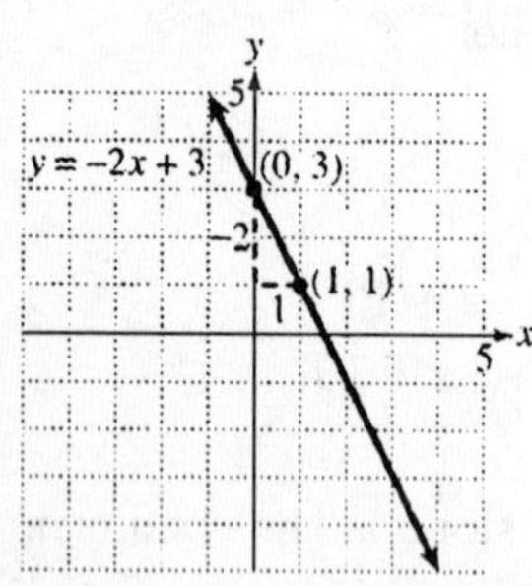

15. Slope $= -2$; passing through $(-1, 4)$
$y - 4 = -2[x - (-1)]$
point-slope form: $y - 4 = -2(x + 1)$
$y - 4 = -2x - 2$
slope-intercept form: $y = -2x + 2$

16. Passing through $(2, 1)$ and $(-1, -8)$

$$m = \frac{-8 - 1}{-1 - 2} = \frac{-9}{-3} = 3$$

Using the point $(2, 1)$, the point-slope equation is

$$y - 1 = 3(x - 2).$$

Rewrite this equation in slope-intercept form

$$y - 1 = 3x - 6$$
$$y = 3x - 5.$$

17. $3x - 2y < 6$

Graph the line $3x - 2y = 6$ as a dashed line through $(2, 0)$ and $(0, -3)$. Use $(0, 0)$ as a test point. Since $3(0) - 2(0) < 6$ is true, shade the half-plane containing $(0, 0)$.

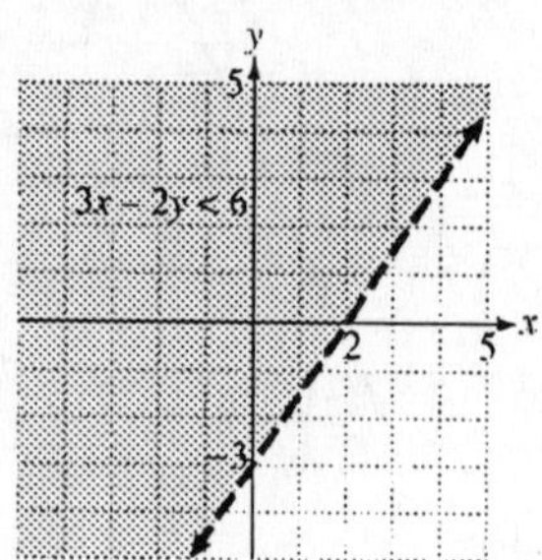

18. $y \geq 2x - 2$

Graph the line $y = 2x - 2$ as a solid line using the slope and y-intercept. Use $(0, 0)$ as a test point. Since $0 \geq 2(0) - 2$ is true, shade the half-plane containing $(0, 0)$.

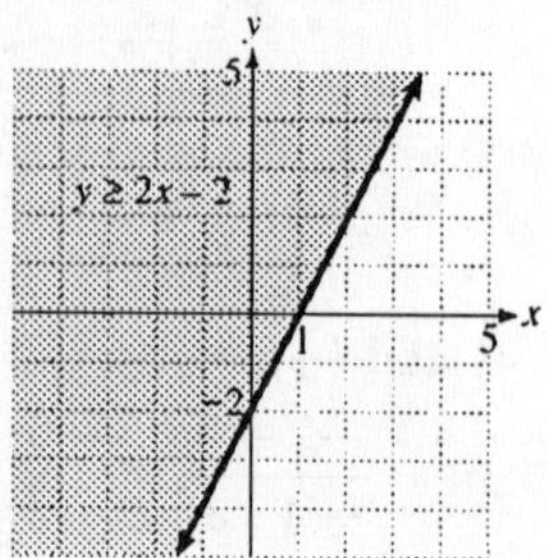

19. $x > -1$

Graph the vertical line $x = -1$ as a dashed line. Use $(0, 0)$ as a test point. Since $0 > -1$ is true, shade the half-plane containing $(0, 0)$, which is the half-plane to the *right* of the line.

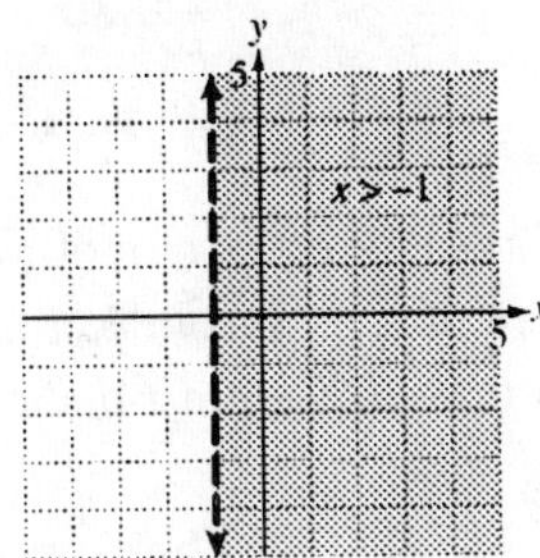

20. Line through $(1970, 2100)$ and $(2000, 5280)$:

$$m = \frac{5280 - 2100}{2000 - 1970} = \frac{3180}{30} = 106$$

This slope indicates that per-pupil spending increases by about \$106 each year.

Cumulative Review Exercises (Chapters 1-4)

1. $\dfrac{10 - (-6)}{3^2 - (4 - 3)} = \dfrac{10 + 6}{9 - 1} = \dfrac{16}{8} = 2$

2.
$$\begin{aligned} 6 - 2[3(x-1)+4] &= 6 - 2(3x - 3 + 4) \\ &= 6 - 2(3x + 1) \\ &= 6 - 6x - 2 \\ &= 4 - 6x \end{aligned}$$

3. The only irrational number in the given set is $\sqrt{5}$.

4.
$$\begin{aligned} 6(2x-1) - 6 &= 11x + 7 \\ 12x - 6 - 6 &= 11x + 7 \\ 12x - 12 &= 11x + 7 \\ 12x - 12 - 11x &= 11x + 7 - 11x \\ x - 12 &= 7 \\ x - 12 + 12 &= 7 + 12 \\ x &= 19 \end{aligned}$$

The solution is 19.

5.
$$\begin{aligned} x - \frac{3}{4} &= \frac{1}{2} \\ x - \frac{3}{4} + \frac{3}{4} &= \frac{1}{2} + \frac{3}{4} \\ x &= \frac{2}{4} + \frac{3}{4} = \frac{5}{4} \end{aligned}$$

The solution is $\frac{5}{4}$.

6. $y = mx + b$ for x

$$\begin{aligned} y &= mx + b \\ y - b &= mx + b - b \\ y - b &= mx \\ \frac{y - b}{m} &= \frac{mx}{m} \\ \frac{y - b}{m} &= x \quad \text{or} \quad x = \frac{y - b}{m} \end{aligned}$$

7. $A = PB$; $A = 120$; $P = 15\% = 0.15$

$$\begin{aligned} A &= PB \\ 120 &= 0.15 \cdot B \\ \frac{120}{0.15} &= \frac{0.15B}{0.15} \\ 800 &= B \end{aligned}$$

120 is 15% of 800.

8. $y = 4.5x - 46.7$; $y = 133.3$

$$\begin{aligned} 133.3 &= 4.5x - 46.7 \\ 133.3 + 46.7 &= 4.5x - 46.7 + 46.7 \\ 180 &= 4.5x \\ \frac{180}{4.5} &= \frac{4.5x}{4.5} \\ 40 &= x \end{aligned}$$

The car is traveling 40 miles per hour.

9.

$$2 - 6x \geq 2(5 - x)$$
$$2 - 6x \geq 10 - 2x$$
$$2 - 6x + 2x \geq 10 - 2x + 2x$$
$$2 - 4x \geq 10$$
$$2 - 4x - 2 \geq 10 - 2$$
$$-4x \geq 8$$
$$\frac{-4x}{-4} \leq \frac{8}{-4}$$
$$x \leq -2$$

$\{x|x \leq -2\}$

-5 -4 -3 -2 -1 0 1 2 3 4 5

10.

$$6(2 - x) > 12$$
$$12 - 6x > 12$$
$$12 - 6x - 12 > 12 - 12$$
$$-6x > 0$$
$$\frac{-6x}{-6} < \frac{0}{-6}$$
$$x < 0$$

$\{x|x < 0\}$

-5 -4 -3 -2 -1 0 1 2 3 4 5

11. Let $x =$ the number of hours the plumber worked.

$$18 + 35x = 228$$
$$35x = 210$$
$$x = 6$$

The plumber worked 6 hours.

12.

	Number of Liters ×	Percent of Acid =	Amount of Acid
40% Acid Solution	x	40%	$0.40x$
70% Acid Solution	$12 - x$	70%	$0.70(12 - x)$
50% Acid Solution	12	50%	$0.50(12)$

$$0.40x + 0.70(12 - x) = 0.50(12)$$
$$0.40x + 8.4 - 0.70x = 6$$
$$-0.30x + 8.4 = 6$$
$$-0.30x + 8.4 - 8.4 = 6 - 8.4$$
$$-0.30x = -2.4$$
$$\frac{-0.30x}{-0.30} = \frac{-2.4}{-0.30}$$
$$x = 8$$

To obtain 12 liters of a 50% acid solution, 8 liters of a 40% solution and $12 - 8 = 4$ liters of a 70% solution should be used.

13.

	Rate ×	Time =	Distance
Slower Car	40	x	$40x$
Faster Car	60	x	$60x$

$$40x + 60x = 350$$
$$100x = 350$$
$$x = 3.5$$

The cars will be 350 miles apart after 3.5 hours.

14. Let $x =$ the measure of the first angle.
Then $x + 20 =$ the measure of the second angle.
$2x =$ the measure of the third angle.

$$x + (x + 20) + 2x = 180$$
$$4x + 20 = 180$$
$$4x = 160$$
$$x = 40$$

Measure of first angle $= x = 40°$
Measure of second angle $= x + 20 = 60°$
Measure of third angle $= 2x = 80°$

15. $\frac{45}{2} = \frac{360}{x}$

$45x = 2 \cdot 360$

$45x = 720$

$\frac{45x}{45} = \frac{720}{45}$

$x = 16$

16. $2x - y = 4$

x-intercept: 2

y-intercept: -4

checkpoint: $(4, 4)$

Draw a line through $(2, 0), (0, -4)$, and $(4, 4)$.

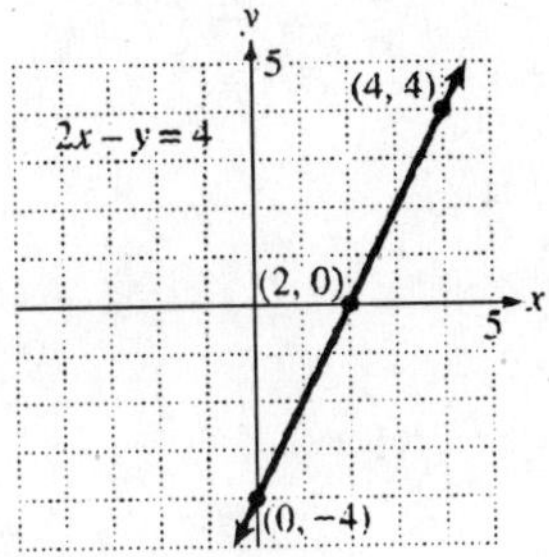

17. $y = x^2 - 5$

x	$y = x^2 - 5$	(x, y)
-3	$y = (-3)^2 - 5 = 4$	$(-3, 4)$
-2	$y = (-2)^2 - 5 = -1$	$(-2, -1)$
-1	$y = (-1)^2 - 5 = -4$	$(-1, -4)$
0	$y = 0^2 - 5 = -5$	$(0, -5)$
1	$y = 1^2 - 5 = -4$	$(1, -4)$
2	$y = 2^2 - 5 = -1$	$(2, -1)$
3	$y = 3^2 - 5 = 4$	$(3, 4)$

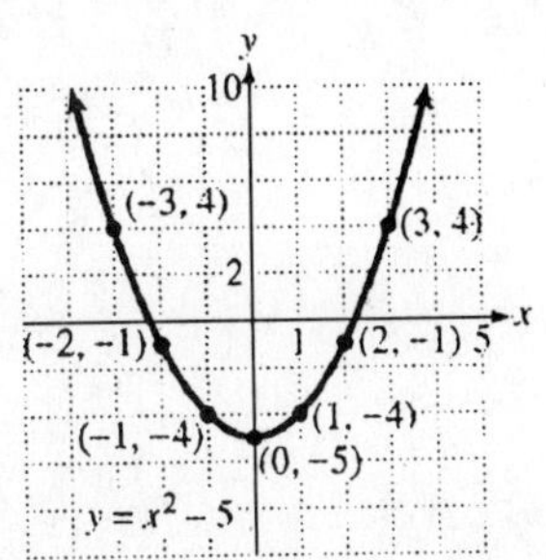

18. $y = -4x + 3$

slope $= -4 = \frac{-4}{1}$; y-intercept $= 3$

Plot $(0, 3)$. Move 4 units *down* and 1 unit to the *right* to reach the point $(3, -1)$. Draw a line through $(0, 3)$ and $(1, -1)$.

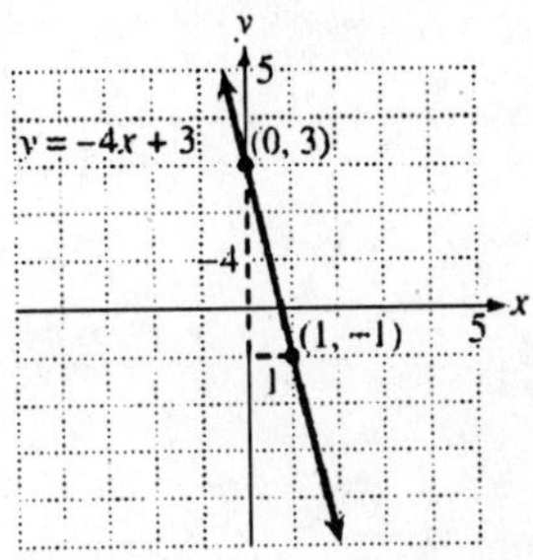

19. $3x - 2y < -6$

Graph the equation $3x - 2y = -6$ as a dashed line through $(-2, 0)$ and $(0, 3)$. Use $(0, 0)$ as a test point. Since $3(0) - 2(0) < -6$ is false, shade the half-plane not containing $(0, 0)$.

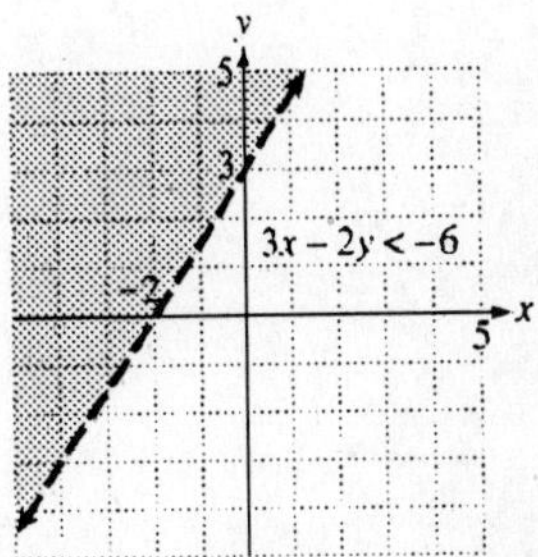

20. $y \geq -1$

Graph the horizontal line $y = -1$ as a solid line. Use $(0, 0)$ as a test point. Since $0 \geq -1$ is true, shade the half-plane containing $(0, 0)$.

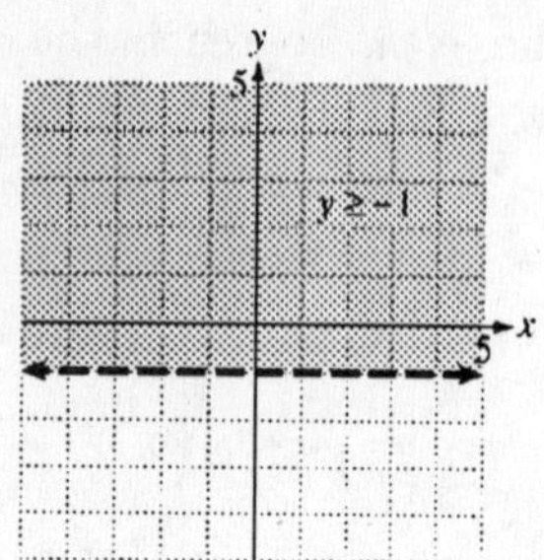

Chapter 5

SYSTEMS OF LINEAR EQUATIONS AND INEQUALITIES

5.1 Solving Systems of Linear Equations by Graphing

5.1 CHECK POINTS

CHECK POINT 1

$$2x - 3y = -4$$
$$2x + y = 4$$

a. $(1, 2)$

To determine if $(1, 2)$ is a solution of the system, replace x with 1 and y with 2 in both equations.

$2x - 3y = -4$	$2x + y = 4$
$2(1) - 3(2) \stackrel{?}{=} -4$	$2(1) + 2 \stackrel{?}{=} 4$
$2 - 6 \stackrel{?}{=} -4$	$2 + 2 \stackrel{?}{=} 4$
$-4 = -4$ true	$4 = 4$ true

The ordered pair $(1, 2)$ satisfies both equations, so it is a solution of the system.

b. $(7, 6)$

$2x - 3y = -4$	$2x + y = 4$
$2(7) - 3(6) \stackrel{?}{=} -4$	$2(7) + 6 \stackrel{?}{=} 4$
$14 - 18 \stackrel{?}{=} -4$	$14 + 6 \stackrel{?}{=} 4$
$-4 = -4$ true	$20 = 4$ false

The ordered pair $(7, 6)$ satisfies the first equation of the system, but not the second one. Because it fails to satisfy *both* equations, $(7, 6)$ is not a solution of the system.

CHECK POINT 2

$$2x + y = 6$$
$$2x - y = -2$$

Step 1 Graph the first equation.
Use intercepts to graph $2x + y = 6$.

x-intercept: Set $y = 0$.	y-intercept: Set $x = 0$.
$2x + 0 = 6$	$2 \cdot 0 + y = 6$
$2x = 6$	$y = 6$
$x = 3$	

The x-intercept is 3, so the line passes through $(3, 0)$. The y-intercept is 6, so the graph passes through $(0, 6)$.

Step 2 Graph the second equation on the same axes.
Use intercepts to graph $2x - y = -2$.

x-intercept:	y-intercept:
$2x - 0 = -2$	$2 \cdot 0 - y = -2$
$2x = -2$	$-y = -2$
$x = -1$	$y = 2$

The x-intercept is -1, so the line passes through $(-1, 0)$. The y-intercept is $(0, 2)$, so the line passes through $(0, 2)$.

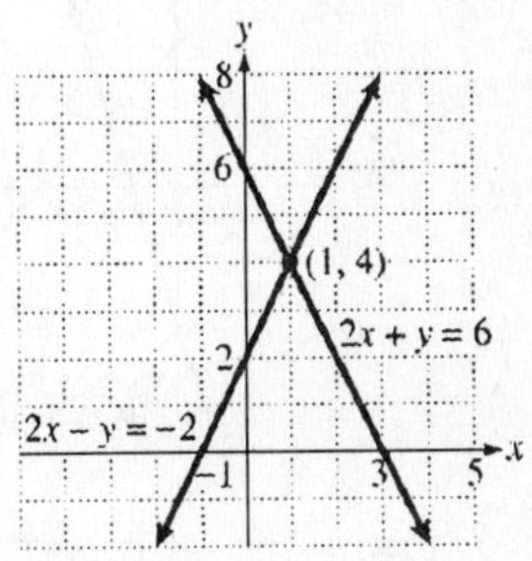

Step 3 Determine the coordinates of the intersection point.
From the graph, it appears that the lines intersect at $(1,4)$, so the apparent solution of the system is $(1,4)$.

Step 4 Check the solution in both equations.

$$\begin{aligned} 2x+y&=6 \\ 2(1)+4&\stackrel{?}{=}6 \\ 2+4&\stackrel{?}{=}6 \\ 6&=6 \text{ true} \end{aligned} \qquad \begin{aligned} 2x-y&=-2 \\ 2(1)-4&\stackrel{?}{=}-2 \\ 2-4&\stackrel{?}{=}-2 \\ -2&=-2 \text{ true} \end{aligned}$$

Because both equations are satisfied $(1,4)$ is the solution of the system.

CHECK POINT 3

$y=-x+6$
$y=3x-6$

Step 1 Graph $y=-x+6$ using the slope, $-1=\frac{-1}{1}$, and y-intercept, 6. Start at $(0,6)$ and move 1 unit down and 1 unit to the right to reach the point $(1,5)$. Draw a line through $(0,6)$ and $(1,5)$.

Step 2 Graph $y=3x-6$ on the same axes, using the slope, $3=\frac{3}{1}$, and the y-intercept, -6. Start at $(0,-6)$ and move 3 units up and 1 unit to the right to reach the point $(1,-3)$. Draw a line through $(0,-6)$ and $(1,-3)$.

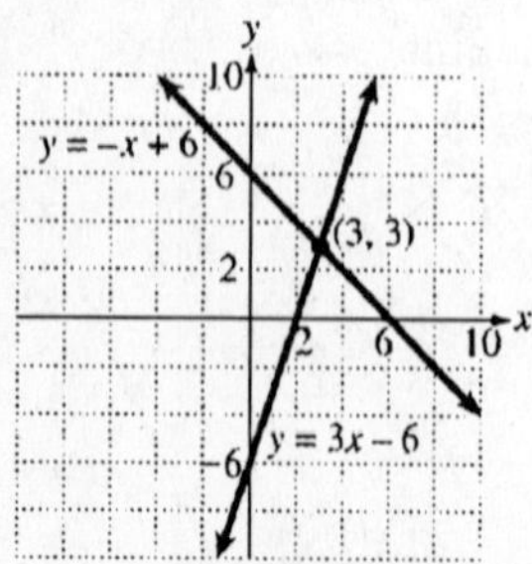

Step 3 From the graph, it appears that the lines intersect at $(3,3)$.

Step 4 Check the solution in both equations.

$$\begin{aligned} y&=-x+6 \\ 3&\stackrel{?}{=}-3+6 \\ 3&=3 \text{ true} \end{aligned} \qquad \begin{aligned} y&=3x-6 \\ 3&\stackrel{?}{=}3\cdot3-6 \\ 3&\stackrel{?}{=}9-6 \\ 3&=3 \text{ true} \end{aligned}$$

Because both equations are satisfied, $(3,3)$ is the solution.

CHECK POINT 4

$y=3x-2$
$y=3x+1$

Graph $y=3x-2$ using its slope, 3, and y-intercept, -2. Graph $y=3x+1$ on the same axes using its slope, 3, and y-intercept, 1.

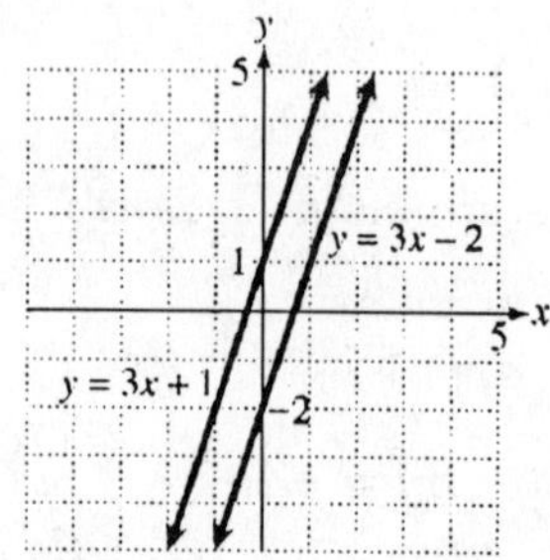

Because the two lines have the same slope, but different y-intercepts, they are parallel. The system is inconsistent and has no solution.

CHECK POINT 5

$x+y=3$
$2x+2y=6$

Use intercepts to graph each equation.

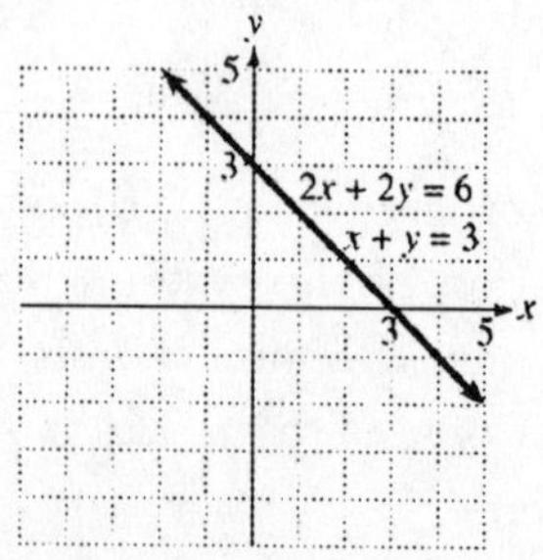

$x + y = 3$
x-intercept: 3, y-intercept: 3

$2x + 2y = 6$
x-intercept: 3, y-intercept: 3

Both lines have the same x-intercept, 3, and the same y-intercept, 3. Thus, the graphs of the two equations are the same line, and the equations have the same equations. Because there are infinitely many points on this line, the system has infinitely many solutions.

EXERCISE SET 5.1

1. $(2, 3)$

$$\begin{aligned} x + 3y &= 11 \\ 2 + 3(3) &\stackrel{?}{=} 11 \\ 2 + 9 &\stackrel{?}{=} 11 \\ 11 &= 11 \text{ true} \end{aligned}$$

$$\begin{aligned} x - 5y &= -13 \\ 2 - 5(3) &\stackrel{?}{=} -13 \\ 2 - 15 &\stackrel{?}{=} -13 \\ -13 &= -13 \text{ true} \end{aligned}$$

Since the ordered pair $(2, 3)$ satisfies both equations, it is solution of the given system of equations.

3. $(-3, -1)$

$$\begin{aligned} 5x - 11y &= -4 \\ 5(-3) - 11(-1) &\stackrel{?}{=} -4 \\ -15 + 11 &\stackrel{?}{=} -4 \\ -4 &= -4 \text{ true} \end{aligned}$$

$$\begin{aligned} 6x - 8y &= -10 \\ 6(-3) - 8(-1) &\stackrel{?}{=} -10 \\ -18 + 8 &\stackrel{?}{=} -10 \\ -10 &= -10 \text{ true} \end{aligned}$$

$(-3, -1)$ is a solution of the given system.

5. $(2, 5)$

$$\begin{aligned} 2x + 3y &= 17 \\ 2(2) + 3(5) &\stackrel{?}{=} 17 \\ 4 + 15 &\stackrel{?}{=} 17 \\ 19 &= 17 \text{ false} \end{aligned}$$

$$\begin{aligned} x + 4y &= 16 \\ 2 + 4(5) &\stackrel{?}{=} 16 \\ 2 + 20 &\stackrel{?}{=} 16 \\ 22 &= 16 \text{ false} \end{aligned}$$

Since $(2, 5)$ fails to satisfy either equation, it is not a solution of the given system. *Note:* Since $(2, 5)$ does not satisfy the first equation, it is not necessary to test it in the second one.

7. $\left(\frac{1}{3}, 1\right)$

$$\begin{aligned} 6x - 9y &= -7 \\ 6\left(\tfrac{1}{3}\right) - 9(1) &\stackrel{?}{=} -7 \\ 2 - 9 &\stackrel{?}{=} -7 \\ -7 &= -7 \text{ true} \end{aligned}$$

$$\begin{aligned} 9x + 5y &= 8 \\ 9\left(\tfrac{1}{3}\right) + 5(1) &\stackrel{?}{=} 8 \\ 3 + 5 &\stackrel{?}{=} 8 \\ 8 &= 8 \text{ true} \end{aligned}$$

$\left(\frac{1}{3}, 1\right)$ is a solution of the given system.

9. $(8, 5)$

$$\begin{aligned} 5x - 4y &= 20 \\ 5(8) - 4(5) &\stackrel{?}{=} 20 \\ 40 - 20 &\stackrel{?}{=} 20 \\ 20 &= 20 \text{ true} \end{aligned}$$

$$\begin{aligned} 3y &= 2x + 1 \\ 3(5) &\stackrel{?}{=} 2(8) + 1 \\ 15 &\stackrel{?}{=} 16 + 1 \\ 15 &= 17 \text{ false} \end{aligned}$$

$(8, 5)$ fails to satisfy *both* equations; it is not a solution of the given system.

11. $x + y = 6$
$x - y = 2$

Graph both equations on the same axes.

$x + y = 6$:

x-intercept $= 6$; y-intercept $= 6$

$x - y = 2$:

x-intercept $= 2$; y-intercept $= -2$

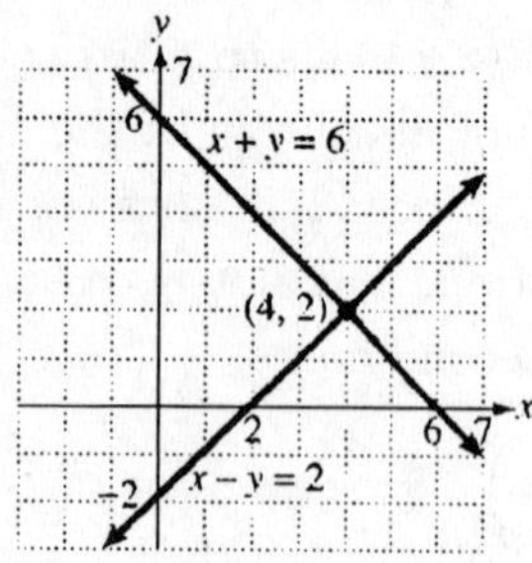

The lines appear to intersect at $(4, 2)$. Check this solution in both equations of the system.

$$\begin{array}{ll} x + y = 6 & x - y = 2 \\ 4 + 2 \stackrel{?}{=} 6 & 4 - 2 \stackrel{?}{=} 2 \\ 6 = 6 \text{ true} & 2 = 2 \text{ true} \end{array}$$

Because both equations are satisfied, $(4, 2)$ is the solution of the system.

In Exercises 13–41, all apparent solutions found from the graphs should be checked in both equations of the given system, as illustrated in the solution for Exercise 1. The checks will not be shown here.

13. $x + y = 1$
$y - x = 3$

Graph both equations on the same axes.

$x + y = 1$:

x-intercept $= 1$; y-intercept $= 1$

$y - x = 3$

x-intercept $= -3$; y-intercept $= 3$

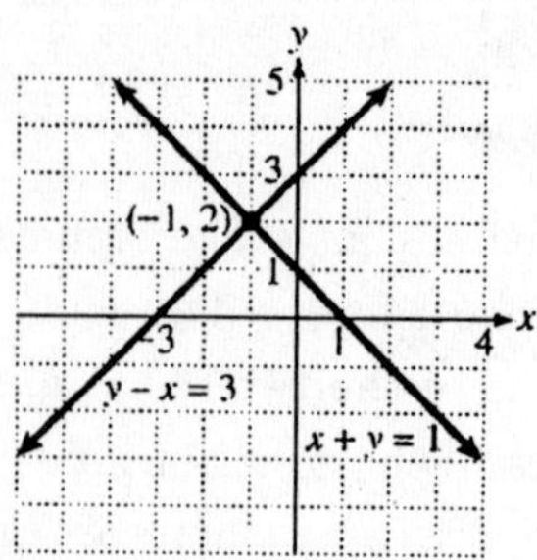

The lines intercept at $(-1, 2)$. $(-1, 2)$ is the solution of the system.

15. $2x - 3y = 6$
$4x + 3y = 12$

Graph both equations.

$2x - 3y = 6$:

x-intercept $= 3$; y-intercept $= -2$

$4x + 3y = 12$:

x-intercept $= 3$; y-intercept $= 4$

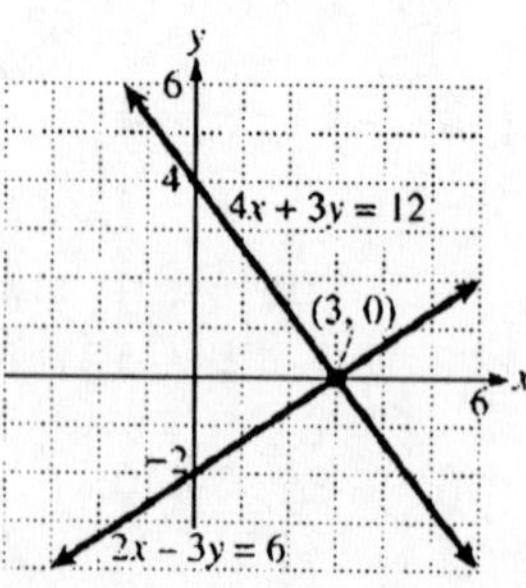

Solution: $(3, 0)$

17. $4x + y = 4$
$3x - y = 3$

Graph both equations.

x-intercept $= 1$; y-intercept $= 4$

$3x - y = 3$:

x-intercept $= 1$; y-intercept $= -3$

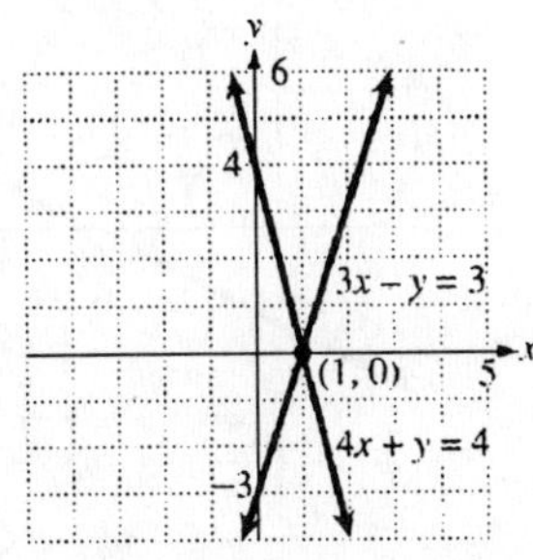

Solution: $(1, 0)$

19. $y = x + 5$
$y = -x + 3$

Graph both equations.

$y = x + 5$:

slope $= 1$; y-intercept $= 5$

$y = -x + 3$:

slope $= -1$; y-intercept $= 3$

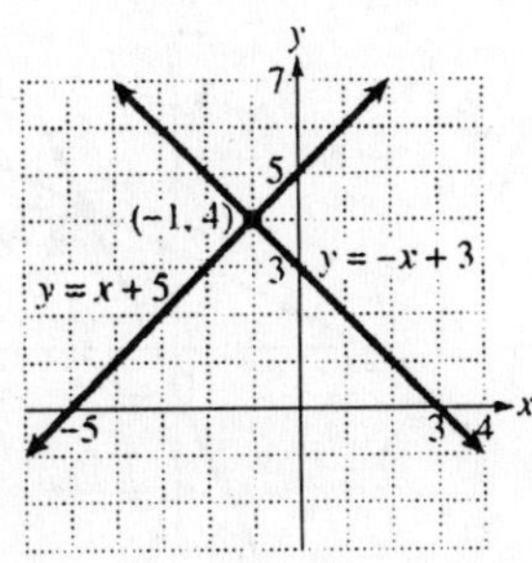

Solution: $(-1, 4)$

21. $y = 2x$
$y = -x + 6$

Graph both equations.

$y = 2x$:

slope $= 2$; y-intercept $= 0$

$y = -x + 6$:

slope $= -1$; y-intercept $= 6$

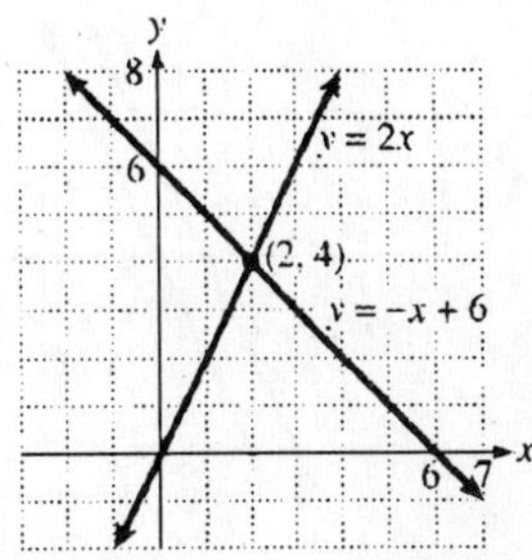

Solution: $(2, 4)$

23. $y = -2x + 3$
$y = -x + 1$

Graph both equations.

$y = -2x + 3$:

slope $= -2$; y-intercept $= 3$

$y = -x + 1$:

slope $= -1$; y-intercept $= 1$

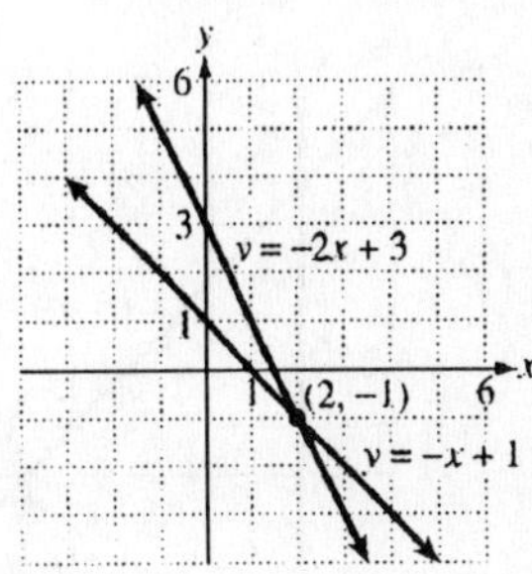

Solution: $(2, -1)$

25. $y = 2x - 1$
$y = 2x + 1$

Graph both equations.

$y = 2x - 1$:

slope $= 2$; y-intercept $= -1$

$y = 2x + 1$:

slope $= 2$; y-intercept $= 1$

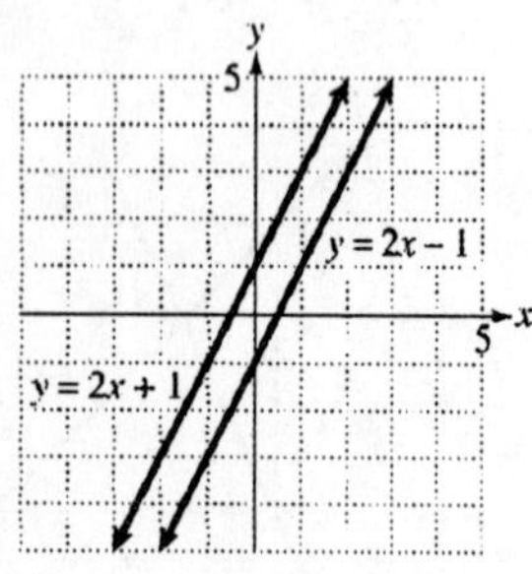

The two lines are parallel. (Note that they have the same slope but different y-intercepts.) The system as no solution.

27. $x + y = 4$
$x = -2$

Graph each equation.

$x + y = 4$

x-intercept $= 4$; y-intercept $= 4$

$x = -2$

vertical line with x-intercept -2

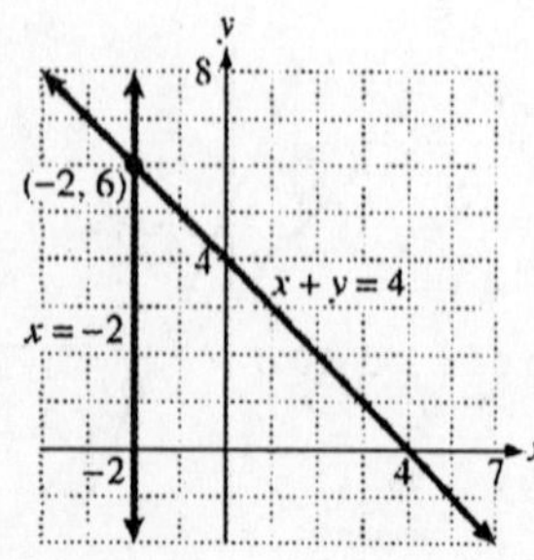

Solution: $(-2, 6)$

29. $x - 2y = 4$
$2x - 4y = 8$

Graph each equation.

$x - 2y = 4$

x-intercept $= 4$; y-intercept $= -2$

$2x - 4y = 8$

x-intercept $= 4$; y-intercept $= -2$

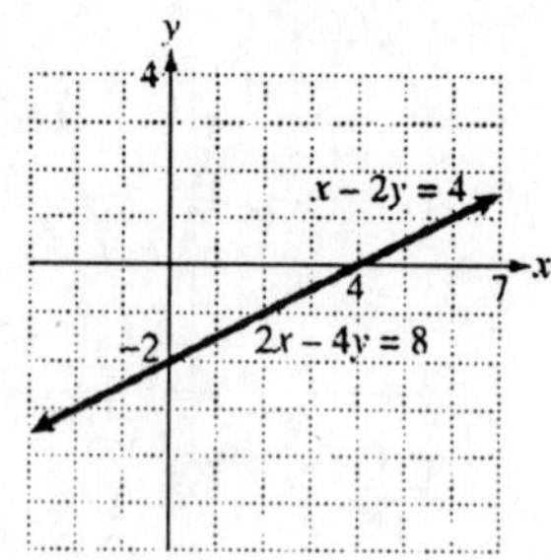

The graph of the two equations are the same line. (Note that they have the same slope and same y-intercept.)
Because the lines coincide, the system has infinitely many solutions.

31. $y = 2x - 1$
$x - 2y = -4$

Graph both lines.

$y = 2x - 1$

slope $= 2$; y-intercept $= -1$

$x - 2y = -4$

x-intercept $= -4$; y-intercept $= 2$

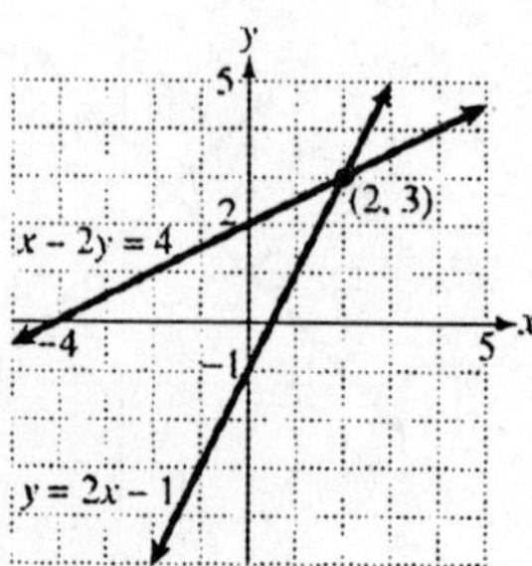

Solution: $(2, 3)$

33. $x + y = 5$
$2x + 2y = 12$

Graph both lines.

$x + y = 5$

x-intercept $= 5$; y-intercept $= 5$

$2x + 2y = 12$

x-intercept $= 6$; y-intercept $= 6$

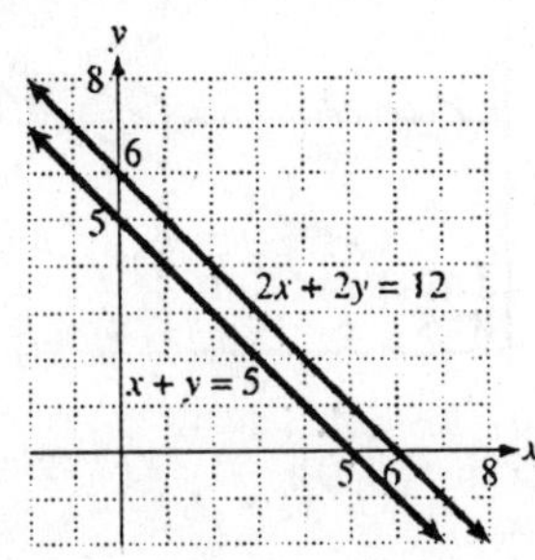

The lines are parallel, so the system has no solution.

35. $x - y = 0$
$y = x$

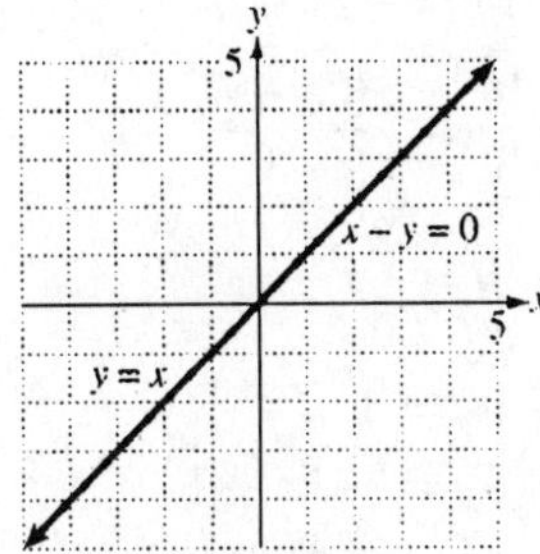

Because the lines coincide, the system has an infinite number of solutions.

37. $x = 2$
$y = 4$

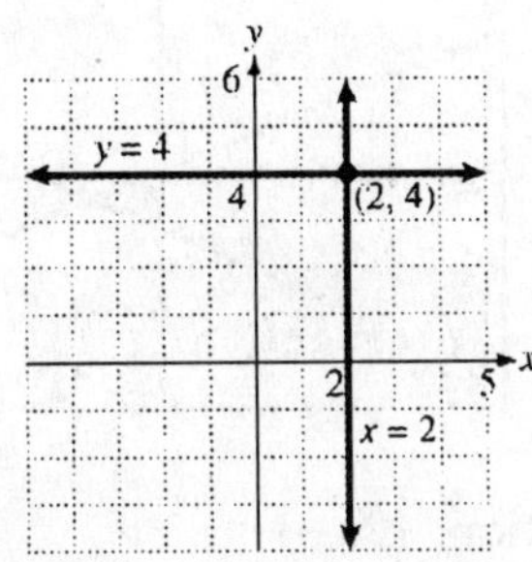

The vertical and horizontal line intersect at $(2, 4)$.
Solution: $(2, 4)$

39. $x = 2$
$x = -1$

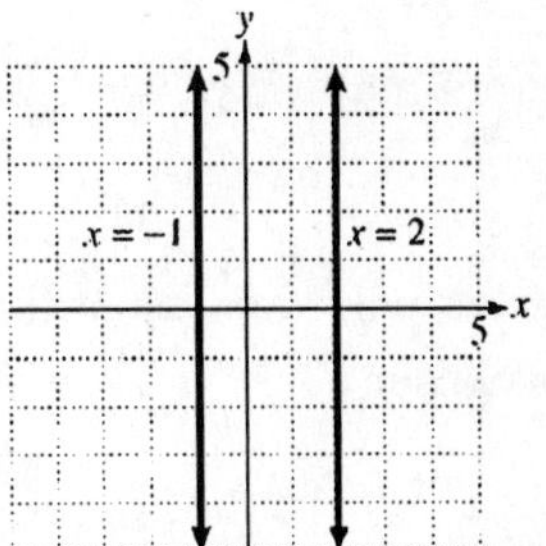

The two vertical lines are parallel, so the system has no solution.

41. $y = 0$
$y = 4$

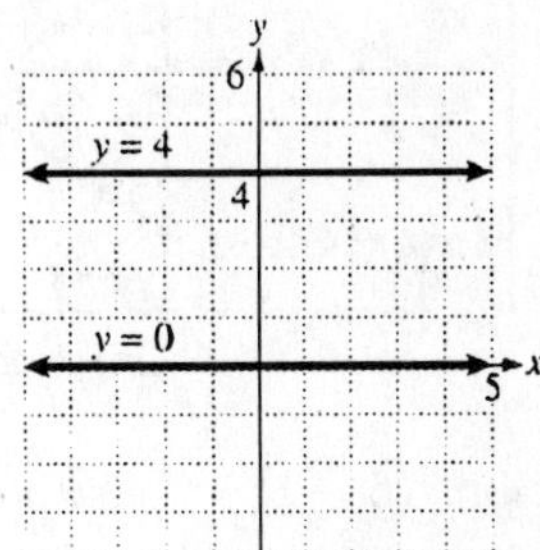

The two horizontal lines are parallel, so the system has no solution.

43. **a.** The intersection point is approximately $(1996, 40)$. This means that mothers 30 years old and older in Massachusetts had about 40 thousand (40,000) births in 1996.

b. Since 1996, there have been more births in Massachusetts to mothers 30 years old and older than to those under 30 years old.

For Exercises 45–51, answers may vary.

53. Statement c is true.
If two lines have two points in common, they must coincide (be the same line), so they will have equal slopes and equal y-intercepts.

55. Answers may vary.

57. Answers will vary according to the exercises chosen.

59. $y = -x + 5$
$y = x - 7$

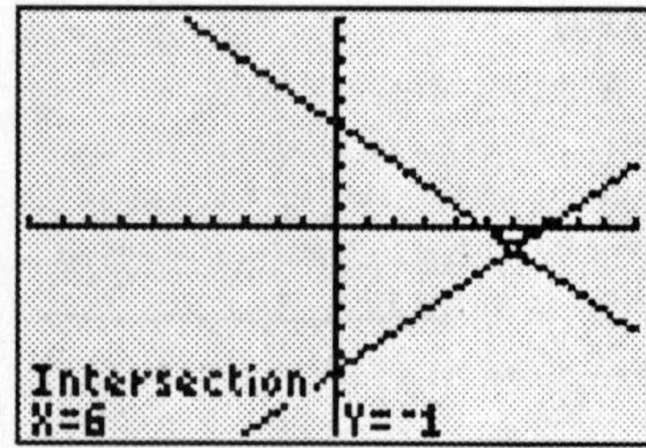

Solution: $(6, -1)$

61. $2x - 3y = 6$
$4x + 3y = 12$

In order to enter the equations into a graphing calculator, each of them must be solved for y.

$$2x - 3y = 6$$
$$-3y = -2x + 6$$
$$\frac{-3y}{-3} = \frac{-2x + 6}{-3}$$
$$y = \frac{2}{3}x - 2$$

$$4x + 3y = 12$$
$$3y = -4x + 12$$
$$\frac{3y}{3} = \frac{-4x + 12}{3}$$
$$y = -\frac{4}{3}x + 4$$

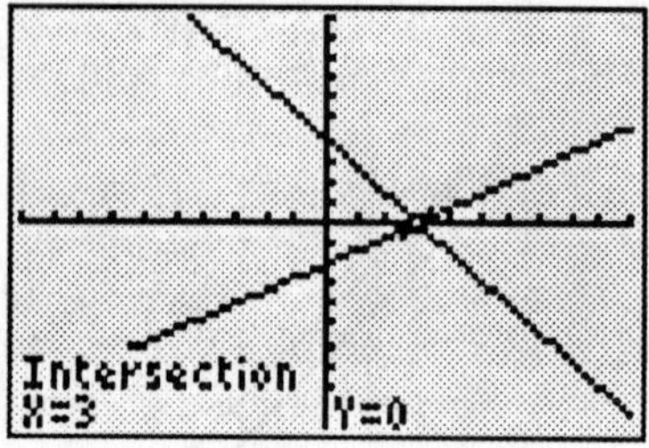

Solution: $(3, 0)$

63. $2x - 3y = 7$
$3x + 5y = 1$

Solve each equation for y.

$$2x - 3y = 7$$
$$-3y = -2x + 7$$
$$\frac{-3y}{-3} = \frac{-2x + 7}{-3}$$
$$y = \frac{2}{3}x - \frac{7}{3}$$

$$3x + 5y = 1$$
$$5y = -3x + 1$$
$$\frac{5y}{5} = \frac{-3x + 1}{5}$$
$$y = -\frac{3}{5}x + \frac{1}{5}$$

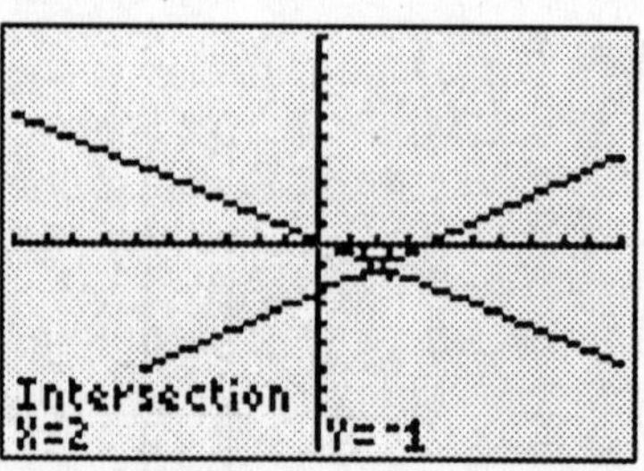

Solution: $(2, -1)$

65. $y = -\frac{1}{2}x + 2$

$y = \frac{3}{4}x + 7$

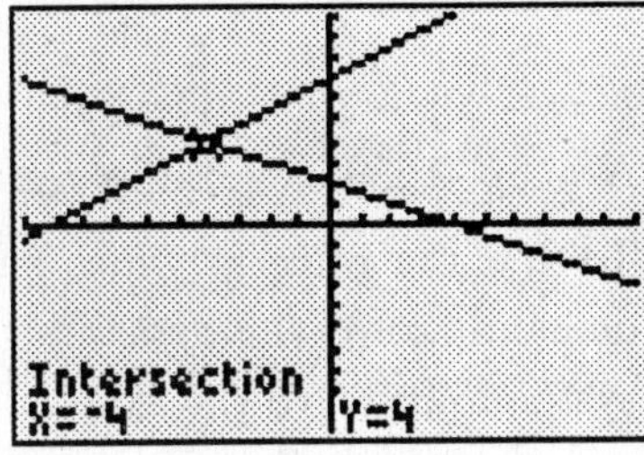

Solution: $(-4, 4)$

Review Exercises

66. $-3 - (-9) = -12$

67. $-3 - (-9) = -3 + 9 = 6$

68. $-3(-9) = 27$

5.2 Solving Systems of Linear Equations by the Substitution Method

5.2 CHECK POINTS

CHECK POINT 1

$$y = 5x - 13$$
$$2x + 3y = 12$$

Step 1 Solve either of the equations for one variable in terms of the other.
This step has already been done. The first equation has y solved in terms of x.

Step 2 Substitute the expression from step 1 into the other equation.

$$2x + 3(5x - 13) = 12$$

The variable y has been eliminated.

Step 3 Solve the resulting equation containing one variable.

$$2x + 15x - 39 = 12$$
$$17x - 39 = 12$$
$$17x = 51$$
$$x = 3$$

Step 4 Back-substitute the obtained value into the equation from Step 1.

$$y = 5x - 13$$
$$y = 5(3) - 13$$
$$y = 15 - 13 = 2$$

With $x = 3$ and $y = 2$, the proposed solution is $(3, 2)$.

Step 5 Check the proposed solution in both of the system's given equations.

$y = 5x - 13$	$2x + 3y = 12$
$2 \stackrel{?}{=} 5(3) - 13$	$2(3) + 3(2) \stackrel{?}{=} 12$
$2 \stackrel{?}{=} 15 - 13$	$6 + 6 \stackrel{?}{=} 12$
$2 = 2$ true	$12 = 12$

The ordered pair $(3, 2)$ satisfies both equations, so the system's solution is $(3, 2)$.

CHECK POINT 2

$$3x + 2y = -1$$
$$x - y = 3$$

Step 1 Solve the second equation for x.

$$x - y = 3$$
$$x = y + 3$$

Step 2 Substitute $y + 3$ for x in the first equation.

$$3x + 2y = -1$$
$$3(y + 3) + 2y = -1$$

Step 3 Solve the resulting equation.

$$3(y + 3) + 2y = -1$$
$$3y + 9 + 2y = -1$$
$$5y + 9 = -1$$
$$5y = -10$$
$$y = -2$$

Step 4 Back-substitute -2 for y in $3x + 2y = -1$ and solve for x.

$$3x + 2y = -1$$
$$3x + 2(-2) = -1$$
$$3x - 4 = -1$$
$$3x = 3$$
$$x = 1$$

With $x = 1$ and $y = -2$, the proposed solution is $(1, -2)$.

Step 5 Substitute 1 for x and -2 for y in both equations of the original system to verify that the solution is $(1, -2)$.

CHECK POINT 3

$$3x + y = -5$$
$$y = -3x + 3$$

The variable y is isolated in the second equation. Substitute $-3x + 3$ for y in the first equation.

$$3x + y = -5$$
$$3x + (-3x + 3) = -5$$
$$3x - 3x - 3 = -5$$
$$-3 = -5 \text{ false}$$

The false statement $-3 = -5$ indicates that the system is inconsistent and has no solution.

CHECK POINT 4

$$y = 3x - 4$$
$$9x - 3y = 12$$

The variable y is isolated in the first equation. Substitute $3x - 4$ for y in the second equation.

$$9x - 3y = 12$$
$$9x - 3(3x - 4) = 12$$
$$9x - 9x + 12 = 12$$
$$12 = 12 \text{ true}$$

The true statement $12 = 12$ indicates that the system contains dependent equations and has infinitely many solutions.

CHECK POINT 5

$N = -20p + 1000$ Demand model
$N = 5p + 250$ Supply model

To find the price at which supply equals demand, solve the demand-supply linear system. To solve the system by the substitution method, substitute $5p + 250$ for N in the first equation.

$$N = -20p + 1000$$
$$5p + 250 = -20p + 1000$$
$$25p + 250 = 1000$$
$$25p = 750$$
$$p = 30$$

The price at which supply and demand are equal is \$30.
To find the value of N, back substitute into either equation of the system.
Using the supply model,

$$N = 5p + 250$$
$$N = 5 \cdot 30 + 250 = 400.$$

Thus, at \$30, 400 units will be supplied and sold each week.

EXERCISE SET 5.2

1. $x + y = 4$
$y = 3x$

Step 1 The second equation is already solved for y.

Step 2 Substitute $3x$ for y in the first equation.

$$x + y = 4$$
$$x + (3x) = 4$$

Step 3 Solve this equation of x.

$$4x = 4$$
$$x = 1$$

Step 4 Back-substitute 1 for x into the second equation

$$y = 3x$$
$$y = 3(1) = 3$$

The proposed solution is $(1, 3)$.

Step 5 Check $(1, 3)$ in both of equations of the system.

$$\begin{array}{ll} x + y = 4 & y = 3x \\ 1 + 3 \stackrel{?}{=} 4 & 3 \stackrel{?}{=} 3(1) \\ 4 = 4 \text{ true} & 3 = 3 \text{ true} \end{array}$$

The ordered pair $(1, 3)$ satisfies both equations, so is the solution of the system.

In Exercises 3–31, the five-step method illustrated in the solution for Exercise 1 should be used. In the remaining solutions, these steps will not be listed and the checks will not be shown.

3. $x + 3y = 8$
$y = 2x - 9$

Substitute $2x-9$ for y in the first equation and solve for x.

$$\begin{aligned} x + 3y &= 8 \\ x + 3(2x - 9) &= 8 \\ x + 6x - 27 &= 8 \\ 7x - 27 &= 8 \\ 7x &= 35 \\ x &= 5 \end{aligned}$$

Back-substitute 5 for x into the second equation and solve for y.

$$y = 2x - 9$$
$$y = 2(5) - 9 = 1$$

Solution: $(5, 1)$

5. $x + 3y = 5$
$4x + 5y = 13$

Solve the first equation for x.

$$x + 3y = 5$$
$$x = 5 - 3y$$

Substitute $5-3y$ for x in the second equation and solve for y.

$$\begin{aligned} 4x + 5y &= 13 \\ 4(5 - 3y) + 5y &= 13 \\ 20 - 12y + 5y &= 13 \\ 20 - 7y &= 13 \\ -7y &= -7 \\ y &= 1 \end{aligned}$$

Back-substitute 1 for y in the equation $x = 5 - 3y$ and solve for x.

$$x = 5 - 3y$$
$$x = 5 - 3(1) = 2$$

Solution: $(2, 1)$

7. $2x - y = -5$
$x + 5y = 14$

Solve the second equation for x.

$$x + 5y = 14$$
$$x = 14 - 5y$$

Substitute $14-5y$ for x in the first equation.

$$\begin{aligned} 2(14 - 5y) - y &= -5 \\ 28 - 10y - y &= -5 \\ 28 - 11y &= -5 \\ -11y &= -33 \\ y &= 3 \end{aligned}$$

Back-substitute.

$$x = 14 - 5y$$
$$x = 14 - 5(3) = -1$$

Solution: $(-1, 3)$

9. $2x - y = 3$
$5x - 2y = 10$

Solve the first equation for y.

$$\begin{aligned} 2x - y &= 3 \\ -y &= -2x + 3 \\ y &= 2x - 3 \end{aligned}$$

Substitute $2x-3$ for y in the second equation.

$$\begin{aligned} 5x - 2(2x - 3) &= 10 \\ 5x - 4x + 6 &= 10 \\ x + 6 &= 10 \\ x &= 4 \end{aligned}$$

Back-substitute.

$$\begin{aligned} y &= 2x - 3 \\ y &= 2(4) - 3 = 5 \end{aligned}$$

Solution: $(4, 5)$

11. $x + 8y = 6$
$2x + 4y = -3$

Solve the first equation for x.

$$\begin{aligned} x + 8y &= 6 \\ x &= 6 - 8y \end{aligned}$$

$$\begin{aligned} 2x + 4y &= -3 \\ 2(6 - 8y) + 4y &= -3 \\ 12 - 16y + 4y &= -3 \\ 12 - 12y &= -3 \\ -12y &= -15 \\ y &= \frac{15}{12} = \frac{5}{4} \end{aligned}$$

Back-substitute

$$\begin{aligned} x &= 6 - 8y \\ x &= 6 - 8\left(\frac{5}{4}\right) \\ x &= 6 - 10 = -4 \end{aligned}$$

Solution: $(-4, \frac{5}{4})$

13. $x = 9 - 2y$
$x + 2y = 13$

The first equation is already solve for x. Substitute $9-2y$ for x in the second equation.

$$\begin{aligned} x + 2y &= 13 \\ (9 - 2y) + 2y &= 13 \\ 9 &= 13 \text{ false} \end{aligned}$$

The false statement $9 = 13$ indicates that the system is inconsistent and has no solution.

15. $y = 3x - 5$
$21x - 35 = 7y$

Substitute $3x-5$ for y in the second equation.

$$\begin{aligned} 21x - 35 &= 7y \\ 21x - 35 &= 7(3x - 5) \\ 21x - 35 &= 21x - 35 \\ 21x - 35 - 21x &= 21x - 35 - 21x \\ -35 &= -35 \text{ true} \end{aligned}$$

The true statement $-35 = -35$ indicates that the system contains dependent equation and has infinitely many solutions.

17. $5x + 2y = 0$
$x - 3y = 0$

Solve the second equation for x.

$$\begin{aligned} x - 3y &= 0 \\ x &= 3y \end{aligned}$$

Substitute $3y$ for x in the first equation.

$$\begin{aligned} 5x + 2y &= 0 \\ 5(3y) + 2y &= 0 \\ 15y + 2y &= 0 \\ 17y &= 0 \\ y &= 0 \end{aligned}$$

Back-substitute.

$$\begin{aligned} x &= 3y \\ x &= 3(0) = 0 \end{aligned}$$

Solution: $(0, 0)$

19. $2x + 5y = -4$
$3x - y = 11$

Solve the second equation for y.

$$\begin{aligned} 3x - y &= 11 \\ -y &= -3x + 11 \\ y &= 3x - 11 \end{aligned}$$

Substitute $3x-11$ for y in the first equation.

$$\begin{aligned} 2x + 5(3x - 11) &= -4 \\ 2x + 15x - 55 &= -4 \\ 17x - 55 &= -4 \\ 17x &= 51 \\ x &= 3 \end{aligned}$$

Back-substitute.

$$\begin{aligned} y &= 3x - 11 \\ y &= 3(3) - 11 = -2 \end{aligned}$$

Solution: $(3, -2)$

21. $2(x - 1) - y = -3$
$y = 2x + 3$

Substitute $2x+3$ for y in the first equation..

$$\begin{aligned} 2(x - 1) - (2x + 3) &= -3 \\ 2x - 2 - 2x - 3 &= -3 \\ -5 &= -3 \text{ false} \end{aligned}$$

The false statement $-5 = -3$ indicates that the system has no solution.

23. $x = 4y - 2$
$x = 6y + 8$

Substitute $4y-2$ for x in the second equation.

$$\begin{aligned} 4y - 2 &= 6y + 8 \\ -2y - 2 &= 8 \\ -2y &= 10 \\ y &= -5 \end{aligned}$$

Back-substitute in the first equation.

$$\begin{aligned} x &= 4y - 2 \\ x &= 4(-5) - 2 = -22 \end{aligned}$$

Solution: $(-22, -5)$

25. $y = 2x - 8$
$y = 3x - 13$

Substitute $2x-8$ for y in the second equation.

$$\begin{aligned} 2x - 8 &= 3x - 13 \\ -x - 8 &= -13 \\ -x &= -5 \\ x &= 5 \end{aligned}$$

Back-substitute in the first equation.

$$\begin{aligned} y &= 2x - 8 \\ y &= 2(5) - 8 = 2 \end{aligned}$$

Solution: $(5, 2)$

27. $y = \frac{1}{3}x + \frac{2}{3}$
$y = \frac{5}{7}x - 2$

First, clear both equations of fractions. Multiply the first equation by the LCD, 3.

$$\begin{aligned} 3y &= 3\left(\frac{1}{3}x + \frac{2}{3}\right) \\ 3y &= 3x + 2 \end{aligned}$$

Multiply the second equation by the LCD, 7.

$$\begin{aligned} 7y &= 7\left(\frac{5}{7}x - 2\right) \\ 7y &= 5x - 14 \end{aligned}$$

Now solve the new system

$$\begin{aligned} 3y &= x + 2 \\ 7y &= 5x - 14 \end{aligned}$$

Solve the first of these equations for x.

$$3y - 2 = x \quad \text{or} \quad x = 3y - 2$$

Substitute $3y - 2$ for x in the second equation of the new system.

$$\begin{aligned} 7y &= 5x - 14 \\ 7y &= 5(3y - 2) - 14 \\ 7y &= 15y - 10 - 14 \\ 7y &= 25y - 24 \\ -8y &= -24 \\ y &= 3 \end{aligned}$$

Back-substitute.

$$x = 3y - 2$$
$$x = 3(3) - 2 = 7$$

Solution: $(7, 3)$

29. $\dfrac{x}{6} - \dfrac{y}{2} = \dfrac{1}{3}$

$x + 2y = -3$

Clear the first equation of fractions by multiplying 6.

$$6\left(\frac{x}{6} - \frac{y}{2}\right) = 6\left(\frac{1}{3}\right)$$
$$x - 3y = 3y = 2$$

Solve this equation for x.

$$x = 3y + 2$$

Substitute $3y+2$ for x in the second equation of the system.

$$(3y + 2) + 2y = -3$$
$$5y + 2 = -3$$
$$5y = -5$$
$$y = -1$$

Back-substitute.

$$x = 3y + 2$$
$$x = 3(-1) + 2 = -1$$

Solution: $(-1, -1)$

31. $2x - 3y = 8 - 2x$

$3x + 4y = x + 3y + 14$

Simplify the first equation.

$$2x - 3y = 8 - 2x$$
$$2x - 3y + 2x = 8 - 2x + 2x$$
$$4x - 3y = 8$$

Simplify the second equation.

$$3x + 4y = x + 3y + 14$$
$$3x + 4y - x - 3y = x + 3y + 14 - x - 3y$$
$$2x + y = 14$$

Solve the last equation for y.

$$y = 14 - 2x$$

Substitute $14 - 2x$ for y in the equation $4x - 3y = 8$.

$$4x - 3y = 8$$
$$4x - 3(14 - 2x) = 8$$
$$4x - 42 + 6x = 8$$
$$10x - 42 = 8$$
$$10x = 50$$
$$x = 5$$

Back-substitute.

$$y = 14 - 2x$$
$$y = 14 - 2(5) = 4$$

Solution: $(5, 4)$

33. $N = -25p + 7500$ Demand model

$N = 5p + 6000$ Supply model

a. Substitute 40 for p in both models.

$$N = -25p + 7500;\ p = 40$$
$$N = -25(40) + 7500 = 6500$$
$$N = 5p + 6000;\ p = 40$$
$$N = 5(40) + 6000 = 6200$$

At \$40 per ticket, 6500 tickets can be sold, but only 6200 tickets w ill be supplied.

b. To find the price at which supply and demand are equal, solve the demand-supply linear system. Substitute $-25p+7500$ for N in the supply equation.

$$N = 5p + 6000$$
$$-25p + 7500 = 5p + 6000$$
$$-30 + 7500 = 6000$$
$$-30p = -1500$$
$$p = 50$$

If $p = 50$,

$$N = 5(50) + 6000 = 6250.$$

Supply and demand are equation when the ticket price is \$50. At this price, 6250 tickets are supplied and sold.

35. $y = 1.2x + 1080$ Weekly costs
$y = 1.6x$ Weekly revenue

The station will break even when costs = revenue. Solve the cost-revenue linear system. Substitute $1.6x$ for y in the cost equation.

$$\begin{aligned} 1.6x &= 1.2x + 1080 \\ 0.4x &= 1080 \\ \frac{0.4x}{0.4} &= \frac{1080}{0.4} \\ x &= 2700 \end{aligned}$$

The station will break even if 2700 gallons of gasoline are sold weekly.

37. $M = -0.41x + 22$ Whites
$M = -0.18x + 10$ Blacks

To find out when infant mortality will be the same for blacks and whites, solve this system. Substitute $-0.41x + 22$ for M in the second equation.

$$\begin{aligned} M &= -0.18x + 10 \\ -0.41x + 22 &= -0.18x + 10 \\ -0.41x + 0.18x &= -0.18x + 10 + 0.18x \\ -0.23x + 22 &= 10 \\ -0.23x + 22 - 22 &= 10 - 22 \\ -0.23x &= -12 \\ \frac{-0.23x}{-0.23} &= \frac{-12}{-0.23} \\ x &\approx 52 \end{aligned}$$

$x = 52$ corresponds to the year $1980 + 52 = 2032$.
Substitute 52 for x in either equation of the system.

$$M = -0.18(52) + 10 = 0.6$$

The model projects that the infant mortality for both groups will be about 0.6 deaths per 1000 live births in the year 2032.

For Exercises 39–43, answers may vary.

45. $x = 3 - y - z$
$2x + y - z = -6$
$3x - y + z = 11$

This is a system of three linear equations with three variables. It can be solved by the substitution method.
First substitute $3 - y - z$ for x in the second equation.

$$\begin{aligned} 2x + y - z &= -6 \\ 2(3 - y - z) + y - z &= -6 \\ 6 - 2y - 2z + y - z &= -6 \\ 6 - y - 3z &= -6 \\ 6 - y - 3z - 6 &= -6 - 6 \\ -y - 3z &= -12 \end{aligned}$$

Solve this equation for y.

$$\begin{aligned} -y &= -12 + 3z \\ y &= 12 - 3z \end{aligned}$$

Now substitute $3 - y - z$ in the third equation of the given system.

$$\begin{aligned} 3x - y + z &= 11 \\ 3(3 - y - z) - y + z &= 11 \\ 9 - 3y - 3z - y + z &= 11 \\ 9 - 4y - 2z &= 11 \end{aligned}$$

Substitute $12 - 3z$ in the last equation.

$$\begin{aligned} 9 - 4y - 2z &= 11 \\ 9 - 4(12 - 3z) - 2z &= 11 \\ 9 - 48 + 12z - 2z &= 11 \\ -39 + 10z &= 11 \\ 10z &= 50 \\ z &= 5 \end{aligned}$$

Now back-substitute in the equation $y = 12 - 3z$ to find the value of y.

$$y = 12 - 3z$$
$$y = 12 - 3(5) = -3$$

Finally, back-substitute in the equation $x = 3 - y - z$ to find the value of x.

$$x = 3 - y - z$$
$$x = 3 - (-3) - 5 = 1$$

Thus, $x = 1, y = -3$, and $z = 5$. The solution should be checked by verifying that these values satisfy all three equations of the given system.

Review Exercises

47. $4x + 6y = 12$
x-intercept: 3
y-intercept: 2
checkpoint: $(-3, 4)$
Draw a line through $(3, 0), (0, 2)$, and $(-3, 4)$.

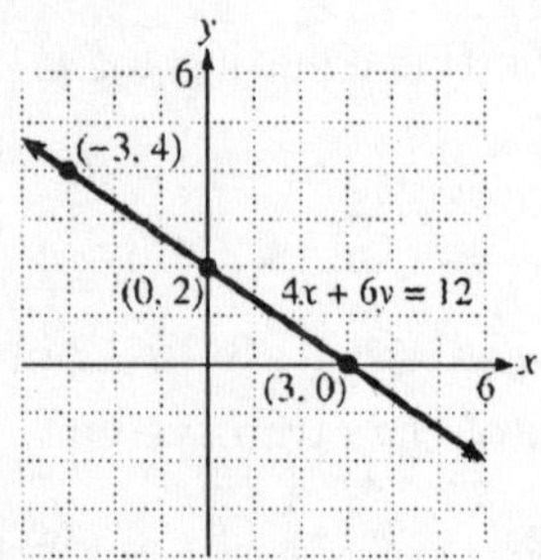

48. $4(x + 1) = 25 + 3(x - 3)$
$$4x + 4 = 25 + 3x - 9$$
$$x + 4 = 16$$
$$x = 12$$

The solution is 12.

49. The integers in the given set are $-73, 0$, and $\frac{3}{1}$ $(= 3)$.

5.3 Solving Systems of Linear Equations by the Addition Method

5.3 CHECK POINTS

CHECK POINT 1

$$x + y = 5$$
$$x - y = 9$$

To solve this system by the addition method, add the two left sides and two right sides. This will eliminate the y-terms.

$$\begin{aligned} x + y &= 5 \\ \underline{x - y} &= \underline{9} \\ 2x + 0y &= 14 \\ 2x &= 14 \\ x &= 7 \end{aligned}$$

Back-substitute 7 for x into either of the original equations to find y.

$$x + y = 5$$
$$7 + y = 5$$
$$y = -2$$

Check the proposed solution, $(7, -2)$, in both equations of the original system. This will verify that the solution is $(7, -2)$.

CHECK POINT 2

$$4x - y = 22$$
$$3x + 4y = 26$$

To eliminate y, multiply each term of the first equation by 4 and then add the equations.

$$\begin{aligned} 16x - 4y &= 88 \\ \underline{3x + 4y} &= \underline{26} \\ 19x + 0y &= 114 \\ 19x &= 114 \\ x &= 6 \end{aligned}$$

Back-substitute 6 for x into either one of the given equations.

$$\begin{aligned} 4x - y &= 22 \\ 4 \cdot 6 - y &= 22 \\ 24 - y &= 22 \\ -y &= -2 \\ y &= 2 \end{aligned}$$

Check to verify that the solution is $(6, 2)$.

CHECK POINT 3

$4x + 5y = 3$
$2x - 3y = 7$

To eliminate x, multiply the second equation by -2 and then add the equations.

$$\begin{array}{r} 4x + 5y = 3 \\ \underline{-4x + 6y = -14} \\ 11y = -11 \\ y = -1 \end{array}$$

Back-substitute into the first equation.

$$\begin{aligned} 4x + 5y &= 3 \\ 4x + 5(-1) &= 3 \\ 4x - 5 &= 3 \\ 4x &= 8 \\ x &= 2 \end{aligned}$$

Check to verify that the solution is $(2, -1)$.

CHECK POINT 4

$2x = 9 + 3y$
$4y = 8 - 3x$

First, rewrite both equations in the form $Ax + By = C$.

$$\begin{aligned} 2x - 3y &= 9 \\ 3x + 4y &= 8 \end{aligned}$$

To eliminate y, multiply the first equation by 4 and the second equation by 3. Then add the equations.

$$\begin{array}{r} 8x - 12y = 36 \\ \underline{9x + 12y = 24} \\ 17x \qquad = 60 \\ x = \dfrac{60}{17} \end{array}$$

To avoid working with fractions, instead of substituting $\frac{60}{17}$ for x in one of the given equations, use the addition method again, this time to eliminate x. Go back to the system

$$\begin{aligned} 2x - 3y &= 9 \\ 3x + 4y &= 8 \end{aligned}$$

and multiply the first equation by 3 and the second equation by -2. Then add the equations.

$$\begin{array}{r} 6x - 9y = 27 \\ \underline{-6x - 8y = -16} \\ -17y = 11 \\ x = -\dfrac{11}{17} \end{array}$$

Check by hand or with a calculator to verify that the solution of the system is $\left(\frac{60}{17}, -\frac{11}{17}\right)$.

CHECK POINT 5

$x + 2y = 4$
$3x + 6y = 13$

To eliminate x, multiply first equation by -3 and then add the equations.

$$\begin{array}{r} -3x - 6y = -12 \\ \underline{3x + 6y = 13} \\ 0 = 1 \end{array}$$

Notice that y has also been eliminated. The false statement $0 = 1$ indicates that the system is inconsistent and has no solution.

CHECK POINT 6

$$\begin{aligned} x - 5y &= 7 \\ 3x - 15y &= 21 \end{aligned}$$

To eliminate x, multiply first equation by -3 and then add the equations.

$$\begin{aligned} -3x + 15y &= 7 \\ \underline{3x - 15y} &= \underline{21} \\ 0 &= 0 \end{aligned}$$

Notice that y has also been eliminated. The true statement $0 = 0$ indicates that the system contains dependent equations and has infinitely many solutions.

EXERCISE SET 5.3

1. $x + y = 1$
$x - y = 3$

Add the equations to eliminate the y-terms.

$$\begin{aligned} x + y &= 1 \\ \underline{x - y} &= \underline{3} \\ 2x \quad &= 4 \end{aligned}$$

Now solve for x.

$$\begin{aligned} 2x &= 4 \\ x &= 2 \end{aligned}$$

Back-substitute into either of the original equations to solve for y.

$$\begin{aligned} x + y &= 1 \\ 2 + y &= 1 \\ y &= -1 \end{aligned}$$

The proposed solution, $(2, -1)$, satisfies both equations of the system since $2 + (-1) = 1$ and $2 - (-1) = 3$.
Solution: $(2, -1)$

3.
$$\begin{aligned} 2x + 3y &= 6 \\ \underline{2x - 3y} &= \underline{6} \\ 4x &= 12 \\ x &= 3 \end{aligned}$$

$$\begin{aligned} 2(3) + 3y &= 6 \\ 3y &= 0 \\ y &= 0 \end{aligned}$$

Solution: $(3, 0)$

5.
$$\begin{aligned} x + 2y &= 7 \\ \underline{-x + 3y} &= \underline{18} \\ 5y &= 25 \\ y &= 5 \end{aligned}$$

$$\begin{aligned} x + 2(5) &= 7 \\ x + 10 &= 7 \\ x &= -3 \end{aligned}$$

Solution: $(-3, 5)$

7.
$$\begin{aligned} 5x - y &= 14 \\ \underline{-5x + 2y} &= \underline{-13} \\ y &= 1 \end{aligned}$$

$$\begin{aligned} 5x - 1 &= 14 \\ 5x &= 15 \\ x &= 3 \end{aligned}$$

Solution: $(3, 1)$

9.
$$\begin{aligned} x + 2y &= 2 \\ -4x + 3y &= 25 \end{aligned}$$

Multiply equation 1 by 4.
Don't change equation 2.

$$\begin{aligned} 4x + 8y &= 8 \\ \underline{-4x + 3y} &= \underline{25} \\ 11y &= 33 \\ y &= 3 \end{aligned}$$

$$\begin{aligned} x + 2(3) &= 2 \\ x + 6 &= 2 \\ x &= -4 \end{aligned}$$

Solution: $(-4, 3)$

11. $2x - 7y = 2$
$3x + y = -20$

No change to equation 1.
Multiply equation 2 by 7.

$$\begin{aligned} 2x - 7y &= 2 \\ 21x + 7y &= -140 \\ \hline 23x &= -138 \\ x &= -6 \end{aligned}$$

$$\begin{aligned} 3(-6) + y &= -20 \\ -18 + y &= -20 \\ y &= -2 \end{aligned}$$

Solution: $(-6, -2)$

13. $x + 5y = -1$
$2x + 7y = 1$

Multiply equation 1 by -2.
No change to equation 2.

$$\begin{aligned} -2x - 10y &= 2 \\ 2x + 7y &= 1 \\ \hline -3y &= 3 \\ y &= -1 \end{aligned}$$

$$\begin{aligned} x + 5(-1) &= -1 \\ x - 5 &= -1 \\ x &= 4 \end{aligned}$$

Solution: $(4, -1)$

15. $4x + 3y = 15$
$2x - 5y = 1$

No change to equation 1.
Multiply equation 2 by -2.

$$\begin{aligned} 4x + 3y &= 15 \\ -4x + 10y &= -2 \\ \hline 13y &= 13 \\ y &= 1 \end{aligned}$$

$$\begin{aligned} 2x - 5(1) &= 1 \\ 2x &= 6 \\ x &= 3 \end{aligned}$$

Solution: $(3, 1)$

17. $3x - 4y = 11$
$2x + 3y = -4$

Multiply equation 1 by 3.
Multiply equation 2 by 4.

$$\begin{aligned} 9x - 12y &= 33 \\ 8x + 12y &= -16 \\ \hline 17x &= 17 \\ x &= 1 \end{aligned}$$

$$\begin{aligned} 2(1) + 3y &= -4 \\ 3y &= -6 \\ y &= -2 \end{aligned}$$

Solution: $(1, -2)$

19. $3x + 2y = -1$
$-2x + 7y = 9$

Multiply equation 1 by 2.
Multiply equation 2 by 3.

$$\begin{aligned} 6x + 4y &= -2 \\ -6x + 21y &= 27 \\ \hline 25y &= 25 \\ y &= 1 \end{aligned}$$

$$\begin{aligned} 3x + 2(1) &= -1 \\ 3x &= -3 \\ x &= -1 \end{aligned}$$

Solution: $(-1, 1)$

21. $3x = 2y + 7$
$5x = 2y + 13$

Rewrite:

$$\begin{aligned} 3x - 2y &= 7 \\ 5x - 2y &= 13 \end{aligned}$$

Multiply equation 1 by -1.
No change to equation 2.

$$\begin{aligned} -3x + 2y &= -7 \\ 5x - 2y &= 13 \\ \hline 2x &= 6 \\ x &= 3 \end{aligned}$$

$$\begin{aligned} 3(3) &= 2y + 7 \\ 2 &= 2y \\ 1 &= y \end{aligned}$$

Solution: $(3, 1)$

23. $2x = 3y - 6$
$-6x + 12y = 6$

Rewrite equation 1.

$$2x - 3y = -4$$

Multiply this equation by 3 and add to equation 2 of the original system.

$$\begin{aligned} 6x - 9y &= -12 \\ -6x + 12y &= 6 \\ \hline 3y &= -6 \\ y &= -2 \end{aligned}$$

$$\begin{aligned} 2x - 3(-2) &= -4 \\ 2x + 6 &= -4 \\ 2x &= -10 \\ x &= -5 \end{aligned}$$

Solution: $(-5, -2)$

25. $2x - y = 3$
$4x + 4y = -1$

Multiply equation 1 by 4.
No change to equation 2.

$$\begin{aligned} 8x - 4y &= 12 \\ 4x + 4y &= -1 \\ \hline 12x &= 11 \\ x &= \frac{11}{12} \end{aligned}$$

Instead of back-substituting $\frac{11}{12}$ and working with fractions, go back to the original system. Multiply equation 1 by -2 and add the result to equation 2 to eliminate x.

$$\begin{aligned} -4x + 2y &= -6 \\ 4x + 4y &= -1 \\ \hline 6y &= -7 \\ y &= -\frac{7}{6} \end{aligned}$$

Solution: $(\frac{11}{12}, -\frac{7}{6})$

27. $4x = 5 + 2y$
$2x + 3y = 4$

Rewrite equation 1.
Multiply equation 2 by -2.

$$\begin{aligned} 4x - 2y &= 5 \\ -4x - 6y &= -8 \\ \hline -8x &= -3 \\ y &= \frac{3}{8} \end{aligned}$$

Instead of back-substituting $\frac{3}{8}$ and working with fractions, go back to the original system, with rewritten equation 1.

$$\begin{aligned} 4x - 2y &= 5 \\ -4x - 6y &= -8 \end{aligned}$$

Multiply the first of these equations by -3 and add to the second.

$$\begin{aligned} -12x + 6y &= -15 \\ -4x - 6y &= -8 \\ \hline -16x &= -23 \\ x &= \frac{23}{16} \end{aligned}$$

Solution: $(\frac{23}{16}, \frac{3}{8})$

29. $3x - y = 1$
$3x - y = 2$

Multiply equation 1 by -1.
No change to equation 2.

$$\begin{aligned} 3x + y &= -1 \\ 3x - y &= 2 \\ \hline 0 &= 1 \text{ false} \end{aligned}$$

The false statement $0 = 1$ indicates that the system is inconsistent and has no solution.

31. $$\begin{aligned} x + 3y &= 2 \\ 3x + 9y &= 6 \end{aligned}$$

Multiply equation 1 by -3.
No change to equation 2.

$$\begin{aligned} -3x - 9y &= -6 \\ 3x + 9y &= 6 \\ \hline 0 &= 0 \text{ true} \end{aligned}$$

The true statement $0 = 0$ indicates that the system has infinitely many solutions.

33. $$\begin{aligned} 7x - 3y &= 4 \\ -14x + 6y &= -7 \end{aligned}$$

Multiply equation 1 by 2.
No change to equation 2.

$$\begin{aligned} 14x - 6y &= 8 \\ -14x + 6y &= -7 \\ \hline 0 &= 1 \end{aligned}$$

The false statement $0 = 1$ indicates that the system has no solution.

35. $$\begin{aligned} 5x + y &= 2 \\ 3x + y &= 1 \end{aligned}$$

No change to equation 1.
Multiply equation 2 by -1.

$$\begin{aligned} 5x + y &= 2 \\ -3x - y &= -2 \\ \hline 2x &= 1 \\ x &= \frac{1}{2} \end{aligned}$$

$$3\left(\frac{1}{2}\right) + y = 1$$

$$y = -\frac{1}{2}$$

Solution: $(\frac{1}{2}, -\frac{1}{2})$

37. $$\begin{aligned} x &= 5 - 3y \\ 2x + 6y &= 10 \end{aligned}$$

Rewrite equation 1.

$$x + 3y = 5$$

Multiply this equation by -2.
No change to equation 2.

$$\begin{aligned} -2x - 6y &= -10 \\ 2x + 6y &= 10 \\ 0 &= 0 \end{aligned}$$

The true statement $0 = 0$ indicates that the system has infinitely many solutions.

39. $$\begin{aligned} 4(3x - y) &= 0 \\ 3(x + 3) &= 10y \end{aligned}$$

Rewrite both equations.
First equation:

$$12x - 4y = 0$$

Second equation:

$$\begin{aligned} 3x + 9 &= 10y \\ 3x - 10y &= -9 \end{aligned}$$

Now solve the system

$$\begin{aligned} 12x - 4y &= 0 \\ 3x - 10y &= -9. \end{aligned}$$

Multiply the second equation by -4 and add the result to the first equation.

$$\begin{aligned} 12x - 4y &= 0 \\ -12x + 40y &= 36 \\ \hline 36y &= 36 \\ y &= 1 \end{aligned}$$

$$\begin{aligned} 12x - 4y &= 0 \\ 12x - 4(1) &= 0 \\ 12x &= 4 \\ x &= \frac{1}{3} \end{aligned}$$

Solution: $(\frac{1}{3}, 1)$

41. $x + y = 11$

$\frac{x}{5} + \frac{y}{7} = 1$

Multiply the second equation by the LCD, 35, to clear fractions.

$$35\left(\frac{x}{5} + \frac{y}{7}\right) = 35(1)$$
$$7x + 5y = 35$$

Now solve the system

$$\begin{aligned} x + y &= 11 \\ 7x + 5y &= 35. \end{aligned}$$

Multiply the first equation by -5 and add the result to the second equation.

$$\begin{aligned} -5x - 5y &= -55 \\ 7x + 5y &= 35 \\ \hline 2x &= -20 \\ x &= -10 \end{aligned}$$

$$\begin{aligned} -10 + y &= 11 \\ y &= 21 \end{aligned}$$

Solution: $(-10, 21)$

43. $\frac{4}{5}x - y = -1$

$\frac{2}{5}x + y = 1$

Multiply equation 1 by 5.
Multiply equation 2 by 5.

$$\begin{aligned} 4x - 5y &= -5 \\ 2x + 5y &= 5 \\ \hline 6x &= 0 \\ x &= 0 \end{aligned}$$

$$\frac{2}{5}(0) + y = 1$$
$$y = 1$$

Solution: $(0, 1)$

45. $3x - 2y = 8$

$x = -2y$

The substitution method is a good choice because the second equation is already solved for x.
Substitute $-2y$ for x in the first equation.

$$\begin{aligned} 3x - 2y &= 8 \\ 3(-2y) - 2y &= 8 \\ -6y - 2y &= 8 \\ -8y &= 8 \\ y &= -1 \end{aligned}$$

Back-substitute -1 for y into the second equation.

$$\begin{aligned} x &= -2y \\ x &= -2(-1) = 2 \end{aligned}$$

Solution: $(2, -1)$

47. $3x + 2y = -3$

$2x - 5y = 17$

The addition method is a good choice because both equations are written in the form $Ax + By = C$.
Multiply equation 1 by 2.
Multiply equation 2 by -3.

$$\begin{aligned} 6x + 4y &= {-6} \\ -6x + 15y &= -51 \\ \hline 19y &= -57 \\ y &= -3 \end{aligned}$$

$$\begin{aligned} 3x + 2(-3) &= -3 \\ 3x - 6 &= -3 \\ 3x &= 3 \\ x &= 1 \end{aligned}$$

Solution: $(1, -3)$

49. $3x - 2y = 6$
$y = 3$

The substitution method is a good choice because the second equation is already solved for y.
Substitute 3 for y in the first equation.

$$\begin{aligned} 3x - 2y &= 6 \\ 3x - 2(3) &= 6 \\ 3x - 6 &= 6 \\ 3x &= 12 \\ x &= 4 \end{aligned}$$

It is not necessary to back-substitute to find the value of y because $y = 3$ is one of the equations of the given system.
Solution: $(4, 3)$

51. $y = 2x + 1$
$y = 2x - 3$

The substitution method is a good choice, because both equations are already solved for y.
Substitute $2x+1$ for y in the second equation.

$$\begin{aligned} y &= 2x - 3 \\ 2x + 1 &= 2x - 3 \\ 2x + 1 - 2x &= 2x - 3 - 2x \\ 1 &= -3 \text{ false} \end{aligned}$$

The false statement $1 = -3$ indicates that the system has no solution.

53. $2(x + 2y) = 6$
$3(x + 2y - 3) = 0$

The addition method is a good choice since the left-hand sides of the equation can easily be simplified to give equations of the form $Ax + By = C$.
First equation:

$$2x + 4y = 6$$

Second equation:

$$\begin{aligned} 3x + 6y - 9 &= 0 \\ 3x + 6y &= 9 \end{aligned}$$

Now solve the system

$$\begin{aligned} 2x + 4y &= 6 \\ 3x + 6y &= 9. \end{aligned}$$

Multiply the first equation by -3 and the second by 2. Add the results.

$$\begin{array}{r} -6x - 12y = -18 \\ \underline{6x + 12y = 18} \\ 0 = 0 \text{ true} \end{array}$$

The true statement $0 = 0$ indicates that the original system has infinitely many solutions.

55. $3y = 2x$
$2x + 9y = 24$

The substitution method is a good choice because the first equation can easily be solved for one of the variables. Solve this equation for y.

$$\begin{aligned} 3y &= 2x \\ y &= \frac{2}{3}x \end{aligned}$$

Substitute $\frac{2}{3}x$ for y in the second equation.

$$\begin{aligned} 2x + 9y &= 24 \\ 2x + 9\left(\frac{2}{3}x\right) &= 24 \\ 2x + 6x &= 24 \\ 8x &= 24 \\ x &= 3 \end{aligned}$$

Back-substitute 3 for x in the equation $y = \frac{2}{3}x$.

$$\begin{aligned} y &= \frac{2}{3}x \\ y &= \frac{2}{3}(3) = 2 \end{aligned}$$

Solution: $(3, 2)$

For Exercises 57–61, answers may vary.

63. $\frac{3x}{5} + \frac{4y}{5} = 1$
$\frac{x}{4} - \frac{3y}{8} = -1$

Multiply the first equation by the LCD, 5.

$$5\left(\frac{3x}{5} + \frac{4y}{5}\right) = 5(1)$$
$$3x + 4y = 5$$

Multiply the second equation by the LCD, 8.

$$8\left(\frac{x}{4} - \frac{3y}{8}\right) = 8(-1)$$
$$2x - 3y = -8$$

Now solve the system

$$3x + 4y = 5$$
$$2x - 3y = -8.$$

Multiply the first of these equations by 3 and the second by 4. Then add the equations.

$$\begin{aligned} 9x + 12y &= 15 \\ 8x - 12y &= -32 \\ \hline 17x \quad &= -17 \\ x &= -1 \end{aligned}$$

Back-substitute -1 for x into the equation that was obtained when the first equation was cleared of fractions.

$$\begin{aligned} 3x + 4y &= 5 \\ 3(-1) + 4y &= 5 \\ -3 + 4y &= 5 \\ 4y &= 8 \\ y &= 2 \end{aligned}$$

Solution: $(-1, 2)$

65. $0.5x - 0.2y = 0.5$
$0.4x + 0.7y = 0.4$

Each equation can be "cleared of decimals" by multiplying by 10.
First equation:

$$\begin{aligned} 10(0.5x - 0.2y) &= 10(0.5) \\ 5x - 2y &= 5 \end{aligned}$$

Second equation:

$$\begin{aligned} 10(0.4x + 0.7y) &= 10(0.4) \\ 4x + 7y &= 4 \end{aligned}$$

Now solve the system

$$5x - 2y = 5$$
$$4x + 7y = 4.$$

Multiply the first of these equations by 4 and the second by -5. Then add the equations.

$$\begin{aligned} 20x - \ 8y &= \ 20 \\ -20x - 35y &= -20 \\ \hline -43y &= \ 0 \\ y &= 0 \end{aligned}$$

Back-substitute 0 for y into the equation obtained when the first equation was cleared of decimals.

$$\begin{aligned} 5x - 2y &= 5 \\ 5x - 2(0) &= 5 \\ 5x &= 5 \\ x &= 1 \end{aligned}$$

Solution: $(1, 0)$

67. Answers will vary according to the exercises chosen.

69. $x = 5y$
$2x - 3y = 7$

Rewrite the first equation in $Ax+By = C$ form.

$$x - 5y = 0$$

Then solve the system

$$x - 5y = 0$$
$$2x - 3y = 7.$$

Enter 2 for two equations in two variables, then the coefficients and constant term for the equations, one equation at a time.
After entering all the numbers, press SOLVE and read the solutions displayed on the screen.
Note: This feature is only available on the TI-85 and higher-numbered TI calculators.
Solution: $(5, 1)$

Review Exercises

71. Let $x =$ the unknown number.

$$5x = x + 40$$
$$40x = 40$$
$$x = 10$$

The number is 10.

72. Because the x-coordinate is negative and the y-coordinate is positive, $(-\frac{3}{2}, 15)$ is located in quadrant II.

73.
$$29{,}700 + 150x = 5000 + 1100x$$
$$29{,}700 + 150x - 1100x = 5000 + 1100x - 1100x$$
$$29{,}700 - 950x = 5000$$
$$29{,}700 - 950x - 29{,}700 = 5000 - 29{,}700$$
$$-950x = -24{,}700$$
$$\frac{-950x}{-950} = \frac{-24{,}700}{-950}$$
$$x = 26$$

The solution is 26.

5.4 Problem Solving Using Systems of Equations

5.4 CHECK POINTS

CHECK POINT 1

Step 1 Use variables to represent unknown quantities.
Let x represent the weight of a bustard.
Let y represent the weight of a condor.

Step 2 Write a system of equations describing the problem's conditions.
Because two bustards and three condors weigh 173 pounds,

$$2x + 3y = 173.$$

Because the bustard's weight increased by double the condor's weight is 100 pounds,

$$x + 2y = 100.$$

Step 3 Solve the system and answer the problem's question. The system

$$2x + 3y = 173$$
$$x + 2y = 100$$

can be solved by substitution or addition. Either method will work well. We will use the addition method.
Multiply the second equation by -2.
Then add the equations.

$$\begin{array}{r} 2x + 3y = 173 \\ \underline{-2x - 4y = -200} \\ -y = {-27} \\ y = 27 \end{array}$$

Back-substitute 27 for y in the second equation of the original system.

$$x + 2y = 100$$
$$x + 2(27) = 100$$
$$x + 54 = 100$$
$$x = 46$$

A bustard weighs 46 pounds and a condor weighs 27 pounds.
This solution should be checked in the original wording of the problem.

CHECK POINT 2

Let x represent the number of calories in a Quarter Pounder and y represent the number of calories in a Whopper.
The conditions in the problem can be described by the system

$$\begin{aligned} 2x + 3y &= 2607 \\ x + y &= 1009. \end{aligned}$$

To solve this system by the addition method, multiply the second equation by -2; then add the equations.

$$\begin{aligned} 2x + 3y &= 2607 \\ -2x - 2y &= -2018 \\ \hline y &= 589 \end{aligned}$$

To find x, back-substitute into the second equation of the second equation.

$$\begin{aligned} x + y &= 1009 \\ x + 589 &= 1009 \\ x &= 420 \end{aligned}$$

A Quarter Pounder has 420 calories and a Whopper has 589 calories.

CHECK POINT 3

Let x represent the length of the lot and y represent the width.

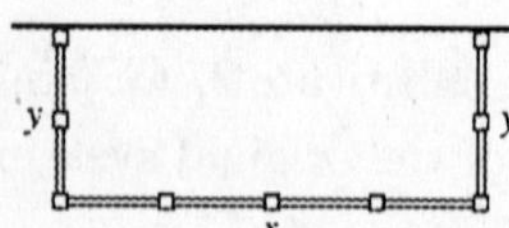

The perimeter of the lot is 360 feet, so

$$2x + 2y = 360.$$

The cost of fencing three sides is 3280, so

$$20x + 8(2y) = 3280$$

or

$$20x + 16y = 3280.$$

We now have the system

$$\begin{aligned} 2x + 2y &= 360 \\ 20x + 16y &= 3280. \end{aligned}$$

To solve this system by the addition method, multiply the first equation by -10, then add the equations.

$$\begin{aligned} -20x - 20y &= -3600 \\ 20x + 16y &= 3280 \\ \hline -4y &= -320 \\ y &= 80 \end{aligned}$$

To find x, back-substitute in the first equation of the original system.

$$\begin{aligned} 2x + 2y &= 360 \\ 2x + 2(80) &= 360 \\ 2x + 160 &= 360 \\ 2x &= 200 \\ x &= 100 \end{aligned}$$

The lot is 100 feet long and 80 feet wide. Its dimensions are 100 feet by 80 feet.

CHECK POINT 4

Let x represent the number of years the heating system is used. Let y represent the total cost for the heating system.

Electric system:

$$y = 5000 + 1100x$$

Gas system:

$$y = 12{,}000 + 700x$$

To find how long it will take for the heating costs to be equal, solve the system formed by these two equations.
The substitution method will work well because y is isolated in second equation. Substitute $5000 + 1100x$ for y in the second equation.

$$\begin{aligned} 5000 + 1100x &= 12{,}000 + 700x \\ 5000 + 400x &= 12{,}000 \\ 400 &= 7000 \\ x &= 17.5 \end{aligned}$$

To find y, back-substitute 17.5 for x in the first equation.

$$\begin{aligned} y &= 5000 + 1100(17.5) \\ y &= 5000 + 19{,}250 \\ y &= 24{,}250 \end{aligned}$$

The total cost for electric and gas heating will be the same after 17.5 years. At the time, the cost for each system will be \$24,250.

EXERCISE SET 5.4

1. $x + y = 7$
$x - y = -1$

Solve the system by the addition method.

$$\begin{array}{rl} x + y &= \ \ 7 \\ x - y &= -1 \\ \hline 2x \quad &= \ \ 6 \\ x &= 3 \end{array}$$

$$\begin{aligned} 3 + y &= 7 \\ y &= 4 \end{aligned}$$

The numbers are 3 and 4.

3. $3x - y = 1$
$x + 2y = 12$

Solve the system by the addition method. Multiply the first equation by 2 and add the result to the second equation.

$$\begin{array}{rl} 6x - 2y &= \ \ 2 \\ x + 2y &= 12 \\ \hline 7x \quad &= 14 \\ x &= \ \ 2 \end{array}$$

$$\begin{aligned} 3(2) - y &= 1 \\ 6 - y &= 1 \\ -y &= -5 \\ y &= 5 \end{aligned}$$

The numbers 2 and 5.

5. Let x = the number of millions of pounds of potato chips.
Let y = the number of pounds of tortilla chips.

$$\begin{array}{rl} x + y &= 10.4 \\ x - y &= \ \ 1.2 \\ \hline 2x \quad &= 11.6 \\ x &= 5.8 \end{array}$$

$$\begin{aligned} y + 5.8 &= 10.4 \\ y &= 4.6 \end{aligned}$$

On Super Bowl Sunday, 5.8 million pounds of potato chips and 4.6 million pounds of tortilla chips are consumed.

7. Let x = the number of calories in one pan pizza.
Let y = the number of calories in one beef burrito.

$$\begin{aligned} x + 2y &= 1980 \\ 2x + y &= 2670 \end{aligned}$$

To solve this system by the addition method, multiply the first equation by -2 and add the result to the second equation.

$$\begin{aligned} -2x - 4y &= -3960 \\ 2x + \ \ y &= \ \ 2670 \\ \hline -3y &= -1290 \\ y &= 430 \end{aligned}$$

$$\begin{aligned} x + 2y &= 1980 \\ x + 2(430) &= 1980 \\ x + 860 &= 1980 \\ x &= 1120 \end{aligned}$$

A pan pizza has 1120 calories and a beef burrito has 430 calories.

9. Let $x =$ number of milligrams of cholesterol in scrambled eggs.
Let $y =$ number of milligrams of cholesterol in Whopper.

$$\begin{aligned} x + y &= -300 + 241 \\ 2x + 3y &= 1257 \end{aligned}$$

$$\begin{aligned} x + y &= 541 \\ 2x + 3y &= 1257 \end{aligned}$$

Multiply the first equation by -2 and add to second equation.

$$\begin{aligned} -2x - 2y &= -1082 \\ 2x + 3y &= \ \ 1257 \\ \hline y &= \ \ 175 \end{aligned}$$

Back-substitute.

$$\begin{aligned} x + 175 &= 541 \\ x &= 366 \end{aligned}$$

The scrambled eggs have 366 mg of cholesterol, and the Double Beef Whopper has 175 mg of cholesterol.

11. Let $x =$ the price of one sweater.
Let $y =$ the price of one shirt.

$$\begin{aligned} x + 3y &= 42 \\ 3x + 2y &= 56 \end{aligned}$$

Multiply the first equation by -3 and add the result to the second equation.

$$\begin{aligned} -3x - 9y &= -126 \\ 3x + 2y &= \ \ 56 \\ \hline -7y &= \ \ -70 \\ y &= 10 \end{aligned}$$

$$\begin{aligned} x + 3(10) &= 42 \\ x + 30 &= 42 \\ x &= 12 \end{aligned}$$

The price of one sweater is \$12 and the price of one shirt is \$10.

13. Let $x =$ the length of a badminton court.
Let $y =$ the width of a badminton court.
Use the formula for the perimeter of a rectangle to write the first equation.

$$\begin{aligned} P &= 2l + 2w \\ 128 &= 2x + 2y \end{aligned}$$

Use the other information in the problem to write the second equation.

$$6x + 9y = 444$$

These two equations form the system

$$\begin{aligned} 2x + 2y &= 128 \\ 6x + 9y &= 444. \end{aligned}$$

Multiply the first equation by -3 and add the result to the second equation.

$$\begin{aligned} -6x - 6y &= -384 \\ 6x + 9y &= \ \ 444 \\ \hline 3y &= \ \ 60 \\ y &= 20 \end{aligned}$$

$$2x + 2(20) = 128$$
$$2x + 40 = 128$$
$$2x = 88$$
$$x = 44$$

The length is 44 feet and the width is 20 feet, so the dimensions of a standard badminton court are 44 feet by 20 feet.

15. Let $x =$ the length of the lot.
Let $y =$ the width of the lot.

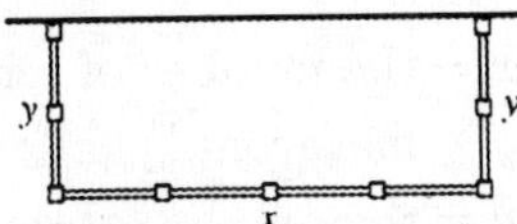

Use the formula for the perimeter of a rectangle to write the first equation.

$$2x + 2y = 320$$

Use the other information in the problem to write the second equation.

$$16x + 5(2y) = 2140$$

These two equations form the system

$$2x + 2y = 320$$
$$16x + 10y = 2140.$$

Multiply the first equation by -5 and add the result to the second equation.

$$\begin{array}{r} -10x - 10y = -1600 \\ 16x + 10y = 2140 \\ \hline 6x = 540 \end{array}$$
$$x = 90$$

$$2(90) + 2y = 320$$
$$180 + 2y = 320$$
$$2y = 140$$
$$y = 70$$

The length is 90 feet and the width is 70 feet, so the dimensions of the lot are 90 feet by 70 feet.

17. a. Let $x =$ the number of minutes of long-distance calls.
Let $y =$ the monthly cost of a telephone plan.

Plan A: $y = 20 + 0.05x$
Plan B: $y = 5 + 0.10x$

To solve this system by the substitution method, substitute $5 + 0.10x$ for y in the first equation.

$$5 + 0.10x = 20 + 0.05x$$
$$5 + 0.05x = 20$$
$$0.05x = 15$$
$$\frac{0.05x}{0.05} = \frac{15}{0.05}$$
$$x = 300$$

If $x = 300$,

$$y = 20 + 0.05(300) = 35.$$

The costs for the two plans will be equal for 300 minutes of long-distance calls per month. The cost of each plan will be \$35.

b. $x = 10(20) = 200$

Plan A: $y = 20 + 0.05(200) = 30$
Plan B: $y = 5 + 0.10(200) = 25$

The monthly cost would be \$30 for Plan A and \$25 for Plan B, so you should select Plan B to get the lower cost.

19. Let $x =$ the number of dollars of merchandise purchased in a year.
Let $y =$ the total cost for a year.
Plan A: $y = 100 + 0.80x$
Plan B: $y = 40 + 0.90x$

Substitute $40 + 0.90x$ for y in the first equation.

$$\begin{aligned}40 + 0.90x &= 100 + 0.80x\\ 40 + 0.10x &= 100\\ 0.10x &= 60\\ \frac{0.10x}{0.10} &= \frac{60}{0.10}\\ x &= 600\end{aligned}$$

If $x = 600$,

$$y = 100 + 0.80(600) = 580.$$

If you purchase \$600 worth of merchandise, you will pay the \$580 under both plans.

21. Let $x =$ the number of years after 1985.
Let $y =$ the average high school graduate's weekly earnings.

We are interested in the year in which the average college graduate earns twice as much as a high school graduate, so the average college graduate's earnings will be $2y$.

College graduates:

$$2y = 508 + 25x$$

High school graduates:

$$y = 345x + 9x$$

Substitute $345+9x$ into the first equation.

$$\begin{aligned}2(345 + 9x) &= 508 + 25x\\ 690 + 18x &= 508 + 25x\\ 690 - 7x &= 508\\ -7x &= -182\\ x &= 26\end{aligned}$$

$1985 + 26 = 2011$
If $x = 26$,

$$y = 345 + 9(26) = 579$$

and

$$2y = 2(579) = 1158.$$

In 26 years after 1985, which is the year 2011, the average college graduate will earn \$1158 per week and the average high school graduate will earn \$579 per week.

23. Let $x =$ the number of servings of macaroni.
Let $y =$ the number of servings of broccoli.

$$\begin{aligned}3x + 2y &= 14\\ 16x + 4y &= 48\end{aligned}$$

Multiply first equation by -2 and add to second equation.

$$\begin{aligned}-6x - 4y &= -28\\ 16x + 4y &= 48\\ \hline 10x \qquad &= 20\\ x &= 2\end{aligned}$$

Back-substitute.

$$\begin{aligned}3(2) + 2y &= 14\\ 2y &= 8\\ y &= 4\end{aligned}$$

It would take 2 servings of macaroni and 4 servings of broccoli to get 14 grams of protein and 48 graphs of carbohydrate.

25. The sum of the measures of the three angles of any triangle is 180°, so

$$(x + 8y - 1) + (3y + 4) + (7x + 5) = 180.$$

Simplify this equation.

$$\begin{aligned}8x + 11y + 8 &= 180\\ 8x + 11y &= 172\end{aligned}$$

The base angles of an isosceles triangle have equal measures, so

$$3y + 4 = 7x + 5.$$

Rewrite this equation in the form $Ax + By = C$.

$$\begin{aligned} 7x + 5 &= 3y + 4 \\ 7x - 3y &= -1 \end{aligned}$$

Now use the addition method to solve the system

$$\begin{aligned} 8x + 11y &= 172 \\ 7x - 3y &= -1. \end{aligned}$$

Multiply the first equation by 3 and the second equation by 11; then add the results.

$$\begin{array}{rl} 24x + 33y &= 516 \\ \underline{77x - 33y} &\underline{= -11} \\ 101x \qquad &= 505 \\ x &= 5 \end{array}$$

Back-substitute into the equation $7x - 3y = -1$.

$$\begin{aligned} 7(5) - 3y &= -1 \\ 35 - 3y &= -1 \\ -3y &= -36 \\ y &= 12 \end{aligned}$$

Use the values of x and y to find the angle measures.

Angle A: $(x + 8y - 1)^\circ = (5 + 8 \cdot 12 - 1)^\circ = 100^\circ$

Angle B: $(3y + 4)^\circ = (3 \cdot 12 + 4)^\circ = 40^\circ$

Angle C: $(7x + 5)^\circ = (7 \cdot 5 + 5)^\circ = 40^\circ$

27. Use the motion formula to write the equations.

Rowing with current:

$$\begin{aligned} r \cdot t &= d \\ (x + y) \cdot 2 &= 16 \end{aligned}$$

Rowing against current:

$$(x - y) \cdot 2 = 8$$

Rewrite each equation in the form $Ax + By = C$.

$$\begin{array}{rl} 2x + 2y &= 16 \\ \underline{2x - 2y} &\underline{= \ 8} \\ 4x \qquad &= 24 \\ x &= 6 \end{array}$$

$$\begin{aligned} 2(6) + 2y &= 16 \\ 12 + 2y &= 16 \\ 2y &= 4 \\ y &= 2 \end{aligned}$$

The rowing rate in still water is 6 miles per hour and the rate of the current is 2 miles per hour.

For Exercises 29–31, answers may vary.

33. Let $x =$ the number of birds.
Let $y =$ the number of lions.

Since each bird has one head and each lion has one head,

$$x + y = 30.$$

Since each bird has two feet and each lion has four feet,

$$2x + 4y = 100.$$

Solve the first equation for y.

$$y = 30 - x$$

Substitute $30-x$ for y in the second equation.

$$\begin{aligned} 2x + 4(30 - x) &= 100 \\ 2x + 120 - 4x &= 100 \\ -2x + 120 &= 100 \\ -2x &= -20 \\ x &= 10 \\ 10 + y &= 30 \\ y &= 20 \end{aligned}$$

There were 10 birds and 20 lions in the zoo.

35. Let $x =$ the number of people in the downstairs apartment.
Let $y =$ the number of people in the upstairs apartment.

If one of the people in the upstairs apartment goes downstairs, there will be the same number of people in both apartments, so

$$y - 1 = x + 1.$$

If one of the people in the downstairs apartment goes upstairs, there will be twice as many people upstairs as downstairs, so

$$y + 1 = 2(x - 1).$$

Solve the first equation for y.

$$y = x + 2$$

Also solve the second equation for y.

$$\begin{aligned} y + 1 &= 2x - 2 \\ y &= 2x - 3 \end{aligned}$$

Substitute $x+2$ for y in the last equation.

$$\begin{aligned} x + 2 &= 2x - 3 \\ -x + 2 &= -3 \\ -x &= -5 \\ x &= 5 \\ y &= 5 + 2 = 7 \end{aligned}$$

There are 5 people downstairs and 7 people upstairs.

37. Answers will vary depending on the problems chosen.

Review Exercises

38. $2x - y < 4$

Graph $2x - y = 4$ as a dashed line with x-intercept 2 and y-intercept -4. Use $(0, 0)$ as a test point. Since $2(0) - 0 < 4$ is true, shade the half-plane containing $(0, 0)$.

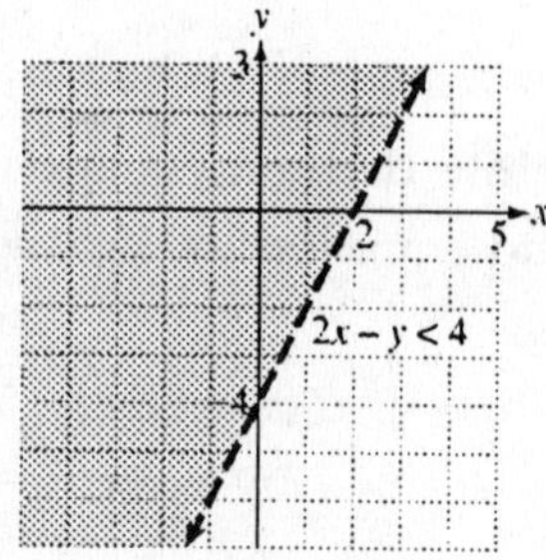

39. $y \geq x + 1$

Graph the line $y = x+1$ using the slope of 1 and y-intercept of 1. Make the line solid because the inequality symbol is $\geq$. Use $(0, 0)$ as a test point. Since $0 \geq 0 + 1$ is false, shade the half-plane *not* containing $(0, 0)$.

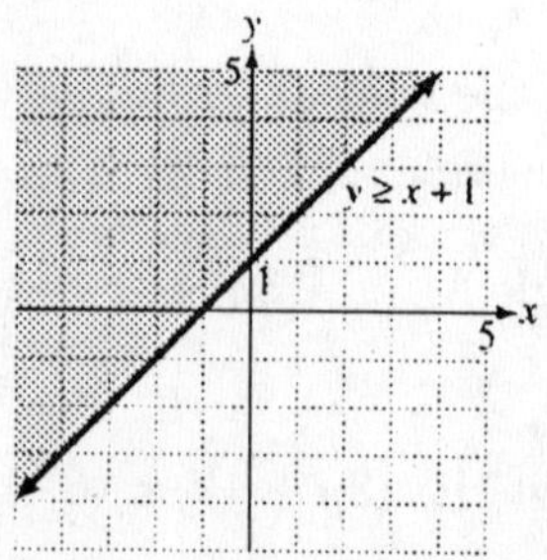

40. $x \geq 2$

Graph $x = 2$ as a solid vertical line. Use $(0, 0)$ as a test point. Since $0 \geq 2$ is false, shade the half-plane *not* containing $(0, 0)$. This is the region to the right of the line $x = 2$.

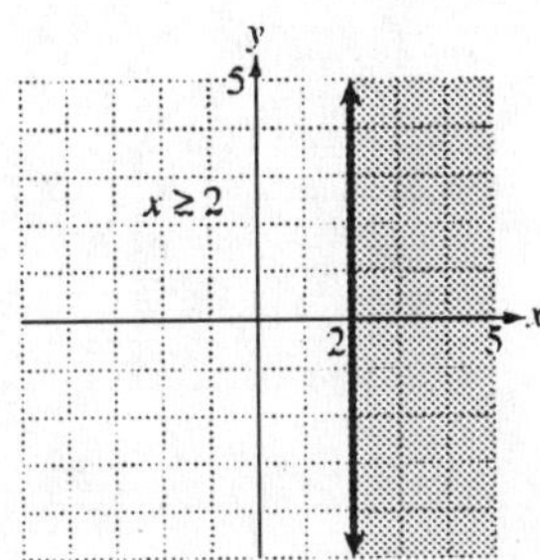

5.5 Systems of Linear Inequalities

5.5 CHECK POINTS

CHECK POINT 1

$x + 2y > 4$
$2x - 3y \leq -6$

Begin by graphing $x + 2y > 4$. Because the inequality symbol is $>$, graph $x + 2y = 4$ as a dashed line. Use the x-intercept, 4, and y-intercept, 2. Because $(0, 0)$ makes the inequality $x + 2y > 4$ false, shade the half-plane *not* containing $(0, 0)$.
Now graph $2x - 3y \leq -6$ in the same rectangular coordinate system. Because the inequality symbol is $\leq$, in which equality is included, graph $2x - 3y = -6$ as a solid line. Use the x-intercept, -3, and the y-intercept, 2. Because $(0, 0)$ makes the inequality $2x - 3y \leq -6$ false, shade the half-plane *not* containing $(0, 0)$.

The solution set of the system is shown graphically by the intersection (overlap) of the two half-planes. The open dot shows that $(0, 2)$ is not in the solution set.

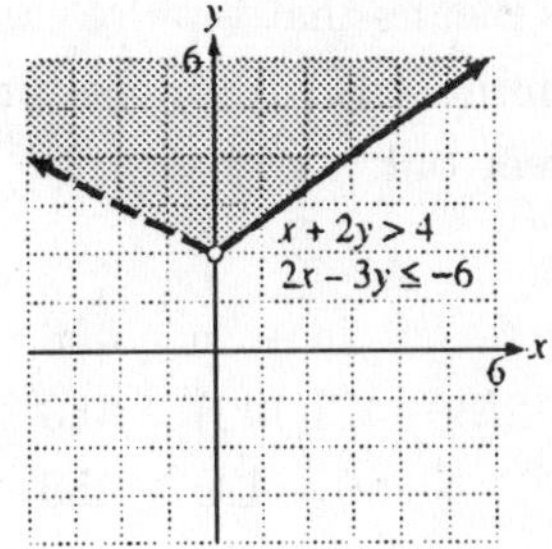

CHECK POINT 2

$y \geq x + 2$
$x \geq 1$

Begin by graphing $y \geq x + 2$. Because the inequality symbol is $\geq$, graph $y = x + 2$ as a solid line. Use the slope, 1, and y-intercept, 2, to graph this line. Because $(0, 0)$ makes $y \geq x + 2$ false, shade the half-plane *not* including $(0, 0)$.
Now graph $x \geq 1$. Because the inequality symbol is $\geq$, graph $x = 1$ as a solid line. This is a vertical line with x-intercept 1. Because $(0, 0)$ makes $x \geq 1$ false, shade the half-plane *not* including $(0, 0)$.
The solution set is shown by the intersection of the two half-planes. The closed dot shows that $(1, 3)$ is part of the solution.

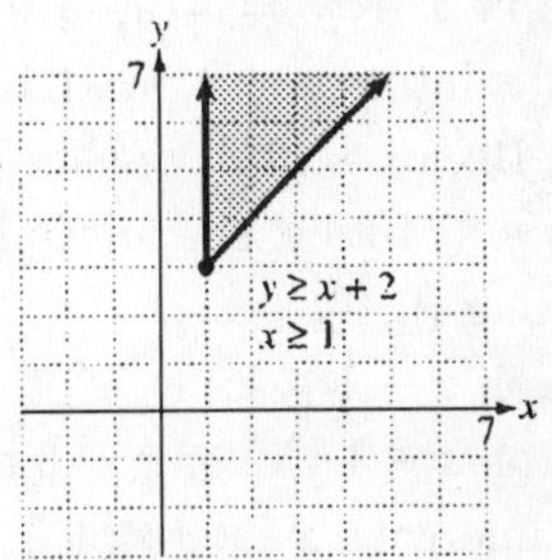

CHECK POINT 3

a. Answers will vary.
One possible choice is the point $(30, 140)$. This means that a pulse rate of 140 beats per minute is within the target zone for a 30-year-old.

b.
$$2a + 3p \geq 450$$
$$\text{Is } 2(30) + 3(140) \geq 450 \text{ ?}$$
$$60 + 420 \geq 450$$
$$480 \geq 450 \text{ true}$$

$$a + p \leq 190$$
$$\text{Is } 30 + 140 \leq 190 \text{ ?}$$
$$170 \leq 190 \text{ true}$$

Therefore $(30, 140)$ satisfies both inequalities and is therefore a solution of the system.

EXERCISE SET 5.5

Note: In the answer graphs in this section, only the solution set of the system will be shaded.

1. $x + y \leq 4$
$x - 1 \leq 2$

Graph $x + y \leq 4$:
Graph $x + y = 4$ as a solid line using the x-intercept, 4, and the y-intercept, 4. Because $(0, 0)$ makes the inequality $x + y \leq 4$ true, shade the half-plane containing $(0, 0)$.
Graph $x - 1 \leq 2$:
Graph $x - 1 = 2$ or $x = 3$ as a solid vertical line with x-intercept 3. Because $(0, 0)$ makes the inequality $x - 1 \leq 2$ true, shade the half-plane containing $(0, 0)$.

The solution set of the system is the intersection (overlap) of the two shaded regions. The closed dot shows that $(3, 1)$ is part of the solution.

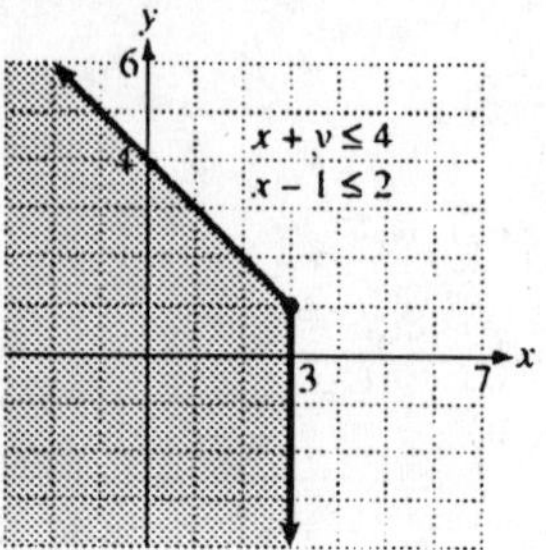

3. $2x - 4y \leq 8$
$x + y \geq -1$

Graph $2x - 4y \leq 8$:
Graph $2x - 4y = 8$ as a solid line using the x-intercept, 4, and the y-intercept, -2. Because $4(0) - 2(0) \leq 8$ is true, shade the half-plane containing $(0, 0)$.
Graph $x + y \geq -1$:
Graph $x + y = -1$ as a solid line using the x-intercept, -1, and the y-intercept, -1. Because $0 + 0 \geq -1$ is true, shade the half-plane containing $(0, 0)$.
The solution set of the system is the intersection of the two shaded regions.

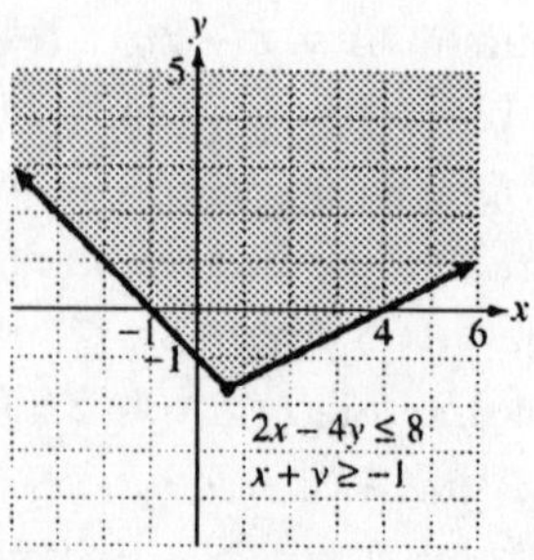

5. $x + 3y \leq 6$
$x - 2y \leq 4$

Graph $x + 3y \leq 6$:
Graph $x + 3y = 6$ as a solid line using the x-intercept, 6, and the y-intercept, 2. Because $0 + 3(0) \leq 6$ is true, shade the half-plane containing $(0, 0)$.
Graph $x - 2y \leq 4$:
Graph $x - 2y = 4$ as a solid line using the x-intercept, 4, and the y-intercept, -2. Because $0 - 2(0) \leq 4$ is true, shade the half-plane containing $(0, 0)$.
The solution set of the system is the intersection of the two shaded regions.

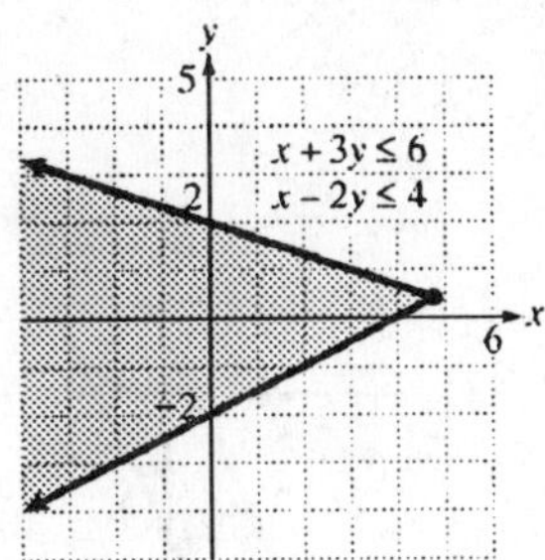

7. $x - 2y > 4$
$2x + y \geq 6$

Graph $x - 2y > 4$:
Graph $x - 2y = 4$ as a dashed line using the x-intercept, 4, and the y-intercept, -2. Because $0 - 2(0) > 4$ is false, shade the half-plane *not* containing $(0, 0)$.
Graph $2x + y \geq 6$:
Graph $2x + y = 6$ as a solid line using the x-intercept, 3, and the y-intercept, 6. Because $2(0) + 0 \geq 6$ is false, shade the half-plane *not* containing $(0, 0)$.

The solution set of the system is the intersection of the two shaded regions.

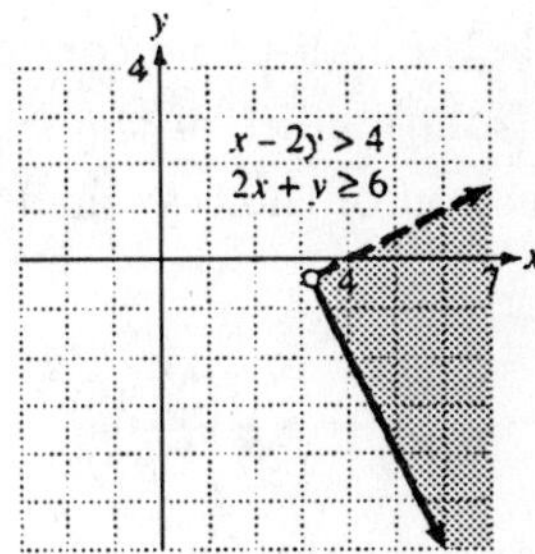

9. $x + y > 1$
$x + y < 4$

Graph $x + y > 1$:
Graph $x+y = 1$ as a dashed line using the x-intercepts. Because $0 + 0 > 1$ is false, shade the half-plane *not* containing $(0, 0)$.
Graph $x + y < 4$:
Graph $x+y = 4$ as a dashed line using the x-intercepts. Because $0 + 0 < 4$ is true, shade the half-plane containing $(0, 0)$.
The solution set is the shaded region between the two dashed parallel lines.

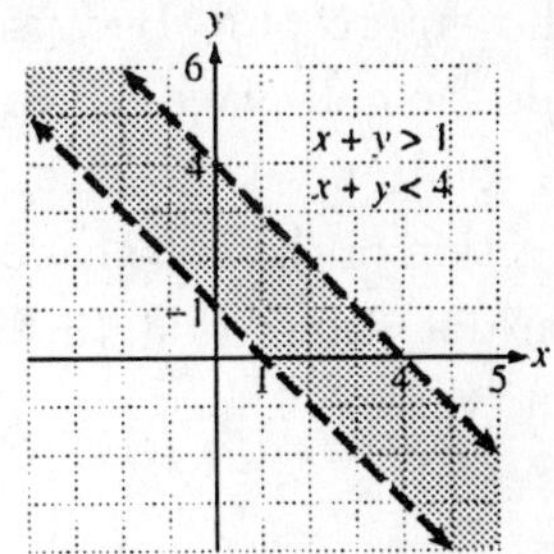

11. $y \geq 2x + 1$
$y \leq 5$

Graph $y \geq 2x + 1$:
Graph $y = 2x + 1$ using the slope, 2, and the y-intercept, 1. Because $0 \geq 2(0) + 1$ is false, shade the half-plane *not* containing $(0, 0)$.

Graph $y = 5$:
Graph $y = 5$ as a solid horizontal line with y-intercept 5. Because $0 \leq 5$ is true, shade the half-plane containing $(0, 0)$.
The solution set of the system is the intersection of the two shaded regions.

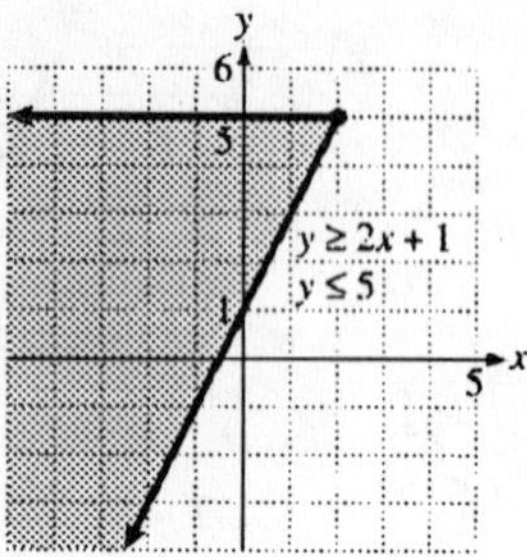

13. $y > x - 1$
$x > 3$

Graph $y > x - 1$:
Graph $y = x - 1$ using the slope, 1, and y-intercept, -1. Because $0 > 0 - 1$ is true, shade the half-plane containing $(0, 0)$.
Graph $x > 3$:
Graph $x = 3$ as a dashed vertical line with x-intercept 3. Because $0 > 3$ is false, shade the half-plane not containing $(0, 0)$.
The solution set of the system is the intersection of the two shaded regions. The open dot shows that $(3, 2)$ is not in the solution set.

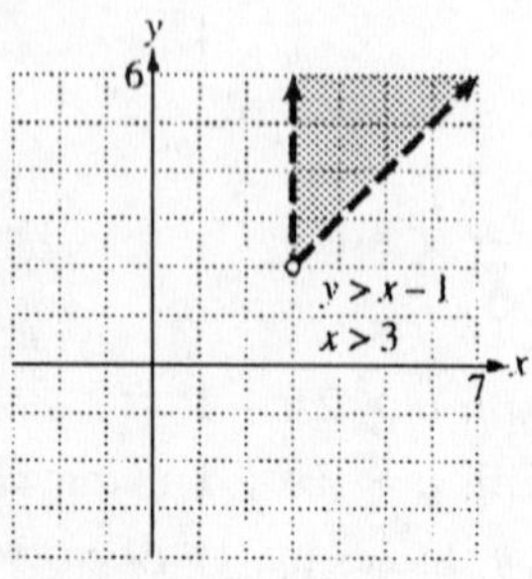

15. $y \geq 2x - 3$
$y \leq 2x + 1$

Graph $y \geq 2x - 3$:
Graph $y = 2x - 3$ as a solid line using slope, 2, and y-intercept, -3. Since $0 \geq 2(0) - 3$ is true, shade the half-plane containing $(0, 0)$.
Graph $y \leq 2x + 1$:
Graph $y = 2x + 1$ as a solid line using its slope, 2, and y-intercept, 1. Since $0 \leq 2(0) + 1$, shade the half-plane containing $(0, 0)$.
The solution set of the system is the intersection of the two shaded regions. Notice that this is the region between two parallel lines, together with the lines themselves.

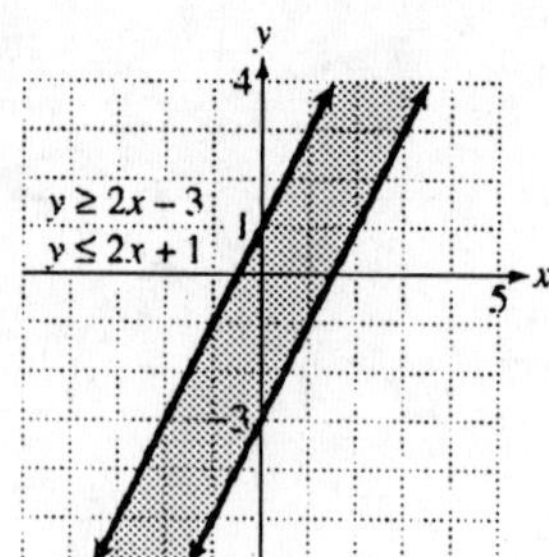

17. $y > 2x + 3$
$y \leq -x + 6$

Graph $y > 2x - 3$:
Graph $y = 2x - 3$ as a dashed line using its slope, 2, and y-intercept, -3. Since $0 > 2(0) - 3$ is true, shade the half-plane containing $(0, 0)$.
Graph $y \leq -x + 6$:
Graph $y = -x + 6$ as a solid line using its slope, -1, and y-intercept, 6. Since $0 \leq -0 + 6$ is true, shade the half-plane containing $(0, 0)$.

The solution set of the system is the intersection of the two shaded regions.

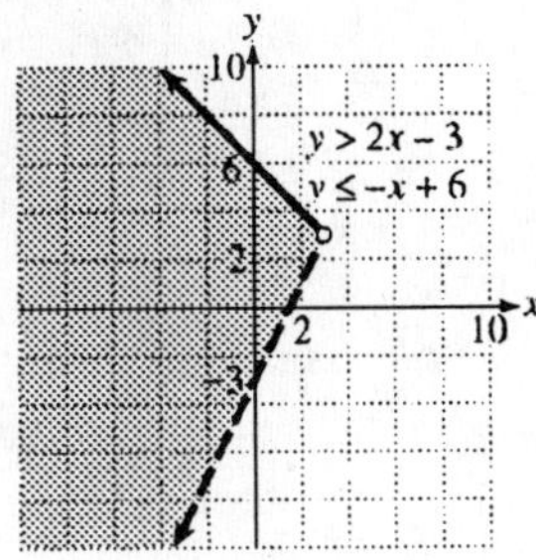

19. $x + 2y \leq 4$
$y \geq x - 3$

Graph $x + 2y \leq 4$:
Graph $x + 2y = 4$ as a solid line using its x-intercept, 4, and y-intercept, 2. Since $0 + 2(0) \leq 4$ is true, shade the half-plane containing $(0, 0)$.
Graph $y \geq x - 3$:
Graph $y = x - 3$ as a solid line, using its slope, 1, and y-intercept, -3. Since $0 \geq 0 - 3$ is true, shade the half-plane containing $(0, 0)$.
The solution set of the system is the intersection of the two shaded regions.

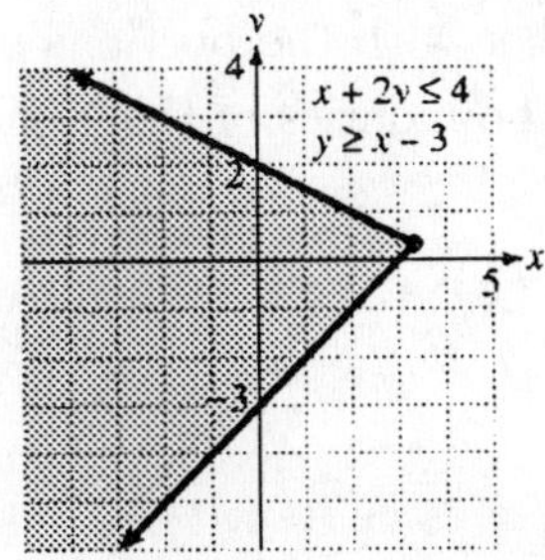

21. $x \leq 2$
$y \geq -1$
Graph $x \leq 2$:
Graph $x = 2$ as a solid vertical line. Since $0 \leq 2$ is true, shade the half-plane containing $(0, 0)$.
Graph $y \geq -1$:
Graph $y = -1$ as a solid horizontal line. Since $0 \geq -1$ is true, shade the half-plane.
The solution set of the system is the intersection of the two shaded regions.

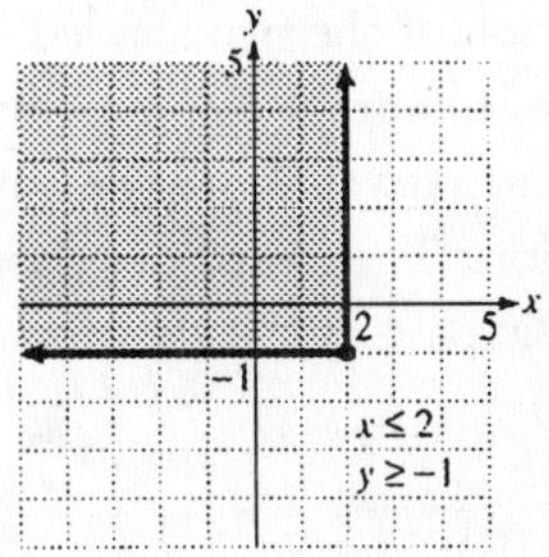

23. $x \geq 2$
$y < 3$
Graph $x \geq 2$:
Graph $x = 2$ as a solid vertical line. Since $0 \geq 2$ is false, shade the half-plane *not* containing $(0, 0)$.
Graph $y < 3$:
Graph $y = 3$ as a dashed horizontal line. Since $0 < 3$ is true, shade the half-plane, shade the half-plane containing $(0, 0)$.
The solution set of the system is the intersection of the two shaded regions. The open dot shows that $(2, 3)$ is not in the solution set.

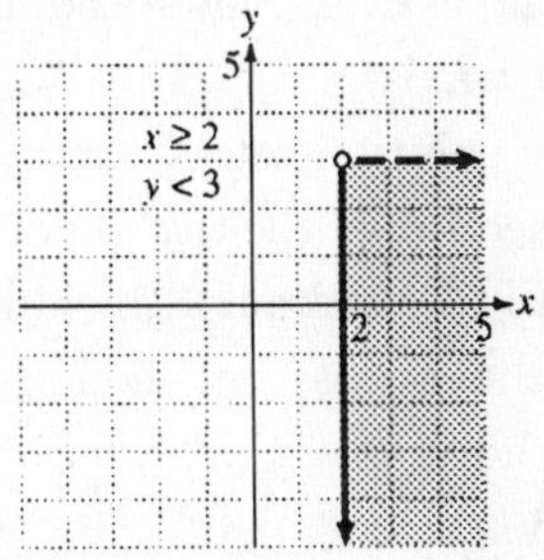

25. $x \geq 0$
$y \leq 0$

Graph $x \geq 0$:
Graph $x = 0$ as a solid vertical line. This is the y-axis. Shade the half-plane to the right of the y-axis.
Graph $y \leq 0$:
Graph $y = 0$ as a solid horizontal line. This is the x-axis. Shade the half-plane below the x-axis.
The solution set of the system is the intersection of the two shaded regions. This is all of quadrant IV, including the portions of the axes that are the boundaries of this region. The closed dot shows that the origin is part of the solution.

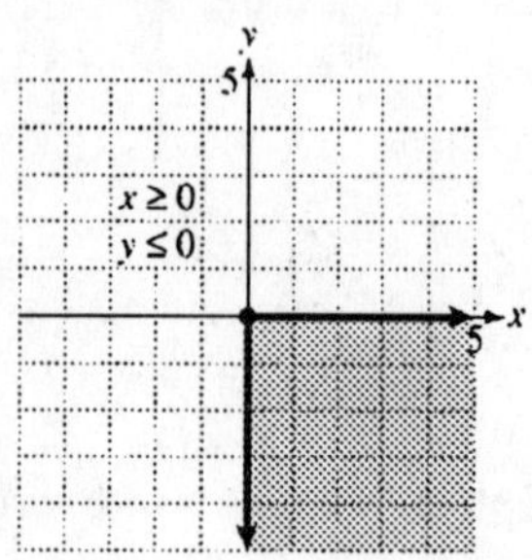

27. $x \geq 0$
$y > 0$

Graph $x \geq 0$:
Graph $x = 0$ as a solid vertical line. This is the y-axis. Shade the half-plane to the right to the y-axis.
Graph $y > 0$:
Graph $y = 0$ as a dashed solid line. This is the x-axis. Shade the half-plane above the x-axis.
The solution set of the system is the intersection of the two shaded regions. This is all of quadrant I, including the portion of the y-axis, but excluding the portion of the x-axis, that are boundaries of this region.

The open dot shows that the origin is not in the solution set.

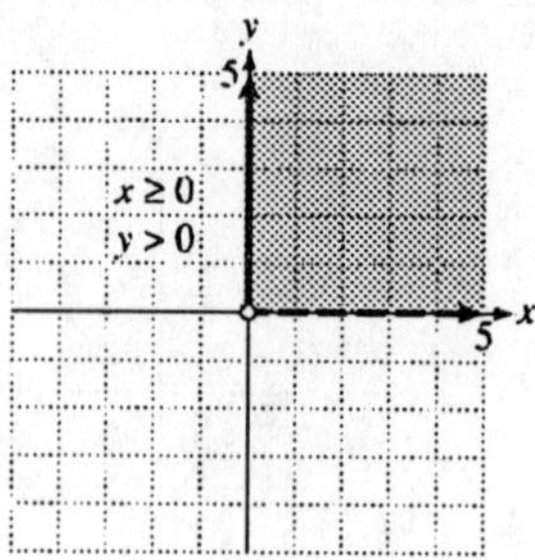

29. $x + y \leq 5$
$x \geq 0$
$y \geq 0$

Graph $x + y \leq 5$:
Graph $x + y = 5$ as a solid line using its x-intercept, 5, and y-intercept, 5. Since $0 + 0 \leq 5$ is true, shade the half-plane containing $(0, 0)$.
Graph $x \geq 0$:
Graph $x = 0$ (the y-axis) as a solid line. Shade the half-plane to the right of the y-axis.
Graph $y \geq 0$:
Graph $y = 0$ (the x-axis) as a solid line. Shade the half-plane above the x-axis.
The solution set of the system is the intersection of the three shaded regions. Notice that this is the set of points satisfying $x + y \leq 5$ that lie in quadrant I, together with the portions of the axes that are boundaries of this region.

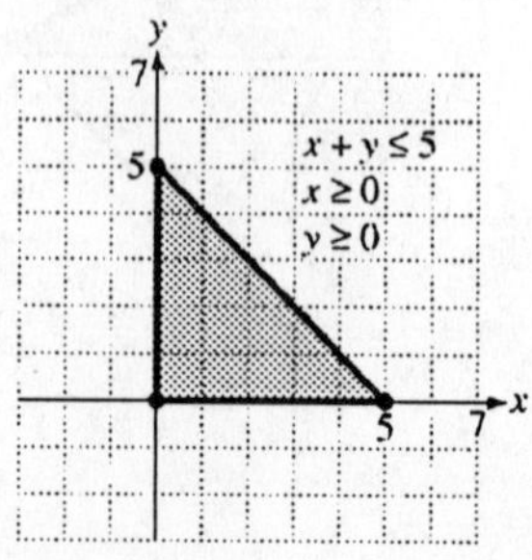

31. $4x - 3y > 12$
$x \geq 0$
$y \leq 0$

Graph $4x - 3y > 12$:
Graph $4x - 3y = 12$ as a dashed line using the x-intercept, 3, and the y-intercept, -4. Since $4(0) - 3(0) > 12$ is false, shade the half-plane *not* including $(0,0)$.
Graph $x \geq 0$:
Graph $x = 0$ (the y-axis) as a solid line and shade the half-plane to the right of it.
Graph $y \leq 0$:
Graph $y = 0$ (the x-axis) as a solid line and shade the half-plane below it.
The solution set of the system is the intersection of the three shaded regions. Notice that this is the set of points satisfying $4x - 3y > 12$ that lie in quadrant IV, together with the portions of the axes that are boundaries of these regions.

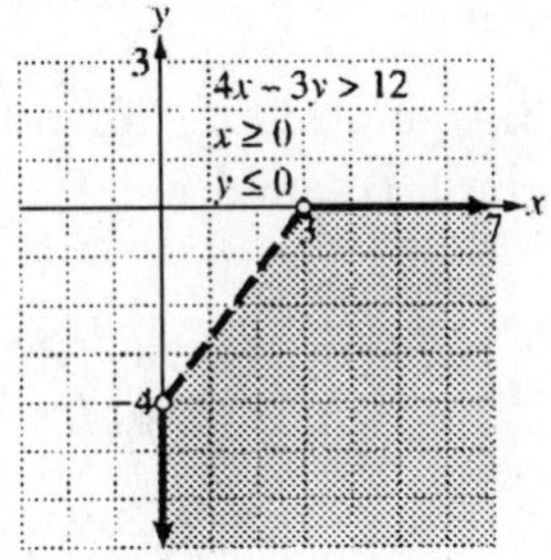

33. $0 \leq x \leq 3$
$0 \leq y \leq 3$

Graph $0 \leq x \leq 3$:
Graph the vertical lines $x = 0$ (the y-axis) and $x = 3$ as solid lines. Shade the region between these parallel lines.
Graph $0 \leq y \leq 3$:
Graph the horizontal lines $y = 0$ (the x-axis) and $y = 3$ as solid lines. Shade the region between these horizontal lines.

The solution set of the system is the intersection of the two shaded regions.

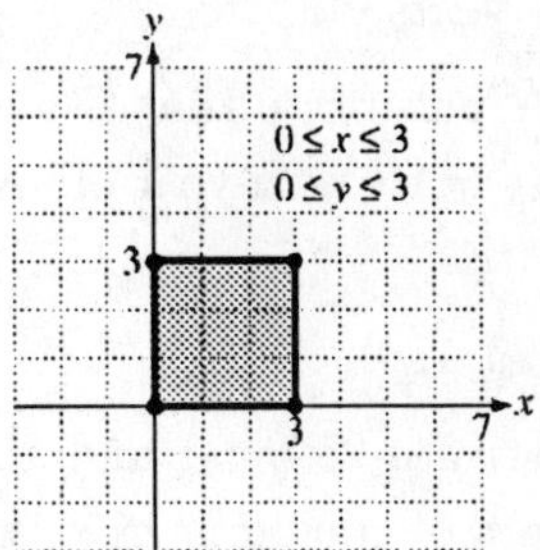

35. $x - y \leq 4$
$x + 2y \leq 4$

Graph $x - y \leq 4$:
Graph $x - y = 4$ as a solid line using the x-intercept, 4, and the y-intercept, -4. Since $0 - 0 \leq 4$ is true, shade the half-plane containing $(0,0)$.
Graph $x + 2y \leq 4$:
Graph $x + 2y = 4$ as a solid line using the x-intercept, 4, and the y-intercept, 2. Since $0 + 2(0) \leq 4$ is true, shade the half-plane containing $(0,0)$.
The solution set of the system is the intersection of the two shaded regions.

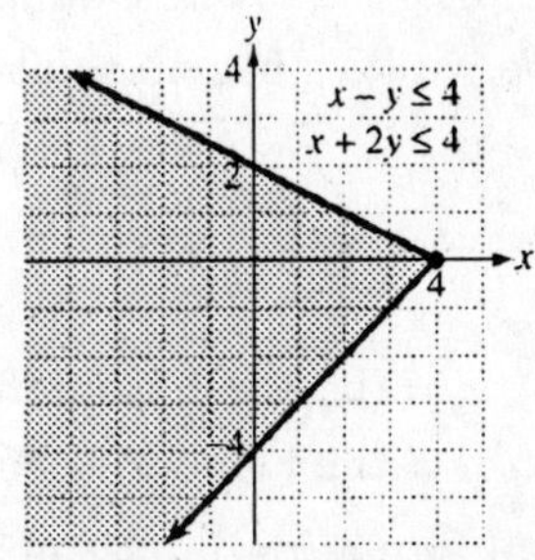

37. Answers will vary according to the student's age and the point chosen. A sample answer is given here for a student who is 25 years old.

a. A pulse rate that lies within the target zone for a 25-year-old is 150 beats per minute.

b. $(25, 150)$

Substitute 25 for a and 150 for p in the system of equations given in Example 3.

$$\begin{aligned} 2a + 3p &\geq 450 \\ \text{Is } \; 2(25) + 3(150) &\geq 450 \quad ? \\ 50 + 450 &\geq 450 \\ 500 &\geq 450 \quad \text{true} \end{aligned}$$

$$\begin{aligned} a + p &\leq 190 \\ \text{Is } \; 25 + 150 &\leq 190 \quad ? \\ 175 &\leq 190 \quad \text{true} \end{aligned}$$

The pair $(25, 150)$ satisfies each inequality of the system.

39. Yes; the point $(175, 70)$ falls in the healthy weight region.

41. The recommended weight range for a person who is 6 ft (72 inches) tall is about 140 to 190 pounds.

43. Answers may vary.

45. The following is one example of a system of inequalities has no solutions:

$$\begin{aligned} x + y &> 0 \\ x + y &< -5. \end{aligned}$$

47. Let $x =$ the number of \$35 tickets sold. Then $y =$ the number of \$50 tickets sold.

The information in the problem leads to the following inequalities:

$$\begin{aligned} x + y &\geq 25{,}000 \\ 35x + 50y &\geq 1{,}025{,}000. \end{aligned}$$

Also, the number of tickets sold and the amount of money in ticket sales cannot be negative, so

$$\begin{aligned} x &\geq 0 \\ y &\geq 0. \end{aligned}$$

The complete system to be graphed is

$$\begin{aligned} x + y &\geq 25{,}000 \\ 35x + 50y &\geq 1{,}025{,}000 \\ x &\geq 0 \\ y &\geq 0. \end{aligned}$$

Graph $x + y \geq 25{,}000$:
Graph $x + y = 25{,}000$ as a solid line using its x-intercept, 25,000, and y-intercept, 25,000. Since $0+0 \geq 25{,}000$ is false, shade the region *not* containing $(0, 0)$.
Graph $35x + 50y \geq 1{,}025{,}000$:
Graph $35x + 50y = 1{,}025{,}000$ using its x-intercept, $\approx$ 29,286 and its y-intercept, 20,500. Since $35(0) + 50(0) \geq 1{,}025{,}000$ is false, shade the region *not* containing $(0, 0)$.
The inequalities $x \geq 0$ and $y \geq 0$ restrict the graph to quadrant I.

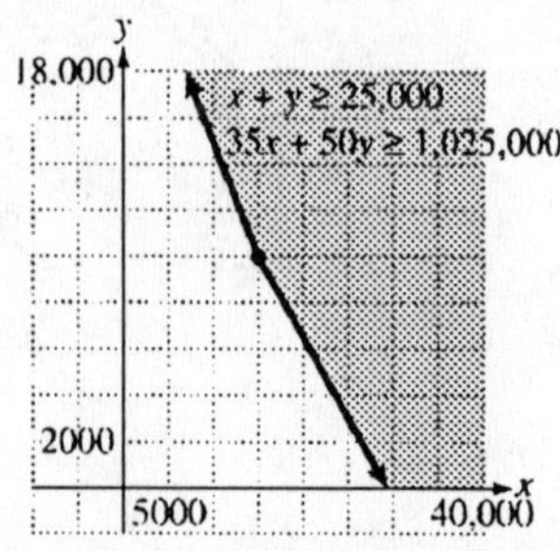

Review Exercises

48. $(-6, 1)$ and $(2, -1)$

$$m = \frac{-1 - 1}{2 - (-6)} = \frac{-2}{8} = -\frac{1}{4}$$

49. $\frac{1}{5} + \left(-\frac{3}{4}\right) = \frac{4}{20} + \left(-\frac{15}{20}\right) = -\frac{11}{20}$

50. $y = x^2$

Make a table of values.

x	$y = x^2$	(x, y)
-3	$y = (-3)^2 = 9$	$(-3, 9)$
-2	$y = (-2)^2 = 4$	$(-2, 4)$
-1	$y = (-1)^2 = 1$	$(-1, 1)$
0	$y = 0^2 = 0$	$(0, 0)$
1	$y = 1^2 = 1$	$(1, 1)$
2	$y = 2^2 = 4$	$(2, 4)$
3	$y = 3^2 = 9$	$(3, 9)$

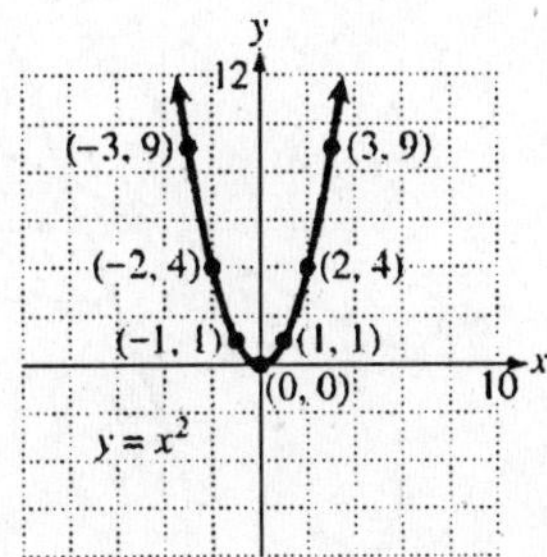

Chapter 5 Review Exercises

1. $(1, -5)$

$$\begin{aligned} 4x - y &= 9 \\ 4(1) - (-5) &\stackrel{?}{=} 9 \\ 4 + 5 &\stackrel{?}{=} 9 \\ 9 &= 9 \text{ true} \end{aligned}$$

$$\begin{aligned} 2x + 3y &= -13 \\ 2(1) + 3(-5) &\stackrel{?}{=} -13 \\ 2 - 15 &\stackrel{?}{=} -13 \\ -13 &= -13 \text{ true} \end{aligned}$$

Since the ordered pair $(1, -5)$ satisfies both equations, it is a solution of the given system.

2. $(-5, 2)$

$$\begin{aligned} 2x + 3y &= -4 \\ 2(-5) + 3(2) &\stackrel{?}{=} -4 \\ -10 + 6 &\stackrel{?}{=} -4 \\ -4 &= -4 \text{ true} \end{aligned}$$

$$\begin{aligned} x - 4y &= -10 \\ -5 - 4(-2) &\stackrel{?}{=} -10 \\ -5 + 8 &\stackrel{?}{=} -10 \\ 3 &= -10 \text{ false} \end{aligned}$$

Since $(-5, 2)$ fails to satisfy *both* equations, it is not a solution of the given system.

3. $(-1, 3)$

$$\begin{aligned} x + y &= 2 \\ -1 + 3 &\stackrel{?}{=} 2 \\ 2 &= 2 \text{ true} \end{aligned}$$

$$\begin{aligned} 2x + y &= -5 \\ 2(-1) + 3 &\stackrel{?}{=} -5 \\ -2 + 3 &\stackrel{?}{=} -5 \\ 1 &= -5 \text{ false} \end{aligned}$$

Since $(-1, 3)$ fails to satisfy *both* equations, it is not a solution of the given system. Also, the second equation in the system, which can be rewritten as $y = -2x - 5$, is a line with slope -2 and y-intercept -5, while the graph shows a line with slope 2 and y-intercept 5.

4. $x + y = 2$
$x - y = 6$

Graph both lines on the same axes.

$x + y = 2$:
x-intercept $= 2$; y-intercept $= 2$

$x - y = 6$:
x-intercept $= 6$; y-intercept $= -6$

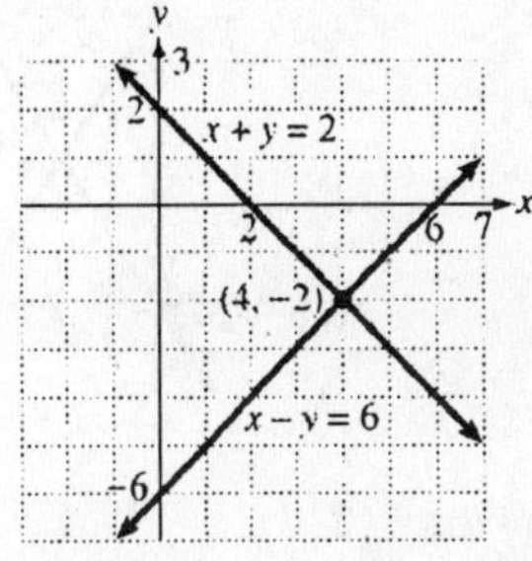

The lines appear to intersect at $(4, -2)$. This apparent solution can be vertified by substituting 4 for x and -2 for y in both equations of the original system.
Solution: $(4, -2)$

5. $2x - 3y = 12$
$-2x + y = -8$

Graph both equations.
$2x - 3y = 12$:
x-intercept $= 6$; y-intercept $= -4$
$-2x + y = -8$
x-intercept $= 4$; y-intercept $= -8$

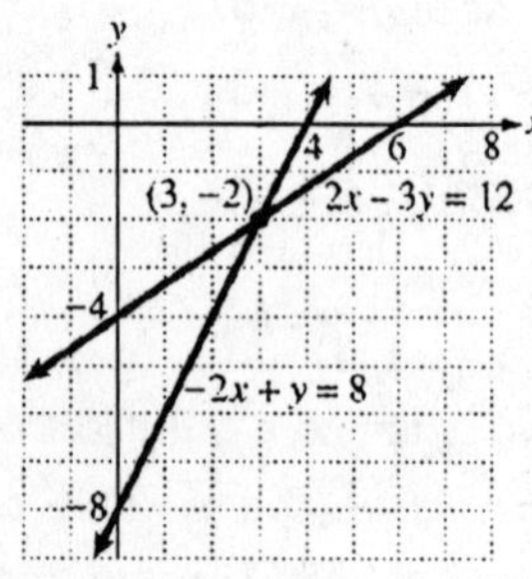

Solution: $(3, -2)$

6. $3x + 2y = 6$
$3x - 2y = 6$

Graph both equations.
$3x + 2y = 6$:
x-intercept $= 2$; y-intercept $= 3$
$3x - 2y = 6$:
x-intercept $= 2$; y-intercept $= -3$

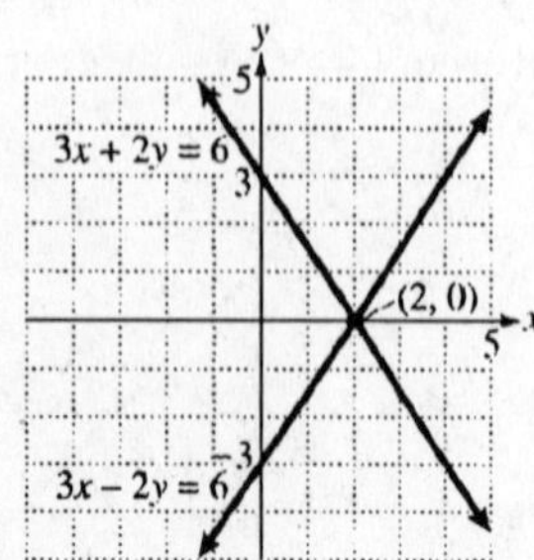

Solution: $(2, 0)$

7. $y = \frac{1}{2}x$
$y = 2x - 3$

Graph both equations.

$y = \frac{1}{2}x$:

slope $= \frac{1}{2}$; y-intercept $= 0$

$y = 2x - 3$:
slope $= 2$; y-intercept $= -3$

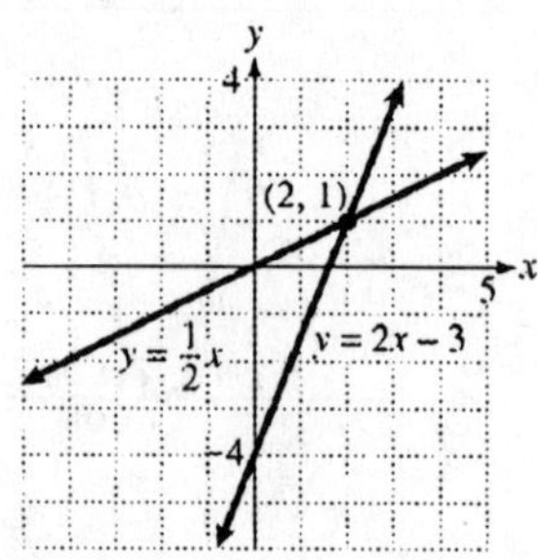

Solution: $(2, 1)$

8. $x + 2y = 2$
$y = x - 5$

Graph both equations.
$x + 2y = 2$:
x-intercept $= 2$; y-intercept $= 1$
$y = x - 5$:
slope $= 1$; y-intercept $= -5$

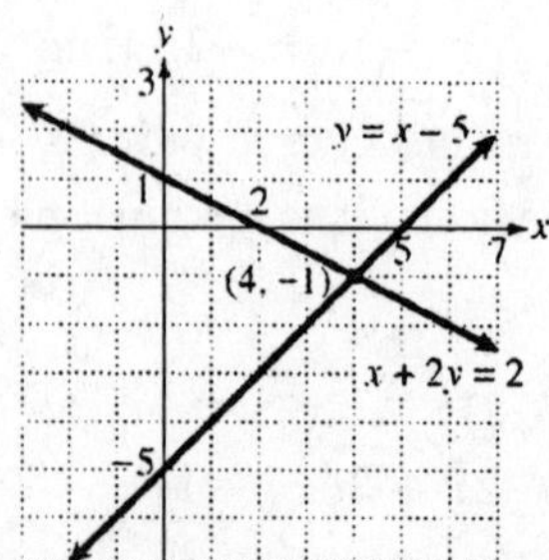

Solution: $(4, -1)$

9. $x + 2y = 8$
$3x + 6y = 12$

Graph both equations.
$x + 2y = 8$:
x-intercept $= 8$; y-intercept $= 4$
$3x + 6y = 12$:
x-intercept $= 4$; y-intercept $= 2$

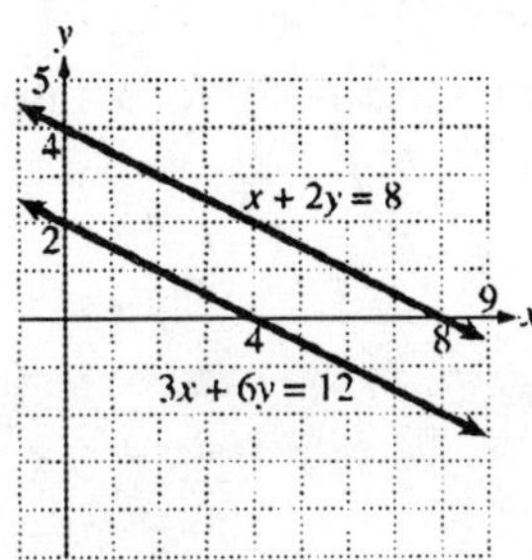

The two lines are parallel. The system has no solution.

10. $2x - 4y = 8$
$x - 2y = 4$

Graph both equations.
$2x - 4y = 8$:
x-intercept: 4; y-intercept $= -2$
$x - 2y = 4$:
x-intercept: 4; y-intercept $= -2$

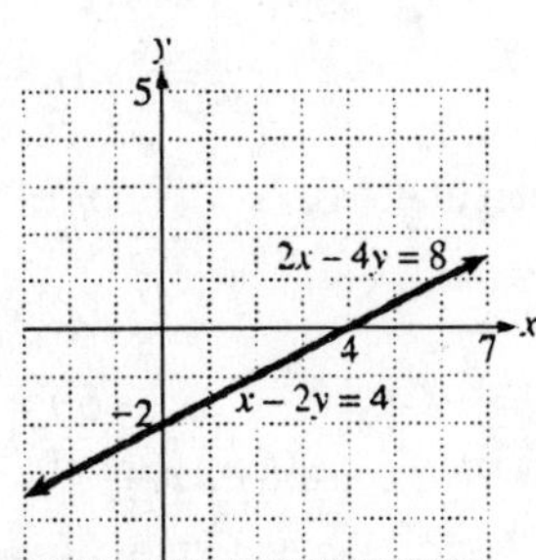

The graphs of the two equations are the same line. The system has infinitely many solutions.

11. $y = 3x - 1$
$y = 3x + 2$

Graph both equations.
$y = 3x - 1$:
slope $= 3$; y-intercept $= -1$
$y = 3x + 2$:
slope $= 3$; y-intercept $= 2$

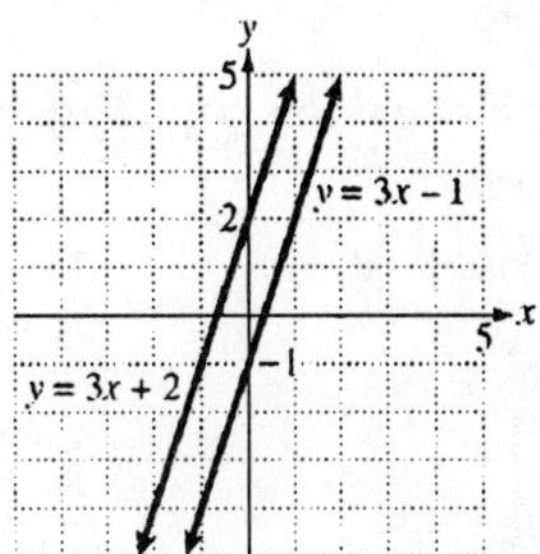

The lines are parallel, so the system has no solution.

12. $x - y = 4$
$x = -2$

Graph both equations:
$x - y = 4$:
x-intercept $= 4$; y-intercept $= -4$
$x = 2$:
vertical line with x-intercept $= -2$

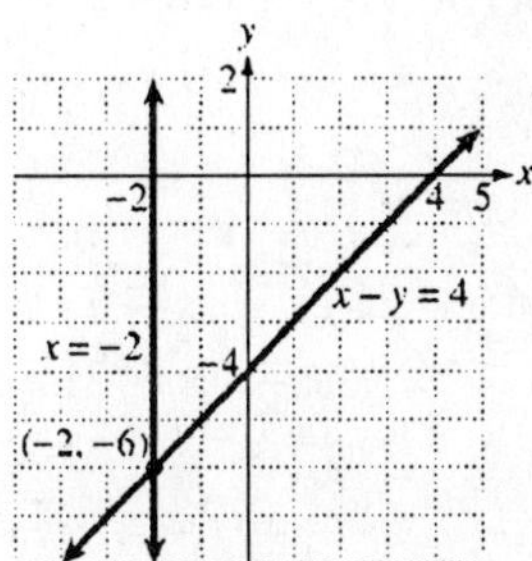

Solution: $(-2, -6)$

13. $x = 2$
$y = 5$

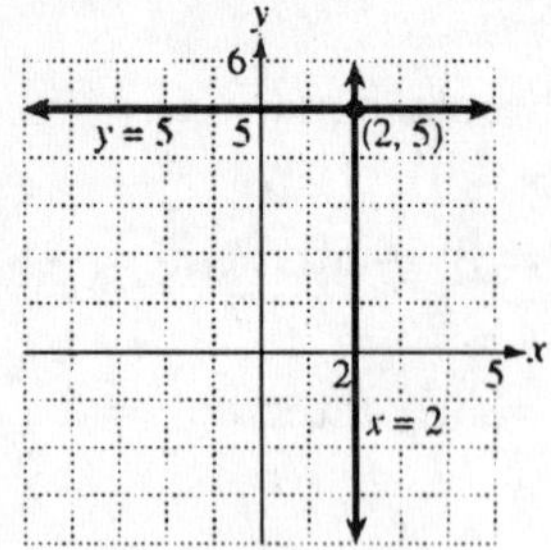

The vertical line and horizontal line intersect at $(2, 5)$.
Solution: $(2, 5)$

14. $x = 2$
$x = 5$

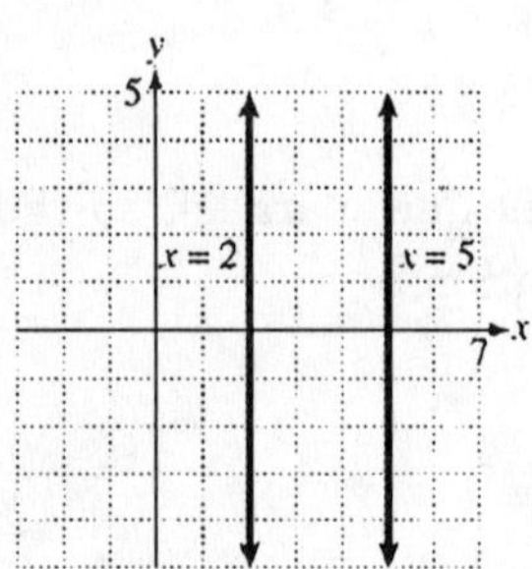

The two vertical lines are parallel, so the system has no solution.

15. $2x - 3y = 7$
$y = 3x - 7$

Substitute $3x - 7$ for y in the first equation.

$$
\begin{aligned}
2x - 3y &= 7 \\
2x - 3(3x - 7) &= 7 \\
2x - 9x + 21 &= 7 \\
-7x + 21 &= 7 \\
-7x &= -14 \\
x &= 2
\end{aligned}
$$

Back-substitute 7 for x into the second equation and solve for y.

$$
\begin{aligned}
y &= 3x - 7 \\
y &= 3(2) - 7 = -1
\end{aligned}
$$

Solution: $(2, -1)$

16. $2x - y = 6$
$x = 13 - 2y$

Substitute $13 - 2y$ for x into the first equation.

$$
\begin{aligned}
2x - y &= 6 \\
2(13 - 2y) - y &= 6 \\
26 - 4y - y &= 6 \\
26 - 5y &= 6 \\
-5y &= -20 \\
y &= 4
\end{aligned}
$$

Back-substitute 4 for y in the second equation.

$$
\begin{aligned}
x &= 13 - 2y \\
x &= 13 - 2(4) = 5
\end{aligned}
$$

Solution: $(5, 4)$

17. $2x - 5y = 1$
$3x + y = -7$

Solve the second equation for y.

$$
\begin{aligned}
3x + y &= -7 \\
y &= -3x - 7
\end{aligned}
$$

Substitute $-3x - 7$ for y in the first equation.

$$
\begin{aligned}
2x - 5y &= 1 \\
2x - 5(-3x - 7) &= 1 \\
2x + 15x + 35 &= 1 \\
17x + 35 &= 1 \\
17x &= -34 \\
x &= -2
\end{aligned}
$$

Back-substitute in the equation $y = -3x - 7$.

$$\begin{aligned} y &= -3x - 7 \\ y &= -3(-2) - 7 = -1 \end{aligned}$$

Solution: $(-2, -1)$

18. $3x + 4y = -13$
$5y - x = -21$

Solve the second equation for x.

$$\begin{aligned} 5y - x &= -21 \\ -x &= -5y - 21 \\ x &= 5y + 21 \end{aligned}$$

Substitute $5y + 21$ for x in the first equation.

$$\begin{aligned} 3x + 4y &= -13 \\ 3(5y + 21) + 4y &= -13 \\ 15y + 63 + 4y &= -13 \\ 19y + 63 &= -13 \\ 19y &= -76 \\ y &= -4 \end{aligned}$$

Back-substitute.

$$\begin{aligned} 3x + 4y &= -13 \\ 3x + 4(-4) &= -13 \\ 3x - 16 &= -13 \\ 3x &= 3 \\ x &= 1 \end{aligned}$$

Solution: $(1, -4)$

19. $y = 39 - 3x$
$y = 2x - 61$

Substitute $2x - 61$ for y in the first equation.

$$\begin{aligned} 2x - 61 &= 39 - 3x \\ 5x - 61 &= 39 \\ 5x &= 100 \\ x &= 20 \end{aligned}$$

Back-substitute.

$$\begin{aligned} y &= 2x - 1 \\ y &= 2(20) - 61 = -21 \end{aligned}$$

Solution: $(20, -21)$

20. $4x + y = 5$
$12x + 3y = 15$

Solve the first equation for y.

$$\begin{aligned} 4x + y &= 5 \\ y &= -4x + 5 \end{aligned}$$

Substitute $-4x + 5$ for y in the second equation.

$$\begin{aligned} 12x + 3y &= 15 \\ 12x + 3(-4x + 5) &= 15 \\ 12x - 12x + 15 &= 15 \\ 15 &= 15 \text{ true} \end{aligned}$$

The true statement $15 = 15$ indicates that the given system has infinitely many solutions.

21. $4x - 2y = 10$
$y = 2x + 3$

Substitute $2x + 3$ for y in the first equation.

$$\begin{aligned} 4x - 2y &= 10 \\ 4x - 2(2x + 3) &= 10 \\ 4x - 4x - 6 &= 10 \\ -6 &= 10 \text{ false} \end{aligned}$$

The false statement $-6 = 10$ indicates that the system has no solution.

22. $x - 4 = 0$
$9x - 2y = 0$

Solve the first equation for x.

$$\begin{aligned} x - 4 &= 0 \\ x &= 4 \end{aligned}$$

Substitute 4 for x in the second equation.

$$\begin{aligned} 9x - 2y &= 0 \\ 9(4) - 2y &= 0 \\ 36 - 2y &= 0 \\ -2y &= -36 \\ y &= 18 \end{aligned}$$

Solution: $(4, 18)$

23. $8y = 4x$
$7x + 2y = -8$

Solve the first equation for y.

$$\begin{aligned} 8y &= 4x \\ y &= \frac{1}{2}x \end{aligned}$$

Substitute $\frac{1}{2}x$ for y in the second equation.

$$\begin{aligned} 7x + 2y &= -8 \\ 7x + 2\left(\frac{1}{2}x\right) &= -8 \\ 7x + x &= -8 \\ 8x &= -8 \\ x &= -1 \end{aligned}$$

Back-substitute.

$$\begin{aligned} y &= \frac{1}{2}x \\ y &= \frac{1}{2}(-1) = -\frac{1}{2} \end{aligned}$$

Solution: $(-1, -\frac{1}{2})$

24. $N = -60p + 1000$ Demand model
$N = 4p + 200$ Supply model

Substitute $4p + 200$ for N in the demand equation.

$$\begin{aligned} N &= -60p + 1000 \\ 4p + 200 &= -60p + 1000 \\ 64p + 200 &= 1000 \\ 64p &= 800 \\ p &= 12.5 \end{aligned}$$

If $p = 12.5$,

$$N = 4(12.5) + 200 = 250.$$

Supply and demand are equal when the price of the video is \$12.50. At this price, 250 copies are supplied and sold.

25. $x + y = 6$
$2x + y = 8$

Multiply the first equation by -1 and add the result to the second equation to eliminate the y-terms.

$$\begin{array}{rcr} -x - y &=& -6 \\ 2x + y &=& 8 \\ \hline x \quad &=& 2 \end{array}$$

Back-substitute into either of the original equations to solve for y.

$$\begin{aligned} x + y &= 6 \\ 2 + y &= 6 \\ y &= 4 \end{aligned}$$

Solution: $(2, 4)$

26. $3x - 4y = 1$
$12x - y = -11$

Multiply the first equation by -4 and add the result to the second equation.

$$\begin{aligned} -12x + 16y &= -4 \\ 12x - y &= -11 \\ \hline 15y &= -15 \\ y &= -1 \end{aligned}$$

Back-substitute.

$$\begin{aligned} 3x - 4y &= 1 \\ 3x - 4(-1) &= 1 \\ 3x + 4 &= 1 \\ 3x &= -3 \\ x &= -1 \end{aligned}$$

Solution: $(-1, -1)$

27. $3x - 7y = 13$
$6x + 5y = 7$

Multiply the first equation by -2. Don't change the second equation.

$$\begin{aligned} -6x + 14y &= -26 \\ 6x - 5y &= 7 \\ \hline 19y &= -19 \\ y &= -1 \end{aligned}$$

Back-substitute.

$$\begin{aligned} 3x - 7y &= 13 \\ 3x - 7(-1) &= 13 \\ 3x + 7 &= 13 \\ 3x &= 6 \\ x &= 2 \end{aligned}$$

Solution: $(2, -1)$

28. $8x - 4y = 16$
$4x + 5y = 22$

Multiply the second equation by -2. Don't change the first equation.

$$\begin{aligned} 8x - 4y &= 16 \\ 8x - 10y &= -44 \\ \hline -14y &= -28 \\ y &= 2 \end{aligned}$$

Back-substitute.

$$\begin{aligned} 8x - 4y &= 16 \\ 8x - 4(2) &= 16 \\ 8x - 8 &= 16 \\ 8x &= 24 \\ x &= 3 \end{aligned}$$

Solution: $(3, 2)$

29. $5x - 2y = 8$
$3x - 5y = 1$

Multiply the first equation by 3. Multiply the second equation by -5.

$$\begin{aligned} -15x - 6y &= 24 \\ 15x + 25y &= -5 \\ \hline 19y &= 19 \\ y &= 1 \end{aligned}$$

Back-substitute.

$$\begin{aligned} 5x - 2y &= 8 \\ 5x - 2(1) &= 8 \\ 5x - 2 &= 8 \\ 5x &= 10 \\ x &= 2 \end{aligned}$$

Solution: $(2, 1)$

30. $2x + 7y = 0$
$7x + 2y = 0$

Multiply the first equation by 7.
Multiply the second equation by -2.

$$\begin{aligned} 14x + 49y &= 0 \\ 14x - 4y &= 0 \\ \hline 45y &= 0 \\ y &= 0 \end{aligned}$$

Back-substitute.

$$\begin{aligned} 2x + 7y &= 0 \\ 2x + 7(0) &= 0 \\ 2x &= 0 \\ x &= 0 \end{aligned}$$

Solution: $(0, 0)$

31. $x + 3y = -4$
$3x + 2y = 3$

Multiply the first equation by -3.
Don't change the second equation.

$$\begin{aligned} -3x - 9y &= 12 \\ 3x + 2y &= 3 \\ \hline -7y &= 15 \\ y &= -\frac{15}{7} \end{aligned}$$

Instead of back-substituting $-\frac{15}{7}$ and working with fractions, go back to the original system. Multiply the first equation by 2 and the second equation by -3.

$$\begin{aligned} 2x + 6y &= -8 \\ 9x - 6y &= -9 \\ \hline -7x \qquad &= -17 \\ x &= \frac{17}{7} \end{aligned}$$

Solution: $\left(\frac{17}{7}, -\frac{15}{7}\right)$

32. $2x + y = 5$
$2x + y = 7$

Multiply the first equation by -1.
Don't change the second equation.

$$\begin{aligned} -2x - y &= -5 \\ 2x + y &= 7 \\ \hline 0 &= 2 \text{ false} \end{aligned}$$

The false statement $0 = 2$ indicates that the system has no solution.

33. $3x - 4y = -1$
$-6x + 8y = 2$

Multiply the first equation by 2.
Don't change the second equation.

$$\begin{aligned} 6x - 8y &= -2 \\ -6x + 8y &= 2 \\ \hline 0 &= 0 \text{ true} \end{aligned}$$

The true statement $0 = 0$ indicates that the system has infinitely many solutions.

34. $2x = 8y + 24$
$3x + 5y = 2$

Rewrite the first equation in the form $Ax + By = C$.

$$2x - 8y = 24$$

Multiply this equation by 3.
Multiply the second equation by -2.

$$\begin{aligned} 6x - 24y &= 72 \\ -6x - 10y &= -4 \\ \hline -34y &= 68 \\ y &= -2 \end{aligned}$$

Back-substitute.

$$\begin{aligned} 3x + 5y &= 2 \\ 3x + 5(-2) &= 2 \\ 3x - 10 &= 2 \\ 3x &= 12 \\ x &= 4 \end{aligned}$$

Solution: $(4, -2)$

35. $5x - 7y = 2$
$3x = 4y$

Rewrite the second equation in the form $Ax + By = C$.

$$3x - 4y = 0$$

Multiply this equation by -5.
Multiply the first equation by 3.

$$\begin{aligned} 15x - 21y &= 6 \\ -15x + 20y &= 0 \\ \hline -y &= 6 \\ y &= -6 \end{aligned}$$

Back-substitute.

$$\begin{aligned} 3x - 4y &= 0 \\ 3x - 4(-6) &= 0 \\ 3x + 24 &= 0 \\ 3x &= -24 \\ x &= -8 \end{aligned}$$

Solution: $(-8, -6)$

36. $3x + 4y = -8$
$2x + 3y = -5$

Multiply the first equation by 2.
Multiply the second equation by -3.

$$\begin{aligned} 6x + 8y &= -16 \\ -6x - 9y &= 15 \\ \hline -y &= -1 \\ y &= 1 \end{aligned}$$

Back-substitute.

$$\begin{aligned} 3x + 4y &= -8 \\ 3x + 4(1) &= -8 \\ 3x + 4 &= -8 \\ 3x &= -12 \\ x &= -4 \end{aligned}$$

Solution: $(-4, 1)$

37. $6x + 8y = 39$
$y = 2x - 2$

Substitute $2x - 2$ for y in the first equation.

$$\begin{aligned} 6x + 8y &= 39 \\ 6x + 8(2x - 2) &= 39 \\ 6x + 16x - 16 &= 39 \\ 22x - 16 &= 39 \\ 22x &= 55 \\ x &= \frac{55}{22} = \frac{5}{2} \end{aligned}$$

Back-substitute $\frac{5}{2}$ for x into the second equation of the system.

$$y = 2x - 2$$
$$y = 2\left(\frac{5}{2}\right) - 2 = 5 - 2 = 3$$

Solution: $\left(\frac{5}{2}, 3\right)$

38. $x + 2y = 7$
$2x + y = 8$

Multiply the first equation by -2.
Don't change the second equation.

$$\begin{aligned} -2x - 4y &= -14 \\ 2x + y &= 8 \\ \hline -3y &= -6 \\ y &= 2 \end{aligned}$$

Back-substitute.

$$\begin{aligned} x + 2y &= 7 \\ x + 2(2) &= 7 \\ x + 4 &= 7 \\ x &= 3 \end{aligned}$$

Solution: $(3, 2)$

39. $y = 2x - 3$
$y = -2x - 1$

Substitute $-2x - 1$ for y in the first equation.

$$\begin{aligned} -2x - 1 &= 2x - 3 \\ -4x - 1 &= -3 \\ -4x &= -2 \\ x &= \frac{1}{2} \end{aligned}$$

Back-substitute.

$$\begin{aligned} y &= 2x - 3 \\ y &= 2\left(\frac{1}{2}\right) - 3 = -2 \end{aligned}$$

Solution: $(\frac{1}{2}, -2)$

40. $3x - 6y = 7$
$3x = 6y$

Solve the second equation for x.

$$\begin{aligned} 3x &= 6y \\ x &= 2y \end{aligned}$$

Substitute $3y$ for x in the first equation.

$$\begin{aligned} 3x - 6y &= 7 \\ 3(2y) - 6y &= 7 \\ 6y - 6y &= 7 \\ 0 &= 7 \end{aligned}$$

The false statement $0 = 7$ indicates that the system has no solution.

41. $y - 7 = 0$
$7x - 3y = 0$

Solve the first equation for y.

$$\begin{aligned} y - 7 &= 0 \\ y &= 7 \end{aligned}$$

Substitute 7 for y in the second equation.

$$\begin{aligned} 7x - 3y &= 0 \\ 7x - 3(7) &= 0 \\ 7x - 21 &= 0 \\ 7x &= 21 \\ x &= 3 \end{aligned}$$

Solution: $(3, 7)$

42. Let $x =$ the average life span for a horse
Let $y =$ the average life span for a lion.

$$\begin{aligned} x + y &= 35 \\ x - y &= 5 \\ \hline 2x \qquad &= 40 \\ x &= 20 \end{aligned}$$

$$\begin{aligned} 20 + y &= 35 \\ y &= 15 \end{aligned}$$

The average life span is 20 years for a horse and 15 years for a lion.

43. Let $x =$ the weight of a gorilla.
Let $y =$ the weight of an orangutan.

$$\begin{aligned} 2x + 3y &= 1465 \\ x + 2y &= 815 \end{aligned}$$

Multiply the second equation by -2. Don't change the first equation.

$$\begin{aligned} 2x + 3y &= 1465 \\ -2x - 4y &= -1630 \\ \hline -y &= -165 \\ y &= 165 \end{aligned}$$

$$\begin{aligned} x + 2(165) &= 815 \\ x + 330 &= 815 \\ x &= 485 \end{aligned}$$

The weight of a gorilla is 485 pounds and the weight of an orangutan is 165 pounds.

44. Let $x =$ the cholesterol content of one ounce of shrimp (in milligrams).
Let $y =$ the cholesterol content in one ounce of scallops.

$$\begin{aligned} 3x + 2y &= 156 \\ 5x + 3y &= 300 - 45 \end{aligned}$$

Simplify the second equation.

$$5x + 3y = 255$$

Multiply this equation by -2.
Multiply the first equation by 3.

$$\begin{array}{r} 9x + 6y = 468 \\ \underline{-10x - 6y = -510} \\ -x \qquad = -42 \\ x = 42 \end{array}$$

Back-substitute.

$$\begin{aligned} 3x + 2y &= 156 \\ 3(42) + 2y &= 156 \\ 126 + 2y &= 156 \\ 2y &= 30 \\ y &= 15 \end{aligned}$$

There are 42 mg of cholesterol in an ounce of shrimp and 15 mg in an ounce of scallops.

45. Let $x =$ the length of a tennis table top.
Let $y =$ the width.
Use the formula for the perimeter of a rectangle to write the first equation and the other information in the problem to write the second equation.

$$\begin{aligned} 2x + 2y &= 28 \\ 4x - 3y &= 21 \end{aligned}$$

Multiply the first equation by -2.

$$\begin{array}{r} -4x - 4y = -56 \\ \underline{4x - 3y = 21} \\ -7y = -35 \\ y = 5 \end{array}$$

$$\begin{aligned} 2x + 2(5) &= 28 \\ 2x + 10 &= 28 \\ 2x &= 18 \\ x &= 9 \end{aligned}$$

The length is 9 feet and the width is 5 feet, so the dimensions of the table are 9 feet by 5 feet.

46. Let $x =$ the length of the garden.
Let $y =$ the width of the garden.

The perimeter of the garden is 24 yards, so

$$2x + 2y = 24.$$

Since there are two lengths and two widths to be fenced, the information about the cost of fencing leads to the equation

$$3(2x) + 2(2y) = 62.$$

Simplify the second equation.

$$6x + 4y = 62.$$

Multiply the first equation by -2.

$$\begin{array}{r} -4x - 4y = -48 \\ \underline{6x + 4y = 62} \\ 2x \qquad = 14 \\ x = 7 \end{array}$$

$$\begin{aligned} 2(7) + 2y &= 24 \\ 14 + 2y &= 24 \\ 2y &= 10 \\ y &= 5 \end{aligned}$$

The length of the garden is 7 yards and the width is 5 yards.

47. Let x = daily cost for room.
Let $150 - x$ = daily cost for car.

First plan: $3x + 2y = 360$
Second plan: $4x + 3y = 500$

Multiply the first equation by 3.
Multiply the second equation by -2.

$$\begin{array}{r} 9x + 6y = 1080 \\ -8x - 6y = -1000 \\ \hline x \quad = 80 \end{array}$$

$$\begin{aligned} 3(80) + 2y &= 360 \\ 240 + 2y &= 360 \\ 2y &= 120 \\ y &= 60 \end{aligned}$$

The cost per day is \$80 for the room and \$60 for the car.

48. Let x = the number of minutes of long-distance calls.
Let y = the monthly cost of a telephone plan.

Plan A: $y = 15 + 0.05x$
Plan B: $y = 10 + 0.075x$

To determine the amount of calling time that will result in the same cost for both plans, solve this system by the substitution method. Substitute $15 + 0.05x$ for x in the first equation.

$$\begin{aligned} 15 + 0.05x &= 10 + 0.075x \\ 15 - 0.025x &= 10 \\ -0.025x &= -5 \\ \frac{-0.025x}{-0.025} &= \frac{-5}{-0.025} \\ x &= 200 \end{aligned}$$

If $x = 200$,

$$y = 15 + 0.05(200) = 25.$$

The costs for the two plans will be equal for 200 minutes of long-distance calls per month. The cost of each plan will be \$25.

Note: In the answer graphs for Exercises 49–55, only the solution set of the system is shaded.

49. $3x - y \le 6$
$x + y \ge 2$

Graph $3x - y \le 6$:
Graph $3x - y = 6$ as a solid line using the x-intercept 2 and y-intercept -6. Because $(0, 0)$ makes the inequality true, shade the half-plane containing $(0, 0)$.
Graph $x + y \ge 2$:
Graph $x + y = 2$ as a solid line using the x-intercept 2 and y-intercept 2. Because $(0, 0)$ makes the inequality false, shade the half-plane *not* containing $(0, 0)$.
The solution set of the system is the intersection (overlap) of the two shaded regions. The closed dot shows that $(0, 2)$ is part of the solution set.

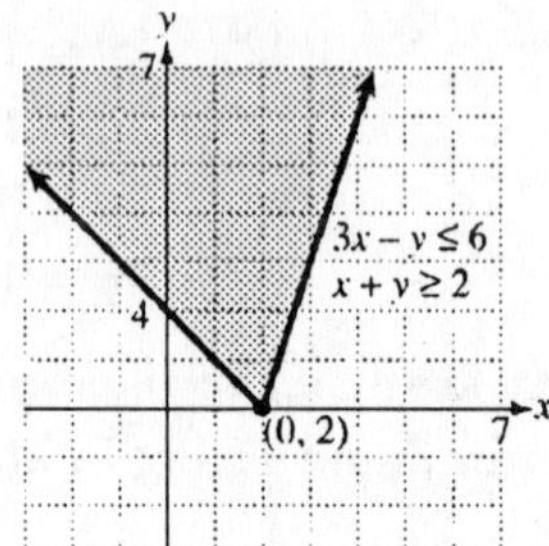

50. $x + y < 4$
$x - y < 4$

Graph $x + y < 4$:
Graph $x+y = 4$ as a dashed line using the x-intercept 4 and y-intercept 4. Because $0+0 < 4$ is true, shade the half-plane containing $(0, 0)$.

$x - y < 4$:
Graph $x - y = 4$ as a dashed line using the x-intercept 4 and y-intercept -4. Because $0 - 0 < 4$ is true, shade the half-plane containing $(0, 0)$.
The solution set of the system is the intersection of the two shaded regions. The open dot shows that $(4, 0)$ is not part of the solution set.

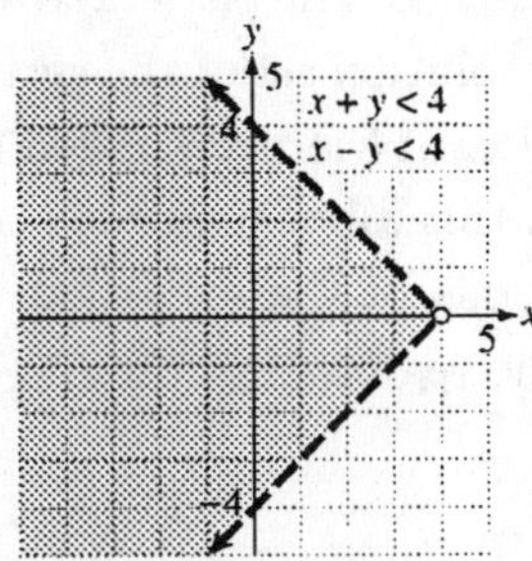

51. $y < 2x - 2$
$x \geq 3$

Graph $y < 2x - 2$:
Graph $y = 2x - 3$ as a dashed line using the slope 2 and y-intercept -2. Since $0 < 2(0) - 2$ is false, shade the half-plane *not* containing $(0, 0)$.
Graph $x \geq 3$:
Graph $x = 3$ as a solid vertical line with x-intercept 3. Since $0 \geq 3$ is false, shade the half-plane *not* containing $(0, 0)$.
The solution set of the system is the intersection of the two shaded regions. The open dot shows that $(3, 4)$ is not part of the solution set.

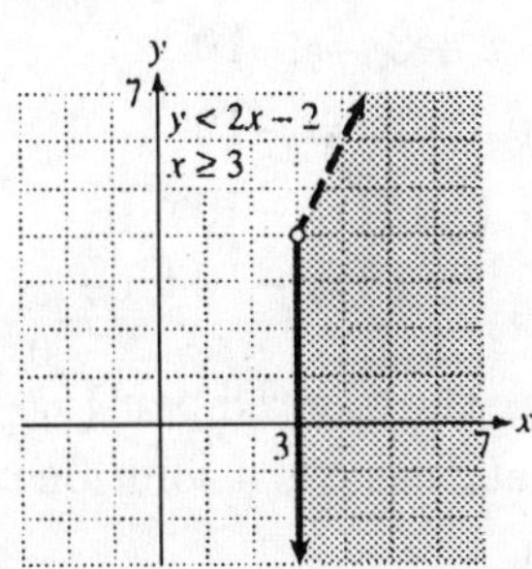

52. $4x + 6y \leq 24$
$y > 2$

Graph $4x + 6y \leq 24$:
Graph $4x + 6y = 24$ as a solid line with x-intercept 6 and y-intercept 4. Since $4(0) + 6(0) \leq 24$ is true, shade the half-plane containing $(0, 0)$.
Graph $y > 2$:
Graph $0 < 2$ is false, shade the half-plane *not* containing$(0, 0)$, which is the half-plane above the line.
The solution set of the system is the intersection of the two shaded regions. The open dot shows that $(3, 2)$ is not part of the solutlion set.

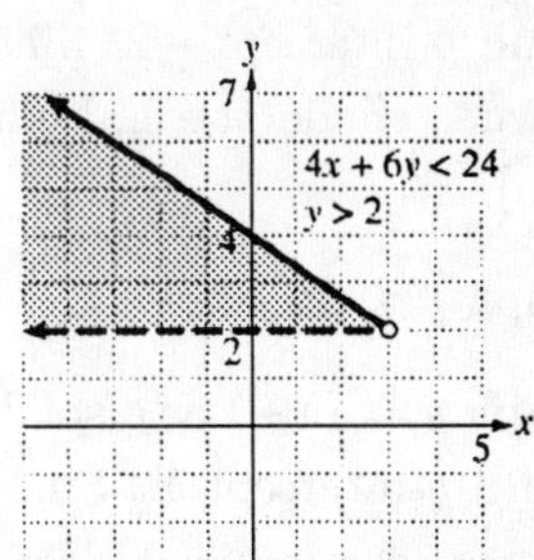

53. $x \leq 3$
$y \geq -2$

Graph $x \leq 3$:
Shade $x = 3$ as a solid vertical line. Since $0 \leq 3$ is true, shade the half-plane containing $(0, 0)$.
Graph $y \geq -2$:
Shade $y = -2$ as a solid vertical line. Since $0 \geq -2$ is true, shade the half-plane containing $(0, 0)$.

The solution set of the system is the intersection of the two shaded regions.

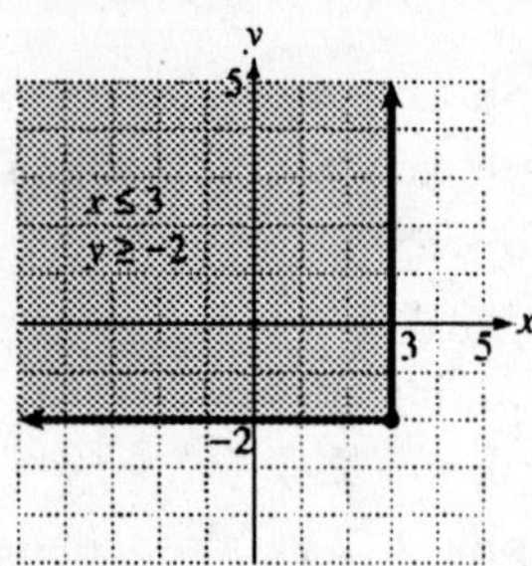

54. $y \geq \dfrac{1}{2}x - 2$

$y \leq \dfrac{1}{2}x + 1$

Graph $y \geq \frac{1}{2}x - 2$:

Graph $y = \frac{1}{2}x - 2$ as a solid line with slope $\frac{1}{2}$ and y-intercept -2. Since $0 \geq \frac{1}{2}(0) - 2$ is true, shade the half-plane containing $(0, 0)$.

Graph $y \leq \frac{1}{2}x + 1$:

Graph $y = \frac{1}{2}x + 1$ as a solid line with slope $\frac{1}{2}$ and y-intercept 1. Since $0 \leq \frac{1}{2}(0) + 1$ is true, shade the half-plane containing $(0, 0)$.

The solution set of the system is the intersection of the two shaded regions. This is region between and including the two parallel lines.

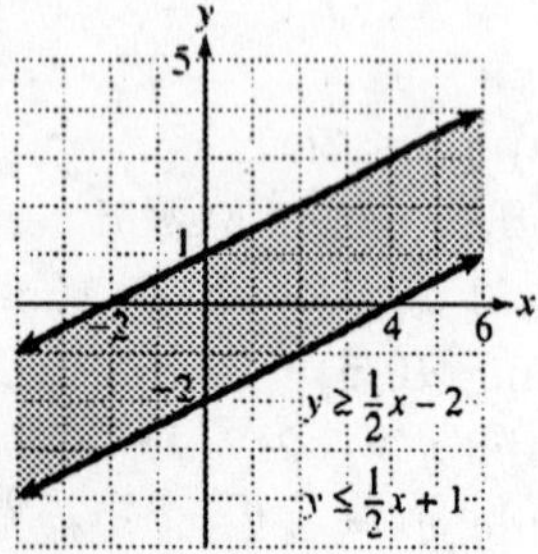

55. $x \leq 0$

$y \geq 0$

Graph $x \leq 0$:
Graph $x = 0$ (the y-axis) as a solid line. Shade the half-plane to the left of the y-axis.
Graph $y \geq 0$:
Graph $y = 0$ (the x-axis) as a solid line. Shade the half-plane above the x-axis.
The solution set of the system is the intersection of the two shaded regions. Notice that this all of quadrant II, including the portions of the axes that are boundaries of the region.

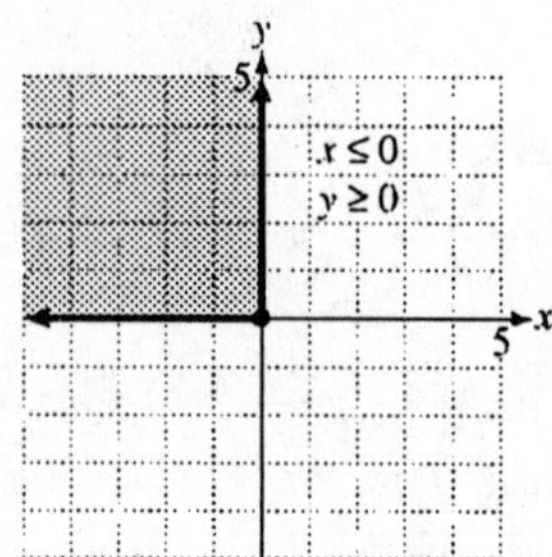

Chapter 5 Test

1. $(5, -5)$

$$\begin{aligned} 2x + y &= 5 \\ 2(5) + (-5) &\stackrel{?}{=} 5 \\ 10 + (-5) &\stackrel{?}{=} 5 \\ 5 &= 5 \text{ true} \end{aligned}$$

$$\begin{aligned} x + 3y &= -10 \\ 5 + 3(-5) &\stackrel{?}{=} -10 \\ 5 + (-15) &\stackrel{?}{=} -10 \\ -10 &= -10 \text{ true} \end{aligned}$$

Since the ordered pair $(5, -5)$ satisfies both equations, it is a solution of the given system.

2. $(-3, 2)$

$$x + 5y = 7$$
$$-3 + 5(2) \stackrel{?}{=} 7$$
$$-3 + 10 \stackrel{?}{=} 7$$
$$7 = 7 \text{ true}$$

$$3x - 4y = 1$$
$$3(-3) - 4(2) \stackrel{?}{=} 1$$
$$-9 - 8 \stackrel{?}{=} 1$$
$$-17 = 1 \text{ false}$$

Since the ordered pair $(-3, 2)$ fails to satisfy *both* equations, it is not a solution of the given system.

3. $x + y = 6$
$4x - y = 4$

Graph both lines on the same axes.
$x + y = 6$:
x-intercept $= 6$; y-intercept $= 6$
$4x - y = 4$:
x-intercept: 1; y-intercept $= -4$

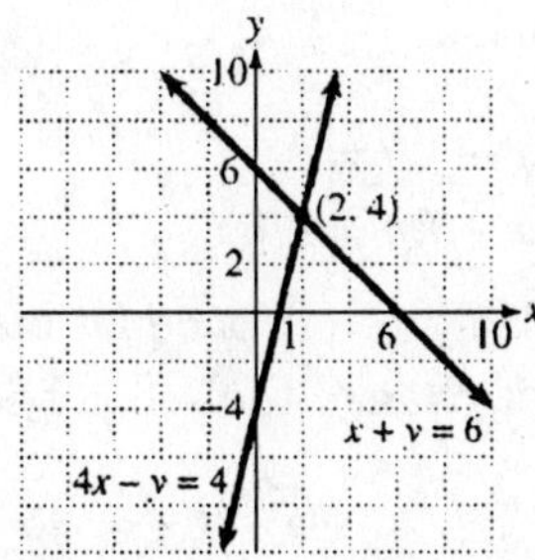

Solution: $(2, 4)$

4. $2x + y = 8$
$y = 3x - 2$

Graph both lines on the same axes.
$2x + y = 8$:
x-intercept $= 4$; y-intercept $= 8$
$y = 3x - 2$:
slope $= 3$; y-intercept $= -2$

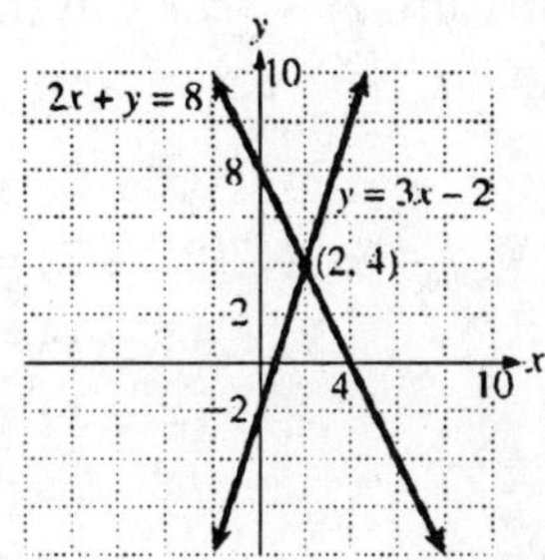

Solution: $(2, 4)$

5. $x = y + 4$
$3x + 7y = -18$

Substitute $y + 4$ for x in the second equation.

$$3x + 7y = -18$$
$$3(y + 4) + 7y = -18$$
$$3y + 12 + 7y = -18$$
$$10y + 12 = -18$$
$$10y = -30$$
$$y = -3$$

Back-substitute -3 for y in the first equation.

$$x = y + 4$$
$$x = -3 + 4 = 1$$

Solution: $(1, -3)$

6. $2x - y = 7$
$3x + 2y = 0$

Solve the first equation for y.

$$\begin{aligned} 2x - y &= 7 \\ -y &= -2x + 7 \\ y &= 2x - 7 \end{aligned}$$

Substitute $2x - 7$ for y in the second equation.

$$\begin{aligned} 3x + 2y &= 0 \\ 3x + 2(2x - 7) &= 0 \\ 3x + 4x - 14 &= 0 \\ 7x - 14 &= 0 \\ 7x &= 14 \\ x &= 2 \end{aligned}$$

Back-substitute 2 for x in the equation $3x + 2y = 0$.

$$\begin{aligned} 3x + 2y &= 0 \\ 3(2) + 2y &= 0 \\ 6 + 2y &= 0 \\ 2y &= -6 \\ y &= -3 \end{aligned}$$

Solution: $(2, -3)$

7. $2x - 4y = 3$
$x = 2y + 4$

Substitute $2y + 4$ for x in the first equation.

$$\begin{aligned} 2x - 4y &= 3 \\ 2(2y + 4) - 4y &= 3 \\ 4y + 8 - 4y &= 3 \\ 8 &= 3 \text{ false} \end{aligned}$$

The false statement $8 = 3$ indicates that the system has no solution.

8.

$$\begin{array}{r} 2x + y = 2 \\ \underline{4x - y = -8} \\ 6x = -6 \\ x = -1 \end{array}$$

Back-substitute.

$$\begin{aligned} 2x + y &= 2 \\ 2(-1) + y &= 2 \\ -2 + y &= 2 \\ y &= 4 \end{aligned}$$

Solution: $(-1, 4)$

9. $2x + 3y = 1$
$3x + 2y = -6$

Multiply the first equation by 3.
Multiply the second equation by -2.

$$\begin{array}{r} 6x + 9y = 3 \\ \underline{-6x - 4y = 12} \\ 5y = 15 \\ y = 3 \end{array}$$

Back-substitute.

$$\begin{aligned} 2x + 3y &= 1 \\ 2x + 3(3) &= 1 \\ 2x + 9 &= 1 \\ 2x &= -8 \\ x &= -4 \end{aligned}$$

Solution: $(-4, 3)$

10. $3x - 2y = 2$
$-9x + 6y = -6$

Multiply the first equation by 3.
Don't change the second equation.

$$\begin{array}{r} 9x - 6y = 6 \\ \underline{-9x + 6y = -6} \\ 0 = 0 \text{ true} \end{array}$$

The true statement $0 = 0$ indicates that the equation has infinitely many solutions.

11. Let $x =$ the cost of World War II (in billions of dollars).
Let $y =$ the cost of the Vietnam War.

$$\begin{aligned} x + y &= 500 \\ x - y &= 120 \\ \hline 2x \quad &= 620 \\ x &= 310 \end{aligned}$$

$$\begin{aligned} 310 + y &= 500 \\ y &= 190 \end{aligned}$$

The cost of World War II was \$310 billion and the cost of the Vietnam War was \$190 billion (in current dollars).

12. Let $x =$ the length of the garden.
Let $y =$ the width of the garden.

The perimeter of the garden is 34 yards, so

$$2x + 2y = 34.$$

Since there are two lengths and two widths to be fenced, the information about the cost of fencing leads to the equation

$$2(2x) + 1(2y) = 58.$$

Simplify the second equation.

$$4x + 2y = 58$$

Multiply this equation by -1 and add the result to the first equation.

$$\begin{aligned} 2x + 2y &= 34 \\ -4x - 2y &= -58 \\ \hline -2x \quad &= -24 \\ x &= 12 \end{aligned}$$

$$\begin{aligned} 2(12) + 2y &= 34 \\ 24 + 2y &= 34 \\ 2y &= 10 \\ y &= 5 \end{aligned}$$

The length of the garden is 12 yards and the width is 5 yards.

13. Let $x =$ the number of minutes of long-distance calls.
Let $y =$ the monthly cost of a telephone plan.

Plan A: $y = 15 + 0.05x$
Plan B: $y = 5 + 0.07x$

To determine the amount of calling time that will result in the same cost for both plans, solve this system by the substitution method. Substitute $5 + 0.07x$ for y in the first equation.

$$\begin{aligned} 5 + 0.07x &= 15 + 0.05x \\ 5 + 0.02x &= 15 \\ 0.02x &= 10 \\ \frac{0.02x}{0.02} &= \frac{10}{0.02} \\ x &= 500 \end{aligned}$$

If $x = 500$,

$$y = 15 + 0.05(500) = 40.$$

The costs of the two plans will be equal for 500 calls per month. The cost of each plan will be \$40.

In the answer graphs for Exercises 14 and 15, only the solution set of the system is shaded.

14. $x - 3y > 6$
$2x + 4y \leq 8$

Graph $x - 3y > 6$:
Graph $x - 3y > 6$ as a dashed line using the x-intercept 6 and y-intercept -2. Because $0 - 3(0) > 6$ is false, shade the half-plane *not* containing $(0, 0)$.
Graph $2x + 4y \leq 8$:
Graph $2x + 4y = 8$ as a solid line using the x-intercept 4 and y-intercept 2. Because $2(0) + 4(0) \leq 8$ is true, shade the half-plane containing $(0, 0)$.

The solution set of the system is the intersection (overlap) of the two shaded regions.

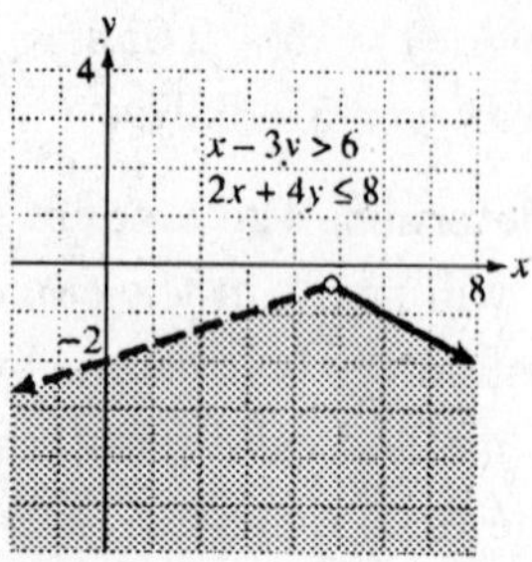

15. $y \geq 2x - 4$
$x < 2$

Graph $y \geq 2x - 4$:
Graph $y = 2x - 4$ as a solid line using the slope 2 and y-intercept -4. Since $0 \geq 2(0) - 4$ is true, shade the half-plane containing $(0,0)$.
Graph $x < 2$:
Graph $x = 2$ as a dashed vertical line with x-intercept 2. Since $0 < 2$ is true, shade the half-plane containing $(0,0)$.
The solution set of the system is the intersection (overlap) of the two shaded regions. The open dot shows that $(2,0)$ is not part of the solution set.

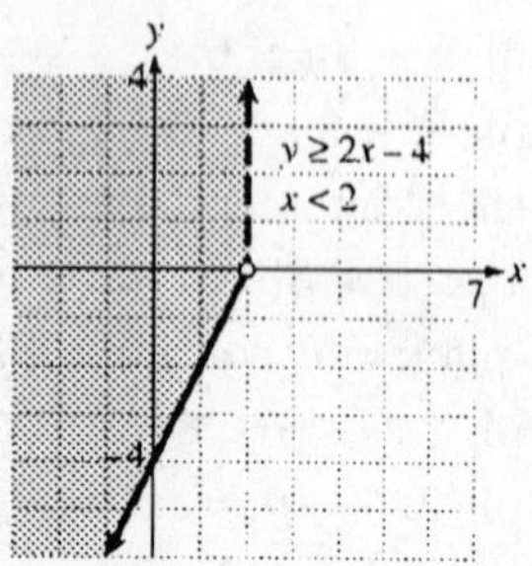

Chapter 5 Cumulative Review Exercises (Chapters 1-5)

1. $$\begin{aligned} -14 - [18 - (6 - 10)] &= -14 - [18 - (-4)] \\ &= -14 - 22 \\ &= -14 + (-22) \\ &= -36 \end{aligned}$$

2. $$\begin{aligned} 6(3x - 2) - (x - 1) &= 18x - 12 - x + 1 \\ &= 17x - 11 \end{aligned}$$

3. $$\begin{aligned} 17(x + 3) &= 13 + 4(x - 10) \\ 17x + 51 &= 13 + 4x - 40 \\ 17x + 51 &= 4x - 27 \\ 13x + 51 &= -27 \\ 13x &= -78 \\ x &= -6 \end{aligned}$$

The solution is -6.

4. $$\frac{x}{4} - 1 = \frac{x}{5}$$

To clear fractions, multiply both sides by 20.

$$\begin{aligned} 20\left(\frac{x}{4} - 1\right) &= 20\left(\frac{x}{5}\right) \\ 5x - 20 &= 4x \\ x - 20 &= 0 \\ x &= 20 \end{aligned}$$

The solution is 20.

5. $A = P + Prt$ for t

$$\begin{aligned} A &= P + Prt \\ A - P &= P + Prt - P \\ A - P &= Prt \\ \frac{A - P}{Pr} &= \frac{Prt}{Pr} \\ \frac{A - P}{Pr} &= t \quad \text{or} \quad t = \frac{A - P}{Pr} \end{aligned}$$

6.
$$2x - 5 < 5x - 11$$
$$2x - 5 - 5x < 5x - 11$$
$$-3x - 5 < -11$$
$$-3x - 5 + 5 < -11 + 5$$
$$-3x < -6$$
$$\frac{-3x}{-3} > \frac{-6}{-3}$$
$$x > 2$$

$\{x|x > 2\}$

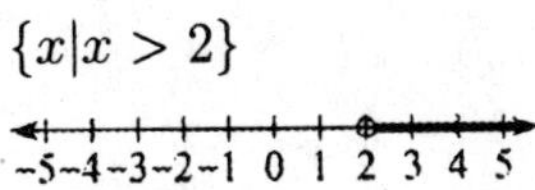

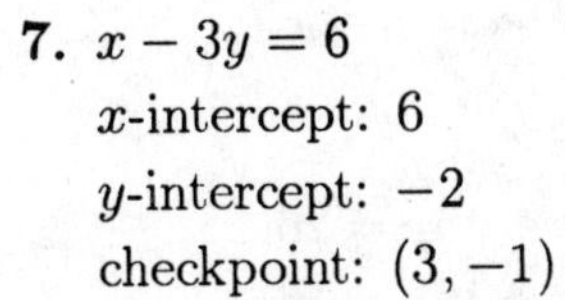

7. $x - 3y = 6$
x-intercept: 6
y-intercept: -2
checkpoint: $(3, -1)$

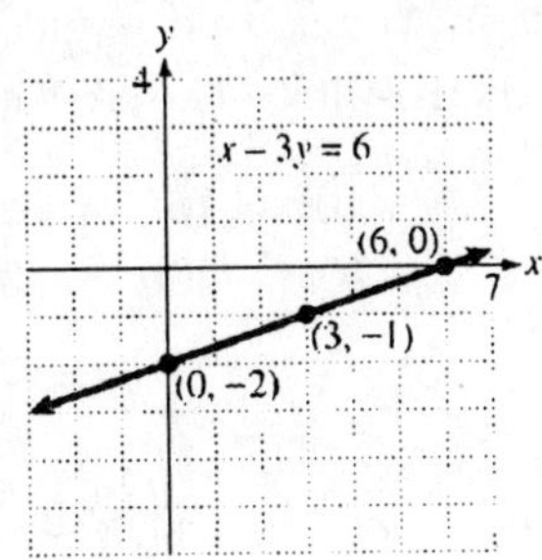

8. $y = 4 - x^2$

Construct a table of values.

x	$y = 4 - x^2$	(x, y)
-3	$y = 4 - (-3)^2 = -5$	$(-3, -5)$
-2	$y = 4 - (-2)^2 = 0$	$(-2, 0)$
-1	$y = 4 - (-1)^2 = 3$	$(-1, 3)$
0	$y = 4 - 0^2 = 4$	$(0, 4)$
1	$y = 4 - 1^2 = 3$	$(1, 3)$
2	$y = 4 - 2^2 = 0$	$(2, 0)$
3	$y = 4 - 3^2 = -5$	$(3, -5)$

Plot the ordered pairs from the table and draw a smooth curve through them.

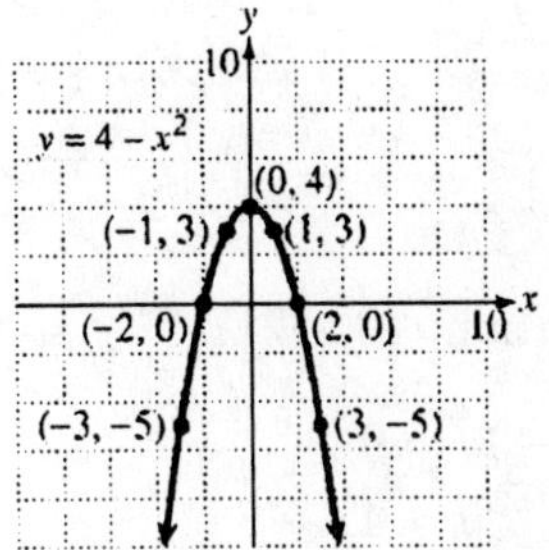

9. $y = -\frac{3}{5}x + 2$

slope $= -\frac{3}{5} = \frac{-3}{5}$; y-intercept $= 2$

Plot the point $(0, 2)$. From this point, move 3 units down (because -3 is negative) and 5 units to the right to reach the point $(5, -1)$. Draw a line through $(0, 2)$ and $(5, -1)$.

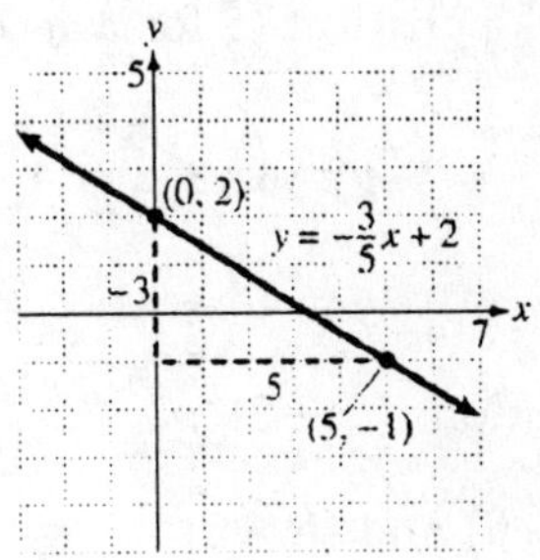

10. $3x - 4y = 8$
$4x + 5y = -10$

To solve this system by the addition method, multiply the first equation by 4 and the second equation by -3. Then add the results.

$$\begin{aligned} 12x - 16y &= 32 \\ -12x - 15y &= 30 \\ \hline -31y &= 62 \\ y &= -2 \end{aligned}$$

Back-substitute.

$$\begin{aligned} 3x - 4y &= 8 \\ 3x - 4(-2) &= 8 \\ 3x + 8 &= 8 \\ 3x &= 0 \\ x &= 0 \end{aligned}$$

Solution: $(0, -2)$

11. $2x - 3y = 9$
$y = 4x - 8$

To solve this system by the substitution method, substitute $4x - 8$ for y in the first equation.

$$\begin{aligned} 2x - 3y &= 9 \\ 2x - 3(4x - 8) &= 9 \\ 2x - 12x + 24 &= 9 \\ -10x + 24 &= 9 \\ -10x &= -15 \\ x &= \frac{15}{10} = \frac{3}{2} \end{aligned}$$

Back-substitute $\frac{3}{2}$ for x in the second equation.

$$y = 4x - 8$$

$$y = 4\left(\frac{3}{2}\right) - 8 = -2$$

Solution: $(\frac{3}{2}, -2)$

12. $(5, -6)$ and $(6, -5)$

$$m = \frac{y_2 - y_1}{x_2 - x_1} = \frac{-5 - (-6)}{6 - 5} = \frac{1}{1} = 1$$

13. Passing through $(-1, 6)$ with slope $= -4$

point-slope form:

$$\begin{aligned} y - y_1 &= m(x - x_1) \\ y - 6 &= -4[x - (-1)] \\ y - 6 &= -4(x + 1) \end{aligned}$$

slope-intercept form:

$$\begin{aligned} y - 6 &= -4x - 4 \\ y &= -4x + 2 \end{aligned}$$

14. Let $x =$ the length of the altitude of the triangle.

Use the formula for the area of a triangle.

$A = \frac{1}{2}bh$; $A = 80, b = 16$

$$\begin{aligned} A &= \frac{1}{2}bh \\ 80 &= \frac{1}{2} \cdot 16 \cdot h \\ 80 &= 8h \\ 10 &= h \end{aligned}$$

The altitude is 10 feet.

15. Let $x =$ the cost of one pen.
Then $y =$ the cost of one pad.

$$\begin{aligned} 10x + 15y &= 26 \\ 5x + 10y &= 16 \end{aligned}$$

Multiply the second equation by -2 and add the result to the first equation.

$$\begin{aligned} 10x + 15y &= 26 \\ -10x - 20y &= -32 \\ \hline -5y &= -6 \end{aligned}$$

$$y = \frac{6}{5} = 1.2$$

$$10x + 15\left(\frac{6}{5}\right) = 26$$

$$\begin{aligned} 10x + 18 &= 26 \\ 10x &= 8 \\ x &= \frac{8}{10} = 0.8 \end{aligned}$$

On pen costs \$0.80 and one pad costs \$1.20.

16. The integers in the given set are $-93, 0$, $\frac{7}{1}$ $(= 7)$ and $\sqrt{100}$ $(= 10)$.

17. In 2000, 20% of U.S. households had multiple computers.

Note: In Exercises 17–20, "one computer" means "at least one computer."

18. Both lines are rising from left to right, and the line for one computer is steeper, so the graph for one computer has the greater slope. This means that the percentage of U.S. households with one computer increased at a faster rate than the percentage with multiple computers over the years 1997–2001.

19. Let $x =$ the number of years after 1997.
Then $y =$ the percentage of households having one computer.

$y = 42 + 6x$; $y = 84$

$$\begin{aligned} 84 &= 42 + 6x \\ 42 &= 6x \\ 7 &= x \end{aligned}$$

84% of U.S. households will have one computer 7 years after 1997, which will be in the year 2004.

20. $y = \frac{8}{3}x + 12$; $y = 52$

$$\begin{aligned} 52 &= \frac{8}{3}x + 12 \\ 40 &= \frac{8}{3}x \\ \frac{3}{8}(40) &= \frac{3}{8}\left(\frac{8}{3}\right) \\ 15 &= x \end{aligned}$$

52% of U.S. households will have multiple computers 15 years after 1997, which will be in the year 2012.

Chapter 6

EXPONENTS AND POLYNOMIALS

6.1 Adding and Subtracting Polynomials

6.1 CHECK POINTS

CHECK POINT 1

$$\begin{aligned}&(-11x^3+7x^2-11x-5)\\&\quad+(16x^3-3x^2+3x-15)\\&\quad=(-11x^3+16x^3)+(7x^2-3x^2)\\&\qquad+(-11x+3x)+(-5-15)\\&\quad=5x^3+4x^2-8x-20\end{aligned}$$

CHECK POINT 2

$$\begin{array}{r}-11x^3\quad 7x^2-11x-\ \ 5\\ \underline{16x^3-3x^2\qquad 3x-15}\\ 5x^3\quad 4x^2-\ \ 8x-20\end{array}$$

$$\begin{aligned}&5x^3+4x^2+(-8x)+(-20)\\&\quad=5x^3+4x^2-8x-20\end{aligned}$$

CHECK POINT 3

$$\begin{aligned}&(9x^2+7x-2)-(2x^2-4x-6)\\&\quad=(9x^2+7x-2)+(-2x^2+4x+6)\\&\quad=(9x^2-2x^2)+(7x+4x)+(-2+6)\\&\quad=7x^2+11x+4\end{aligned}$$

CHECK POINT 4

$$\begin{aligned}&(10x^3-5x^2+7x-2)\\&\quad-(3x^3-8x^2-5x+6)\\&\quad=(10x^3-5x^2+7x-2)\\&\qquad+(-3x^3+8x^2+5x-6)\\&\quad=(10x^3-3x^3)+(-5x^2+8x^2)\\&\qquad+(7x+5x)+(-2-6)\\&\quad=7x^3+3x^2+12x-8\end{aligned}$$

CHECK POINT 5

$$\begin{array}{r}8y^3-10y^2-14y-2\\ \underline{-(5y^3\qquad\qquad-\ \ 3y+6)}\end{array}$$

$$\begin{array}{r}8y^3-10y^2-14y-2\\ \underline{+-5y^3\qquad\qquad+\ \ 3y-6}\\ 3y^3-10y^2-11y-8\end{array}$$

CHECK POINT 6

$y=0.036x^2-28.x+58.14$; $x=40$

$$\begin{aligned}y&=0.036x^2-28x+58.14\\y&=0.036(40)^2-2.8(40)+58.14\\y&=0.036(1600)-2.8(40)+58.14\\y&=57.6-112+58.14\\y&=3.74\approx 4\end{aligned}$$

Approximately 4 people per thousand who are 40 years old die each year. This corresponds to the point $(40, 3.74)$ on the graph, or approximately $(40, 4)$.

EXERCISE SET 6.1

1. $3x+7$ is a binomial of degree 1.

3. x^3-2x is a binomial of degree 3.

5. $8x^2$ is a monomial of degree of 2.

7. 5 is a monomial. Because it is a nonzero constant, its degree is 0.

9. x^2-3x+4 is a trinomial of degree 2.

11. $7y^2-9y^4+5$ is a trinomial of degree 4.

13. $15x-7x^3$ is a binomial of degree 3.

15. $-9y^{23}$ is a monomial of degree of 23.

17.
$$\begin{aligned}&(5x+7)+(-8x+3)\\&=(5x-8x)+(7+3)\\&=-3x+10\end{aligned}$$

19.
$$\begin{aligned}&(3x^2+7x-9)+(7x^2+8x-2)\\&=(3x^2+7x^2)+(7x+8x)+(-9-2)\\&=10x^2+15x-11\end{aligned}$$

21.
$$\begin{aligned}&(5x^2-3x)+(2x^2-x)\\&=(5x^2+2x^2)+(-3x-x)\\&=7x^2-4x\end{aligned}$$

23.
$$\begin{aligned}&(3x^2-7x+10)+(x^2+6x+8)\\&=(3x^2+x^2)+(-7x+6x)+(10+8)\\&=4x^2-x+18\end{aligned}$$

25.
$$\begin{aligned}&(4y^3+7y-5)+(10y^2-6y+3)\\&=4y^3+10y^2+(7y-6y)+(-5+3)\\&=4y^3+10y^2+y-2\end{aligned}$$

27.
$$\begin{aligned}&(2x^2-6x+7)+(3x^3-3x)\\&=3x^3+2x^2+(-6x-3x)+7\\&=3x^3+2x^2-9x+7\end{aligned}$$

29.
$$\begin{aligned}&(4y^2+8y+11)+(-2y^3+5y+2)\\&=-2y^3+4y^2+(8y+5y)+(11+2)\\&=-2y^3+4y^2+13y+13\end{aligned}$$

31.
$$\begin{aligned}&(-2y^6+3y^4-y^2)+(-y^6+5y^4+2y^2)\\&=(-2y^6-y^6)+(3y^4+5y^4)+(-y^2+2y^2)\\&=-3y^6+8y^4+y^2\end{aligned}$$

33.
$$\begin{aligned}&\left(9x^3-x^2-x-\frac{1}{3}\right)+\left(x^3+x^2+x+\frac{4}{3}\right)\\&=(9x^3+x^3)+(-x^2+x^2)+(-x+x)\\&\quad+\left(-\frac{1}{3}+\frac{4}{3}\right)\\&=10x^2+\frac{3}{3}=10x^2+1\end{aligned}$$

35.
$$\begin{aligned}&\left(\frac{1}{5}x^4+\frac{1}{3}x^3+\frac{3}{8}x^2+6\right)\\&\quad+\left(-\frac{3}{5}x^4+\frac{2}{3}x^3-\frac{1}{2}x^2-6\right)\\&=\left[\frac{1}{5}x^4+\left(-\frac{3}{5}x^4\right)\right]+\left(\frac{1}{3}x^2+\frac{2}{3}x^3\right)\\&\quad+\left[\frac{3}{8}x^2+\left(-\frac{1}{2}x^2\right)\right]+[6+(-6)]\\&=-\frac{2}{5}x^4+x^3-\frac{1}{8}x^2\end{aligned}$$

37.
$$\begin{aligned}&(0.03x^5-0.1x^3+x+0.03)\\&\quad+(-0.02x^5+x^4-0.7x+0.3)\\&=(0.03x^5-0.02x^5)+x^4-0.1x^3\\&\quad+(x-0.07x)+(0.03+0.3)\\&=0.01x^5+x^4-0.1x^3+0.3x+0.33\end{aligned}$$

39. Add:

$$\begin{array}{r}5y^3-7y^2\\ \underline{6y^3+4y^2}\\ 11y^3-3y^2\end{array}$$

41. Add:

$$\begin{array}{r}3x^2-7x+4\\ \underline{-5x^2+6x-3}\\ -2x^2-\ x+1\end{array}$$

43. Add:

$$\begin{array}{r}\frac{1}{4}x^4-\ \frac{2}{3}x^3-5\\ \underline{-\frac{1}{4}x^4+\ \frac{1}{5}x^3+4.7}\end{array}\rightarrow$$

$$\begin{array}{r}\frac{1}{4}x^4-\frac{10}{15}x^3-5.0\\ \underline{-\frac{2}{4}x^3+\frac{3}{15}x^3+4.7}\\ -\frac{1}{4}x^4-\frac{7}{15}x^3-0.3\end{array}$$

45. Add:

$$\begin{array}{r}y^3+5y^2-7y-\ 3\\ \underline{-2y^3+3y^2+4y-11}\\ -y^3+8y^2+4y-14\end{array}$$

47. Add:

$$\begin{array}{r} 4x^3 - 6x^2 + 5x - 7 \\ \underline{-9x^3 \qquad\quad - 4x + 3} \\ -5x^3 - 6x^2 + \ x - 4 \end{array}$$

49. Add:

$$\begin{array}{r} 7x^4 - 3x^3 + x^2 \qquad\qquad \\ \underline{x^3 - x^2 + 4x - 2} \\ 7x^4 - 2x^3 \qquad\quad + 4x - 2 \end{array}$$

51. Add:

$$\begin{array}{r} 7x^2 - \ 9x + 3 \\ 4x^2 + 11x - 2 \\ \underline{-3x^2 + \ 5x - 6} \\ 8x^2 + \ 7x - 6 \end{array}$$

53.

$$\begin{array}{r} 1.2x^3 - \ 3x^2 + \ 9.1 \\ 7.8x^3 - 3.1x^2 + \ 8 \\ \underline{1.2x^2 - \ 6} \\ 9x^3 - 4.9x^2 + 11.1 \end{array}$$

55.

$$\begin{aligned} (x - 8) - (3x + 2) &= (x - 8) + (-3x - 2) \\ &= (x - 3x) + (-8 - 2) \\ &= -2x - 10 \end{aligned}$$

57.

$$\begin{aligned} &(x^2 - 5x - 3) - (6x^2 + 4x + 9) \\ &= (x^2 - 5x - 3) + (-6x^2 - 4x - 9) \\ &= (x^2 - 6x^2) + (-5x - 4x) + (-3 - 9) \\ &= -5x^2 - 9x - 12 \end{aligned}$$

59.

$$\begin{aligned} &(x^2 - 5x) - (6x^2 - 4x) \\ &= (x^2 - 5x) + (-6x^2 + 4x) \\ &= (x^2 - 6x^2) + (-5x + 4x) \\ &= -5x^2 - x \end{aligned}$$

61.

$$\begin{aligned} &(x^2 - 8x - 9) - (5x^2 - 4x - 3) \\ &= (x^2 - 8x - 9) + (-5x^2 + 4x + 3) \\ &= -4x^2 - 4x - 6 \end{aligned}$$

$$\begin{aligned} (y - 8) - (3y - 2) &= (y - 8) + (-3y + 2) \\ &= -2y - 6 \end{aligned}$$

65.

$$\begin{aligned} &(6y^3 + 2y^2 - y - 11) - (y^2 - 8y + 9) \\ &= (6y^3 + 2y^2 - y - 11) \\ &\quad + (-y^2 + 8y - 9) \\ &= 6y^3 + y^2 + 7y - 20 \end{aligned}$$

67.

$$\begin{aligned} &(7n^3 - n^7 - 8) - (6n^3 - n^7 - 10) \\ &= (7n^3 - n^7 - 8) + (-6n^3 + n^7 + 10) \\ &= (7n^3 - 6n^3) + (-n^7 + n^7) + (-8 + 10) \\ &= n^3 + 2 \end{aligned}$$

69.

$$\begin{aligned} &(y^6 - y^3) - (y^2 - y) \\ &= (y^6 - y^3) + (-y^2 + y) \\ &= y^6 - y^3 - y^2 + y \end{aligned}$$

71.

$$\begin{aligned} &(7x^4 + 4x^2 + 5x) - (-19x^4 - 5x^2 - x) \\ &= (7x^4 + 4x^2 + 5x) + (19x^4 + 5x^2 + x) \\ &= 26x^4 + 9x^2 + 6x \end{aligned}$$

73.

$$\begin{aligned} &\left(\frac{3}{7}x^3 - \frac{1}{5}x - \frac{1}{3}\right) - \left(-\frac{2}{7}x^3 + \frac{1}{4}x - \frac{1}{3}\right) \\ &= \left(\frac{3}{7}x^3 - \frac{1}{5}x - \frac{1}{3}\right) + \left(\frac{2}{7}x^3 - \frac{1}{4}x + \frac{1}{3}\right) \\ &= \left(\frac{3}{7}x^3 + \frac{2}{7}x^3\right) + \left(-\frac{1}{5}x - \frac{1}{4}x\right) \\ &\quad + \left(-\frac{1}{3} + \frac{1}{3}\right) \\ &= \left(\frac{3}{7}x^3 + \frac{2}{7}x^3\right) + \left(-\frac{4}{20}x - \frac{5}{20}x\right) \\ &= \frac{5}{7}x^3 - \frac{9}{20}x \end{aligned}$$

75. Subtract:

$$\begin{array}{rcr} 7x + 1 & & 7x + 1 \\ \underline{-(3x + 5)} & \rightarrow + & \underline{-3x + 5} \\ & & 4x + 6 \end{array}$$

77. Subtract:

$$\begin{array}{rcr} 7x^2 - 3 & & 7x^2 - 3 \\ \underline{-(-3x + 4)} & \rightarrow + & \underline{3x^2 - 4} \\ & & 10x^2 - 7 \end{array}$$

79. Subtract:

$$\begin{array}{r} 7y^2-5y+2 \\ \underline{-(11y^2+2y-3)} \end{array} \rightarrow + \begin{array}{r} 7y^2-5y+2 \\ \underline{-11y^2-2y+3} \\ -4y^2-7y+5 \end{array}$$

81. Subtract:

$$\begin{array}{r} 7x^3+5x^2-3 \\ \underline{-(-2x^3-6x^2+5)} \end{array} \rightarrow + \begin{array}{r} 7x^3+\ 5x^2-3 \\ \underline{2x^3+\ 6x^2-5} \\ 9x^3+11x^2-8 \end{array}$$

83. Subtract:

$$\begin{array}{r} 5y+6y^2-3y+10 \\ \underline{-(6y^3-2y^2-4y-4)} \end{array} \rightarrow$$

$$\begin{array}{r} 5y^3+6y^2-3y+10 \\ +\ \underline{-6y^3+2y^2+4y+\ 4} \\ -y^3+8y^2+\ y+14 \end{array}$$

85. Subtract:

$$\begin{array}{r} 7x^4-3x^3+2x^2 \\ \underline{-(\qquad -x^3-\ x^2+x-2)} \end{array} \rightarrow$$

$$\begin{array}{r} 7x^4-3x^3+2x^2 \\ +\ \underline{x^3+\ x^2-x+2} \\ 7x^4-2x^3+3x^2-x+2 \end{array}$$

87.

$$\begin{array}{r} 0.07x^3-0.01x^2+0.02x \\ \underline{-(0.02x^3-0.03x^2-\qquad x)} \end{array} \rightarrow$$

$$\begin{array}{r} 0.07x^3-0.01x^2+0.02x \\ +\ \underline{-0.02x^3+0.03x^2+\qquad x} \\ 0.05x^3+0.02x^2+1.02x \end{array}$$

89. $-0.02A^2+2A+22$

$A=20$:

$$-0.02(20)^2+2(2)+22=54$$

$A=50$:

$$-0.02(50)^2+2(50)+22=72$$

$A=80$:

$$-0.02(80)^2+2(80)+22=54$$

As the level of enthusiasm increases, the level of performance first increases up to a maximum level and then decreases.

91. $y=0.022x^2-0.4x+60.07$

The year 2000 corresponds to $x=40$.

$$\begin{aligned} y &= 0.022(40)^2-0.4(40)+60.07 \\ &= 35.2-16+60.07 \\ &\approx 79.3 \end{aligned}$$

In 2000, women's earnings were 79.3% of men's.

93. $y=-3.1x^2+51.4x+4024.5$

The year 2000 corresponds to $x=40$.

$$\begin{aligned} y &= -3.1(40)^2+51.4(40)+4024.5 \\ &= -4960+2056+4024.5 \\ &= 1120.5 \end{aligned}$$

According to the formula, the consumption per adult in 2000 was 1120.5 cigarettes. This is a little less than the number shown on the graph, which is approximately 1400 cigarettes.

95. If a dog is 6 years old, the equivalent age is 42 human years.

97. If a person is 25 years old, the equivalent age is 3 dog years.

For Exercises 99–107, answers may vary.

109. $5x^3-2x+1-(-3x^2-x-2)$

$$\begin{aligned} &= (5x^2-2x+1)+(3x^2+x+2) \\ &= 8x^2-x-3, \end{aligned}$$

so the polynomial is $-3x^2-x-2$.

111. In a polynomial of degree 3, the highest degree term has an exponent of 3. The highest degree term of the sum will be the sum of two terms of degree 3, which will be a term of degree 3 or could be 0. It is impossible to get a term of degree 4, so it is impossible to get a polynomial of degree 4.

Review Exercises

112. $(-10)(-7) \div (1-8) = (-10)(-7) \div (-7)$
$= 70 \div (-7) = -10$

113. $-4.6 - (-10.2) = -4.6 + 10.2 = 5.6$

114.
$$\begin{aligned} 3(x-2) &= 9(x+2) \\ 3x - 6 &= 9x + 18 \\ 3x - 6 - 9x &= 9x + 18 - 9x \\ -6x - 6 &= 18 \\ -6x - 6 + 6 &= 18 + 6 \\ -6x &= 24 \\ \frac{-6x}{-6} &= \frac{24}{-6} \\ x &= -4 \end{aligned}$$

The solution is -4.

6.2 Multiplying Polynomials

6.2 CHECK POINTS

CHECK POINT 1

a. $2^2 \cdot 2^4 = 2^{2+4} = 2^6$ or 64

b. $x^6 \cdot x^4 = x^{6+4} = x^{10}$

c. $y \cdot y^7 = y^1 \cdot y^7 = y^{1+7} = y^8$

d. $y^4 \cdot y^3 \cdot y^2 = y^{4+3+2} = y^9$

CHECK POINT 2

a. $(3^4)^5 = 3^{4\cdot 5} = 3^{20}$

b. $(x^9)^{10} = (x^9)^{10} = x^{90}$

c. $[(-5)^7]^3 = (-5)^{7\cdot 3} = (-5)^{21}$

CHECK POINT 3

a. $(2x)^4 = 2^4x^4 = 16x^4$

b. $(-4y^3)^3 = (-4)^3(y^2)^3 = (-4)^3y^{2\cdot 3} = -64y^6$

CHECK POINT 4

a. $(7x^2)(10x) = (7 \cdot 10)(x^2 \cdot x) = 70x^{2+1}$
$= 70x^3$

b. $(-5x^4)(4x^5) = (-5 \cdot 4)(x^4 \cdot x^5)$
$= -20x^{4+5} = -20x^9$

CHECK POINT 5

a. $3x(x+5) = 3x \cdot x + 3x \cdot 5$
$= 3x^2 + 15x$

b. $6x^2(5x^3 - 2x + 3)$
$= 6x^2 \cdot 5x^3 - 6x^2 \cdot 2x + 6x^2 \cdot 3$
$= 30x^5 - 6x^3 + 18x^2$

CHECK POINT 6

a. $(x+4)(x+5)$
$= x(x+5) + 4(x+5)$
$= x \cdot x + x \cdot 5 + 4 \cdot x + 4 \cdot 5$
$= x^2 + 5x + 4x + 20$
$= x^2 + 9x + 20$

b. $(5x+3)(2x-7)$
$= 5x(2x-7) + 3(2x-7)$
$= 5x \cdot 2x - 5x \cdot 7 + 3 \cdot 2x - 3 \cdot 7$
$= 10x^2 - 35x + 6x - 21$
$= 10x^2 - 29x - 21$

CHECK POINT 7

$$\begin{aligned}(5x+2)(x^2-4x+3)\\ &= 5x(x^2-4x+3)+2(x^2-4x+3)\\ &= 5x\cdot x^2-5x\cdot 4x+5x\cdot 3+2\cdot x^2\\ &\quad -2\cdot 4x+2\cdot 3\\ &= 5x^3-20x^2+15x+2x^2-8x+6\\ &= 5x^3-18x^2+7x+6\end{aligned}$$

CHECK POINT 8

$(3x^2-2x)(2x^3-5x^2+4x)$

$$\begin{array}{r} 2x^3-5x^2+4x \\ 3x^2-2x \\ \hline -4x^4+10x^3-8x^2 \\ 6x^5-15x^4+12x^3 \qquad\qquad \\ \hline 6x^5-19x^4+22x^3-8x^2 \end{array}$$

EXERCISE SET 6.2

1. $x^{10}\cdot x^5$

To multiply exponential expressions with the same base, use the product rule: $b^m\cdot b^n=b^{m+n}$.

$$x^{10}\cdot x^5=x^{10+5}=x^{15}$$

3. $y\cdot y^7=y^1\cdot y^7=y^{1+7}=y^8$

5. $x^2\cdot x^5\cdot x^4=x^{2+5+4}=x^{11}$

7. $3^9\cdot 3^{10}=3^{19}$

9. $(3^9)^{10}$

To raise an exponential expression to a power, use the power rule: $(b^m)^n=b^{mn}$.

$$(3^9)^{10}=3^{9\cdot 10}=3^{90}$$

11. $(x^4)^5=x^{4\cdot 5}=x^{20}$

13. $[(-2)^3]^3=(-2)^9$

15. $(2x)^3$

To raise a product to a power, use the products-to-powers rule: $(ab)^n=a^nb^n$.

$$(2x)^3=2^3\cdot x^3=8x^3$$

17. $(-5x)^2=(-5)^2x^2=25x^2$

19. $(4x^3)^2=4^2(x^3)^2=16x^6$

21. $(-2y^6)^4=(-2)^4(y^6)^4=16y^{24}$

23. $(-2x^7)^5=(-2)^5(x^7)^5=-32x^{35}$

25. $(7x)(2x)=(7\cdot 2)(x\cdot x)=14x^2$

27. $(6x)(4x^2)=(6\cdot 4)(x\cdot x^2)=24x^3$

29. $(-5y^4)(3y^3)=(-5\cdot 3)(y^4\cdot y^3)=-15y^7$

31. $$\begin{aligned}\left(-\frac{1}{2}a^3\right)\left(-\frac{1}{4}a^2\right) &= \left(-\frac{1}{2}\cdot -\frac{1}{4}\right)(a^3\cdot a^2)\\ &= \frac{1}{8}a^5\end{aligned}$$

33. $(2x^2)(-3x)(8x^4)=-48x^7$

35. $4x(x+3)$

To multiply a monomial by a binomial, use the distributive property. (Multiply each term of the polynomial by the monomial.)

$$\begin{aligned}4x(x+3) &= 4x\cdot x+4x\cdot 3\\ &= 4x^2+12x\end{aligned}$$

37. $$\begin{aligned}x(x-3) &= x\cdot x-x\cdot 3\\ &= x^2-3x\end{aligned}$$

39. $$\begin{aligned}2x(x-6) &= 2x\cdot x-2x\cdot 6\\ &= 2x^2-12x\end{aligned}$$

41. $$\begin{aligned}-4y(3y+5) &= -4y\cdot 3y-4y\cdot 5\\ &= -12y^2-20y\end{aligned}$$

43. $$\begin{aligned}4x^2(x+2) &= 4x^2\cdot x+4x^2\cdot 2\\ &= 4x^3+8x^2\end{aligned}$$

45. $2y^2(y^2+3y) = 2y^2 \cdot y^2 + 2y^2 \cdot 3y$
$= 2y^4 + 6y^3$

47. $2y^2(3y^2-4y+7)$
$= 2y^2(3y^2) + 2y^2(-4y) + 2y^2(7)$
$= 6y^4 - 8y^3 + 14y^2$

49. $(3x^3+4x^2)(2x) = 3x^3 \cdot 2x + 4x^2 \cdot 2x$
$= 6x^4 + 8x^3$

51. $(x^2+5x-3)(-2x)$
$= x^2(-2x) + 5x(-2x) - 3(-2x)$
$= -2x^3 - 10x^2 + 6x$

53. $-3x^2(-4x^2+x-5)$
$= -3x^2(-4x^2) - 3x^2(x) - 3x^2(-5)$
$= 12x^4 - 3x^3 + 15x^2$

55. $(x+3)(x+5)$
$= x(x+5) + 3(x+5)$
$= x \cdot x + x \cdot 5 + 3 \cdot x + 3 \cdot 5$
$= x^2 + 5x + 3x + 15$
$= x^2 + 8x + 15$

57. $(2x+1)(x+4)$
$= 2x(x+4) + 1(x+4)$
$= 2x^2 + 8x + x + 4$
$= 2x^2 + 9x + 4$

59. $(x+3)(x-5)$
$= x(x-5) + 3(x-5)$
$= x^2 - 5x + 3x - 15$
$= x^2 - 2x - 15$

61. $(x-11)(x+9)$
$= x(x+9) - 11(x+9)$
$= x^2 + 9x - 11x - 99$
$= x^2 - 2x - 99$

63. $(2x-5)(x+4)$
$= 2x(x+4) - 5(x+4)$
$= 2x^2 + 8x - 5x - 20$
$= 2x^2 + 3x - 20$

65. $\left(\frac{1}{4}x+4\right)\left(\frac{3}{4}x-1\right)$
$= \frac{1}{4}x\left(\frac{3}{4}x-1\right) + 4\left(\frac{3}{4}x-1\right)$
$= \frac{1}{4}x \cdot \frac{3}{4}x + \frac{1}{4}x(-1)$
$+ 4\left(\frac{3}{4}x\right) + 4(-1)$
$= \frac{3}{16}x^2 - \frac{1}{4}x + \frac{12}{4}x - 4$
$= \frac{3}{16}x^2 + \frac{11}{4}x - 4$

67. $(x+1)(x^2+2x+3)$
$= x(x^2+2x+3) + 1(x^2+2x+3)$
$= x^3 + 2x^3 + 3x + x^2 + 2x + 3$
$= x^3 + 3x^2 + 5x + 3$

69. $(y-3)(y^2-3y+4)$
$= y(y^2-3y+4) - 3(y^2-3y+4)$
$= y^3 - 3y^2 + 4y - 3y^2 + 9y - 12$
$= y^3 - 6y^2 + 13y - 12$

71. $(2a-3)(a^2-3a+5)$
$= 2a(a^2-3a+5) - 3(a^2-3a+5)$
$= 2a^3 - 6a^2 + 10a - 3a^2 + 9a - 15$
$= 2a^3 - 9a^2 + 19a - 15$

73. $(x+1)(x^3+2x^2+3x+4)$
$= x(x^3+2x^2+3x+4)$
$+ 1(x^3+2x^2+3x+4)$
$= x^4 + 2x^3 + 3x^2 + 4x + x^3 + 2x^2$
$+ 3x + 4$
$= x^4 + (2x^3 + x^3) + (3x^2 + 2x^2)$
$+ (4x + 3x) + 4$
$= x^4 + 3x^3 + 5x^2 + 7x + 4$

75. $\left(x-\frac{1}{2}\right)(4x^3-2x^2+5x-6)$

$$= x(4x^3-2x^2+5x-6) - \frac{1}{2}(4x^3-2x^2+5x-6)$$
$$= 4x^4-2x^3+5x^2-6x-2x^3+x^2 - \frac{5}{2}x+3$$
$$= 4x^4-4x^3+6x^2-\frac{17}{2}x+3$$

77. $(x^2+2x+1)(x^2-x+2)$

$$= x^2(x^2-x+2)+2x(x^2-x+2) + 1(x^2-x+2)$$
$$= x^4-x^3+2x^2+2x^3-2x^2+4x + x^2-x+2$$
$$= x^4+x^3+x^2+3x+2$$

79.

$$\begin{array}{r} x^2-5x+3 \\ x+8 \\ \hline 8x^2-40x+24 \\ x^3-5x^2+3x \qquad \\ \hline x^3+3x^2-37x+24 \end{array}$$

81.

$$\begin{array}{r} x^2-3x+9 \\ 2x-3 \\ \hline -3x^2+9x-27 \\ 2x^3-6x^2+18x \qquad \\ \hline 2x^3-6x^2+27x-27 \end{array}$$

83.

$$\begin{array}{r} 2x^3+x^2+2x+3 \\ x+4 \\ \hline 8x^3+4x^2+8x+12 \\ 2x^4+x^3+2x^2+3x \qquad \\ \hline 2x^4+9x^3+6x^2+11x+12 \end{array}$$

85.

$$\begin{array}{r} 4z^3-2z^2+5z-4 \\ 3z-2 \\ \hline -8z^3+4z^2-10z+8 \\ 12z^4-6z^3+15z^2-12z \qquad \\ \hline 12z^4-14z^3+19z^2-22z+8 \end{array}$$

87.

$$\begin{array}{r} 7x^3-5x^2+6x \\ 3x^2-4x \\ \hline -28x^4+20x^3-24x^2 \\ 21x^5-15x^4+18x^3 \qquad \\ \hline 21x^5-43x^4+38x^3-24x^2 \end{array}$$

89.

$$\begin{array}{r} 2y^5 \qquad -3y^3+y^2-2y+3 \\ 2y-1 \\ \hline -2y^5 \qquad +3y^3-y^2+2y-3 \\ 4y^6 - \qquad 6y^4+2y^3-4y^2+6y \qquad \\ \hline 4y^6-2y^5-6y^4+5y^3-5y^2+8y-3 \end{array}$$

91.

$$\begin{array}{r} x^2+7x-3 \\ x^2-x-1 \\ \hline -x^2-7x+3 \\ -x^3-7x^2+3x \qquad \\ x^4+7x^3-3x^2 \qquad\qquad \\ \hline x^4+6x^3-11x^2-4x+3 \end{array}$$

93. Use the formula for the area of a rectangle.

$$A = l \cdot w$$
$$A = (x+5)(2x-3)$$
$$= x(2x-3)+5(2x-3)$$
$$= 2x^2-3x+10x-15$$
$$= 2x^2+7x-15$$

The area of the rug is $(2x^2+7x-15)$ feet.

95. **a.** $(x+2)(2x+1)$

b. $x\cdot 2x+2\cdot 2x+x\cdot 1+2\cdot 1$
$$= 2x^2+4x+x+2$$
$$= 2x^2+5x+2$$

c. $(x+2)(2x+1) = x(2x+1)+2(2x+1)$
$$= 2x^2+x+4x+2$$
$$= 2x^2+5x+2$$

For Exercises 97–105, answers may vary.

107. The area of the outer square is

$$\begin{aligned}(x+4)(x+4) &= x(x+4)+4(x+4)\\ &= x^2+4x+4x+16\\ &= x^2+8x+16.\end{aligned}$$

The area of the inner square is x^2. The area of the shaded region is the difference between the areas of the two squares, which is

$$(x^2+8x+16)-x^2 = 8x+16.$$

109. $(-8x^4)\left(-\frac{1}{4}xy^3\right) = 2x^5y^3$, so the missing factor is $-8x^4$.

Review Exercises

110.
$$\begin{aligned}4x-7 &> 9x-2\\ 4x-7-9x &> 9x-2-9x\\ -5x-7 &> -2\\ -5x-7+7 &> -2+7\\ -5x &> 5\\ \frac{-5x}{-5} &< \frac{5}{-5}\\ x &< -1\end{aligned}$$

Solution: $\{x|x<-1\}$

111. $3x-2y=6$

x-intercept: 2
y-intercept: -3
checkpoint: $(4,3)$

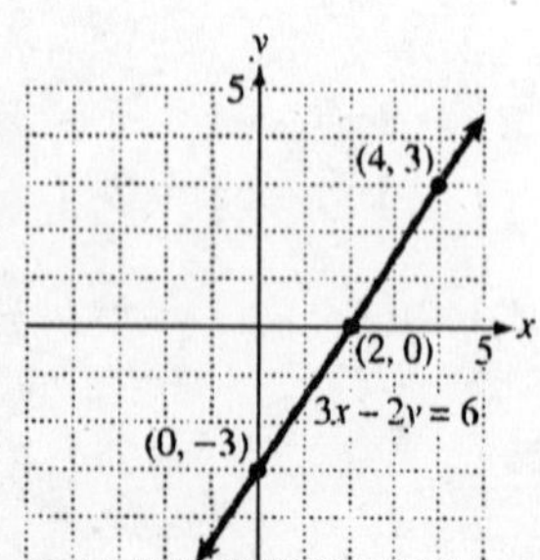

112. $(-2,8)$ and $(1,6)$

$$\begin{aligned}m &= \frac{y_2-y_1}{x_2-x_2}\\ &= \frac{6-8}{1-(-2)} = \frac{-2}{3} = -\frac{2}{3}\end{aligned}$$

6.3 Special Products

6.3 CHECK POINTS

CHECK POINT 1

$$\begin{aligned}&(x+5)(x+6)\\ &= \overset{\text{F}}{x\cdot x} + \overset{\text{O}}{x\cdot 6} + \overset{\text{I}}{5\cdot x} + \overset{\text{L}}{5\cdot 6}\\ &= x^2+6x+5x+30\\ &= x^2+11x+30\end{aligned}$$

CHECK POINT 2

$$\begin{aligned}&(7x+5)(4x-3)\\ &= \overset{\text{F}}{7x\cdot 4x} + \overset{\text{O}}{7x(-3)} + \overset{\text{I}}{5\cdot 4x} + \overset{\text{L}}{5(-3)}\\ &= 28x^2-21x+20x-15\\ &= 28x^2-x-15\end{aligned}$$

CHECK POINT 3

$$\begin{aligned}&(4x-2x)(5x-3x)\\ &= \overset{\text{F}}{4\cdot 5} + \overset{\text{O}}{4(-3x)} + \overset{\text{I}}{(-2x)(5)} + \overset{\text{L}}{(-2x)(-3x)}\\ &= 20-12x-10x+6x^2\\ &= 20-22x+6x^2\\ &\text{or } 6x^2-22x+20\end{aligned}$$

CHECK POINT 4

a. $\begin{aligned}(7y+8)(7y-8) &= (7y^2)^2-8^2\\ &= 49y^2-64\end{aligned}$

b. $\begin{aligned}(4x-5)(4x+5) &= (4x)^2-5^2\\ &= 16x^2-25\end{aligned}$

c. $\begin{aligned}(2a^3+3)(2a^3-3) &= (2a^3)^2-3^2\\ &= 4a^6-9\end{aligned}$

CHECK POINT 5

a. $(x+10)^2 = x^2 + 2 \cdot x \cdot 10 + 10^2$
$= x^2 + 20x + 100$

b. $(5x+4)^2 = (5x)^2 + 2 \cdot 5x \cdot 4 + 4^2$
$= 25x^2 + 40x + 16$

CHECK POINT 6

a. $(x-9)^2 = x^2 - 2 \cdot x + 9 + 9^2$
$= x^2 - 18x + 81$

b. $(7x-3)^2 = (7x)^2 - 2 \cdot 7x \cdot 3 + 3^2$
$= 49x^2 - 42x + 9$

EXERCISE SET 6.3

1. $(x+3)(x+5)$
$= \overset{\text{F}}{x \cdot x} + \overset{\text{O}}{x \cdot 5} + \overset{\text{I}}{3 \cdot x} + \overset{\text{L}}{3 \cdot 5}$
$= x^2 + 5x + 3x + 15$
$= x^2 + 8x + 15$

3. $(y-5)(y+3) = y \cdot y + y \cdot 3 - 5 \cdot y - 5 \cdot 3$
$= y^2 + 3y - 5y - 15$
$= y^2 - 2y - 15$

5. $(2x-1)(x+2)$
$= 2x \cdot x + 2x \cdot 2 - 1 \cdot x - 1 \cdot 2$
$= 2x^2 + 4x - x - 2$
$= 2x^2 + 3x - 2$

7. $(2y-3)(y+1)$
$= 2y \cdot y + 2y \cdot 1 - 3 \cdot y - 3 \cdot 1$
$= 2y^2 + 2y - 3y - 3$
$= 2y^2 - y - 3$

9. $(2x-3)(5x+3) = 10x^2 + 6x - 15x - 9$
$= 10x^2 - 9x - 9$

11. $(3y-7)(4y-5) = 12y^2 - 15y - 28y + 35$
$= 12y^2 - 43y + 35$

13. $(7+3x)(1-5x) = 7 - 35x + 3x - 15x^2$
$= 7 - 32x - 15x^2$
$= -15x^2 - 32x + 7$

15. $(5-3y)(6-2y) = 30 - 10y - 18y + 6y^2$
$= 30 - 28y + 6y^2$
$= 6y^2 - 28y + 30$

17. $(5x^2-4)(3x^2-7)$
$= (5x^2)(3x^2) + (5x^2)(-7)$
$+ (-4)(3x^2) + (-4)(-7)$
$= 15x^4 - 35x^2 - 12x^2 + 28$
$= 15x^4 - 47x^2 + 28$

19. $(6x-5)(2-x) = 12x - 6x^2 - 10 + 5x$
$= -6x^2 + 17x - 10$

21. $(x+5)(x^2+3) = x^3 + 3x + 5x^2 + 15$
$= x^3 + 5x^2 + 3x + 15$

23. $(8x^3+3)(x^2+5) = 8x^5 + 40x^3 + 3x^2 + 15$

In Exercises 25–43, use the rule

$$(A+B)(A-B) + A^2 - B^2.$$

25. $(x+3)(x-3) = x^2 - 3^2 = x^2 - 9$

27. $(3x+2)(3x-2) = (3x)^2 - 2^2 = 9x^2 - 4$

29. $(3r-4)(3r+4) = (3r)^2 - 4^2$
$= 9r^2 - 16$

31. $(3+r)(3-r) = 3^2 - r^2 = 9 - r^2$

33. $(5-7x)(5+7x) = 5^2 - (7x^2) = 25 - 49x^2$

35. $\left(2x+\frac{1}{2}\right)\left(2x-\frac{1}{2}\right) = (2x)^2 - \left(\frac{1}{2}\right)^2$
$= 4x^2 - \frac{1}{4}$

37. $(y^2+1)(y^2-1) = (y^2)^2 - 1^2 = y^4 - 1$

39. $(r^3+2)(r^3-2) = (r^3)^2 - 2^2 = r^6 - 4$

41. $(1-y^4)(1+y^4) = 1^2 - (y^4)^2 = 1 - y^8$

43. $(x^{10}+5)(x^{10}-5) = (x^{10})^2 - 5^2$
$= x^{20} - 25$

In Exercises 45–61, use the rules

$$(A+B)^2 = A^2 + 2AB + B^2$$
$$(A-B)^2 = A^2 - 2AB + B^2.$$

45. $(x+2)^2 = x^2 + 2(2x) + 2^2$
$= x^2 + 4x + 4$

47. $(2x+5)^2 = (2x)^2 + 2(2x)(5) + 5^2$
$= 4x^2 + 20x + 25$

49. $(x-3)^2 = x^2 - 2(3x) + 3^2$
$= x^2 - 6x + 9$

51. $(3y-4)^2 = (3y)^2 - 2(3y)(4) + 4^2$
$= 9y^2 - 24y + 16$

53. $(4x^2-1)^2 = (4x^2)^2 - 2(4x^2)(1) + 1^2$
$= 16x^4 - 8x^2 + 1$

55. $(7-2x)^2 = 7^2 - 2(7)(2x) + (2x)^2$
$= 49 - 28x + 4x^2$

57. $\left(2x+\frac{1}{2}\right)^2 = 4x^2 + 2(2x)\left(\frac{1}{2}\right) + \left(\frac{1}{2}\right)^2$
$= 4x^2 + 2x + \frac{1}{4}$

59. $\left(4y-\frac{1}{4}\right)^2 = 16y^2 - 2(4y)\left(\frac{1}{4}\right) + \left(\frac{1}{4}\right)^2$
$= 16y^2 - 2y + \frac{1}{16}$

61. $(x^8+3)^2 = (x^8)^2 + 2(x^8)(3) + 3^2$
$= x^{16} + 6x^8 + 9$

63. $(x-1)(x^2+x+1)$
$= x(x^2+x+1) - 1(x^2+x+1)$
$= x^3 + x^2 + x - x^2 - x - 1$
$= x^3 - 1$

65. $(x-1)^2 = x^2 - 2(x)(1) + 1^2$
$= x^2 - 2x + 1$

67. $(3y+7)(3y-7) = (3y^2) - 7^2$
$= 9y^2 - 49$

69. $3x^2(4x^2+x+9)$
$= 3x^2(4x^2) + 3x^2(x) + 3x^2(9)$
$= 12x^4 + 3x^3 + 27x^2$

71. $(7y+3)(10y-4)$
$= 70y^2 - 28y + 30y - 12$
$= 70y^2 + 2y - 12$

73. $(x^2+1)^2 = (x^2)^2 + 2(x^2)(1) + 1^2$
$= x^4 + 2x^2 + 1$

75. $(x^2+1)^2(x^2+2)$
$= x^2 \cdot x^2 + x^2 \cdot 2 + 1 \cdot x^2 + 1 \cdot 2$
$= x^4 + 3x^2 + 2$

77. $(x^2+4)(x^2-4) = (x^2)^2 - 4^2$
$= x^4 - 16$

79. $(2-3x^5)^2 = 2^2 - 2(2)(3x^5) + (3x^5)^2$
$= 4 - 12x^5 + 9x^{10}$

81. $\left(\frac{1}{4}x^2+12\right)\left(\frac{3}{4}x^2-8\right)$
$= \frac{1}{4}x^2\left(\frac{3}{4}x^2\right) + \frac{1}{4}x^2(-8) + 12\left(\frac{3}{4}x^2\right)$
$+ 12(-8)$
$= \frac{3}{16}x^4 - 2x^2 + 9x^2 - 96$
$= \frac{3}{16}x^2 + 7x^2 - 96$

83. $A = (x+1)^2 = x^2 + 2x + 1$

85. $A = (2x-3)(2x+3) = (2x)^2 - 3^2$
$= 4x^2 - 9$

87. Area of outer rectangle:

$$(x+9)(x+3) = x^2 + 12x + 27$$

Area of inner rectangle:

$$(x+5)(x+1) = x^2 + 6x + 5$$

Area of shaded region:

$$(x^2+12x+27) - (x^2+6x+5) = 6x + 22$$

89. $(x+1)(x+2)$ yards^2

91. $(x+1)(x+2) = (6+1)(6+2) = 7 \cdot 8 = 56$

If the original garden measures 6 yards on a side, the area of the larger garden will be 56 yards^2. This relationship corresponds to the point $(6, 56)$ on the graph.

93. The outer square (square including painting and frame) measures $(x+2)$ inches.

$$(x+2)^2 = x^2 + 4x + 4$$

The area is $(x^2 + 4x + 4)$ square inches.

For Exercises 95–99, answers may vary.

101. To find the correct binomial factors, try different combinations of constants in the binomials that will give a product of -20 as the last term until you find the combination that gives the correct middle term.

$$\begin{aligned}(x-10)(x+2) &= x^2 + 2x - 10x - 20 \\ &= x^2 - 8x - 20,\end{aligned}$$

so the two binomials are $(x-10)$ and $(x+2)$.

103. Divide the figure into two rectangles.

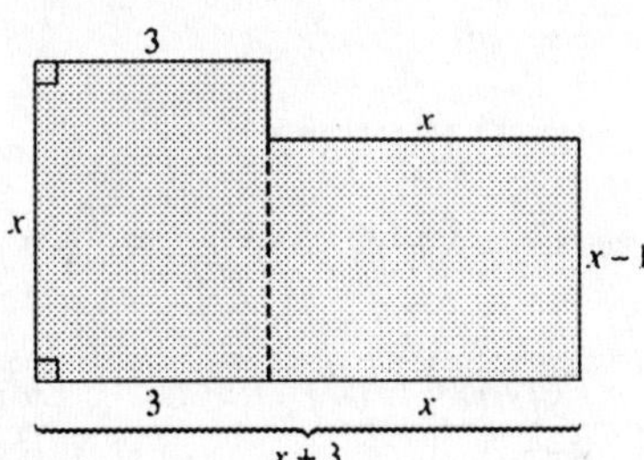

The area of the figure is the sum of the areas of the two rectangles.

$$\begin{aligned}A &= 3 \cdot x + x(x-1) \\ &= 3x + x^2 - x \\ &= x^2 + 2x.\end{aligned}$$

105.

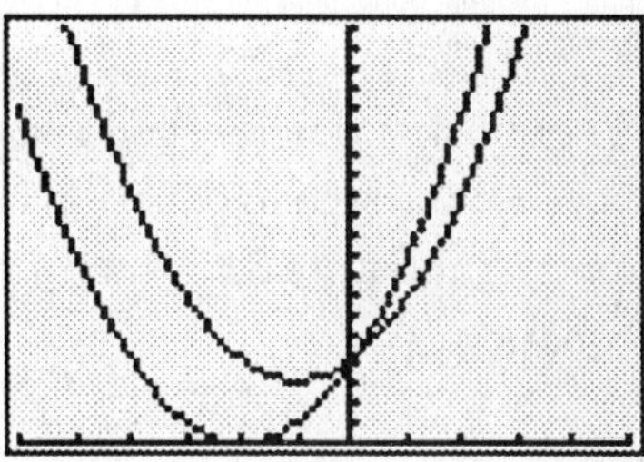

The graphs do not coincide. $(x+2)^2 = x^2 + 4x + 4$, so $x^2 + 2x + 4$ should be changed to $x^2 + 4x + 4$.

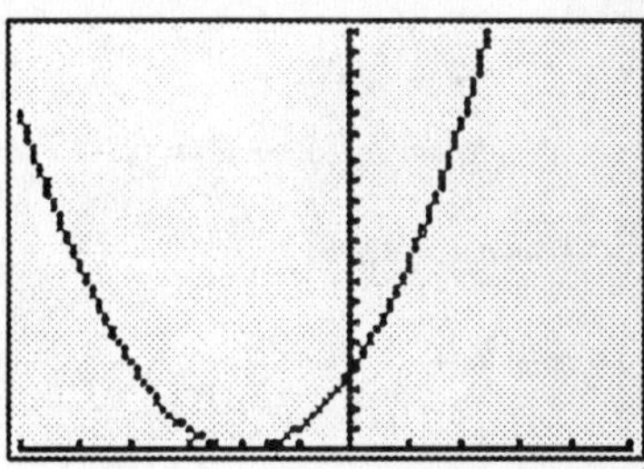

Now the graphs coincide.

107.

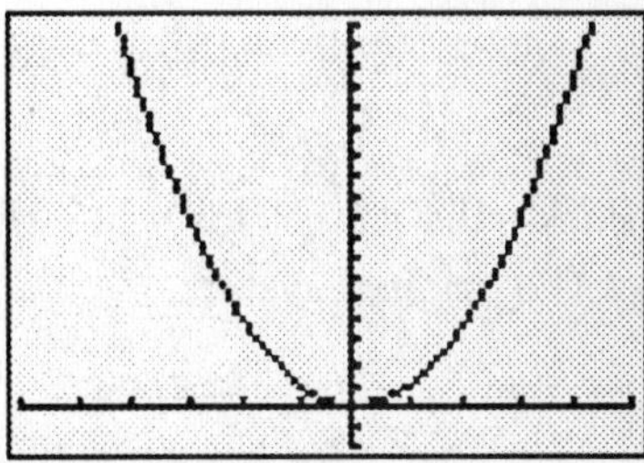

The graphs coincide. This verifies that $(x-2)(x+2) + 4 = x^2$.

Review Exercises

108. $2x + 3y = 1$
$y = 3x - 7$

The substitution method is a good choice because the second equation is already solved for y. Substitute $3x - 7$ for y into the first equation.

$$\begin{aligned} 2x + 3y &= 1 \\ 2x + 3(3x - 7) &= 1 \\ 2x + 9x - 21 &= 1 \\ 11x - 21 &= 1 \\ 11x &= 22 \\ x &= 2 \end{aligned}$$

Back-substitute.

$$\begin{aligned} y &= 3x - 7 \\ y &= 3(2) - 7 = 6 - 7 = -1 \end{aligned}$$

Solution: $(2, -1)$

109. $3x + 4y = 7$
$2x + 7y = 9$

The addition method is a good choice because both equations are written in the form $Ax+By = C$. To eliminate x, multiply the first equation by 2 and the second equation by -3. Then add the results.

$$\begin{aligned} 6x + \ 8y &= \ 14 \\ -6x - 21y &= -27 \\ \hline -13y &= -13 \\ y &= 1 \end{aligned}$$

Back-substitute 1 for y in either equation of the original system.

$$\begin{aligned} 3x + 4y &= 7 \\ 3x + 4(1) &= 7 \\ 3x + 4 &= 7 \\ 3x &= 3 \\ x &= 1 \end{aligned}$$

Solution: $(1, 1)$

110. $y \leq \frac{1}{3}x$

Graph $y = \frac{1}{3}x$ as a solid line using its slope, $\frac{1}{3}$, and y-intercept, 0. Since $(0, 0)$ is on the line, chose a different point as a test point, for example, $(3, 2)$. Since $2 \leq \frac{1}{3}(3)$ is false, shade the half-plane *not* containing $(3, 2)$.

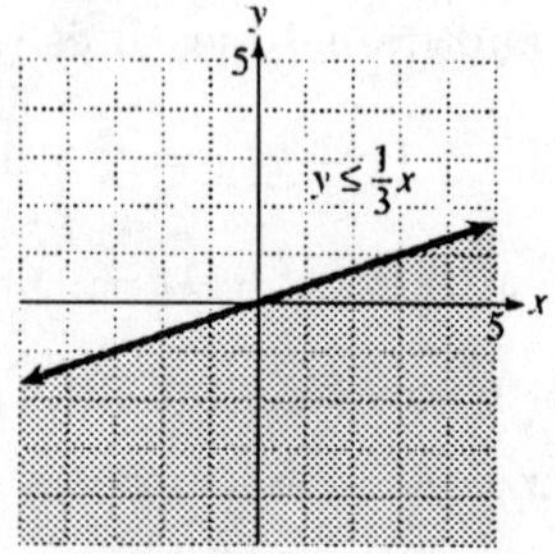

6.4 Polynomials in Several Variables

6.4 CHECK POINTS

CHECK POINT 1

$3x^3y + xy^2 + 5y + 6$ for $x = -1$ and $y = 5$

$$\begin{aligned} &3x^3y + xy^2 + 5y + 6 \\ &= 3(-1)^3 \cdot 5 + (-1)(5)^2 + 5 \cdot 5 + 6 \\ &= 3(-1) \cdot 5 + (-1) \cdot 25 + 5 \cdot 5 + 6 \\ &= -15 - 25 + 25 + 6 \\ &= -9 \end{aligned}$$

CHECK POINT 2

$8x^4y^5 - 7x^3y^2 - x^2y - 5x + 11$

Term	*Coefficient*	*Degree*
$8x^4y^5$	8	$4 + 5 = 9$
$-7x^3y^2$	-7	$3 + 2 = 5$
$-x^2y$	-1	$2 + 1 = 3$
$-5x$	-5	1
11	11	0

The degree of the polynomial is the highest degree of all its terms, which is 9.

CHECK POINT 3

$$\begin{aligned}(-8x^2y - 3xy + 6) &+ (10x^2 + 5xy - 10)\\ &= (-8x^2y + 10x^2y) + (-3xy + 5xy)\\ &\quad + (6 - 10)\\ &= 2x^2y + 2xy - 4\end{aligned}$$

CHECK POINT 4

$$\begin{aligned}(7x^3 &- 10x^2y + 2xy^2 - 5)\\ &- (4x^3 - 12x^2y - 3xy^2 + 5)\\ &= (7x^3 - 10x^2y + 2xy^2 - 5)\\ &\quad + (-4x^3 + 12x^2y + 3xy^2 - 5)\\ &= (7x^3 - 4x^3) + (-10x^2y + 12x^2y)\\ &\quad + (2xy^2 + 3xy^2) + (-5 - 5)\\ &= 3x^3 + 2x^2y + 5xy^2 - 10\end{aligned}$$

CHECK POINT 5

$$\begin{aligned}(6xy^3)(10x^4y^2) &= (6 \cdot 10)(x \cdot x^4)(y^3 \cdot y^2)\\ &= 60x^{1+4}y^{3+2}\\ &= 60x^5y^5\end{aligned}$$

CHECK POINT 6

$$\begin{aligned}6xy^2(10x^4y^5 &- 2x^2y + 3)\\ &= 6xy^2 \cdot 10x^4y^5 - 6xy^2 \cdot 2x^2y\\ &\quad + 6xy^2 \cdot 3\\ &= 60x^{1+4}y^{2+5} - 12x^{1+3}y^{2+1} + 18xy^2\\ &= 60x^5y^7 - 12x^4y^3 + 18xy^2\end{aligned}$$

CHECK POINT 7

a. $(7x - 6y)(3x - y)$
$$\begin{aligned}&= (7x)(3x) + (7x)(-y) - 6y(3x)\\ &\quad + (-6y)(-y)\\ &= 21x^2 - 7xy - 18xy + 6y^2\\ &= 21x^2 - 25xy + 6y^2\end{aligned}$$

b. $(2x + 4y)^2$
$$\begin{aligned}&= (2x)^2 + 2 \cdot 2x \cdot 4y + (4y)^2\\ &= 4x^2 + 16xy + 16y^2\end{aligned}$$

CHECK POINT 8

a. $(6xy^2 + 5x)(6xy^2 - 5x)$
$$\begin{aligned}&= (6xy^2)^2 - (5x)^2\\ &= 36x^2y^4 - 25x^2\end{aligned}$$

b. $(x - y)(x^2 + xy + y^2)$
$$\begin{aligned}&= x(x^2 + xy + y^2)\\ &\quad - y(x^2 + xy + y^2)\\ &= x \cdot x^2 + x \cdot xy + x \cdot y^2 - y \cdot x^2\\ &\quad - y \cdot xy - y \cdot y^2\\ &= x^3 + x^2y + xy^2 - x^2y - xy^2 - y^3\\ &= x^3 - y^3\end{aligned}$$

EXERCISE SET 6.4

1. $x^2 + 2xy + y^2;\ x = 2, y = -3$

$$\begin{aligned}x^2 + 2xy + y^2 &= 2^2 + 2(2)(-3) + (-3)^2\\ &= 4 - 12 + 9 = 1\end{aligned}$$

3. $$\begin{aligned}xy^3 - xy + 1 &= 2(-3)^3 - 2(-3) + 1\\ &= 2(-27) + 6 + 1\\ &= -54 + 6 + 1 = -47\end{aligned}$$

5. $2x^2y - 5y + 3$
$$\begin{aligned}&= 2(2^2)(-3) - 5(-3) + 3\\ &= 2(4)(-3) - 5(-3) + 3\\ &= -24 + 15 + 3 = -6\end{aligned}$$

7.

Term	Coefficient	Degree
x^3y^2	1	$3 + 2 = 5$
$-5x^2y^7$	-5	$2 + 7 = 9$
$6y^2$	6	2
-3	-3	0

The degree of the polynomial is the highest degree of all its terms, which is 9.

9. $(5x^2y - 3xy) + (2x^2y - xy)$
$$\begin{aligned}&= (5x^2y + 2x^2y) + (-3xy - xy)\\ &= 7x^2y - 4xy\end{aligned}$$

11. $(4x^2y + 8xy + 11) + (-2x^2y + 5xy + 2)$
$= (4x^2y - 2x^2y) + (8xy + 5xy) + (11 + 2)$
$= 2x^2y + 13xy + 13$

13. $(7x^4y^2 - 5x^2y^2 + 3xy)$
$+ (-18x^4y^2 - 6x^2y^2 - xy)$
$= (7x^4y^2 - 18x^4y^2) + (-5x^2y^2 - 6x^2y^2)$
$+ (3xy - xy)$
$= -11x^4y^2 - 11x^2y^2 + 2xy$

15. $(x^3 + 7xy - 5y^2) - (6x^3 - xy + 4y^2)$
$= (x^3 + 7xy - 5y^2) + (-6x^3 + xy - 4y^2)$
$= (x^3 - 6x^3) + (7xy + xy) + (-5y^2 - 4y^2)$
$= -5x^3 + 8xy - 9y^2$

17. $(3x^4y^2 + 5x^3y - 3y)$
$- (2x^4y^2 - 3x^3y - 4y + 6x)$
$= (3x^4y^2 + 5x^3y - 3y)$
$+ (-2x^4y^2 + 3x^3y + 4y - 6x)$
$= (3x^4y^2 - 2x^4y^2) + (5x^3y + 3x^3y)$
$+ (-3y + 4y) + (-6x)$
$= x^4y^2 + 8x^3y + y - 6x$

19. $(x^3 - y^3) - (-4x^3 - x^2y + xy^2 + 3y^3)$
$= (x^3 - y^3) + (4x^3 + x^2y - xy^2 - 3y^3)$
$= (x^3 + 4x^3) + x^2y - xy^2 + (-y^3 - 3y^3)$
$= 5x^3 + x^2y - xy^2 - 4y^3$

21. Add:

$$\begin{array}{r} 5x^2y^2 - 4xy^2 + 6y^2 \\ \underline{-8x^2y^2 + 5xy^2 - y^2} \\ -3x^2y^2 + xy^2 + 5y^2 \end{array}$$

23. Subtract:

$$\begin{array}{r} 3a^2b^4 - 5ab^2 + 7ab \\ \underline{-(-5a^2b^4 - 8ab^2 - ab)} \end{array}$$

Add:

$$\begin{array}{l} 3a^2b^4 - 5ab^2 + 7ab \\ \underline{5a^2b^4 + 8ab^2 + ab} \\ 8a^2b^4 + 3ab^2 + 8ab \end{array}$$

25. $[(7x + 13y) + (-26x + 19y)] - (11x - 5y)$
$= [(7x - 26x) + (13y + 19y)]$
$- (11x - 5y)$
$= (-19x + 32y) - (11x - 5y)$
$= (-19x + 32y) + (-11x + 5y)$
$= (-19x - 11x) + (32y + 5y)$
$= -30x + 37y$

27. $(6x^2y)(3xy) = (6 \cdot 3)(x^2 \cdot x)(y \cdot y)$
$= 18x^{2+1}y^{1+1}$
$= 18x^3y^2$

29. $(-7x^3y^4)(2x^2y^5) = (-7)(2)x^{3+2}y^{4+5}$
$= -14x^5y^9$

31. $5xy(2x + 3y) = 5xy(2x) + 5xy(3y)$
$= 10x^2y + 15xy^2$

33. $3xy^2(6x^2 - 2y) = 3xy^2(6x^2) + 3xy^2(-2y)$
$= 18x^3y^2 - 6xy^3$

35. $3ab^2(6a^2b^3 + 5ab)$
$= 3ab^2(6a^2b^3) + 3ab^2(5ab)$
$= 18a^3b^5 + 15a^2b^3$

37. $-b(a^2 - ab + b^2) = -b(a^2) - b(-ab) - b(b^2)$
$= -a^2b + ab^2 - b^3$

39. $(x + 5y)(7x + 3y)$
$= x(7x) + x(3y) + 5y(7x) + 5y(3y)$
$= 7x^2 + 3xy + 35xy + 15y^2$
$= 7x^2 + 38xy + 15y^2$

41. $(x - 3y)(2x + 7y)$
$= x(2x) + x(7y) - 3y(2x) - 3y(7y)$
$= 2x^2 + 7xy - 6xy - 21y^2$
$= 2x^2 + xy - 21y^2$

43. $(3xy - 1)(5xy + 2)$
$= 3xy(5xy) + 3xy(2) - 1(5xy) - 1(2)$
$= 15x^2y^2 + 6xy - 5xy - 2$
$= 15x^2y^2 + xy - 2$

45. $(2x + 3y)^2 = (2x)^2 + 2(2x)(3y) + (3y)^2$
$= 4x^2 + 12xy + 9y^2$

47. $(xy-3)^2 = (xy)^2 - 2(xy)(3) + (-3)^2$
$= x^2y^2 - 6xy + 9$

49. $(x^2+y^2)^2 = (x^2)^2 + 2(x^2)(y^2) + (y^2)^2$
$= x^4 + 2x^2y^2 + y^4$

51. $(x^2 - 2y^2)^2$
$= (x^2) - 2(x^2)(2y^2) + (-2y^2)^2$
$= x^4 - 4x^2y^2 + 4y^4$

53. $(3x+y)(3x-y) = (3x)^2 - y^2 = 9x^2 - y^2$

55. $(ab+1)(ab-1) = (ab)^2 - 1^2 = a^2b^2 - 1$

57. $(x+y^2)(x-y^2) = x^2 - (y^2)^2 = x^2 - y^4$

59. $(3a^2b+a)(3a^2b-a) = (3a^2b)^2 - a^2$
$= 9a^4b^2 - a^2$

61. $(3xy^2-4y)(3xy^2+4y) = (3xy^2)^2 - (4y)^2$
$= 9x^2y^4 - 16y^2$

63. $(a+b)(a^2-b^2)$
$= a(a^2) + a(-b^2) + b(a^2) + b(-b^2)$
$= a^3 - ab^2 + a^2b - b^3$

65. $(x+y)(x^2+3xy+y^2)$
$= x(x^2+3xy+y^2) + y(x^2+3xy+y^2)$
$= x^3 + 3x^2 + xy^2 + x^2y + 3xy^2 + y^3$
$= x^3 + 4x^2y + 4xy^2 + y^3$

67. $(x-y)(x^2-3xy+y^2)$
$= x(x^2-3xy+y^2) - y(x^2-3xy+y^2)$
$= x^3 - 3x^2y + xy^2 - x^2y + 3xy^2 - y^3$
$= x^3 - 4x^2y + 4xy^2 - y^3$

69. $(xy+ab)(xy-ab) = (xy)^2 - (ab)^2$
$= x^2y^2 - a^2b^2$

71. $(x^2+1)(x^4y+x^2+1)$
$= x^2(x^4y+x^2+1) + 1(x^4y+x^2+1)$
$= x^6y + x^4 + x^2 + x^4y + x^2 + 1$
$= x^6y + x^4y + x^4 + 2x^2 + 1$

73. $(x^2y^2-3)^2$
$= (x^2y^2)^2 - 2(x^2y^2)(3) + (-3)^2$
$= x^4y^4 - 6x^2y^2 + 9$

75. $(x+y+1)(x+y-1)$
$= x(x+y-1) + y(x+y-1)$
$+ 1(x+y-1)$
$= x^2 + xy - x + yx + y^2 - y + x + y - 1$
$= x^2 + 2xy + y^2 - 1$

77. $A = (3x+5y)(x+y)$
$= 3x(x) + 3x(y) + 5y(x) + 5y(y)$
$= 3x^2 + 3xy + 5xy + 5y^2$
$= 3x^2 + 8xy + 5y^2$

79. Area of larger square $= (x+y)^2$
$= x^2 + 2xy + y^2$

Area of smaller square $= x^2$

Area of shaded region $= (x^2+2xy+y^2) - x^2$
$= 2xy + y^2$

81. $N = \frac{1}{4}x^2y - 2xy + 4y;\ x = 10, y = 16$

$$N = \frac{1}{4}x^2y - 2xy + 4y$$
$$= \frac{1}{4}(10)^2(16) - 2(10)(16) + 4(16)$$
$$= \frac{1}{4}(100)(16) - 2(10)(16) + 4(16)$$
$$= 400 - 320 + 64$$
$$= 144$$

Each tree provides 144 board feet of lumber, so 20 trees will provide 20(144) = 2880 board feet. This is not enough lumber to complete the job. Since 3000 − 2880 = 120, the contractor will need 120 more board feet.

83. $s = -16t^2 + v_0t + s_0$; $t = 2$; $v_0 = 80$, $s_0 = 96$

$$\begin{aligned} s &= -16t^2 + v_0t + s_0 \\ &= -16(2)^2 + 80(2) + 96 \\ &= -64 + 160 + 96 = 192 \end{aligned}$$

The ball will be 192 feet above the ground 2 seconds after being thrown.

85. $s = -16t^2 + v_0t + s_0 = t = 6$, $v_0 = 80$, $s_0 = 96$

$$\begin{aligned} s &= -16t^2 + v_0t + s_0 \\ &= -16(6)^2 + 80(60) + 96 \\ &= -16(36) + 80(6) + 96 \\ &= -576 + 480 + 96 = 0 \end{aligned}$$

The ball will be 0 feet above the ground after 6 seconds. This means that the ball hits the ground 6 seconds after being thrown.

87. The ball is falling from 2.5 seconds to 6 seconds.

89. $(2, 192)$

91. The ball reaches its maximum height 2.5 seconds after it is thrown. From the graph, a reasonable estimate of the maximum height is 96 feet.

For Exercise 93, answer may vary.

95. Statement c is true.

$$\begin{aligned} &(2x + 3 - 5y)(2x + 3 + 5y) \\ &= [(2x - 3) - 5y][(2x + 3) + 5y] \\ &= (2x + 3)^2 - (5y)^2 \\ &= 4x^2 + 12x + 9 - 25y^2 \end{aligned}$$

97. Area of large rectangle $= (4y)(2y) = 8y^2$

Area of small (unshaded) rectangle $= (2x)(x) = 2x^2$

Area of shaded region $= 8y^2 - 2x^2$

99. The storage building is made up of half of a cylinder sitting on top of a rectangular solid.

Rectangular solid:

$$\begin{aligned} V &= lwh \\ &= y \cdot 2x \cdot x \\ &= 2x^2y \end{aligned}$$

Half-cylinder:

$$\begin{aligned} V &= \frac{1}{2}\pi r^2 h \\ &= \frac{1}{2}\pi(x)^2 \cdot y \\ &= \frac{1}{2}\pi x^2 y \end{aligned}$$

Volume of storage building $= 2x^2y + \frac{1}{2}\pi x^2 y$

Review Exercises

100. $R = \dfrac{L + 3W}{2}$; for W

$$\begin{aligned} R &= \frac{L + 3W}{2} \\ 2R &= 2\left(\frac{L + 3W}{2}\right) \\ 2R &= L + 3W \\ 2R - L &= L + 3W - L \\ 2R - L &= 3W \\ \frac{2R - L}{3} &= \frac{3W}{3} \\ \frac{2R - L}{3} &= W \quad \text{or} \quad W = \frac{2R - L}{3} \end{aligned}$$

101. $-6.4 - (-10.2) = -6.4 + 10.2 = 3.8$

102. $\dfrac{63}{x} = \dfrac{3}{5}$

$$\begin{aligned} 3x &= 63 \cdot 5 \\ 3x &= 315 \\ \frac{3x}{3} &= \frac{315}{3} \\ x &= 105 \end{aligned}$$

The solution is 105.

6.5 Dividing Polynomials

6.5 CHECK POINTS

CHECK POINT 1

a. $\frac{5^{12}}{5^4} = 5^{12-4} = 5^8$

b. $\frac{x^9}{x^2} = x^{9-2} = x^7$

c. $\frac{y^{20}}{y} = \frac{y^{20}}{y^1} = y^{20-1} = y^{19}$

CHECK POINT 2

a. $14^0 = 1$

b. $(-10)^0 = 1$

c. $-10^0 = -1$

Only 10 is raised to the 0 power.

d. $20x^0 = 20 \cdot 1 = 20$

e. $(20x)^0$

The entire expression, $20x$, is raised to the 0 power.

CHECK POINT 3

a. $\left(\frac{x}{5}\right)^2 = \frac{x^2}{5^2} = \frac{x^2}{25}$

b. $\left(\frac{x^4}{2}\right)^3 = \frac{(x^4)^3}{2^3} = \frac{x^{4\cdot3}}{2^3} = \frac{x^{12}}{8}$

c. $\left(\frac{2a^{10}}{b^3}\right)^4 = \frac{(2a^{10})^4}{(b^3)^4} = \frac{2^4(a^{10})^4}{(b^3)^4}$

$$= \frac{2^4a^{40}}{b^{12}} = \frac{16a^{40}}{b^{12}}$$

CHECK POINT 4

a. $\frac{-20x^{12}}{10x^4} = \frac{-20}{10}x^{12-4} = -2x^8$

b. $\frac{3x^4}{15x^4} = \frac{3}{15}x^{4-4} = \frac{1}{5}x^0 = \frac{1}{5}\cdot 1 = \frac{1}{5}$

c. $\frac{9x^6y^5}{3xy^2} = \frac{9}{3}x^{6-1}y^{5-2} = 3x^5y^3$

CHECK POINT 5

$(-15x^9 + 6x^5 - 9x^3) \div 3x^2$

$$\frac{-15x^9 + 6x^5 - 9x^3}{3x^2}$$
$$= \frac{-15x^9}{3x^2} + \frac{6x^5}{3x^2} - \frac{9x^3}{3x^2}$$
$$= \frac{-15}{3}x^{9-7} + \frac{6}{3}x^{5-2} - \frac{9}{3}x^{3-2}$$
$$= -5x^2 + 2x^3 - 3x$$

CHECK POINT 6

$$\frac{25x^9 - 7x^4 + 10x^3}{5x^3}$$
$$= \frac{25x^9}{5x^3} - \frac{7x^4}{5x^3} + \frac{10x^3}{5x^3}$$
$$= \frac{25}{5}x^{9-3} - \frac{7}{5}x^{4-3} + \frac{10}{5}x^{3-3}$$
$$= 5x^6 - \frac{7}{5}x^1 + 2x^0$$
$$= 5x - \frac{7}{5}x + 2$$

CHECK POINT 7

$(18x^7y^6 - 6x^2y^3 + 60xy^2) \div 6xy^2$

$$\frac{18x^7y^6 - 6x^2y^3 + 60xy^2}{6xy^2}$$
$$= \frac{18x^7y^6}{6xy^2} - \frac{6x^2y^3}{6xy^2} + \frac{60xy^2}{6xy^2}$$
$$= 3x^5y^4 - xy + 10$$

EXERCISE SET 6.5

1. $\frac{3^{20}}{3^5}$

To divide exponential expressions with the same nonzero base, use the quotient rule

$$\frac{b^m}{b^n} = b^{m-n},\ b \neq 0.$$

$$\frac{3^{20}}{3^5} = 3^{20-5} = 3^{15}$$

3. $\dfrac{x^6}{x^2} = x^{6-2} = x^4$

5. $\dfrac{y^{13}}{y^5} = y^{13-5} = y^8$

7. $\dfrac{5^6 \cdot 2^8}{5^3 \cdot 2^4} = 5^{6-3} \cdot 2^{8-4} = 5^3 \cdot 2^4$

9. $\dfrac{x^{100}y^{50}}{x^{25}y^{10}} = x^{100-25}y^{50-10} = x^{75}y^{40}$

11. $2^0 = 1$

13. $(-2)^0 = 1$

15. $-2^0 = -(-1) = -1$

17. $100y^0 = 100 \cdot 1 = 100$

19. $(100y^0) = 1$

21. $-5^0 + (-5)^0 = -1 + 1 = 0$

23. $-\pi^0 - (-\pi)^0 = -1 - 1 = -2$

25. $\left(\dfrac{x}{3}\right)^2 = \dfrac{x^2}{9}$

To raise a quotient to a power, use the quotients-to-powers rule

$$\left(\frac{a}{b}\right)^n = \frac{a^n}{b^n}.$$

$$\left(\frac{x}{3}\right)^2 = \frac{x^2}{3^2} = \frac{x^2}{9}$$

27. $\left(\dfrac{x^2}{4}\right)^3 = \dfrac{(x^2)^3}{4^3} = \dfrac{x^{2 \cdot 3}}{4^3} = \dfrac{x^6}{64}$

29. $\left(\dfrac{2x^3}{5}\right)^2 = \dfrac{2^2(x^3)^2}{5^2} = \dfrac{4x^6}{25}$

31. $\left(\dfrac{-4}{3a^3}\right)^3 = \dfrac{(-4)^3}{3^3(a^3)^3} = \dfrac{-64}{27a^9} = -\dfrac{64}{27a^9}$

33. $\left(\dfrac{-2a^7}{b^4}\right)^5 = \dfrac{(-2a^7)^5}{(b^4)^5} = \dfrac{(-2)^5(a^7)^5}{(b^4)^5}$

$$= \frac{-32a^{35}}{b^{20}} = -\frac{32a^{35}}{b^{20}}$$

35. $\left(\dfrac{x^2y^3}{2z}\right)^4 = \dfrac{(x^2)^4(y^3)^4}{2^4z^4} = \dfrac{x^8y^{12}}{16z^4}$

In Exercises 37–51, each answer should be checked by showing that the product of the divisor and the quotient is the dividend. The check is shown here only for Exercise 37.

37. $\dfrac{30x^{10}}{10x^5} = \dfrac{30}{10}x^{10-5} = 3x^5$

Check: $10x^5(3x^5) = (10 \cdot 3)x^{5+5} = 30x^{10}$

39. $\dfrac{-8x^{22}}{4x^2} = \dfrac{-8}{4}x^{22-2} = -2x^{20}$

41. $\dfrac{-9y^8}{18y^5} = \dfrac{-9}{18}y^{8-5} = -\dfrac{1}{2}y^3$

43. $\dfrac{7y^{17}}{5y^5} = \dfrac{7}{5}y^{12}$

45. $\dfrac{30x^7y^5}{5x^2y} = \dfrac{30}{5}x^{7-2}y^{5-1} = 6x^5y^4$

47. $\dfrac{-18x^{14}y^2}{36x^2y^2} = \dfrac{-18}{36}x^{14-2}y^{2-2}$

$$= -\frac{1}{2}x^{12}y^0 = -\frac{1}{2}x^{12} \cdot 1$$

$$= -\frac{1}{2}x^{12}$$

49. $\dfrac{9x^{20}y^{20}}{7x^{20}y^{20}} = \dfrac{9}{7}x^0y^0 = \dfrac{9}{7} \cdot 1 \cdot 1 = \dfrac{9}{7}$

51. $\dfrac{-5x^{10}y^{12}z^6}{50x^2y^3z^2} = -\dfrac{1}{10}x^8y^9z^4$

In Exercises 53–77, each answer should be checked by showing that the product of the divisor and the quotient is the dividend. The check is shown here only for Exercise 53.

53. $\dfrac{6x^4+2x^3}{2}=\dfrac{6x^4}{2}+\dfrac{2x^3}{2}=3x^4+x^3$

Check: $2(3x^4+x^3)=2\cdot 3x^4+2\cdot x^3$
$=6x^4+2x^3$

55. $\dfrac{6x^4-2x^3}{2x}=\dfrac{6x^4}{2x}-\dfrac{2x^3}{2x}=3x^3-x^2$

57. $\dfrac{y^5-3y^2+y}{y}=\dfrac{y^5}{y}-\dfrac{3y^2}{y}+\dfrac{y}{y}$
$=y^4-3y+1$

59. $\dfrac{15x^3-24x^2}{-3x}=\dfrac{15x^3}{-3x}-\dfrac{24x^2}{-3x}$
$=-5x^2+8x$

61. $\dfrac{18x^5+6x^4+9x^3}{3x^2}=\dfrac{18x^5}{3x^2}+\dfrac{6x^4}{3x^2}+\dfrac{9x^3}{3x^2}$
$=6x^3+2x^2+3x$

63. $\dfrac{12x^4-8x^3+40x^2}{4x}=\dfrac{12x^4}{4x}-\dfrac{8x^3}{4x}+\dfrac{40x^2}{4x}$
$=3x^3-2x^2+10x$

65. $(4x^2-6x)\div x=\dfrac{4x^2-6x}{x}=\dfrac{4x^2}{x}-\dfrac{6x}{x}$
$=4x-6$

67. $\dfrac{30z^3+10z^2}{-5z}=\dfrac{30z^3}{-5z}+\dfrac{10z^2}{-5z}=-6z^2-2z$

69. $\dfrac{8x^3+6x^2-2x}{2}=\dfrac{8x^3}{2x}+\dfrac{6x^2}{2x}-\dfrac{2x}{2x}$
$=4x^2+3x-1$

71. $\dfrac{25x^7-15x^5-5x^4}{5x^3}=\dfrac{25x^7}{5x^3}-\dfrac{15x^5}{5x^3}-\dfrac{5x^4}{5x^3}$
$=5x^4-3x^2-x$

73. $\dfrac{18x^7-9x^6+20x^5-10x^4}{-2x^4}$
$=\dfrac{18x^7}{-2x^4}-\dfrac{9x^6}{-2x^4}+\dfrac{20x^5}{-2x^4}-\dfrac{10x^4}{-2x^4}$
$=-9x^3+\dfrac{9}{2}x^2-10x+5$

75. $\dfrac{12x^2y^2+6x^2y-15xy^2}{3xy}$
$=\dfrac{12x^2y^2}{3xy}+\dfrac{6x^2y}{3xy}-\dfrac{15xy^2}{3xy}$
$=4xy+2x-5y$

77. $\dfrac{20x^7y^4-15x^3y^2-10x^2y}{-5x^2y}$
$=\dfrac{20x^7y^4}{-5x^2y}+\dfrac{-15x^3y^2}{-5x^2y}+\dfrac{-10x^2y}{-5x^2y}$
$=-4x^5y^3+3xy+2$

For Exercises 79–85, answers may vary.

87. $\dfrac{18x^8-27x^6+36x^4}{3x^2}=6x^6-9x^4+12x^2,$

so the required polynomial is

$$18x^8-27x^6+36x^4.$$

One way to find this polynomial is to use the relationship between division and multiplication:

$$3x^2(6x^6-9x^4+12x^2)=18x^8-36x^6+36x^4.$$

89. $\dfrac{3x^{14}-6x^{12}-?x^7}{?x^7}=-x^7+2x^5+3$

To get 2 as the coefficient of the middle term of the quotient, the coefficient in the divisor must be -3. To get the exponents shown in the three terms of the quotient, the exponent in the divisor must be 7. Since we now know that the divisor is $-3x^7$, the coefficient of the last term of the dividend must be -9.
Therefore,

$$\frac{3x^{14}-6x^{12}-?x^7}{?x^?}=\frac{3x^{14}-6x^{12}-9x^7}{-3x^7}.$$

Review Exercises

90. $|-20.3| = 20.3$

91.
$$\begin{array}{r} 0.875 \\ 8\overline{)7.000} \\ \underline{6\,4} \\ 60 \\ \underline{56} \\ 40 \\ \underline{40} \\ 0 \end{array}$$

$\frac{7}{8} = 0.875$

92. $y = \frac{1}{3}x + 2$

slope $= \frac{1}{3}$; y-intercept $= 2$

Plot $(0, 2)$. From this point move 1 unit *up* and 3 units to the *right* to reach the point $(3, 3)$. Draw a line through $(0, 2)$ and $(3, 3)$.

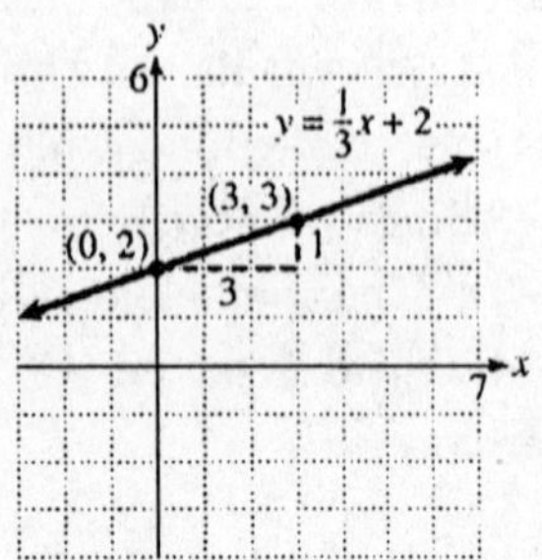

6.6 Dividing Polynomials by Binomials

6.6 CHECK POINTS

CHECK POINT 1

Divide $x^2 + 14x + 45$ by $x + 9$.

$$\begin{array}{r} x + 5 \\ x+9\overline{)x^2 + 14x + 45} \\ \underline{x^2 + 9x}\phantom{{}+45} \\ 5x + 45 \\ \underline{5x + 45} \\ 0 \end{array}$$

The quotient is $x+5$ and the remainder is 0. Thus, $(x^2+14x+45) \div (x+9) = x+5$. To check, multiply the divisor and the quotient and add the remainder, 0:

$$\begin{aligned} &(x+9)(x+5)+0 \\ &= x^2 + 5x + 9x + 45 + 0 \\ &= x^2 + 14x + 45. \end{aligned}$$

CHECK POINT 2

$$\frac{6x + 8x^2 - 12}{2x + 3}$$

Rewrite the dividend in descending powers of x.

$$6x + 8x^2 - 12 = 8x^2 + 6x - 12$$

$$\begin{array}{r} 4x - 3 \\ 2x+3\overline{)8x^2 + 6x - 12} \\ \underline{8x^2 + 12x}\phantom{{}-12} \\ -6x - 12 \\ \underline{-6x - 9} \\ -3 \end{array}$$

The quotient is $4x - 3$ and the remainder is 0. Thus,

$$\frac{6x + 8x^2 - 12}{2x + 3} = 4x - 3 + \frac{-3}{2x + 3}$$

or

$$\frac{6x + 8x^2 - 12}{2x + 3} = 4x - 3 - \frac{3}{2x + 3}.$$

Check:

$$\begin{aligned} &(2x + 3)(4x - 3) + (-3) \\ &= 8x^2 - 6x + 12x - 9 - 3 \\ &= 8x^2 + 6x - 12 \\ &\text{or} \quad 6x + 8x^2 - 12 \end{aligned}$$

CHECK POINT 3

$$\frac{x^3 - 1}{x - 1}$$

Use a coefficient of 0 for the missing x^2- and x-terms in the dividend.

$$\begin{array}{r} x^2 + x + 1 \\ x - 1\overline{)x^3 + 0x^2 + 0x - 1} \\ \underline{x^3 - x^2} \\ x^2 + 0x \\ \underline{x^2 - x} \\ x - 1 \\ \underline{x - 1} \\ 0 \end{array}$$

The quotient is $x^2 + x + 1$ and the remainder is 0. Thus,

$$\frac{x^3 - 1}{x - 1} = x^2 + x + 1.$$

Check:

$$\begin{aligned} &(x - 1)(x^2 + x + 1) \\ &= x(x^2 + x + 1) - 1(x^2 + x + 1) \\ &= x^3 + x^2 + x - x^2 - x - 1 \\ &= x^3 - 1 \end{aligned}$$

EXERCISE SET 6.6

In Exercises 1–35, each answer should be checked by showing that the product of the divisor and the quotient, plus the remainder, is the dividend. Checks will be shown here only for Exercises 1 and 9.

1.
$$\begin{array}{r} x + 4 \\ x + 2\overline{)x^2 + 6x + 8} \\ \underline{x^2 + 2x} \\ 4x + 8 \\ \underline{4x + 8} \\ 0 \end{array}$$

$$\frac{x^2 + 6x + 8}{x + 2} = x + 4$$

Check: $(x + 2)(x + 4) = x^2 + 4x + 2x + 8$
$= x^2 + 6x + 8$

3.
$$\begin{array}{r} 2x + 5 \\ x - 2\overline{)2x^2 + x - 10} \\ \underline{2x^2 - 4x} \\ 5x - 10 \\ \underline{5x - 10} \\ 0 \end{array}$$

$$\frac{2x^2 + x - 10}{x - 2} = 2x + 5$$

5.
$$\begin{array}{r} x - 2 \\ x - 3\overline{)x^2 - 5x + 6} \\ \underline{x^2 - 3x} \\ -2x + 6 \\ \underline{-2x + 6} \\ 0 \end{array}$$

$$\frac{x^2 - 5x + 6}{x - 3} = x - 2$$

7.

$$
\begin{array}{r}
2y+1 \\
y+2\overline{)2y^2+5y+2} \\
\underline{2y^2+4y} \\
y+2 \\
\underline{y+2} \\
0
\end{array}
$$

$$\frac{2y^2+5y+2}{y+2} = 2y+1$$

9.

$$
\begin{array}{r}
x-2 \\
x-3\overline{)x^2-5x+8} \\
\underline{x^2-3x} \\
-2x+8 \\
\underline{-2x+6} \\
2
\end{array}
$$

$$\frac{x^2-5x+8}{x-3} = x-2+\frac{2}{x-3}$$

Check: $(y+2)(y+3)+4 = (y^2+5y+6)+4$
$= y^2+5y+10$

11.

$$
\begin{array}{r}
y+3 \\
y+2\overline{)y^2+5y+10} \\
\underline{y^2+2y} \\
3y+10 \\
\underline{3y+\ \ 6} \\
4
\end{array}
$$

$$\frac{5y+10+y^2}{y+2} = \frac{y^2+5y+10}{y+2}$$

$$= y+3+\frac{4}{y+2}$$

13.

$$
\begin{array}{r}
x^2-5x+2 \\
x-1\overline{)x^3-6x^2+7x-2} \\
\underline{x^3-\ \ x^2} \\
-5x^2+7x \\
\underline{-5x^2+5x} \\
2x-2 \\
\underline{2x-2} \\
0
\end{array}
$$

$$\frac{x^3-6x^2+7x-2}{x-1} = x^2-5x+2$$

15.

$$
\begin{array}{r}
6y-1 \\
2y-3\overline{)12y^2-20y+3} \\
\underline{12y^2-18y} \\
-2y+3 \\
\underline{-2y+3} \\
0
\end{array}
$$

$$\frac{12y^2-20y+3}{2y-3} = 6y-1$$

17.

$$
\begin{array}{r}
2a+3 \\
2a-1\overline{)4a^2+4a-3} \\
\underline{4a^2-2a} \\
6a-3 \\
\underline{6a-3} \\
0
\end{array}
$$

$$\frac{4a^2+4a-3}{2a-1} = 2a+3$$

19.

$$
\begin{array}{r}
y^2-\ \ y+2 \\
2y+1\overline{)2y^3-y^2+3y+2} \\
\underline{2y^3+y^2} \\
-2y^2+3y \\
\underline{-2y^2-\ \ y} \\
4y+2 \\
\underline{4y+2} \\
0
\end{array}
$$

$$\frac{3y-y^2+2y^3+2}{2y+1}$$

$$= \frac{2y^3-y^2+3y+2}{2y+1} = y^2-y+2$$

21.

$$
\begin{array}{r}
x-\ \ 6 \\
2x+3\overline{)2x^2-\ \ 9x+\ \ 8} \\
\underline{2x^2+\ \ 3x} \\
-12x+\ \ 8 \\
\underline{-12x-18} \\
26
\end{array}
$$

$$\frac{2x^2-9x+8}{2x+3} = x-6+\frac{26}{2x+3}$$

23.

$$\begin{array}{r} x^2 + 2x + 8 \\ x-2\overline{)x^3 + 0x^2 + 4x - 3} \\ \underline{x^3 - 2x^2} \qquad\qquad \\ 2x^2 + 4x \qquad \\ \underline{2x^2 - 4x} \qquad \\ 8x - 3 \\ \underline{8x - 16} \\ 13 \end{array}$$

$$\frac{x^3 + 4x - 3}{x - 2} = x^2 + 2x + 8 + \frac{13}{x - 2}$$

25.

$$\begin{array}{r} 2y^2 + y + 1 \\ 2y+3\overline{)4y^3 + 8y^2 + 5y + 9} \\ \underline{4y^3 + 6y^2} \qquad\qquad \\ 2y^2 + 5y \qquad \\ \underline{2y^2 + 3y} \qquad \\ 2y + 9 \\ \underline{2y + 3} \\ 6 \end{array}$$

$$\frac{4y^3 + 8y^2 + 5y + 9}{2y + 3}$$

$$= 2y^2 + y + 1 + \frac{6}{2y + 3}$$

27.

$$\begin{array}{r} 2y^2 - 3y + 2 \\ 3y+2\overline{)6y^3 - 5y^2 + 0y + 5} \\ \underline{6y^3 + 4y^2} \qquad\qquad \\ -9y^2 + 0y \qquad \\ \underline{-9y^2 - 6y} \qquad \\ 6y + 5 \\ \underline{6y + 4} \\ 1 \end{array}$$

$$\frac{6y^3 - 5y^2 + 5}{3y + 2} = 2y^2 - 3y + 2 + \frac{1}{3y + 2}$$

29.

$$\begin{array}{r} 9x^2 + 3x + 1 \\ 3x-1\overline{)27x^3 + 0x^2 + 0x - 1} \\ \underline{27x^3 - 9x^2} \qquad\qquad \\ 9x^2 + 0x \qquad \\ \underline{9x^2 - 3x} \qquad \\ 3x - 1 \\ \underline{3x - 1} \\ 0 \end{array}$$

$$\frac{27x^3 - 1}{3x - 1} = 9x^2 + 3x + 1$$

31.

$$\begin{array}{r} y^3 - 9y^2 + 27y - 27 \\ y-3\overline{)y^4 - 12y^3 + 54y^2 - 108y + 81} \\ \underline{y^4 - 3y^3} \qquad\qquad\qquad\qquad \\ -9y^3 + 54y^2 \qquad\qquad \\ \underline{-9y^3 + 27y^2} \qquad\qquad \\ 27y^2 - 108y \qquad \\ \underline{27y^2 - 81y} \qquad \\ -27y + 81 \\ \underline{-27y + 81} \\ 0 \end{array}$$

$$\frac{81 - 12y^3 + 54y^2 + y^4 - 108y}{y - 3}$$

$$= \frac{y^4 - 12y^3 + 54y^2 - 108y + 81}{y - 3}$$

$$= y^3 - 9y^2 + 27y - 27$$

33.

$$\begin{array}{r} 2y+4 \\ 2y-1\overline{)4y^2+6y+0} \\ \underline{4y^2-2y} \\ 8y+0 \\ \underline{8y-4} \\ 4 \end{array}$$

$$\frac{4y^2+6y}{2y-1} = 2y+4+\frac{4}{2y-1}$$

35.

$$\begin{array}{r} y^3+y^2-y-1 \\ y-1\overline{)y^4+0y^3-2y^2+0y+5} \\ \underline{y^4-y^3} \\ y^3-2y^2 \\ \underline{y^3-y^2} \\ -y^2+0y \\ \underline{-y^2+y} \\ -y+5 \\ \underline{-y+1} \\ 4 \end{array}$$

$$\frac{y^4-2y^2+5}{y-1} = y^3+y^2-y-1+\frac{4}{y-1}$$

37. Solve the formula for the area of rectangle for w. Then substitute the given expressions for A and l.

$$A = lw$$

$$w = \frac{A}{l} = \frac{2x^2+5x-3}{2x-1}$$

$$\begin{array}{r} x+3 \\ 2x-1\overline{)2x^2+5x-3} \\ \underline{2x^2-x} \\ 6x-3 \\ \underline{6x-3} \\ 0 \end{array}$$

The width is $(x+3)$ inches.

39. a. $\dfrac{x+25}{x+20} = 1 + \dfrac{5}{x+20}$

$$\begin{array}{r} 1 \\ x+20\overline{)x+25} \\ \underline{x+20} \\ 5 \end{array}$$

b.

x	0	5	10	25	50	75
$\frac{x+25}{x+20}$	$\frac{5}{4}$	$\frac{6}{5}$	$\frac{7}{6}$	$\frac{10}{9}$	$\frac{15}{14}$	$\frac{20}{19}$

c. As x increases, the ratio is decreasing and approaching 1.

For Exercises 41–43, answers may vary.

45. Multiply the divisor by the quotient and add the remainder to get the dividend, which is the required polynomial:

$$\begin{aligned} &(2x+4)(x-3)+17 \\ &= (2x^2-6x+4x-12)+17 \\ &= 2x^2-2x-12+17 \\ &= 2x^2-2x+5. \end{aligned}$$

47. The quotient starts with x to the power that is one less than the power in the dividend. It is made up of terms that are all the powers of x down to 1, but with alternating signs. The remainder is always -2.

Following this pattern,

$$\frac{x^2-1}{x+1} = x^6 - x^5 + x^4 - x^3 + x^2 - x + 1 + \frac{-2}{x+1} \quad \text{or} \quad x^6 - x^5 + x^4 - x^3 - x + 1 - \frac{2}{x+1}.$$

Long division gives the same result.

$$\begin{array}{r}
x^6 - x^5 + x^4 - x^3 + x^2 - x + 1 \\
x+1\overline{)x^7 + 0x^6 + 0x^5 + 0x^4 + 0x^3 + 0x^2 + 0x - 1} \\
\underline{x^7 + x^6} \qquad\qquad\qquad\qquad\qquad\qquad\qquad \\
-x^6 + 0x^5 \qquad\qquad\qquad\qquad\qquad\quad \\
\underline{-x^6 - x^5} \qquad\qquad\qquad\qquad\qquad\quad \\
x^5 + 0x^4 \qquad\qquad\qquad\qquad \\
\underline{x^5 + x^4} \qquad\qquad\qquad\qquad \\
-x^4 + 0x^3 \qquad\qquad\qquad \\
\underline{-x^4 - x^3} \qquad\qquad\qquad \\
x^3 + 0x^2 \qquad\quad\;\; \\
\underline{x^3 + x^2} \qquad\quad\;\; \\
-x^2 + 0x \qquad \\
\underline{-x^2 - x} \qquad \\
x - 1 \\
\underline{x + 1} \\
-2
\end{array}$$

49.

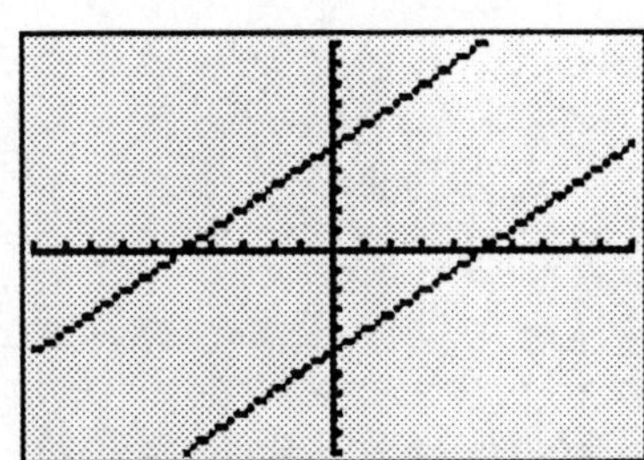

The graphs do not coincide.

$$\begin{array}{r}
x + 5 \\
x-5\overline{)x^2 + 0x - 25} \\
\underline{x^2 - 5x} \qquad\;\; \\
5x - 25 \\
\underline{5x - 25} \\
0
\end{array}$$

$$\frac{x^2-25}{x-5} = x + 5$$

The expression on the right should be changed to $x+5$.

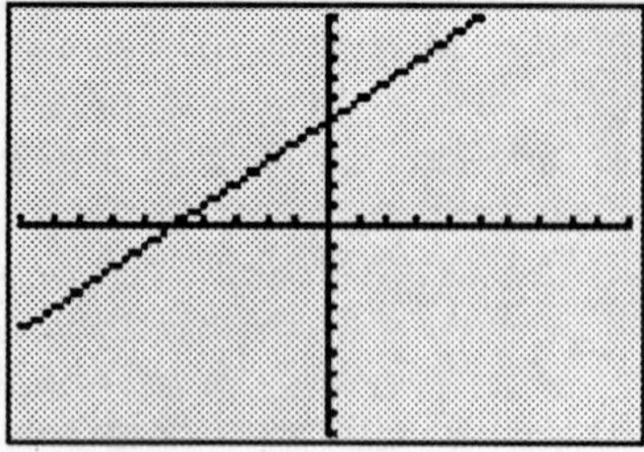

Now the graphs coincide.

51.

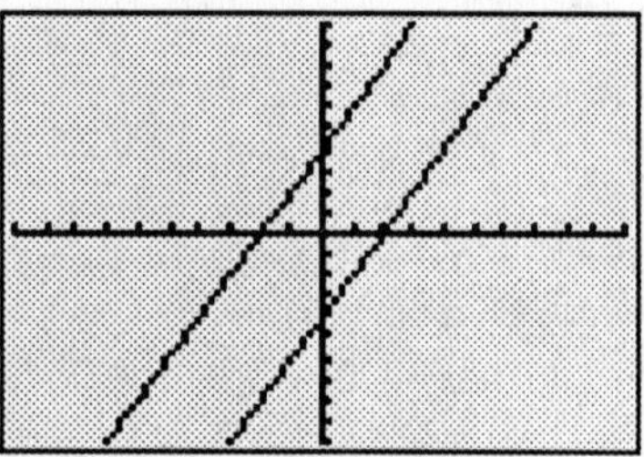

The graphs do not coincide.

$$\begin{array}{r} 2x+4 \\ 3x+2\overline{)6x^2+16x+8} \\ \underline{6x^2+\ \ 4x} \\ 12x+8 \\ \underline{12x+8} \\ 0 \end{array}$$

$$\frac{6x^2+16x+8}{3x+2}=2x+4$$

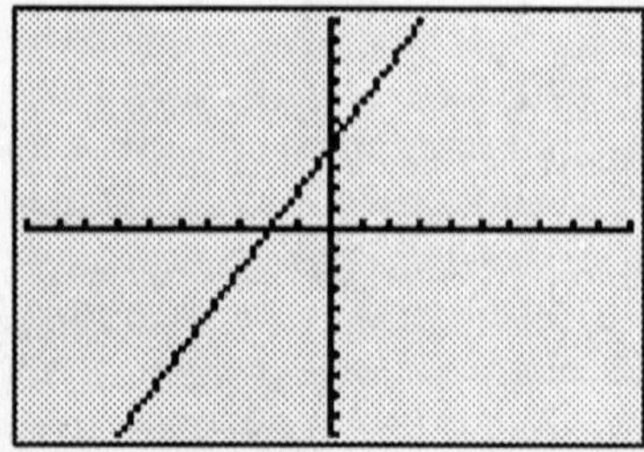

Now the graphs coincide.

Review Exercises

53. $2x-y\geq 4$
$x+y\leq -1$

Graph $2x-y\geq 4$:
Graph $2x-y=4$ as a solid line with x-intercept 2 and y-intercept -4. Since $2(0)-0\geq 4$ is false, shade the half-plane *not* containing $(0,0)$.
Graph $x+y\leq -1$:
Graph $x+y=-1$ as a solid line with x-intercept 1 and y-intercept 1. Since $0+0\leq -1$ is false, shade the half-plane not containing $(0,0)$.
The solution set of the system is the intersection (overlap) of the two shaded regions.

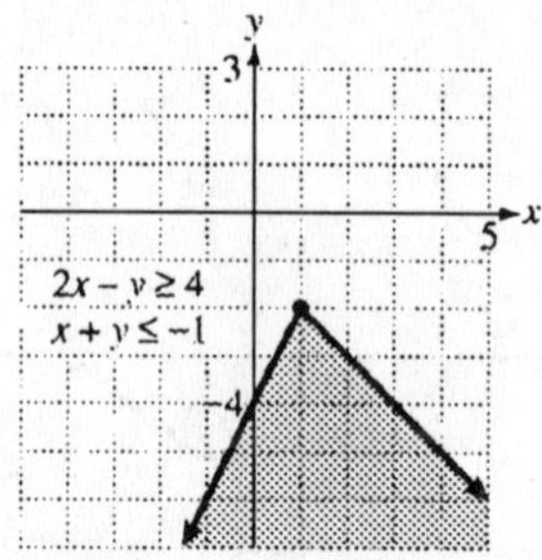

54. $A=PB$; $P=6\%=0.06, B=20$

$$\begin{aligned} A&=PB \\ A&=(0.06)(20) \\ &=1.2 \end{aligned}$$

1.1 is 60% of 20.

55. $\frac{x}{3}+\frac{2}{5}=\frac{x}{5}-\frac{2}{5}$

To clear fractions, multiply by the LCD, 15.

$$15\left(\frac{x}{3}+\frac{2}{5}\right)=15\left(\frac{x}{5}-\frac{2}{5}\right)$$
$$15\left(\frac{x}{3}\right)+15\left(\frac{2}{5}\right)=15\left(\frac{x}{5}\right)-15\left(\frac{2}{5}\right)$$
$$5x+6=3x-6$$
$$2x+6=-6$$
$$2x=-12$$
$$x=-6$$

The solution is -6.

6.7 Negative Exponents and Scientific Notation

6.7 CHECK POINTS

CHECK POINT 1

a. $6^{-2}=\frac{1}{6^2}=\frac{1}{6\cdot 6}=\frac{1}{36}$

b. $5^{-3}=\frac{1}{5^3}=\frac{1}{5\cdot 5\cdot 5}=\frac{1}{125}$

c. $(-4)^{-3}=\frac{1}{(-4)^3}=\frac{1}{(-4)(-4)(-4)}$
$=\frac{1}{-64}=-\frac{1}{64}$

d. $8^{-1}=\frac{1}{8^1}=\frac{1}{8}$

CHECK POINT 2

a. $\frac{2^{-3}}{7^{-2}}=\frac{7^2}{2^3}=\frac{7\cdot 7}{2\cdot 2\cdot 2}=\frac{49}{8}$

b. $\left(\frac{4}{5}\right)^{-2}=\frac{4^{-2}}{5^{-2}}=\frac{5^2}{4^2}=\frac{5\cdot 5}{4\cdot 4}=\frac{25}{16}$

c. $\frac{1}{7y^{-2}}=\frac{y^2}{7}$

d. $\frac{x^{-1}}{y^{-8}}=\frac{y^8}{x^1}=\frac{y^8}{x}$

CHECK POINT 3

$x^{-12}\cdot x^2=x^{-12+2}=x^{-10}=\frac{1}{x^{10}}$

CHECK POINT 4

a. $\frac{x^2}{x^{10}}=x^{2-10}=x^{-8}=\frac{1}{x^8}$

b. $\frac{75x^3}{5x^9}=\frac{75}{5}\cdot x^{3-9}=15x^{-6}=\frac{15}{x^6}$

c. $\frac{50y^8}{-25y^{14}}=\frac{50}{-25}y^{8-14}=-2y^{-6}=-\frac{2}{y^6}$

CHECK POINT 5

$$\frac{(6x^4)^2}{x^{11}}=\frac{6^2(x^4)^2}{x^{11}}=\frac{6^2x^{4\cdot 2}}{x^{11}}$$
$$=\frac{36x^8}{x^{11}}=36x^{8-11}$$
$$=36x^{-3}=\frac{36}{x^3}$$

CHECK POINT 6

$$\left(\frac{x^8}{x^4}\right)^{-5}=\frac{(x^8)^{-5}}{(x^4)^{-5}}=\frac{x^{8(-5)}}{x^{4(-5)}}=\frac{x^{-40}}{x^{-20}}$$
$$=x^{-40-(-20)}=x^{-20}=\frac{1}{x^{20}}$$

CHECK POINT 7

a. 7.4×10^9

Move the decimal point in 7.4 nine places to the right. This requires adding eight zeros.

$$7.4\times 10^9=7{,}400{,}000{,}000$$

b. 3.07×10^{-6}

Move the decimal point in 3.017 six places to the left. This requires adding five zeros to the right of the decimal point.

$$3.017\times 10^{-6}=0.000003017$$

CHECK POINT 8

a. 7,410,000,000

To write this number in scientific notation, move the decimal point nine places to the left. The exponent is positive because the given number is greater than 10.

$$7{,}410{,}000{,}000 = 7.41 \times 10^9$$

b. 0.000000092

To write this number in scientific notation, move the decimal point eight places to the right. The exponent is negative because the given number is between 1 and 10.

CHECK POINT 9

a. $(3 \times 10^8)(2 \times 10^2) = 3 \cdot 2 \cdot 10^8 \cdot 10^2$
$= 6 \times 10^{8+2}$
$= 6 \times 10^{10}$

b. $\dfrac{8.4 \times 10^7}{4 \times 10^{-4}} = \dfrac{8.4}{4} \times \dfrac{10^7}{10^{-4}}$
$= 2.1 \times 10^{7-(-4)}$
$= 2.1 \times 10^{11}$

c. $(4 \times 10^{-2})^3 = 4^3 \times (10^{-2})^3$
$= 4^3 \times 10^{-6}$
$= 64 \times 10^{-6}$
$= 6.4 \times 10^1 \times 10^{-6}$
$= 6.4 \times 10^{-5}$

CHECK POINT 10

$(2 \times 10^4) \times 26 = (2 \times 26) \times 10^4$
$= 5.2 \times 10^4$
$= 5.2 \times 10^1 \times 10^4$
$= 5.2 \times 10^5$

The total distance covered by all the runners was 5.2×10^6 miles.

EXERCISE SET 6.7

1. $5^{-2} = \dfrac{1}{5^2} = \dfrac{1}{25}$

3. $2^{-3} = \dfrac{1}{2^3} = \dfrac{1}{8}$

5. $(-2)^{-2} = \dfrac{1}{(-2)^2} = \dfrac{1}{4}$

7. $(-3)^{-3} = \dfrac{1}{(-3)^3} = \dfrac{1}{-27} = -\dfrac{1}{27}$

9. $4^{-1} = \dfrac{1}{4^1} = \dfrac{1}{4}$

11. $2^{-1} + 3^{-1} = \dfrac{1}{2^1} + \dfrac{1}{3^1} = \dfrac{1}{2} + \dfrac{1}{3}$
$= \dfrac{3}{6} + \dfrac{2}{6} = \dfrac{5}{6}$

13. $\dfrac{1}{3^{-2}} = 3^2 = 9$

15. $\dfrac{1}{(-3)^{-2}} = (-3)^2 = 9$

17. $\dfrac{2^{-3}}{8^{-2}} = \dfrac{8^2}{2^3} = \dfrac{64}{8} = 8$

19. $\left(\dfrac{1}{4}\right)^{-2} = \dfrac{1^{-2}}{4^{-2}} = \dfrac{4^2}{1^2} = \dfrac{16}{1} = 16$

21. $\left(\dfrac{3}{5}\right)^{-3} = \dfrac{3^{-3}}{5^{-3}} = \dfrac{5^3}{3^3} = \dfrac{125}{27}$

23. $\dfrac{1}{6x^{-5}} = \dfrac{1 \cdot x^5}{6} = \dfrac{x^5}{6}$

25. $\dfrac{x^{-8}}{y^{-1}} = \dfrac{y^1}{x^8} = \dfrac{y}{x^8}$

27. $\dfrac{3}{(-5)^{-3}} = 3 \cdot (-5)^3 = 5(-125) = -375$

29. $x^{-8} \cdot x^3 = x^{-8+3} = x^{-5} = \dfrac{1}{x^5}$

31. $(4x^{-5})(2x^2) = 8x^{-5+2} = 8x^{-3} = \dfrac{8}{x^3}$

33. $\dfrac{x^3}{x^9} = x^{3-9} = x^{-6} = \dfrac{1}{x^6}$

35. $\dfrac{y}{y^{100}} = \dfrac{y^1}{y^{100}} = y^{1-100} = y^{-99} = \dfrac{1}{y^{99}}$

37. $\dfrac{30z^5}{10z^{10}} = \dfrac{30}{10} \cdot \dfrac{z^5}{z^{10}} = 3z^{5-10}$
$= 3z^{-5} = \dfrac{3}{z^5}$

39. $\dfrac{-8x^3}{2x^7} = \dfrac{-8}{2} \cdot \dfrac{x^3}{x^7} = -4x^{-4} = -\dfrac{4}{x^4}$

41. $\dfrac{-9a^5}{27a^8} = \dfrac{-9}{27} \cdot \dfrac{a^5}{a^8} = -\dfrac{1}{3}a^{-3} = -\dfrac{1}{3a^3}$

43. $\dfrac{7w^5}{5w^{13}} = \dfrac{7}{5} \cdot \dfrac{w^5}{w^{13}} = \dfrac{7}{5}w^{-8} = \dfrac{7}{5w^8}$

45. $\dfrac{x^3}{(x^4)^2} = \dfrac{x^3}{x^{4\cdot 2}} = \dfrac{x^3}{x^8} = x^{-5} = \dfrac{1}{x^5}$

47. $\dfrac{y^{-3}}{(y^4)^2} = \dfrac{y^{-3}}{y^8} = y^{-3-8} = y^{-11} = \dfrac{1}{y^{11}}$

49. $\dfrac{(4x^3)^2}{x^8} = \dfrac{4^2x^6}{x^8} = 16x^{-2} = \dfrac{16}{x^2}$

51. $\dfrac{(6y^4)^3}{y^{-5}} = \dfrac{6^3y^{12}}{y^{-5}} = 216y^{12-(-5)} = 216y^{17}$

53. $\left(\dfrac{x^4}{x^2}\right)^{-3} = (x^2)^{-3} = x^{-6} = \dfrac{1}{x^6}$

55. $\left(\dfrac{4x^5}{2x^2}\right)^{-4} = (2x^3)^{-4} = 2^{-4}x^{-12} = \dfrac{1}{2^4x^{12}}$
$= \dfrac{1}{16x^{12}}$

57. $(3x^{-1})^{-2} = 3^{-2}(x^{-1})^{-2} = 3^{-2}x^2$
$= \dfrac{x^5}{3^2} = \dfrac{x^2}{9}$

59. $(-2y^{-1})^{-3} = (-2)^{-3}(y^{-1})^{-3} = \dfrac{y^3}{(-2)^3}$
$= \dfrac{y^3}{-8} = -\dfrac{y^3}{8}$

61. $\dfrac{2x^5 \cdot 3x^7}{15x^6} = \dfrac{6x^{12}}{15x^6} = \dfrac{6}{15} \cdot \dfrac{x^{12}}{x^6}$
$= \dfrac{2}{5} \cdot x^6 = \dfrac{2x^6}{5}$

63. $(x^3)^5 \cdot x^{-7} = x^{15} \cdot x^{-7} = x^{15+(-7)} = x^8$

65. $(2y^3)^4y^{-6} = 2^4(y^3)^4y^{-6} = 16y^{12}y^{-6}$
$= 16y^6$

67. $\dfrac{(y^3)^4}{(y^2)^7} = \dfrac{y^{12}}{y^{14}} = y^{-2} = \dfrac{1}{y^2}$

69. $(y^{10})^{-5} = y^{(10)(-5)} = y^{-50} = \dfrac{1}{y^{50}}$

71. $(a^4b^5)^{-3} = (a^4)^{-3}(b^5)^{-3} = a^{-12}b^{-15}$
$= \dfrac{1}{a^{12}b^{15}}$

73. $(a^{-2}b^6)^{-4} = a^8b^{-24} = \dfrac{a^8}{b^{24}}$

75. $\left(\dfrac{x^2}{2}\right)^{-2} = \dfrac{x^{-4}}{2^{-2}} = \dfrac{2^2}{x^4} = \dfrac{4}{x^4}$

77. $\left(\dfrac{x^2}{y^3}\right)^{-3} = \dfrac{(x^2)^{-3}}{(y^3)^{-3}} = \dfrac{x^{-6}}{y^{-9}} = \dfrac{y^9}{x^6}$

79. $2.7 \times 10^2 = 270$ (Move decimal point 2 places right.)

81. $9.12 \times 10^5 = 912{,}000$ (Move right 5.)

83. $3.4 \times 10^0 = 3.4$ (Don't move decimal point.)

85. $7.9 \times 10^{-1} = 0.79$ (Move left 1.)

87. $2.15 \times 10^{-2} = 0.0215$ (Move left 2.)

89. $7.86 \times 10^{-4} = 0.000786$ (Move left 4.)

91. $32{,}400 = 3.24 \times 10^4$

93. $220{,}000{,}000 = 2.2 \times 10^8$

95. $713 = 7.13 \times 10^2$

97. $6751 = 6.751 \times 10^3$

99. $0.0027 = 2.7 \times 10^{-3}$

101. $0.000020 = 2.02 \times 10^{-5}$

103. $0.005 = 5 \times 10^{-3}$

105. $3.14159 = 3.14159 \times 10^0$

106. $(2 \times 10^3)(3 \times 10^2) = 6 \times 10^{3+2} = 6 \times 10^5$

109. $(2 \times 10^5)(8 \times 10^3) = 16 \times 10^{5+3} = 16x^8$
$= 1.6 \times 10^9$

111. $\dfrac{12 \times 10^6}{4 \times 10^2} = 3 \times 10^{6-2} = 3 \times 10^4$

113. $\dfrac{15 \times 10^4}{5 \times 10^{-2}} = 3 \times 10^{4+2} = 3 \times 10^6$

115. $\dfrac{15 \times 10^{-4}}{5 \times 10^2} = 3 \times 10^{-4-2} = 3 \times 10^{-6}$

117. $\dfrac{180 \times 10^6}{2 \times 10^3} = 90 \times 10^{6-3} = 90 \times 10^3$
$= 9 \times 10^4$

119. $\dfrac{3 \times 10^4}{12 \times 10^{-3}} = 0.25 \times 10^{4+3} = 0.25 \times 10^7$
$= 2.5 \times 10^6$

121. $(5 \times 10^2)^3 = 5^3 \times 10^{2(3)} = 125 \times 10^6$
$= 1.25 \times 10^8$

123. $(3 \times 10^{-2})^4 = 3^4 \times 10^{-2(4)} = 81 \times 10^{-8}$
$= 8.1 \times 10^{-7}$

125. $(4 \times 10^6)^{-1} = 4^{-1} \times 10^{6(-1)} = 0.25 \times 10^{-6}$
$= 2.5 \times 10^{-7}$

127. $9200 = 9.2 \times 10^3$

129. $0.00000000000000025 = 2.5 \times 10^{-16}$

131. $1{,}694{,}300 = 1.6943 \times 10^6$
1 million $= 10^6$

1,694,300 million $= (1.6943 \times 10^6)(10^6)$
$= 1.6943 \times 10^{12}$

133. $60 = 6 \times 10^1$
1 billion $= 10^9$
60 billion $= (6 \times 10^1)(10^9) = 6 \times 10^{10}$

135. 1.6 trillion $= 1.6 \times 10^{12}$

25% of 1.6 trillion $= 0.25(1.6 \times 10^{12})$
$= 0.4 \times 10^{12} = 4 \times 10^{11}$

The United States government spends approximately $\$4 \times 10^{11}$ per year on Social Security.

137. $120(2.7 \times 10^8) = 324 \times 10^8 = 3.2410^{10}$

The total annual spending in the United States on ice cream is about $\$3.24 \times 10^{10}$.

For Exercises 139–143, answers may vary.

145. Statement b is true.

$5^{-2} = \frac{1}{25}$ and $2^{-5} = \frac{1}{32}$.

Since $\frac{1}{25} > \frac{1}{32}$, $5^{-2} > 2^{-5}$.

147. There is no advantage in using scientific notation to represent a number greater than or equal to 1 and less than 10 because the decimal point will not be moved and it is simpler to write it without the zero exponent.

Example: $7.75 = 7.75 \times 10^0$

149. Students will check their work with a calculator. Results will depend on the exercises chosen.

151. Students will check their work with a calculator. Results will depend on the exercises chosen.

Review Exercises

153. Let $x =$ the number of deer in the park.

$$\frac{\text{Original number of tagged deer}}{\text{Total number of deer}} = \frac{\text{Number of tagged deer in sample}}{\text{Number of deer in sample}}$$

$$\frac{25}{x} = \frac{4}{36}$$
$$4x = 900$$
$$x = 225$$

There are approximately 225 deer in the park.

154. $24 \div 8 \cdot 3 + 28 \div (-7) = 3 \cdot 3 + 28 \div (-7)$
$= 9 + (-4) = 5$

155. The whole numbers in the given set are 0 and $\sqrt{16}$ $(= 4)$.

Chapter 6 Review Exercises

1. $7x^4 + 9x$ is a binomial of degree 4.

2. $3x + 5x^2 - 2$ is a trinomial of degree 2.

3. $16x$ is a monomial of degree 1.

4. $(-6x^2 + 7x^2 - 9x + 3)$
$+ (14x^3 + 3x^2 - 11x - 7)$
$= (-6x^3 + 14x^3) + (7x^2 + 3x^2)$
$+ (-9x - 11x) + (3 - 7)$
$= 8x^3 + 10x^2 - 20x - 4$

5. $(9y^3 - 7y^2 + 5) + (4y^3 - y^2 + 7y - 10)$
$= (9y^3 + 4y^3) + (-7y^2 - y^2) + 7y$
$+ (5 - 10)$
$= 13y^3 - 8y^2 + 7y - 5$

6. $(5y^2 - y - 8) - (-6y^2 + 3y - 4)$
$= (5y^2 - y - 8) + (6y^2 - 3y + 4)$
$= (5y^2 + 6y^2) + (-y - 3y) + (-8 + 4)$
$= 11y^2 - 4y - 4$

7. $(13x^4 - 8x^3 + 2x^2) - (5x^4 - 3x^3 + 2x^2 - 6)$
$= (13x^4 - 8x^3 + 2x^2)$
$+ (-5x^4 + 3x^3 - 2x^2 + 6)$
$= (13x^4 - 5x^4) + (-8x^3 + 3x^3)$
$+ (2x^2 - 2x^2) + 6$
$= 8x^4 - 5x^3 + 6$

8. $(-13x^4 - 6x^2 + 5x) - (x^4 + 7x^2 - 11x)$
$= (-13x^4 - 6x^2 + 5x)$
$+ (-x^4 - 7x^2 + 11x)$
$= (-13x^4 - x^4) + (-6x^2 - 7x^2)$
$+ (5x + 11x)$
$= -14x^4 - 13x^2 + 16x$

9. Add:

$$\begin{array}{r} 7y^4 - 6y^3 + 4y^2 - 4y \\ y^3 - y^2 + 3y - 4 \\ \hline 7y^4 - 5y^3 + 3y^2 - y - 4 \end{array}$$

10. Subtract:

$$\begin{array}{r} 7x^2 - 9x + 2 \\ -(4x^2 - 2x - 7) \\ \hline \end{array}$$

Add:

$$\begin{array}{r} 7x^2 - 9x + 2 \\ -4x^2 + 2x + 7 \\ \hline 3x^2 - 7x + 9 \end{array}$$

11.

$$\begin{array}{r} 5x^3 - 6x^2 - 9x + 14 \\ -(-5x^3 + 3x^2 - 11x + 3) \\ \hline \end{array}$$

Add:

$$\begin{array}{r} 5x^3 - 6x^2 - 9x + 14 \\ 5x^3 - 3x^2 + 11x - 3 \\ \hline 10x^3 - 9x^2 + 2x + 11 \end{array}$$

12. $104.5x^2 - 1501.5x + 6016$; $x = 10$

$104.5x^2 - 1501.5x + 6016$
$= 104.5(10^2) - 1501.5(10) + 6016$
$= 10{,}450 - 15{,}015 + 6016$
$= 1451$

The death rate for men averaging 10 hours of sleep per night is 1451 men per 10,000 men.

13. $x^{20} \cdot x^3 = x^{20+3} = x^{23}$

14. $y \cdot y^5 \cdot y^8 = y^1 \cdot y^5 \cdot y^8 = y^{1+5+8} = y^{14}$

15. $(x^{20})^5 = x^{20 \cdot 5} = x^{100}$

16. $(10y)^2 = 10^2 y^2 = 100y^2$

17. $(-4x^{10})^3 = (-4)^3(x^{10})^3 = -64x^{30}$

18. $(5x)(10x^3) = (5 \cdot 10)(x^1 \cdot x^3) = 50x^4$

19. $(-12y^7)(3y^4) = -36y^{11}$

20. $(-2x^5)(-3x^4)(5x^3) = 30x^{12}$

21. $7x(3x+9) = 7x(3x) + (7x)(9) = 21x^2 + 63x$

22. $5x^3(4x^2 - 11x) = 5x^3(4x^2) - 5x^3(11x)$
$= 20x^5 - 55x^4$

23. $3y^2(-7y^2 + 3y - 6)$
$= 3y^2(-7y^2) + 3y^2(3y) + 3y^2(-6)$
$= -21y^4 + 9y^3 - 18y^2$

24. $2y^5(8y^3 - 10y^2 + 1)$
$= 2y^5(8y^3) + 2y^5(-10y^2) + 2y^5(1)$
$= 16y^8 - 20y^7 + 2y^5$

25. $(x+3)(x^2 - 5x + 2)$
$= x(x^2 - 5x + 2) + 3(x^2 - 5x + 2)$
$= x^3 - 5x^2 + 2x + 3x^2 - 15x + 6$
$= x^3 - 2x^2 - 13x + 6$

26. $(3y-2)(4y^2 + 3y - 5)$
$= 3y(4y^2 + 3y - 5) - 2(4y^2 + 3y - 5)$
$= 12y^3 + 9y^2 - 15y - 8y^2 - 6y + 10$
$= 12y^3 + y^2 - 21y + 10$

27.
$$\begin{array}{r} y^2 - 4y + 7 \\ 3y - 5 \\ \hline -5y^2 + 20y - 35 \\ 3y^3 - 12y^2 + 21y \\ \hline 3y^3 - 17y^2 + 41y - 35 \end{array}$$

28.
$$\begin{array}{r} 4x^3 - 2x^2 - 6x - 1 \\ 2x + 3 \\ \hline 12x^3 - 6x^2 - 18x - 3 \\ 8x^4 - 4x^3 - 12x^2 - 2x \\ \hline 8x^4 + 8x^3 - 18x^2 - 20x - 3 \end{array}$$

29. $(x+6)(x+2)$
$= x \cdot x + x \cdot 2 + 6 \cdot x + 6 \cdot 2$
$= x^2 + 2x + 6x + 12$
$= x^2 + 8x + 12$

30. $(3y-5)(2y+1) = 6y^2 + 3y - 10y - 5$
$= 6y^2 - 7y - 5$

31. $(4x^2 - 2)(x^2 - 3)$
$= 4x^2 \cdot x^2 + 4x^2(-3) - 2 \cdot x^2 - 2(-3)$
$= 4x^4 - 12x^2 - 2x^2 + 6$
$= 4x^4 - 14x^2 + 6$

32. $(5x+4)(5x-4) = (5x)^2 - 4^2$
$= 25x^2 - 16$

33. $(7-2y)(7+2y) = 7^2 - (2y)^2 = 49 - 4y^2$

34. $(y^2+1)(y^2-1) = (y^2)^2 - 1^2 = y^4 - 1$

35. $(x+3)^2 = x^2 + 2(x)(3) + 3^2$
$= x^2 + 6x + 9$

36. $(3y+4)^2 = (3y)^2 + 2(3y)(4) + 16$
$= 9y^2 + 24y + 16$

37. $(y-1)^2 = y^2 - 2y + 1$

38. $(5y-2)^2 = (5y)^2 - 2(5y)(2) + 2^2$
$= 25y^2 - 20y + 4$

39. $(x^2+4)^2 = (x^2)^2 + 2(x^2)(4) + 4^2$
$= x^4 + 8x^2 + 16$

40. $(x^2+4)(x^2-4) = (x^2)^2 - 4^2 = x^4 - 16$

41. $(x^2+4)(x^2-5) = (x^2)^2 - 5x^2 + 4x^2 - 20$
$= x^4 - x^2 - 20$

42. $A = (x+3)(x+4)$
$= x^2 + 4x + 3x + 12$
$= x^2 + 7x + 12$

43. $A = (x+30)(x+20)$
$= x^2 + 20x + 30x + 600$
$= x^2 + 50x + 600$

The area of the expanded garage is $(x^2 + 50x + 600)$ yards^2.

44. $2x^3y - 4xy^2 + 5y + 6$; $x = -1, y = 2$

$2x^3y - 4xy^2 + 5y + 6$
$= 2(-1)^3(2) - 4(-1)(2)^2 + 5(2) + 6$
$= 2(-1)(2) - 4(1)(4) + 5(2) + 6$
$= -4 + 16 + 10 + 6 = 28$

45.

Term	Coefficient	Degree
$4x^2y$	4	$2+1=3$
$9x^3y^2$	9	$3+2=5$
$-17x^4$	-17	4
-12	-12	0

Degree of the polynomial = 5

46. $(7x^2 - 8xy + y^2) + (-8x^2 - 9xy + 4y^2)$
$= (7x^2 - 8x^2) + (-8xy - 9xy)$
$+ (y^2 + 4y^2)$
$= -x^2 - 17xy + 5y^2$

47. $(13x^3y^2 - 5x^2y - 9x^2)$
$- (11x^3y^2 - 6x^2y - 3x^2 + 4)$
$= (13x^3y^2 - 5x^2y - 9x^2)$
$+ (-11x^3y^2 + 6x^2y + 3x^2 - 4)$
$= (13x^3y^2 - 11x^3y^2) + (-5x^2y + 6x^2y)$
$+ (-9x^2 + 3x^2) - 4$
$= 2x^3y^3 + x^2y - 6x^2 - 4$

48. $(-7x^2y^3)(5x^4y^6)$
$= (-7)(-5)x^{2+4}y^{3+6}$
$= -35x^6y^9$

49. $5ab^2(3a^2b^3 - 4ab)$
$= 5ab^2(3a^2b^3) + 5ab^2(-4ab)$
$= 15a^3b^5 - 20a^2b^3$

50. $(x+7y)(3x-5y)$
$= x(3x) + x(-5y) + 7y(3x) + 7y(-5y)$
$= 3x^2 - 5xy + 21xy - 35y^2$
$= 3x^2 + 16xy - 35y^2$

51. $(4xy-3)(9xy-1)$
$= 4xy(9xy) + 4xy(-1) - 3(9xy) - 3(-1)$
$= 36x^2y^2 - 4xy - 27xy + 3$
$= 36x^2y^2 - 31xy + 3$

52. $(3x+5y)^2 = (3x)^2 + 2(3x)(5y) + (5y)^2$
$= 9x^2 + 30xy + 25y^2$

53. $(xy-7)^2 = (xy)^2 - 2(xy)(7) + 7^2$
$= x^2y^2 - 14xy + 49$

54. $(7x+4y)(7x-4y) = (7x)^2 - (4y)^2$
$= 49x^2 - 16y^2$

55. $(a-b)(a^2 + ab + b^2)$
$= a(a^2 + ab + b^2) - b(a^2 + ab + b^2)$
$= a^3 + a^2b + ab^2 - a^2b - ab^2 - b^3$
$= a^3 + (a^2b - a^2b) + (ab^2 - ab^2) - b^3$
$= a^3 - b^3$

56. $\dfrac{6^{40}}{6^{10}} = 6^{40-10} = 6^{30}$

57. $\dfrac{x^{18}}{x^3} = x^{18-x} = x^{15}$

58. $(-10)^0 = 1$

59. $-10^0 = -(1) = -1$

60. $400x^0 = 400 \cdot 1 = 400$

61. $\left(\dfrac{x^4}{2}\right)^3 = \dfrac{(x^4)^3}{2^3} = \dfrac{x^{4\cdot 3}}{8} = \dfrac{x^2}{8}$

62. $\left(\dfrac{-3}{2y^6}\right)^4 = \dfrac{(-3)^4}{(2y^6)^4} = \dfrac{81}{(2^4y^6)^4} = \dfrac{81}{16y^{24}}$

63. $\dfrac{-15y^8}{3y^2} = \dfrac{-15}{3} \cdot \dfrac{y^8}{y^2} = -5y^6$

64. $\dfrac{40x^8y^6}{5xy^3} = \dfrac{40}{5} \cdot \dfrac{x^8}{x^1} \cdot \dfrac{y^6}{y^3} = 5x^7y^3$

65. $\dfrac{18x^4 - 12x^2 + 36x}{6x} = \dfrac{18x^4}{6x} - \dfrac{12x^2}{6x} + \dfrac{36x}{6x}$

$= 3x^3 - 2x + 6$

66. $\dfrac{30x^8 - 25x^7 - 40x^5}{-5x^3}$

$= \dfrac{30x^8}{-5x^3} - \dfrac{25x^7}{-5x^3} - \dfrac{40x^5}{-5x^3}$

$= -6x^5 + 5x^4 + 8x^2$

67. $\dfrac{27x^3y - 9x^2y - 18xy^2}{3xy}$

$= \dfrac{27x^3y}{3xy} - \dfrac{9x^2y}{3xy} - \dfrac{18xy^2}{3xy}$

$= 9x^2 - 3x - 6y$

68.

$$\begin{array}{r}
2x + 7 \\
x - 2\,\overline{)\,2x^2 + 3x - 14} \\
\underline{2x^2 - 4x} \\
7x - 14 \\
\underline{7x - 14} \\
0
\end{array}$$

$\dfrac{2x^2 + 3x - 14}{x - 2} = 2x + 7$

69.

$$\begin{array}{r}
y^2 - 3y + 5 \\
2y + 1\,\overline{)\,2y^3 - 5y^2 + 7y + 5} \\
\underline{2y^3 + y^2} \\
-6y^2 + 7y \\
\underline{-6y^2 - 3y} \\
10y + 5 \\
\underline{10y + 5} \\
0
\end{array}$$

$\dfrac{2y^3 - 5y^2 + 7y + 5}{2y + 1} = y^2 - 3y + 5$

70.

$$\begin{array}{r}
z^2 + 5z + 2 \\
z - 7\,\overline{)\,z^3 - 2z^2 - 33z - 7} \\
\underline{z^3 - 7z^2} \\
5z^2 - 33z \\
\underline{5z^2 - 35z} \\
2z - 7 \\
\underline{2z - 14} \\
7
\end{array}$$

$\dfrac{z^3 - 2z^2 - 33z - 7}{z - 7} = z^2 + 5z + 2 + \dfrac{7}{z - 7}$

71.

$$\begin{array}{r}
y^2 + 3y + 9 \\
y - 3\,\overline{)\,y^3 + 0y^2 + 0y - 27} \\
\underline{y^3 - 3y^2} \\
3y^2 + 0y \\
\underline{3y^2 - 9y} \\
9y - 27 \\
\underline{9y - 27} \\
0
\end{array}$$

$\dfrac{y^3 - 27}{y - 3} = y^2 + 3y + 9$

72. $7^{-2} = \dfrac{1}{7^2} = \dfrac{1}{49}$

73. $(-4)^{-3} = \dfrac{1}{(-4)^3} = \dfrac{1}{-64} = -\dfrac{1}{64}$

74. $2^{-1} + 4^{-1} = \dfrac{1}{2} + \dfrac{1}{4} = \dfrac{3}{4}$

75. $\dfrac{1}{5^{-2}} = 5^2 = 25$

76. $\left(\dfrac{2}{5}\right)^{-3} = \dfrac{2^{-3}}{5^{-3}} = \dfrac{5^3}{2^3} = \dfrac{125}{8}$

77. $\dfrac{x^3}{x^9} = x^{3-9} = x^{-6} = \dfrac{1}{x^6}$

78. $\dfrac{30y^6}{5y^8} = \dfrac{30}{5} \cdot \dfrac{y^6}{y^8} = 6y^{-2} = \dfrac{6}{y^2}$

79. $(5x^{-7})(6x^2) = (5 \cdot 6)(x^{-7+2})$

$= 30x^{-5} = \dfrac{30}{x^5}$

80. $\frac{x^4 \cdot x^{-2}}{x^{-6}} = \frac{x^{4+(-2)}}{x^{-6}} = \frac{x^2}{x^{-6}}$
$= x^{2-(-6)} = x^8$

81. $\frac{(3y^3)^4}{y^{10}} = \frac{3^4 y^{3(4)}}{y^{10}} = \frac{81y^{12}}{y^{10}}$
$= 81y^{12-10} = 81y^2$

82. $\frac{y^{-7}}{(y^4)^3} = \frac{y^{-7}}{y^{12}} = y^{-7-12} = y^{-19} = \frac{1}{y^{19}}$

83. $(2x^{-1})^{-3} = 2^{-3}(x^{-1})^{-3} = 2^{-3}x^3$
$= \frac{x^3}{2^{-3}} = \frac{x^3}{8}$

84. $\left(\frac{x^7}{x^4}\right)^{-2} = (x^3)^{-2} = x^{-6} = \frac{1}{x^6}$

85. $\frac{(y^3)^4}{(y^{-2})^4} = \frac{y^{12}}{y^{-8}} = y^{12-(-8)} = y^{20}$

86. $2.3 \times 10^4 = 23{,}000$

(Move decimal point to right 4 places.)

87. $1.76 \times 10^{-3} = 0.00176$ (Move left 3 places.)

88. $9 \times 10^{-1} = 0.9$

89. $73{,}900{,}000 = 7.39 \times 10^7$

90. $0.00062 = 6.2 \times 10^{-4}$

91. $0.38 = 3.8 \times 10^{-1}$

92. $3.8 = 3.8 \times 10^0$

93. $(6 \times 10^{-3})(1.5 \times 10^6) = 6(1.5) \times 10^{-3+6}$
$= 9 \times 10^3$

94. $\frac{2 \times 10^2}{4 \times 10^{-3}} = \frac{10^{2+3}}{2} = 0.5 \times 10^5$
$= 5 \times 10^{-1} \times 10^5$
$= 5.0 \times 10^4$

95. $(4 \times 10^{-2})^2 = 4^2 \times 10^{-2(2)} = 16 \times 10^{-4}$
$= 1.6 \times 10^{-4} = 1.6 \times 10^{1-4}$
$= 1.6 \times 10^{-3}$

96. $\frac{10^{-6}}{10^{-9}} = \frac{10^9}{10^6} = 10^{9-6} = 10^3 = 1000$

There are 1000 nanoseconds in a mircosecond..

97. $2(6.1 \times 10^9) = 12.2 \times 10^9 = 1.22 \times 10^{10}$

In 40 years, there will be approximately 1.22×10^{10} people in the world.

Chapter 6 Test

1. $9x + 6x^2 - 4$ is a trinomial of degree 2.

2. $(7x^3 + 3x^2 - 5x - 11)$
$+ (6x^3 - 2x^2 + 4x - 13)$
$= (7x^3 + 6x^3) + (3x^2 - 2x^2)$
$+ (-5x + 4x) + (-11 - 13)$
$= 13x^3 + x^2 - x - 24$

3. $(9x^3 - 6x^2 - 11x - 4)$
$- (4x^3 - 8x^2 - 13x + 5)$
$= (9x^3 - 6x^2 - 11x - 4)$
$+ (-4x^3 + 8x^2 + 13x - 5)$
$= (9x^3 - 4x^3) + (-6x^2 + 8x^2)$
$+ (-11x + 13x) + (-4 - 5)$
$= 5x^3 + 2x^2 + 2x - 9$

4. $(-7x^3)(5x^8) = (-7 \cdot 5)(x^{3+8}) = -35x^{11}$

5. $6x^2(8x^3 - 5x - 2)$
$= 6x^2(8x^3) + 6x^2(-5x) + 6x^2(-2)$
$= 48x^5 - 30x^3 - 12x^2$

6. $(3x + 2)(x^2 - 4x - 3)$
$= 3x(x^2 - 4x - 3) + 2(x^2 - 4x - 3)$
$= 3x^3 - 12x^2 - 9x + 2x^2 - 8x - 6$
$= 3x^3 - 10x^2 - 17x - 6$

7. $(3y + 7)(2y - 9) = 6y^2 + 14y - 27y - 63$
$= 6y^2 - 13y - 63$

8. $(7x + 5)(7x - 5) = (7x)^2 - 5^2 = 49x^2 - 25$

9. $(x^2+3)^2 = (x^2)^2 + 2(x^2)(3) + 3^2$
$= x^4 + 6x^2 + 9$

10. $(5x-3)^2 = (5x)^2 - 2(5x)(3) + 3^2$
$= 25x^2 - 30x + 9$

11. $4x^2 + 5xy - 6x;\ x = -2, y = 3$

$4x^2 + 5xy - 6x$
$= 4(-2)^2(3) + 5(-2)(3) - 6(-2)$
$= 4(4)(3) + 5(-2)(3) - 6(-2)$
$= 48 - 30 + 12 = 30$

12. $(8x^2y^3 - xy + 2y^2) - (6x^2y^3 - 4xy - 10y^2)$
$= (8x^2y^3 - xy + 2y^2)$
$+ (-6x^2y^3 + 4xy + 10y^2)$
$= (8x^2y^3 - 6x^2y^3) + (-xy + 4xy)$
$+ (2y^2 + 10y^2)$
$= 2x^2y^3 + 3xy + 12y^2$

13. $(3a-7b)(4a+5b)$
$= (3a)(4a) + (3a)(5b) - (7b)(4a)$
$- (7b)(5b)$
$= 12a^2 + 15ab - 28ab - 35b^2$
$= 12a^2 - 13ab - 35b^2$

14. $(2x+3y)^2 = (2x)^2 + 2(2x)(3y) + (3y)^2$
$= 4x^2 + 12xy + 9y^2$

15. $\dfrac{-25x^{16}}{5x^4} = \dfrac{-25}{5} \cdot \dfrac{x^{16}}{x^4} = -5x^{16-4}$
$= -5x^{12}$

Check by multiplication:

$5x^4(-5x^{12}) = -25x^{4+12} = -25x^{16}$

16. $\dfrac{15x^4 - 10x^3 + 25x^2}{5x}$
$= \dfrac{15x^4}{5x} - \dfrac{10x^3}{5x} + \dfrac{25x^2}{5x}$
$= 3x^3 - 2x^2 + 5x$

Check by multiplication:

$5x(3x^3 - 2x^2 + 5x)$
$= 5x(3x^3) + 5x(-2x^2) + 5x(5x)$
$= 15x^4 - 10x^3 + 25x^2$

17.

$$\begin{array}{r} x^2 - 2x + 3 \\ 2x+1\overline{)2x^3 - 3x^2 + 4x + 4} \\ \underline{2x^3 + \ \ x^2} \qquad\qquad \\ -4x^2 + 4x \qquad \\ \underline{-4x^2 - 2x} \qquad \\ 6x + 4 \\ \underline{6x + 3} \\ 1 \end{array}$$

$$\frac{2x^3 - 3x^2 + 4x + 4}{2x+1} = x^2 - 2x + 3 + \frac{1}{2x+1}$$

Check by multiplication:

$(2x+1)(x^2 - 2x + 3) + 1$
$= [2x(x^2 - 2x + 3) + 1(x^2 - 2x + 3)] + 1$
$= (2x^3 - 4x^2 + 6x + x^2 - 2x + 3) + 1$
$= (2x^3 - 3x^2 + 4x + 3) + 1$
$= 2x^3 - 3x^2 + 4x + 4$

18. $10^{-2} = \dfrac{1}{10^2} = \dfrac{1}{100}$

19. $\dfrac{1}{4^{-3}} = 1 \cdot 4^3 = 4^3 = 64$

20. $(-3x^2)^3 = (-3)^3(x^2)^3 = -27x^6$

21. $\dfrac{20x^3}{5x^8} = \dfrac{4}{x^5}$

22. $(-7x^{-8})(3x^2) = -21x^{-6} = -\dfrac{21}{x^6}$

23. $\dfrac{(2x^3)^4}{x^8} = \dfrac{2^4(x^3)^4}{x^8} = \dfrac{16x^{12}}{x^8} = 16x^4$

24. $(5x^{-4})^{-2} = 5^{-2}(x^{-4})^{-2} = 5^{-2}x^8$
$= \dfrac{x^8}{5^2} = \dfrac{x^8}{25}$

25. $\left(\dfrac{x^{10}}{x^5}\right)^{-3} = (x^{10-5})^{-3} = (x^5)^{-3}$
$= x^{-15} = \dfrac{1}{x^{15}}$

26. $3.7 \times 10^{-4} = 0.00037$

27. $7{,}600{,}000 = 7.6 \times 10^{6}$

28. $$\begin{aligned}&(4.1 \times 10^{2})(3 \times 10^{-5})\\ &= (4.1 \cdot 3)(10^{2} \cdot 10^{-5})\\ &= 12.3 \times 10^{-3}\\ &= 1.23 \times 10^{-2}\end{aligned}$$

29. $$\begin{aligned}\frac{8.4 \times 10^{6}}{4 \times 10^{-2}} &= \frac{8.4}{4} \times \frac{10^{6}}{10^{-2}}\\ &= 2.1 \times 10^{6-(-2)}\\ &= 2.1 \times 10^{8}\end{aligned}$$

30. $$\begin{aligned}A &= (x+8)(x+2)\\ &= x^2 + 2x + 8x + 16\\ &= x^2 + 10x + 16\end{aligned}$$

Chapter 6 Cumulative Review Exercises (Chapters 1-6)

1. $$\begin{aligned}(-7)(-5) \div (12-3) &= (-7)(-5) \div 9\\ &= 35 \div 9 = \frac{35}{9}\end{aligned}$$

2. $$\begin{aligned}(3-7)^2(9-11)^3 &= (-4)^2(-2)^3\\ &= 16(-8) = -128\end{aligned}$$

3. $$\begin{aligned}14{,}300 - (-750) &= 14{,}300 + 750\\ &= 15{,}050\end{aligned}$$

The difference in elevation between the plane and the submarine is 15,050 feet.

4. $$\begin{aligned}2(x+3) + 2x &= x + 4\\ 2x + 6 + 2x &= x + 4\\ 4x + 6 &= x + 4\\ 3x + 6 &= 4\\ 3x &= -2\\ x &= -\frac{2}{3}\end{aligned}$$

The solution is $-\frac{2}{3}$.

5. $\frac{x}{5} - \frac{1}{3} = \frac{x}{10} - \frac{1}{2}$

To clear fractions, multiply by the LCD $= 30$.

$$\begin{aligned}30\left(\frac{x}{5} - \frac{1}{3}\right) &= 30\left(\frac{x}{10} - \frac{1}{2}\right)\\ 30\left(\frac{x}{5}\right) - 30\left(\frac{1}{3}\right) &= 30\left(\frac{x}{10}\right) - 30\left(\frac{1}{2}\right)\\ 6x - 10 &= 3x - 15\\ 3x - 10 &= -15\\ 3x &= -5\\ x &= -\frac{5}{3}\end{aligned}$$

The solution is $-\frac{5}{3}$.

6. Let x = width of sign.
Then $3x - 2$ = length of sign.

$$\begin{aligned}2x + 2(3x-2) &= 28\\ 2x + 6x - 4 &= 28\\ 8x - 4 &= 28\\ 8x &= 32\\ x &= 4\\ 3x - 2 &= 3(4) - 2 = 10\end{aligned}$$

The length of the sign is 10 feet and the width is 4 feet, so the dimensions are 10 feet by 4 feet.

7. $$\begin{aligned}7 - 8x &\le -6x - 5\\ 7 - 8x + 6x &\le -6x - 5 + 6x\\ -2x + 7 &\le -5\\ -2x + 7 - 7 &\le -5 - 7\\ -2x &\le -12\\ \frac{-2x}{-2} &\ge \frac{-12}{-2}\\ x &\ge 6\end{aligned}$$

$\{x|x \ge 6\}$

0 1 2 3 4 5 6 7 8 9 10

8.

	Rate ×	Time =	Distance
You	13	x	$13x$
Friend	11	x	$11x$

$$\begin{aligned} 13x + 11x &= 72 \\ 24x &= 72 \\ x &= 3 \end{aligned}$$

It will take 3 hours to meet.

9. Let $x =$ the number of pounds of fertilizer needed to cover 26,000 square feet.

$$\frac{20 \text{ pounds}}{5000 \text{ square feet}} = \frac{x \text{ pounds}}{26{,}000 \text{ square feet}}$$

$$\begin{aligned} \frac{20}{5000} &= \frac{x}{26{,}000} \\ 5000x &= 20(26{,}000) \\ 5000x &= 520{,}000 \\ \frac{5000x}{5000} &= \frac{520{,}000}{5000} \\ x &= 104 \end{aligned}$$

To cover an area of 26,000 square feet, 104 pounds of fertilizer are needed.

$$\frac{104}{20} = 5.2$$

Since the fertilizer is sold in 20-pound bags and you cannot buy a fraction of a bag, 6 bags of fertilizer are needed.

10. $y = -\frac{2}{5}x + 2$

slope $= -\frac{2}{5} = \frac{-2}{5}$; y-intercept $= 2$

Plot $(0, 2)$. Move 2 units *down* (since -2 is negative) and 5 units to the *right* to reach the point $(5, 0)$.

Draw a line through $(0, 2)$ and $(5, 0)$.

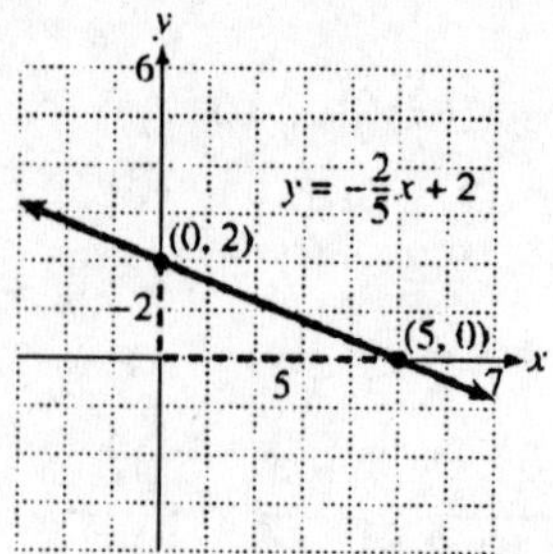

11. $x - 2y = 4$

x-intercept: 4
y-intercept: -2
checkpoint: $(-2, -3)$

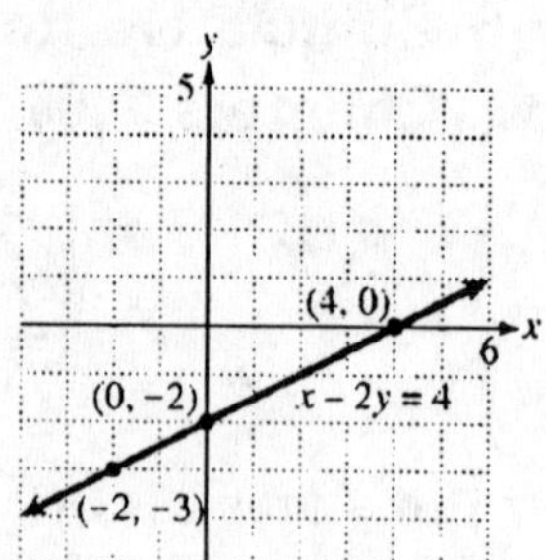

12. $(-3, 2)$ and $(2, -4)$

$$\begin{aligned} m &= \frac{y_2 - y_1}{x_2 - x_1} \\ &= \frac{-4 - 2}{2 - (-3)} = \frac{-6}{5} = -\frac{6}{5} \end{aligned}$$

Because the slope is negative, the line is falling.

13. Slope = -2; passing through $(3, -1)$
Substitute -2 for m, 3 for x_1, and -1 for y_1 in the point-slope form.

$$\begin{aligned} y - y_1 &= m(x - x_1) \\ y - (-1) &= -2(x - 3) \\ y + 1 &= -2(x - 3) \end{aligned}$$

Now rewrite the equation in slope-intercept from.

$$\begin{aligned} y + 1 &= -2x + 6 \\ y &= -2x + 5 \end{aligned}$$

14. $3x + 2y = 10$
$4x - 3y = -15$

The addition method is a good choice because both equations are written in the form $Ax + By = C$. Multiply the first equation by 3 and the second equation by 2; then add the equations.

$$\begin{aligned} 9x + 6y &= 30 \\ \underline{8x - 6y} &\underline{= -30} \\ 17x &= 0 \\ x &= 0 \end{aligned}$$

Back-substitute into the first equation of the given system.

$$\begin{aligned} 3x + 2y &= 10 \\ 3(0) + 2y &= 10 \\ 2y &= 10 \\ y &= 5 \end{aligned}$$

Solution: $(0, 5)$

15. $2x + 3y = -6$
$y = 3x - 13$

The substitution methods is a good choice since the second equation is already solved for y. Substitute $3x - 13$ for y in the first equation.

$$\begin{aligned} 2x + 3y &= -6 \\ 2x + 3(3x - 13) &= -6 \\ 2x + 9x - 39 &= -6 \\ 11x - 39 &= -6 \\ 11x &= 33 \\ x &= 3 \end{aligned}$$

Back-substitute.

$$\begin{aligned} y &= 3x - 13 \\ y &= 3(3) - 13 = -4 \end{aligned}$$

Solution: $(3, -4)$

16. Let x = the number of minutes of long-distance calls.
Then y = the monthly cost of a telephone plan.

First plan: $y = 15 + 0.05x$
Second plan: $y = 5 + 0.07x$

To solve this system by the substitution method, substitute $5 + 0.07x$ for y in the first equation.

$$\begin{aligned} 5 + 0.07x &= 15 + 0.05x \\ 5 + 0.07x - 0.05x &= 15 + 0.05x - 0.05x \\ 5 + 0.02x &= 15 \\ 0.02x &= 10 \\ \frac{0.02x}{0.02} &= \frac{10}{0.02} \\ x &= 500 \end{aligned}$$

If $x = 500$,

$$y = 15 + 0.05(500) = 40.$$

The plans will cost the same for 500 minutes of long-distance calls per month. The cost of each plan will be \$40.

17. $2x + 5y \leq 10$
$x - y \geq 4$

Graph $2x + 5y \leq 10$:
Graph $2x + 5y = 10$ as a solid line using its x-intercept, 5, and y-intercept, 2. Since $2(0) + 5(0) \leq 10$ is true, shade the half-plane containing $(0, 0)$.
Graph $x - y \geq 4$:
Graph $x - y = 4$ as a solid line using its x-intercept, 4, and y-intercept, 4. Since $0 - 0 \geq 4$ is false, shade the half-plane *not* containing $(0, 0)$.
The solution set of the system is the intersection of the two shaded regions.

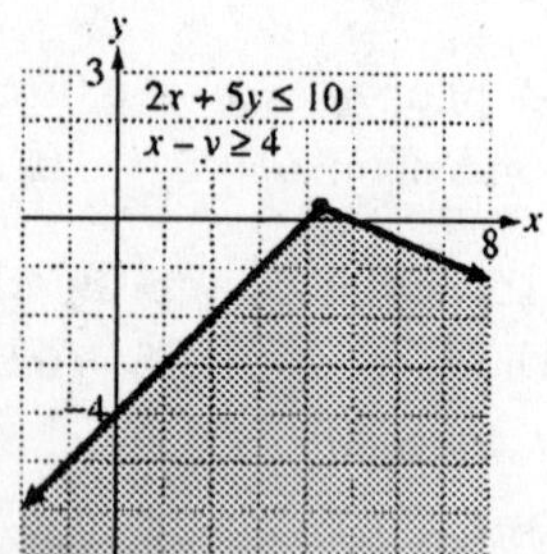

18. $(9x^5 - 3x^3 + 2x - 7) - (6x^5 + 3x^3 - 7x - 9)$
$= (9x^5 - 3x^3 + 2x - 7)$
$\quad + (-6x^5 - 3x^3 + 7x + 9)$
$= (9x^5 - 6x^5) + (-3x^3 - 3x^3) + (2x + 7x)$
$\quad + (-7 + 9)$
$= 3x^5 - 6x^3 + 9x + 2$

19.
$$\begin{array}{r} x^2 + 2x + 3 \\ x+1\overline{)x^3 + 3x^2 + 5x + 3} \\ \underline{x^3 + x^2} \\ 2x^2 + 5x \\ \underline{2x^2 + 2x} \\ 3x + 3 \\ \underline{3x + 3} \\ 0 \end{array}$$

$$\frac{x^3 + 3x^2 + 5x + 3}{x + 1} = x^2 + 2x + 3$$

20. $\dfrac{(3x^2)^4}{x^{10}} = \dfrac{3^4(x^2)^4}{x^{10}} = \dfrac{81x^8}{x^{10}}$
$= 81x^{8-10} = 81x^{-2} = \dfrac{81}{x^2}$

Chapter 7

FACTORING POLYNOMIALS

7.1 The Greatest Common Factor and Factoring by Grouping

7.1 CHECK POINTS

CHECK POINT 1

a. $18x^3$ and $15x^2$

The greatest integer that divides 18 and 15 is 3. The variable, x, raised to the smallest exponent, is x^2. Therefore, the GCF (greatest common factor) of $18x^3$ and $15x^2$ is $3x^2$.

b. The GCF of $-20x^2, 12x^4$, and $40x^3$ is $4x^2$.

c. The GCF of x^4y, x^3y^2, and x^2y is x^2y. Notice that all three terms have a numerical coefficient of 1.

CHECK POINT 2

$6x^2 + 18$

The GCF of $6x^2$ and 18 is 6.

$$6x^2 + 18 = 6(x^2 + 3)$$

CHECK POINT 3

$25x^2 + 35x^3$

The GCF of $25x^2$ and $35x^3$ is $5x^2$.

$$25x^2 + 35x^3 = 5x^2(5 + 7x)$$

CHECK POINT 4

$15x^2 + 12x^4 - 27x^3$

The GCF is $3x^3$.

$$15x^7 + 12x^4 - 27x^3 = 3x^3(5x^2 + 4x - 9)$$

CHECK POINT 5

$8x^3y^2 - 14x^2y + 2xy$

The GCF is $2xy$.

$$8x^3y^2 - 14x^2y + 2xy = 2xy(4x^2y - 7x + 1)$$

CHECK POINT 6

a. $x^2(x + 1) + 7(x + 1)$

The greatest common factor is the binomial $x + 1$. Factor out this common binomial factor.

$$x^2(x + 1) + 7(x + 1) = (x + 1)(x^2 + 7)$$

b. $x(y + 4) - 7(y + 4)$

The greatest common factor is the binomial $y + 4$.

$$x(y + 4) - 7(y + 4) = (y + 4)(x - 7)$$

CHECK POINT 7

$x^3 + 5x^2 + 2x + 10$

First, group terms with common factors.

$$(x^3 + 5x^2) + (2x + 10)$$

Factor out the common monomial factor from each group.

$$x^2(x + 5) + 2(x + 5)$$

Factor out the common binomial factor, $x + 5$.

$$(x + 5)(x^2 + 2)$$

Thus,

$$x^3 + 5x^2 + 2x + 10 = (x + 5)(x^2 + 2).$$

CHECK POINT 8

$$\begin{aligned} xy + 3x - 5y - 15 &= (xy + 3x) + (-5y - 15) \\ &= x(y-3) - 5(y+3) \\ &= (y+3)(x-5) \end{aligned}$$

EXERCISE SET 7.1

1. Possible answers:

$$8x^3 = (2x)(4x^2)$$
$$8x^3 = (4x)(2x^2)$$
$$8x^3 = (8x)(x^2)$$

3. Possible answers:

$$-12x^5 = (-4x^3)(3x^2)$$
$$-12x^5 = (2x^2)(-6x^3)$$
$$-12x^5 = (-3)(4x^5)$$

5. Possible answers:

$$36x^4 = (6x^2)(6x^2)$$
$$36x^4 = (-2x)(-18x^3)$$
$$36x^4 = (4x^3)(9x)$$

7. The GCF (greatest common factor) of 4 and $8x$ is 4.

9. $12x^2 + 8x$

Since 4 is the numerical coefficient of the GCF, and x is the variable factor of the GCF, the GCF of $12x^2$ and $8x$ is $4x$.

11. The GCF of $-2x^4$ and $6x^3$ is $2x^3$.

13. The GCF of $9y^5, 18y^2$, and $-3y$ and $3y$.

15. The GCF of xy, xy^2, and xy^3 is xy.

17. The GCF of $16x^5y^4$, $8x^6y^3$, and $20x^4y^5$ is $4x^4y^3$.

19. $5x + 5 = 5 \cdot x + 5 \cdot 1 = 5(x+1)$

21. $3y - 3 = 3 \cdot y - 3 \cdot 1 = 3(y-1)$

23. $8x + 16 = 8 \cdot x + 8 \cdot 2 = 8(x+2)$

25. $25x - 10 = 5(5x) - 5(2) = 5(5x-2)$

27. $x^2 + x = x \cdot x + x \cdot 1 = x(x+1)$

29. $$\begin{aligned} 18y^2 + 24 &= 6(3y^2) + 6(4) \\ &= 6(3y^2 + 4) \end{aligned}$$

31. $$\begin{aligned} 36x^3 + 24x^2 &= 6x^2(6x) + 6x^2(4) \\ &= 6x^2(6x+4) \end{aligned}$$

33. $$\begin{aligned} 25y^2 - 13y &= y(25y) - y(13) \\ &= y(25y - 13) \end{aligned}$$

35. $$\begin{aligned} 9y^4 + 27y^6 &= 9y^4 \cdot 1 + 9y^4 \cdot 3y^3 \\ &= 9y^4(1 + 3y^3) \end{aligned}$$

37. $$\begin{aligned} 8x^2 - 4x^4 &= 4x^2(2) - 4x^2(x^2) \\ &= 4x^2(2 - x^2) \end{aligned}$$

39. $$\begin{aligned} 12y^2 + 16y - 8 &= 4(3y^2) + 4(4y) - 4(2) \\ &= 4(3y^2 + 4y - 2) \end{aligned}$$

41. $$\begin{aligned} &9x^4 + 18x^3 + 6x^2 \\ &= 3x^2(3x^2) + 3x^2(6x) + 3x^2(2) \\ &= 3x^2(3x^2 + 6x + 2) \end{aligned}$$

43. $$\begin{aligned} &100y^5 - 50y^3 + 100y^2 \\ &= 50y^2(2y^3) - 50y^2(y) + 50y^2(2) \\ &= 50y^2(2y^3 - y + 2) \end{aligned}$$

45. $$\begin{aligned} &10x - 20x^2 + 5x^3 \\ &= 5x(2) - 5x(4x) + 5x(x^2) \\ &= 5x(2 - 4x + x^2) \end{aligned}$$

47. $11x^2 - 23$ cannot be factored because the two terms have no common factor other than 1.

49. $$\begin{aligned} 6x^3y^2 + 9xy &= 3xy(2x^2y) + 3xy(3) \\ &= 3xy(2x^2y + 3) \end{aligned}$$

51. $$\begin{aligned} &30x^2y^2 - 10xy^2 + 20xy \\ &= 10xy(3xy^2) - 10xy(y) + 10xy(2) \\ &= 10xy(3xy^2 - y + 2) \end{aligned}$$

53. $32x^3y^2 - 24x^3y - 16x^2y$
$= 8x^2y(4xy) - 8x^2y(3x) - 8x^2y(2)$
$= 8x^2y(4xy - 3x - 2)$

55. $x(x+5) + 3(x+5) = (x+5)(x+3)$

Here, $(x+5)$ is the greatest common binomial factor.

57. $x(x+2) - 4(x+2) = (x+2)(x-4)$

59. $x(y+6) - 7(y+6) = (y+6)(x-7)$

61. $3x(x+y) - (x+y) = 3x(x+y) - 1(x+y)$
$= (x+y)(3x-1)$

63. $4x(3x+1) + 3x + 1 = 4x(3x+1) + 1(3x+1)$
$= (3x+1)(4x+1)$

65. $7x^2(5x+4) + 5x + 4$
$= 7x^2(5x+4) + 1(5x+4)$
$= (5x+4)(7x^2+1)$

67. $x^2 + 2x + 4x + 8 = (x^2+2x) + (4x+8)$
$= x(x+2) + 4(x+2)$
$= (x+2)(x+4)$

69. $x^2 + 3x - 5x - 15 = (x^2+3x) + (-5x-15)$
$= x(x+3) - 5(x+3)$
$= (x-5)(x+3)$

71. $x^3 - 2x^2 + 5x - 10 = (x^3 - 2x^2) + (5x - 10)$
$= x^2(x-2) + 5(x-2)$
$= (x-2)(x^2+5)$

73. $x^3 - x^2 + 2x - 2 = x^2(x-1) + 2(x-1)$
$= (x-1)(x^2+2)$

75. $xy + 5x + 9y + 45 = x(y+5) + 9(y+5)$
$= (y+5)(x+9)$

77. $xy - x + 5y - 5 = x(y-1) + 5(y-1)$
$= (y-1)(x+5)$

79. $3x^2 - 6xy + 5xy - 10y^2$
$= 3x(x-2y) + 5y(x-2y)$
$= (x-2y)(3x+5y)$

81. $3x^3 - 2x^2 - 6x + 4$
$= x^2(3x-2) - 2(3x-2)$
$= (3x-2)(x^2-2)$

83. $x^2 - ax - bx + ab = x(x-a) - b(x-a)$
$= (x-a)(x-b)$

85. $8x^2 + 20x + 2488$

a. The year 2003 corresponds to $x = 10$.

$8x^2 + 20x + 2488$
$= 8(10)^2 + 20(1) + 2488$
$= 800 + 200 + 2488$
$= 3488$

According to the model, 3488 thousand (or 3,488,000) students will graduate from U.S. high schools in 2003.

b. The greatest common factor of the three terms is 4, so

$$8x^2 + 20x + 2488 = 4(2x^2 + 5x + 622).$$

c. $4(2x^2 + 5x + 622)$; $x = 10$

$4(2x^2 + 5x + 622) = 4[2(10)^2 + 5(10) + 622]$
$= 4[200 + 50 + 622]$
$= 4(872)$
$= 3488$

The factored form also predicts that 3488 thousand (or 3,488,000) students will graduate from U.S. high schools in 2003. Getting the same answer in parts (a) and (b) suggests that the factorization is correct. However, it only *proves* that the two expressions (unfactored and factored forms) are equal when $x = 10$. To prove that the two expressions are equal, you need to show they are equal for *all* possible values of x (all real numbers).

87. Use the formula for the area of a rectangle. Substitute $5x^4 - 10x$ for A and $5x$ for w.

$$A = l \cdot w$$
$$5x^4 - 10x = l(5x)$$

To find a polynomial representing l, factor $5x^4 - 10x$.

$$5x^4 - 10x = 5x(x^3 - 2)$$
$$\text{or } (x^3 - 2)5x$$

Therefore, the length is $(x^3 - 2)$ units.

For Exercises 89–93, answers may vary.

95. Statement d is true.
Either $-4x$ or $4x$ can be used as the GCF.

97. $x^{4n} + x^{2n} + x^{3n}$

Because n is a natural number (positive integer), $4n, 2n,$ and $3n$ are all natural numbers with $4n > 3n > 2n$. Therefore, the GCF is x^{2n}.

$$x^{4n} + x^{2n} + x^{3n} = x^{2n}(x^{2n} + 1 + x^n)$$

99. Answers will vary. One example is

$$5x^2 + 10x - 4x - 8.$$

101.

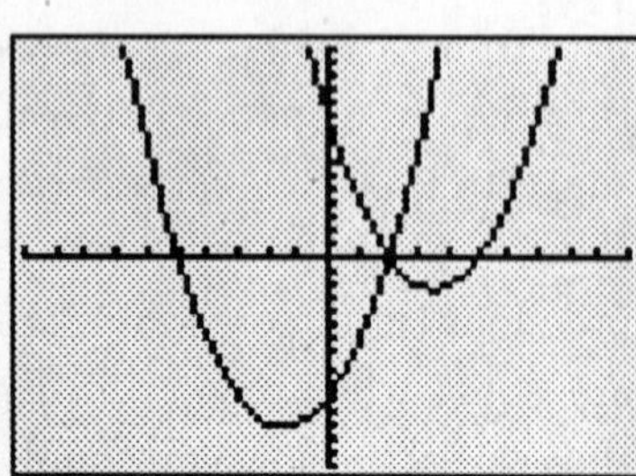

The graphs do not coincide.

Factor by grouping.

$$x^2 - 2x + 5x - 10 = x(x - 2) + 5(x - 2)$$
$$= (x - 2)(x + 5)$$

Change the expression on the right side to $(x - 2)(x + 5)$.

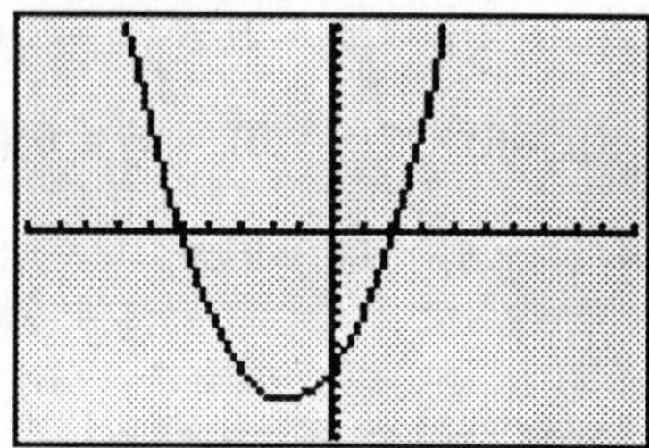

Now the graphs coincide.

Review Exercises

103. $(x + 7)(x + 10) = x^2 + 10x + 7x + 70$
$= x^2 + 17x + 70$

104. $2x - y = -4$
$x - 3y = 3$

Graph both equations on the same axes.

$2x - y = -4$:
x-intercept: -2; y-intercept: 4
$x - 3y = 3$:
x-intercept: 3; y-intercept: -1

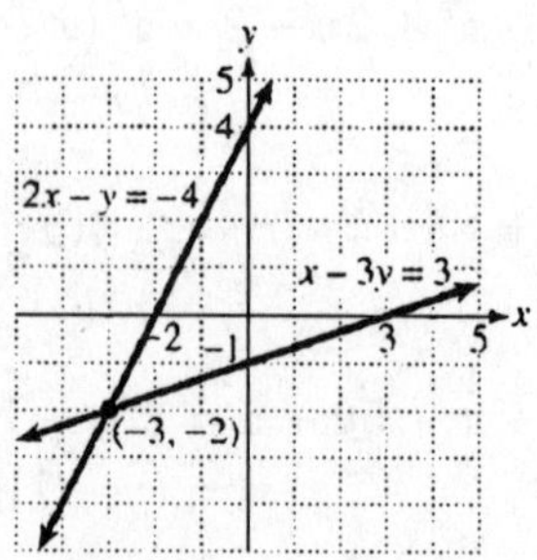

The lines interseect as $(-3, -2)$.
Solution: $(-3, -2)$

105. Line through $(-7,2)$ and $(-4,5)$
First, find the slope.

$$m = \frac{5-2}{-4-(-7)} = \frac{3}{3} = 1$$

Write the point-slope equation using $m = 1$ and $(x_1, y_1) = (-7, 2)$.

$$y - y_1 = m(x - x_1)$$
$$y - 2 = 1[x - (-7)]$$
$$y - 2 = 1(x + 7)$$

Now rewrite this equation in slope-intercepet form.

$$y - 2 = x + 7$$
$$y = x + 9$$

Note: If $(-4, 5)$ is used as (x_1, y_1), the point-slope equation will be

$$y - 5 = 1[x - (-4)]$$
$$y - 5 = x + 4.$$

This also leads to the slope-intercept equation $y = x + 9$.

7.2 Factoring Trinomials Whose Leading Coefficient Is One

7.2 CHECK POINTS

CHECK POINT 1

$x^2 + 5x + 6 = (x + 2)(x + 3)$

The product of the First terms is $x \cdot x = x^2$.
The product of the Last terms is $2 \cdot 3 = 6$.
The sum of the Outside and inside products is $3x + 2x = 5x$.

CHECK POINT 2

$x^2 - 6x + 8$

Factors of 8	$1, 8$	$2, 4$	$-1, -8$	$-2, -4$
Sum of Factors	9	6	-9	-6

The factors of 8 whose sum is -6, the coefficient of the middle term of the binomial, are -2 and -4. Thus,

$$x^2 - 6x + 8 = (x - 2)(x - 4).$$

CHECK POINT 3

$x^2 + 3x - 10$

Factors of -10	$-10, 1$	$-5, 2$	$5, -2$	$10, -1$
Sum of Factors	-9	-3	3	9

$$x^2 + 3x - 10 = (x + 5)(x - 2)$$

CHECK POINT 4

$y^2 - 6y - 27$

Factors of -27	$-27, 1$	$-9, 3$	$-3, 9$	$-1, 27$
Sum of Factors	-26	-6	6	26

$$y^2 - 6y - 27 = (y - 9)(y + 3)$$

CHECK POINT 5

$x^2 + x - 7$

Factors of -7	$-7, 1$	$7, -1$
Sum of Factors	-6	6

Because neither pair has a sum of 1, $x^2 + x - 7$ cannot be factored using integers. This trinomial is prime.

CHECK POINT 6

$x^2 - 4xy + 3y^2$

The factors will have the form $(x \quad ?y) \cdot (x \quad ?y)$.

Factors of 3	$3, 1$	$-3, -1$
Sum of Factors	4	-4

$$x^2 - 4xy + 3y^2 = (x - 3y)(x - y)$$

CHECK POINT 7

$2x^3 + 6x^2 - 56x$

First factor out the GCF, $2x$.

$$2x^3 + 6x^2 - 56x = 2x(x^2 + 3x - 28)$$

Now factor $x^2 + 3x - 28$ by finding two intergers whose product is -28 and whose sum is 3.

$$x^2 + 3x - 28 = (x - 4)(x + 7)$$

Thus, the complete factorization is

$$2x^3 + 6x^2 - 56x = 2x(x - 4)(x + 7).$$

EXERCISE SET 7.2

In Exercises 1–61, each factorization should be checked using FOIL multiplication. The check will only be shown here for Exercise 1.

1. $x^2 + 6x + 5$

Factors of 5	$5, 1$	$-5, -1$
Sum of Factors	6	-6

The factors of 5 whose sum is 6 are 5 and 1. Thus,

$$x^2 + 6x + 5 = (x + 5)(x + 1).$$

Check:

$$\begin{aligned}(x + 5)(x + 1) &= x^2 + x + 5x + 5 \\ &= x^2 + 6x + 5\end{aligned}$$

3. $x^2 + 8x + 15 = (x + 3)(x + 5)$
$(3)(5) = 15$; $3 + 5 = 8$

5. $x^2 + 12x + 11 = (x + 1)(x + 11)$
$(1)(11) = 11$; $1 + 11 = 12$

7. $x^2 - 8x + 15 = (x - 5)(x - 3)$
$(-5)(-3) = 15$; $(-5) + (-3) = -8$

9. $x^2 - 14x + 49 = (x - 7)(x - 7)$
$(-7)(-7) = 49$; $(-7) + (-7) = -14$

11. $y^2 - 15y + 36 = (y - 3)(y - 12)$
$(-3)(-12) = 36$; $(-3) + (-12) = -15$

13. $x^2 + 3x - 10 = (x + 5)(x - 2)$
$(5)(-2) = -10$; $5 + (-2) = 3$

15. $y^2 + 10y - 39 = (y + 13)(y - 3)$
$(13)(-3) = -39$; $13 + (-3) = 10$

17. $x^2 - 2x - 15 = (x - 5)(x + 3)$
$(-5)(3) = -15$; $-5 + 3 = -2$

19. $x^2 - 2x - 8 = (x-4)(x+2)$
$(-4)(2) = -8;\ -4 + 2 = -2$

21. $x^2 + 4x + 12$ is prime because there is no pair of integers whose product is 12 and whose sum is 4.

23. $y^2 - 16y + 48 = (y-4)(y-12)$
$(-4)(-12) = 48;\ (-4) + (-12) = -16$

25. $x^2 - 3x + 6$ is prime because there is no pair of integers whose product is 6 and whose sum is -3.

27. $w^2 - 30w - 64 = (w-32)(w+2)$
$(-32)(2) = -64;\ -32 + 2 = -30$

29. $y^2 - 18y + 65 = (y-5)(y-13)$
$(-5)(-13) = 65;\ (-5) + (-13) = -18$

31. $r^2 + 12r + 27 = (r+3)(r+9)$
$(3)(9) = 27;\ 3 + 9 = 12$

33. $y^2 - 7y + 5$ is prime because there is no pair of integers whose product is 5 and whose sum is -7.

35. $x^2 + 7xy + 6y^2 = (x+6y)(x+y)$
$(6)(1) = 6;\ 6 + 1 = 7$

37. $x^2 - 8xy + 15y^2 = (x-3y)(x-5y)$
$(-3)(-5) = 15;\ (-3) + (-5) = -8$

39. $x^2 - 3xy - 18y^2 = (x-6y)(x+3y)$
$(-6)(3) = -18;\ (-6) + 3 = -3$

41. $a^2 - 18ab + 45b^2 = (a-15b)(a-3b)$
$(-15)(-3) = 45;\ (-15) + (-3) = -18$

43. $3x^2 + 15x + 18$

First factor out the GCF, 3. Then factor the resulting binomial.

$$\begin{aligned} 3x^2 + 15x + 18 &= 3(x^2 + 5x + 6) \\ &= 3(x+2)(x+3) \end{aligned}$$

45. $\begin{aligned} 4y^2 - 4y - 8 &= 4(y^2 - y - 2) \\ &= 4(y-2)(y+1) \end{aligned}$

47. $\begin{aligned} 10x^2 - 40x - 600 &= 10(x^2 - 4x - 60) \\ &= 10(x-10)(x+6) \end{aligned}$

49. $\begin{aligned} 3x^2 - 33x + 54 &= 3(x^2 - 11x + 18) \\ &= 3(x-2)(x-9) \end{aligned}$

51. $\begin{aligned} 2r^3 + 6r^2 + 4r &= 2r(r^2 + 3r + 2) \\ &= 2r(r+2)(r+1) \end{aligned}$

53. $\begin{aligned} 4x^3 + 12x^2 - 72x &= 4x(x^2 + 3x - 18) \\ &= 4x(x+6)(x-3) \end{aligned}$

55. $\begin{aligned} 2r^3 + 8r^2 - 64r &= 2r(r^2 + 4r - 32) \\ &= 2r(r+8)(r-4) \end{aligned}$

57. $\begin{aligned} y^4 + 2y^3 - 80y^2 &= y^2(y^2 + 2y - 80) \\ &= y^2(y+10)(y-8) \end{aligned}$

59. $\begin{aligned} x^4 - 3x^3 - 10x^2 &= x^2(x^2 - 3x - 10) \\ &= x^2(x-5)(x+2) \end{aligned}$

61. $\begin{aligned} 2w^4 - 26w^3 - 96w^2 &= 2w^2(w^2 - 13w - 48) \\ &= 2w^2(w-16)(w+3) \end{aligned}$

63. $\begin{aligned} -16t^2 + 16t + 32 &= -16(t^2 - t - 2) \\ &= -16(t-2)(t+1) \end{aligned}$

For Exercises 65–67, answers may vary.

69. Statement c is true.

$$y^2 + 5y - 24 = (y-3)(y+8)$$

71. In order for $x^2 + 4x + b$ to be factorable, b must be an integer with two positive factors whose sum is 4. The only such pairs are 3 and 1, or 2 and 2.

$$\begin{aligned} (x+3)(x+1) &= x^2 + 4x + 3 \\ (x+2)(x+2) &= x^2 + 4x + 4 \end{aligned}$$

Therefore, the possible values of b are 3 and 4.

73. $4x^3 - 28x^2 + 48x = 4x(x^2 - 7x + 12)$
$= 4x(x-4)(x-3)$

The box has the following dimensions:

$$\begin{aligned} \text{length} &= 8 - 2x = 2(4 - x) \\ \text{width} &= 6 - 2x = 2(3 - x) \\ \text{height} &= x. \end{aligned}$$

Therefore, the volume is

$$\begin{aligned} V &= lwh \\ &= 2(4-x) \cdot 2(3-x) \cdot x \\ &= 4[(-1)(x-4) \cdot (-1)(x-3)]x \\ &= 4x(x-4)(x-3), \end{aligned}$$

which is the factored form obtained above.

75.

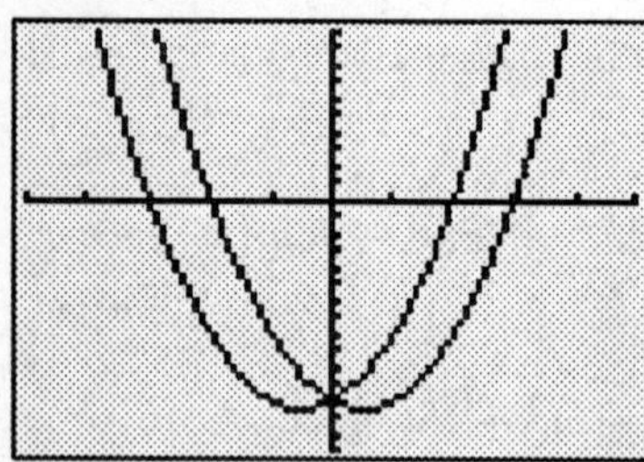

$$\begin{aligned} 2x^2 + 2x - 12 &= 2(x^2 + x - 6) \\ &= 2(x+3)(x-2) \end{aligned}$$

Change the polynomial on the right to $2(x+3)(x-2)$.

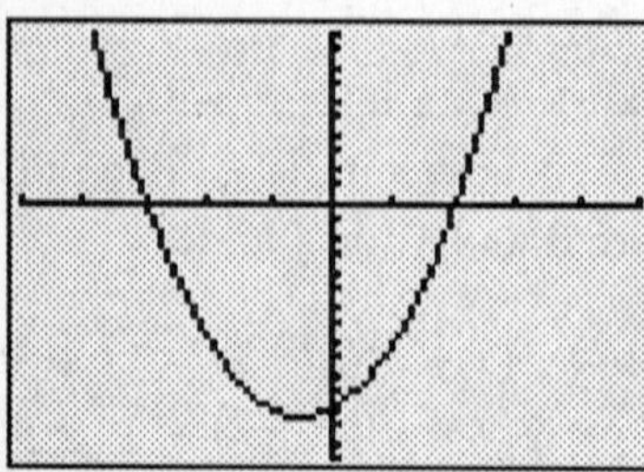

Now the graphs coincide.

77.

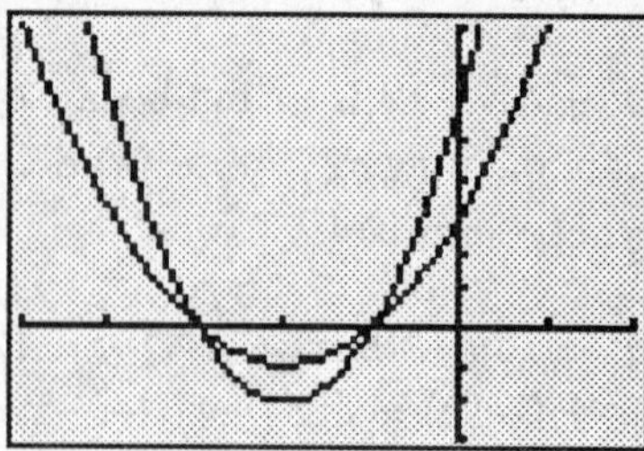

$$\begin{aligned} 2x^2 + 8x + 6 &= 2(x^2 + 4x + 3) \\ &= 2(x+3)(x+1) \end{aligned}$$

Change the polynomial on the right to $2(x+3)(x+1)$.

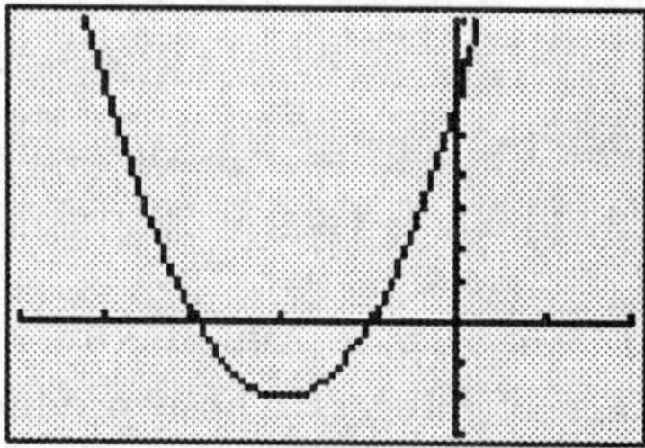

Now the graphs coincide.

Review Exercises

78. $(2x+3)(x-2) = 2x^2 - 4x + 3x - 6$
$= 2x^2 - x - 6$

79. $(3x+4)(3x+1) = 9x^2 + 3x + 12x + 4$
$= 9x^2 + 15x + 4$

80.
$$\begin{aligned} 4(x-2) &= 3x + 5 \\ 4x - 8 &= 3x + 5 \\ x - 8 &= 5 \\ x &= 13 \end{aligned}$$

The solution is 13.

7.3 Factoring Trinomials Whose Leading Coefficient Is Not One

7.3 CHECK POINTS

CHECK POINT 1

$5x^2 - 14x + 8$

Step 1 Find two First terms whose product is $5x^2$.

$$5x^2 - 14x + 8 = (5x \quad)(x \quad)$$

Step 2 Find two Last terms whose product is 8. The number 8 has pairs of factors that are either both positive or both negative. Because the middle term, $-14x$, is negative, both factors must be negative. The negative factorizations of 8 are $-1(-8)$ and $-2(-4)$.

Step 3 Try various combinations of these factors to find the one in which the sum of the Outside and Inside products is equal to $-14x$.

Possible Factors of $5x^2 - 14x + 8$	Sum of Outside and Inside Products
$(5x-1)(x-8)$	$-40x - x = -41x$
$(5x-8)(x-1)$	$-5x - 8x = -13x$
$(5x-2)(x-4)$	$-20x - 2x = -22x$
$(5x-4)(x-2)$	$-10x - 4x = -14x$

Thus,

$$5x^2 - 14x + 8 = (5x - 4)(x - 2).$$

CHECK POINT 2

$6x^2 + 19x - 7$

Step 1 There are two possiblities of the first terms.

$$6x^2 + 19x - 7 \stackrel{?}{=} (6x \quad)(x \quad)$$
$$6x^2 + 19x - 7 \stackrel{?}{=} (6x \quad)(x \quad)$$

Step 2 The only possible factorizations of -7 are $1(-7)$ and $-1(7)$.

Step 3

Possible Factors of $6x^2 + 19x - 7$	Sum of Outside and Inside Products
$(6x+7)(x-1)$	$-6x + 7x = x$
$(6x-7)(x+1)$	$6x - 7x = -x$
$(6x+1)(x-7)$	$-42x + x = -41x$
$(6x-1)(x+7)$	$42x - x = 41x$
$(3x+7)(2x-1)$	$-3x + 14x = 11x$
$(3x-7)(2x+1)$	$3x - 14x = -11x$
$(3x+1)(2x-7)$	$-21x + 2x = -19x$
$(3x-1)(2x+7)$	$21x - 2x = 19x$

Thus,

$$6x^2 + 19x - 7 = (3x - 1)(2x + 7).$$

CHECK POINT 3

$3x^2 - 13xy + 4y^2$

Step 1 Find two First terms whose product is $3x^2$.

$$3x^2 - 13xy + 4y^2 = (3x \quad)(x \quad)$$

Step 2 Find two Last terms whose product is $4y^2$. The possible factorizations are $(y)(4y), (-y)(-4y), (2y)(2y)$, and $(-2y)(-2y)$. Because the middle term is negative, the factors must be $(-y)(-4y)$ and $(-2y)(-2y)$.

Step 3 Try various combinations of these factors.

Possible Factors of $3x^2 - 13xy + 4y^2$	Sum of Outside and Inside Products
$(3x - 4y)(3x - y)$	$-3xy - 4xy = -7xy$
$(3x - y)(x - 4y)$	$-12xy - xy = -13xy$
$(3x - 2y)(x - 2y)$	$-6xy - 2xy = -8xy$

Thus,

$$3x^2 - 13xy + 4y^2 = (3x - y)(x - 4y).$$

CHECK POINT 4

$3x^2 - x - 10$

Step 1 Multiply the leading coefficient, a, and the constant, c.

$$ac = 3(-10) = -30$$

Step 2 Find the factors of ac whose sum is b.
The factors of $ac = -30$ whose sum is $b = -1$ are -6 and 5.

Step 3 Rewrite the middle term, $-x$, using the factors -6 and 5.

$$3x^2 - x - 10 = 3x^2 - 6x + 5x - 10$$

Step 4 Factor by grouping.

$$\begin{aligned} 3x^2 - x - 10 &= 3x^2 - 6x + 5x - 10 \\ &= 3x(x-2) + 5(x-2) \\ &= (x-2)(3x+5) \\ \text{or} \quad &(3x+5)(x-2) \end{aligned}$$

CHECK POINT 5

$8x^2 - 10x + 3$

Here, $ac = 8(3) = 24$. Find the factors of 24 whose sum is -10. These factors are -6 and -4. Rewrite $-10x$ as $-6x - 4x$; then factor by grouping.

$$\begin{aligned} 8x^2 - 10x + 3 &= 8x^2 - 6x - 4x + 3 \\ &= 2x(4x-3) - 1(4x-3) \\ &= (4x-3)(2x-1) \\ \text{or} \quad &(2x-1)(4x-3) \end{aligned}$$

CHECK POINT 6

$5y^4 + 13y^3 + 6y^2$

First factor out the GCF, y^2. Then factor the resulting trinomial using trial and error or grouping.

$$\begin{aligned} 5y^4 + 13y^3 + 6y^2 &= y^2(5y^2 + 13y + 6) \\ &= y^2(5y+3)(y+2) \end{aligned}$$

EXERCISE SET 7.3

In Exercises 1–57, each trinomial may be factored by either trial and error or by factoring. Both methods will be illustrated here. Each factorization should be checked by FOIL multiplication. The check will be shown here only for Exercise 1. In all answers, the factors maybe written either order.

1. $2x^2 + 7x + 3$

Factor by trial and error.

Step 1 $2x^2 + 7x + 3 = (2x \quad)(x \quad)$

Step 2 The number 3 has pairs of factors that are either both positive or both negative. Because the middle term, $7x$, is positive, both factors must be positive. The only positive factorization is (1)(3).

Step 3

Possible Factors of $2x^2+7x+3$	Sum of Outside and Inside Products
$(2x+1)(x+3)$	$6x+x=7x$
$(2x+3)(x+1)$	$2x+3x=5x$

Thus,

$$2x^2+7x+3=(2x+1)(x+3).$$

Check:

$$\begin{aligned}(2x+1)(x+3)&=2x^2+6x+x+3\\&=2x^2+7x+3\end{aligned}$$

3. $3x^2+8x+4$

Factor by trial and error.
The only possibility for the First terms is $(3x)(x)=3x^2$.
Because the middle term is positive and the last term is also positive, the possible factorizations of 4 are (1)(4) and (2)(2).

Possible Factors of $3x^2+8x+4$	Sum of Outside and Inside Products
$(3x+1)(x+4)$	$12x+x=13x$
$(3x+4)(x+1)$	$3x+4x=7x$
$(3x+2)(x+2)$	$6x+2x=8x$

Thus,

$$3x^2+8x+4=(3x+2)(x+2).$$

5. $2x^2+13x+20$

Factor by grouping.
$a=2$ and $c=20$, so $ac=2(20)=40$.
The factors of 40 whose sum is 13 are 8 and 5.

$$\begin{aligned}2x^2+13x+20&=2x^2+8x+5x+20\\&=2x(x+4)+5(x+4)\\&=(x+4)(2x+5)\end{aligned}$$

7. $5y^2-8y+3$

Factor by trial and error. The First terms must be $5y$ and y. Beause the middle term is negative, the factors of 3 must be -3 and -1.

$$\begin{aligned}(5y-1)(y-3)&=5y^2-16y+3\\(5y-3)(y-1)&=5y^2-8y+3\end{aligned}$$

Thus,

$$(5y-3)(y-1)=y^2-8y+3.$$

9. $3y^2-y-2$

Factor of trial and error.

$$\begin{aligned}(3y+1)(y-2)&=3y^2-5y+2\\(3y-1)(y+2)&=3y^2-5y-2\\(3y+2)(y-1)&=3y^2-y-2\\(3y-2)(y+1)&=3y^2+y-2\end{aligned}$$

Thus,

$$3y^2-y-2=(3y+2)(y-1).$$

11. $3x^2+x-10$

Factor by grouping.
$a=3$ and $c=-10$, so $ac=-30$.
The factors of -30 whose sum is 1 are 6 and -5.

$$\begin{aligned}3x^2+x-10&=3x^2+6x-5x-10\\&=3x(x+2)-5(x+2)\\&=(x+2)(3x-5)\end{aligned}$$

13. $3x^2-22x+7$

Factor by trial and error.

$$\begin{aligned}(3x-7)(x-1)&=3x^2-10x+7\\(3x-1)(x-7)&=3x^2-22x+7\end{aligned}$$

Thus,

$$3x^2-22x+7=(3x-1)(x-7).$$

15. $5y^2 - 16y + 3$

Factor by trial and error.

$$(5y-3)(y-1) = 5y^2 - 8y + 3$$
$$(5y-1)(y-3) = 5y^2 - 16y + 3$$

Thus,

$$5y^2 - 16y + 3 = (5y-1)(y-3).$$

17. $3x^2 - 17x + 10$

Factor by grouping.
$a = 3$ and $c = 10$, so $ac = 10$.
The factors of 30 whose sum is -17 are -15 and -2.

$$\begin{aligned} 3x^2 - 17x + 10 &= 3x^2 - 15x - 2x + 10 \\ &= 3x(x-5) - 2(x-5) \\ &= (x-5)(3x-2) \end{aligned}$$

19. $6w^2 - 11w + 4$

Factor by grouping.
$a = 6$ and $c = 4$, so $ac = 24$.
The factors of 24 whose sum is -11 are -3 and -8.

$$\begin{aligned} 6w^2 - 11w + 4 &= 6w^2 - 3w - 8w + 4 \\ &= 3w(2w-1) - 4(2w-1) \\ &= (2w-1)(3w-4) \end{aligned}$$

21. $8x^2 + 33x + 4$

Factor by grouping.
$a = 8$ and $c = 4$, so $ac = 32$.
The factors of 32 whose sum is 33 are 32 and 1.

$$\begin{aligned} 8x^2 + 33x + 4 &= 8x^2 + 32x + x + 4 \\ &= 8x(x+4) + 1(x+4) \\ &= (x+4)(8x+1) \end{aligned}$$

23. $5x^2 + 33x - 14$

Factor by trial and error.

$$(5x-7)(x+2) = 5x^2 + 3x - 14$$
$$(5x+7)(x-2) = 5x^2 - 3x - 14$$
$$(5x-2)(x+7) = 5x^2 + 33x - 14$$

Because the correct factorization has been found, there is no need to try additional possibilities.

$$5x^2 + 33x - 14 = (5x-2)(x+7).$$

25. $14y^2 + 15y - 9$

Factor by trial and error. Try various combinations until the correct one is obtained.

$$(7y+9)(2y-1) = 14y^2 + 11y - 9$$
$$(7y+1)(2y-9) = 14y^2 - 61y - 9$$
$$(7y+3)(2y-3) = 14y^2 - 15y - 9$$
$$(7y-3)(2y+3) = 14y^2 + 15y - 9$$

Thus,

$$14y^2 + 15y - 9 = (7y-3)(2y+3).$$

27. $6x^2 - 7x + 3$

Use trial and error. List all of the possiblilities in which both signs are negative.

$$(6x-1)(x-3) = 6x^2 - 19x + 3$$
$$(6x-3)(x-1) = 6x^2 - 9x + 3$$
$$(3x-1)(2x-3) = 6x^2 - 11x + 3$$
$$(3x-3)(2x-1) = 6x^2 - 9x + 3$$

None of these possibilities gives the required middle term, $-7x$, and there are no more possibilities to try, so $6x^2 - 7x + 3$ is prime.

29. $25z^2 - 30z + 9$

Use trial and error until the correct factorization is obtained. The signs in both factors must be negative.

$$(5z-1)(5z-9) = 25z^2 - 50z + 9$$
$$(5z-3)(5z-3) = 25z^2 - 30z + 9$$

Thus,

$$25z^2 - 30z + 9 = (5z-3)(5z-3).$$

31. $15y^2 - y - 2$

Factor by grouping.
$a = 15$ and $c = -2$, so $ac = -30$.
The factors of -30 whose sum is -1 are -6 and 5.

$$\begin{aligned} 15y^2 - y - 2 &= 15y^2 - 6y + 5y - 2 \\ &= 3y(5y-2) + 1(5y-2) \\ &= (5y-2)(3y+1) \end{aligned}$$

33. $5x^2 + 2x + 9$

Use trial and error. The signs in both factors must be positive.

$$(5x+3)(x+3) = 5x^2 + 18x + 9$$
$$(5x+9)(x+1) = 5x^2 + 14x + 9$$
$$(5x+1)(x+9) = 5x^2 + 46x + 9$$

None of these possiblities gives the required middle term, $2x$, and there are no more possibilities to try, so $5x^2+2x+9$ is prime.

35. $10y^2 + 43y - 9$

Factor by grouping.
$a = 10$ and $c = -9$, so $ac = -90$.
The factors of -90 whose sum is 43 are 45 and -2.

$$\begin{aligned} 10y^2 + 43y - 9 &= 10y^2 + 45y - 2y - 9 \\ &= 5y(2y+9) - 1(2y+9) \\ &= (2y+9)(5y-1) \end{aligned}$$

37. $8x^2 - 2x - 1$

Use trial and error until the correct factorization is obtained. The sign just be negative in one factor and positive in the other.

$$(4x-1)(2x+1) = 8x^2 + 2x - 1$$
$$(4x+1)(2x-1) = 8x^2 - 2x - 1$$

Thus,

$$8x^2 - 2x - 1 = (4x+1)(2x-1).$$

39. $9y^2 - 9y + 2$

Factor by grouping.
$a = 9$ and $c = 2$, so $ac = 18$.
The factors of 18 whose sum is -9 are -3 and -6.

$$\begin{aligned} 9y^2 - 9y + 2 &= 9y^2 - 3y - 6y + 2 \\ &= 3y(3y-1) - 2(3y-1) \\ &= (3y-1)(3y-2) \end{aligned}$$

41. $20x^2 + 27x - 8$

Factor by grouping.
$a = 20$ and $c = -8$, so $ac = -160$.
The factors of -160 whose sum is 27 are -5 and 32.

$$\begin{aligned} 20x^2 + 27x - 8 &= 20x^2 - 5x + 32x - 8 \\ &= 5x(4x-1) + 8(4x-1) \\ &= (4x-1)(5x+8) \end{aligned}$$

43. $2x^2 + 3xy + y^2 = (2x+y)(x+y)$

(In this case, there are no other combinations to try.)

45. $3x^2 + 5xy + 2y^2$

Factor by trial and error.

$$(3x+y)(x+2y) = 3x^2 + 7xy + 2y^2$$
$$(3x+2y)(x+y) = 3x^2 + 5xy + 2y^2$$

Thus,

$$3x^2 + 5xy + 2y^2 = (3x+2y)(x+y).$$

47. $2x^2 - 9xy + 9y^2 = (2x - 3y)(x - 3y)$

49. $6x^2 - 5xy - 6y^2 = (2x - 3y)(3x + 2y)$

51. $15x^2 + 11xy - 14y^2 = (3x - 2y)(5x + 7y)$

53. $2a^2 + 7ab + 5b^2 = (2a + 5b)(a + b)$

55. $15a^2 - ab - 6b^2 = (3a - 2b)(5a + 3b)$

57. $12x^2 - 25xy + 12y^2 = (3x - 4y)(4x - 3y)$

59. $4x^2 + 26x + 30$

First factor out the GCF, 2. Then factor the resulting trinomial by trial and error or grouping.

$$\begin{aligned} 4x^2 + 26x + 30 &= 2(2x^2 + 13x + 15) \\ &= 2(2x + 3)(x + 5) \end{aligned}$$

61. $9x^2 - 6x - 24$
The GCF is 3.

$$\begin{aligned} 9x^2 - 6x - 24 &= 3(3x^2 - 2x - 8) \\ &= 3(3x + 4)(x - 2) \end{aligned}$$

63. $\begin{aligned}[t] 4y^2 + 2y - 30 &= 2(2y^2 + y - 15) \\ &= 2(2y - 5)(y + 3) \end{aligned}$

65. $\begin{aligned}[t] 9y^2 + 33y - 60 &= 3(3y^2 + 11y - 20) \\ &= 3(3y - 4)(y + 5) \end{aligned}$

67. $3x^3 + 4x^2 + x$
The GCF is x.

$$\begin{aligned} 3x^3 + 4x^2 + x &= x(3x^2 + 4x + 1) \\ &= x(3x + 1)(x + 1) \end{aligned}$$

69. $\begin{aligned}[t] 2x^3 - 3x^2 - 5x &= x(2x^2 - 3x - 5) \\ &= x(2x - 5)(x + 1) \end{aligned}$

71. $9y^3 - 39y^2 + 12y$
The GCF is $3y$.

$$\begin{aligned} 9y^3 - 39y^2 + 12y &= 3y(3y^2 - 13y + 4) \\ &= 3y(3y - 1)(y - 4) \end{aligned}$$

73. $\begin{aligned}[t] 60z^3 + 40z^2 + 5z &= 5z(12z^2 + 8z + 1) \\ &= 5z(6z + 1)(2z + 1) \end{aligned}$

75. $\begin{aligned}[t] 15x^4 - 39x^3 + 18x^2 &= 3x^2(5x^2 - 13x + 6) \\ &= 3x^2(5x - 3)(x - 2) \end{aligned}$

77. $\begin{aligned}[t] 10x^5 - 17x^4 + 3x^3 &= x^3(10x^2 - 17x + 3) \\ &= x^3(2x - 3)(5x - 1) \end{aligned}$

79. $\begin{aligned}[t] 6x^2 - 3xy - 18y^2 &= 3(2x^2 - xy - 6y^2) \\ &= 3(2x + 3y)(x - 2y) \end{aligned}$

81. $\begin{aligned}[t] 12x^2 + 10xy - 8y^2 &= 2(6x^2 + 5xy - 4y^2) \\ &= 2(2x - y)(3x + 4y) \end{aligned}$

83. $\begin{aligned}[t] 8x^2y + 34xy - 84y &= 2y(4x^2 + 17x - 42) \\ &= 2y(4x - 7)(x + 6) \end{aligned}$

85. $\begin{aligned}[t] &12a^2b - 46ab^2 + 14b^3 \\ &= 2b(6a^2 - 23ab + 7b^2) \\ &= 2b(2a - 7b)(3a - b) \end{aligned}$

87. **a.** $x^2 + 3x + 2$

b. $(x + 2)(x + 1)$

c. Yes, the pieces are the same in both figures: one large square, three long rectangles, and two small squares. This geometric model illustrates the factorization

$$x^2 + 3x + 2 = (x + 2)(x + 1).$$

For Exercises 89–91, answers may vary.

93. Statement a is true.

$18y^2 - 6y + 6 = 9(y^2 - 3y + 3)$, and $y^2 - 3y + 3$ is prime.

95. $2x^2 + bx + 3$

The possible factorizations that will give $2x^2$ as the first term and 3 as the last term are:

$$\begin{aligned}(2x+3)(x+1) &= 2x^2+5x+3\\(2x+1)(x+3) &= 2x^2+7x+3\\(2x-3)(x-1) &= 2x^2-5x+3\\(2x-1)(x-3) &= 2x^2-7x+3.\end{aligned}$$

The possible middle terms are $5x, 7x, -5x$, and $-7x$, so $2x^2 + bx + 3$ can be factored if b is $5, 7, -5$, or -7.

97. $2x^{2n} - 7x^n - 4$

Since $x^n \cdot x^n = x^{n+n} = x^{2n}$, the first terms of the factors will be $2x^n$ and x^n. Use trial and error or grouping to obtain the correct factorization.

$$2x^{2n} - 7x^n - 4 = (2x^n + 1)(x^n - 4)$$

Review Exercises

98. $$\begin{aligned}(9x+10)(9x-10) &= (9x)^2 - 10^2\\ &= 81x^2 - 100\end{aligned}$$

99. $$\begin{aligned}(4x+5y)^2 &= (4x)^2 + 2(4x)(5y) + (5y)^2\\ &= 16x^2 + 40xy + 25y^2\end{aligned}$$

100. $$\begin{aligned}&(x+2)(x^2-2x+4)\\ &= x(x^2-2x+4) + 2(x^2-2x+4)\\ &= x^3 - 2x^2 + 4x + 2x^2 - 4x + 8\\ &= x^3 + 8\end{aligned}$$

7.4 Factoring Special Forms

7.4 CHECK POINTS

CHECK POINT 1

Use the formula for factoring the difference of two squares:

$$A^2 - B^2 = (A+B)(A-B).$$

a. $x^2 - 81 = x^2 - 9^2 = (x+9)(x-9)$

b. $$\begin{aligned}36x^2 - 25 &= (6x)^2 - 5^2\\ &= (6x+5)(6x-5)\end{aligned}$$

CHECK POINT 2

a. $$\begin{aligned}25 - 4x^{10} &= 5^2 - (2x^5)^2\\ &= (5+2x^5)(2-2x^5)\end{aligned}$$

b. $$\begin{aligned}100x^2 - 9y^2 &= (10x)^2 - (3y)^2\\ &= (10x+3y)(10x-3y)\end{aligned}$$

CHECK POINT 3

Factor out the GCF, then factor the resulting polynomial as the difference of two squares.

a. $$\begin{aligned}18x^3 - 2x &= 2x(9x^2-1)\\ &= 2x[(3x)^2 - 1^2]\\ &= 2x(3x+1)(3x-1)\end{aligned}$$

b. $$\begin{aligned}72 - 18x^2 &= 18(4-x^2) = 18(2^2 - x^2)\\ &= 18(2+x)(2-x)\end{aligned}$$

CHECK POINT 4

$$\begin{aligned} 81x^4 - 16 &= (9x^2)^2 - 4^2 \\ &= (9x^2+4)(9x^2-4) \end{aligned}$$

Notice that $9x^2 - 4$ is also the difference of two squares, so the factorizations must be continued. The complete factorization is

$$\begin{aligned} 81x^4 - 16 &= (9x^2+4)(9x^2-4) \\ &= (9x^2+4)[(3x)^2-2^2] \\ &= (9x^2+4)(3x+2)(3x-2). \end{aligned}$$

CHECK POINT 5

Use the formulas for factoring perfect square trinomials:

$$\begin{aligned} A^2 + 2AB + B^2 &= (A+B)^2 \\ A^2 - 2AB + B^2 &= (A-B)^2. \end{aligned}$$

a. $x^2 + 14x + 49 = x^2 + 2 \cdot x \cdot 7 + 7^2$
$= (x+7)^2$

b. $x^2 - 6x + 9 = x^2 - 2 \cdot x \cdot 3 + 3^2$
$= (x-3)^2$

c. $16x^2 - 56x + 49 = (4x)^2 - 2 \cdot 4x \cdot 7 + 7^2$
$= (4x-7)^2$

CHECK POINT 6

$$\begin{aligned} &4x^2 + 12xy + 9y^2 \\ &= (2x)^2 + 2 \cdot 2x \cdot 3y + (3y)^2 \\ &= (2x+3y)^2 \end{aligned}$$

CHECK POINT 7

Use the formula for factoring the sum of two cubes:

$$\begin{aligned} A^3 + B^3 &= (A+B)(A^2 - AB + B^2) \\ x^3 + 27 &= x^3 + 3^3 \\ &= (x+3)(x^2 - x \cdot 3 + 3^2) \\ &= (x+3)(x^2 - 3x + 9) \end{aligned}$$

CHECK POINT 8

Use the formula for factoring the difference of two cubes:

$$\begin{aligned} A^3 - B^3 &= (A-B)(A^2 + AB + B^2) \\ 1 - y^3 &= 1^3 - y^3 \\ &= (1-y)(1^2 + 1 \cdot y + y^2) \\ &= (1-y)(1 + y + y^2) \end{aligned}$$

CHECK POINT 9

Use the formula for factoring the sum of two cubes.

$$\begin{aligned} &125x^3 + 8 \\ &= (5x)^3 + 2^3 \\ &= (5x+2)[(5x)^2 - 5x \cdot 2 + 2^2] \\ &= (5x+2)(25x^2 - 10x + 4) \end{aligned}$$

EXERCISE SET 7.4

1. $x^2 - 25 = x^2 - 5^2 = (x+5)(x-5)$

3. $y^2 - 1 = y^2 - 1^2 = (y+1)(y-1)$

5. $4x^2 - 9 = (2x)^2 - 3^2 = (2x+3)(2x-3)$

7. $25 - x^2 = 5^2 - x^2 = (5+x)(5-x)$

9. $1 - 49x^1 = 1^2 - (7x)^2 = (1+7x)(1-7x)$

11. $9 - 25y^2 = 3^2 - (5y)^2 = (3+5y)(3-5y)$

13. $x^4 - 9 = (x^2)^2 - 3^2 = (x^2+3)(x^2-3)$

15. $49y^4 - 16 = (7y^2) - 4^2 = (7y^2+4)(7y^2-4)$

17. $x^{10} - 9 = (x^5) - 3^2 = (x^5+3)(x^5-3)$

19. $25x^2 - 16y^2 = (5x)^2 - (4y)^2$
$= (5x+4y)(5x-4y)$

21. $x^4 - y^{10} = (x^2)^2 - (y^5)^2$
$= (x^2+y^5)(x^2-y^5)$

23. $x^4 - 16 = (x^2)^2 - 4^2 = (x^2+4)(x^2-4)$

Because $x^2 - 4$ is also the difference of two squares, the factorization must be continued. The complete factorization is

$$\begin{aligned} x^4 - 16 &= (x^2+4)(x^2-4) \\ &= (x^2+4)(x^2-2^2) \\ &= (x^2+4)(x+2)(x-2). \end{aligned}$$

25. $\begin{aligned}[t] 16x^4 - 81 &= (4x^2) - 9^2 \\ &= (4x^2+9)(4x^2-9) \\ &= (4x^2+9)[(2x)^2-3^2] \\ &= (4x^2+9)(2x+3)(2x-3) \end{aligned}$

27. $2x^2 - 18 = 2(x^2-9) = 2(x+3)(x-3)$

29. $\begin{aligned}[t] 2x^3 - 72x &= 2x(x^2-36) \\ &= 2x(x+6)(x-6) \end{aligned}$

31. $x^2 + 36$ is prime because it is the sum of two squares with no common factor other than 1.

33. $2x^3 + 72x = 2x(x^2+36)$

35. $50 - 2y^2 = 2(25-y^2) = 2(5+y)(5-y)$

37. $\begin{aligned}[t] 8y^3 - 2y &= 2y(4y^2-1) \\ &= 2y(2y+1)(2y-1) \end{aligned}$

39. $2x^3 - 2x = 2x(x^2-1) = 2x(x+1)(x-1)$

41. $\begin{aligned}[t] x^2 + 2x + 1 &= x^2 + 2 \cdot x \cdot 1 + 1^2 \\ &= (x+1)^2 \end{aligned}$

43. $\begin{aligned}[t] x^2 - 14x + 49 &= x^2 - 2 \cdot x \cdot 7 + 7 + 7^2 \\ &= (x-7)^2 \end{aligned}$

45. $\begin{aligned}[t] x^2 - 2x + 1 &= x^2 - 2 \cdot x + 1 + 1^2 \\ &= (x-1)^2 \end{aligned}$

47. $\begin{aligned}[t] x^2 + 22x + 121 &= x^2 + 2 \cdot x \cdot 11 + 11^2 \\ &= (x+11)^2 \end{aligned}$

49. $\begin{aligned}[t] 4x^2 + 4x + 1 &= (2x)^2 + 2 \cdot 2x \cdot 1 \\ &= (2x+1)^2 \end{aligned}$

51. $\begin{aligned}[t] 25y^2 - 10y + 1 &= (5y)^2 - 2 \cdot 5y \cdot 1 + 1^2 \\ &= (5y-1)^2 \end{aligned}$

53. $x^2 - 10x + 100$ is prime.

To be a perfect square trinomial, the middle term would have to be $-20x$, rather than $-10x$.

55. $\begin{aligned}[t] x^2 + 14xy + 49y^2 &= x^2 + 2 \cdot x \cdot 7y + (7y)^2 \\ &= (x+7y)^2 \end{aligned}$

57. $\begin{aligned}[t] x^2 - 12xy + 36y^2 &= x^2 - 2 \cdot x \cdot 6y + (6y)^2 \\ &= (x-6y)^2 \end{aligned}$

59. $x^2 - 8xy + 64y^2$ is prime.

To be a perfect square trinomial, the middle term would have to be $-16xy$ rather than $-8xy$.

61. $\begin{aligned}[t] &16x^2 - 40xy + 25y^2 \\ &= (4x)^2 - 2 \cdot 4x \cdot 5y + (5y)^2 \\ &= (4x-5y)^2 \end{aligned}$

63. $\begin{aligned}[t] 12x^2 - 12x + 3 &= 3(4x^2-4x+1) \\ &= 3[(2x)^2 - 2 \cdot 2x \cdot 1 + 1^2] \\ &= 3(2x-1)^2 \end{aligned}$

65. $\begin{aligned}[t] &9x^3 + 6x^2 + x \\ &= x(9x^2+6x+1) \\ &= x[(3x)^2 + 2 \cdot 3x \cdot 1 + 1^2] \\ &= x(3x+1)^2 \end{aligned}$

67. $\begin{aligned}[t] 2y^2 - 4y + 2 &= 2(y^2-2y+1) \\ &= 2(y-1)^2 \end{aligned}$

69. $\begin{aligned}[t] 2y^3 + 28y^2 + 98y &= 2y(y^2+14y+49) \\ &= 2y(y+7)^2 \end{aligned}$

71. $\begin{aligned}[t] &x^3 + 1 \\ &= x^3 + 1^3 \\ &= (x+1)(x^2 - x \cdot 1 + 1^2) \\ &= (x+1)(x^2-x+1) \end{aligned}$

73. $x^3 - 27$
$= x^3 - 3^3$
$= (x-3)(x^2 + x \cdot 3 + 3^2)$
$= (x-3)(x^2 + 3x + 9)$

75. $8y^3 - 1$
$= (2y)^3 - 1$
$= (2y-1)[(2y)^2 + 2y + 1]$
$= (2y-1)(4y^2 + 2y + 1)$

77. $27x^3 + 8$
$= (3x)^3 + 2^3$
$= (3x+2)[(3x)^2 - 3x \cdot 2 + 2^2]$
$= (3x+2)(9x^2 - 6x + 4)$

79. $x^3y^3 - 64$
$= (xy)^3 - 4^3$
$= (xy-4)[(xy)^2 + xy \cdot 4 + 4^2]$
$= (xy-4)(x^2y^2 + 4xy + 16)$

81. $27y^4 + 8y$
$= y(27y^3 + 8)$
$= y[(3y)^3 + 2^3]$
$= y(3y+2)[(3y)^2 - 3y \cdot 2 + 2^2]$
$= y(3y+2)(9y^2 - 6y + 4)$

83. $54 - 16y^3$
$= 2(27 - 8y^3)$
$= 2[3^3 - (2y)^3]$
$= 2(3-2y)[3^2 + 3 \cdot 2y + (2y)^2]$
$= 2(3-2y)(9 + 6y + 4y^2)$

85. $64x^3 + 27y^3$
$= (4x)^3 + (3y)^3$
$= (4x+3y)(4x)^2 - 4x \cdot 3y + (3y)^2]$
$= (4x+3y)(16x^2 - 12xy + 9y^2)$

87. $125x^3 - 64y^3$
$= (5x)^3 - (4y)^3$
$= (5x-4y)[(5x)^2 + 5x \cdot 4y + (4y)^2]$
$= (5x-4y)(25x^2 + 20xy + 16y^2)$

89. Area of outer square $= x^2$
Area of inner square $= 5^2 = 25$
Area of shaded region $= x^2 - 25$
$= (x+5)(x-5)$

91. Area of large square $= x^2$
Area of each small (corner) square $= 2^2$
$= 4$
Area of four corner squares $= 4 \cdot 4 = 16$
Area of shaded region $= x^2 - 16$
$= (x+4)(x-4)$

For Exercises 93–95, answers may vary.

97. Statement b is true.

99. $(x+1)^2 - 25$
$= (x+1)^2 - 5^2$
$= [(x+1)+5][(x+1)-5]$
$= (x+6)(x-4)$

101. $4x^{2n} + 12x^n + 9$
$= (2x^n)^2 + 2 \cdot 2x^n \cdot 3 + 3^2$
$= (2x^n + 3)^2$

103. $(x+3)^2 - 2(x+3) + 1$
$= [(x+3) - 1]^2$
$= (x+2)^2$

105. $64x^2 - 16x + k$

Let r be the number such that $r^2 = k$. Then

$$64x^2 - 16x + k = (8x)^2 - 2 \cdot 8x \cdot r + r^2.$$

Comparing the middle terms, we see that

$$-2 \cdot 8x \cdot r = -16x$$
$$-16xr = -16x$$
$$r = 1.$$

Therefore, $k = r^2 = 1^2 = 1$.

107.

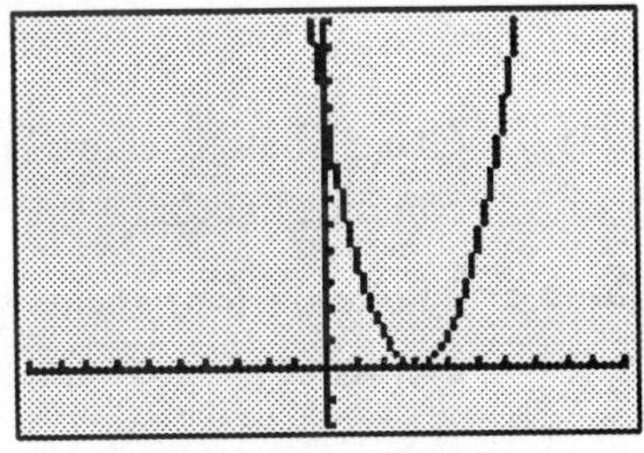

The graphs coincide. This verfies that

$$x^2 - 6x + 9 = (x - 3)^2.$$

109.

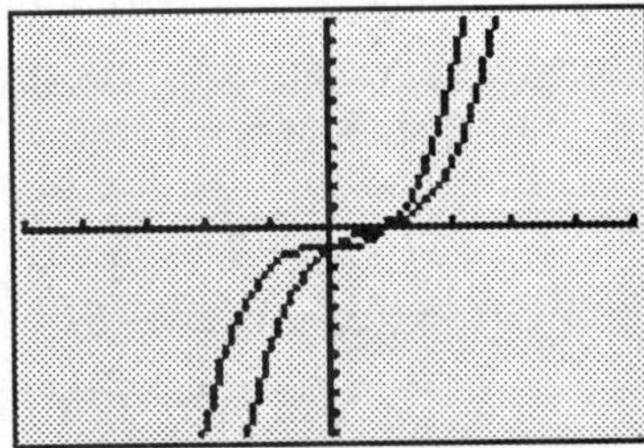

The graphs do not coincide.

$$x^3 - 1 = x^3 - 1^3 = (x + 1)(x^2 + 1)$$

The polynomial on the right should be changed to $(x - 1)(x^2 - x + 1)$.

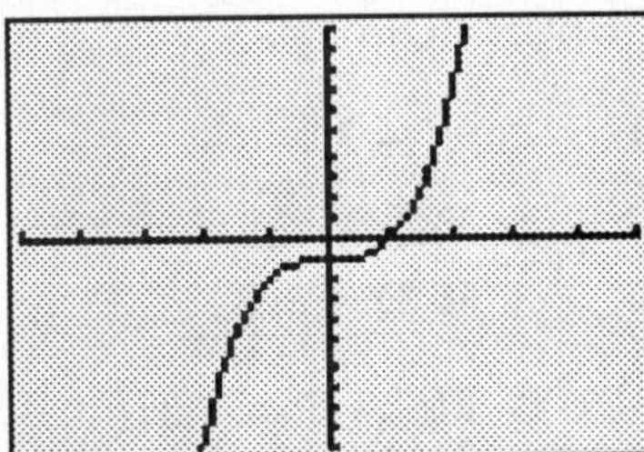

Now the graphs coincide.

Review Exercises

110. $(2x^2y^3)^4(5xy^2)$

$$\begin{aligned} &= [2^4(x^2)^4(y^3)^4] \cdot (5xy^2) \\ &= (16x^8y^{12})(5xy^2) \\ &= (16 \cdot 5)(x^8 \cdot x^1)(y^{12} \cdot y^2) \\ &= 80x^9y^{14} \end{aligned}$$

111. $(10x^2 - 5x + 2) - (14x^2 - 5x - 1)$

$$\begin{aligned} &= (10x^2 - 5x + 2) + (-14x^2 + 5x + 1) \\ &= (10x^2 - 14x^2) + (-5x + 5x) + (2 - 1) \\ &= -4x^2 + 3 \end{aligned}$$

112.

$$\begin{array}{r} 2x + 5 \\ 3x - 2\overline{)6x^2 + 11x - 10} \\ \underline{6x^2 - 4x} \\ 15x - 10 \\ \underline{15x - 10} \\ 0 \end{array}$$

$$\frac{6x^2 + 11x - 10}{3x - 2} = 2x + 5$$

7.5 A General Factoring Strategy

7.5 CHECK POINTS

CHECK POINT 1

$5x^4 - 45x^2$

Step 1 Factor out the GCF, which is $5x^2$.

$$5x^4 - 45x^2 = 5x^2(x^2 - 9)$$

Step 2 The factor $x^2 - 9$ has two terms and is the difference of two squares.

$$\begin{aligned} 5x^4 - 45x^2 &= 5x^2(x^2 - 9) \\ &= 5x^2(x + 3)(x - 3) \end{aligned}$$

Step 3 No factor with more than one term can be factored further.

Step 4 Check by multiplying.

$$\begin{aligned} 5x^2(x + 3)(x - 3) &= 5x^2(x^2 - 9) \\ &= 5x^4 - 45x^2 \end{aligned}$$

CHECK POINT 2

$4x^2 - 16x - 48$

Step 1 Factor out the GCF, which is 4.

$$4x^2 - 16x - 48 = 4(x^2 - 4x - 12)$$

Step 2 The factor $x^2 - 4x - 12$ has three terms, but it is not a perfect square trinomial. Factor it by using trial and error.

$$\begin{aligned} 4x^2 - 16x - 48 &= 4(x^2 - 4x - 12) \\ &= 4(x - 6)(x + 2) \end{aligned}$$

Step 3 No factor with more than one term can be factored further.

Step 4 Check by multiplying.

$$\begin{aligned} 4(x - 6)(x + 2) &= 4(x^2 - 4x - 12) \\ &= 4x^2 - 16x - 48 \end{aligned}$$

CHECK POINT 3

$4x^5 - 64x$

Step 1 Factor out the GCF, which is $4x$.

$$4x^5 - 64x = 4x(x^4 - 16)$$

Step 2 The factor $x^4 - 16$ has two terms. This binomial can be expressed as the difference of two squares, $(x^2)^2 - 4^2$, so it can be factored as the difference of two squares.

$$\begin{aligned} 4x^5 - 64x &= 4x(x^4 - 16) \\ &= 4x(x^2 + 4)(x^2 - 4) \end{aligned}$$

Step 3 $x^2 - 4$ is also the difference of two squares, so continue factoring.

$$\begin{aligned} 4x^5 - 64x &= 4x(x^4 - 16) \\ &= 4x(x^2 + 4)(x^2 - 4) \\ &= 4x(x^2 + 4)(x + 2)(x - 2) \end{aligned}$$

Step 4 Check by multiplying.

$$\begin{aligned} &4x(x^2 + 4)(x + 2)(x - 2) \\ &= 4x(x^2 + 4)(x^2 - 4) \\ &= 4x(x^4 - 16) \\ &= 4x^5 - 64x \end{aligned}$$

CHECK POINT 4

$x^3 - 4x^2 - 9x + 36$

Step 1 Other than 1, there is no common factor.

Step 2 There are four terms. Try factoring by grouping.

$$\begin{aligned} &x^3 - 4x^2 - 9x + 36 \\ &= (x^3 - 4x^2) + (-9x + 36) \\ &= x^2(x - 4) - 9(x - 4) \\ &= (x - 4)(x^2 - 9) \end{aligned}$$

Step 3 Since $x^2 - 9$ is the difference of two squares, continue factoring.

$$\begin{aligned} &x^3 - 4x^2 - 9x + 36 \\ &= (x - 4)(x^2 - 9) \\ &= (x - 4)(x + 3)(x - 3) \end{aligned}$$

Step 4

$$\begin{aligned} &(x - 4)(x + 3)(x - 3) \\ &= (x - 4)(x^2 - 9) \\ &= x^3 - 9x - 4x^2 + 36 \\ &= x^3 - 4x^2 - 9x + 36 \end{aligned}$$

CHECK POINT 5

$3x^3 - 30x^2 + 75x$

Step 1 Factor out the GCF, which is $3x$.

$$3x^3 - 30x^2 + 75x = 3x(x^2 - 10x + 25)$$

Step 2 The factor $x^2 - 10x + 25$ has three terms and is a perfect square trinomial.

$$\begin{aligned} &3x^3 - 30x^2 + 75x \\ &= 3x(x^2 - 10x + 25) \\ &= 3x(x^2 - 2 \cdot x \cdot 5 + 5^2) \\ &= 3x(x - 5)^2 \end{aligned}$$

Step 3 The factorization is complete.

Step 4 Check by multiplying.

$$\begin{aligned} 3x(x-5)^2 &= 3x(x^2-10x+25) \\ &= 3x^3-30x^2+75x \end{aligned}$$

CHECK POINT 6

$2x^5+54x^2$

Step 1 Factor out the GCF, which is $2x^2$.

$$2x^5+54x^2 = 2x^2(x^3+27)$$

Step 2 The factor x^3+27 has two terms and is the sum of two cubes.

$$\begin{aligned} 2x^5+54x^2 &= 2x^2(x^3+3^3) \\ &= 2x^2(x+3)(x^2-3x+9) \end{aligned}$$

Step 3 The factorization is complete.

Step 4 Check by multiplyling.

$$\begin{aligned} 2x^2(x+3)(x^2-3x+9) &= 2x^2(x^3+27) \\ &= 2x^5+54x^2 \end{aligned}$$

CHECK POINT 7

$3x^4y-48y^5$

Step 1 Factor out the GCF, which is $3y$.

$$3x^4y-48y^5 = 3y(x^4-16y^4)$$

Step 2 The factor x^4-16y^4 has two terms and is the difference of two squares.

$$\begin{aligned} 3x^4-48y^5 &= 3y(x^4-16y^4) \\ &= 3y[(x^2)^2-(4y^2)^2] \\ &= 3y(x^2+4y^2)(x^2-4y^2) \end{aligned}$$

Step 3 The last factor, x^2-4y^2, is also the difference of two squares, so continue factoring.

$$\begin{aligned} &3x^2y-48y^5 \\ &= 3y(x^2+4y^2)(x^2-4y^2) \\ &= 3y(x^2+4y^2)(x+2y)(x-2y) \end{aligned}$$

Step 4 Check by multiplying.

$$\begin{aligned} &3y(x^2+4y^2)(x+2y)(x-2y) \\ &= 3y(x^2+4y^2)(x^2-4y^2) \\ &= 3y(x^4-16y^4) \\ &= 3x^4y-48y^5 \end{aligned}$$

CHECK POINT 8

$12x^3+36x^2y+27xy^2$

Step 1 Factor out the GCF, which is $3x$.

$$\begin{aligned} &12x^3+36y^2+27xy^2 \\ &= 3x(4x^2+12xy+9y^2) \end{aligned}$$

Step 2 The factor $4x^2+12xy+9y^2$ has three terms and is a perfect square trinomial.

$$\begin{aligned} &12x^3+36x^2y+27xy^2 \\ &= 3x(4x^2+12xy+9y^2) \\ &= 3x[(2x)^2+2\cdot 2x\cdot 3y+(3y)^2] \\ &= 3x(2x+3y)^2 \end{aligned}$$

Step 3 The factorization is complete.

Step 4 Check by multiplying.

$$\begin{aligned} &3x(2x+3y)^2 \\ &= 3x[(2x)^2+2\cdot 2x\cdot 3y+(3y)^2] \\ &= 3x(4x^2+12xy+9y^2) \\ &= 12x^3+36x^2y+27xy^2 \end{aligned}$$

EXERCISE SET 7.5

In Exercises 1–61, all factorizations should be checked using multiplication or a graphing utility. Checks will not be shown here.

1. $3x^3 - 3x = 3x(x^2 - 1)$
$= 3x(x + 1)(x - 1)$

3. $3x^3 + 3x = 3x(x^2 + 1)$

5. $4x^2 - 4x - 24 = 4(x^2 - x - 6)$
$= 4(x - 3)(x + 2)$

7. $2x^4 - 162 = 2(x^4 - 81)$
$= 2(x^2 + 9)(x^2 - 9)$
$= 2(x^2 + 9)(x + 3)(x - 3)$

9. $x^3 + 2x^2 - 9x - 18$
$= (x^3 + 2x^2) + (-9x - 18)$
$= x^2(x + 2) - 9(x + 2)$
$= (x + 2)(x^2 - 9)$
$= (x + 2)(x + 3)(x - 3)$

11. $3x^3 - 24x^2 + 48x = 3x(x^2 - 8x + 16)$
$= 3x(x - 4)^2$

13. $2x^5 + 2x^2 = 2x^2(x^3 + 1)$
$= 2x^2(x + 1)(x^2 - x + 1)$

15. $6x^2 + 8x = 2x(3x + 4)$

17. $2y^2 - 2y - 112 = 2(y^2 - y - 56)$
$= 2(y - 8)(y + 7)$

19. $7y^4 + 14y^3 + 7y^2 = 7y^2(y^2 + 2y + 1)$
$= 7y^2(y + 1)^2$

21. $y^2 + 8y - 16$ is prime because there are no two integers whose product is -16 and whose sum is 8.

23. $16y^2 - 4y - 2 = 2(8y^2 - 2y - 1)$
$= 2(4y + 1)(2y - 1)$

25. $r^2 - 25r = r(r - 25)$

27. $4w^2 + 8w - 5 = (2w + 5)(2w - 1)$

29. $x^3 - 4x = x(x^2 - 4) = x(x + 2)(x - 2)$

31. $x^2 + 64$ is prime because it is the sum of two squares with no common fator other than 1.

33. $9y^2 + 13y + 4 = (9y + 4)(y + 1)$

35. $y^3 + 2y^2 - 4y - 8$
$= (y^3 + 2y^2) + (-4y - 8)$
$= y^2(y + 2) - 4(y + 2)$
$= (y + 2)(y^2 - 4)$
$= (y + 2)(y + 2)(y - 2)$
or $(y + 2)^2(y - 2)$

37. $9y^2 + 24y + 16$
$= (3y)^2 + 2 \cdot 3y \cdot 4 + 4^2$
$= (3y + 4)^2$

39. $5y^3 - 45y^2 + 70y$
$= 5y(y^2 - 9y + 14)$
$= 5y(y - 7)(y - 2)$

41. $y^5 - 81y$
$= y(y^4 - 81)$
$= y(y^2 + 9)(y^2 - 9)$
$= y(y^2 + 9)(y + 3)(y - 3)$

43. $20a^4 - 45a^2$
$= 5a^2(4a^2 - 9)$
$= 5a^2(2a + 3)(2a - 3)$

45. $12y^2 - 11y + 2 = (4y - 1)(3y - 2)$

47. $9y^2 - 64 = (3y)^2 - 8^2$
$= (3y + 8)(3y - 8)$

49. $9y^2 + 64$ is prime because it is the sum of two squares with no common factor other than 1.

51. $2y^3 + 3y^2 - 50y - 75$
$= (2y^3 + 3y^2) + (-50y - 75)$
$= y^2(2y + 3) - 25(2y + 3)$
$= (2y + 3)(y^2 - 25)$
$= (2y + 3)(y + 5)(y - 5)$

53. $2r^3 + 30r^2 - 68r$
$= 2r(r^2 + 15r - 34)$
$= 2r(r + 17)(r - 2)$

55. $8x^5 - 2x^3 = 2x^3(4x^2 - 1)$
$= 2x^2[(2x)^2 - 1^2]$
$= 2x^2(2x + 1)(2x - 1)$

57. $3x^2 + 243 = 3(x^2 + 81)$

59. $x^4 + 8x = x(x^3 + 8)$
$= x(x^3 + 2^3)$
$= x(x + 2)(x^2 - 2x + 4)$

61. $2y^5 - 2y^2$
$= 2y^2(y^3 - 1)$
$= 2y^2(y - 1)(y^2 + y + 1)$

63. $6x^2 + 8xy = 2x(3x + 4y)$

65. $xy - 7x + 3y - 21$
$= (xy - 7x) + (3y - 21)$
$= x(y - 7) + 3(y - 7)$
$= (y - 7)(x + 3)$

67. $x^2 - 3xy - 4y^2 = (x - 4y)(x + y)$

69. $72a^3b^2 + 12a^2 - 24a^4b^2$
$= 12a^2(6ab^2 + 1 - 2a^2b^2)$

71. $3a^2 + 27ab + 54b^2$
$= 3(a^2 + 9ab + 18b^2)$
$= 3(a + 6b)(a + 3b)$

73. $48x^4y - 3x^2y$
$= 3x^2y(16x^2 - 1)$
$= 3x^2y(4x + 1)(4x - 1)$

75. $6a^2b + ab - 2b$
$= b(6a^2 + a - 2)$
$= b(3a + 2)(2a - 1)$

77. $7x^5y - 7xy^5$
$= 7xy(x^4 - y^4)$
$= 7xy(x^2 + y^2)(x^2 - y^2)$
$= 7xy(x^2 + y^2)(x + y)(x - y)$

79. $10x^3y - 14x^2y^2 + 4xy^3$
$= 2xy(5x^2 - 7xy + 2y^2)$
$= 2xy(5x - 2y)(x - y)$

81. $2bx^2 + 44bx + 242b$
$= 2b(x^2 + 22x + 121)$
$= 2b(x^2 + 2 \cdot x \cdot 11 + 11^2)$
$= 2b(x + 11)^2$

83. $15a^2 + 11ab - 14b^2 = (5a + 7b)(3a - 2b)$

85. $36x^3y - 62x^2y^2 + 12xy^3$
$= 2xy(18x^2 - 31xy + 6y^2)$
$= 2xy(9x - 2y)(2x - 3y)$

87. $a^2y - b^2y - a^2x + b^2x$
$= (a^2y - b^2y) + (-a^2x + b^2x)$
$= y(a^2 - b^2) - x(a^2 - b^2)$
$= (a^2 - b^2)(y - -x)$
$= (a + b)(a - b)(y - x)$

89. $9ax^3 + 15ax^2 - 14ax$
$= ax(9x^2 + 15x - 14)$
$= ax(3x + 7)(3x - 2)$

91. $81x^4y - y^5$
$= y(81x^4 - y^4)$
$= y(9x^2 + y^2)(9x^2 - y^2)$
$= y(9x^2 + y^2)(3x + y)(3x - y)$

93. $256 - 16t^2 = 16(16 - t^2)$
$= 16(4 + t)(4 - t)$

95. Area of outer circle $= \pi b^2$
Area of inner circle $= \pi a^2$
Area of shaded ring $= \pi b^2 - \pi a^2$

$$\pi b^2 - \pi a^2 = \pi(b^2 - a^2) = \pi(b + a)(b - a)$$

97. Answers may vary.

99. Statement d is true.

$$3x^2y^3 + 9xy^2 + 21xy = 3xy(xy^2 + 3y + 7),$$

and $xy^2 + 3y + 7$ cannot be factored further.

101. $5y^5 - 5y^4 - 20y^3 + 20y^2$
$= 5y^2(y^3 - y^2 - 4y + 4)$
$= 5y^2[y^2(y - 1) - 4(y - 1)]$
$= 5y^2(y - 1)(y^2 - 4)$
$= 5y^2(y - 1)(y + 2)(y - 2)$

103. $(x + 5)^2 - 20(x + 5) + 100$

This is a perfect square trinomial.

$$(x + 5)^2 - 20(x + 5) + 100 = (x + 5)^2 - 2(x + 5)(10) + 10^2 = [(x + 5) - 10]^2 = (x - 5)^2$$

105.

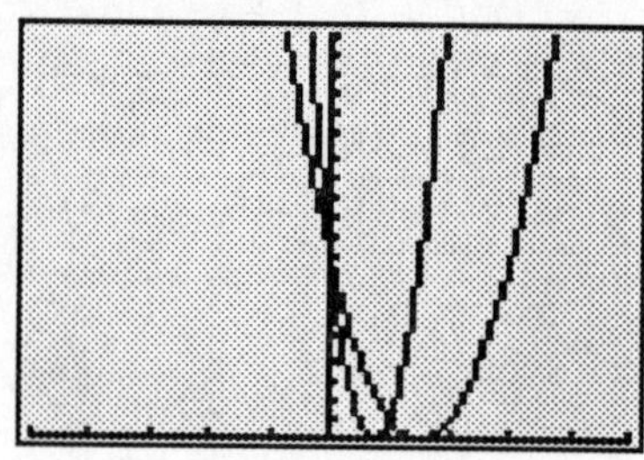

The graphs do not coincide.

$$4x^2 - 12x + 9 = (2x)^2 - 2 \cdot 2x \cdot 3 + 3^2 = (2x - 3)^2$$

Change the polynomial on the right side to $(4x - 3)^2$.

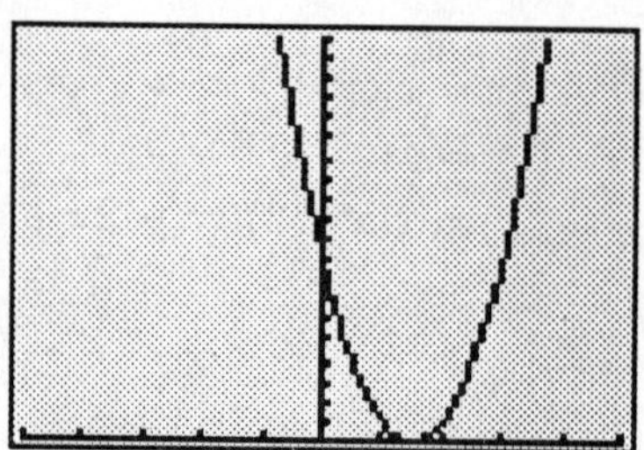

Now the graphs coincide.

107.

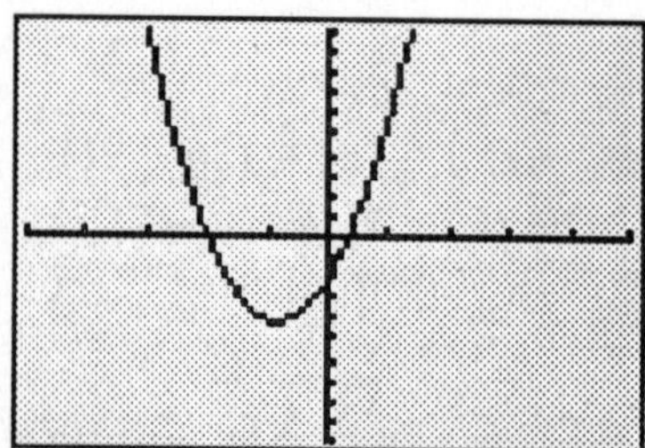

The graphs coincide.
This verifies that the factorization

$$6x^2 + 10x - 4 = 2(3x - 1)(x + 2)$$

is correct.

109.

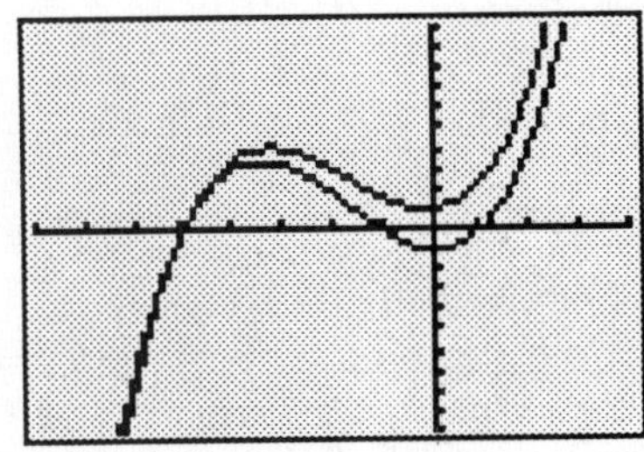

The graphs do not coincide.

$$\begin{aligned}&2x^3 + 10x^2 - 2x - 10\\ &= 2(x^3 + 5x^2 - x - 5)\\ &= 2[(x^3 + 5x^2) + (-x - 5)\\ &= 2[x^2(x + 5) - 1(x + 5)]\\ &= 2(x + 5)(x^2 - 1)\\ &= 2(x + 5)(x + 1)(x - 1)\end{aligned}$$

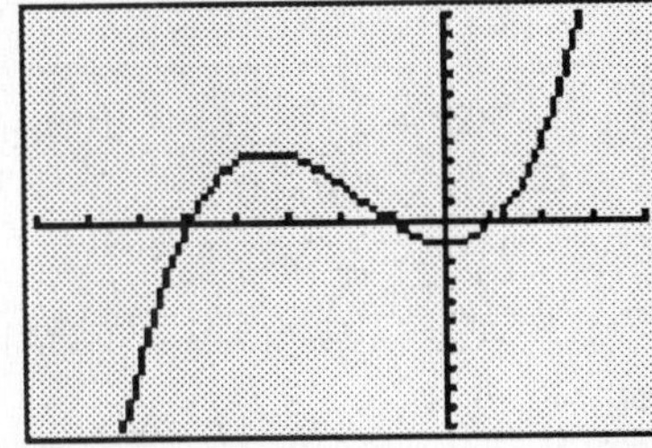

Review Exercises

110. $9x^2 - 16 = (3x)^2 - 4^2$
$= (3x + 4)(3x - 4)$

111. $5x - 2y = 10$
x-intercept: 2
y-intercept: -5
checkpoint: $(4, 5)$

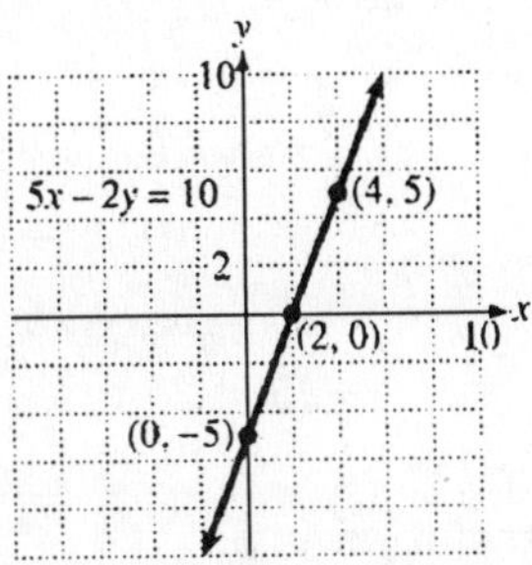

112. Let x = the measure of the first angle.
Then $3x$ = the measure of the second angle;
$x + 80$ = the measure of the third angle.

$$\begin{aligned}x + 3x + (x + 80) &= 180\\ 5x + 80 &= 180\\ 5x &= 100\\ x &= 20\end{aligned}$$

Measure of first angle $= x = 20°$
Measure of second angle $= 3x = 60°$
Measure of third angle $= x + 80 = 100°$

7.6 Solving Quadratic Equations by Factoring

7.6 CHECK POINTS

CHECK POINT 1

$(2x + 1)(x - 4) = 0$

Set each factor equal to zero and solve each resulting equation for x.

$$(2x + 1)(x - 4) = 0$$
$$2x + 1 = 0 \quad \text{or} \quad x - 4 = 0$$
$$2x = -1 \qquad x = 4$$
$$x = -\frac{1}{2}$$

Check each of these solutions in the equation $(2x+1)(x-4)$. The equation has two solutions, $-\frac{1}{2}$ and 4.

CHECK POINT 2

$x^2 - 6x + 5 = 0$

Step 1 The equation is already written in standard form.

Step 2 Factor the trinomial.

$$x^2 - 6x + 5 = 0$$
$$(x - 5)(x - 1) = 0$$

Step 3 and 4 Set each factor equal to zero and solve the resulting equation.

$$x - 5 = 0 \quad \text{or} \quad x - 1 = 0$$
$$x = 5 \qquad\qquad x = 1$$

Step 5 Check the solutions in the original equation.

Check 5:

$$x^2 - 6x + 5 = 0$$
$$5^2 - 6 \cdot 5 + 5 \stackrel{?}{=} 0$$
$$25 - 30 + 5 \stackrel{?}{=} 0$$
$$-5 + 5 \stackrel{?}{=} 0$$
$$0 = 0 \text{ true}$$

Check 1:

$$x^2 - 6x + 5 = 0$$
$$1^2 - 6 \cdot 1 + 5 \stackrel{?}{=} 0$$
$$1 - 6 + 5 \stackrel{?}{=} 0$$
$$-5 + 5 \stackrel{?}{=} 0$$
$$0 = 0 \text{ true}$$

The solutions are 5 and 1.

CHECK POINT 3

$4x^2 = 2x$

Step 1 Write the equation in standard form.

$$4x^2 = 2x$$
$$4x^2 - 2x = 0$$

Step 2 Factor the binomial by factoring out the GCF, $2x$.

$$2x(2x - 1) = 0$$

Step 3 and 4 Set each factor equal to zero and solve the resulting equations.

$$2x = 0 \quad \text{or} \quad 2x - 1 = 0$$
$$x = 0 \qquad\qquad 2x = 1$$
$$x = \frac{1}{2}$$

Step 5 Check the solutions in the original equation:

Check 0:

$$4x^2 = 2x$$
$$4 \cdot 0^2 = 2 \cdot 0$$
$$0 = 0 \text{ true}$$

Check: $\frac{1}{2}$:

$$4x^2 = 2x$$
$$4\left(\frac{1}{2}\right)^2 = 2\left(\frac{1}{2}\right)$$
$$4 \cdot \frac{1}{4} = 1$$
$$1 = 1 \text{ true}$$

The solutions are 0 and $\frac{1}{2}$.

CHECK POINT 4

$x^2 = 10x - 25$

Step 1

$$x^2 - 10x + 25 = 10x - 10x - 25 + 25$$
$$x^2 - 10x + 25 = 0$$

Step 2 $x^2 - 10x + 25$ is a perfect square trinomial.

$$(x - 5)^2 = 0$$

Step 3 and 4 Because both factors are the same, it is only necessary to set one of them equal to zero.

$$x - 5 = 0$$
$$x = 5$$

Step 5 Check 5:

$$x^2 = 10x - 25$$
$$5^2 \stackrel{?}{=} 10 \cdot 5 - 25$$
$$25 \stackrel{?}{=} 50 - 25$$
$$25 = 25 \text{ true}$$

The solution is 5.

CHECK POINT 5

$16x^2 = 25$

Step 1

$$\begin{aligned} 16x^2 - 25 &= 25 - 25 \\ 16x^2 - 25 &= 0 \end{aligned}$$

Step 2 $16x^2 - 25$ is the difference of two squares.

$$(4x+5)(4x-5) = 0$$

Step 3 and 4

$$\begin{aligned} 4x + 5 &= 0 \quad \text{or} \quad & 4x - 5 &= 0 \\ 4x &= -5 & 4x &= 5 \\ x &= -\frac{5}{4} & x &= \frac{5}{4} \end{aligned}$$

Step 5

Check $-\frac{5}{4}$:

$$\begin{aligned} 16x^2 &= 25 \\ 16\left(-\frac{5}{4}\right)^2 &\stackrel{?}{=} 25 \\ 16 \cdot \frac{25}{16} &\stackrel{?}{=} 25 \\ 25 &= 25 \text{ true} \end{aligned}$$

Check: $\frac{5}{4}$:

$$\begin{aligned} 16x^2 &= 25 \\ 16\left(\frac{5}{4}\right)^2 &\stackrel{?}{=} 25 \\ 16 \cdot \frac{25}{16} &\stackrel{?}{=} 25 \\ 25 &= 25 \text{ true} \end{aligned}$$

The solutions are $-\frac{5}{4}$ and $\frac{5}{4}$.

CHECK POINT 6

$(x-5)(x-2) = 28$

Step 1

$$\begin{aligned} x^2 - 2x - 5x + 10 &= 28 \\ x^2 - 7x + 10 &= 28 \\ x^2 - 7x + 10 - 28 &= 28 - 28 \\ x^2 - 7x - 8 &= 0 \end{aligned}$$

Step 2

$$(x-9)(x+2) = 0$$

Step 3 and 4

$$\begin{aligned} x - 9 &= 0 \quad \text{or} \quad & x + 2 &= 0 \\ x &= 9 & x &= -2 \end{aligned}$$

Step 5

Check 9:

$$\begin{aligned} (x-5)(x-2) &= 28 \\ (9-5)(9-2) &\stackrel{?}{=} 28 \\ 4 \cdot 7 &\stackrel{?}{=} 28 \\ 28 &= 28 \text{ true} \end{aligned}$$

Check -2:

$$\begin{aligned} (x-5)(x-2) &= 28 \\ (-2-5)(-2-2) &\stackrel{?}{=} 28 \\ (-7)(-4) &\stackrel{?}{=} 28 \\ 28 &= 28 \text{ true} \end{aligned}$$

The solutions are 9 and -2.

CHECK POINT 7

$h = -16t^2 + 48t + 160$

Substitute 192 for h and solve for t.

$$\begin{aligned} 192 &= -16t^2 + 48t + 160 \\ 16t^2 + 48t + 192 - 160 &= -16t^2 + 16t^2 + 48t \\ &\quad - 48t + 160 - 160 \\ 16t^2 - 48t + 32 &= 0 \\ 16(t^2 - 3t + 2) &= 0 \\ 16(t-1)(t-2) &= 0 \end{aligned}$$

$$\begin{aligned} t - 1 &= 0 \quad \text{or} \quad & t - 2 &= 0 \\ t &= 1 & t &= 0 \end{aligned}$$

The ball's height is 192 feet after 1 second and after 2 seconds. These solutionss correspond to the points $(1, 192)$ and $(2, 192)$ on the graph.

CHECK POINT 8

Let x = the width of the sign.
Then $x+3$ = the length of the floor.

Use the formula for the area of a rectangle.

$$\begin{aligned} l \cdot w &= A \\ (x+3)(x) &= 54 \\ x^2+3x &= 54 \\ x^2+3x-54 &= 0 \\ (x+9)(x-6) &= 0 \end{aligned}$$

$$\begin{aligned} x+9=0 \quad &\text{or} \quad x-6=0 \\ x=-9 \quad & \qquad\quad x=6 \end{aligned}$$

A rectangle cannot have a negative length. Thus, $x=6$ and $x+3=9$. The length of the sign is 9 feet and the width is 6 feet. This solution checks because

$$\begin{aligned} A = lw &= (9 \text{ feet})(6 \text{ feet}) \\ &= 54 \text{ square feet.} \end{aligned}$$

EXERCISE SET 7.6

1. $x(x+3)=0$

$$\begin{aligned} x=0 \quad \text{or} \quad x+3&=0 \\ x&=-3 \end{aligned}$$

The solutions are 0 and -3.

3. $(x-8)(x+5)=0$

$$\begin{aligned} x-8=0 \quad &\text{or} \quad x+5=0 \\ x=8 \quad & \qquad\quad x=-5 \end{aligned}$$

The solutions are 8 and -5.

5. $(x-2)(4x+5)=0$

$$\begin{aligned} x-2=0 \quad &\text{or} \quad 4x+5=0 \\ x=2 \quad & \qquad\quad 4x=-5 \\ & \qquad\quad x=-\frac{5}{4} \end{aligned}$$

The solutions are 2 and $-\frac{5}{4}$.

7. $4(x-3)(2x+7)=0$

$$\begin{aligned} x-3=0 \quad &\text{or} \quad 2x+7=0 \\ x=3 \quad & \qquad\quad 2x=-7 \\ & \qquad\quad x=-\frac{7}{2} \end{aligned}$$

The solutions are 3 and $-\frac{7}{2}$.

In Exercises 9–55, all solutions should be checked by substitution or by using a graphing utility and identifying x-intercepts. The check by substitution will be shown here for Exercise 9 only.

9. $x^2+8x+15=0$

$$\begin{aligned} (x+5)(x+3)&=0 \\ x+5=0 \quad \text{or} \quad x+3&=0 \\ x=5 \qquad\quad x&=-3 \end{aligned}$$

Check -5:

$$\begin{aligned} x^2+8x+15&=0 \\ (-5)^2+8(-5)+15 &\stackrel{?}{=} 0 \\ 25-40+15 &\stackrel{?}{=} 0 \\ -15+15 &\stackrel{?}{=} 0 \\ 0&=0 \text{ true} \end{aligned}$$

Check 3:

$$\begin{aligned} x^2+8x+15&=0 \\ (-3)^2+8(-3)+15 &\stackrel{?}{=} 0 \\ 9-24+15 &\stackrel{?}{=} 0 \\ -15+15 &\stackrel{?}{=} 0 \\ 0&=0 \text{ true} \end{aligned}$$

The solutions are -5 and -3.

11. $x^2-2x-15=0$

$$\begin{aligned} (x+3)(x-5)&=0 \\ x+3=0 \quad \text{or} \quad x-5&=0 \\ x=-3 \qquad\quad x&=5 \end{aligned}$$

The solutions are -3 and 5.

13.
$$\begin{aligned} x^2 - 4x &= 21 \\ x^2 - 4x - 21 &= 0 \\ (x+3)(x-7) &= 0 \end{aligned}$$
$$x + 3 = 0 \quad \text{or} \quad x - 7 = 0$$
$$x = -3 \qquad\qquad x = 7$$

The solutions are -3 and 7.

15.
$$\begin{aligned} x^2 + 9x &= -8 \\ x^2 + 9x + 8 &= 0 \\ (x+8)(x+1) &= 0 \end{aligned}$$
$$x + 8 = 0 \quad \text{or} \quad x + 1 = 0$$
$$x = -8 \qquad\qquad x = -1$$

The solutions are -8 and -1.

17.
$$\begin{aligned} x^2 + 4x &= 0 \\ x(x+4) &= 0 \end{aligned}$$
$$x = 0 \quad \text{or} \quad x + 4 = 0$$
$$x = -4$$

The solutions are 0 and -4.

19.
$$\begin{aligned} x^2 - 5x &= 0 \\ x(x-5) &= 0 \end{aligned}$$
$$x = 0 \quad \text{or} \quad x - 5 = 0$$
$$x = 5$$

The solutions are 0 and 5.

21.
$$\begin{aligned} x^2 &= 4x \\ x^2 - 4x &= 0 \\ x(x-4) &= 0 \end{aligned}$$
$$x = 0 \quad \text{or} \quad x - 4 = 0$$
$$x = 4$$

The solutions are 0 and 4.

23.
$$\begin{aligned} 2x^2 &= 5x \\ 2x^2 - 5x &= 0 \\ x(2x-5) &= 0 \end{aligned}$$
$$x = 0 \quad \text{or} \quad 2x - 5 = 0$$
$$2x = 5$$
$$x = \frac{5}{2}$$

The solutions are 0 and $\frac{5}{2}$.

25.
$$\begin{aligned} 3x^2 &= -5x \\ 3x^2 + 5x &= 0 \\ x(3x+5) &= 0 \end{aligned}$$
$$x = 0 \quad \text{or} \quad 3x + 5 = 0$$
$$3x = -5$$
$$x = -\frac{5}{3}$$

The only solution is 0 and $-\frac{5}{3}$.

27.
$$\begin{aligned} x^2 + 4x + 4 &= 0 \\ (x-2)^2 &= 0 \\ x + 2 &= 0 \\ x &= -2 \end{aligned}$$

The only solution is -2.

29.
$$\begin{aligned} x^2 &= 12x - 36 \\ x^2 - 12x + 36 &= 0 \\ (x-6)^2 &= 0 \\ x - 6 &= 0 \\ x &= 6 \end{aligned}$$

The only solution is 6.

31.
$$\begin{aligned} 4x^2 &= 12x - 9 \\ 4x^2 - 12x + 9 &= 0 \\ (2x-3)^2 &= 0 \\ 2x - 3 &= 0 \\ 2x &= 3 \\ x &= \frac{3}{2} \end{aligned}$$

The only solution is $\frac{3}{2}$.

33.
$$\begin{aligned} 2x^2 &= 7x + 4 \\ 2x^2 - 7x - 4 &= 0 \\ (2x+1)(x-4) &= 0 \end{aligned}$$
$$2x + 1 = 0 \quad \text{or} \quad x - 4 = 0$$
$$2x = -1 \qquad\qquad x = 4$$
$$x = -\frac{1}{2}$$

The solutions are $-\frac{1}{2}$ and 4.

35.
$$5x^2 = 18 - x$$
$$5x^2 + x - 18 = 0$$
$$(5x-9)(x+2) = 0$$
$$5x - 9 = 0 \quad \text{or} \quad x + 2 = 0$$
$$5x = 9 \qquad x = -2$$
$$x = \frac{9}{5}$$

The solutions are $\frac{9}{5}$ and -2.

37.
$$x^2 - 49 = 0$$
$$(x+7)(x-7) = 0$$
$$x + 7 = 0 \quad \text{or} \quad x - 7 = 0$$
$$x = -7 \qquad x = 7$$

The solutions are -7 and 7.

39.
$$4x^2 - 25 = 0$$
$$(2x+5)(2x-5) = 0$$
$$2x + 5 = 0 \quad \text{or} \quad 2x - 5 = 0$$
$$2x = -5 \qquad 2x = 5$$
$$x = -\frac{5}{2} \qquad x = \frac{5}{2}$$

The solutions are $-\frac{5}{2}$ and $\frac{5}{2}$.

41.
$$81x^2 = 25$$
$$81x^2 - 25 = 0$$
$$(9x+5)(9x-5) = 0$$
$$9x + 5 = 0 \quad \text{or} \quad 9x - 5 = 0$$
$$9x = -5 \qquad 9x = 5$$
$$x = -\frac{5}{9} \qquad x = \frac{5}{9}$$

The solutions are $-\frac{5}{9}$ and $\frac{5}{9}$.

43.
$$x(x-4) = 21$$
$$x^2 - 4x = 21$$
$$x^2 - 4x - 21 = 0$$
$$(x+3)(x-7) = 0$$
$$x + 3 = 0 \quad \text{or} \quad x - 7 = 0$$
$$x = -3 \qquad x = 7$$

The solutions are -3 and 7.

45.
$$4x(x+1) = 15$$
$$4x^2 + 4x = 15$$
$$4x^2 + 4x - 15 = 0$$
$$(2x+5)(2x-3) = 0$$
$$2x + 5 = 0 \quad \text{or} \quad 2x - 3 = 0$$
$$2x = -5 \qquad 2x = 3$$
$$x = -\frac{5}{2} \qquad x = \frac{3}{2}$$

The solutions are $-\frac{5}{2}$ and $\frac{3}{2}$.

47.
$$(x-1)(x+4) = 14$$
$$x^2 + 3x - 4 = 14$$
$$x^2 + 3x - 18 = 0$$
$$(x+6)(x-3) = 0$$
$$x + 6 = 0 \quad \text{or} \quad x - 3 = 0$$
$$x = -6 \qquad x = 3$$

The solutions are -6 and 3.

49.
$$(x+1)(2x+5) = -1$$
$$2x^2 + 7x + 5 = -1$$
$$2x^2 + 7x + 6 = 0$$
$$(2x+3)(x+2) = 0$$
$$2x + 3 = 0 \quad \text{or} \quad x + 2 = 0$$
$$2x = -3 \qquad x = -2$$
$$x = -\frac{3}{2}$$

The solutions are $-\frac{3}{2}$ and -2.

51.
$$y(y+8) = 16(y-1)$$
$$y^2 + 8y = 16y - 16$$
$$y^2 - 8y + 16 = 0$$
$$(y-4)^2 = 0$$
$$y - 4 = 0$$
$$y = 4$$

The only solution is 4.

53. $4y^2 + 20y + 25 = 0$

$$\begin{aligned}(2y+5)^2 &= 0\\ 2y+5 &= 0\\ 2y &= -5\\ y &= -\frac{5}{2}\end{aligned}$$

The only solution is $-\frac{5}{2}$.

55.

$$\begin{aligned}64w^2 &= 48w - 9\\ 64w^2 - 48w + 9 &= 0\\ (8w-3)^2 &= 0\\ 8w - 3 &= 0\\ 8w &= 3\\ w &= \frac{3}{8}\end{aligned}$$

The only solution is $\frac{3}{8}$.

57. $h = -16t^2 + 20t + 300$

Substitute 0 for h and solve for t.

$$\begin{aligned}0 &= -16t^2 + 20t + 300\\ 16t^2 - 20t - 300 &= 0\\ 4t(4t^2 - 5t - 75) &= 0\\ 4t(4t+15)(t-5) &= 0\end{aligned}$$

$$4t + 15 = 0 \quad \text{or} \quad t - 5 = 0$$
$$4t = -15 \qquad t = 5$$
$$t = -\frac{15}{4}$$

Discard $t = -\frac{15}{4}$ since time cannot be negative. It will take 5 seconds for the ball to reach the ground.

59. Substitute 276 for h and solve for t.

$$\begin{aligned}276 &= -16t^2 + 20t + 300\\ 16t^2 - 20t - 24 &= 0\\ 4(4t^2 - 5t - 6) &= 0\\ 4(4t+3)(t-2) &= 0\end{aligned}$$

$$4t + 3 = 0 \quad \text{or} \quad t - 2 = 0$$
$$4t = -3 \qquad t = 2$$
$$t = -\frac{3}{4}$$

Discard $t = \frac{3}{4}$ since time cannot be negative. The ball's height will be 276 feet 2 seconds after it is thrown. This corresponds to the point $(2, 276)$ on the graph.

61. $h = -16t^2 + 72t$

Substitute 32 for h and solve for t.

$$\begin{aligned}32 &= -16t^2 + 72t\\ 16t^2 + 72t + 32 &= 0\\ 8(2t^2 + 9t + 4) &= 0\\ 8(2t-1)(t-4) &= 0\end{aligned}$$

$$2t - 1 = 0 \quad \text{or} \quad t - 4 = 0$$
$$t = \frac{1}{2} \qquad t = 4$$

The debris will be 32 feet above the ground $\frac{1}{2}$ second after the explosion and 4 seconds after the explosion.

63. $N = 2x^2 + 22x + 320$

Substitute 1100 for N and solve for x.

$$\begin{aligned}1100 &= 2x^2 + 22x + 320\\ 0 &= 2x^2 + 22x - 780\\ 0 &= 2(x^2 + 11x - 390)\\ 0 &= 2(x+26)(x-15)\end{aligned}$$

$$x + 26 = 0 \quad \text{or} \quad x - 15 = 0$$
$$x = -26 \qquad x = 15$$

Discard $x = -26$ because the model starts at $x = 0$ to represent 1980. Since $x = 15$ represents the year 1995, the model shows that there were 1100 thousand inmates in U.S state and federal prisons in 1995. This corresponds to the point $(15, 1100)$ on the graph.

65. $P = -10x^2 + 475x + 3500$

Substitute 7250 for P and solve for x.

$$
\begin{aligned}
7250 &= -10x^2 + 475x + 3500\\
10x^2 - 475x + 3750 &= 0\\
5(2x^2 - 95x + 750) &= 0\\
5(x-10)(2x-75) &= 0
\end{aligned}
$$

$$x - 10 = 0 \quad \text{or} \quad 2x - 75 = 0$$
$$x = 10 \qquad 2x = 75$$
$$x = \frac{75}{2} \text{ or } 37.5$$

The alligator population will have increased to 7250 after 10 years. (Discard 37.5 because this value is outside of $0 \le x \le 12$.)

67. The solution in Exercise 65 corresponds to the point $(10, 7250)$ on the graph.

69. $N = \dfrac{t^2 - t}{2}$

Substitute 45 for N and solve for t.

$$
\begin{aligned}
45 &= \frac{t^2 - t}{2}\\
2 \cdot 45 &= 2\left(\frac{t^2 - t}{2}\right)\\
90 &= t^2 - t\\
0 &= t^2 - t - 90\\
0 &= (t-10)(t+9)
\end{aligned}
$$

$$t - 10 = 0 \quad \text{or} \quad t + 9 = 0$$
$$t = 10 \qquad t = -9$$

Discard $t = -9$ since the number of teams cannot be negative. If 45 games are scheduled, there are 10 teams in the league.

71. Let $x =$ the width of the parking lot.
Then $x + 3 =$ the length.

$$
\begin{aligned}
l \cdot w &= A\\
(x+3)(x) &= 180\\
x^2 + 3x &= 180\\
x^2 + 3x - 180 &= 0\\
(x+15)(x-12) &= 0
\end{aligned}
$$

$$x + 15 = 0 \quad \text{or} \quad x - 12 = 0$$
$$x = -15 \qquad x = 12$$

Discard $x = -15$ since the width cannot be negative. Then $x = 12$ and $x+3 = 15$, so the length is 15 yards and the width is 12 yards.

73. Use the formula for the area of a triangle where x is the base and $x+1$ is the height.

$$
\begin{aligned}
\frac{1}{2}bh &= A\\
\frac{1}{2}x(x+1) &= 15\\
2\left[\frac{1}{2}x(x+1)\right] &= 2 \cdot 15\\
x(x+1) &= 30\\
x^2 + x &= 30\\
x^2 + x - 30 &= 0\\
(x+6)(x-5) &= 0
\end{aligned}
$$

$$x + 6 = 0 \quad \text{or} \quad x - 5 = 0$$
$$x = -6 \qquad x = 5$$

Discard $x = -6$ since the length of the base cannot be negative. Then $x = 5$ and $x+1 = 6$, so the base is 5 centimeters and the height is 6 centimeters.

75. a. Area of large rectangle

$$\begin{aligned}&(2x+12)(2x+10)\\&= 4x^2+20x+24x+120\\&= 4x^2+44x+120\end{aligned}$$

Area of flower bed $= 10 \cdot 12 = 120$

Area of border

$$\begin{aligned}&= (4x^2+44x+120)-120\\&= 4x^2+44x\end{aligned}$$

b. Find the width of the border for which the area of the border would be 168 square feet.

$$\begin{aligned}4x^2+44x &= 168\\4x^2+44x-168 &= 0\\4(x^2+11x-42) &= 0\\4(x+14)(x-3) &= 0\end{aligned}$$

$$x+14=0 \quad \text{or} \quad x-3=0$$
$$x=-14 \qquad\qquad x=3$$

Discard $x = -14$ since the width of the border cannot be negative. You should prepare a strip that is 3 feet wide for the border.

For Exercises 77–79, answers may vary.

81. If -3 and 5 are solutions of the quadratic equation, then $x-(-3) = x+3$ and $x-5$ must be factors of the polynomial on the left side when the quadratic equation is written in standard form.

$$\begin{aligned}(x+3)(x-5) &= 0\\x^2-5x+3x-15 &= 0\\x^2-2x-15 &= 0\end{aligned}$$

Thus, $x^2-2x-15=0$ is a quadratic equation in standard form whose solutions are -3 and 5.

83. $x^3+3x^2-10x=0$

This is a cubic equation (equation of degree 3), rather than a quadratic equation, but it can be solved by factoring following the same method that is used with quadratic equations.

$$\begin{aligned}x^3+3x^2-10x &= 0\\x(x^2+3x-10) &= 0\\x(x+5)(x-2) &= 0\end{aligned}$$

$$x=0 \quad \text{or} \quad x+5=0 \quad \text{or} \quad x-2=0$$
$$x=-5 \qquad\qquad x=2$$

The equation has three solutions, $0, -5$, and 2.

85. $(x^2-5x+5)^3 = 1$

The only number that can be cubed (raised to the third power) to give 1 is 1. Therefore, the given equation is equivalent to the quadratic equation

$$x^2-5x+5=1.$$

Solve this equation.

$$\begin{aligned}x^2-5x+4 &= 0\\(x-1)(x-4) &= 0\end{aligned}$$

$$x-1=0 \quad \text{or} \quad x-4=0$$
$$x=1 \qquad\qquad x=4$$

The solutions are 1 and 4.

87. $y = x^2 + x - 2$

To match this equation with its graph find the intercepts.

y-intercept:
Let $x = 0$ and solve for y.

$$y = 0^2 + 0 - 2$$
$$y = -2$$

The y-intercept is -2.

x-intercepts:
Let $y = 0$ and solve for x.

$$0 = x^2 + x - 2$$
$$0 = (x + 2)(x - 1)$$

$$x + 2 = 0 \quad \text{or} \quad x - 1 = 0$$
$$x = -2 \qquad\qquad x = 1$$

The x-intercepts are -2 and 1.
The only graph with y-intercept -2 and x-intercepts -2 and 1 is graph a.

89. $y = x^2 - 4x$

To match this equation with its graph, find the intercepts.

y-intercept:
Let $x = 0$ and solve for y.

$$y = 0^2 - 4(0) = 0$$

The y-intercept is 0, which means that the graph passes through the origin.

x-intercepts:
Let $y = 0$ and solve for x.

$$0 = x^2 - 4x$$
$$0 = x(x - 4)$$
$$x = 0 \quad \text{or} \quad x - 4 = 0$$
$$x = 4$$

The x-intercepts are 0 and 4.
The only graph with y-intercept 0 and x-intercepts 0 and 4 is graph b.

91. $y = x^2 + x - 6$
$x^2 + x - 6 = 0$

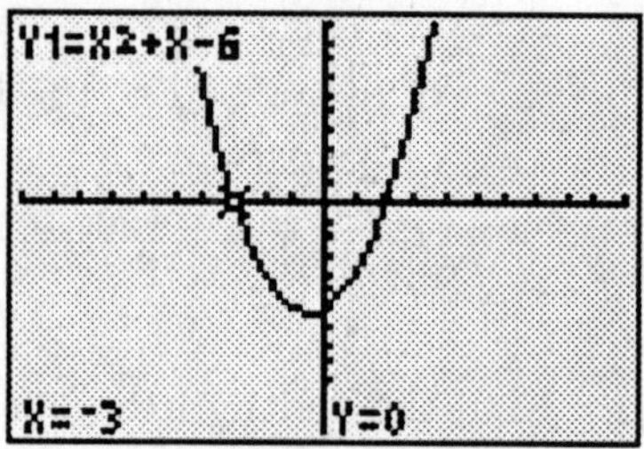

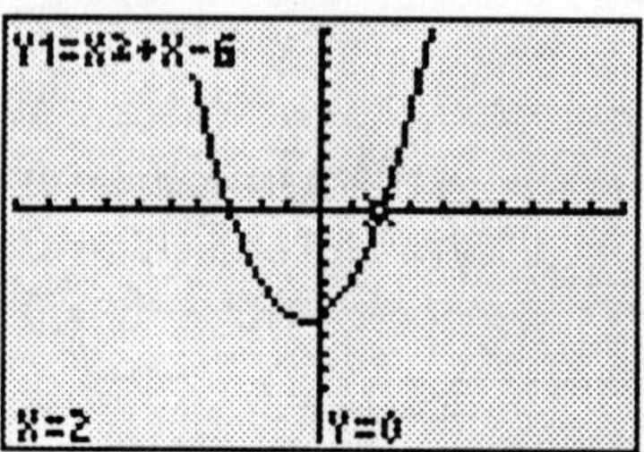

The calculator shows that the x-intercepts for the graph are -3 and 2. This means that the solutions of the equation $x^2 + x - 6 = 0$ are -3 and 2.

Check -3:

$$x^2 + x - 6 = 0$$
$$(-3)^2 + (-3) - 6 \stackrel{?}{=} 0$$
$$9 - 3 - 6 \stackrel{?}{=} 0$$
$$6 - 6 = 0$$
$$0 = 0 \text{ true}$$

Check 2:

$$x^2 + x - 6 = 0$$
$$2^2 + 2 - 6 \stackrel{?}{=} 0$$
$$4 + 2 - 6 \stackrel{?}{=} 0$$
$$6 - 6 \stackrel{?}{=} 0$$
$$0 = 0 \text{ true}$$

The check verify that the solutions of $x^2 + x - 6 = 0$ are -3 and 2.

93. $y = x^2 - 2x + 1$
$x^2 - 2x + 1 = 0$

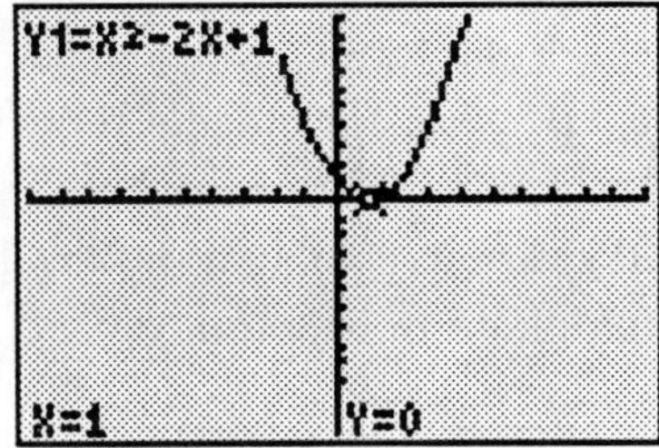

The calculator shows that the graph has one x-intercept, 1. This means that the only solution of the equation $x^2-2x+1 = 0$ is 1.

Check 1:

$$\begin{aligned} x^2 - 2x + 1 &= 0 \\ 1^2 - 2(1) + 1 &\stackrel{?}{=} 0 \\ 1 - 2 + 1 &\stackrel{?}{=} 0 \\ -1 + 1 &\stackrel{?}{=} 0 \\ 0 &= 0 \text{ true} \end{aligned}$$

The check verifies that the solution of $x^2 + 2x + 1$ is 1.

95. Answers will vary depending on the exercises chosen.

Review Exercises

96. $y > -\dfrac{2}{3}x + 1$

Graph $y = -\frac{2}{3}x + 1$ as a dashed line using the slope $-\frac{2}{3} = \frac{-2}{3}$ and y-intercept 1. (Plot $(0, 1)$ and move 2 units *down* and 3 units to the *right* to reach the point $(3, -1)$. Draw a line through $(0, 1)$ and $(3, -1)$.)

Use $(0, 0)$ as a test point. Since $0 > -\frac{2}{3}(0)+1$ is false, shade the half-plane *not* containing $(0, 0)$.

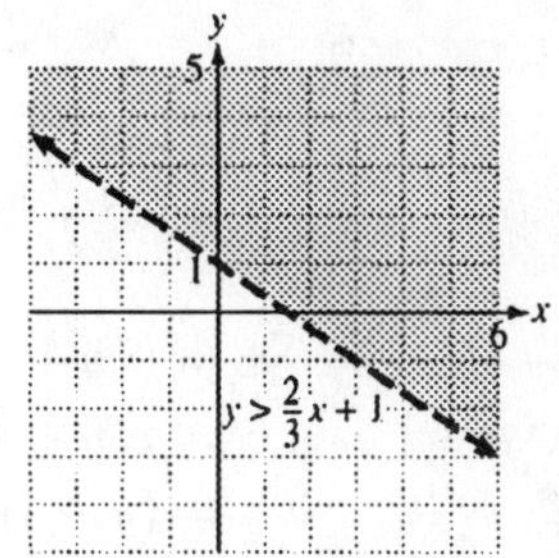

97. $\left(\dfrac{8x^4}{4x^7}\right)^2 = \left(\dfrac{8}{4} \cdot x^{4-7}\right) = (2x^{-3})^2$

$$= 2^2 \cdot (x^{-3})^2 = 4x^{-6} = \frac{4}{x^6}$$

98.

$$\begin{aligned} 5x + 28 &= 6 - 6x \\ 5x + 6x + 28 &= 6 - 6x + 6x \\ 11x + 28 &= 6 \\ 11x + 28 - 28 &= 6 - 28 \\ 11x &= -22 \\ \frac{11x}{11} &= \frac{-22}{11} \\ x &= -2 \end{aligned}$$

Chapter 7 Review Exercises

1. $30x - 45 = 15(2x - 3)$

2. $12x^3 + 16x^2 - 400x = 4x(3x^2 + 4x - 100)$

3. $30x^4y + 15x^3y + 5x^2y = 5x^2(6x^2 + 3x + 1)$

4. $\begin{aligned}[t] 7(x + 3) - 2(x + 3) &= (x + 3)(7 - 2) \\ &= (x + 3) \cdot 5 \text{ or } 5(x + 3) \end{aligned}$

5. $\begin{aligned}[t] 7x^2(x + y) - (x + y) &= 7x^2(x + y) - 1(x + y) \\ &= (x + y)(7x^2 - 1) \end{aligned}$

6. $\begin{aligned}[t] x^3 + 3x^2 + 2x + 6 &= (x^3 + 3x^2) + (2x + 6) \\ &= x^2(x + 3) + 2(x + 3) \\ &= (x + 3)(x^2 + 2) \end{aligned}$

7. $$\begin{aligned} xy + y + 4x + 4 &= (xy + y) + (4x + 4) \\ &= y(x+1) + 4(x+1) \\ &= (x+1)(y+4) \end{aligned}$$

8. $$\begin{aligned} x^3 + 5x + x^2 + 5 &= (x^3 + 5x) + (x^2 + 5) \\ &= x(x^2+5) + 1(x^2+5) \\ &= (x^2+5)(x+1) \end{aligned}$$

9. $$\begin{aligned} xy + 4x - 2y - 8 &= (xy + 4x) + (-2y - 8) \\ &= x(y+4) - 2(y+4) \\ &= (y+4)(x-2) \end{aligned}$$

10. $x^2 - 3x + 2 = (x-2)(x-1)$

11. $x^2 - x - 20 = (x-5)(x+4)$

12. $x^2 + 19x + 48 = (x+3)(x+16)$

13. $x^2 - 6xy + 8y^2 = (x-4y)(x-2y)$

14. $x^2 + 5x - 9$ is prime because there is no pair of integers whose product is -9 and whose sum is 5.

15. $x^2 + 16xy - 17y^2 = (x+17y)(x-y)$

16. $$\begin{aligned} 3x^2 + 6x - 24 &= 3(x^2 + 2x - 8) \\ &= 3(x+4)(x-2) \end{aligned}$$

17. $$\begin{aligned} 3x^3 - 36x^2 + 33x &= 3x(x^2 - 12x + 11) \\ &= 3x(x-11)(x-1) \end{aligned}$$

18. $3x^2 + 17x + 10$

Factor by trial and error or by grouping. To factor by grouping, find two integers whose product is $ac = 3 \cdot 10 = 30$ and whose sum is $b = 17$. These integers are 15 and 2.

$$\begin{aligned} 3x^2 + 17x + 10 &= 3x^2 + 15x + 2x + 10 \\ &= 3x(x+5) + 2(x+5) \\ &= (x+5)(3x+2) \end{aligned}$$

19. $5y^2 - 17y + 6$

Factor by trial and error or by grouping. To factor by trial and error, start with the First terms, which must be $5y$ and y. Because the middle term is negative, the factors of 6 must both be negative. Try various combinations until the correct middle term is obtained.

$$\begin{aligned} (5y-1)(y-6) &= 5y^2 - 31y + 6 \\ (5y-6)(y-1) &= 5y^2 - 11y + 6 \\ (5y-3)(y-2) &= 5y^2 - 13y + 6 \\ (5y-2)(y-3) &= 5y^2 - 17y + 6 \end{aligned}$$

Thus,

$$5y^2 - 17y + 6 = (5y-2)(y-3).$$

20. $4x^2 + 4x - 15 = (2x+5)(2x-3)$

21. $5y^2 + 11y + 4$

Use trial and error. The First terms must be $5y$ and 4. Because the middle term is positive, the factors of 4 must both be positive. Try various combinations.

$$\begin{aligned} (5y+2)(y+2) &= 5y^2 + 12y + 4 \\ (5y+4)(y+1) &= 5y^2 + 9y + 4 \\ (5y+1)(y+4) &= 5y^2 + 21y + 4 \end{aligned}$$

None of these possibilities gives the required middle term, $11x$, and there are no more possibilities to try, so $5y^2 + 11y + 4$ is prime.

22. $8x^2 + 8x - 6$

First factor out the GCF, 2. Then factor the resulting trinomial by trial and error or by grouping.

$$\begin{aligned} 8x^2 + 8x - 6 &= 2(4x^2 + 4x - 3) \\ &= 2(2x+3)(2x-1) \end{aligned}$$

23. $2x^3 + 7x^2 - 72x = x(2x^2 + 7x - 72)$
$= x(2x - 9)(x + 8)$

24. $12y^3 + 28y^2 + 8y = 4y(3y^2 + 7y + 2)$
$= 4y(3y + 1)(y + 2)$

25. $2x^2 - 7xy + 3y^2 = (2x - y)(x - 3y)$

26. $5x^2 - 6xy - 8y^2 = (5x + 4y)(x - 2y)$

27. $4x^2 - 1 = (2x)^2 - 1^2 = (2x + 1)(2x - 1)$

28. $81 - 100y^2 = 9^2 - (10y)^2$
$= (9 + 10y)(9 - 10y)$

29. $25a^2 - 49b^2 = (5a)^2 - (7b)^2$
$= (5a + 7b)(5a - 7b)$

30. $z^4 - 16 = (z^2)^2 - 4^2$
$= (z^2 + 4)(z^2 - 4)$
$= (z^2 + 4)(z + 2)(z - 2)$

31. $2x^2 - 18 = 2(x^2 - 9) = 2(x + 3)(x - 3)$

32. $x^2 + 1$ is prime because it is the sum of two squares with no common factor other than 1.

33. $9x^3 - x = x(9x^2 - 1) = x(3x + 1)(3x - 1)$

34. $18xy^2 - 8x = 2x(9y^2 - 4)$
$= 2x(3y + 2)(3y - 2)$

35. $x^2 + 22x + 121 = x^2 + 2 \cdot x \cdot 11 + 11^2$
$= (x + 11)^2$

36. $x^2 - 16x + 64 = x^2 - 2 \cdot x \cdot 8 + 8^2$
$= (x - 8)^2$

37. $9y^2 + 48y + 64 = (3y)^2 + 2 \cdot 3y \cdot 8 + 8^2$
$= (3y + 8)^2$

38. $16x^2 - 40x + 25 = (4x)^2 - 2 \cdot 4x \cdot 5 + 5^2$
$= (4x - 5)^2$

39. $25x^2 + 15x + 9$ is prime.
(To be a perfect square trinomial, the middle term would have to be $30x$.)

40. $36x^2 + 60xy + 25y^2$
$= (6x)^2 + 2 \cdot 6x \cdot 5y + (5y)^2$
$= (6x + 5y)^2$

41. $25x^2 - 40xy + 16y^2$
$= (5x)^2 - 2 \cdot 5x \cdot 4y + (4y)^2$
$= (5x - 4y)^2$

42. $x^3 - 27 = x^3 - 3^2 = (x - 3)(x^2 + 3x + 9)$

43. $64x^3 + 1$
$= (4x)^3 + 1^3$
$= (4x + 1)[(4x)^2 - 4x \cdot 1 + 1^2]$
$= (4x + 1)(16x^2 - 4x + 1)$

44. $54x^3 - 16y^3$
$= 2(27x^3 - 8y^3)$
$= 2[(3x)^3 - (2y)^3]$
$= 2(3x - 2y)[(3x)^2 + 3x \cdot 2y + (2y)^2]$
$= 2(3x - 2y)(9x^2 + 6xy + 4y^2)$

45. $27x^3y + 8y$
$= y(27x^3 + 8)$
$= y[(3x)^3 + 2^3]$
$= y(3x + 2)[(3x)^2 - 3x \cdot 2 + 2^2]$
$= y(3x + 2)(9x^2 - 6x + 4)$

46. Area of outer square $= a^2$
Area of inner square $= 3^2 = 9$
Area of shaded region $= a^2 - 9$
$= (a + 3)(a - 3)$

47. Area of large square $= a^2$
Area of each small (corner) square $= b^2$
Area of four corner squares $= 4b^2$
Area of shaded region $= a^2 - 4b^2$
$= (a + 2b)(a - 2b)$

48. Area on the left:
Area of large square $= A^2$
Area of each rectangle: $A \cdot 1 = A$
Area of two rectangles $= 2A$
Area of small square $= 1^2 = 1$

On the right:
Area of square $= (A+1)^2$

This geometric model illustrates the factorization

$$A^2 + 2A + 1 = (A+1)^2.$$

49. $x^3 - 8x^2 + 7x = x(x^2 - 8x + 7)$
$= x(x-7)(x-1)$

50. $10y^2 + 9y + 2 = (5y+2)(2y+1)$

51. $128 - 2y^2 = 2(64 - y^2)$
$= 2(8+y)(8-y)$

52. $9x^2 + 6x + 1 = (3x)^2 + 2 \cdot 3x \cdot 1 + 1^2$
$= (3x+1)^2$

53. $20x^7 - 36x^3 = 4x^3(5x^4 - 9)$

54. $x^3 - 3x^2 - 9x + 27$
$= (x^3 - 3x^2) + (-9x + 27)$
$= x^2(x-3) - 9(x-3)$
$= (x-3)(x^2-9)$
$= (x-3)(x+3)(x-3)$
$= (x-3)^2(x+3)$

55. $y^2 + 16$ is prime because it is the sum of two squares with no common factor other than 1.

56. $2x^3 + 19x^2 + 35x = x(2x^2 + 19x + 35)$
$= x(2x+5)(x+7)$

57. $3x^3 - 30x^2 + 75x = 3x(x^2 - 10x + 25)$
$= 3x(x-5)^2$

58. $3x^5 - 24x^2 = 3x^2(x^3 - 8)$
$= 3x^2(x^3 - 2^3)$
$= 3x^2(x-2)(x^2 + 2x + 4)$

59. $4y^4 - 36y^2 = 4y^2(y^2 - 9)$
$= 4y^2(y+3)(y-3)$

60. $5x^2 + 20x - 105 = 5(x^2 + 4x - 21)$
$= 5(x+7)(x-3)$

61. $9x^2 + 8x - 3$ is prime.

62. $10x^5 - 44x^2 + 16x^3 = 2x^3(5x^2 - 22x + 8)$
$= 2x^3(5x-2)(x-4)$

63. $100y^2 - 49 = (10y)^2 - 7^2$
$= (10y+7)(10y-7)$

64. $9x^5 - 18x^4 = 9x^4(x-2)$

65. $x^4 - 1 = (x^2)^2 - 1^2$
$= (x^2+1)(x^2-1)$
$= (x^2+1)(x+1)(x-1)$

66. $2y^3 - 16 = 2(y^3 - 8)$
$= 2(y^3 - 2^3)$
$= 2(y-2)(y^2 + 2y + 2^2)$
$= 2(y-2)(y^2 + 2y + 4)$

67. $x^3 + 64 = x^3 + 4^3$
$= (x+4)(x^2 - 4x + 4^2)$
$= (x+4)(x^2 - 4x + 16)$

68. $6x^2 + 11x - 10 = (3x-2)(2x+5)$

69. $3x^4 - 12x^2 = 3x^2(x^2 - 4)$
$= 3x^2(x+2)(x-2)$

70. $x^2 - x - 90 = (x-10)(x+9)$

71. $25x^2 + 25xy + 6y^2 = (5x+2y)(5x+3y)$

72. $x^4 + 125x = x(x^3 + 125)$
$= x(x^3 + 5^3)$
$= x(x+5)(x^2 - 5x + 5^2)$
$= x(x+5)(x^2 - 5x + 25)$

73. $32y^3 + 32y^2 + 6y = 2y(16y^2 + 16y + 3)$
$= 2y(4y+3)(4y+1)$

74. $2y^2 - 16y + 32 = 2(y^2 - 8y + 16)$
$= 2(y-4)^2$

75. $x^2 - 2xy - 35y^2 = (x+5y)(x-7y)$

76. $x^2 + 7x + xy + 7y = x(x+7) + y(x+7)$
$= (x+7)(x+y)$

77. $9x^2 + 24xy + 16y^2$
$= (3x)^2 + 2 \cdot 3x \cdot 4y + (4y)^2$
$= (3x+4y)^2$

78. $2x^4y - 2x^2y = 2x^2y(x^2-1)$
$= 2x^2y(x+1)(x-1)$

79. $100y^2 - 49z^2 = (10y)^2 - (7z)^2$
$= (10y+7z)(10y-7z)$

80. $x^2 + xy + y^2$ is prime.
(To be a perfect square trinomial, the middle term would have to be $2xy$.)

81. $3x^4y^2 - 12x^2y^4 = 3x^2y^2(x^2 - 4y^2)$
$= 3x^2y^2(x+2y)(x-2y)$

82. $x(x-12) = 0$
$x = 0$ or $x - 12 = 0$
$x = 12$

The solutions are 0 and 12.

83. $3(x-7)(4x+9) = 0$
$x - 7 = 0$ or $4x + 9 = 0$
$x = 7$ $\quad 4x = -9$
$x = -\frac{9}{4}$

The solutions are 7 and $-\frac{9}{4}$.

84. $x^2 + 5x - 14 = 0$
$(x+7)(x-2) = 0$
$x + 7 = 0$ or $x - 2 = 0$
$x = -7$ $\quad x = 2$

The solutions are -7 and 2.

85. $5x^2 + 20x = 0$
$5x(x+4) = 0$
$5x = 0$ or $x + 4 = 0$
$x = 0$ $\quad x = -4$

The solutions are 0 and -4.

86. $2x^2 + 15x = 8$
$2x^2 + 15x - 8 = 0$
$(2x-1)(x+8) = 0$
$2x - 1 = 0$ or $x + 8 = 0$
$2x = 1$ $\quad x = -8$
$x = \frac{1}{2}$

The solutions are $\frac{1}{2}$ and -8.

87. $x(x-4) = 32$
$x^2 - 4x = 32$
$x^2 - 4x - 32 = 0$
$(x+4)(x-8) = 0$
$x + 4 = 0$ or $x - 8 = 0$
$x = -4$ $\quad x = 8$

The solutions are -4 and 8.

88. $(x+3)(x-2) = 50$
$x^2 + x - 6 = 50$
$x^2 + x - 56 = 0$
$(x+8)(x-7) = 0$
$x + 8 = 0$ or $x - 7 = 0$
$x = -8$ $\quad x = 7$

The solutions are -8 and 7.

89. $x^2 = 14x - 49$
$x^2 - 14x + 49 = 0$
$(x-7)^2 = 0$
$x - 7 = 0$
$x = 7$

The only solution is 7.

90.
$$9x^2 = 100$$
$$9x^2 - 100 = 0$$
$$(3x+10)(3x-10) = 0$$
$$3x + 10 = 0 \quad \text{or} \quad 3x - 10 = 0$$
$$3x = -10 \qquad 3x = 10$$
$$x = -\frac{10}{3} \qquad x = \frac{10}{3}$$

The solutions are $-\frac{10}{3}$ and $\frac{10}{3}$.

91.
$$3x^2 + 21x + 30 = 0$$
$$3(x^2 + 7x + 10) = 0$$
$$3(x+5)(x+2) = 0$$
$$x + 5 = 0 \quad \text{or} \quad x + 2 = 0$$
$$x = -5 \qquad x = -2$$

The solutions are -5 and -2.

92.
$$3x^2 = 22x - 7$$
$$3x^2 - 22x + 7 = 0$$
$$(3x - 1)(x - 7) = 0$$
$$3x - 1 = 0 \quad \text{or} \quad x - 7 = 0$$
$$3x = 1 \qquad x = 7$$
$$x = \frac{1}{3}$$

The solutions are $\frac{1}{3}$ and 7.

93. $h = -16t^2 + 16t + 32$

Substitute 0 for h and solve for t.

$$0 = -16t^2 + 16t + 32$$
$$16t^2 - 16t - 32 = 0$$
$$16(t^2 - t - 2) = 0$$
$$16(t+1)(t-2) = 0$$

$$t = 1 = 0 \quad \text{or} \quad t - 2 = 0$$
$$t = -1 \qquad t = 2$$

Because time cannot be negative, discard the solution $t = -1$. The solution $t = 2$ indicates that you will hit the water after 2 seconds.

94. Let $x =$ the width of the sign.
Then $x + 3 =$ the length of the floor.

Use the formula for the area of a rectangle.

$$l \cdot w = A$$
$$(x+3)(x) = 40$$
$$x^2 + 3x = 40$$
$$x^2 + 3x - 40 = 0$$
$$(x+8)(x-5) = 0$$
$$x + 8 = 0 \quad \text{or} \quad x - 5 = 0$$
$$x = -8 \qquad x = 5$$

A rectangle cannot have a negative length. Thus, $x = 5$ and $x + 3 = 8$. The length of the sign is 8 feet and the width is 5 feet. This solution checks because

$$A = lw = (9 \text{ feet})(6 \text{ feet})$$
$$= 54 \text{ square feet.}$$

95. Area of garden $= x(x-3) = 88$

$$x(x-3) = 88$$
$$x^2 - 3x = 88$$
$$x^2 - 3x - 88 = 0$$
$$(x - 11)(x + 8) = 0$$
$$x - 11 = 0 \quad \text{or} \quad x + 8 = 0$$
$$x = 11 \qquad x = -8$$

Because a length cannot be negative, discard $x = -8$. Each side of the square lot is 11 meters, that is, the dimensions of the square lot are 11 meters by 11 meters.

Chapter 7 Test

1. $x^2 - 9x + 18 = (x-3)(x-6)$

2. $$\begin{aligned} x^2 - 14x + 49 &= x^2 - 2 \cdot x \cdot 7 + 7^2 \\ &= (x-7)^2 \end{aligned}$$

3. $$\begin{aligned} 15y^4 - 35y^3 + 10y^2 &= 5y^2(3y^2 - 7y + 2) \\ &= 5y^2(3y-1)(y-2) \end{aligned}$$

4. $$\begin{aligned} x^3 + 2x^2 + 3x + 6 &= (x^3 + 2x^2) + (3x + 6) \\ &= x^2(x+2) + 3(x+2) \\ &= (x+2)(x^2+3) \end{aligned}$$

5. $x^2 - 9x = x(x-9)$

6. $$\begin{aligned} x^3 + 6x^2 - 7x &= x(x^2 + 6x - 7) \\ &= x(x+7)(x-1) \end{aligned}$$

7. $$\begin{aligned} 14x^2 + 64x - 30 &= 2(7x^2 + 32x - 15) \\ &= 2(7x-3)(x+5) \end{aligned}$$

8. $$\begin{aligned} 25x^2 - 9 &= (5x)^2 - 3^2 \\ &= (5x+3)(5x-3) \end{aligned}$$

9. $$\begin{aligned} x^3 + 8 = x^3 + 2^3 &= (x+2)(x^2 - 2x + 2^2) \\ &= (x+2)(x^2 - 2x + 4) \end{aligned}$$

10. $x^2 - 4x - 21 = (x+3)(x-7)$

11. $x^2 + 4$ is prime.

12. $$\begin{aligned} 6y^3 + 9y^2 + 3y &= 3y(2y^2 + 3y + 1) \\ &= 3y(2y+1)(y+1) \end{aligned}$$

13. $4y^2 - 36 = 4(y^2 - 9) = 4(y+3)(y-3)$

14. $$\begin{aligned} &16x^2 + 48x + 36 \\ &= 4(4x^2 + 12x + 9) \\ &= 4[(2x)^2 + 2 \cdot 4x \cdot 3 + 3^2] \\ &= 4(2x+3)^2 \end{aligned}$$

15. $$\begin{aligned} 2x^4 - 32 &= 2(x^4 - 16) \\ &= 2(x^2+4)(x^2-4) \\ &= 2(x^2+4)(x+2)(x-2) \end{aligned}$$

16. $$\begin{aligned} 36x^2 - 84x + 49 &= (6x)^2 - 2 \cdot 6x \cdot 7 + 7^2 \\ &= (6x-7)^2 \end{aligned}$$

17. $7x^2 - 50x + 7 = (7x-1)(x-7)$

18. $$\begin{aligned} x^3 + 2x^2 - 5x - 10 &= (x^3 + 2x^2) + (-5x - 10) \\ &= x^2(x+2) - 5(x+2) \\ &= (x+2)(x^2-5) \end{aligned}$$

19. $$\begin{aligned} 12y^3 - 12y^2 - 45y &= 3y(4y^2 - 4y - 15) \\ &= 3y(2y+3)(2y-5) \end{aligned}$$

20. $$\begin{aligned} y^3 - 125 &= y^3 - 5^3 \\ &= (y-5)(y^2 + 5y + 5^2) \\ &= (y-5)(y^2 + 5y + 25) \end{aligned}$$

21. $$\begin{aligned} 5x^2 - 5xy - 30y^2 &= 5(x^2 - xy - 6y^2) \\ &= 5(x-3y)(x+2y) \end{aligned}$$

22. $$\begin{aligned} x^2 + 2x - 24 &= 0 \\ (x+6)(x-4) &= 0 \\ x + 6 = 0 \quad &\text{or} \quad x - 4 = 0 \\ x = -6 \quad & \quad\quad x = 4 \end{aligned}$$

The solutions are -6 and 4.

23. $$\begin{aligned} 3x^2 - 5x &= 2 \\ 3x^2 - 5x - 2 &= 0 \\ (3x+1)(x-2) &= 0 \\ 3x + 1 = 0 \quad &\text{or} \quad x - 2 = 0 \\ 3x = -1 \quad & \quad\quad x = 2 \\ x = -\frac{1}{3} \quad & \end{aligned}$$

The solutions are $-\frac{1}{3}$ and 2.

24. $$\begin{aligned} x(x-6) &= 16 \\ x^2 - 6x &= 16 \\ x^2 - 6x - 16 &= 0 \\ (x+2)(x-8) &= 0 \\ x + 2 = 0 \quad &\text{or} \quad x - 8 = 0 \\ x = -2 \quad & \quad\quad x = 8 \end{aligned}$$

The solutions are -2 and 8.

25.
$$\begin{aligned}
6x^2 &= 21x\\
6x^2 - 21x &= 0\\
3x(2x-7) &= 0
\end{aligned}$$
$$3x = 0 \quad \text{or} \quad 2x - 7 = 0$$
$$x = 0 \qquad 2x = 7$$
$$x = \frac{7}{2}$$

The solutions are 0 and $\frac{7}{2}$.

26.
$$\begin{aligned}
16x^2 &= 81\\
16x^2 - 81 &= 0\\
(4x+9)(4x-9) &= 0
\end{aligned}$$
$$4x + 9 = 0 \quad \text{or} \quad 4x - 9 = 0$$
$$4x = -9 \qquad 4x = 9$$
$$x = -\frac{9}{4} \qquad x = \frac{9}{4}$$

The solutions are $-\frac{9}{4}$ and $\frac{9}{4}$.

27.
$$\begin{aligned}
(5x+4)(x-1) &= 2\\
5x^2 - x - 4 &= 2\\
5x^2 - x - 6 &= 0\\
(5x-6)(x+1) &= 0
\end{aligned}$$
$$5x - 6 = 0 \quad \text{or} \quad x + 1 = 0$$
$$5x = 6$$
$$x = \frac{6}{5} \qquad x = -1$$

The solutions are $\frac{6}{5}$ and -1.

28. Area of large square $= x^2$
Area of each small (corner) square $= 1^2 = 1$
Area of four corner squares $= 4$
Area of shaded region $= x^2 - 4$
$= (x+2)(x-2)$

29. $h = -16t^2 + 80t + 96$

Substitute 96 for h and solve for t.

$$\begin{aligned}
0 &= -16t^2 + 80t + 96\\
16t^2 - 80t - 96 &= 0\\
16(t^2 - 5t - 6) &= 0\\
16(t-6)(t+1) &= 0
\end{aligned}$$
$$t - 6 = 0 \quad \text{or} \quad t + 1 = 0$$
$$t = 6 \qquad t = -1$$

Since time cannot be negative, discard $t = -1$. The rocket will reach the ground after 6 seconds.

30. Let $x =$ the width of the garden.
Then $x + 6 =$ the width.

$$\begin{aligned}
(x+6)(x) &= 55\\
x^2 + 6x &= 55\\
x^2 + 6x - 55 &= 0\\
(x+11)(x-5) &= 0
\end{aligned}$$
$$x + 11 = 0 \quad \text{or} \quad x - 5 = 0$$
$$x = -11 \qquad x = 5$$

Since the width cannot be negative, discard $x = 11$. Then $x = 5$ and $x + 6 = 11$, so the length is 11 feet and the width is 5 feet.

Chapter 7 Cumulative Review Exercises (Chapters 1-7)

1.
$$\begin{aligned}
6[5 + 2(3-8) - 3] &= 6[5 + 2(-5) - 3]\\
&= 6[5 - 10 - 3]\\
&= 6(-8) = -48
\end{aligned}$$

2.
$$\begin{aligned}
4(x-2) &= 2(x-4) + 3x\\
4x - 8 &= 2x - 8 + 3x\\
4x - 8 &= 5x - 8\\
4x - 5x &= -8 + 8\\
-x &= 0\\
x &= 0
\end{aligned}$$

The solution is 0.

3.
$$\frac{x}{2} - 1 = \frac{x}{3} + 1$$
$$6\left(\frac{x}{2} - 1\right) = 6\left(\frac{x}{3} + 1\right)$$
$$3x - 6 = 2x + 6$$
$$3x - 2x = 6 + 6$$
$$x = 12$$

The solution is 12.

4.
$$5 - 5x > 2(5 - x) + 1$$
$$5 - 5x > 10 - 2x + 1$$
$$5 - 5x > 11 - 2x$$
$$5 - 5x + 2x > 11 - 2x + 2x$$
$$5 - 3x > 11$$
$$5 - 3x - 5 > 11 - 5$$
$$-3x > 6$$
$$\frac{-3x}{-3} < \frac{6}{-3}$$
$$x < -2$$

Solution set: $\{x | x < -2\}$

-5 -4 -3 -2 -1 0 1 2 3 4 5

5. Let x = the measure of each of the base angles.
Then $3x - 10$ = the measure of the three angles of any triangle is 180°, so

$$x + x + (3x - 10) = 180.$$

Solve this equation.

$$5x - 10 = 180$$
$$5x = 190$$
$$x = 38$$

If $x = 38, 3x - 10 = 3(38) - 10 = 104$.
The measures of the three angles of the triangle are 38°, 38°, and 104°.

6. Let x = the cost of the dinner before tax.

$$x + 0.06x = 159$$
$$1.06x = 159$$
$$\frac{1.06x}{1.06} = \frac{159}{1.06}$$
$$x \approx 150$$

The cost of the dinner before tax was \$150.

7. $y = -\frac{3}{5}x + 2$

slope $= -\frac{3}{5} = \frac{-3}{5}$; y-intercept $= 2$
Plot $(0, 3)$. From this point, move 3 units *down* (because -3 is negative) and 5 units to the *right* to reach the point $(5, 0)$. Draw a line through $(0, 3)$ and $(5, 0)$.

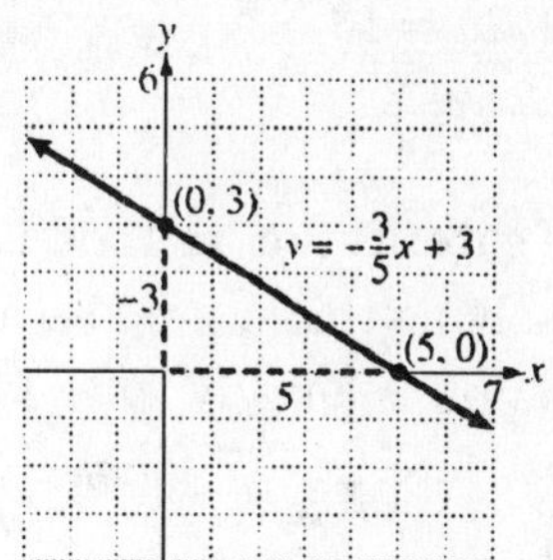

8. Line passing through $(2, -4)$ and $(3, 1)$

$$m = \frac{1 - (-4)}{3 - 2} = \frac{5}{1} = 5$$

Use the point $(2, -4)$ in the point-slope equation.

$$y - y_1 = m(x - x_1)$$
$$y - (-4) = 5(x - 2)$$
$$y + 4 = 5(x - 2)$$

Rewrite this equation in slope-intercept form.

$$y + 4 = 5x - 10$$
$$y = 5x - 14$$

9. $5x - 6y > 30$

Graph $5x - 6y = 30$ as a dashed line through $(6, 0)$ and $(0, -5)$. Use $(0, 0)$ as a test point. Since $0 - 0 > 30$ is false, shade the half-plane *not* containing $(0, 0)$.

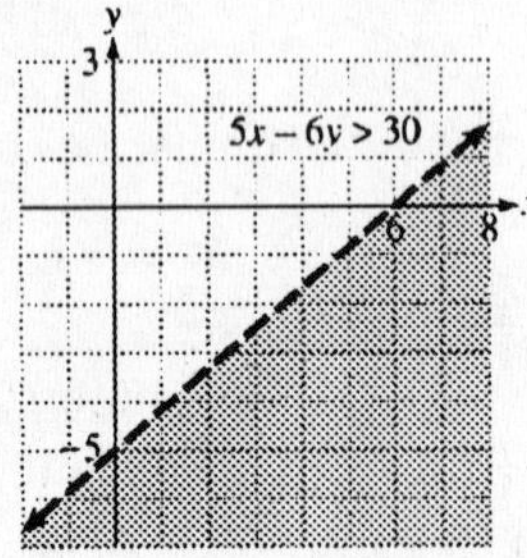

10. $5x + 2y = 13$
$y = 2x - 7$

The substitution method is a good choice for solving this system because the second equation is already solve for y.
Substitute $2x - 7$ for y in the first equation.

$$\begin{aligned} 5x + 2y &= 13 \\ 5x + 2(2x - 7) &= 13 \\ 5x + 4x - 14 &= 13 \\ 9x - 14 &= 13 \\ 9x &= 27 \\ x &= 3 \end{aligned}$$

Back-substitute into the second given equation.

$$y = 2x - 7$$

$$y = 2(3) - 7 = -1$$

Solution: $(3, -1)$

11. $2x + 3y = 5$
$3x - 2y = -4$

The addition method is a good choice for solving this system because both equations are written in the form $Ax + By = C$.
Multiply equation 1 by 2 and equation 2 by 3; then add the results.

$$\begin{aligned} 4x + 6y &= 10 \\ 9x - 6y &= -12 \\ \hline 13x \quad &= -2 \\ x &= -\frac{2}{13} \end{aligned}$$

Instead of back-substituting $-\frac{2}{13}$ and working with fractions, go back to the original system and eliminate x. Multiply equation 1 by 3 and equation 2 by -2; then add the results.

$$\begin{aligned} 6x + 9y &= 15 \\ -6x + 4y &= 8 \\ \hline 13y &= 23 \\ y &= \frac{23}{3} \end{aligned}$$

Solution: $\left(-\frac{2}{13}, \frac{23}{3}\right)$

12. $\frac{4}{5} - \frac{9}{8} = \frac{4}{5} \cdot \frac{8}{8} - \frac{9}{8} \cdot \frac{5}{5}$
$= \frac{32}{40} - \frac{45}{40} = -\frac{13}{40}$

13. $\frac{6x^5 - 3x^4 + 9x^2 + 27x}{3x}$
$= \frac{6x^5}{3x} - \frac{3x^4}{3x} + \frac{9x^2}{3x} + \frac{27x}{3x}$
$= 2x^4 - x^3 + 3x + 9$

14. $(3x - 5y)(2x + 9y)$
$= 6x^2 + 27xy - 10xy - 45y^2$
$= 6x^2 + 17xy - 45y^2$

15.

$$\begin{array}{r} 2x^2 + 5x - 3 \\ 3x-5\overline{)6x^3 + 5x^2 - 34x + 13} \\ \underline{6x^3 - 10x^2} \qquad\qquad \\ 15x^2 - 34x \qquad \\ \underline{15x^2 - 25x} \qquad \\ -9x + 13 \\ \underline{-9x + 15} \\ -2 \end{array}$$

$$\frac{6x^3 + 5x^2 - 34x + 13}{3x - 5} = 2x^2 + 5x + 3 + \frac{-20}{3x - 5}$$

$$\text{or} \quad 2x^2 + 5x + 3 - \frac{20}{3x - 5}$$

16. To write 0.0071 in scienific notation, move the decimal point 3 places to the right. Because the given number is between 0 and 1, the exponent will be negative.

$$0.0071 = 7.1 \times 10^{-3}$$

17. $3x^2 + 11x + 6$

Factor by trial and error by grouping. To factor by grouping, find two integers whose product is $ac = 3 \cdot 6 = 18$ and whose sum is $b = 11$. These integers are 9 and 2.

$$\begin{aligned} 3x^2 + 11x + 6 &= 3x^2 + 9x + 2x + 6 \\ &= 3x(x + 3) + 2(x + 3) \\ &= (x + 3)(3x + 2) \end{aligned}$$

18. $\begin{aligned}[t] y^5 - 16y &= y(y^4 - 16) \\ &= y(y^2 + 4)(y^2 - 4) \\ &= y(y^2 + 4)(y + 2)(y - 2) \end{aligned}$

19. $\begin{aligned}[t] 4x^2 + 12x + 9 &= (2x)^2 + 2 \cdot 2x \cdot 3 + 3^2 \\ &= (2x + 3)^2 \end{aligned}$

20. Let $x =$ the width of the rectangle. Then $x + 2 =$ the length.

Use the formula for the area of a rectangle.

$$\begin{aligned} l \cdot w &= A \\ (x + 2)(x) &= 24 \\ x^2 + 2x &= 24 \\ x^2 + 2x - 24 &= 0 \\ (x + 6)(x - 4) &= 0 \end{aligned}$$

$$x + 6 = 0 \quad \text{or} \quad x - 4 = 0$$
$$x = -6 \qquad\qquad x = 4$$

Discard -6 because the width cannot be negative. Then $x = 4$ and $x + 2 = 6$, so the length is 6 feet and the width is 4 feet. The dimensions of the rectangle are 6 feet by 4 feet.

Chapter 8

RATIONAL EXPRESSIONS

8.1 Rational Expressions and Their Simplification

8.1 CHECK POINTS

CHECK POINT 1

a. $\frac{7x-28}{8x-40}$

Set the denominator equal to 0 and solve for x.

$$8x - 40 = 0$$
$$8x = 40$$
$$x = 5$$

The rational expression is undefined for $x = 5$.

b. $\frac{8x-40}{x^2+3x-28}$

Set the denominator equal to 0 and solve for x.

$$x^2 + 3x - 28 = 0$$
$$(x+7)(x-4) = 0$$

$$x + 7 = 0 \quad \text{or} \quad x - 4 = 0$$
$$x = -7 \qquad\qquad x = 4$$

The rational expression is undefined for $x = -7$ and $x = 4$.

CHECK POINT 2

$$\frac{7x+28}{21x} = \frac{\overset{1}{\cancel{7}}(x+4)}{\underset{1}{\cancel{7}}\cdot 3x} = \frac{x+4}{3x}$$

CHECK POINT 3

$$\frac{x^3-x^2}{7x-7} = \frac{x^2(x-1)}{7(x-1)} = \frac{x^2}{7},\ x \neq 1$$

CHECK POINT 4

$$\frac{x^2-1}{x^2+2x+1} = \frac{(x+1)(x-1)}{(x+1)(x+1)} = \frac{x-1}{x+1}$$

CHECK POINT 5

$$\frac{9x^2-49}{28-12x} = \frac{(3x+7)(3x-7)}{4(7x-3)}$$
$$= \frac{(3x+7)(3x-7)}{4(7x-3)}$$
$$= \frac{-(3x+7)}{4} \quad \text{or} \quad -\frac{3x+7}{4}$$
$$\text{or} \quad \frac{-3x-7}{4}$$

EXERCISE SET 8.1

1. $\frac{7}{2x}$

Set the denominator equal to 0 and solve for x.

$$2x = 0$$
$$x = 0$$

The rational expression is undefined for $x = 0$.

3. $\frac{x}{x-7}$

Set the denominator equal to 0 and solve for x.

$$x - 7 = 0$$
$$x = 7$$

The rational expression is undefined for $x = 7$.

5. $\dfrac{7}{5x-15}$

$$\begin{aligned} 5x - 15 &= 0 \\ 5x &= 15 \\ x &= 3 \end{aligned}$$

The rational expression is undefined for $x = 3$.

7. $\dfrac{x+4}{(x+7)(x-3)}$

$$(x+7)(x-3) = 0$$
$$x + 7 = 0 \quad \text{or} \quad x - 3 = 0$$
$$x = -7 \qquad\qquad x = 3$$

The rational expression is undefined for $x = -7$ and $x = 3$.

9. $\dfrac{13x}{(3x-15)(x+2)}$

$$(3x-15)(x+2) = 0$$
$$3x - 15 = 0 \quad \text{or} \quad x + 2 = 0$$
$$3x = 15 \qquad\qquad x = -2$$
$$x = 5$$

The rational expression is undefined for $x = 5$ and $x = -2$.

11. $\dfrac{x+5}{x^2+x-12}$

$$x^2 + x - 12 = 0$$
$$(x+4)(x-3) = 0$$
$$x + 4 = 0 \quad \text{or} \quad x - 3 = 0$$
$$x = -4 \qquad\qquad x = 3$$

The rational expression is undefined for $x = -4$ and $x = 3$.

13. $\dfrac{x+5}{5}$

Because the denominator, 5, is not zero for any value of x, the rational expression is defined for all real numbers.

15. $\dfrac{y+3}{4y^2+y-3}$

$$4y^2 + y - 3 = 0$$
$$(y+1)(4y-3) = 0$$
$$y + 1 = 0 \quad \text{or} \quad 4y - 3 = 0$$
$$y = -1 \qquad\qquad 4y = 3$$
$$y = \frac{3}{4}$$

The rational expression is undefined for $y = -1$ and $y = \frac{3}{4}$.

17. $\dfrac{y+5}{y^2-25}$

$$y^2 - 25 = 0$$
$$(y+5)(y-5) = 0$$
$$y + 5 = 0 \quad \text{or} \quad y - 5 = 0$$
$$y = -5 \qquad\qquad y = 5$$

The rational expression is undefined for $y = -5$ and $y = 5$.

19. $\dfrac{5}{x^2+1}$

The smallest possible value of x^2 is 0, so $x^2 + 1 \geq 1$ for all real numbers x. This means that there is no real number x for which $x^2 + 1 = 0$. Thus, the rational expression is defined for all real numbers.

21. $\dfrac{14x^2}{7x} = \dfrac{2 \cdot 7 \cdot x \cdot x}{7 \cdot x} = 2x$

23. $\dfrac{5x-15}{25} = \dfrac{5(x-3)}{5 \cdot 5} = \dfrac{x-3}{5}$

25. $\dfrac{2x-8}{4x} = \dfrac{2(x-4)}{2 \cdot 2x} = \dfrac{x-4}{2x}$

27. $\dfrac{3}{3x-9} = \dfrac{3}{3(x-3)} = \dfrac{1}{x-3}$

29. $\dfrac{-15}{3x-9}=\dfrac{-15}{3(x-3)}=\dfrac{-5}{x-3}$ or $-\dfrac{5}{x-3}$

31. $\dfrac{3x+9}{x+3}=\dfrac{3(x+3)}{x+3}=3$

33. $\dfrac{x+5}{x^2-25}=\dfrac{x+5}{(x+5)(x-5)}=\dfrac{1}{x-5}$

35. $\dfrac{2y-10}{3y-15}=\dfrac{2(y-5)}{3(y-5)}=\dfrac{2}{3}$

37. $\dfrac{x+1}{x^2-2x-3}=\dfrac{x+1}{(x+1)(x-3)}=\dfrac{1}{x-3}$

39. $\dfrac{4x-8}{x^2-4x+4}=\dfrac{4(x-2)}{(x-2)(x-2)}=\dfrac{4}{x-2}$

41. $\dfrac{y^2-3y+2}{y^2+7y-18}=\dfrac{(y-1)(y-2)}{(y+9)(y-2)}=\dfrac{y-1}{y+9}$

43. $\dfrac{2y^2-7y+3}{2y^2-5y+2}=\dfrac{(2y-1)(y-3)}{(2y-1)(y-2)}=\dfrac{y-3}{y-2}$

45. $\dfrac{2x+3}{2x+5}$

The numerator and denominator have no common factor (other than 1), so this rational expression cannot be simplified.

47. $\dfrac{x^2+12x+36}{x^2-36}=\dfrac{(x+6)(x+6)}{(x+6)(x-6)}=\dfrac{x+6}{x-6}$

49.
$$\begin{aligned}\frac{x^3-2x^2+x-2}{x-2}&=\frac{x^2(x-2)+1(x-2)}{x-1}\\&=\frac{(x-2)(x^2+1)}{x-2}\\&=x^2+1\end{aligned}$$

51.
$$\begin{aligned}\frac{x^3-8}{x-2}&=\frac{(x-2)(x^2+2x+4)}{x-2}\\&=x^2+2x+4\end{aligned}$$

53. $\dfrac{(x-4)^2}{x^2-16}=\dfrac{(x-4)(x-4)}{(x+4)(x-4)}=\dfrac{x-4}{x+4}$

55. $\dfrac{x}{x+1}$

The numerator and denominator have no common factor (other than 1), so this rational expression cannot be simplified.

57. $\dfrac{x+4}{x^2+16}$

The numerator and denominator are both prime polynomials. They have no common factor (other than 1), so this rational expression cannot be simplified.

59. $\dfrac{x-5}{5-x}=\dfrac{-1(5-x)}{x-5}=-1$

Notice that the numerator and denominator of the given rational expression are additive inverses.

61. $\dfrac{2x-3}{3-2x}$

The numerator and denominator of this rational expression are additive inverses, so

$$\frac{2x-3}{3-2x}=-1.$$

63. $\dfrac{x-5}{x+5}$

The numerator and denominator have no common factor, so this rational expression cannot be simplified.

65. $\dfrac{4x-6}{3-2x}=\dfrac{2(2x-3)}{3-2x}=\dfrac{-2(3-2x)}{3-2x}=-2$

67.
$$\begin{aligned}\frac{4-6x}{3x^2-2x}&=\frac{2(2-3x)}{x(3x-2)}\\&=\frac{-2(3x-2)}{x(3x-2)}\\&=-\frac{2}{x}\end{aligned}$$

69.
$$\begin{aligned}\frac{x^2-1}{1-x}&=\frac{(x+1)(x-1)}{1-x}\\&=\frac{(x+1)\cdot-1(1-x)}{1-x}\\&=-1(x+1)=-x-1\end{aligned}$$

71. $\dfrac{y^2-y-12}{4-y} = \dfrac{(y-4)(y+3)}{4-y}$

$= \dfrac{-1(4-y)(y+3)}{4-y}$

$= -1(y+3) = -y-3$

73. $\dfrac{x^2y-x^2}{x^3-x^3y} = \dfrac{x^2(y-1)}{x^3(1-y)}$

$= \dfrac{x^2 \cdot -1(1-y)}{x^3(1-y)}$

$= -\dfrac{1}{x}$

75. $\dfrac{x^2+2xy-3y^2}{2x^2+5xy-3y^2} = \dfrac{(x-y)(x+3y)}{(2x-y)(x+3y)}$

$= \dfrac{x-y}{2x-y}$

77. The conviction rate is the ratio of the number of drug convictions to the number of drug arrests. Therefore, the conviction rate can be described by the polynomial

$$\frac{6t^4-207t^3+2128t^2-6622t+15{,}220}{28t^4-711t^3+5963t^2-1695t+27{,}424},$$

where t is the number of years after 1984.

79. $\dfrac{130x}{100-x}$

a. $x = 40$:

$$\frac{130x}{100-x} = \frac{130(40)}{100-40} = \frac{5200}{60} \approx 86.67$$

$x = 80$:

$$\frac{130x}{100-x} = \frac{130(80)}{100-80} = \frac{10{,}400}{20} = 520$$

$x = 90$:

$$\frac{130x}{100-x} = \frac{130(90)}{100-90} = \frac{11{,}700}{10} = 1170$$

These results mean that it costs \$86.67 million to inoculate 40% of the population, \$520 million to inoculate 80% of the population, and \$1170 million to inoculate 90% of the population.

b. Set the denominator equal to 0 and solve for x.

$$100 - x = 0$$
$$100 = x$$

The rational expression is undefined for $x = 100$.

c. The cost keeps rising as x approaches 100. No amount of money will be enough to inoculate 100% of the population.

81. $\dfrac{DA}{A+12}$; $D = 1000$, $A = 8$

$$\frac{DA}{A+12} = \frac{1000 \cdot 8}{8+12} = \frac{8000}{20} = 400$$

The correct dosage for an 8-year-old is 400 milligrams.

83. $C = \dfrac{100x+100{,}000}{x}$

a. $x = 500$

$$C = \frac{100(500)+100{,}000}{500} = \frac{150{,}000}{500} = 300$$

The cost per bicycle when manufacturing 500 bicycles is \$300.

b. $x = 4000$

$$\begin{aligned} C &= \frac{100(4000) + 100{,}000}{4000} \\ &= \frac{400{,}000 + 100{,}000}{4000} \\ &= \frac{500{,}000}{4000} = 125 \end{aligned}$$

c. The cost per bicycle decreases as more bicycles are manufactured. One possible reason for this is that there could be fixed costs for equipment, so the more the equipment is used, the lower the cost per bicycle.

85. $y = \dfrac{5x}{x^2+1}$; $x = 3$

$$y = \frac{5 \cdot 3}{3^2 + 1} = \frac{15}{10} = 1.5$$

The equation indicates that the drug's concentration after 3 hours is 1.5 milligram per liter. The point $(3, 1.5)$ on the graph conveys this information.

87. The graph shows that the drug reaches its maximum concentration after 1 hour. If $x = 1$,

$$y = \frac{5 \cdot 1}{1^2 + 1} = \frac{5}{2} = 2.5,$$

so the drug's concentration after 1 hour is 2.5 milligrams per liter.

For Exercises 89–93, answers may vary.

95. Any rational expression in which the numerator and denominator have no common factor other than 1 cannot be simplified. Student examples will vary.

97. $x^2 - x - 6 = (x-3)(x+2)$

Therefore,

$$\frac{x^2 - x - 6}{x + 2} = x - 3,$$

so

$$\frac{x^2 - x - 6}{x + 2}$$

is the desired rational expression.

99.

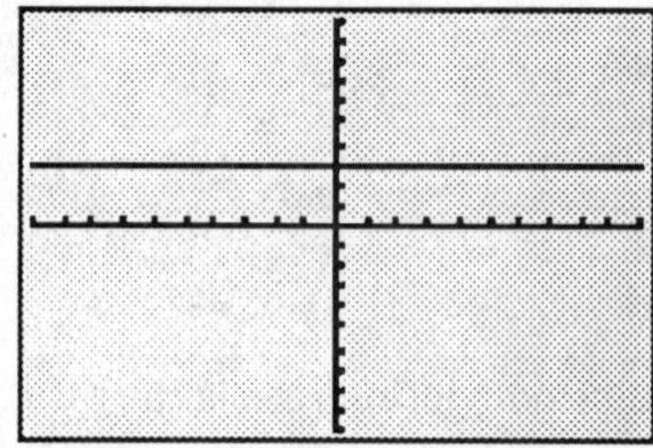

The graphs coincide. This verifies that the simplification

$$\frac{3x + 15}{x + 5} = 3, x \neq -5.$$

is correct.

101.

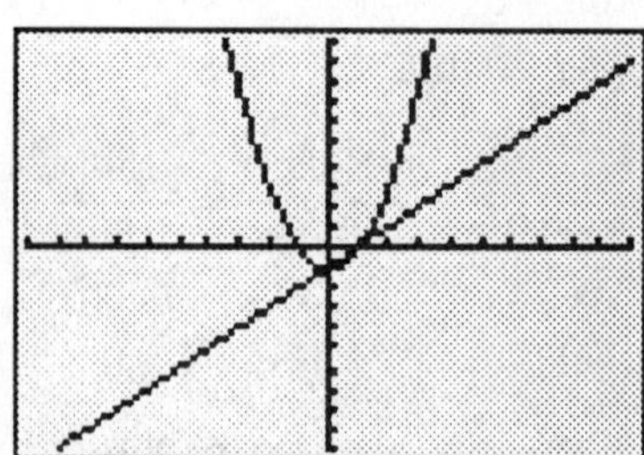

The graphs do not coincide.

$$\begin{aligned} \frac{x^2 - x}{x} &= \frac{x(x-1)}{x} \\ &= x - 1, x \neq 0 \end{aligned}$$

Change the expression on the right from $x^2 - 1$ to $x - 1$.

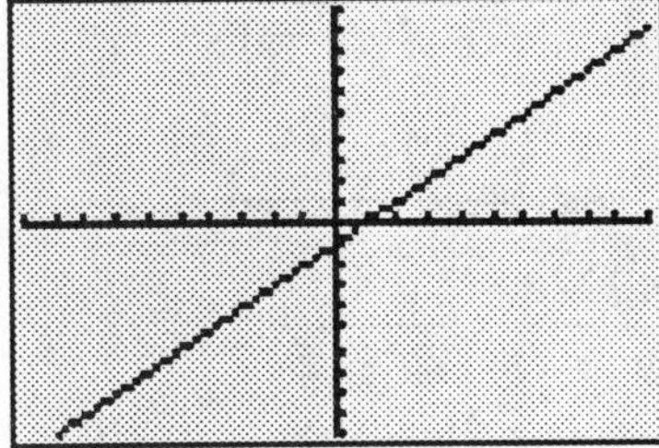

Now the graphs coincide.

Review Exercises

103. $\frac{5}{6} \cdot \frac{9}{25} = \frac{45}{150} = \frac{\cancel{15} \cdot 3}{\cancel{15} \cdot 10} = \frac{3}{10}$

104. $\frac{2}{3} \div 4 = \frac{2}{3} \cdot \frac{1}{4} = \frac{2}{12} = \frac{\cancel{2} \cdot 1}{\cancel{2} \cdot 6} = \frac{1}{6}$

105. $2x - 5y = -2$
$3x + 4y = 20$

Multiply the first equation by 3 and the second equation by -2; then add the results.

$$\begin{aligned} 6x - 15y &= -6 \\ -6x - 8y &= -40 \\ \hline -23y &= -46 \\ y &= 2 \end{aligned}$$

Back-substitute into the first equation of the original system.

$$\begin{aligned} 2x - 5y &= -2 \\ 2x - 5(2) &= -2 \\ 2x - 10 &= -2 \\ 2x &= 8 \\ x &= 4 \end{aligned}$$

Solution: $(4, 2)$

8.2 Multiplying and Dividing Rational Expressions

8.2 CHECK POINTS

CHECK POINT 1

$$\frac{9}{x+4} \cdot \frac{x-5}{2} = \frac{9(x-5)}{(x+4)2} = \frac{9x-45}{2x+8}$$

CHECK POINT 2

$$\frac{x+4}{x-7} \cdot \frac{3x-21}{8x+32} = \frac{x+4}{x-7} \cdot \frac{3(x-7)}{8(x+4)} = \frac{3}{8}$$

CHECK POINT 3

$$\frac{x-5}{x-2} \cdot \frac{x^2-4}{9x-45} = \frac{x-5}{x-2} \cdot \frac{(x+2)(x-2)}{9(x-5)} = \frac{x+2}{9}$$

CHECK POINT 4

$$\begin{aligned} &\frac{5x+5}{7x-7x^2} \cdot \frac{2x^2+x-3}{4x^2-9} \\ &= \frac{5(x+1)}{7x(1-x)} \cdot \frac{(2x+3)(x-1)}{(2x+3)(2x-3)} \\ &= \frac{-5(x+1)}{7x(2x-3)} \text{ or } -\frac{5(x+1)}{7x(2x-3)} \end{aligned}$$

CHECK POINT 5

$$\begin{aligned} (x+3) \div \frac{x-4}{x+7} &= \frac{x+3}{1} \cdot \frac{x+7}{x-4} \\ &= \frac{(x+3)(x+7)}{x-4} \\ &\text{or } \frac{x^2+10x+7}{x-4} \end{aligned}$$

CHECK POINT 6

$$\frac{x^2+5x+6}{x^2-25} \div \frac{x+2}{x+5}$$
$$= \frac{x^2+5x+6}{x^2-25} \cdot \frac{x+5}{x+2}$$
$$= \frac{(x+3)(x+2)}{(x+5)(x-5)} \cdot \frac{x+5}{x+2}$$
$$= \frac{x+3}{x-5}$$

CHECK POINT 7

$$\frac{y^2+3y+2}{y^2+1} \div (5y^2+10y)$$
$$= \frac{y^2+3y+2}{y^2+1} \cdot \frac{1}{5y^2+10y}$$
$$= \frac{(y+2)(y+1)}{y^2+1} \cdot \frac{1}{5y(y+2)}$$
$$= \frac{y+1}{5y(y^2+1)}$$

EXERCISE SET 8.2

1. $\frac{5}{x+2} \cdot \frac{x-3}{7} = \frac{5(x-3)}{(x+2)7} = \frac{5x-15}{7x+14}$

3. $\frac{x}{2} \cdot \frac{4}{x+1} = \frac{4x}{2(x+1)} = \frac{2x}{x+1}$

5. $\frac{3}{x} \cdot \frac{2x}{9} = \frac{6x}{9x} = \frac{2}{3}$

7. $\frac{x-2}{x+3} \cdot \frac{2x+6}{5x-10} = \frac{x-2}{x+3} \cdot \frac{2(x+3)}{5(x-2)}$
$$= \frac{2}{5}$$

9. $\frac{x^2+7x+12}{x+4} \cdot \frac{1}{x+3}$
$$= \frac{(x+4)(x+3)\cdot 1}{(x+4)(x+3)} = 1$$

11. $\frac{x^2-25}{x^2-3x-10} \cdot \frac{x+2}{x}$
$$= \frac{(x+5)(x-5)}{(x+2)(x-5)} \cdot \frac{(x+2)}{x}$$
$$= \frac{x+5}{x}$$

13. $\frac{4y+30}{y^2-3y} \cdot \frac{y-3}{2y+15}$
$$= \frac{2(2y+15)}{y(y-3)} \cdot \frac{(y-3)}{(2y+15)}$$
$$= \frac{2}{y}$$

15. $\frac{y^2-7y-30}{y^2-6y-40} \cdot \frac{2y^2+5y+2}{2y^2+7y+3}$
$$= \frac{(y+3)(y-10)}{(y+4)(y-10)} \cdot \frac{(2y+1)(y+2)}{(2y+1)(y+3)}$$
$$= \frac{y+2}{y+4}$$

17. $(y^2-9) \cdot \frac{4}{y-3}$
$$= \frac{y^2-9}{1} \cdot \frac{4}{y-3}$$
$$= \frac{(y+3)(y-3)}{1} \cdot \frac{4}{y-3}$$
$$= 4(y+3) \quad \text{or} \quad 4y+12$$

19. $\frac{x^2-5x+6}{x^2-2x-3} \cdot \frac{x^2-1}{x^2-4}$
$$= \frac{(x-2)(x-3)}{(x+1)(x-3)} \cdot \frac{(x+1)(x-1)}{(x+2)(x-2)}$$
$$= \frac{x-1}{x+2}$$

21. $\frac{x^3-8}{x^2-4} \cdot \frac{x+2}{3x}$
$$= \frac{(x-2)(x^2+2x+4)}{(x+2)(x-2)} \cdot \frac{(x+2)}{3x}$$
$$= \frac{x^2+2x+4}{3x}$$

23. $\dfrac{(x-2)^3}{(x-1)^2}\cdot\dfrac{x^2-2x+1}{x^2-4x+4}$

$=\dfrac{(x-2)^3}{(x-1)^2}\cdot\dfrac{(x-1)^2}{(x-2)^2}$

$=\dfrac{x-2}{x-1}$

25. $\dfrac{6x+2}{x^2-1}\cdot\dfrac{1-x}{3x^2+x}$

$=\dfrac{2(3x+1)}{(x+1)(x-1)}\cdot\dfrac{(1-x)}{x(3x+1)}$

$=\dfrac{2(3x+1)}{(x+1)(x-1)}\cdot\dfrac{-1(x-1)}{x(3x+1)}$

$=\dfrac{-2}{x(x+1)}$ or $-\dfrac{2}{x(x+1)}$

27. $\dfrac{25-y^2}{y^2-2y-35}\cdot\dfrac{y^2-8y-20}{y^2-3y-10}$

$=\dfrac{(5+y)(5-y)}{(y+5)(y-7)}\cdot\dfrac{(y-10)(y+2)}{(y-5)(y+2)}$

$=\dfrac{-(y-10)}{y-7}$ or $-\dfrac{y-10}{y-7}$

29. $\dfrac{x^2-y^2}{x}\cdot\dfrac{x^2+xy}{x+y}$

$=\dfrac{(x+y)(x-y)}{x}\cdot\dfrac{x(x+y)}{(x+y)}$

$=(x-y)(x+y)$ or x^2-y^2

31. $\dfrac{x^2+2xy+y^2}{x^2-2xy+y^2}\cdot\dfrac{4x-4y}{3x+3y}$

$=\dfrac{(x+y)(x+y)}{(x-y)(x-y)}\cdot\dfrac{4(x-y)}{3(x+y)}$

$=\dfrac{4(x+y)}{3(x-y)}$

33. $\dfrac{x}{7}\div\dfrac{5}{3}=\dfrac{x}{7}\cdot\dfrac{3}{5}=\dfrac{3x}{35}$

35. $\dfrac{3}{x}\div\dfrac{12}{x}=\dfrac{3}{x}\cdot\dfrac{x}{12}=\dfrac{1}{4}$

37. $\dfrac{15}{x}\div\dfrac{3}{2x}=\dfrac{\overset{5}{\cancel{15}}}{\underset{1}{\cancel{x}}}\cdot\dfrac{\overset{1}{2\cancel{x}}}{\underset{1}{\cancel{3}}}=10$

39. $\dfrac{x+1}{3}\div\dfrac{3x+3}{7}=\dfrac{x+1}{3}\cdot\dfrac{7}{3x+3}$

$=\dfrac{x+1}{3}\cdot\dfrac{7}{3(x+1)}$

$=\dfrac{7}{9}$

41. $\dfrac{7}{x-5}\div\dfrac{28}{3x-15}=\dfrac{7}{x-5}\cdot\dfrac{3x-15}{28}$

$=\dfrac{7}{(x-5)}\cdot\dfrac{3(x-5)}{7\cdot 4}$

$=\dfrac{3}{4}$

43. $\dfrac{x^2-4}{x}\div\dfrac{x+2}{x-2}=\dfrac{x^2-4}{x}\cdot\dfrac{x-2}{x+2}$

$=\dfrac{(x+2)(x-2)}{x}\cdot\dfrac{x-2}{x+2}$

$=\dfrac{(x-2)^2}{x}$

45. $(y^2-16)\div\dfrac{y^2+3y-4}{y^2+4}$

$=\dfrac{y^2-16}{1}\cdot\dfrac{y^2+4}{y^2+3y-4}$

$=\dfrac{(y+4)(y-4)}{1}\cdot\dfrac{y^2+4}{(y+4)(y-1)}$

$=\dfrac{(y-4)(y^2+4)}{y-1}$

47. $\dfrac{y^2-y}{15}\div\dfrac{y-1}{4}=\dfrac{y^2-y}{15}\cdot\dfrac{5}{y-1}$

$=\dfrac{y(y-1)}{15}\cdot\dfrac{5}{(y-1)}$

$=\dfrac{y}{3}$

49. $\dfrac{4x^2+10}{x-3}\div\dfrac{6x^2+15}{x^2-9}$

$=\dfrac{4x^2+10}{x-3}\cdot\dfrac{x^2-9}{6x^2+15}$

$=\dfrac{2(2x^2+5)}{(x-3)}\cdot\dfrac{(x+3)(x-3)}{3(2x^2+5)}$

$=\dfrac{2(x+3)}{3}$ or $\dfrac{2x+6}{3}$

51. $\dfrac{x^2-25}{2x-2} \div \dfrac{x^2+10x+25}{x^2+4x-5}$

$$= \frac{x^2-25}{2x-2} \cdot \frac{x^2+4x-5}{x^2+10x+25}$$

$$= \frac{(x+5)(x-5)}{2(x-1)} \cdot \frac{(x+5)(x-1)}{(x+5)(x+5)}$$

$$= \frac{x-5}{2}$$

53. $\dfrac{y^3+y}{y^2-y} \div \dfrac{y^3-y^2}{y^2-2y+1}$

$$= \frac{y^3+y}{y^2-y} \cdot \frac{y^2-2y+1}{y^3-y^2}$$

$$= \frac{y(y^2+1)}{y(y-1)} \cdot \frac{(y-1)(y-1)}{y^2(y-1)}$$

$$= \frac{y^2+1}{y^2}$$

55. $\dfrac{y^2+5y+4}{y^2+12y+32} \div \dfrac{y^2-12y+35}{y^2+3y-40}$

$$= \frac{y^2+5y+4}{y^2+12y+32} \cdot \frac{y^2+3y-40}{y^2-12y+35}$$

$$= \frac{(y+4)(y+1)}{(y+4)(y+8)} \cdot \frac{(y+8)(y-5)}{(y-7)(y-5)}$$

$$= \frac{y+1}{y-7}$$

57. $\dfrac{2y^2-128}{y^2+16y+64} \div \dfrac{y^2-6y-16}{3y^2+30y+48}$

$$= \frac{2y^2-128}{y^2+16y+64} \cdot \frac{3y^2+30y+48}{y^2-6y-16}$$

$$= \frac{2(y^2-64)}{(y+8)(y+8)} \cdot \frac{3(y^2+10y+16)}{(y+2)(y-8)}$$

$$= \frac{2(y+8)(y-8)}{(y+8)(y+8)} \cdot \frac{3(y+2)(y+8)}{(y+2)(y-8)} = 6$$

59. $\dfrac{2x+2y}{3} \div \dfrac{x^2-y^2}{x-y}$

$$= \frac{2x+2y}{3} \cdot \frac{x-y}{x^2-y^2}$$

$$= \frac{2(x+y)}{3} \cdot \frac{x-y}{(x+y)(x-y)} = \frac{2}{3}$$

61. $\dfrac{x^2-y^2}{8x^2-16xy+8y^2} \div \dfrac{4x-4y}{x+y}$

$$= \frac{x^2-y^2}{8x^2-16xy+8y^2} \cdot \frac{x+y}{4x-4y}$$

$$= \frac{(x+y)(x-y)}{8(x^2-2xy+y^2)} \cdot \frac{x+y}{4(x-y)}$$

$$= \frac{(x+y)(x-y)}{8(x-y)(x-y)} \cdot \frac{(x+y)}{4(x-y)}$$

$$= \frac{(x+y)^2}{32(x-y)^2}$$

63. $\dfrac{xy-y^2}{x^2+2x+1} \div \dfrac{2x^2+xy-3y^2}{2x^2+5xy+3y^2}$

$$= \frac{xy-y^2}{x^2+2x+1} \cdot \frac{2x^2+5xy+3y^2}{2x^2+xy-3y^2}$$

$$= \frac{y(x-y)}{(x+1)(x+1)} \cdot \frac{(2x+3y)(x+y)}{(2x+3y)(x-y)}$$

$$= \frac{y(x+y)}{(x+1)^2}$$

65. $\dfrac{1}{2} \cdot \dfrac{250x}{100-x} = \dfrac{125x}{100-x}$

The rational expression

$$\frac{125x}{100-x}$$

represents the reduced cost.

For Exercises 67–69, answers may vary.

71. $$\frac{\square}{\square} \cdot \frac{3x-12}{2x} = \frac{3}{2}$$

$$\frac{\square}{\square} \cdot \frac{3(x-4)}{2x} = \frac{3}{2}$$

The numerator of the unknown rational expression must contain a factor of x. The denominator of the unknown rational expression must contain a factor of $(x-4)$. Therefore, the simplest pair of polynomials that will work are x in the numerator and $x-4$ in the denominator, to give the rational expression $\frac{x}{x-4}$.

Check:

$$\frac{x}{x-4} \cdot \frac{3x-12}{2x} = \frac{x}{x-4} \cdot \frac{3(x-4)}{2x} = \frac{3}{2}$$

73. $$\left(\frac{y-2}{y^2-9y+18} \cdot \frac{y^2-4y-12}{y+2}\right) \div \frac{y^2-4}{y^2+5y+6}$$

$$= \frac{y-2}{y^2-9y+18} \cdot \frac{y^2-4y-12}{y+2} \cdot \frac{y^2+5y+6}{y^2-4}$$

$$= \frac{(y-2)}{(y-3)(y-6)} \cdot \frac{(y-6)(y+2)}{(y+2)} \cdot \frac{(y+2)(y+3)}{(y+2)(y-2)}$$

$$= \frac{y+3}{y-3}$$

75.

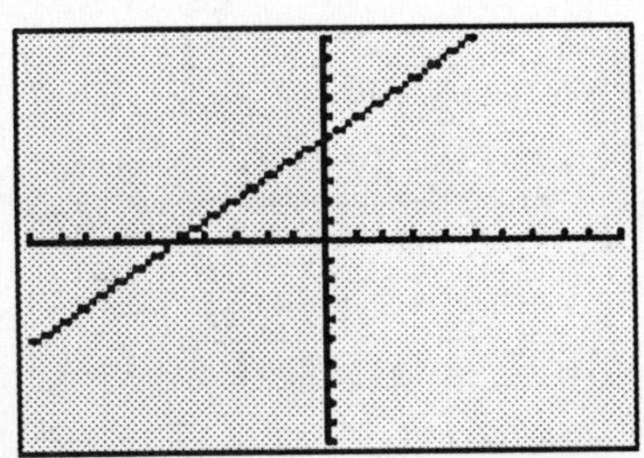

The graph coincides. This verifies that

$$\frac{x^3-25x}{x^2-3x-10} \cdot \frac{x+2}{x} = x+5.$$

77.

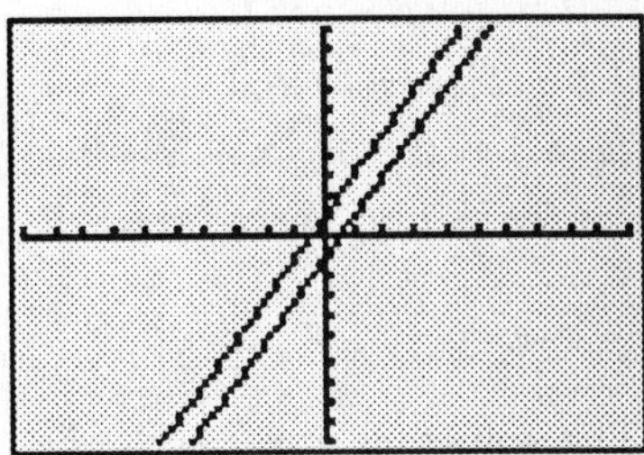

The graphs do not coincide.

$$(x-5) \div \frac{2x^2-11x+5}{4x^2-1}$$

$$= \frac{x-5}{1} \cdot \frac{4x^2-1}{2x^2-11x+5}$$

$$= \frac{x-5}{1} \cdot \frac{(2x+1)(2x-1)}{(2x-1)(x-5)}$$

$$= 2x+1$$

Change the expression on the right from $(2x-1)$ to $(2x+1)$.

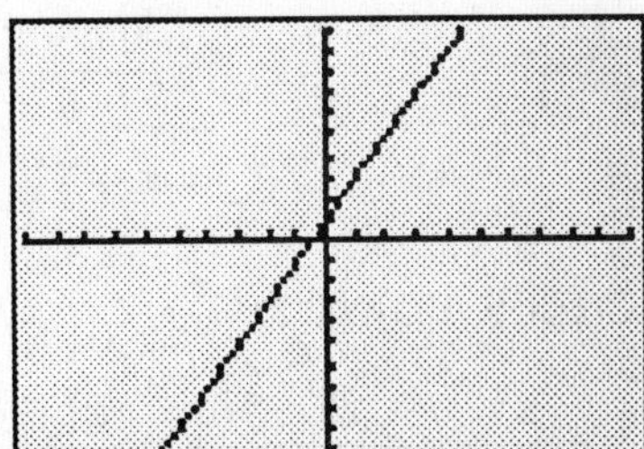

Now the graphs coincide.

Review Exercises

78. $$\begin{aligned} 2x+3 &< 3(x-5) \\ 2x+3 &< 3x-15 \\ -x+3 &< -15 \\ -x &< -18 \\ x &> 18 \end{aligned}$$

$\{x | x > 18\}$

79. $3x^2 - 15x - 42 = 3(x^2 - 5x - 14)$
$= 3(x-7)(x+2)$

80.
$$x(2x+9) = 5$$
$$2x^2 + 9x = 5$$
$$2x^2 + 9x - 5 = 0$$
$$(2x-1)(x+5) = 0$$
$$2x - 1 = 0 \quad \text{or} \quad x + 5 = 0$$
$$2x = 1 \qquad x = -5$$
$$x = \frac{1}{2}$$

The solutions are $\frac{1}{2}$ and -5.

8.3 Adding and Subtracting Rational Expressions with the Same Denominator

8.3 CHECK POINTS

CHECK POINT 1

$$\frac{3x-2}{5} + \frac{2x+12}{5} = \frac{3x-2+2x+12}{5}$$
$$= \frac{5x+10}{5}$$
$$= \frac{5(x+2)}{5}$$
$$= x+2$$

CHECK POINT 2

$$\frac{x^2}{x^2-25} + \frac{25-10x}{x^2-25} = \frac{x^2-10x+25}{x^2-25}$$
$$= \frac{(x-5)(x-5)}{(x+5)(x-5)}$$
$$= \frac{x-5}{x+5}$$

CHECK POINT 3

a. $$\frac{4x+5}{x+7} - \frac{x}{x+7} = \frac{4x+5-x}{x+7}$$
$$= \frac{3x+5}{x+7}$$

b. $$\frac{3x^2+4x}{x-1} - \frac{11x-4}{x-1} = \frac{(3x^2+4x)-(11x-4)}{x-1}$$
$$= \frac{3x^2+4x-11x+4}{x-1}$$
$$= \frac{3x^2-7x+4}{x-1}$$
$$= \frac{(3x-4)(x-1)}{x-1}$$
$$= 3x-4$$

CHECK POINT 4

$$\frac{y^2+3y-6}{y^2-5y+4} - \frac{4y-4-2y^2}{y^2-5y+4}$$
$$= \frac{(y^2+3y-6)-(4y-4-2y^2)}{y^2-5y+4}$$
$$= \frac{y^2+3y-6-4y+4+2y^2}{y^2-5y+4}$$
$$= \frac{3y^2-y-2}{y^2-5y+4}$$
$$= \frac{(3y+2)(y-1)}{(y-4)(y-1)}$$
$$= \frac{3y+2}{y-4}$$

CHECK POINT 5

$$\frac{x^2}{x-7} + \frac{4x+21}{7-x}$$
$$= \frac{x^2}{x-7} + \frac{(-1)}{(-1)} \cdot \frac{(4x+21)}{(7-x)}$$
$$= \frac{x^2}{x-7} + \frac{-4x-21}{-7+x}$$
$$= \frac{x^2+(-4x-21)}{x-7}$$
$$= \frac{x^2-4x-21}{x-7}$$
$$= \frac{(x-7)(x+3)}{x-7}$$
$$= x+3$$

CHECK POINT 6

$$\frac{7x-x^2}{x^2-2x-9}-\frac{5x-3x^2}{9+2x-x^2}$$
$$=\frac{7x-x^2}{x^2-2x-9}-\frac{(-1)}{(-1)}\cdot\frac{5x-3x^2}{9-2x-x^2}$$
$$=\frac{7x-x^2}{x^2-2x-9}-\frac{-5x+3x^2}{x^2-2x-9}$$
$$=\frac{(7x-x^2)-(-5x+3x^2)}{x^2-2x-9}$$
$$=\frac{7x-x^2+5x-3x^2}{x^2-2x-9}$$
$$=\frac{-4x^2+12x}{x^2-2x-9}$$

EXERCISE SET 8.3

1. $\frac{4x}{9}+\frac{3x}{9}=\frac{7x}{9}$

3. $\frac{7x}{12}+\frac{x}{12}=\frac{8x}{12}=\frac{2x}{3}$

5. $$\frac{x-3}{8}+\frac{3x+7}{8}=\frac{4x+4}{8}$$
$$=\frac{4(x+1)}{8}$$
$$=\frac{x+1}{2}$$

7. $\frac{5}{x}+\frac{3}{x}=\frac{8}{x}$

9. $\frac{7}{9x}+\frac{5}{9x}=\frac{12}{9x}=\frac{4}{3x}$

11. $\frac{5}{x+3}+\frac{4}{x+3}=\frac{9}{x+3}$

13. $\frac{x}{x-3}+\frac{4x+5}{x-3}=\frac{5x+5}{x-3}$

15. $$\frac{4x+1}{6x+5}+\frac{8x+9}{6x+5}=\frac{12x+10}{6x+5}$$
$$=\frac{2(6x+5)}{6x+5}=2$$

17. $$\frac{y^2+7y}{y^2-5y}+\frac{y^2-4y}{y^2-5y}=\frac{y^2+7y+y^2-4y}{y^2-5y}$$
$$=\frac{2y^2+3y}{y^2-5y}$$
$$=\frac{y(2y+3)}{y(y-5)}$$
$$=\frac{2y+3}{y-5}$$

19. $$\frac{4y-1}{5y^2}+\frac{3y+1}{5y^2}=\frac{4y-1+3y+1}{5y^2}$$
$$=\frac{7y}{5y^2}=\frac{7}{5y}$$

21. $$\frac{x^2-2}{x^2+x-2}+\frac{2x-x^2}{x^2+x-2}=\frac{x^2-2+2x-x^2}{x^2+x-2}$$
$$=\frac{2x-2}{x^2+x-2}$$
$$=\frac{2(x-1)}{(x+2)(x-1)}$$
$$=\frac{2}{x+2}$$

23. $$\frac{x^2-4x}{x^2-x-6}+\frac{4x-4}{x^2-x-6}$$
$$=\frac{x^2-4x+4x-4}{x^2-x-6}$$
$$=\frac{x^2-4}{x^2-x-6}$$
$$=\frac{(x+2)(x-2)}{(x-3)(x+2)}$$
$$=\frac{x-2}{x-3}$$

25. $\frac{3x}{5x-4}-\frac{4}{5x-4}=\frac{3x-4}{5x-4}$

27. $\frac{4x}{4x-3}-\frac{3}{4x-3}=\frac{4x-3}{4x-3}=1$

29. $$\frac{14y}{7y+2}-\frac{7y-2}{7y+2}=\frac{14y-(7y-2)}{7y+2}=\frac{14y-7y+2}{7y+2}=\frac{7y+2}{7y+2}=1$$

31. $$\frac{3x+1}{4x-2}-\frac{x+1}{4x-2}=\frac{(3x+1)-(x+1)}{4x-2}=\frac{3x+1-x-1}{4x-2}=\frac{2x}{4x-2}=\frac{2x}{2(2x-1)}=\frac{x}{2x-1}$$

33. $$\frac{3y^2-1}{3y^3}-\frac{6y^2-1}{3y^3}=\frac{(3y^2-1)-(6y^2-1)}{3y^3}=\frac{3y^2-1-6y^2+1}{3y^3}=\frac{-3y^2}{3y^3}=-\frac{1}{y}$$

35. $$\frac{4y^2+5}{9y^2-64}-\frac{y^2-y+29}{9y^2-64}=\frac{(4y^2+5)-(y^2-y+29)}{9y^2-64}=\frac{4y^2+5-y^2+y-29}{9y^2-64}=\frac{3y^2+y-24}{9y^2-64}=\frac{(3y-8)(y+3)}{(3y+8)(3y-8)}=\frac{y+3}{3y+8}$$

37. $$\frac{6y^2+y}{2y^2-9y+9}-\frac{2y+9}{2y^2-9y+9}-\frac{4y-3}{2y^2-9y+9}=\frac{(6y^2+y)-(2y+9)-(4y-3)}{2y^2-9y+9}=\frac{6y^2+y-2y-9-4y+3}{2y^2-9y+9}=\frac{6y^2-5y-6}{2y^2-9y+9}=\frac{(2y-3)(3y+2)}{(2y-3)(y-3)}=\frac{3y+2}{y-3}$$

39. $$\frac{4}{x-3}+\frac{2}{3-x}=\frac{4}{x-3}+\frac{(-1)}{(-1)}\cdot\frac{2}{3-x}=\frac{4}{x-3}+\frac{-2}{x-3}=\frac{2}{x-3}$$

41. $$\frac{6x+7}{x-6}+\frac{3x}{6-x}=\frac{6x+7}{x-6}+\frac{(-1)}{(-1)}\cdot\frac{3x}{6-x}=\frac{6x+7}{x-6}+\frac{-3x}{x-6}=\frac{3x+7}{x-6}$$

43. $$\frac{5x-2}{3x-4}+\frac{2x-3}{4-3x}=\frac{5x-2}{3x-4}+\frac{(-1)}{(-1)}\cdot\frac{2x-3}{4-3x}=\frac{5x-2}{3x-4}+\frac{-2x+3}{3x-4}=\frac{5x-2-2x+3}{3x-4}=\frac{3x+1}{3x-4}$$

45. $$\frac{x^2}{x-2}+\frac{4}{2-x}=\frac{x^2}{x-2}+\frac{(-1)}{(-1)}\cdot\frac{4}{2-x}$$
$$=\frac{x^2}{x-2}+\frac{-4}{x-2}$$
$$=\frac{x^2-4}{x-2}$$
$$=\frac{(x+2)(x-2)}{x-2}$$
$$=x+2$$

47. $$\frac{y-3}{y^2-25}+\frac{y-3}{25-y^2}$$
$$=\frac{y-3}{y^2-25}+\frac{(-1)}{(-1)}\cdot\frac{y-3}{25-y^2}$$
$$=\frac{y-3}{y^2-25}+\frac{-y+3}{y^2-25}$$
$$=\frac{y-3-y+3}{y^2-25}$$
$$=\frac{0}{y^2-25}=0$$

49. $$\frac{6}{x-1}-\frac{5}{1-x}=\frac{6}{x-1}-\frac{(-1)}{(-1)}\cdot\frac{5}{1-x}$$
$$=\frac{6}{x-1}-\frac{-5}{x-1}$$
$$=\frac{6+5}{x-1}=\frac{11}{x-1}$$

51. $$\frac{10}{x+3}-\frac{2}{-x-3}=\frac{10}{x+3}-\frac{(-1)}{(-1)}\cdot\frac{2}{-x-3}$$
$$=\frac{10}{x+3}-\frac{-2}{x+3}$$
$$=\frac{10+2}{x+3}=\frac{12}{x+3}$$

53. $$\frac{y}{y-1}-\frac{1}{1-y}=\frac{y}{y-1}-\frac{(-1)}{(-1)}\cdot\frac{1}{1-y}$$
$$=\frac{y}{y-1}-\frac{-1}{y-1}$$
$$=\frac{y+1}{y-1}$$

55. $$\frac{3-x}{x-7}-\frac{2x-5}{7-x}$$
$$=\frac{3-x}{x-7}-\frac{(-1)}{(-1)}\cdot\frac{2x-5}{7-x}$$
$$=\frac{3-x}{x-7}-\frac{-2x+5}{x-7}$$
$$=\frac{(3-x)-(-2x+5)}{x-7}$$
$$=\frac{3-x+2x-5}{x-7}$$
$$=\frac{x-2}{x-7}$$

57. $$\frac{x-2}{x^2-25}-\frac{x-2}{25-x^2}$$
$$=\frac{x-2}{x^2-25}-\frac{(-1)}{(-1)}\cdot\frac{x-2}{x^2-25}$$
$$=\frac{x-2}{x^2-25}-\frac{-x+2}{x^2-25}$$
$$=\frac{(x-2)-(-x+2)}{x^2-25}$$
$$=\frac{x-2+x-2}{x^2-25}$$
$$=\frac{2x-4}{x^2-25}$$

59. $$\frac{x}{x-y}+\frac{y}{y-x}=\frac{x}{x-y}+\frac{(-1)}{(-1)}\cdot\frac{y}{y-x}$$
$$=\frac{x}{x-y}+\frac{-y}{x-y}$$
$$=\frac{x-y}{x-y}=1$$

61. $\dfrac{2x}{x^2-y^2}+\dfrac{2y}{y^2-x^2}$

$$=\frac{2x}{x^2-y^2}+\frac{(-1)}{(-1)}\cdot\frac{2y}{y^2-x^2}$$
$$=\frac{2x}{x^2-y^2}+\frac{-2y}{x^2-y^2}$$
$$=\frac{2x-2y}{x^2-y^2}$$
$$=\frac{2(x-y)}{(x+y)(x-y)}$$
$$=\frac{2}{x+y}$$

63. $\dfrac{x^2-2}{x^2+6x-7}+\dfrac{19-4x}{7-6x-x^2}$

$$=\frac{x^2-2}{x^2+6x-7}+\frac{(-1)}{(-1)}\cdot\frac{19-4x}{7-6x-x^2}$$
$$=\frac{x^2-2}{x^2+6x-7}+\frac{-19+4x}{7-6x-x^2}$$
$$=\frac{x^2-2-19+4x}{x^2+6x-7}$$
$$=\frac{x^2+4x-21}{x^2+6x-7}$$
$$=\frac{(x+7)(x-3)}{(x+7)(x-1)}$$
$$=\frac{x-3}{x-1}$$

65. a. $\dfrac{L+60W}{L}-\dfrac{L-40W}{L}$

$$=\frac{(L+60W)-(L-40W)}{L}$$
$$=\frac{L+60W-L+40W}{L}$$
$$=\frac{100W}{L}$$

b. $\dfrac{100W}{L}$; $W=5, L=6$

$$\frac{100W}{L}=\frac{100\cdot 5}{6}$$
$$\approx 83.3$$

Since this value is over 80, the skull is round.

67. $P=2L+2W$

$$=2\left(\frac{5x+10}{x+3}\right)+2\left(\frac{5}{x+3}\right)$$
$$=\frac{10x+20}{x+3}+\frac{10}{x+3}$$
$$=\frac{10x+30}{x+3}$$
$$=\frac{10(x+3)}{x+3}=10$$

The perimeter is 10 meters.

For Exercises 69–71, answers may vary.

73. Statement d is true.

$$\frac{2x+1}{x-7}+\frac{3x+1}{x-7}-\frac{5x+2}{x-7}$$
$$=\frac{5x+2}{x-7}-\frac{5x+2}{x-7}=0$$

75. $\left(\dfrac{3x-1}{x^2+5x-6}-\dfrac{2x-7}{x^2+5x-6}\right)\div\dfrac{x+2}{x^2-1}$

$$=\left(\frac{(3x-1)-(2x-7)}{x^2+5x-6}\right)\div\frac{x+2}{x^2-1}$$
$$=\frac{3x-1-2x+7}{x^2+5x-6}\div\frac{x+2}{x^2-1}$$
$$=\frac{x+6}{x^2+5x-6}\div\frac{x+2}{x^2-1}$$
$$=\frac{x+6}{x^2+5x-6}\cdot\frac{x^2-1}{x+1}$$
$$=\frac{(x+6)}{(x+6)(x-1)}\cdot\frac{(x+1)(x-1)}{(x+2)}$$
$$=\frac{x+1}{x+2}$$

77. $\frac{2x}{x+3} + \frac{\square}{x+3} = \frac{4x+1}{x+3}$

The sum of numerators on the left side must be $4x+1$, so the missing expression is $2x+1$.

Check:

$$\frac{2x}{x+3} + \frac{2x+1}{x+3} = \frac{2x+2x+1}{x+3} = \frac{4x+1}{x+3}$$

79. $\frac{6}{x-2} + \frac{\square}{2-x} = \frac{13}{x-2}$

$$\frac{6}{x-2} + \frac{(-1)}{(-1)} \cdot \frac{\square}{2-x} = \frac{13}{x-2}$$

$$\frac{6}{x-2} + \frac{(-1)\square}{x-2} = \frac{13}{x-2}$$

Since $6+7=13$, the opposite of the missing expression must be 7, so the missing expression is -7.

Check:

$$\frac{6}{x-2} + \frac{-7}{2-x} = \frac{6}{x-2} + \frac{7}{x-2} = \frac{13}{x-2}$$

81. $\frac{3x}{x-5} + \frac{\square}{5-x} = \frac{7x+1}{x-5}$

$$\frac{3x}{x-5} + \frac{(-1)}{(-1)} \cdot \frac{\square}{5-x} = \frac{7x+1}{x-5}$$

$$\frac{3x}{x-5} + \frac{(-1)\square}{x-5} = \frac{7x+1}{x-5}$$

Since $3x+(4x+1) = 7x+1$, the opposite of the missing expression must be $4x+1$, so the missing expression is $-4x-1$.

Check:

$$\frac{3x}{x-5} + \frac{-4x-1}{5-x} = \frac{3x}{x-5} + \frac{4x+1}{x-5} = \frac{7x+1}{x-5}$$

83.

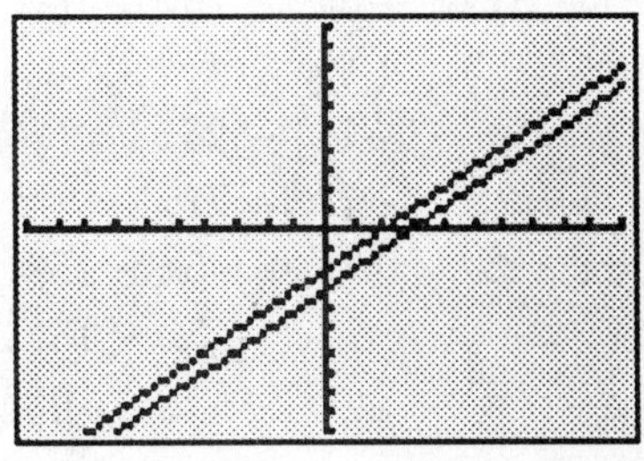

The graphs do not coincide.

$$\frac{x^2+4x+3}{x+2} - \frac{5x+9}{x+2} = \frac{(x^2+4x+3)-(5x+9)}{x+2} = \frac{x^2+4x+3-5x-9}{x+2} = \frac{x^2-x-6}{x+2} = \frac{(x+2)(x-3)}{x+2} = x-3$$

Change $x-2$ to $x-3$.

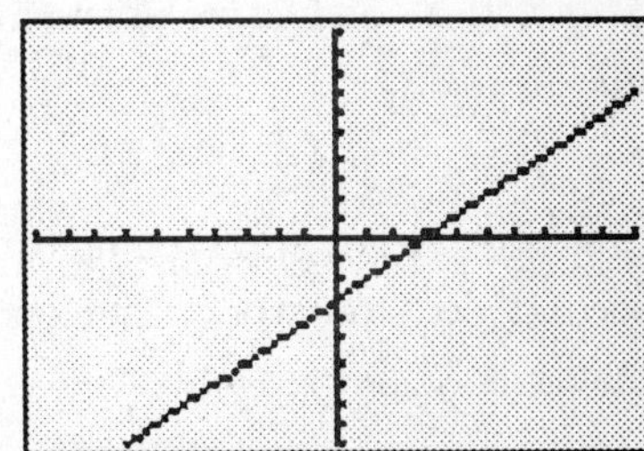

Now the graphs coincide.

Review Exercises

85. $\frac{13}{15} - \frac{8}{45} = \frac{13}{15} \cdot \frac{3}{3} - \frac{8}{45} = \frac{39}{45} - \frac{8}{45} = \frac{31}{45}$

86. $81x^4 - 1 = (9x^2+1)(9x^2-1) = (9x^2+1)(3x+1)(3x-1)$

87.

$$\begin{array}{r} 3x^2 - 7x - 5 \\ x+3 \overline{)3x^3 + 2x^2 - 26x - 15} \\ \underline{3x^3 + 9x^2} \qquad\qquad \\ -7x^2 - 26x \qquad \\ \underline{-7x^2 - 21x} \qquad \\ -5x - 15 \\ \underline{-5x - 15} \\ 0 \end{array}$$

$$\frac{3x^3 + 2x^2 - 26x - 15}{x+3} = 3x^2 - 7x - 5$$

8.4 Adding and Subtracting Rational Expressions with Different Denominators

8.4 CHECK POINTS

CHECK POINT 1

$\frac{3}{10x^2}$ and $\frac{7}{15x}$

Step 1 Factor each denominator completely.

$$10x^2 = 2 \cdot 5x^2$$
$$15x = 3 \cdot 5x$$

Step 2 List the factors of the first denominator.

$$2, 5, x^2$$

Step 3 Add any unlisted factors from the second denominator. The only unlisted factor is 3, giving the list

$$2, 3, 5, x^2.$$

Step 4 The LCD is the product of all factors in the final list. Thus, the LCD is

$$2 \cdot 3 \cdot 5x^2 = 30x^2.$$

CHECK POINT 2

$\frac{2}{x+3}$ and $\frac{4}{x-3}$

The LCD is $(x+3)(x-3)$.

CHECK POINT 3

$\frac{9}{7x^2+28x}$ and $\frac{11}{x^2+8x+16}$

$$7x^2 + 28x = 7x(x+4)$$
$$x^2 + 8x + 16 = (x+4)^2$$

LCD $= 7x(x+4)(x+4)$ or $7(x+4)^2$

CHECK POINT 4

$$\frac{3}{10x^2} + \frac{7}{15x}$$

Step 1 Find the LCD. In CHECK POINT 1, you found that the LCD for these rational expressions is $30x^2$.

Step 2 Write equivalent rational expressions with LCD as denominators.

$$\frac{3}{10x^2} \cdot \frac{3}{3} = \frac{9}{30x^2}$$
$$\frac{7}{15x} \cdot \frac{2x}{2x} = \frac{14x}{30x^2}$$

Thus,

$$\frac{3}{10x^2} + \frac{7}{15x} = \frac{9}{30x^2} + \frac{14x}{30x^2}.$$

Steps 3 and 4

Add numerators, putting this sum over the LCD. Simplify if possible.

$$\frac{9}{30x^2} + \frac{14x}{30x^2} = \frac{9+14x}{30x^2}$$

The numerator is prime and further simplification is not possible.

CHECK POINT 5

$$\frac{2}{x+3}+\frac{4}{x-3}$$

In CHECK POINT 2, you found that the LCD for these rational expressions is $(x+3)(x-3)$.

$$\begin{aligned}&\frac{2}{x+3}+\frac{4}{x-3}\\&=\frac{2(x-3)}{(x+3)(x-3)}+\frac{4(x+3)}{(x+3)(x-3)}\\&=\frac{2(x-3)+4(x+3)}{(x+3)(x-3)}\\&=\frac{2x-6+4x+12}{(x+3)(x-3)}\\&=\frac{6x+6}{(x+3)(x-3)}\end{aligned}$$

CHECK POINT 6

$$\frac{x}{x+5}-1$$

The LCD is $x+5$.

$$\begin{aligned}\frac{x}{x+5}-1&=\frac{x}{x+5}-\frac{1(x+5)}{1(x+5)}\\&=\frac{x-(x+5)}{x+5}\\&=\frac{x-x-5}{x+5}\\&=\frac{-5}{x+5}\text{ or }-\frac{5}{x+5}\end{aligned}$$

CHECK POINT 7

$$\frac{5}{y^2-5y}-\frac{y}{5y-25}$$

First, find the LCD.

$$\begin{aligned}y^2-5y&=y(y-5)\\5y-25&=5(y-5)\end{aligned}$$

The LCD is $5y(y-5)$.

$$\begin{aligned}\frac{5}{y^2-5y}-\frac{y}{5y-25}&=\frac{5}{y(y-5)}-\frac{y}{5(y-5)}\\&=\frac{5\cdot5}{5y(y-5)}-\frac{y\cdot y}{5y(y-5)}\\&=\frac{25-y^2}{5y(y-5)}\\&=\frac{(5+y)(5-y)}{5y(y-5)}\\&=\frac{-1(5+y)}{5y}\\&=-\frac{5+y}{5y}\end{aligned}$$

CHECK POINT 8

$$\frac{4x}{x^2-25}+\frac{3}{5-x}$$

Find the LCD.

$$\begin{aligned}x^2-25&=(x+5)(x-5)\\5-x&=1(5-x)\end{aligned}$$

Notice that $x-5$ and $5-x$ are opposite factors, so either rational expression may be multiplied by $\frac{-1}{-1}$. Here, the second expression will be multiplied by $\frac{-1}{-1}$, and $(x+5)(x-5)$ will be used as the LCD.

$$\begin{aligned}&\frac{4x}{x^2-25}+\frac{3}{5-x}\\&=\frac{4x}{(x+5)(x-5)}+\frac{(-1)}{(-1)}\cdot\frac{3}{5-x}\\&=\frac{4x}{(x+5)(x-5)}+\frac{-3(x+5)}{(x+5)(x-5)}\\&=\frac{4x-3(x+5)}{(x+5)(x-5)}\\&=\frac{4x-3x-15}{(x+5)(x-5)}\\&=\frac{x-15}{(x+5)(x-5)}\end{aligned}$$

EXERCISE SET 8.4

1. $\dfrac{7}{15x^2}$ and $\dfrac{13}{24x}$

$$15x^2 = 3 \cdot 5x^2$$
$$24x = 2^3 \cdot 3x$$

LCD $= 2^3 \cdot 3 \cdot 5x^2 = 120x^2$

3. $\dfrac{8}{15x^2}$ and $\dfrac{5}{6x^5}$

$$15x^2 = 3 \cdot 5x^2$$
$$6x^5 = 2 \cdot 3x^5$$

LCD $= 2 \cdot 3 \cdot 5 \cdot x^5 = 30x^5$

5. $\dfrac{4}{x-3}$ and $\dfrac{7}{x+1}$

LCD $= (x-3)(x+1)$

7. $\dfrac{5}{7(y+2)}$ and $\dfrac{10}{y}$

LCD $= 7y(y+2)$

9. $\dfrac{2}{x+3}$ and $\dfrac{5}{x^2-9}$

$$x+3 = 1(x+3)$$
$$x^2-9 = (x+3)(x-3)$$

LCD $= (x+3)(x-3)$

11. $\dfrac{7}{y^2-4}$ and $\dfrac{15}{y(y+2)}$

$$y^2-4 = (y+2)(y-2)$$
$$y(y+2) = y(y+2)$$

LCD $= y(y+2)(y-2)$

13. $\dfrac{3}{y^2-25}$ and $\dfrac{y}{y^2-10y+25}$

$$y^2-25 = (y+5)(y-5)$$
$$y^2-10y+25 = (y-5)(y-5)$$

LCD $= (y+5)(y-5)(y-5)$

15. $\dfrac{3}{x^2-x-20}$ and $\dfrac{x}{2x^2+7x-4}$

$$x^2-x-20 = (x-5)(x+4)$$
$$2x^2+7x-4 = (2x-1)(x+4)$$

LCD $= (x-5)(x+1)(2x-1)$

17. $\dfrac{3}{x}+\dfrac{5}{x^2}$

LCD $= x^2$

$$\frac{3}{x}+\frac{5}{x^2} = \frac{3}{x}\cdot\frac{x}{x}+\frac{5}{x^2} = \frac{3x+5}{x^2}$$

19. $\dfrac{2}{9x}+\dfrac{11}{6x}$

LCD $= 18x$

$$\frac{2}{9x}+\frac{11}{6x} = \frac{2\cdot 2}{18x}+\frac{11\cdot 3}{18x}$$
$$= \frac{4}{18x}+\frac{33}{18x} = \frac{37}{18x}$$

21. $\dfrac{4}{x}+\dfrac{7}{2x^2}$

LCD $= 2x^2$

$$\frac{4}{x}+\frac{7}{2x^2} = \frac{4\cdot 2x}{2x^2}+\frac{7}{2x^2} = \frac{8x+7}{2x^2}$$

23. $1+\dfrac{1}{x}$

LCD $= x$

$$1+\frac{1}{x} = \frac{1\cdot x}{x}+\frac{1}{x} = \frac{x+1}{x}$$

25. $\dfrac{3}{x}+5$

LCD $= x$

$$\frac{3}{x}+5 = \frac{3}{x}+\frac{5\cdot x}{x} = \frac{3+5x}{x}$$

27. $\dfrac{x-1}{6}+\dfrac{x+2}{3}$

LCD $= 6$

$$\begin{aligned}\frac{x-1}{6}+\frac{x+2}{3}&=\frac{x-1}{6}+\frac{(x+2)(2)}{6}\\&=\frac{x-1+2x+4}{6}\\&=\frac{3x+3}{6}\\&=\frac{3(x+1)}{6}\\&=\frac{x+1}{2}\end{aligned}$$

29. $\dfrac{4}{x}+\dfrac{3}{x-5}$

LCD $= x(x-5)$

$$\begin{aligned}\frac{4}{x}+\frac{3}{x-5}&=\frac{4(x-5)}{x(x-5)}+\frac{3x}{x(x-5)}\\&=\frac{4(x-5)+3x}{x(x-5)}\\&=\frac{4x-20+3x}{x(x-5)}\\&=\frac{7x-20}{x(x-5)}\end{aligned}$$

31. $\dfrac{2}{x-1}+\dfrac{3}{x+2}$

LCD $= (x-1)(x+2)$

$$\begin{aligned}&\frac{2}{x-1}+\frac{3}{x+2}\\&=\frac{2(x+2)}{(x-1)(x+2)}+\frac{3(x-1)}{(x-1)(x+2)}\\&=\frac{2x+4+3x-3}{(x-1)(x+2)}\\&=\frac{5x+1}{(x-1)(x+2)}\end{aligned}$$

33. $\dfrac{2}{y+5}+\dfrac{3}{4y}$

LCD $= 4y(y+5)$

$$\begin{aligned}\frac{2}{y+5}+\frac{3}{4y}&=\frac{2(4y)}{4y(y+5)}+\frac{3(y+5)}{4y(y+5)}\\&=\frac{2(4y)+3(y+5)}{4y(y+5)}\\&=\frac{8y+3y+15}{4y(y+5)}\\&=\frac{11y+15}{4y(y+5)}\end{aligned}$$

35. $\dfrac{x}{x+7}-1$

LCD $= x+7$

$$\begin{aligned}\frac{x}{x+7}-1&=\frac{x}{x+7}-\frac{x+7}{x+7}\\&=\frac{x-(x+7)}{x+7}\\&=\frac{x-x-7}{x+7}\\&=\frac{-7}{x+7}\text{ or }-\frac{7}{x+7}\end{aligned}$$

37. $\dfrac{7}{x+5}-\dfrac{4}{x-5}$

LCD $= (x+5)(x-5)$

$$\begin{aligned}&\frac{7}{x+5}-\frac{4}{x-5}\\&=\frac{7(x-5)}{(x+5)(x-5)}-\frac{4(x+5)}{(x+5)(x-5)}\\&=\frac{7(x-5)-4(x+5)}{(x+5)(x-5)}\\&=\frac{7x-35-4x-20}{(x+5)(x-5)}\\&=\frac{3x-55}{(x+5)(x-5)}\end{aligned}$$

39. $\dfrac{2x}{x^2-16}+\dfrac{x}{x-4}$

$$x^2-16=(x+4)(x-4)$$
$$x-4=1(x-4)$$

LCD $=(x+4)(x-4)$

$$\begin{aligned}&\frac{2x}{x^2-16}+\frac{x}{x-4}\\&=\frac{2x}{(x+4)(x-4)}+\frac{x}{x-4}\\&=\frac{2x}{(x+4)(x-4)}+\frac{x(x+4)}{(x+4)(x-4)}\\&=\frac{2x+x(x+4)}{(x+4)(x-4)}\\&=\frac{2x+x^2+4x}{(x+4)(x-4)}\\&=\frac{x^2+6x}{(x+4)(x-4)}\end{aligned}$$

41. $\dfrac{5y}{y^2-9}-\dfrac{4}{y+3}$

LCD $=(y+3)(y-3)$

$$\begin{aligned}&\frac{5y}{y^2-9}-\frac{4}{y+3}\\&=\frac{5y}{(y+3)(y-3)}-\frac{4}{y+3}\\&=\frac{5y}{(y+3)(y-3)}-\frac{4(y-3)}{(y+3)(y-3)}\\&=\frac{5y-4(y-3)}{(y+3)(y-3)}\\&=\frac{5y-4y+12}{(y+3)(y-3)}\\&=\frac{y+12}{(y+3)(y-3)}\end{aligned}$$

43. $\dfrac{7}{x-1}-\dfrac{3}{(x-1)(x-1)}$

LCD $=(x-1)(x-1)$

$$\begin{aligned}&\frac{7}{x-1}-\frac{3}{(x-1)(x-1)}\\&=\frac{7(x-1)}{(x-1)(x-1)}-\frac{3}{(x-1)(x-1)}\\&=\frac{7x-7-3}{(x-1)(x-1)}\\&=\frac{7x-10}{(x-1)(x-1)}\quad\text{or}\quad\frac{7x-10}{(x-1)^2}\end{aligned}$$

45. $\dfrac{3y}{4y-20}+\dfrac{9y}{6y-30}$

$$4y-20=4(y-5)$$
$$6y-30=6(y-5)$$

LCD $=12(y-5)$

$$\begin{aligned}\frac{3y}{4y-20}+\frac{9y}{6y-30}&=\frac{3y}{4(y-5)}+\frac{9y}{6(y-5)}\\&=\frac{3y\cdot 3}{12(y-5)}+\frac{9y\cdot 2}{12(y-5)}\\&=\frac{9y+18y}{12(y-5)}=\frac{27y}{12(y-5)}\\&=\frac{9y}{4(y-5)}\end{aligned}$$

47. $\dfrac{y+4}{y}-\dfrac{y}{y+4}$

LCD $=y(y+4)$

$$\begin{aligned}&\frac{y+4}{y}-\frac{y}{y+4}\\&=\frac{(y+4)(y+4)}{y(y+4)}-\frac{y\cdot y}{y(y+4)}\\&=\frac{y^2+8y+16-y^2}{y(y+4)}\\&=\frac{8y+16}{y(y+4)}\end{aligned}$$

49. $\dfrac{2x+9}{x^2-7x+12} - \dfrac{2}{x-3}$

$$x^2-7x+12 = (x-3)(x-4)$$
$$x-3 = 1(x-3)$$

$$\text{LCD} = (x-3)(x-4)$$

$$\frac{2x+9}{x^2-7x+12} - \frac{2}{x-3}$$
$$= \frac{2x+9}{(x-3)(x-4)} - \frac{2}{x-3}$$
$$= \frac{2x+9}{(x-3)(x-4)} - \frac{2(x-4)}{(x-3)(x-4)}$$
$$= \frac{2x+9-2(x-4)}{(x-3)(x-4)}$$
$$= \frac{2x+9-2x+8}{(x-3)(x-4)}$$
$$= \frac{17}{(x-3)(x-4)}$$

51. $\dfrac{3}{x^2-1} + \dfrac{4}{(x+1)^2}$

$$x^2-1 = (x+1)(x-1)$$
$$(x+1)^2 = (x+1)(x+1)$$

$$\text{LCD} = (x+1)(x+1)(x-1)$$

$$\frac{3}{x^2-1} + \frac{4}{(x+1)^2}$$
$$= \frac{3}{(x+1)(x-1)} + \frac{4}{(x+1)(x+1)}$$
$$= \frac{3(x+1)}{(x+1)(x+1)(x-1)}$$
$$+ \frac{4(x-1)}{(x+1)(x+1)(x-1)}$$
$$= \frac{3(x+1)+4(x-1)}{(x+1)(x+1)(x-1)}$$
$$= \frac{3x+3+4x-4}{(x+1)(x+1)(x-1)}$$
$$= \frac{7x-1}{(x+1)(x+1)(x-1)}$$

53. $\dfrac{3x}{x^2+3x-10} - \dfrac{2x}{x^2+x-6}$

$$x^2+3x-10 = (x-2)(x+5)$$
$$x^2+x-6 = (x+3)(x-2)$$

$$\text{LCD} = (x+3)(x-2)(x+5)$$

$$\frac{3x}{x^2+3x-10} - \frac{2x}{x^2+x-6}$$
$$= \frac{3x}{(x-2)(x+5)} - \frac{2x}{(x+3)(x-2)}$$
$$= \frac{3x(x+3)}{(x+3)(x-2)(x+5)}$$
$$- \frac{2x(x+5)}{(x+3)(x-2)(x+5)}$$
$$= \frac{3x(x+3)-2x(x+5)}{(x+3)(x-2)(x+5)}$$
$$= \frac{3x^2+9x-2x^2-10x}{(x+3)(x-2)(x+5)}$$
$$= \frac{x^2-x}{(x+3)(x-2)(x+5)}$$

55. $\dfrac{y}{y^2+2y+1} + \dfrac{4}{y^2+5y+4}$

$$y^2+2y+1 = (y+1)(y+1)$$
$$y^2+5y+4 = (y+4)(y+1)$$

$$\text{LCD} = (y+4)(y+1)(y+1)$$

$$\frac{y}{y^2+2y+1} + \frac{4}{y^2+5y+4}$$
$$= \frac{y}{(y+1)(y+1)} + \frac{4}{(y+4)(y+1)}$$
$$= \frac{y(y+4)}{(y+4)(y+1)(y+1)}$$
$$+ \frac{4(y+1)}{(y+4)(y+1)(y+1)}$$
$$= \frac{y(y+4)+4(y+1)}{(y+4)(y+1)(y+1)}$$
$$= \frac{y^2+4y+4y+4}{(y+4)(y+1)(y+1)}$$
$$= \frac{y^2+8y+4}{(y+4)(y+1)(y+1)}$$

57. $\dfrac{x-5}{x+3}+\dfrac{x+3}{x-5}$

LCD $=(x+3)(x-5)$

$$\begin{aligned}\frac{x-5}{x+3}+\frac{x+3}{x-5} &= \frac{(x-5)(x-5)}{(x+3)(x-5)}+\frac{(x+3)(x+3)}{(x+3)(x-5)}\\ &= \frac{(x-5)(x-5)+(x+3)(x+3)}{(x+3)(x-5)}\\ &= \frac{(x^2-10x+25)+(x^2+6x+9)}{(x+3)(x-5)}\\ &= \frac{2x^2-4x+34}{(x+3)(x-5)}\end{aligned}$$

59. $\dfrac{5}{2y^2-2y}-\dfrac{3}{2y-2}$

$$\begin{aligned}2y^2-2y &= 2y(y-1)\\ 2y-2 &= 2(y-1)\end{aligned}$$

LCD $=2y(y-1)$

$$\begin{aligned}\frac{5}{2y^2-2y}-\frac{3}{2y-2} &= \frac{5}{2y(y-1)}-\frac{3}{2(y-1)}\\ &= \frac{5}{2y(y-1)}-\frac{3\cdot y}{2y(y-1)}\\ &= \frac{5-3y}{2y(y-1)}\end{aligned}$$

61. $\dfrac{4x+3}{x^2-9}-\dfrac{x+1}{x-3}$

LCD $=(x+3)(x-3)$

$$\begin{aligned}\frac{4x+3}{x^2-9}-\frac{x+1}{x-3} &= \frac{4x+3}{(x+3)(x-3)}-\frac{(x+1)(x+3)}{(x+3)(x-3)}\\ &= \frac{(4x+3)-(x+1)(x+3)}{(x+3)(x-3)}\\ &= \frac{(4x+3)-(x^2+4x+3)}{(x+3)(x-3)}\\ &= \frac{4x+3-x^2-4x-3}{(x+3)(x-3)}\\ &= \frac{-x^2}{(x+3)(x-3)} = -\frac{x^2}{(x+3)(x-3)}\end{aligned}$$

63. $\dfrac{y^2-39}{y^2+3y-10}-\dfrac{y-7}{y-2}$

$$\begin{aligned}y^2+3y-10 &= (y-2)(y+5)\\ y-2 &= 1(y-2)\end{aligned}$$

LCD $=(y-2)(y+5)$

$$\begin{aligned}\frac{y^2-39}{y^2+3y-10}-\frac{y-7}{y-2} &= \frac{y^2-39}{(y-2)(y+5)}-\frac{y-7}{y-2}\\ &= \frac{y^2-39}{(y-2)(y+5)}-\frac{(y-7)(y+5)}{(y-2)(y+5)}\\ &= \frac{(y^2-39)-(y-7)(y+5)}{(y-2)(y+5)}\\ &= \frac{(y^2-39)-(y^2-2y-35)}{(y-2)(y+5)}\\ &= \frac{y^2-39-y^2+2y+35}{(y-2)(y+5)}\\ &= \frac{2y-4}{(y-2)(y+5)}\\ &= \frac{2(y-2)}{(y-2)(y+5)}\\ &= \frac{2}{y+5}\end{aligned}$$

65. $4+\dfrac{1}{x-3}$

LCD $=x-3$

$$\begin{aligned}4+\frac{1}{x-3} &= \frac{4(x-3)}{x-3}+\frac{1}{x-3}\\ &= \frac{4(x-3)+1}{x-3}\\ &= \frac{4x-12+1}{x-3}\\ &= \frac{4x-11}{x-3}\end{aligned}$$

67. $3 - \dfrac{3y}{y+1}$

LCD $= y+1$

$$3 - \frac{3y}{y+1} = \frac{3(y+1)}{y+1} - \frac{3y}{y+1} = \frac{3(y+1) - 3y}{y+1} = \frac{3y+3-3y}{y+1} = \frac{3}{y+1}$$

69. $\dfrac{9x+3}{x^2-x-6} + \dfrac{x}{3-x}$

$$x^2 - x - 6 = (x-3)(x+2)$$
$$-1(3-x) = x-3$$

LCD $= (x-3)(x+2)$

$$\frac{9x+3}{x^2-x-6} + \frac{x}{3-x} = \frac{9x+3}{(x-3)(x+2)} + \frac{(-1)}{(-1)} \cdot \frac{x}{3-x} = \frac{9x+3}{(x-3)(x+2)} + \frac{-x}{x-3} = \frac{9x+3}{(x-3)(x+2)} + \frac{-x(x+2)}{(x-3)(x+2)} = \frac{9x+3-x(x+2)}{(x-3)(x+2)} = \frac{9x+3-x^2-2x}{(x-3)(x+2)} = \frac{-x^2+7x+3}{(x-3)(x+2)}$$

71. $\dfrac{x+3}{x^2+x-2} - \dfrac{2}{x^2-1}$

$$x^2 + x - 2 = (x-1)(x+2)$$
$$x^2 - 1 = (x+1)(x-1)$$

LCD $= (x+1)(x-1)(x+2)$

$$\frac{x+3}{x^2+x-2} - \frac{2}{x^2-1} = \frac{x+3}{(x-1)(x+2)} - \frac{2}{(x+1)(x-1)} = \frac{(x+3)(x+1)}{(x+1)(x-1)(x+2)} - \frac{2(x+2)}{(x+1)(x-1)(x+2)} = \frac{(x+3)(x+1) - 2(x+2)}{(x+1)(x-1)(x+2)} = \frac{x^2+4x+3-2x-4}{(x+1)(x-1)(x+2)} = \frac{x^2+2x-1}{(x+1)(x-1)(x+2)}$$

73. $\dfrac{y+3}{5y^2} - \dfrac{y-5}{15y}$

LCD $= 15y^2$

$$\frac{y+3}{5y^2} - \frac{y-5}{15y} = \frac{(y+3)(3)}{15y^2} - \frac{(y-5)(y)}{15y^2} = \frac{(3y+9)-(y^2-5y)}{15y^2} = \frac{3y+9-y^2+5y}{15y^2} = \frac{-y^2+8y+9}{15y^2}$$

75. $\dfrac{x+3}{3x+6}+\dfrac{x}{4-x^2}$

$$3x+6=3(x+2)$$
$$4-x^2=(2+x)(2-x)$$

Note that $-1(2-x)=x-2$.
LCD $=3(x+2)(x-2)$

$$\begin{aligned}
&\frac{x+3}{3x+6}+\frac{x}{4-x^2}\\
&=\frac{x+3}{3(x+2)}+\frac{x}{(2+x)(2-x)}\\
&=\frac{x+3}{3(x+2)}+\frac{(-1)}{(-1)}\cdot\frac{x}{(2+x)(2-x)}\\
&=\frac{x+3}{3(x+2)}+\frac{-x}{(x+2)(x-2)}\\
&=\frac{(x+3)(x-2)}{3(x+2)(x-2)}+\frac{-x(3)}{3(x+2)(x-2)}\\
&=\frac{x^2+x-6-3x}{3(x+2)(x-2)}\\
&=\frac{x^2-2x-6}{3(x+2)(x-2)}
\end{aligned}$$

77. $\dfrac{y}{y^2-1}+\dfrac{2y}{y-y^2}$

$$y^2-1=(y+1)(y-1)$$
$$y-y^2=y(1-y)$$

Note that $-1(1-y)=y-1$.
LCD $=y(y+1)(y-1)$

$$\begin{aligned}
&\frac{y}{y^2-1}+\frac{2y}{y-y^2}\\
&=\frac{y}{(y+1)(y-1)}+\frac{2y}{y(1-y)}\\
&=\frac{y}{(y+1)(y-1)}+\frac{(-1)}{(-1)}\cdot\frac{2y}{y(1-y)}\\
&=\frac{y}{(y+1)(y-1)}+\frac{-2y}{y(y-1)}\\
&=\frac{y\cdot y}{y(y+1)(y-1)}+\frac{-2y(y+1)}{y(y+1)(y-1)}\\
&=\frac{y^2-2y(y+1)}{y(y+1)(y-1)}=\frac{y^2-2y^2-2y}{y(y+1)(y-1)}\\
&=\frac{-y^2-2y}{y(y+1)(y-1)}=\frac{-y(y+2)}{y(y+1)(y-1)}\\
&=-\frac{-1(y+2)}{(y+1)(y-1)}=\frac{-y-2}{(y+1)(y-1)}
\end{aligned}$$

79. $\dfrac{x-1}{x}+\dfrac{y+1}{y}$

LCD $=xy$

$$\begin{aligned}
\frac{x-1}{x}+\frac{y+1}{y}&=\frac{(x-1)(y)}{xy}+\frac{(y+1)(x)}{xy}\\
&=\frac{xy-y+xy+x}{xy}\\
&=\frac{x+2xy-y}{xy}
\end{aligned}$$

81. $\dfrac{3x}{x^2-y^2}-\dfrac{2}{y-x}$

$$x^2-y^2=(x+y)(x-y)$$

Note that $y-x=-1(x-y)$.
LCD $=(x+y)(x-y)$

$$\begin{aligned}
&\frac{3x}{x^2-y^2}-\frac{2}{y-x}\\
&=\frac{3x}{(x+y)(x-y)}-\frac{(-1)}{(-1)}\cdot\frac{2}{y-x}\\
&=\frac{3x}{(x+y)(x-y)}-\frac{-2}{x-y}\\
&=\frac{3x}{(x+y)(x-y)}-\frac{-2(x+y)}{(x+y)(x-y)}\\
&=\frac{3x+2(x+y)}{(x+y)(x-y)}=\frac{3x+2x+2y}{(x+y)(x-y)}\\
&=\frac{5x+2y}{(x+y)(x-y)}
\end{aligned}$$

83. Young's Rule: $C = \dfrac{DA}{A+12}$

$A = 8$:

$$C = \frac{D \cdot 8}{8+12} = \frac{8D}{20} = \frac{2D}{5}$$

$A = 3$:

$$C = \frac{D \cdot 3}{3+12} = \frac{3D}{15} = \frac{D}{5}$$

Difference:

$$\frac{2D}{5} - \frac{D}{5} = \frac{D}{5}$$

The difference is dosages for an 8-year-old child and a 3-year-old child is $\frac{D}{5}$. This means that an 8-year-old should be given $\frac{1}{5}$ more of the adult dosage than a 3-year-old.

85. Young's Rule:

$$C = \frac{DA}{A+12}$$

Cowling's Rule:

$$C = \frac{D(A+1)}{24}$$

For $A = 12$, Young's Rule gives

$$C = \frac{D \cdot 12}{12+12} = \frac{12D}{24} = \frac{D}{2}$$

and Cowling's Rule gives

$$C = \frac{D(12+1)}{24} = \frac{13D}{24}.$$

The difference between the dosages given by Cowling's Rule and Young's Rule is

$$\frac{13D}{24} - \frac{12D}{24} = \frac{D}{24}.$$

This means that Cowling's Rule says to give a 12-year-old $\frac{1}{24}$ of the adult dose more than Young's Rule says the dosage should be.

87. No, because the graphs cross, neither formula gives a consistently smaller dosage.

89. The difference in dosage is greatest at 13 years.

91. $P = 2L + 2W$

$$\begin{aligned}
&= 2\left(\frac{x}{x+3}\right) + 2\left(\frac{x}{x+4}\right) \\
&= \frac{2x}{x+3} + \frac{2x}{x+4} \\
&= \frac{2x(x+4)}{(x+3)(x+4)} + \frac{2x(x+3)}{(x+3)(x+4)} \\
&= \frac{2x^2 + 8x + 2x^2 + 6x}{(x+3)(x+4)} \\
&= \frac{4x^2 + 14x}{(x+3)(x+4)}
\end{aligned}$$

93. Answers may vary.

95. Explanations will vary. The right side of the equation should be charged from $\frac{3}{x+5}$ to $\frac{5+2x}{5x}$.

97. Answers may vary.

99. $\dfrac{x+6}{x^2-4}-\dfrac{x+3}{x+2}+\dfrac{x-3}{x-2}$

LCD $=(x+2)(x-2)$

$$\frac{x+6}{x^2-4}-\frac{x+3}{x+2}+\frac{x-3}{x-2}$$
$$=\frac{x+6}{(x+2)(x-2)}-\frac{x+3}{x+2}+\frac{x-3}{x-2}$$
$$=\frac{x+6}{(x+2)(x-2)}-\frac{(x+3)(x-2)}{(x+2)(x-2)}+\frac{(x-3)(x+2)}{(x+2)(x-2)}$$
$$=\frac{(x+6)-(x+3)(x-2)+(x-3)(x+2)}{(x+2)(x-2)}$$
$$=\frac{(x+6)-(x^2+x-6)+(x^2-x-6)}{(x+2)(x-2)}$$
$$=\frac{x+6-x^2-x+6+x^2-x-6}{(x+2)(x-2)}$$
$$=\frac{-x+6}{(x+2)(x-2)}$$

101. $\dfrac{y^2+5y+4}{y^2+2y-3}\cdot\dfrac{y^2+y-6}{y^2+2y-3}-\dfrac{2}{y-1}$

$$=\frac{(y+4)(y+1)}{(y+3)(y-1)}\cdot\frac{(y+3)(y-2)}{(y+3)(y-1)}-\frac{2}{y-1}$$
$$=\frac{(y+4)(y+1)(y-2)}{(y+3)(y-1)(y-1)}-\frac{2}{y-1}$$

LCD $=(y+3)(y-1)(y-1)$

$$=\frac{(y+4)(y+1)(y-2)}{(y+3)(y-1)(y-1)}-\frac{2(y+3)(y-1)}{(y+3)(y-1)(y-1)}$$
$$=\frac{(y+3)(y+1)((y-2)-2(y+3)(y-1)}{(y+3)(y-1)(y-1)}$$
$$=\frac{(y+4)(y^2-y-2)-2(y^2+2y-3)}{(y+3)(y-1)(y-1)}$$
$$=\frac{y^3+3y^2-6y-8-2y^2-4y+6}{(y+3)(y-1)(y-1)}$$
$$=\frac{y^3+y^2-10y-2}{(y+3)(y-1)(y-1)}$$

103. $\dfrac{4}{x-2}-\boxed{}=\dfrac{2x+8}{(x-2)(x+1)}$

The missing rational expression must have $(x+1)$ as a factor in its denominator or as the complete denominator.
Let $x=$ the numerator of the missing rational expression.

$$\frac{4}{x-2}-\frac{y}{x+1}=\frac{2x+8}{(x-2)(x+1)}$$

Then

$$\frac{4(x+1)-y(x-2)}{(x-2)(x+1)}=\frac{2x+8}{(x-2)(x+1)},$$

so

$$4x+4-yx+2y=2x+8,$$

which implies that

$$4x-yx=2x$$

and

$$4+2y=8.$$

Both of these equations give $y=2$. Thus, the missing rational expression is

$$\frac{2}{x+1}.$$

Review Exercises

104. $(3x+5)(2x-7) = 6x^2 - 21x + 10x - 35$
$= 6x^2 - 11x - 35$

105. $3x - y < 3$

Graph $3x - y = 3$ as a dashed line using the x-intercept, 1, and the y-intercept, -3. Use $(0,0)$ as a test point. Since $3 \cdot 0 - 0 < 3$ is a true statement, shade the half-plane including $(0,0)$.

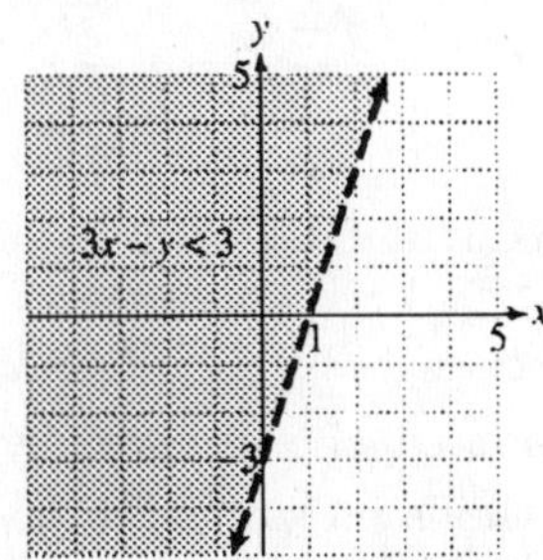

106. Line passing through $(-3,-4)$ and $(1,0)$
First, find the slope.

$$m = \frac{0-(-4)}{1-(-3)} = \frac{4}{4} = 1$$

Use $m = (1,0)$ and $(x_1, y_1) = (1,0)$ in the point-slope form and simplify to find the slope-intercept form.

$$y - y_1 = m(x - x_1)$$
$$y - 0 = 1(x-1)$$
$$y = x - 1$$

8.5 Complex Rational Expressions

8.5 CHECK POINTS

CHECK POINT 1

$$\frac{\frac{1}{4}+\frac{2}{3}}{\frac{2}{3}-\frac{1}{4}}$$

Step 1 Add to get a single rational expression in the numerator.

$$\frac{1}{4}+\frac{2}{3} = \frac{1}{4}\cdot\frac{3}{3}+\frac{2}{3}\cdot\frac{4}{4}$$
$$= \frac{3}{12}+\frac{8}{11} = \frac{11}{12}$$

Step 2 Subtract to get a single rational expression in the denominator.

$$\frac{2}{3}-\frac{1}{4} = \frac{2}{3}\cdot\frac{4}{4}-\frac{1}{4}\cdot\frac{3}{3}$$
$$= \frac{8}{12}-\frac{3}{12} = \frac{5}{12}$$

Step 3 and 4 Perform the division indicated by the main fraction bar: Invert and multiply. If possible, simplify.

$$\frac{\frac{1}{4}+\frac{2}{3}}{\frac{2}{3}-\frac{1}{4}} = \frac{\frac{11}{12}}{\frac{5}{12}} = \frac{11}{12}\cdot\frac{12}{5} = \frac{11}{5}$$

CHECK POINT 2

$$\frac{2-\frac{1}{x}}{2+\frac{1}{x}}$$

Step 1

$$2-\frac{1}{x} = \frac{2\cdot x}{1\cdot x}-\frac{1}{x} = \frac{2x-1}{x}$$

Step 2

$$2+\frac{1}{x} = \frac{2\cdot x}{1\cdot x}+\frac{1}{x} = \frac{2x+1}{x}$$

Step 3 and 4

$$\frac{2-\frac{1}{x}}{2+\frac{1}{x}} = \frac{\frac{2x-1}{x}}{\frac{2x+1}{x}} = \frac{2x-1}{x}\cdot\frac{x}{2x+1}$$
$$= \frac{2x-1}{2x+1}$$

CHECK POINT 3

$$\frac{\frac{1}{x}-\frac{1}{y}}{\frac{1}{xy}}=\frac{\frac{y-x}{xy}}{\frac{1}{xy}}=\frac{y-x}{xy}\cdot\frac{xy}{1}=y-x$$

CHECK POINT 4

$$\frac{\frac{1}{4}+\frac{2}{3}}{\frac{2}{3}-\frac{1}{4}}$$

LCD = 12

$$\frac{\frac{1}{4}+\frac{2}{3}}{\frac{2}{3}-\frac{1}{4}}=\frac{12}{12}\cdot\frac{\left(\frac{1}{4}+\frac{2}{3}\right)}{\left(\frac{2}{3}-\frac{1}{4}\right)}$$

$$=\frac{12\cdot\frac{1}{4}+12\cdot\frac{2}{3}}{12\cdot\frac{2}{3}-12\cdot\frac{1}{4}}$$

$$=\frac{3+8}{8-3}=\frac{11}{5}$$

CHECK POINT 5

$$\frac{2-\frac{1}{x}}{2+\frac{1}{x}}$$

LCD $= x$

$$\frac{2-\frac{1}{x}}{2+\frac{1}{x}}=\frac{x\left(2-\frac{1}{x}\right)}{x\left(2+\frac{1}{x}\right)}$$

$$=\frac{x\cdot 2-x\cdot\frac{1}{x}}{x\cdot 2+x\cdot\frac{1}{x}}$$

$$=\frac{2x-1}{2x+1}$$

CHECK POINT 6

$$\frac{\frac{1}{x}-\frac{1}{y}}{\frac{1}{xy}}$$

LCD $= xy$

$$\frac{\frac{1}{x}-\frac{1}{y}}{\frac{1}{xy}}=\frac{xy}{xy}\cdot\frac{\left(\frac{1}{x}-\frac{1}{y}\right)}{\left(\frac{1}{xy}\right)}=\frac{xy\cdot\frac{1}{x}-xy\cdot\frac{1}{x}}{xy\cdot\frac{1}{xy}}$$

$$=\frac{y-x}{1}=y-x$$

EXERCISE SET 8.5

In Exercises 1–39, each complex rational expression can be simlified by either of the two methods introduced in this section of the textbook. Both methods will be illustrated here.

1. $\dfrac{\frac{1}{2}+\frac{1}{4}}{\frac{1}{2}+\frac{1}{3}}$

Add to get a single rational expression in the numerator.

$$\frac{1}{2}+\frac{1}{4}=\frac{2}{4}+\frac{1}{4}=\frac{3}{4}$$

Add to get a single rational expression in the denominator.

$$\frac{1}{2}+\frac{1}{3}=\frac{3}{6}+\frac{2}{6}=\frac{5}{6}$$

Perform the division indicated by the fraction bar: Invert and multiply.

$$\frac{\frac{1}{2}+\frac{1}{4}}{\frac{1}{2}+\frac{1}{3}}=\frac{\frac{3}{4}}{\frac{5}{6}}=\frac{3}{\cancel{4}_{2}}\cdot\frac{\cancel{6}^{3}}{5}=\frac{9}{10}$$

3. $\dfrac{3+\dfrac{1}{2}}{4-\dfrac{1}{4}}$

$$3+\frac{1}{2}=\frac{6}{2}+\frac{1}{2}=\frac{7}{2}$$

$$4-\frac{1}{4}=\frac{16}{4}-\frac{1}{4}=\frac{15}{4}$$

$$\frac{3+\frac{1}{2}}{4-\frac{1}{4}}=\frac{\frac{7}{2}}{\frac{15}{4}}=\frac{7}{\cancel{2}_1}\cdot\frac{\cancel{4}^2}{15}=\frac{14}{15}$$

5. $\dfrac{\dfrac{2}{5}-\dfrac{1}{3}}{\dfrac{2}{3}-\dfrac{3}{4}}$

LCD = 60

$$\frac{\frac{2}{5}-\frac{1}{3}}{\frac{2}{3}-\frac{3}{4}}=\frac{60}{60}\cdot\frac{\left(\frac{2}{5}-\frac{1}{3}\right)}{\left(\frac{2}{3}-\frac{3}{4}\right)}$$

$$=\frac{60\cdot\frac{2}{5}-60\cdot\frac{1}{3}}{60\cdot\frac{2}{3}-60\cdot\frac{3}{4}}$$

$$=\frac{24-20}{40-45}$$

$$=\frac{4}{-5}=-\frac{4}{5}$$

7. $\dfrac{\dfrac{3}{4}-x}{\dfrac{3}{4}+x}=\dfrac{\dfrac{3}{4}-\dfrac{4x}{x}}{\dfrac{3}{4}+\dfrac{4x}{x}}$

$$=\frac{\frac{3-4x}{4}}{\frac{3+4x}{4}}$$

$$=\frac{3-4x}{4}\cdot\frac{4}{3+4x}$$

$$=\frac{3-4x}{3+4x}$$

9. $\dfrac{5-\dfrac{2}{x}}{3+\dfrac{1}{x}}=\dfrac{\dfrac{5x-2}{x}}{\dfrac{3x+1}{x}}=\dfrac{5x-2}{x}\cdot\dfrac{x}{3x+1}$

$$=\frac{5x-2}{3x+1}$$

11. $\dfrac{2+\dfrac{3}{7}}{1-\dfrac{7}{y}}=\dfrac{\dfrac{2y+3}{y}}{\dfrac{y-7}{y}}$

$$=\frac{2y+3}{y}\cdot\frac{y}{y-7}$$

$$=\frac{2y+3}{y-7}$$

13. $\dfrac{\dfrac{1}{y}-\dfrac{3}{2}}{\dfrac{1}{y}+\dfrac{3}{4}}=\dfrac{\dfrac{2-3y}{2y}}{\dfrac{4+3y}{4y}}$

$$=\frac{2-3y}{2y}\cdot\frac{4y}{4+3y}$$

$$=\frac{2(2-3y)}{4+3y}=\frac{4-6y}{4+3y}$$

15. $\dfrac{\dfrac{x}{5}-\dfrac{5}{x}}{\dfrac{1}{5}+\dfrac{1}{x}}$

LCD = $5x$

$$\frac{\frac{x}{5}-\frac{5}{x}}{\frac{1}{5}+\frac{1}{x}}=\frac{5x}{5x}\cdot\frac{\left(\frac{x}{5}-\frac{5}{x}\right)}{\left(\frac{1}{5}+\frac{1}{x}\right)}$$

$$=\frac{5x\cdot\frac{x}{5}-5x\cdot\frac{5}{x}}{5x\cdot\frac{1}{5}+5x\cdot\frac{1}{x}}$$

$$=\frac{x^2-25}{x+5}$$

$$=\frac{(x+5)(x-5)}{x+5}=x-5$$

17. $\dfrac{1+\dfrac{1}{x}}{1-\dfrac{1}{x^2}} = \dfrac{\dfrac{x+1}{x}}{\dfrac{x^2-1}{x^2}}$

$= \dfrac{x+1}{x} \cdot \dfrac{x}{x^2-1}$

$= \dfrac{x+1}{x} \cdot \dfrac{x^2}{(x+1)(x-1)}$

$= \dfrac{x}{x-1}$

19. $\dfrac{\dfrac{1}{7}-\dfrac{1}{y}}{\dfrac{7-y}{7}}$

LCD = $7y$

$$\frac{\frac{1}{7}-\frac{1}{y}}{\frac{7-y}{7}} = \frac{7y}{7y} \cdot \frac{\left(\frac{1}{7}-\frac{1}{y}\right)}{\left(\frac{7-y}{7}\right)}$$

$$= \frac{7y\left(\frac{1}{7}\right) - 7y\left(\frac{1}{y}\right)}{7y\left(\frac{7-y}{7}\right)}$$

$$= \frac{y-7}{y(7-y)}$$

$$= \frac{-1(7-y)}{y(7-y)} = -\frac{1}{y}$$

21. $\dfrac{x+\dfrac{1}{y}}{\dfrac{x}{y}} = \dfrac{\dfrac{xy+1}{y}}{\dfrac{x}{y}}$

$= \dfrac{xy+1}{y} \cdot \dfrac{y}{x}$

$= \dfrac{xy+1}{x}$

23. $\dfrac{\dfrac{1}{x}+\dfrac{1}{y}}{xy}$

LCD = xy

$$\frac{\frac{1}{x}+\frac{1}{y}}{xy} = \frac{xy}{xy} \cdot \frac{\left(\frac{1}{x}+\frac{1}{y}\right)}{(xy)} = \frac{y+x}{x^2y^2}$$

25. $\dfrac{\dfrac{x}{y}+\dfrac{1}{x}}{\dfrac{y}{x}+\dfrac{1}{x}} = \dfrac{\dfrac{x^2+y}{xy}}{\dfrac{y+1}{x}} = \dfrac{x^2+y}{xy} \cdot \dfrac{x}{y+1}$

$= \dfrac{x^2+y}{y(y+1)}$

27. $\dfrac{\dfrac{1}{y}+\dfrac{2}{y^2}}{\dfrac{2}{y}+1}$

LCD = y^2

$$\frac{\frac{1}{y}+\frac{2}{y^2}}{\frac{2}{y}+1} = \frac{y^2}{y^2} \cdot \frac{\left(\frac{1}{y}+\frac{2}{y^2}\right)}{\left(\frac{2}{y}+1\right)}$$

$$= \frac{y^2\left(\frac{1}{y}\right) + y^2\left(\frac{2}{y^2}\right)}{y^2\left(\frac{2}{y}\right) + y^2(1)}$$

$$= \frac{y+2}{2y+y^2}$$

$$= \frac{(y+2)}{y(2+y)} = \frac{1}{y}$$

29. $\dfrac{\dfrac{12}{x^2}-\dfrac{3}{x}}{\dfrac{15}{x}-\dfrac{9}{x^2}} = \dfrac{\dfrac{12}{x^2}-\dfrac{3x}{x^2}}{\dfrac{15x}{x^2}-\dfrac{9}{x^2}} = \dfrac{\dfrac{12-3x}{x^2}}{\dfrac{15x-9}{x^2}}$

$= \dfrac{12-3x}{x^2} \cdot \dfrac{x^2}{15x-9} = \dfrac{12-3x}{15x-9}$

$= \dfrac{3(4-x)}{3(5x-3)} = \dfrac{4-x}{5x-3}$

31. $\dfrac{2+\dfrac{6}{y}}{1-\dfrac{9}{y^2}}$

$\text{LCD} = y^2$

$$\frac{2+\dfrac{6}{y}}{1-\dfrac{9}{y^2}} = \frac{y^2}{y^2}\cdot\frac{\left(2+\dfrac{6}{y}\right)}{\left(1-\dfrac{9}{y^2}\right)}$$
$$= \frac{2y^2+6y}{y^2-9}$$
$$= \frac{2y(y+3)}{(y+3)(y-3)}$$
$$= \frac{2y}{y-3}$$

33. $\dfrac{\dfrac{1}{x+2}}{1+\dfrac{1}{x+2}}$

$\text{LCD} = x+2$

$$\frac{\dfrac{1}{x+2}}{1+\dfrac{1}{x+2}} = \frac{x+2}{x+2}\cdot\frac{\left(\dfrac{1}{x+2}\right)}{\left(1+\dfrac{1}{x+2}\right)}$$
$$= \frac{1}{x+2+1} = \frac{1}{x+3}$$

35. $\dfrac{x-5+\dfrac{3}{x}}{x-7+\dfrac{2}{x}}$

$\text{LCD} = x$

$$\frac{x-5+\dfrac{3}{x}}{x-7+\dfrac{2}{x}} = \frac{x}{x}\cdot\frac{\left(x-5+\dfrac{3}{x}\right)}{\left(x-7+\dfrac{2}{x}\right)}$$
$$= \frac{x^2-5x+3}{x^2-7x+2}$$

37. $\dfrac{\dfrac{3}{xy^2}+\dfrac{2}{x^2y}}{\dfrac{1}{x^2y}+\dfrac{2}{xy^3}} = \dfrac{\dfrac{3x}{x^2y^2}+\dfrac{2y}{x^2y^2}}{\dfrac{y^2}{x^2y^3}+\dfrac{2x}{x^2y^3}}$

$$= \frac{\dfrac{3x+2y}{x^2y^2}}{\dfrac{y^2+2x}{x^2+y^3}}$$
$$= \frac{3x+2y}{x^2y^2}\cdot\frac{x^2y^3}{y^2+2x}$$
$$= \frac{(3x+2y)(y)}{y^2+2x}$$
$$= \frac{3xy+2y^2}{y^2+2x}$$

39. $\dfrac{\dfrac{3}{x+1}-\dfrac{3}{x-1}}{\dfrac{5}{x^2-1}}$

$$= \frac{\dfrac{3(x-1)-3(x+1)}{(x+1)(x-1)}}{\dfrac{5}{x^2-1}}$$
$$= \frac{\dfrac{3x-3-3x-3}{(x+1)(x-1)}}{\dfrac{5}{x^2-1}}$$
$$= \frac{\dfrac{-6}{(x+1)(x-1)}}{\dfrac{5}{x^2-1}}$$
$$= \frac{-6}{(x+1)(x-1)}\cdot\frac{x^2-1}{5}$$
$$= \frac{-6}{(x+1)(x-1)}\cdot\frac{(x+1)(x-1)}{5}$$
$$= -\frac{6}{5}$$

41. $\dfrac{2d}{\dfrac{d}{r_1}+\dfrac{d}{r_2}}$

LCD $= r_1r_2$

$$\frac{2d}{\dfrac{d}{r_1}+\dfrac{d}{r_2}} = \frac{r_1r_2}{r_1r_2}\cdot\frac{2d}{\left(\dfrac{d}{r_1}+\dfrac{d}{r_2}\right)}$$
$$= \frac{2r_1r_2d}{r_2d+r_1d}$$

If $r_1 = 40$ and $r_2 = 30$, the value of this expression will be

$$\frac{2\cdot 40\cdot 30\cdot d}{30d+40d} = \frac{2400d}{70d}$$
$$= \frac{240}{7}$$
$$= 34\tfrac{2}{7}.$$

Your average speed will be $34\frac{2}{7}$ miles per hour.

For Exercises 43–45, answers may vary.

47. Simplify the given complex fraction
LCD $= x^6$

$$\frac{x^6}{x^6}\cdot\frac{\left(\dfrac{1}{x}+\dfrac{1}{x^2}+\dfrac{1}{x^3}\right)}{\left(\dfrac{1}{x^4}+\dfrac{1}{x^5}+\dfrac{1}{x^6}\right)}$$
$$= \frac{\dfrac{x^6}{x}+\dfrac{x^6}{x^2}+\dfrac{x^6}{x^3}}{\dfrac{x^6}{x^4}+\dfrac{x^6}{x^5}+\dfrac{x^6}{x^6}}$$
$$= \frac{x^5+x^4+x^3}{x^2+x+1}$$
$$= \frac{x^3(x^2+x+1)}{x^3}$$
$$= x^3$$

Because the rational expression can be simplified to x^3, this is what it does it each number x: It cubes x.

49. $\dfrac{1+\dfrac{1}{y}-\dfrac{6}{y^2}}{1-\dfrac{5}{y}+\dfrac{6}{y^2}} - \dfrac{1-\dfrac{1}{y}}{1-\dfrac{2}{y}-\dfrac{3}{y^2}}$

Simplify the first complex rational expression using by the LCD method.

$$\frac{y^2}{y^2}\cdot\frac{\left(1+\dfrac{1}{y}-\dfrac{6}{y^2}\right)}{\left(1-\dfrac{5}{y}+\dfrac{6}{y^2}\right)} = \frac{y^2+y-6}{y^2-5y+6}$$

Simplify the second complex algebraic expression by the LCD method.

$$\frac{y^2}{y^2}\cdot\frac{\left(1-\dfrac{1}{y}\right)}{\left(1-\dfrac{2}{y}-\dfrac{3}{y^2}\right)} = \frac{y^2-y}{y^2-2y-3}$$

Now subtract.

$$\frac{y^2+y-6}{y^2-5y+6} - \frac{y^2-y}{y^2-2y-3}$$
$$= \frac{y^2+y-6}{(y-2)(y-3)} - \frac{y^2-y}{(y-3)(y+1)}$$
$$= \frac{(y-2)(y+3)}{(y-2)(y-3)} - \frac{y^2-y}{(y-3)(y+1)}$$
$$= \frac{y+3}{y-3} - \frac{y^2-y}{(y-3)(y+1)}$$

LCD $= (y-3)(y+1)$

$$= \frac{(y+3)(y+1)}{(y-3)(y+1)} - \frac{y^2-y}{(y-3)(y+1)}$$
$$= \frac{(y+3)(y+1)-(y^2-y)}{(y-3)(y+1)}$$
$$= \frac{(y^2+4y+3)-(y^2-y)}{(y-3)(y+1)}$$
$$= \frac{y^2+4y+3-y^2+y}{(y-3)(y+1)}$$
$$= \frac{5y+3}{(y-3)(y+1)}$$

51.

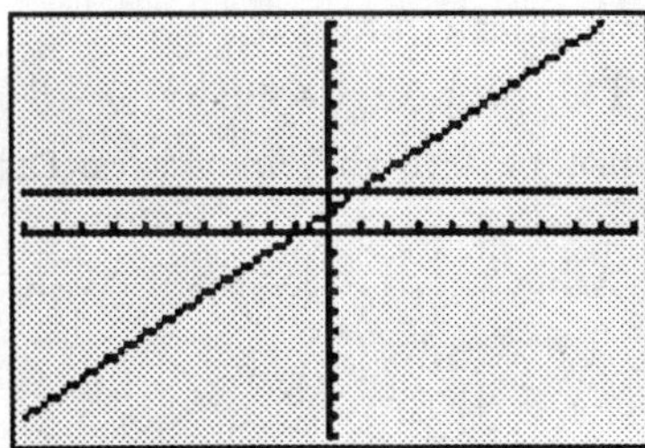

The graphs do not coincide.

$$\frac{\frac{1}{x}+1}{\frac{1}{x}} = \frac{\frac{1}{x}+\frac{x}{x}}{\frac{1}{x}} = \frac{\frac{1+x}{x}}{\frac{1}{x}}$$

$$= \frac{1+x}{x} \cdot \frac{x}{1} = 1+x$$

Change the expression on the right to $1+x$.

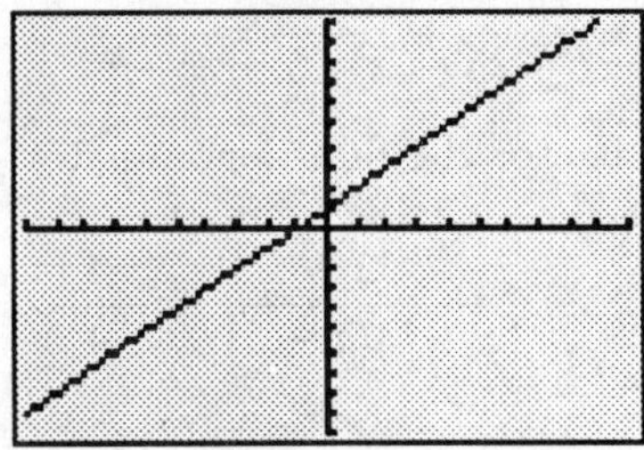

Review Exercises

53. $2x^3 - 20x^2 + 50x = 2x(x^2 - 10x + 25)$
$= 2x(x-5)^2$

54. $2 - 3(x-2) = 5(x+5) - 1$

$$2 - 3x + 6 = 5x + 25 - 1$$
$$8 - 3x = 5x + 24$$
$$8 - 3x - 5x = 5x + 24 - 5x$$
$$8 - 8x = 24$$
$$8 - 8x - 8 = 24 - 8$$
$$-8x = 16$$
$$\frac{-8x}{-8} = \frac{16}{-8}$$
$$x = -2$$

The solution is -2.

55. $(x+y)(x^2 - xy + y^2)$
$= x(x^2 - xy + y^2) + y(x^2 - xy + y^2)$
$= x^3 - x^2y + xy^2 + x^2y - xy^2 + y^3$
$= x^3 + y^3$

8.6 Solving Rational Equations

8.6 CHECK POINTS

CHECK POINT 1

$$\frac{x}{6} = \frac{1}{6} + \frac{x}{8}$$

The LCD is 24. To clear the equation of fractions, multiply both sides by 24.

$$\frac{x}{6} = \frac{1}{6} + \frac{x}{8}$$
$$24\left(\frac{x}{6}\right) = 24\left(\frac{1}{6} + \frac{x}{8}\right)$$
$$24 \cdot \frac{x}{6} = 24 \cdot \frac{1}{6} + 24 \cdot \frac{x}{8}$$
$$4x = 4 + 3x$$
$$x = 4$$

Check by substituting 4 for x in the original equation:

$$\frac{x}{6} = \frac{1}{6} + \frac{x}{8}$$
$$\frac{4}{6} \stackrel{?}{=} \frac{1}{6} + \frac{4}{8}$$
$$\frac{4}{6} \stackrel{?}{=} \frac{1}{6} + \frac{1}{2}$$
$$\frac{4}{6} \stackrel{?}{=} \frac{1}{6} + \frac{3}{6}$$
$$\frac{4}{6} = \frac{4}{6} \text{ true}$$

The solution is 4.

CHECK POINT 2

$$\frac{5}{2x} = \frac{17}{18} - \frac{1}{3x}$$

The denominators are $2x, 18$, and $3x$, so the LCD is $18x$. In this equation, x cannot equal zero because that would make two of the denominator equal to zero.

$$\frac{5}{2x} = \frac{17}{18} - \frac{1}{3x}, x \neq 0$$
$$18x \cdot \frac{5}{2x} = 18x\left(\frac{17}{18} - \frac{1}{3x}\right)$$
$$18x \cdot \frac{5}{2x} = 18x \cdot \frac{17}{18} - 18x \cdot \frac{1}{3x}$$
$$45 = 17x - 6$$
$$51 = 17x$$
$$3 = x$$

Check by substituting 3 for x in the original equation. Note that the original restriction that $x \neq 0$ is met. The solution is 3.

CHECK POINT 3

$$x + \frac{6}{x} = -5$$

Step 1 List restrictions on the variable. The restriction is $x \neq 0$.

Step 2 Multiply both sides by the LCD. The LCD is x.

$$x + \frac{6}{x} = -5, x \neq 0$$
$$x\left(x + \frac{6}{x}\right) = x(-5)$$
$$x \cdot x + x \cdot \frac{6}{x} = x(-5)$$
$$x^2 + 6 = -5x$$

Step 3 Solve the resulting equation.

$$x^2 + 5x + 6 = 0$$
$$(x+3)(x+2) = 0$$
$$x + 3 = 0 \quad \text{or} \quad x + 2 = 0$$
$$x = -3 \qquad\qquad x = -2$$

Step 4 Check proposed solutions in the original equation.
The proposed solutions, -3 and -2, are not part of the restriction that $x \neq 0$.

Check -3:

$$x + \frac{6}{x} = -5$$
$$-3 + \frac{6}{-3} \stackrel{?}{=} -5$$
$$-3 - 2 \stackrel{?}{=} -5$$
$$-5 = -5 \text{ true}$$

Check -2:

$$x + \frac{6}{x} = -5$$
$$-2 + \frac{6}{-2} \stackrel{?}{=} -5$$
$$-3 + (-2) \stackrel{?}{=} -5$$
$$-5 = -5 \text{ true}$$

The solutions are -3 and -2.

CHECK POINT 4

$$\frac{11}{x^2 - 25} + \frac{4}{x+5} = \frac{3}{x-5}$$

Factor the first denominator.

$$\frac{11}{(x+5)(x-5)} + \frac{4}{x+5} = \frac{3}{x-5}$$

The restrictions are $x \neq -5, x \neq 5$.
The LCD is $(x+5)(x-5)$.

$$(x+5)(x-5)\left[\frac{11}{(x+5)(x-5)} + \frac{4}{x+5}\right]$$
$$= (x+5)(x-5) \cdot \frac{3}{x-5}$$
$$11 + 4(x-5) = (x+5) \cdot 3$$
$$11 + 4x - 20 = 3x + 15$$
$$4x - 9 = 3x + 15$$
$$x - 9 = 15$$
$$x = 24$$

The proposed solution, 24, is not part of the restriction that $x \neq -5, x \neq 5$. Substitute 24 for x in the given equation to verify that 24 is the solutions.

CHECK POINT 5

$$\frac{x}{x-3} = \frac{3}{x-3} + 9$$

The restriction is $x \neq 3$.
The LCD is $x - 3$.

$$\frac{x}{x-3} = \frac{3}{x-3} + 9, x \neq 3$$
$$(x-3) \cdot \frac{x}{x-3} = (x-3)\left(\frac{3}{x-3} + 9\right)$$
$$(x-3) \cdot \frac{x}{x-3} = (x-3) \cdot \frac{3}{x-3} + (x-3) \cdot 9$$
$$x = 3 + 9x - 27$$
$$-8x = -24$$
$$x = 3$$

The proposed solution, 3, is *not* a solution because of the restriction $x \neq 3$. Notice that 3 makes two of the denominators zero in the original equation. Therefore, this equation has no solution.

CHECK POINT 6

$$y = \frac{250x}{100-x}; y = 750$$

$$750 = \frac{250x}{100-x}$$
$$(100-x)(750) = (100-x) \cdot \frac{250x}{100-x}$$
$$75{,}000 - 750x = 250x$$
$$75{,}000 = 1000x$$
$$75 = x$$

If the government spends \$750 million, 75% of the pollutants can be removed.

EXERCISE SET 8.6

In Exercises 1–43, all proposed solutions that are on the list of restritions on the variable should be rejected and all other proposed solutions should be checked in the original equation. Checks will not be shown here.

1. $\frac{x}{3} = \frac{x}{2} - 2$

There are no restrictions on the variable because the variable does not appear in any denominator.
The LCD is 6.

$$\frac{x}{3} = \frac{x}{2} - 2$$
$$6\left(\frac{x}{3}\right) = 6\left(\frac{x}{2} - 2\right)$$
$$6 \cdot \frac{x}{3} = 6 \cdot \frac{x}{2} - 6 \cdot 2$$
$$2x = 3x - 12$$
$$0 = x - 12$$
$$12 = x$$

The solution is 12.

3. $\frac{4x}{3} = \frac{x}{18} - \frac{x}{6}$

There are no restrictions.
The LCD is 18.

$$\frac{4x}{3} = \frac{x}{18} - \frac{x}{6}$$
$$18\left(\frac{4x}{3}\right) = 18\left(\frac{x}{18} - \frac{x}{6}\right)$$
$$18 \cdot \frac{4x}{3} = 18 \cdot \frac{x}{18} - 18 \cdot \frac{x}{6}$$
$$24x = x - 3x$$
$$24x = -2x$$
$$26x = 0$$
$$x = 0$$

The solution is 0.

5. $2 - \frac{8}{x} = 6$

The restriction is $x \neq 0$.
The LCD is x.

$$\begin{aligned} 2 - \frac{8}{x} &= 6 \\ x\left(2 - \frac{8}{x}\right) &= x \cdot 6 \\ x \cdot 2 - x \cdot \frac{8}{x} &= x \cdot 6 \\ 2x - 8 &= 6x \\ -8 &= 4x \\ -2 &= x \end{aligned}$$

The solution is -2.

7. $\frac{4}{x} + \frac{1}{2} = \frac{5}{x}$

The restriction is $x \neq 0$.
The LCD is $2x$.

$$\begin{aligned} \frac{4}{x} + \frac{1}{2} &= \frac{5}{x} \\ 2x\left(\frac{4}{x} + \frac{1}{2}\right) &= 2x\left(\frac{5}{x}\right) \\ 2x \cdot \frac{4}{x} + 2x \cdot \frac{1}{2} &= 2x \cdot \frac{5}{x} \\ 8 + x &= 10 \\ x &= 2 \end{aligned}$$

The solution is 2.

9. $\frac{2}{x} + 3 = \frac{5}{2x} + \frac{13}{4}$

The restriction is $x \neq 0$.
The LCD is $4x$.

$$\begin{aligned} \frac{2}{x} + 3 &= \frac{5}{2x} + \frac{13}{4} \\ 4x\left(\frac{2}{x} + 3\right) &= 4x\left(\frac{5}{2x} + \frac{13}{4}\right) \\ 8 + 12x &= 10 + 13x \\ 8 &= 10 + x \\ -2 &= x \end{aligned}$$

The solution is -2.

11. $\frac{2}{3x} + \frac{1}{4} = \frac{11}{6x} - \frac{1}{3}$

The restriction is $x \neq 0$.
The LCD is $12x$.

$$\begin{aligned} \frac{2}{3x} + \frac{1}{4} &= \frac{11}{6x} - \frac{1}{3} \\ 12\left(\frac{2}{3x} + \frac{1}{4}\right) &= 12x\left(\frac{11}{6x} - \frac{1}{3}\right) \\ 8 + 3x &= 22 - 4x \\ 8 + 7x &= 22 \\ 7x &= 14 \\ x &= 2 \end{aligned}$$

The solution is 2.

13. $\frac{6}{x+3} = \frac{4}{x-3}$

Restrictions: $x \neq -3, x \neq 3$
LCD $= (x+3)(x-3)$

$$\begin{aligned} \frac{6}{x+3} &= \frac{4}{x-3} \\ (x-3)(x-3) \cdot \frac{6}{x+3} &= (x+3)(x-3) \cdot \frac{4}{x-3} \\ (x-3) \cdot 6 &= (x+3) \cdot 4 \\ 6x - 18 &= 4x + 12 \\ 2x - 18 &= 12 \\ 2x &= 30 \\ x &= 15 \end{aligned}$$

The solution is 15.

15. $\frac{x-2}{2x} + 1 = \frac{x+1}{x}$

Restriction: $x \neq 0$
LCD $= 2x$

$$\begin{aligned} \frac{x-2}{2x} + 1 &= \frac{x+1}{x} \\ 2x\left(\frac{x-2}{2x} + 1\right) &= 2x\left(\frac{x+1}{x}\right) \\ x - 2 + 2x &= 2(x+1) \\ 3x - 2 &= 2x + 2 \\ x - 2 &= 2 \\ x &= 4 \end{aligned}$$

The solution is 4.

17. $x + \frac{6}{x} = -7$

Restriction: $x \neq 0$
LCD $= x$

$$\begin{aligned} x + \frac{6}{x} &= -7 \\ x\left(x + \frac{6}{x}\right) &= x(-7) \\ x^2 + 6 &= -7x \\ x^2 + 7x + 6 &= 0 \\ (x+6)(x+1) &= 0 \end{aligned}$$

$$x + 6 = 0 \quad \text{or} \quad x + 1 = 0$$
$$x = -6 \qquad\qquad x = -1$$

The solutions are -6 and -1.

19. $\frac{x}{5} - \frac{5}{x} = 0$

Restriction: $x \neq 0$
LCD $= 5x$

$$\begin{aligned} \frac{x}{5} - \frac{5}{x} &= 0 \\ 5x\left(\frac{x}{5} - \frac{5}{x}\right) &= 5x \cdot 0 \\ 5x \cdot \frac{x}{5} - 5x \cdot \frac{5}{x} &= 0 \\ x^2 - 25 &= 0 \\ (x+5)(x-5) &= 0 \end{aligned}$$

$$x + 5 = 0 \quad \text{or} \quad x - 5 = 0$$
$$x = -5 \qquad\qquad x = 5$$

The solutions are -5 and 5.

21. $x + \frac{3}{x} = \frac{12}{x}$

Restriction: $x \neq 0$
LCD $= x$

$$\begin{aligned} x + \frac{3}{x} &= \frac{12}{x} \\ x\left(x + \frac{3}{x}\right) &= x\left(\frac{12}{x}\right) \\ x^2 + 3 &= 12 \\ x^2 - 9 &= 0 \\ (x+3)(x-3) &= 0 \end{aligned}$$

$$x + 3 = 0 \quad \text{or} \quad x - 3 = 0$$
$$x = -3 \qquad\qquad x = 3$$

The solutions are -3 and 3.

23. $\frac{4}{y} - \frac{y}{2} = \frac{7}{2}$

Restrictions: $y \neq 0$
LCD $= 2y$

$$\begin{aligned} \frac{4}{y} - \frac{y}{2} &= \frac{7}{2} \\ 2y\left(\frac{4}{y} - \frac{y}{2}\right) &= 2y\left(\frac{7}{2}\right) \\ 8 - y^2 &= 7y \\ 0 &= y^2 + 7y - 8 \\ 0 &= (y+8)(y-1) \end{aligned}$$

$$y + 8 = 0 \quad \text{or} \quad y - 1 = 0$$
$$y = -8 \qquad\qquad y = 1$$

The solutions are -8 and 1.

25. $\frac{x-4}{x} = \frac{15}{x+4}$

Restrictions: $x \neq 0, x \neq -4$
LCD $= x(x+4)$

$$\begin{aligned} \frac{x-4}{x} &= \frac{15}{x+4} \\ x(x+4)\left(\frac{x-4}{x}\right) &= x(x+4)\left(\frac{15}{x+4}\right) \\ (x+4)(x-4) &= x \cdot 15 \\ x^2 - 16 &= 15x \\ x^2 - 15x - 16 &= 0 \\ (x+1)(x-16) &= 0 \end{aligned}$$

$$x+1=0 \quad \text{or} \quad x-16=0$$
$$x=-1 \qquad\qquad x=16$$

The solutions are -1 and 16.

27. $\dfrac{1}{x-1}+5=\dfrac{11}{x-1}$

Restriction: $x \neq 1$
LCD $= x-1$

$$\frac{1}{x-1}+5=\frac{11}{x-1}$$
$$(x-1)\left(\frac{1}{x-1}+5\right)=(x-1)\left(\frac{11}{x-1}\right)$$
$$1+(x-1)\cdot 5=11$$
$$1+5x-5=11$$
$$5x-4=11$$
$$5x=15$$
$$x=3$$

The solution is 3.

29. $\dfrac{8y}{y+1}=4-\dfrac{8}{y+1}$

Restriction: $y \neq -1$
LCD $= y+1$

$$\frac{8y}{y+1}=4-\frac{8}{y+1}$$
$$(y+1)\left(\frac{8y}{y+1}\right)=(y+1)\left(4-\frac{8}{y+1}\right)$$
$$8y=(y+1)\cdot 4-8$$
$$8y=4y+4-8$$
$$8y=4y-4$$
$$4y=-4$$
$$y=-1$$

The proposed solution, -1, is a solution because of the restriction $x \neq -1$. Notice that -1 makes two of the denominators zero in the original equation. Therefore, the equation has no solution.

31. $\dfrac{3}{x-1}+\dfrac{8}{x}=3$

Restrictions: $x \neq 1, x \neq 0$
LCD $= x(x-1)$

$$\frac{3}{x-1}+\frac{8}{x}=3$$
$$x(x-1)\left(\frac{3}{x-1}+\frac{8}{x}\right)=x(x-1)\cdot 3$$
$$x(x-1)\cdot\frac{3}{x-1}+x(x-1)\cdot\frac{8}{x}=3x(x-1)$$
$$3x+8(x-1)=3x^2-3x$$
$$3x+8x-8=3x^2-3x$$
$$11x-8=3x^2-3x$$
$$0=3x^2-14x+8$$
$$0=(3x-2)(x-4)$$

$$0=3x-2 \text{ or } x-4=0$$
$$3x-2=0 \quad \text{or} \quad x-4=0$$
$$3x=2 \qquad\qquad x=4$$
$$x=\frac{2}{3}$$

The solutions are $\frac{2}{3}$ and 4.

33. $\dfrac{3y}{y-4}-5=\dfrac{12}{y-4}$

Restriction: $y \neq 4$
LCD $= y-4$

$$\frac{3y}{y-4}-5=\frac{12}{y-4}$$
$$(y-4)\left(\frac{3y}{y-4}-5\right)=(y-4)\left(\frac{12}{y-4}\right)$$
$$3y-5(y-4)=12$$
$$3y-5y+20=12$$
$$-2y+20=12$$
$$-2y=-8$$
$$y=4$$

The proposed solution, 4, is *not* a solution because of the restriction $y \neq 4$. Therefore, equation has no solution.

35. $\dfrac{1}{x}+\dfrac{1}{x-3}=\dfrac{x-2}{x-3}$

Restrictions: $x \neq 0, x \neq 3$

LCD $= x(x-3)$

$$\frac{1}{x}+\frac{1}{x-3}=\frac{x-2}{x-3}$$

$$x(x-3)\left(\frac{1}{x}+\frac{1}{x-3}\right)=x(x-3)\cdot\frac{x-2}{x-3}$$

$$x-3+x=x(x-2)$$

$$2x-3=x^2-2x$$

$$0=x^2-4x+3$$

$$0=(x-3)(x-1)$$

$$x-3=0 \quad \text{or} \quad x-1=0$$

$$x=3 \qquad\qquad x=1$$

The proposed solution 3 is *not* a solution because of the restriction $x \neq -3$.

The proposed solution 1 checks in the original equation.

The solution is 1.

37. $\dfrac{x+1}{3x+9}+\dfrac{x}{2x+6}=\dfrac{2}{4x+12}$

To find any restrictions and the LCD, factor the denominators.

$$\frac{x+1}{3(x+3)}+\frac{x}{2(x+3)}=\frac{2}{4(x+3)}$$

Restriction: $x \neq -3$

LCD $= 12(x+3)$

$$12(x+3)\left[\frac{x+1}{3(x+3)}+\frac{x}{2(x+3)}\right]$$

$$=12(x+3)\left[\frac{2}{4(x+3)}\right]$$

$$4(x+1)+6x=6$$

$$4x+4+6x=6$$

$$10x+4=6$$

$$10x=2$$

$$x=\frac{2}{10}=\frac{1}{5}$$

The solution is $\frac{1}{5}$.

39. $\dfrac{4y}{y^2-25}+\dfrac{2}{y-5}=\dfrac{1}{y+5}$

To find any restrictions and the LCD, factor the first denominator.

$$\frac{4y}{(y+5)(y-5)}+\frac{2}{y-5}=\frac{1}{y+5}$$

Restrictions: $y \neq -5, y \neq 5$

LCD $= (y+5)(y-5)$

$$(y+5)(y-5)\left[\frac{4y}{(y+5)(y-5)}+\frac{2}{y-5}\right]$$

$$=(y+5)(y-5)\cdot\frac{1}{y+5}$$

$$4y+2(y+5)=y-5$$

$$4y+2y+10=y-5$$

$$6y+10=y-5$$

$$5y+10=-5$$

$$5y=-15$$

$$y=-3$$

The solution is -3.

41. $\dfrac{1}{x-4}-\dfrac{5}{x+2}=\dfrac{6}{x^2-2x-8}$

Factor the last denominator.

$$\frac{1}{x-4}-\frac{5}{x+2}=\frac{6}{(x-4)(x+2)}$$

Restrictions: $x \neq 4, x \neq -2$

LCD $= (x-4)(x+2)$

$$(x-4)(x+2)\left[\frac{1}{x-4}-\frac{5}{x+2}\right]$$

$$=(x-4)(x+2)\left[\frac{6}{(x-4)(x+2)}\right]$$

$$(x+2)\cdot 1-(x-4)\cdot 5=6$$

$$x+2-5x+20=6$$

$$-4x+22=6$$

$$-4x=-16$$

$$x=4$$

The proposed solution 4 is *not* a solution because of the restriction $x \neq 4$. Therefore, the given equation has no solution.

43. $\dfrac{2}{x+3} - \dfrac{2x+3}{x-1} = \dfrac{6x-5}{x^2+2x-3}$

Factor the last denominator.

$$\frac{2}{x+3} - \frac{2x+3}{x-1} = \frac{6x-5}{(x+3)(x-1)}$$

Restrictions: $x \neq -3, x \neq 1$
LCD $= (x+3)(x-1)$

$$(x+3)(x-1)\left[\frac{2}{x+3} - \frac{2x+3}{x-1}\right]$$
$$= (x+3)(x-1)\left[\frac{6x-5}{(x+3)(x-1)}\right]$$

$$\begin{aligned}(x-1)\cdot 2 - (x+3)(2x+3) &= 6x-5\\ 2x-2-(2x^2+9x+9) &= 6x-5\\ 2x-2-2x^2-9x-9 &= 6x-5\\ -2x^2-7x-11 &= 6x-5\\ 0 &= 2x^2+13x+6\\ 0 &= (x+6)(2x+1)\end{aligned}$$

$x+6=0$ or $2x+1=0$
$x=-6$ $\quad 2x=-1$
$x=-\frac{1}{2}$

The solutions are -6 and $-\frac{1}{2}$.

45. $C = \dfrac{400x+500{,}000}{x}$; $C = 450$

$$450 = \frac{400x+500{,}000}{x}$$

LCD $= x$

$$x \cdot 450 = x\left(\frac{400x+500{,}000}{x}\right)$$

$$\begin{aligned}450x &= 40x + 500{,}000\\ 50x &= 500{,}000\\ x &= 10{,}000\end{aligned}$$

At an average cost of \$450 per wheelchair, 10,000 wheelchairs can be produced.

47. $C = \dfrac{2x}{100-x}$; $C = 2$

$$2 = \frac{2x}{100-x}$$

LCD $= 100 - x$

$$(100-x)\cdot 2 = (100-x)\cdot\frac{2x}{100-x}$$

$$\begin{aligned}200-2x &= 2x\\ 200 &= 4x\\ 50 &= x\end{aligned}$$

For \$2 million, 50% of the contaminants can be removed.

49. $C = \dfrac{DA}{A+12}$; $C = 300, D = 1000$

$$300 = \frac{1000A}{A+12}$$

LCD $= A + 12$

$$(A+12)\cdot 300 = (A+12)\left(\frac{1000A}{A+12}\right)$$

$$\begin{aligned}300A + 3600 &= 1000A\\ 3600 &= 700A\\ \frac{3600}{700} &= A\\ A &= \frac{36}{7} \approx 5.14\end{aligned}$$

To the nearest year, the child is 5 years old.

51. $C = \dfrac{10{,}000}{x} + 3x$; $C = 350$

$$350 = \frac{10{,}000}{x} + 3x$$

LCD $= x$

$$x \cdot 350x = x\left(\frac{10{,}000}{x} + 3x\right)$$

$$\begin{aligned}350x &= 10{,}000 + 3x^2\\ 0 &= 3x^2 - 350x + 10{,}000\\ 0 &= (3x-200)(x-50)\end{aligned}$$

$$
\begin{aligned}
3x - 200 &= 0 \qquad \text{or} \qquad x - 50 = 0 \\
3x &= 200 \qquad\qquad\qquad x = 50 \\
x &= \frac{200}{3} \\
&= 66\tfrac{2}{3} \approx 67
\end{aligned}
$$

For yearly inventory costs to be \$350, the owner should order either 50 or approximately 67 cases. These solutions correspond to the points $(50, 350)$ and $(67, 350)$ on the graph.

53. Let $x =$ the number of additional hits needed.
After x additional consecutive hits, the player's batting average will be

$$\frac{12 + x}{40 + x},$$

so solve the equation

$$\frac{12 + x}{40 + x} = 0.440.$$

Multiply both sides by the LCD, $40 + x$.

$$
\begin{aligned}
(40 + x)\left(\frac{12 + x}{40 + x}\right) &= (40 + x)(0.440) \\
12 + x &= 17.6 + 0.44x \\
12 + x - 12 &= 17.6 + 0.44x - 12 \\
x &= 5.6 + 0.44x \\
x - 0.44x &= 5.6 + 0.44x - 0.44x \\
0.56 &= 5.6 \\
\frac{0.56x}{0.56} &= \frac{5.6}{0.56} \\
x &= 10
\end{aligned}
$$

The player must get 10 additional consecutive hits to achieve a batting average of 0.440.

For Exercises 55–59, answers may vary.

61. Statement b is true.
The given equation is equivalent to the false statement $1 = 0$, so it has no solution.

63. $f = \dfrac{f_1 f_2}{f_1 + f_2}$ for f_2

$$f = \frac{f_1 f_2}{f_1 + f_2}$$

Multiply both sides by the LCD, $f_1 + f_2$.

$$
\begin{aligned}
(f_1 + f_2) \cdot f &= (f_1 + f_2)\left(\frac{f_1 f_2}{f_1 + f_2}\right) \\
f f_1 + f f_2 &= f_1 f_2
\end{aligned}
$$

Get all terms containing f_2 on one side and all terms not containing f_2 on the other side.

$$f f_2 - f_1 f_2 = -f_1 f$$

Factor out the common factor f_2 on the left side.

$$f_2(f - f_1) = -f_1 f$$

Divide both sides by $f - f_1$.

$$
\begin{aligned}
\frac{f_2(f - f_1)}{f - f_1} &= \frac{-f_1 f}{f - f_1} \\
f_2 &= \frac{-f_1 f}{f - f_1} \quad \text{or} \quad \frac{f f_1}{f_1 - f}
\end{aligned}
$$

65. $\left(\dfrac{x+1}{x+7}\right)^2 \div \left(\dfrac{x+1}{x+7}\right)^4 = 0$

$$\left(\frac{x+1}{x+7}\right)^2 \cdot \left(\frac{x+7}{x+1}\right)^4 = 0$$

$$\left(\frac{x+1}{x+7}\right)^2 \cdot \frac{(x+7)^4}{(x+1)^4} = 0$$

Restrictions: $x \neq -7, x \neq -1$

$$\frac{(x+7)^2}{(x+1)^2} = 0$$

Multiply both sides by $(x+1)^2$.

$$(x+1)^2\left[\frac{(x+7)^2}{(x+1)^2}\right] = (x+1)^2 \cdot 0$$

$$(x+7)^2 = 0$$

$$x+7 = 0$$

$$x = -7$$

The proposed solution, -7, *not* a solution of the original equation because it is on the list of restrictions. Therefore, the given equation has no solution.

67. $\dfrac{x}{2} + \dfrac{x}{4} = 6$

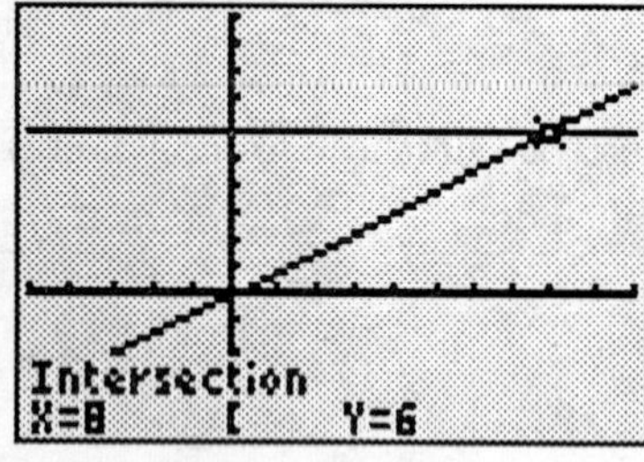

The solution is 8.

Check:

$$\frac{x}{2} + \frac{x}{4} = 6$$

$$\frac{8}{2} + \frac{8}{4} \stackrel{?}{=} 6$$

$$4 + 2 \stackrel{?}{=} 6$$

$$6 = 6 \text{ true}$$

69. $x + \dfrac{6}{x} = -5$

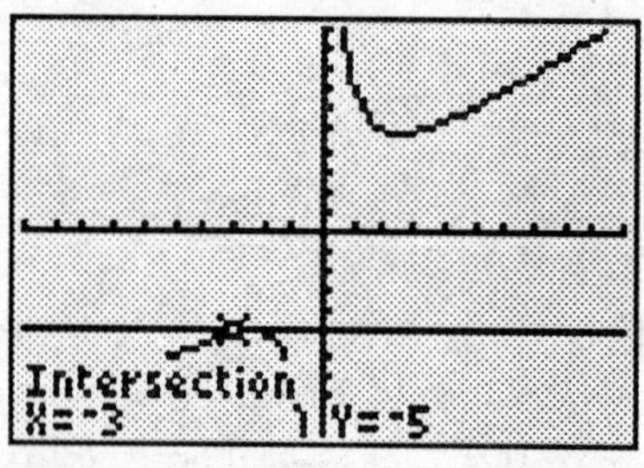

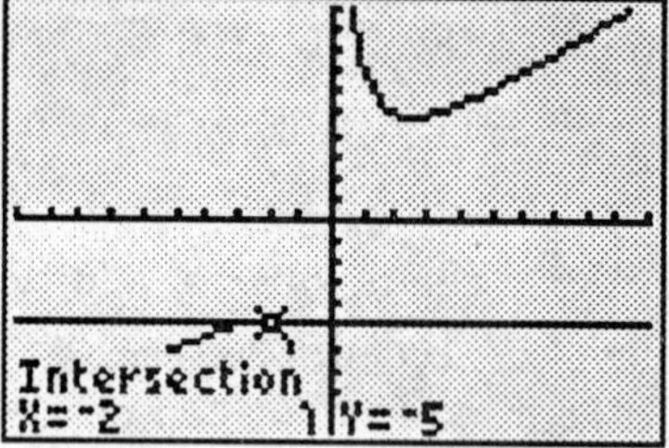

The solutions are -3 and -2.

Check -3:

$$x + \frac{6}{x} = -5$$

$$-3 + \frac{6}{-3} \stackrel{?}{=} -5$$

$$-3 + (-2) \stackrel{?}{=} -5$$

$$-5 = -5 \text{ true}$$

Check -3:

$$x + \frac{6}{x} = -5$$

$$-2 + \frac{6}{-2} \stackrel{?}{=} -5$$

$$-2 + (-3) \stackrel{?}{=} -5$$

$$-5 = -5 \text{ tru}$$

Review Exercises

70. $x^4 + 2x^3 - 3x - 6$

Factor by grouping.

$$\begin{aligned} x^4 + 2x^3 - 3x - 6 &= (x^4 + 2x^3) + (-3x - 6) \\ &= x^3(x+2) - 3(x+2) \\ &= (x+2)(x^3 - 3) \end{aligned}$$

71. $\begin{aligned} (3x^2)(-4x^{-10}) &= (3 \cdot -4)(x^2 \cdot x^{-10}) \\ &= -12x^{2+(-10)} = -12x^{-8} \\ &= -\frac{12}{x^8} \end{aligned}$

72. $\begin{aligned} -5[4(x-2) - 3] &= -5[4x - 8 - 3] \\ &= -5[4x - 11] \\ &= -20x + 55 \end{aligned}$

8.7 Applications Using Rational Equations and Variation

8.7 CHECK POINTS

CHECK POINT 1

Let $x =$ the rate of current.
Then $3 + x =$ the boat's rate with the current
and $3 - x =$ the boat's rate against the current.

	Distance	Rate	Time $= \dfrac{\text{Distance}}{\text{Rate}}$
With the Current	10	$3+x$	$\dfrac{10}{3+x}$
Against the Current	2	$3-x$	$\dfrac{2}{3-x}$

The times are equal, so

$$\frac{10}{3+x} = \frac{2}{3-x}.$$

Multiply both sides by the LCD, $(3+x)(3-x)$.

$$(3+x)(3-x)\cdot\frac{10}{3+x} = (3+x)(3-x)\cdot\frac{2}{3-x}$$
$$10(3-x) = 2(3+x)$$
$$30 - 10x = 6 + 2x$$
$$30 = 6 + 12x$$
$$24 = 12x$$
$$2 = x$$

The rate of the current is 2 miles per hour.
Check the proposed solution in the original wording of the problem.

Time to travel 10 miles with the current $= \dfrac{\text{Distance}}{\text{Time}} = \dfrac{10}{3+2} = \dfrac{10}{5} = 2$ hours

Time to travel 2 miles against the current $= \dfrac{\text{Distance}}{\text{Time}} = \dfrac{2}{3-2} = \dfrac{2}{1} = 2$ hours

The times are the same, which checks with the original conditions of the problem.

CHECK POINT 2

Let $x =$ the time, in hours, for both people to paint the house together.

	Fractional part of job completed in 1 hour	Time working together	Fractional part of job completed in x hours
First Person	$\frac{1}{8}$	x	8
Second Person	$\frac{1}{4}$	x	$\frac{x}{4}$

Working together, the two people complete one whole job, so

$$\frac{x}{8} + \frac{x}{4} = 1.$$

Multiply both sides by the LCD, 8.

$$8\left(\frac{x}{8} + \frac{x}{4}\right) = 8 \cdot 1$$
$$8 \cdot \frac{x}{8} + 8 \cdot \frac{x}{4} = 8$$
$$x + 2x = 8$$
$$3x = 8$$
$$x = \frac{8}{3} = 2\tfrac{2}{3}$$

It will take the two people $2\frac{2}{3}$ hours or 2 hours 40 minutes to paint the house working together.

CHECK POINT 3

$$\frac{3}{8} = \frac{12}{x}$$

Because this equation is a proportion, the cross-products principle can be used. (This method will give the same result as multiplying both sides by the LCD, $12x$, but using the cross-products principle requires one less step.)

$$3x = 8 \cdot 12$$
$$3x = 96$$
$$x = 32$$

The length of the side marked x is 32 inches.

CHECK POINT 4

Use the large and s all similar triangles in the figure to write a proportion.

$$\frac{h}{2} = \frac{56}{3.5}$$
$$3.5h = 112$$
$$h = 32$$

The height of the tower is 32 yards.

CHECK POINT 5

a. $L = kN$

b. $L = 4N$

c. $L = 4(17) = 68$

The length of Sain's moustache was 68 inches.

CHECK POINT 6

a. $W = kL$

b. $75 = k \cdot 6$
$12.5 = k$

c. $W = 12.5L$

d. $W = 12.5(16) = 200$

CHECK POINT 7

Step 1 Write an equation.

$$P = kD$$

Step 2 Use the given values to find k. Substitute 25 for P and 60 for D.

$$25 = k \cdot 60$$
$$\frac{25}{60} = k$$
$$\frac{5}{12} = k$$

Step 3 Substitute the value for k into the equation.

$$P = \frac{5}{12}D$$

Step 4 Answer the problem's question. Substitute 330 for D and solve for P.

$$P = \frac{5}{12}D$$
$$P = \frac{5}{12}(330)$$
$$P = 137.5$$

When the submarine is 330 feet below the surface, it will experience a pressure of 137.5 pounds per square inch.

CHECK POINT 8

Step 1 Write an equation.

$$P = \frac{k}{V}$$

Step 2 Use the given values to find k. Substitute 12 for P and 8 for V.

$$12 = \frac{k}{8}$$
$$12 \cdot 8 = \frac{k}{8} \cdot 8$$
$$96 = k$$

Step 3 Substitute the value of k into the equation.

$$P = \frac{96}{V}$$

Step 4 Answer the problem's question. Substitute 22 for V and solve for P.

$$P = \frac{96}{22} \approx 4.36$$

The new pressure is about 4.36 pounds per square inch.

EXERCISE SET 8.7

1. The times are equal, so

$$\frac{10}{x} = \frac{15}{x+3}.$$

To solve this equation, multiply both sides by the LCD, $x(x+3)$.

$$\begin{aligned} x(x+3)\cdot\frac{10}{x} &= x(x+3)\cdot\frac{15}{x+3} \\ 10(x+3) &= 145 \\ 10x + 30 &= 15x \\ 30 &= 5x \\ 6 &= x \end{aligned}$$

If $x = 6, x + 3 = 9$.
Note: The equation

$$\frac{10}{x} = \frac{15}{x+3}$$

is a proportion, so it can also be solved by using the cross-products principle. This allows you to skip the first step of the solution process shown above.
The walking rate is 6 miles per hour and the car's rate is 9 miles per hour.

3. Let x = the jogger's rate running uphill.
Then $x + 4$ = the jogger's rate running downhill.

	Distance	Rate	Time
Downhill	5	$x+4$	$\frac{5}{x+4}$
Uphill	3	x	$\frac{3}{x}$

The times are equal, so

$$\frac{5}{x+4} = \frac{3}{x}.$$

Use the cross-products principle to solve this equation.

$$\begin{aligned} 5x &= 3(x+4) \\ 5x &= 3x + 12 \\ 2x &= 12 \\ x &= 6 \end{aligned}$$

If $x = 6, x + 4 = 10$.
The jogger runs 10 miles per hour downhill and 6 miles per hour uphill.

5. Let x = the rate of the current.
Then $15 + x$ = the boat's rate with the current.
and $15 - x$ = the boat's rate against the current.

	Distance	Rate	Time
With the Current	20	$15+x$	$\frac{20}{15+x}$
Against the Current	10	$15-x$	$\frac{10}{15-x}$

Use the cross-products principle to solve this equation.

$$\begin{aligned} 20(15-x) &= 10(15+x) \\ 300 - 20x &= 150 + 10x \\ 300 &= 150 + 30x \\ 150 &= 30x \\ 5 &= x \end{aligned}$$

The rate of the current is 5 miles per hour.

7. Let $x =$ walking rate.
Then $2x =$ jogging rate.

	Distance	Rate	Time
Walking	2	x	$\frac{2}{x}$
Jogging	2	$2x$	$\frac{2}{2x}$

The total time is 1 hour, so

$$\frac{2}{x} + \frac{2}{2x} = 1$$

$$\frac{2}{x} + \frac{1}{x} = 1.$$

To solve this equation, multiply both sides by the LCD, x.

$$x\left(\frac{2}{x} + \frac{1}{x}\right) = x \cdot 1$$

$$2 + 1 = x$$

$$3 = x$$

If $x = 3, 2x = 6$.
The walking rate is 3 miles per hour and the jogging rate is 6 miles per hour.

9. Let $x =$ the boat's average rate in still water.
Then $x + 2 =$ the boat's rate with the current.
and $x - 2 =$ the boat's rate against the current.

	Distance	Rate	Time
With the Current	6	$x + 2$	$\frac{6}{x+2}$
Against the Current	4	$x - 2$	$\frac{4}{x-2}$

$$\frac{6}{x+2} = \frac{4}{x-2}$$

$$6(x-2) = 4(x+2)$$

$$6x - 12 = 4x + 8$$

$$2x - 12 = 8$$

$$2x = 20$$

$$x = 10$$

The boat's average rate in still water is 4 miles per hour.

11. Let $x =$ the time, in minutes, for both people to shovel the driveway together.

	Fractional part of job completed in 1 hour	Time working together	Fractional part of job completed in x hours
You	$\frac{1}{20}$	x	$\frac{x}{20}$
Your Brother	$\frac{1}{15}$	x	$\frac{x}{15}$

Working together, the two people complete on whole job, so

$$\frac{x}{20} + \frac{x}{15} = 1.$$

Multiply both sides by the LCD, 60.

$$60\left(\frac{x}{20}+\frac{x}{15}\right)=60\cdot 1$$
$$60\cdot\frac{x}{20}+60\cdot\frac{x}{15}=60$$
$$3x+4x=60$$
$$7x=60$$
$$x=\frac{60}{7}\approx 8.6$$

It will take about 8.6 minutes, which is enough time.

13. Let $x=$ the time, in minutes, for both teams to clean the streets working together.

	Fractional part of job completed in 1 hour	Time working together	Fractional part of job completed in x hours
First Team	$\frac{1}{400}$	x	$\frac{x}{400}$
Second Team	$\frac{1}{300}$	x	$\frac{x}{300}$

Working together, the two teams complete one whole job, so

$$\frac{x}{400}+\frac{x}{300}=1.$$

Multiply both sides by the LCD, 1200.

$$1200\left(\frac{x}{400}+\frac{x}{300}\right)=1200\cdot 1$$
$$3x+4x=1200$$
$$7x=1200$$
$$x=\frac{1200}{7}\approx 171.4$$

It will take about 171.4 hours for both teams to clean the streets working together.
One week is $7\cdot 24=168$ hours, so even if both crews work 24 hours a day, there is not enough time.

15. Let $x =$ the time, in hours, for both pipes to fill in pool.

$$\frac{x}{4} + \frac{x}{6} = 1$$
$$12\left(\frac{x}{4} + \frac{x}{6}\right) = 12 \cdot 1$$
$$3x + 2x = 12$$
$$5x = 12$$
$$x = \frac{12}{5} = 2.4$$

Using both pipes, it will take 2.4 hours or 2 hours 24 minutes to fill the pool.

17. $\frac{18}{9} = \frac{10}{x}$
$$18x = 9 \cdot 10$$
$$18x = 90$$
$$x = 5$$

The length of the side marked x is 5 inches.

19. $\frac{10}{30} = \frac{x}{18}$
$$30x = 10 \cdot 18$$
$$30x = 180$$
$$x = 6$$

The length of the side marked x is 6 meters.

21. $\frac{20}{15} = \frac{x}{12}$
$$15x = 12 \cdot 20$$
$$15x = 240$$
$$x = 16$$

The length of the side marked x is 16 inches.

23. $\frac{8}{6} = \frac{x}{12}$
$$6x = 8 \cdot 12$$
$$6x = 96$$
$$x = 16$$

The tree is 16 feet tall.

25. $g = kh$

27. $w = \frac{k}{v}$

29. $y = kx$

To find k, substitute 75 for y and 3 for x.

$$75 = k \cdot 3$$
$$25 = k$$

The constant of variation is 25.

31. $W = \frac{k}{r}$

To find k, substitute 500 for W and 10 for r.

$$500 = \frac{k}{10}$$
$$500 \cdot 10 = \frac{k}{10} \cdot 10$$
$$5000 = k$$

The constant of variation is 5000.

33. *Step 1* Write an equation.

$$y = kx$$

Step 2 Use the given values to find k. Substitute 35 for y and 5 for x.

$$35 = k \cdot 5$$
$$7 = k$$

Step 3 Substitute the value of k into the equation.

$$y = 7k$$

Step 4 Answer the problem's question. Substitute 12 for x and solve for y.

$$y = 7 \cdot 12 = 84$$

35. *Step 1* $y = \frac{k}{x}$

Step 2 Substitute 10 for y and 5 for x.

$$10 = \frac{k}{5}$$
$$50 = k$$

Step 3 $y = \frac{50}{x}$

Step 4 Substitute 2 for x and solve for y.

$$y = \frac{50}{2}$$
$$y = 25$$

37. **a.** $G = kW$

b. $G = 0.02W$

c. $G = 0.02(52) = 1.04$

Your fingernails would grow 1.04 inches in one year.

39. *Step 1* Write an equation.

$$C = kM$$

Step 2 Use the given values to find k.

$$400 = k \cdot 3000$$
$$\frac{400}{3000} = k$$
$$\frac{2}{15} = k$$

Step 3 Substitute the value of k into the equation.

$$C = \frac{2}{15}M$$

Step 4 Answer the problem's question. Substitute 450 for M and solve for C.

$$C = \frac{2}{15}(450) = 60$$

The cost of a 450-mile trip is \$60.

41. Let $x =$ speed.
Then $M =$ Mach number.

Step 1 $s = kM$

Step 2 To find k, substitute 1502.2 for s and 2.03 for M.

$$1502.2 = k \cdot 2.03$$
$$\frac{150.2}{2.03} = k$$
$$740 = k$$

Step 3 Substitute 3.3 for M and solve for k.

$$s = 740(3.3) = 2442$$

The Blackbird's speed is 2442 miles per hour.

43. *Step 1* $t = \frac{k}{r}$

Step 2

$$1.5 = \frac{k}{20}$$
$$1.5 \cdot 20 = \frac{k}{20} \cdot 20$$
$$30 = k$$

Step 3 $t = \frac{30}{r}$

Step 4 $t = \frac{30}{60} = 0.5$

The trip would take 0.5 hour (or 30 minutes) at an average rate of 60 miles per hour.

45. Let $V =$ volume and $P =$ pressure.

Step 1 $V = \frac{k}{P}$

Step 2

$$32 = \frac{k}{8}$$
$$256 = k$$

Step 3 $V = \frac{256}{P}$

Step 4

$$40 = \frac{256}{P}$$
$$40P = 256$$
$$P = 6.4$$

When the volume is 40 cubic centimeters, the pressure is 6.4 pounds per square centimeter.

47. Let $n =$ the number of pens.
Then $p =$ the price per pen.

Step 1 $n = \frac{k}{p}$

Step 2 To find k, substitute 4000 for n and 1.50 for p.

$$4000 = \frac{k}{1.50}$$
$$4000 \cdot 1.50 = \frac{k}{1.50} \cdot 1.50$$
$$6000 = k$$

Step 3 $n = \frac{6000}{p}$

Step 4 Substitute 1.20 for p and solve for n.

$$n = \frac{6000}{1.20} = 5000$$

There will be 5000 pens sold at $1.20 each.

For Exercises 49–61, answers may vary.

63. Let $x =$ the time, in hours, for the experienced carpenter to panel the room.
Then $3x =$ the time, in hours, for the apprentice to panel the room.

Note: Because the experienced carpenter can do the job 3 times faster, the apprentice takes 3 times as long as the experienced carpenter.

	Fractional part of job completed in 1 hour	**Time working together**	**Fractional part of job completed in x hours**
Experienced Carpenter	$\frac{1}{x}$	6	$\frac{6}{x}$
Apprentice	$\frac{1}{3x}$	6	$\frac{6}{3x}$

Together, the two carpenters complete one whole job, so

$$\frac{6}{x} + \frac{6}{3x} = 1$$

or

$$\frac{6}{x} + \frac{2}{x} = 1.$$

To solve this equation, multiply both sides by the LCD, x.

$$x\left(\frac{6}{x}+\frac{2}{x}\right)=x\cdot 1$$
$$6+2=x$$
$$8=x$$

If $x=8, 3x=24$.
Walking alone, it would take the experienced carpenter 8 hours and the apprentice 24 hours to panel the room.

65. Let $x=$ body-mass index,
Then $w=$ weight (in pounds),
and $h=$ height (in inches).

Step 1 $I=\dfrac{kw}{h}$

Step 2 To find k, substitute 21 for I, 150 for w, and 70 for h.

$$21=\frac{k\cdot 150}{70}$$
$$21\cdot 70=\frac{k\cdot 150}{70}\cdot 70$$
$$1470=k\cdot 150$$
$$\frac{1470}{150}=k$$
$$9.8=k$$

Step 3 $I=\dfrac{9.8w}{k}$

Step 4 Substitute 240 for w and 74 for h, and then solve for I.

$$I=\frac{9.8(240)}{74}\approx 31.8\approx 32$$

The person's body-mass index is 32, which is not in the desirable range.

Review Exercises

66. $25x^2-81=(5x)^2-9^2$
$=(5x+9)(5x-9)$

67. $x^2-12x+36=0$
$(x-6)^2=0$
$x-6=0$
$x=6$

The only solution is 6.

68. $y=-\dfrac{2}{3}x+4$

slope $=-\dfrac{2}{3}=\dfrac{-2}{3}$

y-intercept $=4$
Plot $(0,4)$. From this point, move 2 units *down* and 3 units to the *right* to reach the point $(3,2)$. Draw a line through $(0,4)$ and $(3,2)$.

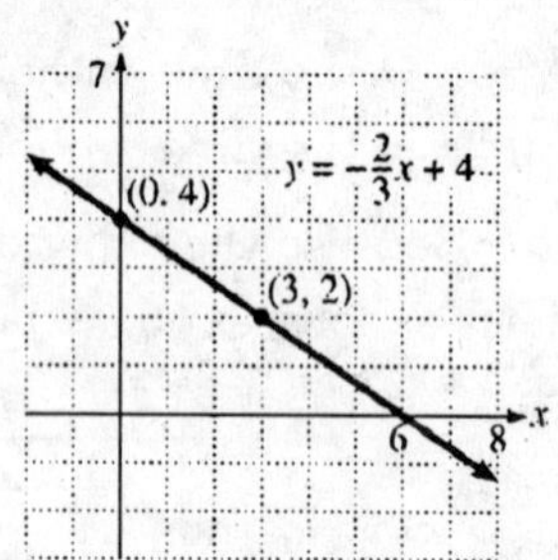

Chapter 8 Review Exercises

1. $\dfrac{5x}{6x-24}$

Set the denominator equal to 0 and solve for x.

$$6x-24=0$$
$$6x=24$$
$$x=4$$

The rational expression is undefined for $x=4$.

2. $\dfrac{x+3}{(x-2)(x+5)}$

Set the denominator equal to 0 and solve for x.

$$\begin{aligned}(x-2)(x+5)&=0\\ x-2=0 \quad &\text{or} \quad x+5=0\\ x=2 \quad & \quad\quad x=-5\end{aligned}$$

The rational expression is undefined for $x=2$ and $x=-5$.

3. $\dfrac{x^2+3}{x^2-3x+2}$

$$\begin{aligned}(x-1)(x-2)&=0\\ x-1=0 \quad &\text{or} \quad x-1=0\\ x=1 \quad & \quad\quad x=2\end{aligned}$$

The rational expression is undefined for $x=1$ and $x=2$.

4. $\dfrac{7}{x^2+81}$

The smallest possible value of x^2 is 0, so $x^2+81 \geq 81$ for all real numbers x. This means that there is no real number x for which $x^2+81=0$. Thus, the rational expression is defined for all real numbers.

5. $\dfrac{16x^2}{12x}=\dfrac{4\cdot 4\cdot x\cdot x}{4\cdot 3\cdot x}=\dfrac{4x}{3}$

6. $\dfrac{x^2-4}{x-2}=\dfrac{(x+2)(x-2)}{(x-2)}=x+2$

7. $\dfrac{x^3+2x^2}{x+2}=\dfrac{x^2(x+2)}{(x+2)}=x^2$

8. $$\begin{aligned}\frac{x^2+3x-18}{x^2-36}&=\frac{(x+6)(x-3)}{(x+6)(x-6)}\\ &=\frac{x-3}{x-6}\end{aligned}$$

9. $$\begin{aligned}\frac{x^2-4x-5}{x^2+8x+7}&=\frac{(x+1)(x-5)}{(x+1)(x+7)}\\ &=\frac{x-5}{x+7}\end{aligned}$$

10. $$\begin{aligned}\frac{y^2+2y}{y^2+4y+4}&=\frac{y(y+2)}{(y+2)(y+2)}\\ &=\frac{y}{y+2}\end{aligned}$$

11. $\dfrac{x^2}{x^2+4}$

The numerator and denominator have no common factor, so this rational expression cannot be simplified.

12. $$\begin{aligned}\frac{2x^2-18y^2}{3y-x}&=\frac{2(x^2-9y^2)}{3y-x}\\ &=\frac{2(x+3y)(x-3y)}{(3y-x)}\\ &=\frac{2(x+3y)(-1)(3y-x)}{(3y-x)}\\ &=-2(x+3y) \text{ or } -2x-6y\end{aligned}$$

13. $$\begin{aligned}\frac{x^2-4}{12x}\cdot\frac{3x}{x+2}&=\frac{(x+2)(x-2)}{12x}\cdot\frac{3x}{(x+2)}\\ &=\frac{x-2}{4}\end{aligned}$$

14. $$\begin{aligned}\frac{5x+5}{6}\cdot\frac{3x}{x^2+x}&=\frac{5(x+1)}{6}\cdot\frac{3x}{x(x+1)}\\ &=\frac{5}{2}\end{aligned}$$

15. $$\begin{aligned}&\frac{x^2+6x+9}{x^2-4}\cdot\frac{x-2}{x+3}\\ &=\frac{(x+3)(x+3)}{(x+2)(x-2)}\cdot\frac{x-2}{x+3}\\ &=\frac{x+3}{x+2}\end{aligned}$$

16. $$\begin{aligned}&\frac{y^2-2y+1}{y^2-1}\cdot\frac{2y^2+y-1}{5y-5}\\ &=\frac{(y-1)(y-1)}{(y+1)(y-1)}\cdot\frac{(2y-1)(y+1)}{5(y-1)}\\ &=\frac{2y-1}{5}\end{aligned}$$

17. $\frac{2y^2+y-3}{4y^2-9}\cdot\frac{3y+3}{5y-5y^2}$

$$= \frac{(2y+3)(y-1)}{(2y+3)(2y-3)}\cdot\frac{3(y+1)}{5y(1-y)}$$

$$= \frac{-3(y+1)}{5y(2y-3)} \text{ or } -\frac{3(y+1)}{5y(2y-3)}$$

18. $\frac{x^2+x-2}{10}\div\frac{2x+4}{5}$

$$= \frac{x^2+x-2}{10}\cdot\frac{5}{2x+4}$$

$$= \frac{(x-1)(x+2)}{10}\cdot\frac{5}{2(x+2)}$$

$$= \frac{x-1}{4}$$

19. $\frac{6x+2}{x^2-1}\div\frac{3x^2+x}{x-1}$

$$= \frac{6x+2}{x^2-1}\cdot\frac{x-1}{3x^2+x}$$

$$= \frac{2(3x+1)}{(x+1)(x-1)}\cdot\frac{(x-1)}{x(3x+1)}$$

$$= \frac{2}{x(x+1)}$$

20. $\frac{1}{y^2+8y+15}\div\frac{7}{y+5}$

$$= \frac{1}{y^2+8y+15}\cdot\frac{y+5}{7}$$

$$= \frac{1}{(y+3)(y+5)}\cdot\frac{(y+5)}{7}$$

$$= \frac{1}{7(y+3)}$$

21. $\frac{y^2+y-42}{y-3}\div\frac{y+7}{(y-3)^2}$

$$= \frac{y^2+y-42}{y-3}\cdot\frac{(y-3)^2}{y+7}$$

$$= \frac{(y+7)(y-6)}{(y-3)}\cdot\frac{(y-3)(y-3)}{y+7}$$

$$= (y-6)(y-3) \text{ or } y^2-9y+18$$

22. $\frac{8x+8y}{x^2}\div\frac{x^2-y^2}{x^2}$

$$= \frac{8x+8y}{x^2}\cdot\frac{x^2}{x^2-y^2}$$

$$= \frac{8(x+y)}{x^2}\cdot\frac{x^2}{(x+y)(x-y)}$$

$$= \frac{8}{x-y}$$

23. $\frac{4x}{x+5}+\frac{20}{x+5}=\frac{4x+20}{x+5}=\frac{4(x+5)}{x+5}=4$

24. $\frac{8x-5}{3x-1}+\frac{4x+1}{3x-1}=\frac{8x-5+4x+1}{3x-1}$

$$= \frac{12x-4}{3x-1}$$

$$= \frac{4(3x-1)}{3x-1}=4$$

25. $\frac{3x^2+2x}{x-1}-\frac{10x-5}{x-1}$

$$= \frac{(3x^2+2x)-(10x-5)}{x-1}$$

$$= \frac{3x^2+2x-10x+5}{x-1}$$

$$= \frac{3x^2-8x+5}{x-1}$$

$$= \frac{(3x-5)(x-1)}{x-1}$$

$$= 3x-5$$

26. $\frac{6y^2-4y}{2y-3}-\frac{12-3y}{2y-3}$

$$= \frac{(6y^2-4y)-(12-3y)}{2y-3}$$

$$= \frac{6y^2-4y-12+3y}{2y-3}$$

$$= \frac{6y^2-y-12}{2y-3}$$

$$= \frac{(2y-3)(3y+4)}{2y-3}$$

$$= 3y+4$$

27. $$\frac{x}{x-2}+\frac{x-4}{2-x}=\frac{x}{x-2}+\frac{(-1)}{(-1)}\cdot\frac{x-4}{x-2}$$
$$=\frac{x}{x-2}+\frac{-x+4}{x-2}$$
$$=\frac{x-x+4}{x-2}=\frac{4}{x-2}$$

28. $$\frac{x+5}{x-3}-\frac{x}{3-x}=\frac{x+5}{x-3}-\frac{(-1)}{(-1)}\cdot\frac{x}{3-x}$$
$$=\frac{x+5}{x-3}+\frac{x}{x-3}$$
$$=\frac{x+5+x}{x-3}=\frac{2x+5}{x-5}$$

29. $\frac{7}{9x^3}$ and $\frac{5}{12x}$

$$9x^3=3^2x^3$$
$$12x=2^2\cdot 3x$$

$\text{LCD}=2^2\cdot 3^2\cdot x^3=36x^3$

30. $\frac{3}{x^2(x-1)}$ and $\frac{11}{x(x-1)^2}$

$\text{LCD}=x^2(x-1)^2$

31. $\frac{x}{x^2+4x+3}$ and $\frac{17}{x^2+10x+21}$

$$x^2+4x+3=(x+3)(x+1)$$
$$x^2+10x+21=(x+3)(x+7)$$

$\text{LCD}=(x+3)(x+1)(x+7)$

32. $\frac{7}{3x}+\frac{5}{2x^2}$

$\text{LCD}=6x^2$

$$\frac{7}{3x}+\frac{5}{2x^2}=\frac{7}{3x}\cdot\frac{2x}{2x}+\frac{5}{2x^2}\cdot\frac{3}{3}$$
$$=\frac{14x+15}{6x^2}$$

33. $\frac{5}{x+1}+\frac{2}{x}$

$\text{LCD}=x(x+1)$

$$\frac{5}{x+1}+\frac{2}{x}=\frac{5x}{x(x+1)}+\frac{2(x+1)}{x(x+1)}$$
$$=\frac{5x+2(x+1)}{x(x+1)}=\frac{5x+2x+2}{x(x+1)}$$
$$=\frac{7x+2}{x(x+1)}$$

34. $\frac{7}{x+3}+\frac{4}{(x+3)^2}$

$\text{LCD}=(x+3)^2$ or $(x+3)(x+3)$

$$\frac{7}{x+3}+\frac{4}{(x+3)^2}$$
$$=\frac{7}{x+3}+\frac{4}{(x+3)(x+3)}$$
$$=\frac{7(x+3)}{(x+3)(x+3)}+\frac{4}{(x+3)(x+3)}$$
$$=\frac{7(x+3)+4}{(x+3)(x+3)}=\frac{7x+21+4}{(x+3)(x+3)}$$
$$=\frac{7x+25}{(x+3)(x+3)}\text{ or }\frac{7x+25}{(x+3)^2}$$

35. $\frac{6y}{y^2-4}-\frac{3}{y+2}$

$$y^2-4=(y+2)(y-2)$$
$$y+2=1(y+2)$$

$\text{LCD}=(y+2)(y-2)$

$$\frac{6y}{y^2-4}-\frac{3}{y+2}$$
$$=\frac{6y}{(y+2)(y-2)}-\frac{3}{y+2}$$
$$=\frac{6y}{(y+2)(y-2)}-\frac{3(y-2)}{(y+2)(y-2)}$$
$$=\frac{6y-3(y-2)}{(y+2)(y-2)}=\frac{6y-3y+6}{(y+2)(y-2)}$$
$$=\frac{3y+6}{(y+2)(y-2)}=\frac{3(y+2)}{(y+2)(y-2)}$$
$$=\frac{3}{y-2}$$

36. $\dfrac{y-1}{y^2+2y+1} - \dfrac{y+1}{y-1}$

$$= \frac{y-1}{(y-1)(y-1)} - \frac{y+1}{y-1}$$
$$= \frac{1}{y-1} - \frac{y+1}{y-1}$$
$$= \frac{1-(y+1)}{y-1} = \frac{1-y-1}{y-1}$$
$$= \frac{-y}{y-1} \text{ or } -\frac{y}{y-1}$$

37. $\dfrac{x+y}{y} - \dfrac{y-x}{x}$

$\text{LCD} = xy$

$\dfrac{x+y}{y} - \dfrac{y-x}{x}$

$$= \frac{(x+y)}{y} \cdot \frac{x}{x} - \frac{(x-y)}{x} \cdot \frac{y}{y}$$
$$= \frac{x^2+xy}{xy} - \frac{xy-y^2}{xy}$$
$$= \frac{(x^2+xy)-(xy-y^2)}{xy}$$
$$= \frac{x^2+xy-xy+y^2}{xy}$$
$$= \frac{x^2+y^2}{xy}$$

38. $\dfrac{2x}{x^2+2x+1} + \dfrac{x}{x^2-1}$

$$x^2+2x+1 = (x+1)(x+1)$$
$$x^2-1 = (x+1)(x-1)$$

$\text{LCD} = (x+1)(x+1)(x-1)$

$\dfrac{2x}{x^2+2x+1} + \dfrac{x}{x^2-1}$

$$= \frac{2x}{(x+1)(x+1)} + \frac{x}{(x+1)(x+1)}$$
$$= \frac{2x(x-1)}{(x+1)(x+1)(x-1)}$$
$$+ \frac{x(x+1)}{(x+1)(x+1)(x-1)}$$
$$= \frac{2x(x-1)+x(x+1)}{(x+1)(x+1)(x-1)}$$
$$= \frac{2x^2-2x+x^2+x}{(x+1)(x+1)(x-1)}$$
$$= \frac{3x^2-x}{(x+1)(x+1)(x-1)}$$
$$= \frac{3x(x-1)}{(x+1)(x+1)(x-1)}$$
$$= \frac{3x}{(x+1)(x+1)} \text{ or } \frac{3x}{(x+1)^2}$$

39. $\dfrac{5x}{x+1} - \dfrac{2x}{1-x^2}$

$$x+1 = 1(x+1)$$
$$1-x^2 = -1(x^2-1) = -(x+1)(x-1)$$

$\text{LCD} = (x+1)(x-1)$

$\dfrac{5x}{x+1} - \dfrac{2x}{1-x^2}$

$$= \frac{5x}{x+1} - \frac{(-1)}{(-1)} \cdot \frac{2x}{1-x^2}$$
$$= \frac{5x}{x+1} - \frac{-2x}{(x+1)(x-1)}$$
$$= \frac{5x(x-1)}{x+1} - \frac{-2x}{(x+1)(x-1)}$$
$$= \frac{5x(x-1)+2x}{(x+1)(x-1)}$$
$$= \frac{5x^2-5x+2x}{(x+1)(x-1)}$$
$$= \frac{5x^2-3x}{(x+1)(x-1)}$$

40. $\dfrac{4}{x^2-x-6}-\dfrac{4}{x^2-4}$

$$x^2-x-6=(x+2)(x-3)$$
$$x^2-4=(x+2)(x-2)$$

$$\text{LCD}=(x+2)(x-3)(x-2)$$

$$\begin{aligned}\frac{4}{x^2-x-6}-\frac{4}{x^2-4} &= \frac{4}{(x+2)(x-3)}-\frac{4}{(x+2)(x-2)}\\ &= \frac{4(x-2)}{(x+2)(x-3)(x-2)} - \frac{4(x-3)}{(x+2)(x-3)(x-2)}\\ &= \frac{4(x-2)-4(x-3)}{(x+2)(x-3)(x-2)}\\ &= \frac{4x-8-4x+12}{(x+2)(x-3)(x-2)}\\ &= \frac{4}{(x+2)(x-3)(x-2)}\end{aligned}$$

41. $\dfrac{7}{x+3}+2$

$$\text{LCD}=x+3$$

$$\begin{aligned}\frac{7}{x+3}+2 &= \frac{7}{x+3}+\frac{2(x+3)}{x+3}\\ &= \frac{7+2(x+3)}{x+3}\\ &= \frac{7+2x+6}{x+3}\\ &= \frac{2x+13}{x+3}\end{aligned}$$

42. $\dfrac{2y-5}{6y+9}-\dfrac{4}{2y^2+3y}$

$$6y+9=3(2y+3)$$
$$2y^2+3y=y(2y+3)$$

$$\text{LCD}=3(2y+3)$$

$$\begin{aligned}\frac{2y-5}{6y+9}-\frac{4}{2y^2+3y} &= \frac{2y-5}{3(2y+3)}-\frac{4}{y(2y+3)}\\ &= \frac{(2y-5)(y)}{3y(2y+3)}-\frac{4\cdot 3}{3y(2y+3)}\\ &= \frac{2y^2-5y-12}{3y(2y+3)}=\frac{(2y+3)(y-4)}{3y(2y+3)}\\ &= \frac{y-4}{3y}\end{aligned}$$

In Exercises 43–47, each complex rational expression can be simplified by either of the two methods introduced in Section 8.5 of the textbook. Both methods will be illustrated here.

43. $\dfrac{\frac{1}{2}+\frac{3}{8}}{\frac{3}{4}-\frac{1}{2}}=\dfrac{\frac{4}{8}+\frac{3}{8}}{\frac{3}{4}-\frac{2}{4}}=\dfrac{\frac{7}{8}}{\frac{1}{4}}=\dfrac{7}{8}\cdot\dfrac{4}{1}=\dfrac{7}{2}$

44. $\dfrac{\frac{1}{x}}{1-\frac{1}{x}}$

$$\text{LCD}=x$$

$$\begin{aligned}\frac{\frac{1}{x}}{1-\frac{1}{x}} &= \frac{x}{x}\cdot\frac{\left(\frac{1}{x}\right)}{\left(1-\frac{1}{x}\right)}\\ &= \frac{x\cdot\frac{1}{x}}{x\cdot 1-x\cdot\frac{1}{x}}=\frac{1}{x-1}\end{aligned}$$

45. $\dfrac{\dfrac{1}{x}+\dfrac{1}{y}}{\dfrac{1}{xy}}$

LCD $= xy$

$$\frac{\frac{1}{x}+\frac{1}{y}}{\frac{1}{xy}} = \frac{xy}{xy}\cdot\frac{\left(\frac{1}{x}+\frac{1}{y}\right)}{\left(\frac{1}{xy}\right)}$$

$$= \frac{xy\cdot\frac{1}{x}+xy\cdot\frac{1}{y}}{xy\cdot\frac{1}{xy}}$$

$$= \frac{y+x}{1} = y+x \text{ or } x+y$$

46. $\dfrac{\dfrac{1}{x}-\dfrac{1}{2}}{\dfrac{1}{3}-\dfrac{x}{6}} = \dfrac{\dfrac{2}{2x}-\dfrac{x}{2x}}{\dfrac{2}{6}-\dfrac{x}{6}} = \dfrac{\dfrac{2-x}{2x}}{\dfrac{2-x}{6}}$

$$= \frac{2-x}{2x}\cdot\frac{6}{2-x} = \frac{3}{x}$$

47. $\dfrac{3+\dfrac{12}{x}}{1-\dfrac{16}{x^2}}$

LCD $= x^2$

$$\frac{3+\frac{12}{x}}{1-\frac{16}{x^2}} = \frac{x^2}{x^2}\cdot\frac{\left(3+\frac{12}{x}\right)}{\left(1-\frac{16}{x^2}\right)}$$

$$= \frac{x^2\cdot 3+x^2\cdot\frac{12}{x}}{x^2\cdot 1-x^2\cdot\frac{16}{x^2}}$$

$$= \frac{3x^2+12x}{x^2-16}$$

$$= \frac{3x(x+4)}{(x+4)(x-4)}$$

$$= \frac{3x}{x-4}$$

48. $\dfrac{3}{x}-\dfrac{1}{6}=\dfrac{1}{x}$

The restriction is $x \neq 0$.

The LCD is $6x$.

$$\frac{3}{x}-\frac{1}{6}=\frac{1}{x}$$

$$6x\left(\frac{3}{x}-\frac{1}{6}\right)=6x\left(\frac{1}{x}\right)$$

$$6x\cdot\frac{3}{x}-6x\cdot\frac{1}{6}=6x\cdot\frac{1}{x}$$

$$18-x=6$$

$$-x=12$$

$$x=12$$

The solution is 12.

49. $\dfrac{3}{4x}=\dfrac{1}{x}+\dfrac{1}{4}$

The restriction is $x \neq 0$.

The LCD is $4x$.

$$\frac{3}{4x}=\frac{1}{x}+\frac{1}{4}$$

$$4x\left(\frac{3}{4x}\right)=4x\left(\frac{1}{x}+\frac{1}{4}\right)$$

$$3=4+x$$

$$-1=x$$

The solution is -1.

50. $x+5=\dfrac{6}{x}$

The restriction is $x \neq 0$.

The LCD is x.

$$x+5=\frac{6}{x}$$

$$x(x+5)=x\left(\frac{6}{x}\right)$$

$$x^2+5x=6$$

$$x^2+5x-6=0$$

$$(x+6)(x-1)=0$$

$$x+6=0 \quad\text{or}\quad x-1=0$$

$$x=-6 \qquad\qquad x=1$$

The equation has two solutions, -6 and 1.

51. $4 - \dfrac{x}{x+5} = \dfrac{5}{x+5}$

The restriction is $x \neq -5$.
The LCD is $x + 5$.

$$(x+5)\left(4 - \frac{x}{x+5}\right) = (x+5)\left(\frac{5}{x+5}\right)$$
$$(x+5)\cdot 4 - (x+5)\left(\frac{x}{x+5}\right) = (x+5)\left(\frac{5}{x+5}\right)$$
$$4x + 20 = 5$$
$$3x + 20 = 5$$
$$3x = -15$$
$$x = -5$$

The only proposed solution, -5, is *not* a solution because of the restriction $x \neq -5$. Notice that -5 makes two of the denominators zero in the original equation. Therefore, the given equation has no solution.

52. $\dfrac{2}{x-3} = \dfrac{4}{x+3} + \dfrac{8}{x^2-9}$

To find any restrictions and the LCD, all denominators should be written in factored form.

$$\frac{2}{x-3} = \frac{4}{x+3} + \frac{8}{(x+3)(x-3)}$$

Restrictions: $x \neq 3, x \neq -3$
LCD $= (x+3)(x-3)$

$$(x+3)(x-3)\cdot\frac{2}{x+3}$$
$$= (x+3)(x-3)\left(\frac{4}{x+3} + \frac{8}{(x+3)(x-3)}\right)$$

$$2(x-3) = 4(x-3) + 8$$
$$2x - 6 = 4x - 12 + 8$$
$$2x - 6 = 4x - 4$$
$$-6 = 2x - 4$$
$$10 = 2x$$

The solution is 5.

53. $\dfrac{2}{x} = \dfrac{2}{3} + \dfrac{x}{6}$

Restriction: $x \neq 0$
LCD $= 6x$

$$6x\left(\frac{2}{x}\right) = 6x\left(\frac{2}{3} + \frac{x}{6}\right)$$
$$12 = 4x + x^2$$
$$0 = x^2 + 4x - 12$$
$$0 = (x+6)(x-2)$$

$$x + 6 = 0 \quad \text{or} \quad x - 2 = 0$$
$$x = -6 \qquad\qquad x = 2$$

The solutions are -6 and 2.

54. $\dfrac{13}{y-1} - 3 = \dfrac{1}{y-1}$

Restriction: $y \neq 1$
LCD $= y - 1$

$$(y-1)\left(\frac{13}{y-1} - 3\right) = (y-1)\left(\frac{1}{y-1}\right)$$
$$13 - 3(y-1) = 1$$
$$13 - 3y + 3 = 1$$
$$16 - 3y = 1$$
$$-3y = -15$$
$$y = 5$$

The solution is 5.

55. $\dfrac{1}{x+3} - \dfrac{1}{x-1} = \dfrac{x+1}{x^2+2x-3}$

$\dfrac{1}{x+3} - \dfrac{1}{x-1} = \dfrac{x+1}{(x+3)(x-1)}$

Restrictions: $x \neq -3, x \neq 1$
LCD $= (x+3)(x-1)$

$$(x+3)(x-1)\left[\frac{1}{x+3} - \frac{1}{x-1}\right]$$
$$= (x+3)(x-1)\cdot\left[\frac{x+1}{(x+3)(x-1)}\right]$$

$$(x-1) - (x+3) = x + 1$$
$$x - 1 - x - 3 = x + 1$$
$$-4 = x + 1$$
$$-5 = x$$

The solution is -5.

56. $P = \dfrac{250(3t+5)}{t+25}$; $P = 125$

$$\begin{aligned} 125 &= \frac{250(3t+5)}{t+25} \\ 125(t+25) &= \frac{250(3t+5)}{t+25} \cdot (t+25) \\ 125t + 3125 &= 250(3t+5) \\ 125t + 3125 &= 750t + 1250 \\ 3125 &= 625t + 1250 \\ 1875 &= 625t \\ 3 &= t \end{aligned}$$

It will take 3 years for the population to reach 125 elk.

57. $S = 1 - r$; $S = 200, C = 140$

$$\begin{aligned} 200 &= \frac{140}{1-r} \\ 200(1-r) &= \frac{140}{1-r} \cdot 1 - r \\ 200 - 200r &= 140 \\ -200r &= -60 \\ r &= \frac{-60}{-200} = \frac{3}{10} = 30\% \end{aligned}$$

The markup is 30%.

58. Let $x =$ the rate of the current.
Then $20 + x =$ the rate of the boat with the current
and $20 - x =$ the rate of the boat against the current.

	Distance	Rate	Time
With the Current	72	$20 + x$	$\frac{72}{20+x}$
Against the Current	48	$20 - x$	$\frac{48}{20-x}$

The times are equal, so

$$\frac{72}{20+x} = \frac{48}{20-x}$$

This equation is a proportion, so it can be solved using the cross-products principle.

$$\begin{aligned} 72(20-x) &= 48(20+x) \\ 1440 - 72x &= 960 + 48x \\ 1440 &= 960 + 120x \\ 480 &= 120x \\ 4 &= x \end{aligned}$$

The rate of the current is 4 miles per hour.

59. Let $x =$ the rate of the slower car.
Then $x + 10 =$ the rate of the faster car.

	Distance	Rate	Time
Slower Car	60	x	$\frac{60}{x}$
Faster Car	90	$x + 10$	$\frac{90}{x+10}$

$$\begin{aligned} \frac{60}{x} &= \frac{90}{x+10} \\ 60(x+10) &= 90x \\ 60x + 600 &= 90x \\ 600 &= 30x \\ 20 &= x \end{aligned}$$

If $x = 20, x + 10 = 30$.
The rate of the slower car is 20 miles per hour and the rate of the faster car is 30 miles per hour.

60. Let $x =$ the time, in hours, for both people to paint the fence together.

	Fractional part of job completed in 1 hour	Time working together	Fractional part of job completed in x hours
Painter	$\frac{1}{6}$	x	$\frac{x}{6}$
Apprentice	$\frac{1}{12}$	x	$\frac{x}{12}$

Working together, the two people complete one whole job, so

$$\frac{x}{6} + \frac{x}{12} = 1.$$

Multiply both sides by the LCD, 12.

$$\begin{aligned} 12\left(\frac{x}{6} + \frac{x}{12}\right) &= 12 \cdot 1 \\ 2x + x &= 12 \\ 3x &= 12 \\ x &= 4 \end{aligned}$$

It would take them 4 hours to paint the fence working together.

61. $\frac{8}{4} = \frac{10}{x}$

$8x = 40$

$x = 5$

The length of the side marked with an x is 5 feet.

62. Write a proportion relating the corresponding sides of the large and small triangle. Notice that the length of the base of the larger triangle is 10 ft + 6 ft = 16 ft.

$$\begin{aligned} \frac{x}{5} &= \frac{16}{6} \\ 6x &= 5 \cdot 16 \\ 6x &= 80 \\ x &= \frac{80}{6} = \frac{40}{3} \text{ or } 13\tfrac{1}{3} \end{aligned}$$

The height of the lamppost is $13\frac{1}{3}$ feet.

63. Let $x =$ electric bill (in dollars)
Then $e =$ number of kilowatts of electricity used.

Step 1 $b = ke$

Step 2 To find k, substitute 98 for b and 1400 for e.

$$98 = k \cdot 1400$$
$$\frac{98}{1400} = k$$
$$0.07 = k$$

Step 3 $b = 0.07e$

Step 4 Substitute 2200 for e and solve for b.

$$b = 0.07(2200) = 154$$

The bill for 2200 kilowatts of electricity is \$154.

64. *Step 1* $t = \frac{k}{r}$

Step 2 To find k, substitute k, substitute 4 for t and 50 for r.

$$4 = \frac{k}{50}$$
$$200 = k$$

Step 3 $t = \frac{200}{r}$

Step 4 Substitute 40 for r and solve for t.

$$t = \frac{200}{40} = 5$$

At 40 miles per hour, the trip will take 5 hours.

Chapter 8 Test

1. $\dfrac{x+7}{x^2+5x-36}$

Set the denominator equal to 0 and solve for x.

$$x^2 + 5x - 36 = 0$$
$$(x+9)(x-4) = 0$$
$$x + 9 = 0 \quad \text{or} \quad x - 4 = 0$$
$$x = -9 \qquad\qquad x = 4$$

The rational expression is undefined for $x = -9$ and $x = 4$.

2. $\dfrac{x^2+2x-3}{x^2-3x+2} = \dfrac{(x-1)(x+3)}{(x-1)(x-2)} = \dfrac{x+3}{x-2}$

3. $\dfrac{4x^2-20x}{x^2-4x-5} = \dfrac{4x(x-5)}{(x+1)(x-5)} = \dfrac{4x}{x+1}$

4. $\dfrac{x^2-16}{10} \cdot \dfrac{5}{x+4} = \dfrac{(x+4)(x-4)}{10} \cdot \dfrac{5}{(x+4)}$

$$= \frac{x-4}{2}$$

5. $\dfrac{x^2-7x+12}{x^2-4x} \cdot \dfrac{x^2}{x^2-9}$

$$= \frac{(x-3)(x-4)}{x(x-4)} \cdot \frac{x^2}{(x+3)(x-3)}$$
$$= \frac{x}{x+3}$$

6. $\dfrac{2x+8}{x-3} \div \dfrac{x^2+5x+4}{x^2-9}$

$$= \frac{2x+8}{x-3} \cdot \frac{x^2-9}{x^2+5x+4}$$
$$= \frac{2(x+4)}{(x-3)} \cdot \frac{(x+3)(x-3)}{(x+4)(x+1)}$$
$$= \frac{2(x+3)}{x+1} = \frac{2x+6}{x+1}$$

7. $$\frac{5y+5}{(y-3)^2} \div \frac{y^2-1}{y-3}$$
$$= \frac{5y+5}{(y-3)^2} \cdot \frac{y-3}{y^2-1}$$
$$= \frac{5(y+1)}{(y-3)(y-3)} \cdot \frac{(y-3)}{(y+1)(y-1)}$$
$$= \frac{5}{(y-3)(y-1)}$$

8. $$\frac{2y^2+5}{y+3} + \frac{6y-5}{y+3}$$
$$= \frac{(2y^2+5)+(6y-5)}{y+3}$$
$$= \frac{2y^2+5+6y-5}{y+3}$$
$$= \frac{2y^2+6y}{y+3}$$
$$= \frac{2y(y+3)}{y+3} = 2y$$

9. $$\frac{y^2-2y+3}{y^2+7y+12} - \frac{y^2-4y-5}{y^2+7y+12}$$
$$= \frac{(y^2-2y+3)-(y^2-4y-5)}{y^2+7y+12}$$
$$= \frac{y^2-2y+3-y^2+4y+5}{y^2+7y+12}$$
$$= \frac{2y+8}{y^2+7y+12}$$
$$= \frac{2(y+4)}{y^2+7y+12}$$
$$= \frac{2(y+4)}{(y+3)(y+4)}$$
$$= \frac{2}{y+3}$$

10. $$\frac{x}{x+3} + \frac{5}{x-3}$$

$\text{LCD} = (x+3)(x-3)$

$$\frac{x}{x+3} + \frac{5}{x-3}$$
$$= \frac{x(x-3)}{(x+3)(x-3)} + \frac{5(x+3)}{(x+3)(x-3)}$$
$$= \frac{x(x-3)+5(x+3)}{(x+3)(x-3)}$$
$$= \frac{x^2-3x+5x+15}{(x+3)(x-3)}$$
$$= \frac{x^2+2x+15}{(x+3)(x-3)}$$

11. $$\frac{2}{x^2-4x+3} + \frac{6}{x^2+x-2}$$

$$x^2-4x+3 = (x-1)(x-3)$$
$$x^2+x-2 = (x-1)(x+2)$$

$\text{LCD} = (x-1)(x-3)(x+2)$

$$\frac{2}{x^2-4x+3} + \frac{6}{x^2+x-2}$$
$$= \frac{2}{(x-1)(x-3)} + \frac{6}{(x-1)(x+2)}$$
$$= \frac{2(x+2)}{(x-1)(x-3)(x+2)}$$
$$+ \frac{6(x-3)}{(x-1)(x-3)(x+2)}$$
$$= \frac{2(x+2)+6(x-3)}{(x-1)(x-3)(x+2)}$$
$$= \frac{2x+4+6x-18}{(x-1)(x-3)(x+2)}$$
$$= \frac{8x-14}{(x-1)(x-3)(x+2)}$$

12. $\dfrac{4}{x-3}+\dfrac{x+5}{3-x}$

$$3-x=-1(x-3)$$

LCD $= x-3$

$$\begin{aligned}\frac{4}{x-3}+\frac{x+5}{3-x}&=\frac{4}{x-3}+\frac{(-1)}{(-1)}\cdot\frac{(x+5)}{(3-x)}\\&=\frac{4}{x-3}+\frac{-x-5}{x-3}\\&=\frac{4-x-5}{x-3}=\frac{-x-1}{x-3}\end{aligned}$$

13. $1+\dfrac{3}{x-1}$

LCD $= x-1$

$$\begin{aligned}1+\frac{3}{x-1}&=\frac{1(x-1)}{x-1}+\frac{3}{x-1}\\&=\frac{x-1+3}{x-1}=\frac{x+2}{x-1}\end{aligned}$$

14. $\dfrac{2x+3}{x^2-7x+12}-\dfrac{2}{x-3}$

$$\begin{aligned}x^2-7x+12&=(x-3)(x-4)\\x-3&=1(x-3)\end{aligned}$$

LCD $= (x-3)(x-4)$

$$\begin{aligned}\frac{2x+3}{x^2-7x+12}-\frac{2}{x-3}&=\frac{2x+3}{(x-3)(x-4)}-\frac{2(x-4)}{(x-3)(x-4)}\\&=\frac{2x+3-2(x-4)}{(x-3)(x-4)}\\&=\frac{2x+3-2x+8}{(x-3)(x-4)}\\&=\frac{11}{(x-3)(x-4)}\end{aligned}$$

15. $\dfrac{8y}{y^2-16}-\dfrac{4}{y-4}$

$$\begin{aligned}y^2-16&=(y+4)(y-4)\\y-4&=1(y-4)\end{aligned}$$

LCD $= (y+4)(y-4)$

$$\begin{aligned}\frac{8y}{y^2-16}-\frac{4}{y-4}&=\frac{8y}{(y+4)(y-4)}-\frac{4}{y-4}\\&=\frac{8y}{(y+4)(y-4)}-\frac{4(y+4)}{(y+4)(y-4)}\\&=\frac{8y-4(y+4)}{(y+4)(y-4)}\\&=\frac{8y-4y-16}{(y+4)(y-4)}\\&=\frac{4y-16}{(y+4)(y-4)}\\&=\frac{4(y-4)}{(y+4)(y-4)}\\&=\frac{4}{y+4}\end{aligned}$$

16.
$$\begin{aligned}\frac{(x-y)^2}{x+y}\div\frac{x^2-xy}{3x+3y}&=\frac{(x-y)^2}{x+y}\cdot\frac{3x+3y}{x^2-xy}\\&=\frac{(x-y)(x-y)}{(x+y)}\cdot\frac{3(x+y)}{x(x-y)}\\&=\frac{3(x-y)}{x}=\frac{3x-3y}{x}\end{aligned}$$

17.
$$\begin{aligned}\frac{5+\frac{5}{x}}{2+\frac{1}{x}}=\frac{\frac{5x}{x}+\frac{5}{x}}{\frac{2x}{x}+\frac{1}{x}}&=\frac{\frac{5x+5}{x}}{\frac{2x+1}{x}}\\&=\frac{5x+5}{x}\cdot\frac{x}{2x+1}\\&=\frac{5x+5}{2x+1}\end{aligned}$$

18. $\dfrac{\frac{1}{x}-\frac{1}{y}}{\frac{1}{x}}$

LCD $= xy$

$$\frac{\frac{1}{x}-\frac{1}{y}}{\frac{1}{x}} = \frac{xy}{xy}\cdot\frac{\left(\frac{1}{x}-\frac{1}{y}\right)}{\left(\frac{1}{x}\right)}$$

$$= \frac{xy\cdot\frac{1}{x} - xy\cdot\frac{1}{y}}{xy\cdot\frac{1}{x}}$$

$$= \frac{y-x}{y}$$

19. $\dfrac{5}{x}+\dfrac{2}{3} = 2 - \dfrac{2}{x} - \dfrac{1}{6}$

Restriction: $x \neq 0$
LCD $= 6x$

$$6x\left(\frac{5}{x}+\frac{2}{3}\right) = 6x\left(2-\frac{2}{x}-\frac{1}{6}\right)$$
$$6x\cdot\frac{5}{x}+6x\cdot\frac{2}{3} = 6x\cdot 2 - 6x\cdot\frac{2}{x} - 6x\cdot\frac{1}{6}$$
$$30+4x = 12x-12-6$$
$$30+4x = 12x-18$$
$$30 = 8x-18$$
$$48 = 8x$$
$$6 = x$$

The solution is 6.

20. $\dfrac{3}{y+5} - 1 = \dfrac{4-y}{2y+10}$

$$\frac{3}{y+5} - 1 = \frac{4-y}{2(y+5)}$$

Restriction: $y \neq -5$
LCD $= 2(y+5)$

$$2(y+5)\left(\frac{3}{y+5}-1\right) = 2(y+5)\left[\frac{4-y}{2(y+5)}\right]$$
$$6-2(y+5) = 4-y$$
$$6-2y-10 = 4-y$$
$$-4-2y = 4-y$$
$$-4 = 4+y$$
$$-8 = y$$

The solution is -8.

21. $\dfrac{2}{x-1} = \dfrac{3}{x^2-1}+1$

$$\frac{2}{x-1} = \frac{3}{(x+1)(x-1)}+1$$

Restrictions: $x \neq 1, x \neq -1$
LCD $= (x+1)(x-1)$

$$(x+1)(x-1)\left(\frac{2}{x-1}\right)$$
$$= (x+1)(x-1)\left[\frac{3}{(x+1)(x-1)}+1\right]$$

$$2(x+1) = 3(x+1)(x-1)$$
$$2x+2 = 3+x^2-1$$
$$2x+2 = 2+x^2$$
$$0 = x^2-2x$$
$$0 = x(x-2)$$
$$x = 0 \quad\text{or}\quad x-2 = 0$$

The equation has two solutions, 0 and 2.

22. Let $x =$ the rate of the current.
Then $30 - x =$ the rate of the boat with the current
and $30 - x =$ the rate of the boat against the current.

	Distance	Rate	Time
With the Current	16	$30 + x$	$\frac{16}{30 + x}$
Against the Current	14	$30 - x$	$\frac{14}{30 - x}$

$$\frac{16}{30 + x} = \frac{14}{30 - x}$$
$$16(30 - x) = 14(30 + x)$$
$$480 - 16x = 420 + 14x$$
$$480 = 420 + 30x$$
$$60 = 30x$$
$$2 = x$$

The rate of the current is 2 miles per hour.

23. Let $x =$ the time (in minutes) for both pipes to fill the hot tub.

$$\frac{x}{20} + \frac{x}{30} = 1$$

LCD = 60

$$60\left(\frac{x}{20} + \frac{x}{30}\right) = 60 \cdot 1$$
$$3x + 2x = 60$$
$$5x = 60$$
$$x = 12$$

It will take 12 minutes for both pipes to fill the hot tub.

24. $\frac{10}{4} = \frac{8}{x}$

$$10x = 8 \cdot 4$$
$$10x = 32$$
$$x = 3.2$$

The length of the side marked with an x is 3.2 inches.

25. Let $C =$ the current (in amperes).
Then $R =$ the resistance (in ohms).

Step 1 $C = \frac{k}{R}$

Step 2 To find k, substitute 42 for C and 5 for R.

$$42 = \frac{k}{5}$$
$$42 \cdot 5 = \frac{k}{5} \cdot 5$$
$$210 = k$$

Step 3 $C = \frac{210}{R}$

Step 4 Substitute 4 for R and solve for C.

$$C = \frac{210}{4} = 52.5$$

When the resistance is 4 ohms, the current is 52.5 amperes.

Chapter 8 Cumulative Review Exercises (Chapters 1-8)

1. $2(x - 3) + 5x = 8(x - 1)$

$$2x - 6 + 5x = 8x - 8$$
$$7x - 6 = 8x - 8$$
$$-6 = x - 8$$
$$2 = x$$

The solution is 2.

2. $-3(2x - 4) > 2(6x - 12)$

$$-6x + 12 > 12x - 24$$
$$-18x + 12 > -24$$
$$-18x > -36$$
$$\frac{-18x}{-18} < \frac{-36}{-18}$$
$$x < 2$$

Solution set: $\{x | x < 2\}$

3.
$$x^2 + 3x = 18$$
$$x^2 + 3x - 18 = 0$$
$$(x+6)(x-3) = 0$$
$$x + 6 = 0 \quad \text{or} \quad x - 3 = 0$$
$$x = -6 \qquad\qquad x = 3$$

The solutions are -6 and 3.

4. $$\frac{2x}{x^2-4} + \frac{1}{x-2} = \frac{2}{x+2}$$

$$x^2 - 4 = (x+2)(x-2)$$

Restrictions: $x \neq -2, x = 2$
LCD $= (x+2)(x-2)$

$$\frac{2x}{(x+2)(x-2)} + \frac{1}{x-2} = \frac{2}{x+2}$$

$$(x+2)(x-2)\left[\frac{2x}{(x+2)(x-2)} + \frac{1}{x-2}\right]$$
$$= (x+2)(x-2) \cdot \frac{2}{x+2}$$

$$2x + (x+2) = 2(x-2)$$
$$3x + 2 = 2x - 4$$
$$x = -6$$

The solution is -6.

5. $y = 2x - 3$
$x + 2y = 9$

To solve this system by the substitution method, substitute $2x - 3$ for y in the second equation.

$$x + 2y = 9$$
$$x + 2(2x-3) = 9$$
$$x + 4x - 6 = 9$$
$$5x - 6 = 9$$
$$5x = 15$$
$$x = 3$$

Back-substitute 3 for x into the first equation.

$$y = 2x - 3$$
$$y = 2 \cdot 3 - 3 = 3$$

Solution: $(3, 3)$

6. $3x + 2y = -2$
$-4x + 5y = 18$

To solve this system by the addition method, multiply the first equation by 4 and the second equation by 3.
Then add the equations.

$$\begin{aligned} 12x + \ \ 8y &= -8 \\ -12x + 15y &= 54 \\ \hline 23y &= 46 \\ y &= 2 \end{aligned}$$

Back-substitute 2 for y in the first equation of the original system.

$$3x + 2y = -2$$
$$3x + 2(2) = -2$$
$$3x + 4 = -2$$
$$3x = -6$$
$$x = -2$$

Solution: $(-2, 2)$

7. $3x - 2y = 6$
x-intercept: 2
y-intercept: -3
checkpoint: $(4, 3)$
Draw a line through $(2, 0)$, $(0, -3)$ and $(4, 3)$.

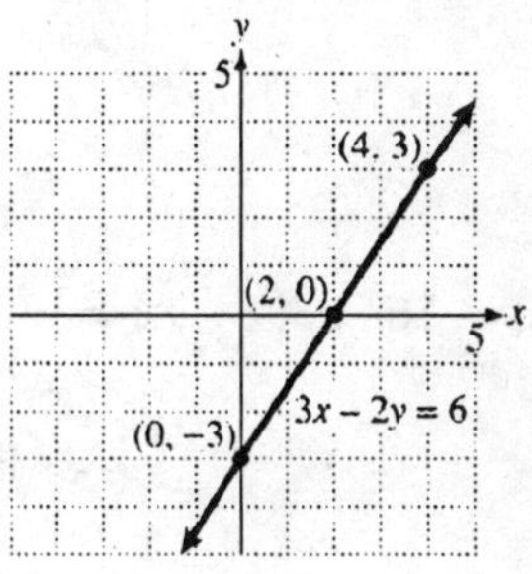

8. $y > -2x + 3$

Graph $y = -2x + 3$ as a dashed line using its slope, $-2 = \frac{-2}{1}$, and its y-intercept, 3. Use $(0, 0)$ as a test point. Because $0 > 2 \cdot 0 + 3$ is false, shade the half-plane *not* containing $(0, 0)$.

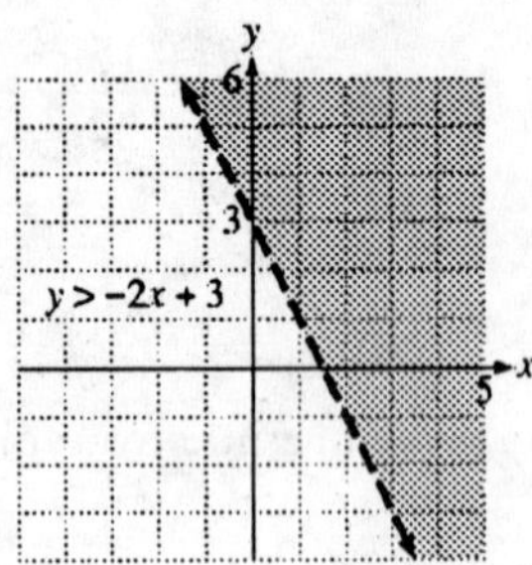

9. $y = -3$

The graph is a horizontal line with y-intercept -3.

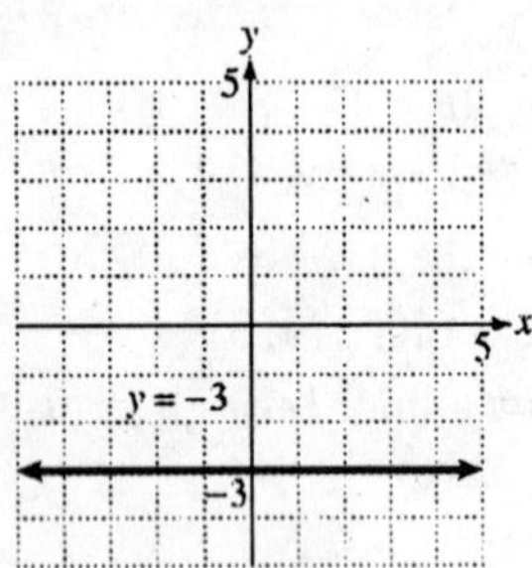

10. $-21 - 16 - 3(2 - 8) = -21 - 16 - 3(-6)$
$= -21 - 16 + 18$
$= -37 + 18 = -19$

11. $\left(\dfrac{4x^5}{2x^2}\right)^3 = (2x^3)^3 = 2^3 \cdot (x^3)^3 = 8x^9$

12. $\dfrac{\frac{1}{x} - 2}{4 - \frac{1}{x}}$

LCD $= x$

$$\frac{\frac{1}{x} - 2}{4 - \frac{1}{x}} = \frac{x\left(\frac{1}{x} - 2\right)}{x\left(4 - \frac{1}{x}\right)} = \frac{x \cdot \frac{1}{x} - x \cdot 2}{x \cdot 4 - x \cdot \frac{1}{x}} = \frac{1 - 2x}{4x - 1}$$

13. $4x^2 - 13x + 3$

Factor by trial and error. Try various combinations until the correct one is found.

$$4x^2 - 13x + 3 = (4x - 1)(x - 3)$$

14. $4x^2 - 20x + 25 = (2x)^2 - 2 \cdot 2x \cdot 5 + 5^2$
$= (2x - 5)^2$

15. $3x^2 - 75 = 3(x^2 - 25)$
$= 3(x + 5)(x - 5)$

16. $(4x^2 - 3x + 2) - (5x^2 - 7x - 6)$
$= (4x^2 - 3x + 2) + (-5x^2 + 7x + 6)$
$= -x^2 + 4x + 8$

17. $\dfrac{-8x^6 + 12x^4 - 4x^2}{4x^2} = \dfrac{-8x^6}{4x^2} + \dfrac{12x^4}{4x^2} - \dfrac{4x^2}{4x^2}$
$= -2x^4 + 3x^2 - 1$

18. $\frac{x+6}{x-2}+\frac{2x+1}{x+3}$

LCD $= (x-2)(x+3)$

$$\begin{aligned}
&\frac{x+6}{x-2}+\frac{2x+1}{x+3}\\
&=\frac{(x+6)(x+3)}{(x-2)(x+3)}+\frac{(2x+1)(x-2)}{(x-2)(x+3)}\\
&=\frac{(x+6)(x+3)+(2x+1)(x-2)}{(x-2)(x+3)}\\
&=\frac{x^2+9x+18+2x^2-3x-2}{(x-2)(x+3)}\\
&=\frac{3x^2+6x+16}{(x-2)(x+3)}
\end{aligned}$$

19. Let $x =$ the amount invested at 5%.

Then $4000 - x =$ the amount invested at 9%.

$$\begin{aligned}
0.05x+0.09(4000-x)&=311\\
0.05x+360-0.09x&=311\\
-0.04x+360&=311\\
-0.04x&=-49\\
x&=\frac{-49}{-0.04}\\
&=1225
\end{aligned}$$

If $x = 1225$, then $4000 - x = 2775$.
\$1225 was invested at 5% and \$2775 at 9%.

20. Let $x =$ the length of the shorter piece.

Then $3x =$ the length of the larger piece.

$$\begin{aligned}
x+3x&=68\\
4x&=68\\
x&=17
\end{aligned}$$

If $x = 17$, then $3x = 51$.
The lengths of the pieces are 17 inches and 51 inches.

Chapter 9

ROOTS AND RADICALS

9.1 Finding Roots

9.1 CHECK POINTS

CHECK POINT 1

a. $\sqrt{81} = 9$

The principal square root of 81 is 9.

b. $-\sqrt{9} = -3$

The negative square root of 9 is -3.

c. $\sqrt{\frac{1}{25}} = \frac{1}{5}$

d. $\sqrt{36+64} = \sqrt{100} = 10$

e. $\sqrt{36} + \sqrt{64} = 6 + 8 = 14$

CHECK POINT 2

$E = \frac{w}{20\sqrt{a}}$; $a = 4, w = 20$

$$E = \frac{20}{20\sqrt{4}} = \frac{20}{20 \cdot 2} = \frac{1}{2}$$

The evaporation is $\frac{1}{2}$ inch on that day.

CHECK POINT 3

$P = 6.85\sqrt{t} + 19$; $t = 2$ (2 years after 1997)

$$P = 6.85\sqrt{2} + 19$$
$$P \approx 28.69$$

According to the formula, about 29% of U.S. households were online in 1999. This is close to the actual data from the table, which shows that 28% of U.S. households were online in 1999.

CHECK POINT 4

a. $\sqrt[3]{1} = 1$ because $1^3 = 1$.

b. $\sqrt[3]{-27} = -3$ because $(-3)^3 = -27$.

c. $\sqrt[3]{\frac{1}{25}} = \frac{1}{5}$ because $\left(\frac{1}{5}\right)^3 = \frac{1}{125}$.

CHECK POINT 5

a. $\sqrt[4]{81} = 3$ because $3^4 = 81$.

b. $\sqrt[4]{-81}$ is not a real number. No real number raised to the fourth power will give a negative result.

c. $-\sqrt[4]{81} = -3$ because $\sqrt[4]{81} = 3$.

d. $\sqrt[5]{-\frac{1}{32}} = -\frac{1}{2}$ because $\left(-\frac{1}{2}\right)^5 = -\frac{1}{32}$.

EXERCISE SET 9.1

1. $\sqrt{36} = 6$

The principal square root of 36 is 6.

3. $-\sqrt{36} = -6$

The negative square root of 36 is -6.

5. $\sqrt{-36}$ is not a real number.
There is no real number whose square is -36.

7. $\sqrt{\frac{1}{9}} = \frac{1}{3}$ because $\left(\frac{1}{3}\right)^2 = \frac{1}{9}$.

9. $\sqrt{\frac{1}{100}} = \frac{1}{10}$ because $\left(\frac{1}{10}\right)^2 = \frac{1}{100}$.

11. $-\sqrt{\frac{1}{36}} = -\frac{1}{6}$ because $\sqrt{\frac{1}{36}} = \frac{1}{6}$.

13. $\sqrt{-\frac{1}{36}}$ is not a real number.

15. $\sqrt{0.04} = 0.2$ because $(0.2)^2 = 0.04$ and 0.2 is positive.

17. $\sqrt{33-8} = \sqrt{25} = 5$

19. $\sqrt{2 \cdot 32} = \sqrt{64} = 8$

21. $\sqrt{144+25} = \sqrt{169} = 13$

23. $\sqrt{144} + \sqrt{25} = 12 + 5 = 17$

25. $\sqrt{25-144} = \sqrt{-119}$, which is not a real number.

27. $y = \sqrt{x-1}$

x	$y = \sqrt{x-1}$	(x, y)
1	$y = \sqrt{1-1} = 0$	$(1, 0)$
2	$y = \sqrt{2-1} = 1$	$(2, 1)$
5	$y = \sqrt{5-1} = 2$	$(5, 2)$
10	$y = \sqrt{10-1} = 3$	$(10, 3)$
17	$y = \sqrt{17-1} = 4$	$(17, 4)$

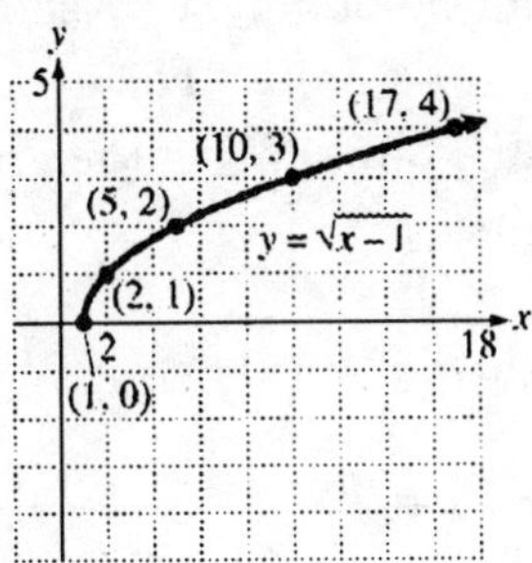

29. Answers may vary.

31. $\sqrt{7} \approx 2.646$

33. $\sqrt{23} \approx 4.796$

35. $-\sqrt{65} \approx -8.062$

37. $9 + \sqrt{5} \approx 11.236$

39. $\dfrac{9+\sqrt{5}}{2} \approx 5.618$

41. $\dfrac{-3+\sqrt{207}}{11} \approx 1.035$

43. $\sqrt{7-2} = \sqrt{5} \approx 2.236$

45. $\sqrt{2-7} = \sqrt{-5}$, which is not a real number.

47. $\sqrt[3]{64} = 4$ because $4^3 = 64$.

49. $\sqrt[3]{-27} = -3$ because $(-3)^3 = -27$.

51. $-\sqrt[3]{8} = 2$ because $\sqrt[3]{8} = 2$.

53. $\sqrt[3]{\frac{1}{125}} = \frac{1}{5}$ because $\left(\frac{1}{5}\right)^3 = \frac{1}{125}$.

55. $\sqrt[3]{-1000} = -10$ because $(-10)^3 = -1000$.

57. $\sqrt[4]{1} = 1$ because $1^4 = 1$.

59. $\sqrt[4]{16} = 2$ because $2^4 = 16$.

61. $-\sqrt[4]{16} = -2$

63. $\sqrt[4]{-16}$ is not a real number.

65. $\sqrt[5]{-1} = -1$ because $(-1)^5 = -1$.

67. $\sqrt[6]{-1}$ is not a real number because the index, 6, is even, and the radicand, -1, is negative.

69. $-\sqrt[4]{256} = -4$ because $\sqrt[4]{256} = 4$.

71. $\sqrt[6]{64} = 2$ because $2^6 = 64$.

73. $-\sqrt[5]{32} = -2$ because $\sqrt[5]{32}$.

75. $v = 4\sqrt{r};\ r = 9$

$$v = 4\sqrt{9} = 4 \cdot 4 = 12$$

The maximum velocity is 12 miles per hour.

77. $v = \sqrt{20L};\ L = 245$

$$v = \sqrt{20 \cdot 245} = \sqrt{4900} = 70$$

The motorist was traveling 70 miles per hour, so she was speeding.

79. $y = 6.75\sqrt{x}+12$; $x = 1$ (1 year after 1993)

$$y = 6.75\sqrt{1} + 12 = 18.75$$

According to the model, \$18.75 billion was loaned in 1994. The actual amount shown in the table is \$18.0 billion dollars, so the model describes the data fairly well.

81. $y = 6.75\sqrt{x} + 12$; $x = 7$ (7 years after 1993)

$$y = 6.75\sqrt{7} + 12 \approx 29.9$$

According to the model, \$29.9 billion was loaned in 1993. The actual amount shown in the table is \$30.0 billion, so the model describes the data very well.

83. $y = 2.9\sqrt{x} + 20.1$; $x = 36$

$$y = 2.9\sqrt{36} + 20.1$$
$$= 2.9 \cdot 6 + 20.1 = 37.5$$

According to the model, the median height of boys who are 36 months old is 37.5 inches. This matches the actual median height in the table exactly.

85. $y = 2.9\sqrt{x} + 20.1$; $x = 48$

$$y = 2.9\sqrt{48} + 20.1 \approx 40.2$$

According to the model, the median height of boys who are 48 months old is 40.2 inches. The actual median height shown in the table is 40.8 inches, so the model describes the actual median height quite well.

For Exercises 87–93, answers may vary.

95. Statement d is true.

$$\sqrt{\frac{1}{4}} + \sqrt{\frac{1}{9}} = \frac{1}{2} + \frac{1}{3} = \frac{5}{6}$$
$$\sqrt{\frac{25}{36}} = \frac{5}{6}$$

97. $\sqrt[3]{-\sqrt{1}} = \sqrt[3]{-1} = -1$

99. $-\sqrt{47} \approx -6.856$

This number is between -7 and -6.

Review Exercises

101. $y_1 = \sqrt{x}$
$y_2 = \sqrt{x} + 4$
$y_3 = \sqrt{x} - 3$

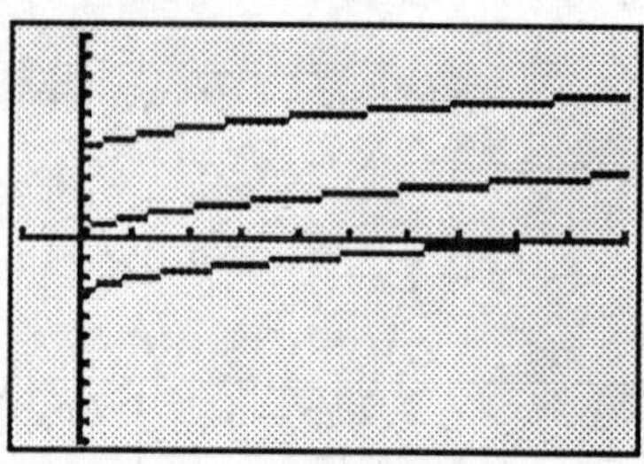

All three graphs have the same shape, but they have different positions. Notice that y_1 has y-intercept 0, y_2 has y-intercept 4, and y_3 has y-intercept -3. The graph of y_2 can be obtained by shifting the graph of y_1 up 4 units. The graph of y_3 can be obtained by shifting the graph of y_1 down 3 units.

Review Exercises

102. $4x - 5y = 20$
x-intercept: 5
y-intercept: -4
checkpoint: $(-5, -8)$

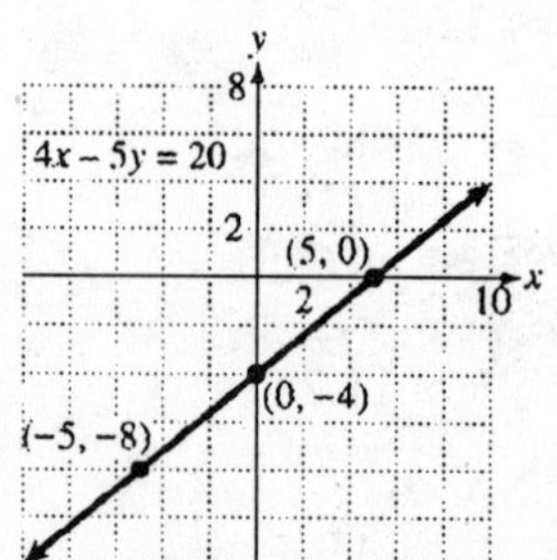

103. $2(x-3) > 4x+10$
$$2x-6 > 4x+10$$
$$-2x-6 > 10$$
$$-2x > 16$$
$$x < -8$$

$\{x|x < -8\}$

−10 −9 −8 −7 −6 −5 −4 −3

104. $\frac{1}{x^2-17x+30} \div \frac{1}{x^2+7x-18}$
$$= \frac{1}{x^2-17x+30} \cdot \frac{x^2+7x-18}{1}$$
$$= \frac{1}{(x-15)(x-2)} \cdot \frac{(x+9)(x-2)}{1}$$
$$= \frac{x+9}{x-15}$$

9.2 Multiplying and Dividing Radicals

9.2 CHECK POINTS

CHECK POINT 1

a. $\sqrt{3} \cdot \sqrt{10} = \sqrt{3 \cdot 10} = \sqrt{30}$

b. $\sqrt{2x} \cdot \sqrt{13y} = \sqrt{2x \cdot 13y} = \sqrt{26y}$

c. $\sqrt{5} \cdot \sqrt{5} = \sqrt{25} = 5$

d. $\sqrt{\frac{3}{2}} \cdot \sqrt{\frac{5}{11}} = \sqrt{\frac{3}{2} \cdot \frac{5}{11}} = \sqrt{\frac{15}{22}}$

CHECK POINT 2

a. $\sqrt{12} = \sqrt{4 \cdot 3} = \sqrt{4}\sqrt{3} = 2\sqrt{3}$

b. $\sqrt{60} = \sqrt{4 \cdot 15} = \sqrt{4}\sqrt{15} = 2\sqrt{15}$

c. $\sqrt{55}$ cannot be simplified because 55 has no perfect square factors other than 1.

CHECK POINT 3

$$\sqrt{40x^{16}} = \sqrt{4x^{16} \cdot 10} = \sqrt{4x^{16}}\sqrt{10}$$
$$= 2x^8\sqrt{10}$$

CHECK POINT 4

$$\sqrt{27x^9} = \sqrt{9x^8 \cdot 3x} = \sqrt{9x^8}\sqrt{3x}$$
$$= 3x^4\sqrt{3x}$$

CHECK POINT 5

$$\sqrt{15x^6} \cdot \sqrt{3x^7} = \sqrt{15x^6 \cdot 3x^7} = \sqrt{45x^{13}}$$
$$= \sqrt{9x^{12} \cdot 5x} = \sqrt{9x^{12}}\sqrt{5x}$$
$$= 3x^6\sqrt{5x}$$

CHECK POINT 6

a. $\sqrt{\frac{49}{25}} = \frac{\sqrt{49}}{\sqrt{25}} = \frac{7}{5}$

b. $\frac{\sqrt{48x^5}}{\sqrt{3x}} = \sqrt{\frac{48x^5}{3x}} = \sqrt{16x^4} = 4x^2$

CHECK POINT 7

a. $\sqrt[3]{40} = \sqrt[3]{8 \cdot 5} = \sqrt[3]{8} \cdot \sqrt[3]{5} = 2\sqrt[3]{5}$

b. $\sqrt[5]{8} \cdot \sqrt[5]{8} = \sqrt[5]{64} = \sqrt[5]{32 \cdot 2}$
$$= \sqrt[5]{32} \cdot \sqrt[5]{2} = 2\sqrt[5]{2}$$

c. $\sqrt[3]{\frac{125}{27}} = \frac{\sqrt[3]{125}}{\sqrt[3]{27}} = \frac{5}{3}$

EXERCISE SET 9.2

1. $\sqrt{2} \cdot \sqrt{3} = \sqrt{2 \cdot 3} = \sqrt{6}$

3. $\sqrt{3x} \cdot \sqrt{11y} = \sqrt{3x \cdot 11y} = \sqrt{33xy}$

5. $\sqrt{2} \cdot \sqrt{2} = \sqrt{4} = 2$

7. $\sqrt{\frac{1}{2}} \cdot \sqrt{\frac{5}{7}} = \sqrt{\frac{1}{2} \cdot \frac{5}{7}} = \sqrt{\frac{5}{14}}$

9. $\sqrt{0.1x} \cdot \sqrt{2y} = \sqrt{0.2xy}$

11. $\sqrt{\frac{1}{3}a} \cdot \sqrt{\frac{1}{3}b} = \sqrt{\frac{1}{9}ab} = \sqrt{\frac{1}{9}} \cdot \sqrt{ab}$
$$= \frac{1}{3}\sqrt{ab}$$

13. $\sqrt{\frac{2x}{3}} \cdot \sqrt{\frac{3}{2}} = \sqrt{\frac{2x \cdot 3}{3 \cdot 2}} = \sqrt{\frac{6x}{6}} = \sqrt{x}$

15. $\sqrt{50} = \sqrt{25 \cdot 2} = \sqrt{25}\sqrt{2} = 5\sqrt{2}$

17. $\sqrt{45} = \sqrt{9 \cdot 5} = \sqrt{9}\sqrt{5} = 3\sqrt{5}$

19. $\sqrt{200} = \sqrt{100 \cdot 2} = \sqrt{100}\sqrt{2} = 10\sqrt{2}$

21. $\sqrt{75x} = \sqrt{25 \cdot 3x} = \sqrt{25}\sqrt{3x} = 5\sqrt{3x}$

23. $\sqrt{9x} = \sqrt{9}\sqrt{x} = 3\sqrt{x}$

25. $\sqrt{35}$ cannot be simplified because 35 has no perfect square factors other than 1.

27. $\sqrt{y^2} = y$

29. $\sqrt{64x^2} = 8x$

31. $\sqrt{11x^2} = \sqrt{x^2}\sqrt{11} = x\sqrt{11}$

33. $\sqrt{8x^2} = \sqrt{4x^2}\sqrt{2} = 2x\sqrt{2}$

35. $\sqrt{x^{20}} = x^{10}$ because $(x^{10})^2 = x^{20}$.

37. $\sqrt{25y^{10}} = 5y^5$

39. $\sqrt{20x^6} - \sqrt{4x^6}\sqrt{5} = 2x^3\sqrt{5}$

41. $\sqrt{72y^{100}} = \sqrt{36y^{100}}\sqrt{2} = 6y^{50}\sqrt{2}$

43. $\sqrt{x^3} = \sqrt{x^2}\sqrt{x} = x\sqrt{x}$

45. $\sqrt{x^7} = \sqrt{x^6}\sqrt{x} = x^3\sqrt{x}$

47. $\sqrt{y^{17}} = \sqrt{y^{16}}\sqrt{y} = y^8\sqrt{y}$

49. $\sqrt{25x^5} = \sqrt{25x^4}\sqrt{x} = 5x^2\sqrt{x}$

51. $\sqrt{8x^{17}} = \sqrt{4x^{16}}\sqrt{2x} = 2x^8\sqrt{2x}$

53. $\sqrt{90y^{19}} = \sqrt{9y^{18}}\sqrt{10y} = 3y^9\sqrt{10y}$

55. $\sqrt{3} \cdot \sqrt{15} = \sqrt{45} = \sqrt{9}\sqrt{5} = 3\sqrt{5}$

57. $\sqrt{5x} \cdot \sqrt{10y} = \sqrt{50xy} = \sqrt{25}\sqrt{2xy}$
$= 5\sqrt{2xy}$

59. $\sqrt{12x} \cdot \sqrt{3x} = \sqrt{36x^2} = 6x$

61. $\sqrt{15x^2} \cdot \sqrt{3x} = \sqrt{45x^3} = \sqrt{9x^2}\sqrt{5x}$
$= 3x\sqrt{5x}$

63. $\sqrt{15x^4} \cdot \sqrt{5x^9} = \sqrt{75x^{13}} = \sqrt{25x^{12}}\sqrt{3x}$
$= 5x^6\sqrt{3x}$

65. $\sqrt{7x} \cdot \sqrt{3y} = \sqrt{21xy}$

67. $\sqrt{50xy} \cdot \sqrt{4xy^2} = \sqrt{200x^2y^3}$
$= \sqrt{100x^2y^2}\sqrt{2y}$
$= 10xy\sqrt{2y}$

69. $\sqrt{\frac{49}{16}} = \frac{\sqrt{49}}{\sqrt{16}} = \frac{7}{4}$

71. $\sqrt{\frac{3}{4}} = \frac{\sqrt{3}}{\sqrt{4}} = \frac{\sqrt{3}}{2}$

73. $\sqrt{\frac{x^2}{36}} = \frac{\sqrt{x^2}}{36} = \frac{x}{6}$

75. $\sqrt{\frac{7}{x^4}} = \frac{\sqrt{7}}{\sqrt{x^4}} = \frac{\sqrt{7}}{x^2}$

77. $\sqrt{\frac{72}{y^{20}}} = \frac{\sqrt{72}}{\sqrt{y^{20}}} = \frac{\sqrt{36}\sqrt{2}}{y^{10}} = \frac{6\sqrt{2}}{y^{10}}$

79. $\frac{\sqrt{54}}{\sqrt{6}} = \sqrt{\frac{54}{6}} = \sqrt{9} = 3$

81. $\frac{\sqrt{24}}{\sqrt{3}} = \sqrt{\frac{24}{3}} = \sqrt{8} = \sqrt{4}\sqrt{2} = 2\sqrt{2}$

83. $\frac{\sqrt{75}}{\sqrt{15}} = \sqrt{\frac{75}{15}} = \sqrt{5}$

85. $\frac{\sqrt{48x}}{\sqrt{3x}} = \sqrt{\frac{48x}{3x}} = \sqrt{16} = 4$

87. $\frac{\sqrt{32x^3}}{\sqrt{8x}} = \sqrt{\frac{32x^3}{8x}} = \sqrt{4x^2} = 2x$

89. $\frac{\sqrt{150x^4}}{\sqrt{3x}} = \sqrt{\frac{150x^4}{3x}} = \sqrt{50x^3}$
$= \sqrt{25x^2}\sqrt{2x} = 5x\sqrt{2x}$

91. $\dfrac{\sqrt{400x^{10}}}{\sqrt{10x^3}} = \sqrt{\dfrac{400x^{10}}{10x^3}} = \sqrt{40x^7}$
$= \sqrt{4x^6}\sqrt{10x} = 2x^3\sqrt{10x}$

93. $\sqrt[3]{16} = \sqrt[3]{8 \cdot 2} = \sqrt[3]{8} \cdot \sqrt[3]{2} = 2\sqrt[3]{2}$

95. $\sqrt[3]{54} = \sqrt[3]{27 \cdot 2} = \sqrt[3]{27} \cdot \sqrt[3]{2} = 3\sqrt[3]{2}$

97. $\sqrt[4]{32} = \sqrt[4]{16 \cdot 2} = \sqrt[4]{16} \cdot \sqrt[4]{2} = 2\sqrt[4]{2}$

99. $\sqrt[3]{4} \cdot \sqrt[3]{2} = \sqrt[3]{8} = 2$

101. $\sqrt[3]{9} \cdot \sqrt[3]{6} = \sqrt[3]{54} = \sqrt[3]{27}\sqrt[3]{2} = 3\sqrt[3]{2}$

103. $\sqrt[4]{4} \cdot \sqrt[4]{8} = \sqrt[4]{32} = \sqrt[4]{16} \cdot \sqrt[4]{2} = 2\sqrt[4]{2}$

105. $\sqrt[3]{\dfrac{27}{8}} = \dfrac{\sqrt[3]{27}}{\sqrt[3]{8}} = \dfrac{3}{2}$

107. $\sqrt[3]{\dfrac{3}{8}} = \dfrac{\sqrt[3]{3}}{\sqrt[3]{8}} = \dfrac{\sqrt[3]{3}}{2}$

109. $2\sqrt{5L}$; $L = 40$

$$2\sqrt{5 \cdot 40} = 2\sqrt{200} = 2\sqrt{100}\sqrt{2}$$
$$= 2 \cdot 10\sqrt{2} = 20\sqrt{2}$$

The speed of the car was $20\sqrt{2}$ miles per hour.

111. $A = l \cdot w$
$= \sqrt{15} \cdot \sqrt{5} = \sqrt{75}$
$= \sqrt{25}\sqrt{3} = 5\sqrt{3}$

The area is $5\sqrt{3}$ square feet.

For Exercises 113–119, answers may vary.

121. $\sqrt{\square x^{\square}} = 5x^7$

Since $(5x^7)^2 = 5^2(x^7)^2 = 25x^{14}$, the radicand is $25x^{14}$. The missing coefficient is 25 and the missing exponent is 14.

123. Results will vary depending on the exercises chosen.

125.

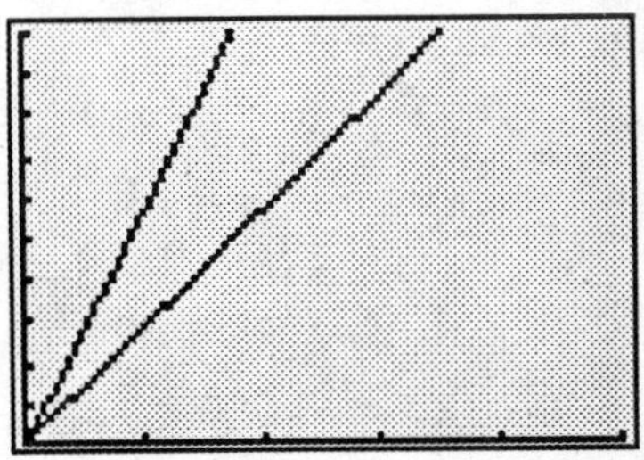

The graphs do not coincide.

$$\sqrt{8x^2} = \sqrt{4x^2 \cdot 2} = \sqrt{4x^2}\sqrt{2} = 2x\sqrt{2}$$

Change the expression on the right from $4x\sqrt{2}$ to $2x\sqrt{2}$.

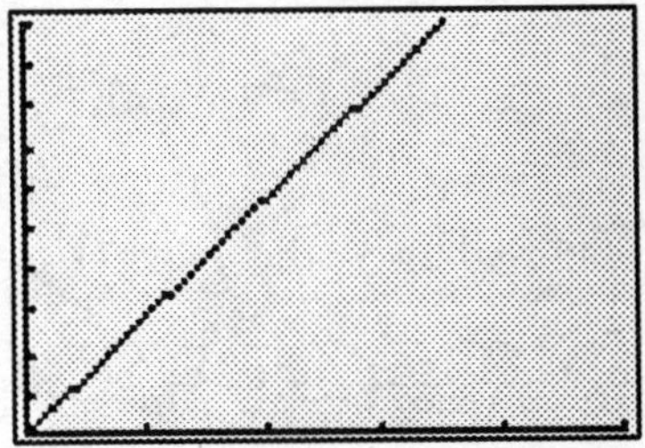

Now the graphs coincide.

Review Exercises

127. $4x + 3y = 18$
$5x - 9y = 48$

To solve this system but the addition method, multiply the first equation by 3 and add the result to the second equation.

$$\begin{aligned} 12x + 9y &= 54 \\ 5x - 9y &= 48 \\ \hline 17x \quad &= 102 \\ x &= 6 \end{aligned}$$

Back-substitute into the first equation of the original system.

$$\begin{aligned}4x+3y&=18\\4(6)+3y&=18\\24+3y&=18\\3y&=-6\\y&=-2\end{aligned}$$

Solution: $(6,-2)$

128. $\dfrac{6x}{x^2-4}-\dfrac{3}{x+2}$

Factor the first denominator.

$$x^2-4=(x+2)(x-2)$$

The LCD is $(x+2)(x-2)$.

$$\begin{aligned}&\frac{6x}{(x+2)(x-2)}-\frac{3}{x+2}\\&=\frac{6x}{(x+2)(x-2)}-\frac{3(x-2)}{(x+2)(x-2)}\\&=\frac{6x-3(x-2)}{(x+2)(x-2)}\\&=\frac{6x-3x+6}{(x+2)(x-2)}\\&=\frac{3x+6}{(x+2)(x-2)}\\&=\frac{3(x+2)}{(x+2)(x-2)}\\&=\frac{3}{x-2}\end{aligned}$$

129. $\begin{aligned}[t]2x^3-16x^2+30x&=2(x^2-8x+15)\\&=2(x-3)(x-5)\end{aligned}$

9.3 Operations with Radicals

9.3 CHECK POINTS

CHECK POINT 1

a. $8\sqrt{13}+9\sqrt{13}=(8+9)\sqrt{13}=17\sqrt{13}$

b. $\begin{aligned}[t]\sqrt{17x}-20\sqrt{17x}&=1\sqrt{17x}-20\sqrt{17x}\\&=(1-20)\sqrt{17x}\\&=-19\sqrt{17x}\end{aligned}$

CHECK POINT 2

a. $\begin{aligned}[t]5\sqrt{27}+\sqrt{12}&=5\sqrt{9\cdot 3}+\sqrt{4\cdot 3}\\&=5\cdot 3\sqrt{3}+2\sqrt{3}\\&=15\sqrt{3}+2\sqrt{13}\\&=(15+2)\sqrt{3}=17\sqrt{3}\end{aligned}$

b. $\begin{aligned}[t]6\sqrt{18x}-4\sqrt{8x}&=6\sqrt{9\cdot 2x}-4\sqrt{4\cdot 2x}\\&=6\cdot 3\sqrt{2x}-4\cdot 2\sqrt{2x}\\&=18\sqrt{2x}-8\sqrt{2x}\\&=(18-8)\sqrt{2x}=10\sqrt{2x}\end{aligned}$

CHECK POINT 3

a. $\begin{aligned}[t]\sqrt{2}(\sqrt{5}+\sqrt{11})&=\sqrt{2}\cdot\sqrt{5}+\sqrt{2}\cdot\sqrt{11}\\&=\sqrt{10}+\sqrt{22}\end{aligned}$

b. $\begin{aligned}[t]&(4+\sqrt{3})(2+\sqrt{3})\\&=4\cdot 2+4\cdot\sqrt{3}+\sqrt{3}\cdot 2+\sqrt{3}\cdot\sqrt{3}\\&=8+4\sqrt{3}+2\sqrt{3}+3\\&=(8+3)+(4+2)\sqrt{3}=11+6\sqrt{3}\end{aligned}$

c. $\begin{aligned}[t]&(3+\sqrt{5})(8-4\sqrt{5})\\&=3\cdot 8+3(-4\sqrt{5})+\sqrt{5}\cdot 8+\sqrt{5}(-4\sqrt{5})\\&=24-12\sqrt{5}+8\sqrt{5}-4\cdot 5\\&=24-12\sqrt{5}+8\sqrt{5}-20\\&=(24-20)+(-12\sqrt{5}+8\sqrt{5})\\&=4-4\sqrt{5}\end{aligned}$

CHECK POINT 4

a. $(3+\sqrt{11})(3-\sqrt{11}) = 3^2 - (\sqrt{11})^2$
$= 9 - 11 = -2$

b. $(\sqrt{7}-\sqrt{2})(\sqrt{7}+\sqrt{2}) = (\sqrt{7})^2 - (\sqrt{2})^2$
$= 7 - 2 = 5$

EXERCISE SET 9.3

1. $7\sqrt{3}+2\sqrt{3} = (7+2)\sqrt{3} = 9\sqrt{3}$

3. $9\sqrt{6}-2\sqrt{6} = (9-2)\sqrt{6} = 7\sqrt{6}$

5. $4\sqrt{13}-6\sqrt{13} = (4-6)\sqrt{13} = -2\sqrt{13}$

7. $3\sqrt{x}+5\sqrt{x} = (3+5)\sqrt{x} = 8\sqrt{x}$

9. $7\sqrt{y}-12\sqrt{y} = (7-12)\sqrt{y} = -5\sqrt{y}$

11. $7\sqrt{5x}+3\sqrt{5x} = (7+3)\sqrt{5x} = 10\sqrt{5x}$

13. $7\sqrt{5y}-\sqrt{5y} = 7\sqrt{5y}-1\sqrt{5y}$
$= (7-1)\sqrt{5y} = 6\sqrt{5y}$

15. $\sqrt{5}+\sqrt{5} = 1\sqrt{5}+1\sqrt{5} = (1+1)\sqrt{5}$
$= 2\sqrt{5}$

17. $4\sqrt{2}+3\sqrt{2}+5\sqrt{2} = (4+3+5)\sqrt{2}$
$= 12\sqrt{2}$

19. $4\sqrt{7}-5\sqrt{7}+8\sqrt{7} = (4-5+8)\sqrt{7} = 7\sqrt{7}$

21. $4\sqrt{11}-6\sqrt{11}+2\sqrt{11} = (4-6+2)\sqrt{11}$
$= 0\sqrt{11} = 0$

23. $\sqrt{5}+\sqrt{20} = \sqrt{5}+\sqrt{4\cdot 5} = \sqrt{5}+2\sqrt{5}$
$= 1\sqrt{5}+2\sqrt{5} = 3\sqrt{5}$

25. $\sqrt{8}-\sqrt{2} = \sqrt{4\cdot 2}-\sqrt{2} = \sqrt{4}\sqrt{2}-\sqrt{2}$
$= 2\sqrt{2}-1\sqrt{2} = (2-1)\sqrt{2} = \sqrt{2}$

27. $\sqrt{50}+\sqrt{18} = \sqrt{25}\sqrt{2}+\sqrt{9}\sqrt{2}$
$= 5\sqrt{2}+3\sqrt{2} = 8\sqrt{2}$

29. $7\sqrt{12}+\sqrt{75} = 7\sqrt{4}\sqrt{3}+\sqrt{25}\sqrt{3}$
$= 7\cdot 2\sqrt{3}+5\sqrt{3}$
$= 14\sqrt{3}+5\sqrt{3} = 19\sqrt{3}$

31. $3\sqrt{27}-2\sqrt{18} = 3\sqrt{9\cdot 3}-2\sqrt{9\cdot 2}$
$= 3\cdot 3\sqrt{3}-2\cdot 3\sqrt{2}$
$= 9\sqrt{3}-6\sqrt{2}$

Because $\sqrt{3}$ and $\sqrt{2}$ are unlike radicals, it is not possible to combine terms and simplify further.

33. $2\sqrt{45x}-2\sqrt{20x}$
$= 2\sqrt{9}\sqrt{5x}-2\sqrt{4}\sqrt{5x}$
$= 2\cdot 3\sqrt{5x}-2\cdot 2\sqrt{5x}$
$= 6\sqrt{5x}-4\sqrt{5x}$
$= (6-4)\sqrt{5x} = 2\sqrt{5x}$

35. $\sqrt{8}+\sqrt{16}+\sqrt{18}+\sqrt{25}$
$= \sqrt{4}\sqrt{2}+4+\sqrt{9}\sqrt{2}+5$
$= 2\sqrt{2}+4+3\sqrt{2}+5$
$= (4+5)+(2\sqrt{2}+3\sqrt{2})$
$= 9+5\sqrt{2}$

37. $\sqrt{2}+\sqrt{11}$

These are unlike radicals, so the terms cannot be combined.

39. $2\sqrt{80}+3\sqrt{75} = 2\sqrt{16}\sqrt{5}+3\sqrt{25}\sqrt{3}$
$= 2\cdot 4\sqrt{5}+3\cdot 5\sqrt{3}$
$= 8\sqrt{5}+15\sqrt{3}$

Because $\sqrt{5}$ and $\sqrt{3}$ are unlike radials, is not possible to combine terms.

41. $3\sqrt{54}-2\sqrt{20}+4\sqrt{45}-\sqrt{24}$
$= 3\sqrt{9}\sqrt{6}-2\sqrt{4}\sqrt{5}+4\sqrt{9}\sqrt{5}-\sqrt{4}\sqrt{6}$
$= 3\cdot 3\sqrt{6}-2\cdot 2\sqrt{5}+4\cdot 3\sqrt{5}-2\sqrt{6}$
$= 9\sqrt{6}-4\sqrt{5}+12\sqrt{5}-2\sqrt{6}$
$= (9-2)\sqrt{6}+(-4+12)\sqrt{5}$
$= 7\sqrt{6}+8\sqrt{5}$

43. $\sqrt{2}(\sqrt{3}+\sqrt{5})$

Use the distributive property.

$$\sqrt{2}(\sqrt{3}+\sqrt{5}) = \sqrt{2}\cdot\sqrt{3}+\sqrt{2}\cdot\sqrt{5} = \sqrt{6}+\sqrt{10}$$

45. $\sqrt{7}(\sqrt{6}-\sqrt{10}) = \sqrt{7}\cdot\sqrt{6}-\sqrt{7}\cdot\sqrt{10}$
$= \sqrt{42}-\sqrt{70}$

47. $\sqrt{3}(5+\sqrt{3}) = \sqrt{3}\cdot 5+\sqrt{3}\cdot\sqrt{3}$
$= 5\sqrt{3}+3$

49. $\sqrt{3}(\sqrt{6}-\sqrt{3}) = \sqrt{3}\cdot\sqrt{6}-\sqrt{3}\cdot\sqrt{3}$
$= \sqrt{18}-3 = \sqrt{9}\sqrt{2}-3$
$= 3\sqrt{2}-3$

51. $(5+\sqrt{2})(6+\sqrt{2})$

Use the FOIL method.

$$\begin{aligned}&(5+\sqrt{2})(6+\sqrt{2})\\&= 5\cdot 6+5\sqrt{2}+6\sqrt{2}+\sqrt{2}\cdot\sqrt{2}\\&= 30+5\sqrt{2}+6\sqrt{2}+2\\&= (30+2)+(5+6)\sqrt{2}\\&= 32+11\sqrt{2}\end{aligned}$$

53. $(4+\sqrt{5})(10-3\sqrt{5})$
$= 4\cdot 10+4(-3\sqrt{5})+\sqrt{5}\cdot 10$
$+\sqrt{5}(-3\sqrt{5})$
$= 40-12\sqrt{5}+10\sqrt{5}-3\cdot 5$
$= 40-12\sqrt{5}+10\sqrt{5}-15$
$= (40-15)+(-12+10)\sqrt{5}$
$= 25-2\sqrt{5}$

55. $(6-3\sqrt{7})(2-5\sqrt{7})$
$= 6\cdot 2+6(-5\sqrt{7})-3\sqrt{7}(2)$
$-3\sqrt{7}(-5\sqrt{7})$
$= 12-30\sqrt{7}-6\sqrt{7}+15\cdot 7$
$= 12-30\sqrt{7}-6\sqrt{7}+105$
$= (12+105)+(-30-6)\sqrt{7}$
$= 117-36\sqrt{7}$

57. $(\sqrt{10}-3)(\sqrt{10}-5)$
$= \sqrt{10}\cdot\sqrt{10}+\sqrt{10}(-5)-3\sqrt{10}-3(-5)$
$= 10-5\sqrt{10}-3\sqrt{10}+15$
$= 25-8\sqrt{10}$

59. $(\sqrt{3}+\sqrt{6})(\sqrt{3}+2\sqrt{6})$
$= \sqrt{3}\cdot\sqrt{3}+\sqrt{3}\cdot 2\sqrt{6}+\sqrt{6}\cdot\sqrt{3}$
$+\sqrt{6}\cdot 2\sqrt{6}$
$= 3+2\sqrt{18}+\sqrt{18}+2\cdot 6$
$= 3+2\sqrt{18}+\sqrt{18}+12$
$= 15+3\sqrt{18} = 15+3\sqrt{9}\sqrt{2}$
$= 15+3\cdot 3\sqrt{2}$
$= 15+9\sqrt{2}$

61. $(\sqrt{2}+1)(\sqrt{3}-6)$
$= \sqrt{2}\cdot\sqrt{3}+\sqrt{2}(-6)+1\cdot\sqrt{3}+1(-6)$
$= \sqrt{6}-6\sqrt{2}+\sqrt{3}-6$

63. $(3+\sqrt{5})(3-\sqrt{5})$

These two radical expressions are conjugates. Use the special-product formula

$$(A+B)(A-B) = A^2-B^2.$$

$$\begin{aligned}(3+\sqrt{5})(3-\sqrt{5}) &= 3^2-(\sqrt{5})^2\\&= 9-5\\&= 4\end{aligned}$$

65. $(1-\sqrt{6})(1+\sqrt{6}) = 1^2-(\sqrt{6})^2$
$= 1-6$
$= -5$

67. $(\sqrt{11}+5)(\sqrt{11}-5) = (\sqrt{11})^2-5^2$
$= 11-25 = -14$

69. $(\sqrt{7}-\sqrt{5})(\sqrt{7}+\sqrt{5}) = (\sqrt{7})^2-(\sqrt{5})^2$
$= 7-5 = 2$

71. $(2\sqrt{3}+7)(2\sqrt{3}-7) = (2\sqrt{3})^2-7^2$
$= 12-49$
$= -37$

73. $(2\sqrt{3}+\sqrt{5})(2\sqrt{3}-\sqrt{5}) = (2\sqrt{3})^2-(\sqrt{5})^2$
$= 12-5$
$= 7$

75. $(\sqrt{2}+\sqrt{3})^2$

Use the special product formula

$$(A+B)^2 = A^2 + 2AB + B^2.$$

$$\begin{aligned}(\sqrt{2}+\sqrt{3})^2 &= (\sqrt{2})^2 + 2\cdot\sqrt{2}\cdot\sqrt{3} + (\sqrt{3})^2\\ &= 2 + 2\sqrt{6} + 3 = 5 + 2\sqrt{6}\end{aligned}$$

77. $(\sqrt{x}-\sqrt{10})^2$

Use the special-product formula

$$(A+B)^2 = A^2 - 2AB + B^2.$$

$$\begin{aligned}&(\sqrt{x}-\sqrt{10})^2\\ &= (\sqrt{x})^2 - 2\cdot\sqrt{x}\cdot\sqrt{10} + (\sqrt{10})^2\\ &= x - 2\sqrt{10x} + 10\end{aligned}$$

79. Use the formulas for the perimeter and area of a square with $s = \sqrt{3}+\sqrt{5}$.

$$\begin{aligned}P = 4s &= 4(\sqrt{3}+\sqrt{5})\\ &= 4\sqrt{3} + 4\sqrt{5}\end{aligned}$$

The perimeter is $(4\sqrt{3}+4\sqrt{5})$ inches.

$$\begin{aligned}A = s^2 &= (\sqrt{3}+\sqrt{5})^2\\ &= (\sqrt{3})^2 + 2\sqrt{3}\sqrt{5} + (\sqrt{5})^2\\ &= 3 + 2\sqrt{15} + 5\\ &= 8 + 2\sqrt{15}\end{aligned}$$

The area is $(8+2\sqrt{15})$ square inches.

81. Use the formulas for the perimeter and area of a rectangle with $l = \sqrt{6}+1$ and $w = \sqrt{6}-1$.

$$\begin{aligned}P = 2l + 2w &= 2(\sqrt{6}+1) + 2(\sqrt{6}-1)\\ &= 2\sqrt{6} + 2 + 2\sqrt{6} - 2\\ &= 4\sqrt{6}\end{aligned}$$

The perimeter is $4\sqrt{6}$ inches.

$$\begin{aligned}A = lw &= (\sqrt{6}+1)(\sqrt{6}-1)\\ &= (\sqrt{6})^2 - 1^2\\ &= 6 - 1 = 5\end{aligned}$$

The area is 5 square inches.

83. To find the perimeter of a triangle, add the lengths of the three sides.

$$P = \sqrt{2} + \sqrt{2} + 2 = 2 + 2\sqrt{2}$$

The perimeter is $(2+2\sqrt{2})$ inches.
Use the formula for the area of a triangle with $b = \sqrt{2}$ and $h = \sqrt{2}$.

$$\begin{aligned}A = \frac{1}{2}bh &= \frac{1}{2}(\sqrt{2})(\sqrt{2})\\ &= \frac{1}{2}\cdot 2 = 1\end{aligned}$$

The area is 1 square inch.

85. $\sqrt{2}+\sqrt{8}$; $a = 2, b = 8$

$$\begin{aligned}\sqrt{a}+\sqrt{b} &= \sqrt{(a+b)+2\sqrt{ab}}\\ \sqrt{2}+\sqrt{8} &= \sqrt{(2+8)+2\sqrt{2\cdot 8}}\\ &= \sqrt{10+2\sqrt{16}}\\ &= \sqrt{10+2\cdot 4}\\ &= \sqrt{18} = \sqrt{9}\sqrt{2} = 3\sqrt{2}\end{aligned}$$

$$\begin{aligned}\sqrt{2}+\sqrt{8} &= \sqrt{2}+\sqrt{4\cdot 2}\\ &= \sqrt{2}+\sqrt{4}\sqrt{2}\\ &= \sqrt{2}+2\sqrt{2}\\ &= (1+2)\sqrt{2} = 3\sqrt{2}\end{aligned}$$

Explanations of preferences will vary.

For Exercises 87–93, answers may vary.

95. $$\begin{aligned}\sqrt{5}\cdot\sqrt{15}+6\sqrt{3} &= \sqrt{75}+6\sqrt{3}\\ &= \sqrt{25}\sqrt{3}+6\sqrt{3}\\ &= 5\sqrt{3}+6\sqrt{3}\\ &= 11\sqrt{3}\end{aligned}$$

97. $$\begin{aligned}&(\sqrt[3]{4}+1)(\sqrt[3]{2}-3)\\ &= \sqrt[3]{4}\cdot\sqrt[3]{2} - 3\sqrt[3]{4} + 1\sqrt[3]{2} + 1(-3)\\ &= \sqrt[3]{8} - 3\sqrt[3]{4} + \sqrt[3]{2} - 3\\ &= 2 - 3\sqrt[3]{4} + \sqrt[3]{2} - 3\\ &= -1 - 3\sqrt[3]{4} + \sqrt[3]{2}\end{aligned}$$

99. $(4\sqrt{3x}+\sqrt{2y})(4\sqrt{3x}-\sqrt{2y})$
$= (4\sqrt{3x})^2 - (\sqrt{2y})^2$
$= 16 \cdot 3x - 2y$
$= 48x - 2y$

101.

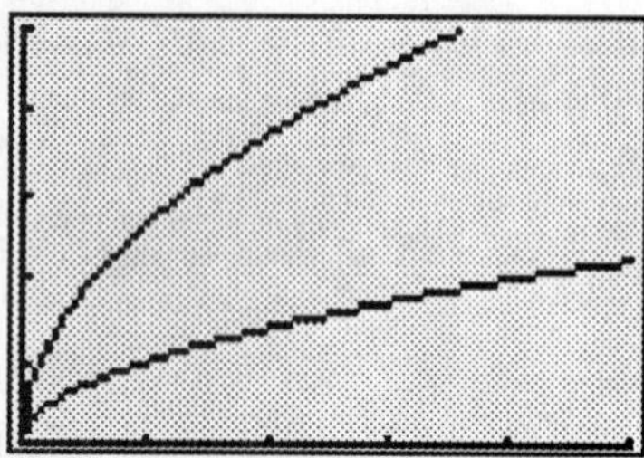

The graphs do not coincide.

$$\sqrt{16x}-\sqrt{9x} = \sqrt{16x}\sqrt{x}-\sqrt{9}\sqrt{x}$$
$$= 4\sqrt{x}-3\sqrt{x}$$
$$= (4-3)\sqrt{x} = \sqrt{x}$$

Change the expression on the right from $\sqrt{7x}$ to $\sqrt{x}$.

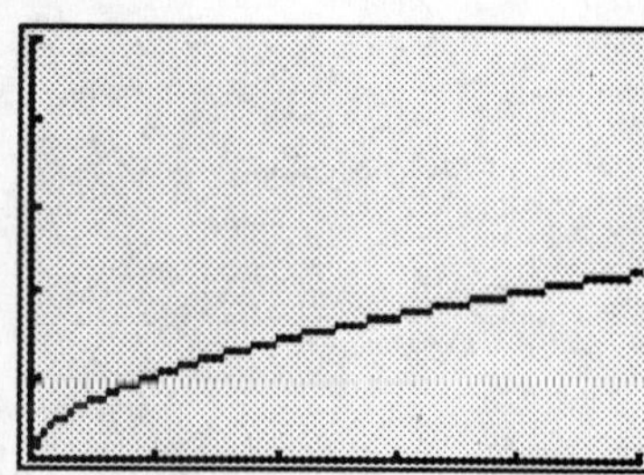

Now the graphs coincide.

103.

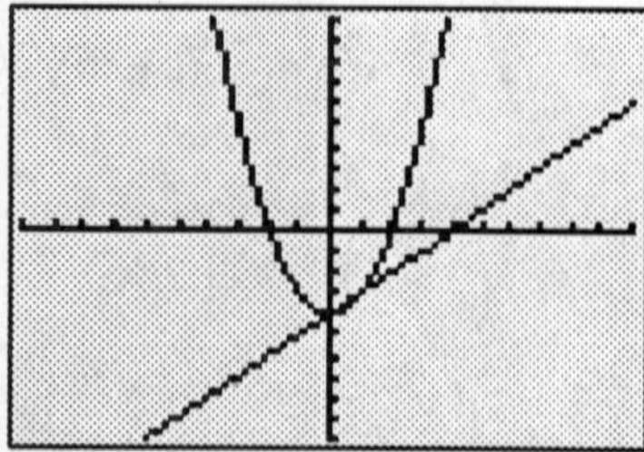

The graphs do not coincide.

$$(\sqrt{x}+2)(\sqrt{x}-2) = (\sqrt{x})^2 - 2^2 = x-4$$

Change the expression on the right from x^2-4 to $x-4$.

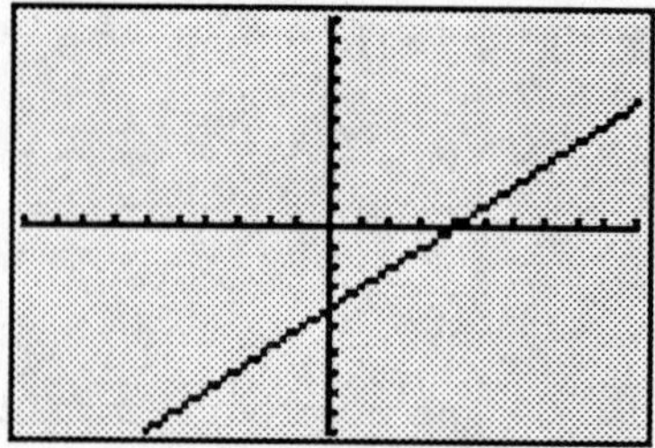

Now the graphs coincide.

Review Exercises

104. $(5x+3)(5x-3) = (5x)^2 - 3^2$
$= 25x^2 - 9$

105. $64x^3 - x = x(64x^2-1)$
$= x[(8x)^2 - 1^2]$
$= x(8x+1)(8x-1)$

106. $y = -\frac{1}{4}x + 3$

slope $= -\frac{1}{4} = \frac{-1}{4}$; y-intercept $= 3$

Plot $(0,3)$. From this point, move 1 unit *down* and 4 units to the *right* to reach the point $(4,2)$. Draw a line through $(0,3)$ and $(4,2)$.

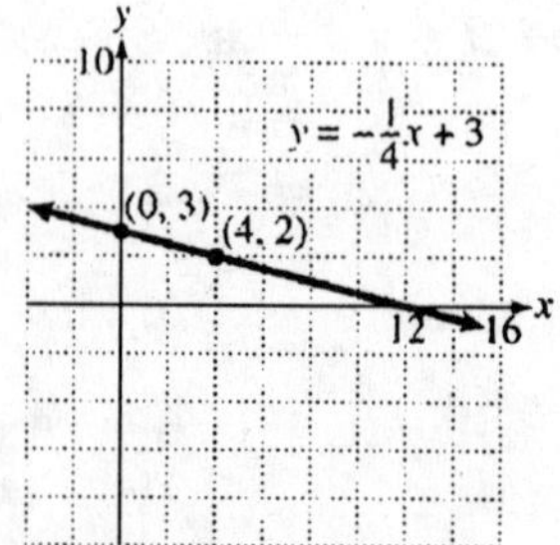

9.4 Rationalizing the Denominator

9.4 CHECK POINTS

CHECK POINT 1

a. $\frac{25}{\sqrt{10}} = \frac{25}{\sqrt{10}} \cdot \frac{\sqrt{10}}{\sqrt{10}} = \frac{25\sqrt{10}}{10} = \frac{5\sqrt{10}}{2}$

b. $\sqrt{\frac{2}{7}} = \frac{\sqrt{2}}{\sqrt{7}} = \frac{\sqrt{2}}{\sqrt{7}} \cdot \frac{\sqrt{7}}{\sqrt{7}} = \frac{\sqrt{14}}{\sqrt{7}}$

CHECK POINT 2

a. $\frac{15}{\sqrt{18}} = \frac{15}{\sqrt{9 \cdot 2}} = \frac{15}{3\sqrt{2}} = \frac{15}{\sqrt{2}}$

$= \frac{5}{\sqrt{2}} \cdot \frac{\sqrt{2}}{\sqrt{2}} = \frac{5\sqrt{2}}{2}$

b. $\sqrt{\frac{7x}{20}} = \sqrt{\frac{7x}{20}} = \frac{\sqrt{7x}}{\sqrt{4 \cdot 5}} = \frac{\sqrt{7x}}{2\sqrt{5}}$

$= \frac{\sqrt{7x}}{2\sqrt{5}} \cdot \frac{\sqrt{5}}{\sqrt{5}} = \frac{\sqrt{35x}}{2 \cdot 5}$

$= \frac{\sqrt{35x}}{10}$

CHECK POINT 3

$\frac{8}{4+\sqrt{5}} = \frac{8}{4+\sqrt{5}} \cdot \frac{4-\sqrt{5}}{4-\sqrt{5}}$

$= \frac{8(4-\sqrt{5})}{4^2-(\sqrt{5})^2} = \frac{8(4-\sqrt{5})}{16-5}$

$= \frac{8(4-\sqrt{5})}{11}$ or $\frac{32-8\sqrt{5}}{11}$

CHECK POINT 4

$\frac{8}{\sqrt{7}-\sqrt{3}} = \frac{8}{\sqrt{7}-\sqrt{3}} \cdot \frac{\sqrt{7}+\sqrt{3}}{\sqrt{7}+\sqrt{3}}$

$= \frac{8(\sqrt{7}+\sqrt{3})}{(\sqrt{7})^2-(\sqrt{3})^2}$

$= \frac{8(\sqrt{7}+\sqrt{3})}{7-3}$

$= \frac{\overset{2}{\cancel{8}}(\sqrt{7}+\sqrt{3})}{\underset{1}{\cancel{4}}}$

$= 2(\sqrt{7}+\sqrt{3})$
$= 2\sqrt{7}+2\sqrt{3}$

EXERCISE SET 9.4

1. $\frac{1}{\sqrt{5}} = \frac{1}{\sqrt{5}} \cdot \frac{\sqrt{5}}{\sqrt{5}} = \frac{\sqrt{5}}{5}$

3. $\frac{3}{\sqrt{3}} = \frac{3}{\sqrt{3}} \cdot \frac{\sqrt{3}}{\sqrt{3}} = \frac{3\sqrt{3}}{3} = \sqrt{3}$

5. $\frac{2}{\sqrt{6}} = \frac{2}{\sqrt{6}} \cdot \frac{\sqrt{6}}{\sqrt{6}} = \frac{2\sqrt{6}}{6} = \frac{\sqrt{6}}{3}$

7. $\frac{21}{\sqrt{7}} = \frac{21}{\sqrt{7}} \cdot \frac{\sqrt{7}}{\sqrt{7}} = \frac{21\sqrt{7}}{7} = 3\sqrt{7}$

9. $\sqrt{\frac{2}{5}} = \frac{\sqrt{2}}{\sqrt{5}} = \frac{\sqrt{2}}{\sqrt{5}} \cdot \frac{\sqrt{5}}{\sqrt{5}} = \frac{\sqrt{10}}{5}$

11. $\sqrt{\frac{7}{3}} = \frac{\sqrt{7}}{\sqrt{3}} = \frac{\sqrt{7}}{\sqrt{3}} \cdot \frac{\sqrt{3}}{\sqrt{3}} = \frac{\sqrt{21}}{3}$

13. $\sqrt{\frac{x^2}{3}} = \frac{\sqrt{x^2}}{\sqrt{3}} = \frac{x}{\sqrt{3}} = \frac{x}{\sqrt{3}} \cdot \frac{\sqrt{3}}{\sqrt{3}} = \frac{x\sqrt{3}}{3}$

15. $\sqrt{\frac{11}{x}} = \frac{\sqrt{11}}{\sqrt{x}} = \frac{\sqrt{11}}{\sqrt{x}} \cdot \frac{\sqrt{x}}{\sqrt{x}} = \frac{\sqrt{11x}}{x}$

17. $\sqrt{\frac{x}{y}} = \frac{\sqrt{x}}{\sqrt{y}} = \frac{\sqrt{x}}{\sqrt{y}} \cdot \frac{\sqrt{y}}{\sqrt{y}} = \frac{\sqrt{xy}}{y}$

19. $\sqrt{\dfrac{x^4}{2}} = \dfrac{\sqrt{x^4}}{\sqrt{2}} = \dfrac{x^2}{\sqrt{2}} = \dfrac{x^2}{\sqrt{2}} \cdot \dfrac{\sqrt{2}}{\sqrt{2}} = \dfrac{x^2\sqrt{2}}{2}$

21. $\dfrac{\sqrt{7}}{\sqrt{5}} = \dfrac{\sqrt{7}}{\sqrt{5}} \cdot \dfrac{\sqrt{5}}{\sqrt{5}} = \dfrac{\sqrt{35}}{5}$

23. $\dfrac{\sqrt{3x}}{\sqrt{14}} = \dfrac{\sqrt{3x}}{\sqrt{14}} \cdot \dfrac{\sqrt{14}}{\sqrt{14}} = \dfrac{\sqrt{42x}}{14}$

25. $\dfrac{1}{\sqrt{20}} = \dfrac{1}{\sqrt{4}\sqrt{5}} = \dfrac{1}{2\sqrt{5}} = \dfrac{1}{2\sqrt{5}} \cdot \dfrac{\sqrt{5}}{\sqrt{5}}$

$= \dfrac{\sqrt{5}}{2 \cdot 5} = \dfrac{\sqrt{5}}{10}$

27. $\dfrac{12}{\sqrt{32}} = \dfrac{12}{\sqrt{6}\sqrt{2}} = \dfrac{12}{4\sqrt{2}} = \dfrac{3}{\sqrt{2}}$

$= \dfrac{3}{\sqrt{2}} \cdot \dfrac{\sqrt{2}}{\sqrt{2}} = \dfrac{3\sqrt{2}}{2}$

29. $\dfrac{15}{\sqrt{12}} = \dfrac{15}{\sqrt{4}\sqrt{3}} = \dfrac{15}{2\sqrt{3}} = \dfrac{15}{2\sqrt{3}} \cdot \dfrac{\sqrt{3}}{\sqrt{3}}$

$= \dfrac{15\sqrt{3}}{2 \cdot 3} = \dfrac{15\sqrt{3}}{6} = \dfrac{5\sqrt{3}}{2}$

31. $\sqrt{\dfrac{5}{18}} = \dfrac{\sqrt{5}}{\sqrt{18}} = \dfrac{\sqrt{5}}{\sqrt{9}\sqrt{2}} = \dfrac{\sqrt{5}}{3\sqrt{2}}$

$= \dfrac{\sqrt{5}}{3\sqrt{2}} \cdot \dfrac{\sqrt{2}}{\sqrt{2}} = \dfrac{\sqrt{10}}{3 \cdot 2} = \dfrac{\sqrt{10}}{6}$

33. $\sqrt{\dfrac{x}{32}} = \dfrac{\sqrt{x}}{\sqrt{32}} = \dfrac{\sqrt{x}}{\sqrt{16}\sqrt{2}} = \dfrac{\sqrt{x}}{4\sqrt{2}}$

$= \dfrac{\sqrt{x}}{4\sqrt{2}} \cdot \dfrac{\sqrt{2}}{\sqrt{2}} = \dfrac{\sqrt{2x}}{4 \cdot 2} = \dfrac{\sqrt{2x}}{8}$

35. $\sqrt{\dfrac{1}{45}} = \dfrac{\sqrt{1}}{\sqrt{45}} = \dfrac{1}{\sqrt{45}} = \dfrac{1}{\sqrt{9}\sqrt{5}} = \dfrac{1}{3\sqrt{5}}$

$= \dfrac{1}{3\sqrt{5}} \cdot \dfrac{\sqrt{5}}{\sqrt{5}} = \dfrac{\sqrt{5}}{3 \cdot 5} = \dfrac{\sqrt{5}}{15}$

37. $\dfrac{\sqrt{7}}{\sqrt{12}} = \dfrac{\sqrt{7}}{\sqrt{4}\sqrt{3}} = \dfrac{\sqrt{7}}{2\sqrt{3}} \cdot \dfrac{\sqrt{3}}{\sqrt{3}}$

$= \dfrac{\sqrt{21}}{2 \cdot 3} = \dfrac{\sqrt{21}}{6}$

39. $\dfrac{8x}{\sqrt{8}} = \dfrac{8x}{\sqrt{4}\sqrt{2}} = \dfrac{8x}{2\sqrt{2}} = \dfrac{4x}{\sqrt{2}}$

$= \dfrac{4x}{\sqrt{2}} \cdot \dfrac{\sqrt{2}}{\sqrt{2}} = \dfrac{4x\sqrt{2}}{2}$

$= 2x\sqrt{2}$

41. $\dfrac{\sqrt{7y}}{\sqrt{8}} = \dfrac{\sqrt{7y}}{\sqrt{4}\sqrt{2}} = \dfrac{\sqrt{7y}}{2\sqrt{2}} \cdot \dfrac{\sqrt{2}}{\sqrt{2}}$

$= \dfrac{\sqrt{14y}}{2 \cdot 2} = \dfrac{\sqrt{14y}}{4}$

43. $\sqrt{\dfrac{7x}{12}} = \dfrac{\sqrt{7x}}{\sqrt{12}} = \dfrac{\sqrt{7x}}{\sqrt{4}\sqrt{3}} = \dfrac{\sqrt{7x}}{2\sqrt{3}}$

$= \dfrac{\sqrt{7x}}{2\sqrt{3}} \cdot \dfrac{\sqrt{3}}{\sqrt{3}} = \dfrac{\sqrt{21x}}{2 \cdot 3}$

$= \dfrac{\sqrt{21x}}{6}$

45. $\sqrt{\dfrac{45}{x}} = \dfrac{\sqrt{45}}{\sqrt{x}} = \dfrac{\sqrt{9}\sqrt{5}}{\sqrt{x}} = \dfrac{3\sqrt{5}}{\sqrt{x}}$

$= \dfrac{3\sqrt{5}}{\sqrt{x}} \cdot \dfrac{\sqrt{x}}{\sqrt{x}} = \dfrac{3\sqrt{5x}}{x}$

47. $\dfrac{5}{\sqrt{x^3}} = \dfrac{5}{\sqrt{x^2}\sqrt{x}} = \dfrac{5}{x\sqrt{x}} = \dfrac{5}{x\sqrt{x}} \cdot \dfrac{\sqrt{x}}{\sqrt{x}}$

$= \dfrac{5\sqrt{x}}{x \cdot x} = \dfrac{5\sqrt{x}}{x^2}$

49. $\sqrt{\dfrac{27}{y^3}} = \dfrac{\sqrt{27}}{\sqrt{y^3}} = \dfrac{\sqrt{9}\sqrt{3}}{\sqrt{y^2}\sqrt{y}}$

$= \dfrac{3\sqrt{3}}{y\sqrt{y}} = \dfrac{3\sqrt{3}}{y\sqrt{y}} \cdot \dfrac{\sqrt{y}}{\sqrt{y}}$

$= \dfrac{3\sqrt{3y}}{y \cdot y} = \dfrac{3\sqrt{3y}}{y^2}$

51. $\dfrac{\sqrt{50x^2}}{\sqrt{12y^3}} = \dfrac{\sqrt{25x^2}\sqrt{2}}{\sqrt{4y^2}\sqrt{3y}} = \dfrac{5x\sqrt{2}}{2y\sqrt{3y}}$

$= \dfrac{5x\sqrt{2}}{2y\sqrt{3y}} \cdot \dfrac{\sqrt{3y}}{\sqrt{3y}} = \dfrac{5x\sqrt{6y}}{2y \cdot 3y}$

$= \dfrac{5x\sqrt{6y}}{6y^2}$

53. $\dfrac{1}{4+\sqrt{3}}$

Multiply the numerator and denominator by the conjugate of the denominator, $4-\sqrt{3}$.

$$\frac{1}{4+\sqrt{3}} \cdot \frac{4-\sqrt{3}}{4-\sqrt{3}} = \frac{1(4-\sqrt{3})}{4^2-(\sqrt{3})^2} = \frac{4-\sqrt{3}}{16-3} = \frac{4-\sqrt{3}}{13}$$

55. $$\frac{9}{2-\sqrt{7}} = \frac{9}{2-\sqrt{7}} \cdot \frac{2+\sqrt{7}}{2+\sqrt{7}} = \frac{9(2+\sqrt{7})}{2^2-(\sqrt{7})^2} = \frac{9(2+\sqrt{7})}{4-7} = \frac{9(2+\sqrt{7})}{-3} = -3(2+\sqrt{7}) = -6-3\sqrt{7}$$

57. $$\frac{16}{\sqrt{11}+3} = \frac{16}{\sqrt{11}+3} \cdot \frac{\sqrt{11}-3}{\sqrt{11}-3} = \frac{16(\sqrt{11}-3)}{(\sqrt{11})^2-3^2} = \frac{16(\sqrt{11}-3)}{11-9} = \frac{16(\sqrt{11}-3)}{2} = 8(\sqrt{11}-3) = 8\sqrt{11}-24$$

59. $$\frac{18}{3-\sqrt{3}} = \frac{18}{3-\sqrt{3}} \cdot \frac{3+\sqrt{3}}{3+\sqrt{3}} = \frac{18(3+\sqrt{3})}{3^2-(\sqrt{3})^2} = \frac{18(3+\sqrt{3})}{9-3} = \frac{18(3+\sqrt{3})}{6} = 3(3+\sqrt{3}) = 9+3\sqrt{3}$$

61. $$\frac{\sqrt{2}}{\sqrt{2}+1} = \frac{\sqrt{2}}{\sqrt{2}+1} \cdot \frac{\sqrt{2}-1}{\sqrt{2}-1} = \frac{\sqrt{2}(\sqrt{2}-1)}{(\sqrt{2})^2-1^2} = \frac{\sqrt{2}(\sqrt{2}-1)}{2-1} = \frac{\sqrt{2}(\sqrt{2}-1)}{1} = 2-\sqrt{2}$$

63. $$\frac{\sqrt{10}}{\sqrt{10}-\sqrt{7}} = \frac{\sqrt{10}}{\sqrt{10}-\sqrt{7}} \cdot \frac{\sqrt{10}+\sqrt{7}}{\sqrt{10}+\sqrt{7}} = \frac{\sqrt{10}(\sqrt{10}+\sqrt{7})}{(\sqrt{10})^2-(\sqrt{7})^2} = \frac{\sqrt{10}(\sqrt{10}+\sqrt{7})}{10-7} = \frac{\sqrt{10}(\sqrt{10}+\sqrt{7})}{3} = \frac{10+\sqrt{70}}{3}$$

65. $$\frac{6}{\sqrt{6}+\sqrt{3}} = \frac{6}{\sqrt{6}+\sqrt{3}} \cdot \frac{\sqrt{6}-\sqrt{3}}{\sqrt{6}-\sqrt{3}} = \frac{6(\sqrt{6}-\sqrt{3})}{(\sqrt{6})^2-(\sqrt{3})^2} = \frac{6(\sqrt{6}-\sqrt{3})}{6-3} = \frac{6(\sqrt{6}-\sqrt{3})}{3} = 2(\sqrt{6}-\sqrt{3}) = 2\sqrt{6}-2\sqrt{3}$$

67. $$\frac{2}{\sqrt{5}-\sqrt{3}} = \frac{2}{\sqrt{5}-\sqrt{3}} \cdot \frac{\sqrt{5}+\sqrt{3}}{\sqrt{5}+\sqrt{3}} = \frac{2(\sqrt{5}+\sqrt{3})}{(\sqrt{5})^2-(\sqrt{3})^2} = \frac{2(\sqrt{5}+\sqrt{3})}{5-3} = \frac{2(\sqrt{5}+\sqrt{3})}{2} = \sqrt{5}+\sqrt{3}$$

69. $\dfrac{2}{4+\sqrt{x}} = \dfrac{2}{4+\sqrt{x}} \cdot \dfrac{4-\sqrt{x}}{4-\sqrt{x}} = \dfrac{2(4-\sqrt{x})}{4^2-(\sqrt{x})^2}$

$= \dfrac{2(4-\sqrt{x})}{16-x} = \dfrac{8-2\sqrt{x}}{16-x}$

71. $\dfrac{2\sqrt{3}}{\sqrt{15}+2} = \dfrac{2\sqrt{3}}{\sqrt{15}+2} \cdot \dfrac{\sqrt{15}-2}{\sqrt{15}-2}$

$= \dfrac{2\sqrt{3}(\sqrt{15}-2)}{(\sqrt{15})^2-2^2}$

$= \dfrac{2\sqrt{3}(\sqrt{15}-2)}{15-4}$

$= \dfrac{2\sqrt{3}(\sqrt{15}-2)}{11}$

$= \dfrac{2\sqrt{45}-4\sqrt{3}}{11}$

$= \dfrac{2\sqrt{9}\sqrt{5}-4\sqrt{3}}{11}$

$= \dfrac{2\cdot 3\sqrt{5}-4\sqrt{3}}{11}$

$= \dfrac{6\sqrt{5}-4\sqrt{3}}{11}$

73. $\dfrac{\sqrt{5}+\sqrt{2}}{\sqrt{5}-\sqrt{2}} = \dfrac{\sqrt{5}+\sqrt{2}}{\sqrt{5}-\sqrt{2}} \cdot \dfrac{\sqrt{5}+\sqrt{2}}{\sqrt{5}+\sqrt{2}}$

$= \dfrac{(\sqrt{5}+\sqrt{2})^2}{(\sqrt{5})^2-(\sqrt{2})^2}$

$= \dfrac{(\sqrt{5})^2+2\sqrt{5}\sqrt{2}+(\sqrt{2})^2}{(\sqrt{5})^2-(\sqrt{2})^2}$

$= \dfrac{5+2\sqrt{10}+2}{5-2}$

$= \dfrac{7+2\sqrt{10}}{3}$

75. a. $P = \dfrac{x(13+\sqrt{x})}{5\sqrt{x}}$; $x = 25$

$P = \dfrac{25(13+\sqrt{25})}{5\sqrt{25}}$

$= \dfrac{25(13+5)}{5\cdot 5}$

$= \dfrac{25\cdot 18}{25} = 18$

According to the formula, 18% of 25-year-olds must pay more taxes.

b. $\dfrac{x(13+\sqrt{x})}{5\sqrt{x}} \cdot \dfrac{\sqrt{x}}{\sqrt{x}} = \dfrac{x\sqrt{x}(13+\sqrt{x})}{5\sqrt{x}\sqrt{x}}$

$= \dfrac{x\sqrt{x}\cdot 13 + x\sqrt{x}\sqrt{x}}{5\sqrt{x}\sqrt{x}}$

$= \dfrac{13x\sqrt{x}+x\cdot x}{5x}$

$= \dfrac{x(13\sqrt{x}+x)}{5x}$

$= \dfrac{13\sqrt{x}+x}{5}$

77. $\dfrac{7\sqrt{2\cdot 2\cdot 3}}{6} = \dfrac{7\sqrt{2}\cdot 2\sqrt{3}}{6}$

$= \dfrac{7\cdot 2\sqrt{3}}{6} = \dfrac{14\sqrt{3}}{6}$

$= \dfrac{7\sqrt{3}}{3} = \dfrac{7}{3}\sqrt{3}$

For Exercises 79–81, answers may vary.

83. $P = \dfrac{x(13+\sqrt{x})}{5\sqrt{x}}$

$x = 30$:

$P = \dfrac{30(13+\sqrt{30})}{5\sqrt{30}} \approx 20$

$x = 40$:

$P = \dfrac{40(13+\sqrt{40})}{5\sqrt{40}} \approx 24$

$x = 50$:

$P = \dfrac{50(13+\sqrt{50})}{5\sqrt{50}} \approx 28$

These results show that about 20% of 30-year-old taxpayers, 24% of 40-year-old taxpayers, and 28% of 50-year-old taxpayers must pay more taxes. The trend is for an increasing percentage of taxpayers to pay more taxes as the taxpayers get older. Explanations may vary.

85. $\dfrac{1}{\sqrt[3]{2}}$

Because the denominator is a cube root rather than a square root, multiply numerator and denominator by a radical that will make the radicand a perfect cube rather than a perfect square. Since 8 is a perfect cube, multiply numerator and denominator by $\sqrt[3]{4}$.

$$\frac{1}{\sqrt[3]{2}} \cdot \frac{\sqrt[3]{4}}{\sqrt[3]{4}} = \frac{\sqrt[3]{4}}{\sqrt[3]{8}} = \frac{\sqrt[3]{4}}{2}$$

87. $\sqrt{13+\sqrt{2}+\dfrac{7}{3+\sqrt{2}}}$

$$= \sqrt{13+\sqrt{2}+\frac{7}{3+\sqrt{2}} \cdot \frac{3-\sqrt{2}}{3-\sqrt{2}}}$$
$$= \sqrt{13+\sqrt{2}+\frac{7(3-\sqrt{2})}{3^2-(\sqrt{2})^2}}$$
$$= \sqrt{13+\sqrt{2}+\frac{7(3-\sqrt{2})}{9-2}}$$
$$= \sqrt{13+\sqrt{2}+\frac{7(3-\sqrt{2})}{7}}$$
$$= \sqrt{13+\sqrt{2}+3-\sqrt{2}}$$
$$= \sqrt{16} = 4$$

Review Exercises

89. $2x - 1 = x^2 - 4x + 4$

$$0 = x^2 - 6x + 5$$
$$0 = (x-5)(x-1)$$
$$x - 5 = 0 \quad \text{or} \quad x - 1 = 0$$
$$x = 5 \qquad\qquad x = 1$$

The solutions are 5 and 1.

90. $(2x^2)^{-3} = \dfrac{1}{(2x^2)^3} = \dfrac{1}{2^3(x^2)^3} = \dfrac{1}{8x^6}$

91. $\dfrac{x^2-6x+9}{12} \cdot \dfrac{3}{x^2-9}$

$$= \frac{(x-3)(x-3)}{12} \cdot \frac{3}{(x+3)(x-3)}$$
$$= \frac{x-3}{4(x+3)}$$

9.5 Radical Equations

9.5 CHECK POINTS

CHECK POINT 1

$\sqrt{2x+3} = 5$

Step 1 Isolate the radical.
In this equation, the radical is already isolated, so this step can be skipped.

Step 2 Square both sides.

$$\sqrt{2x+3} = 5$$
$$(\sqrt{2x+3}) = 5^2$$
$$2x + 3 = 25$$

Step 3 Solve the resulting equation.

$$2x = 22$$
$$x = 11$$

Step 4 Check the proposed solution in the original equation.
Check 11:

$$\sqrt{2x+3} = 5$$
$$\sqrt{2 \cdot 11 + 3} \stackrel{?}{=} 5$$
$$\sqrt{22+3} \stackrel{?}{=} 5$$
$$\sqrt{25} \stackrel{?}{=} 5$$
$$5 = 5 \text{ true}$$

The solution is 11.

CHECK POINT 2

$\sqrt{x+32}-3\sqrt{x}=0$

Step 1 Isolate each radical by adding $\sqrt{3x}$ to both sides.

$$\begin{aligned}\sqrt{x+32}-3\sqrt{x}&=0\\ \sqrt{x+32}&=3\sqrt{x}\end{aligned}$$

Step 2 Square both sides.

$$\begin{aligned}(\sqrt{x+32})^2&=(3\sqrt{x})^2\\ x+32&=9x\end{aligned}$$

Step 3 Solve the resulting equation.

$$\begin{aligned}32&=8x\\ 4&=x\end{aligned}$$

Step 4 Check the proposed solution in the original equation.
Check 4:

$$\begin{aligned}\sqrt{x+32}-3\sqrt{x}&=0\\ \sqrt{4+32}-3\sqrt{4}&\stackrel{?}{=}0\\ \sqrt{36}-3\cdot 2&\stackrel{?}{=}0\\ 6-6&\stackrel{?}{=}0\\ 0&=0 \text{ true}\end{aligned}$$

The solution is 4.

CHECK POINT 3

$\sqrt{x}+1=0$

Step 1 Isolate the radical by subtracting 5 from both sides.

$$\begin{aligned}\sqrt{x}+1&=0\\ \sqrt{x}&=-1\end{aligned}$$

Step 2 Square both sides.

$$\begin{aligned}(\sqrt{x})^2&=(-1)^2\\ x&=1\end{aligned}$$

Step 3 The equation obtained in Step 2 shows that 1 is the proposed solution.

Step 4 Check the proposed solution in the original equation.
Check 1:

$$\begin{aligned}\sqrt{x}+1&=0\\ \sqrt{1}+1&\stackrel{?}{=}0\\ 1+1&\stackrel{?}{=}0\\ 2&=0 \text{ false}\end{aligned}$$

This false statement indicates that 1 is not a solution. Thus, the given equation has no solution.

CHECK POINT 4

$\sqrt{x+3}+3=x$

Step 1 Isolate the radical.

$$\begin{aligned}\sqrt{x+3}+3&=x\\ \sqrt{x+3}&=x-3\end{aligned}$$

Step 2 Square both sides.

$$\begin{aligned}(\sqrt{x+3})^2&=(x-3)^2\\ x+3&=x^2-6x+9\end{aligned}$$

Step 3 Solve the resulting quadratic equation.

$$\begin{aligned}0&=x^2-7x+6\\ 0&=(x-1)(x-6)\\ x-1=0 \quad &\text{or} \quad x-6=0\\ x=1 \quad & \quad\quad x=6\end{aligned}$$

Step 4 Check the proposed solutions in the original equation.

Check 1:

$$\begin{aligned}\sqrt{x+3}+3&=x\\ \sqrt{1+3}+3&\stackrel{?}{=}1\\ \sqrt{4}+3&\stackrel{?}{=}1\\ 2+3&\stackrel{?}{=}1\\ 5&=1 \text{ false}\end{aligned}$$

Check 1:

$$\begin{aligned}\sqrt{x+3}+3&=x\\ \sqrt{6+3}+3&\stackrel{?}{=}6\\ \sqrt{9}+3&\stackrel{?}{=}6\\ 3+3&\stackrel{?}{=}6\\ 6&=6 \text{ true}\end{aligned}$$

Thus, 1 is an extraneous solution. The only solution is 6.

CHECK POINT 5

$S = 4\sqrt{t} + 280$; $S = 300$

$$\begin{aligned} 300 &= 4\sqrt{t} + 280 \\ 20 &= 4\sqrt{t} \\ 5 &= \sqrt{t} \\ 5^2 &= (\sqrt{t})^2 \\ 25 &= t \end{aligned}$$

The model indicates that the average science score will be 300 25 years after 1982. Because $1982 + 25 = 2007$, this will occur in 2007.

EXERCISE SET 9.5

In Exercises 1–43, it is *essential* to check all proposed solutions in the original equation in order to eliminate extraneous solutions.

1. $$\begin{aligned} \sqrt{x} &= 4 \\ (\sqrt{x})^2 &= 4^2 \\ x &= 16 \end{aligned}$$

Check 16:

$$\begin{aligned} \sqrt{x} &= 4 \\ \sqrt{16} &\stackrel{?}{=} 4 \\ 4 &= 4 \text{ true} \end{aligned}$$

The solution is 4.

3. $$\begin{aligned} \sqrt{x} - 5 &= 0 \\ \sqrt{x} &= 5 \\ (\sqrt{x})^2 &= 5^2 \\ x &= 25 \end{aligned}$$

Check 25:

$$\begin{aligned} \sqrt{x} - 5 &= 0 \\ \sqrt{25} - 5 &\stackrel{?}{=} 0 \\ 5 - 5 &\stackrel{?}{=} 0 \\ 0 &= 0 \text{ true} \end{aligned}$$

The solution is 25.

5. $$\begin{aligned} \sqrt{x+4} &= 3 \\ (\sqrt{x+4})^2 &\stackrel{?}{=} 3^2 \\ x + 4 &\stackrel{?}{=} 9 \\ x &= 5 \end{aligned}$$

Substitute 5 for x in the original equation to verify that the solution is 5.

7. $$\begin{aligned} \sqrt{x-4} - 11 &= 0 \\ \sqrt{x-4} &= 11 \\ (\sqrt{x-4})^2 &= 11^2 \\ x - 4 &= 121 \\ x &= 125 \end{aligned}$$

Substitute 125 for x in the original equation to verify that the solution is 125.

9. $$\begin{aligned} \sqrt{3x-2} &= 4 \\ (\sqrt{3x-2})^2 &= 4^2 \\ 3x - 2 &= 16 \\ 3x &= 18 \\ x &= 6 \end{aligned}$$

Substitute 6 for x in the original equation to verify that 6 is the solution.

11. $$\begin{aligned} \sqrt{x+5} + 2 &= 5 \\ \sqrt{x+5} &= 3 \\ (\sqrt{x+5})^2 &= 3^2 \\ x + 5 &= 9 \\ x &= 4 \end{aligned}$$

Substitute 4 for x in the original equation to verify that the solution is 4.

13. $$\begin{aligned} \sqrt{x+3} &= \sqrt{4x-3} \\ (\sqrt{x+3})^2 &= (\sqrt{4x-3})^2 \\ x + 3 &= 4x - 3 \\ -3x + 3 &= -3 \\ -3x &= -6 \\ x &= 2 \end{aligned}$$

Substitute 2 for x in the original equation to verify that the solution is 2.

15. $\sqrt{6x-2} = \sqrt{4x+4}$

$$(\sqrt{6x-2})^2 = (\sqrt{4x+4})^2$$
$$6x - 2 = 4x + 4$$
$$2x - 2 = 4$$
$$2x = 6$$
$$x = 3$$

Substitute 3 for x in the original equation to verify that the solution is 3.

17. $11 = 6 + \sqrt{x+1}$

$$5 = \sqrt{x+1}$$
$$5^2 = (\sqrt{x+1})^2$$
$$25 = x + 1$$
$$24 = x$$

Substitute 24 for x in the original equation to verify that the solution is 24.

19. $\sqrt{x} + 10 = 0$

$$\sqrt{x} = -10$$
$$(\sqrt{x})^2 = (-10)^2$$
$$x = 100$$

Check 100:

$$\sqrt{x} + 10 = 0$$
$$\sqrt{100} + 10 \stackrel{?}{=} 0$$
$$10 + 10 \stackrel{?}{=} 0$$
$$20 = 0 \text{ false}$$

This false statement indicates that 100 is not a solution. Since the only proposed solution is extraneous, the given equation has no solution.

21. $\sqrt{x-1} = -3$

$$(\sqrt{x-1})^2 = (-3)^2$$
$$x - 1 = 9$$
$$x = 10$$

Check 10:

$$\sqrt{x-1} = -3$$
$$\sqrt{10-x} \stackrel{?}{=} -3$$
$$\sqrt{9} \stackrel{?}{=} -3$$
$$3 = -3 \text{ false}$$

The false statement shows that 10 is an extraneous solution. Since it is the only proposed solution, the given equation has no solution.

23. $3\sqrt{x} = \sqrt{8x+16}$

$$(3\sqrt{x}) = (\sqrt{8x+16})^2$$
$$9x = 8x + 16$$
$$x = 16$$

Check 16:

$$3\sqrt{x} = \sqrt{8x+16}$$
$$3\sqrt{16} \stackrel{?}{=} \sqrt{8 \cdot 16 + 16}$$
$$3 \cdot 4 \stackrel{?}{=} \sqrt{128+16}$$
$$12 \stackrel{?}{=} \sqrt{144}$$
$$12 = 12 \text{ true}$$

The solution is 16.

25. $\sqrt{2x-3} + 5 = 0$

$$\sqrt{2x-3} = -5$$
$$(\sqrt{2x-3})^2 = (-5)^2$$
$$2x - 3 = 25$$
$$2x = 28$$
$$x = 14$$

Check 14:

$$\sqrt{2x-3} + 5 = 0$$
$$\sqrt{2 \cdot 14 - 3} + 5 \stackrel{?}{=} 0$$
$$\sqrt{28-3} + 5 \stackrel{?}{=} 0$$
$$\sqrt{25} + 5 \stackrel{?}{=} 0$$
$$5 + 5 \stackrel{?}{=} 0$$
$$10 = 0 \text{ false}$$

The false statement shows that 14 is an extraneous solution, so the given equation has no solution.

27. $\sqrt{3x+4}-2=3$

$$\begin{aligned}\sqrt{3x+4}&=5\\(\sqrt{3x+4})^2&=5^2\\3x+4&=25\\3x&=21\\x&=7\end{aligned}$$

Substitute 7 for x in the original equation to verify that the solution is 7.

29.

$$\begin{aligned}3\sqrt{x-1}&=\sqrt{3x+3}\\(3\sqrt{x-1})^2&=(\sqrt{3x+3})^2\\9(x-1)&=3x+3\\9x-9&=3x+3\\6x&=12\\x&=2\end{aligned}$$

Substitute 2 for x in the original equation to verify that the solution is 2.

31. $\sqrt{x+7}=x+5$

Square both sides,

$$(\sqrt{x+7})^2=(x+5)^2$$

Square the binomial on the right.

$$x+7=x^2+10x+25$$

Simplify and solve this quadratic equation.

$$\begin{aligned}0&=x^2+9x+18\\0&=(x+3)(x+6)\\x+3=0 \quad &\text{or} \quad x+6=0\\x=-3 \quad & \quad\quad x=-6\end{aligned}$$

There are two proposed solutions. Each must checked separately in the original equation.

Check -3:

$$\begin{aligned}\sqrt{x+7}&=x+5\\\sqrt{-3+7}&\stackrel{?}{=}-3+5\\\sqrt{4}&\stackrel{?}{=}2\\2&=2 \text{ true}\end{aligned}$$

Check -6:

$$\begin{aligned}\sqrt{x+7}&=x+5\\\sqrt{-6+7}&\stackrel{?}{=}-6+5\\\sqrt{1}&\stackrel{?}{=}-1\\1&=-1 \text{ false}\end{aligned}$$

Thus, -6 is an extraneous solution, while -3 satisfies the equation. The only solution is -3.

33.

$$\begin{aligned}\sqrt{2x+13}&=x+7\\(\sqrt{2x+13})^2&=(x+7)^2\\2x+13&=x^2+14x+49\\0&=x^2+12x+36\\0&=(x+6)^2\\0&=x+6\\-6&=x\end{aligned}$$

Check -6:

$$\begin{aligned}\sqrt{2x+13}&=x+7\\\sqrt{2(-6)+13}&\stackrel{?}{=}-6+7\\\sqrt{-12+13}&\stackrel{?}{=}1\\\sqrt{1}&\stackrel{?}{=}1\\1&=1 \text{ true}\end{aligned}$$

The solution is -6.

35.

$$\begin{aligned}\sqrt{9x^2+2x-4}&=3x\\(\sqrt{9x^2+2x-4})^2&=(3x)^2\\9x^2+2x-4&=9x^2\\2x-4&=0\\2x&=4\\x&=2\end{aligned}$$

Substitute 2 for x in the original equation to verify that the solution is 2.

37.

$$\begin{aligned} x &= \sqrt{2x-2}+1 \\ x-1 &= \sqrt{2x-2} \\ (x-1)^2 &= (\sqrt{2x-2})^2 \\ x^2+2x+1 &= 2x-2 \\ x^2-4x+3 &= 0 \\ (x-1)(x-3) &= 0 \\ x-1=0 \quad &\text{or} \quad x-3=0 \\ x=1 \quad & \quad\quad x=3 \end{aligned}$$

Check 1:

$$\begin{aligned} x &= \sqrt{2x-2}+1 \\ 1 &\stackrel{?}{=} \sqrt{2\cdot 1-2}+1 \\ 1 &\stackrel{?}{=} \sqrt{2-2}+1 \\ 1 &\stackrel{?}{=} 0+1 \\ 1 &= 1 \text{ true} \end{aligned}$$

Check 3:

$$\begin{aligned} x &= \sqrt{2x-2}+1 \\ 3 &\stackrel{?}{=} \sqrt{2\cdot 3-2}+1 \\ 3 &\stackrel{?}{=} \sqrt{6-2}+1 \\ 3 &\stackrel{?}{=} \sqrt{4}+1 \\ 3 &\stackrel{?}{=} 2+1 \\ 3 &= 3 \text{ true} \end{aligned}$$

Both proposed solutions, 1 and 3, satisfy the original equation, so the equation has two solutions, 1 and 3.

39.

$$\begin{aligned} x &= \sqrt{8-7x}+2 \\ x-2 &= \sqrt{8-7x} \\ (x-2)^2 &= (\sqrt{8-7x})^2 \\ x^2-4x+4 &= 8-7x \\ x^2+3x-4 &= 0 \\ (x+4)(x-1) &= 0 \\ x+4=0 \quad &\text{or} \quad x-1=0 \\ x=-4 \quad & \quad\quad x=1 \end{aligned}$$

Check −4:

$$\begin{aligned} x &= \sqrt{8-7x}+2 \\ -4 &\stackrel{?}{=} \sqrt{8-7(-4)}+2 \\ -4 &\stackrel{?}{=} \sqrt{8+28}+2 \\ -4 &\stackrel{?}{=} \sqrt{36}+2 \\ -4 &\stackrel{?}{=} 6+2 \\ -4 &= 8 \text{ false} \end{aligned}$$

Check 1:

$$\begin{aligned} x &= \sqrt{8-7x}+2 \\ -4 &\stackrel{?}{=} \sqrt{8-7\cdot 1}+2 \\ -4 &\stackrel{?}{=} \sqrt{8-7}+2 \\ -4 &\stackrel{?}{=} \sqrt{1}+2 \\ -4 &\stackrel{?}{=} 1+2 \\ -4 &= 3 \text{ false} \end{aligned}$$

Both of the proposed solutions, −4 and 1, are extraneous, so the given equation has no solution.

41.

$$\begin{aligned} \sqrt{3x}+10 &= x+4 \\ \sqrt{3x} &= x-6 \\ (\sqrt{3x})^2 &= (x-6)^2 \\ 3x &= x^2-12x+36 \\ 0 &= x^2-15x+36 \\ 0 &= (x-3)(x-12) \\ x-3=0 \quad &\text{or} \quad x-12=0 \\ x=3 \quad & \quad\quad x=12 \end{aligned}$$

Check 3:

$$\begin{aligned} \sqrt{3x}+10 &= x+4 \\ \sqrt{3\cdot 3}+10 &\stackrel{?}{=} 3+4 \\ \sqrt{9}+10 &\stackrel{?}{=} 7 \\ 3+10 &\stackrel{?}{=} 7 \\ 13 &= 7 \text{ false} \end{aligned}$$

Check 12:

$$\begin{aligned} \sqrt{3x}+10 &= x+4 \\ \sqrt{3\cdot 12}+10 &\stackrel{?}{=} 12+4 \\ \sqrt{36}+10 &\stackrel{?}{=} 16 \\ 6+10 &\stackrel{?}{=} 16 \\ 16 &= 16 \text{ true} \end{aligned}$$

The proposed solution 3 is extraneous, while 12 satisfies the equation. Therefore, the solution is 12.

43. $3\sqrt{x}+5=2$

$$\begin{aligned}3\sqrt{x}&=-3\\(3\sqrt{x})^2&=(-3)^2\\9x&=9\\x&=1\end{aligned}$$

Check 1:

$$\begin{aligned}3\sqrt{x}+5&=2\\3\sqrt{1}+5&\stackrel{?}{=}2\\3\cdot1+5&\stackrel{?}{=}2\\3+5&\stackrel{?}{=}2\\8&=2 \text{ false}\end{aligned}$$

The proposed solution 1 is extraneous, so the equation has no solution.

45. $y=2.6\sqrt{x}+11;\ y=26.6$

$$\begin{aligned}26.6&=2.6\sqrt{x}+11\\15.6&=2.6\sqrt{x}\\6&=\sqrt{x}\\6^2&=(\sqrt{x})^2\\36&=x\end{aligned}$$

Substitute 36 for x in the original equation to verify that the solution is 36. According to the formula, there will be 26.6 million Americans living alone 36 years after 1970. Because 1970 + 36 = 2006, this will occur in the year 2006.

47. $y=2.6\sqrt{x}+11;\ y=28$

$$\begin{aligned}28&=2.6\sqrt{x}+11\\17&=2.6\sqrt{x}\\\frac{17}{2.6}&=\sqrt{x}\\\left(\frac{17}{2.6}\right)^2&=(\sqrt{x})^2\\42.75&\approx x\end{aligned}$$

To the nearest year, $x=43$.
Because 1970 + 43 = 2013, the model predicts that there will be about 28 million people living alone in 2013.

49. $y=6.75\sqrt{x}+12;\ y=32.25$

$$\begin{aligned}32.25&=6.75\sqrt{x}+12\\20.25&=6.75\sqrt{x}\\3&=\sqrt{x}\\3^2&=(\sqrt{x})^2\\9&=x\end{aligned}$$

The amount loaned is expected to reach \$32.25 billion years after 1993. Because 1993 + 9 = 2002, this will occur in 2002.

51. $N=5000\sqrt{100-x};\ N=40{,}000$

$$\begin{aligned}40{,}000&=5000\sqrt{100-x}\\8&=\sqrt{100-x}\\8^2&=\sqrt{100-x})^2\\64&=100-x\\-36&=-x\\36&=x\end{aligned}$$

According to the formula, 40,000 people in the group will survive to 36 years old.

53. $d=3.5\sqrt{h};\ d=200$

$$\begin{aligned}200&=3.5\sqrt{h}\\\frac{200}{3.5}&=\sqrt{h}\\\left(\frac{200}{3.5}\right)^2&=h\\h&\approx3265\end{aligned}$$

After losing altitude, the plane's altitude is about 3265 meters or 3.265 kilometers. Because the plane was flying at an altitude of 8 kilometers and dropped to an altitude of about 3 kilometers, it lost about 5 kilometers in altitude.

55. $R = \sqrt{A^2 + B^2}$; $R = 500, A = 300$

$$\begin{aligned} 500 &= \sqrt{300^2 + B^2} \\ 500 &= \sqrt{90{,}000 + B^2} \\ 500^2 &= (\sqrt{90{,}000 + B^2})^2 \\ 250{,}000 &= 90{,}000 + B^2 \\ 160{,}000 &= B^2 \\ 0 &= B^2 - 160{,}000 \\ 0 &= (B + 400)(B - 400) \end{aligned}$$

$$B + 400 = 0 \quad \text{or} \quad B - 400 = 0$$
$$B = -400 \qquad\qquad B = 400$$

Although both proposed solutions satisfy the given equation, reject -400 because the size of a force cannot be negative. Tractor B is exerting a force of 400 pounds.

For Exercises 57–59, answers may vary.

61. Statement b is true.
This can be seen simply by looking at the equation because the square root of a real number can never be negative.

63. $\sqrt{x - 8} = 5 - \sqrt{x + 7}$

Each radical is already isolated on one side of the equation, so the first step is to square both sides.

$$(\sqrt{x - 8})^2 = (5 - \sqrt{x + 7})^2$$

To square the binomial on the right, use the formula

$$(A - B)^2 = A^2 - 2AB + B^2$$

with $A = 5$ and $B = \sqrt{x + 7}$.

$$\begin{aligned} x - 8 &= 5^2 - 2 \cdot 5 \cdot \sqrt{x + 7} + (\sqrt{x + 7})^2 \\ x - 8 &= 25 - 10\sqrt{x + 7} + x + 7 \\ x - 8 &= 32 + x - 10\sqrt{x + 7} \end{aligned}$$

The last equation still contains a radical, so it is necessary to repeat the steps done up to this point.
First, isolate the radical by moving the other terms to the left side.

$$\begin{aligned} x - 8 - x - 32 &= 32 + x - x - 32 \\ &\quad - 10\sqrt{x + 7} \\ -40 &= -10\sqrt{x + 7} \end{aligned}$$

Simplify the equation by multiplying both sides by -10.

$$\begin{aligned} \frac{-40}{-10} &= \frac{-10\sqrt{x + 7}}{-10} \\ 4 &= \sqrt{x + 7} \end{aligned}$$

Now square both sides again.

$$\begin{aligned} 4^2 &= (\sqrt{x + 7})^2 \\ 16 &= x + 7 \\ 9 &= x \end{aligned}$$

Check the proposed solution in the original equation.
Check 9:

$$\begin{aligned} \sqrt{x - 8} &= 5 - \sqrt{x + 7} \\ \sqrt{9 - 8} &\stackrel{?}{=} 5 - \sqrt{9 + 7} \\ \sqrt{1} &\stackrel{?}{=} 5 - \sqrt{16} \\ 1 &\stackrel{?}{=} 5 - 4 \\ 1 &= 1 \end{aligned}$$

The solution is 9.

65. $y = \sqrt{x-2} + 2$
$z = \sqrt{y-2} + 2$
$w = \sqrt{z-2} + 2$
$w = 2$

Substitute 2 for w in the third equation and solve for z.

$$\begin{aligned} 2 &= \sqrt{z-2} + 2 \\ 0 &= \sqrt{z-2} \\ 0^2 &= (\sqrt{z-2})^2 \\ 0 &= z - 2 \\ z &= 2 \end{aligned}$$

Now substitute 2 for z in the second equation.

$$2 = \sqrt{y-2} + 2$$

This is the same as the equation $2 = \sqrt{z-2} + 2$ with just the variable changed, so from the previous work we know that $y = 2$. Similarly, substituting 2 for y in the first equation gives

$$y = \sqrt{x-2} + 2,$$

which leads to $x = 2$.
Thus, $x = 2, y = 2$, and $z = 2$.

67. $\sqrt{x} + 3 = 5$

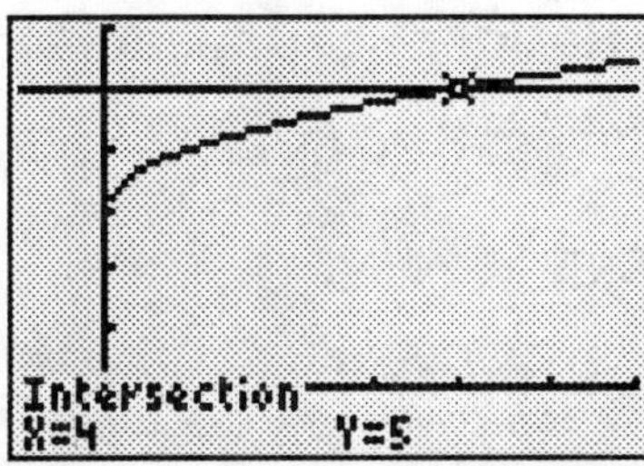

The graphs intersect at one point, $(4, 5)$, so the x-intercept of the intersection point is 4.

Therefore, the solution of the given equation is 4.

Check 4:

$$\begin{aligned} \sqrt{x} + 3 &= 5 \\ \sqrt{4} + 3 &\stackrel{?}{=} 5 \\ 2 + 3 &\stackrel{?}{=} 5 \\ 5 &= 5 \text{ true} \end{aligned}$$

69. $4\sqrt{x} = x + 3$

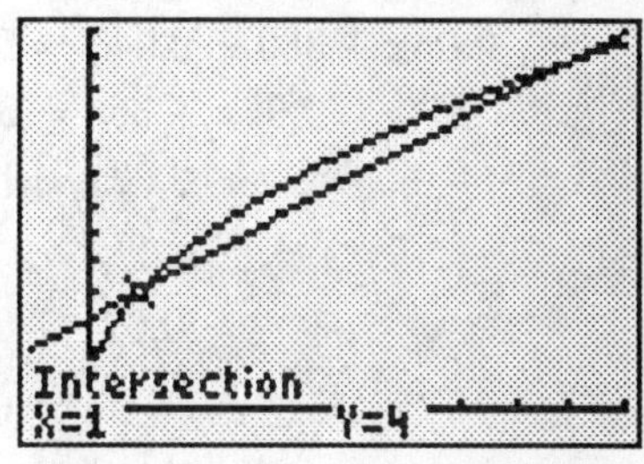

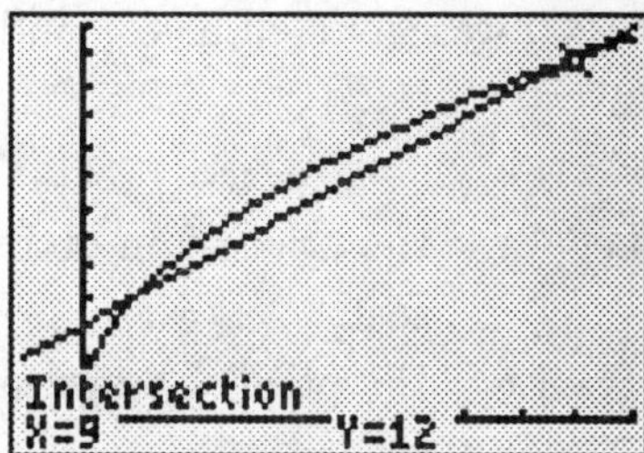

The graphs intersect at $(1, 4)$ and $(9, 12)$. Therefore, the x-intercepts of the intersection point are 9 and 12 and the solutions of the equation are also 9 and 12.

Check 1:	Check 9:
$4\sqrt{x} = x + 3$	$4\sqrt{x} = x + 3$
$4\sqrt{1} \stackrel{?}{=} 1 + 3$	$4\sqrt{9} \stackrel{?}{=} 9 + 3$
$4 \cdot 1 \stackrel{?}{=} 1 + 3$	$4 \cdot 3 \stackrel{?}{=} 9 + 3$
$4 = 4$ true	$12 = 12$ true

Review Exercises

71. Let $x =$ the amount invested at 6%.
Then $9000 - x =$ the amount invested at 4%.

The investments earned a total of $500 in interest, so

$$0.06x + 0.04(9000 - x) = 500.$$

Solve this equation.

$$\begin{aligned} 0.06x + 360 - 0.04x &= 500 \\ 0.02x + 360 &= 500 \\ 0.02x &= 140 \\ \frac{0.02x}{0.02} &= \frac{140}{0.02} \\ x &= 7000 \\ 9000 - x &= 2000 \end{aligned}$$

$7000 was invested at 6% and $2000 was invested at 4%.

72. Let $x =$ the price of an orchestra seat.
Then $y =$ the price of a mezzanine seat.

The given information leads to the system

$$\begin{aligned} 4x + 2y &= 22 \\ 2x + 3y &= 16. \end{aligned}$$

Because both equations are written in the form $Ax+By = C$, the addition method is a good choice for solving this system. Because the problem only asks for the price of an orchestra seat, it is only necessary to solve the system for x. To do this, it is necessary to eliminate y.

Multiply the first equation by 3 and the second equation by -2. Then add the results.

$$\begin{aligned} 12x + 6y &= 66 \\ -4x - 6y &= -32 \\ \hline 8x \quad &= 34 \end{aligned}$$

$$x = \frac{34}{8} = 4.25$$

The price of an orchestra seat is $4.25.

73. $2x + y = -4$
$x + y = -3$

Graph $2x + y = -4$ using its x-intercept -2 and its y-intercept -4.
Graph $x + y = -3$ using its x-intercept -3 and y-intercept -3.

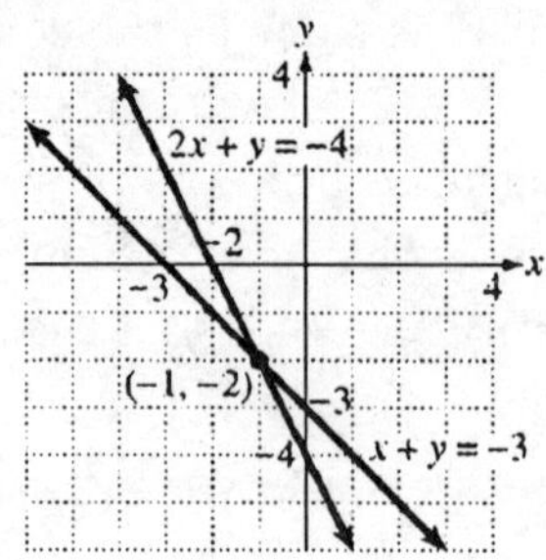

The two lines intersect at the point $(-1, -2)$, so the solution of the system is $(-1, -2)$.

9.6 Rational Exponents

9.6 CHECK POINTS

CHECK POINT 1

a. $25^{\frac{1}{2}} = \sqrt{25} = 5$

b. $8^{\frac{1}{3}} = \sqrt[8]{3} = 2$

c. $-81^{\frac{1}{4}} = -(\sqrt[4]{81}) = -3$

d. $(-8)^{\frac{1}{3}} = \sqrt[3]{-8} = -2$

CHECK POINT 2

a. $27^{\frac{4}{3}} = (\sqrt[3]{27})^4 = 3^4 = 81$

b. $4^{\frac{3}{2}} = (\sqrt{4})^3 = 2^3 = 8$

c. $-16^{\frac{3}{4}} = -(\sqrt[4]{16})^3 = -2^3 = -8$

CHECK POINT 3

a. $25^{-\frac{1}{2}} = \frac{1}{25^{\frac{1}{2}}} = \frac{1}{\sqrt{25}} = \frac{1}{5}$

b. $64^{-\frac{1}{3}} = \frac{1}{64^{\frac{1}{3}}} = \frac{1}{\sqrt[3]{64}} = \frac{1}{4}$

c. $32^{-\frac{4}{5}} = \frac{1}{32^{\frac{4}{5}}} = \frac{1}{(\sqrt[5]{32})^4} = \frac{1}{2^4} = \frac{1}{16}$

CHECK POINT 4

$S = 63.25x^{\frac{1}{4}}$; $x = 16$ (for 1997)

$$\begin{aligned} S &= 63.25 \cdot 16^{\frac{1}{4}} \\ &= 63.25\sqrt[4]{16} \\ &= 63.25 \cdot 2 = 126.5 \end{aligned}$$

According to the formula, the average sale price for a single-family home in the U.S. Midwest in 1997 was \$126.5 thousand (or \$126,500).

EXERCISE SET 9.6

1. $49^{\frac{1}{2}} = \sqrt{49} = 7$

3. $121^{\frac{1}{2}} = \sqrt{121} = 11$

5. $27^{\frac{1}{3}} = \sqrt[3]{27} = 3$

7. $-125^{\frac{1}{3}} = -(\sqrt[3]{125}) = -5$

9. $16^{\frac{1}{4}} = \sqrt[4]{16} = 2$

11. $-32^{\frac{1}{5}} = -(\sqrt[5]{32}) = -2$

13. $\left(\frac{1}{9}\right)^{\frac{1}{2}} = \sqrt{\frac{1}{9}} = \frac{1}{3}$

15. $\left(\frac{27}{64}\right)^{\frac{1}{3}} = \sqrt[3]{\frac{27}{64}} = \frac{\sqrt[3]{27}}{\sqrt[3]{64}} = \frac{3}{4}$

17. $81^{\frac{3}{2}} = (\sqrt{81})^3 = 9^3 = 729$

19. $125^{\frac{2}{3}} = (\sqrt[3]{125})^2 = 5^2 = 25$

21. $9^{\frac{3}{2}} = (\sqrt{9})^3 = 3^3 = 27$

23. $(-32)^{\frac{3}{5}} = (\sqrt[5]{-32})^3 = (-2)^3 = -8$

25. $9^{-\frac{1}{2}} = \frac{1}{9^{\frac{1}{2}}} = \frac{1}{\sqrt{9}} = \frac{1}{3}$

27. $125^{-\frac{1}{3}} = \frac{1}{125^{\frac{1}{3}}} = \frac{1}{\sqrt[3]{125}} = \frac{1}{5}$

29. $32^{-\frac{1}{5}} = \frac{1}{32^{\frac{1}{5}}} = \frac{1}{\sqrt[5]{32}} = \frac{1}{2}$

31. $\left(\frac{1}{4}\right)^{-\frac{1}{2}} = \frac{1}{\left(\frac{1}{4}\right)^{\frac{1}{2}}} = \frac{1}{\sqrt{\frac{1}{4}}} = \frac{1}{\frac{1}{2}} = 2$

33. $16^{-\frac{3}{4}} = \frac{1}{16^{\frac{3}{4}}} = \frac{1}{(\sqrt[4]{16})^3} = \frac{1}{2^3} = \frac{1}{8}$

35. $81^{-\frac{5}{4}} = \frac{1}{81^{\frac{5}{4}}} = \frac{1}{(\sqrt[4]{81})^5} = \frac{1}{3^5} = \frac{1}{243}$

37. $8^{-\frac{2}{3}} = \frac{1}{8^{\frac{2}{3}}} = \frac{1}{(\sqrt[3]{8})^2} = \frac{1}{2^2} = \frac{1}{4}$

39. $\left(\frac{4}{25}\right)^{-\frac{1}{2}} = \frac{1}{\left(\frac{4}{25}\right)^{\frac{1}{2}}} = \frac{1}{\sqrt{\frac{4}{25}}} = \frac{1}{\frac{2}{5}} = \frac{5}{2}$

41. $\left(\frac{8}{125}\right)^{-\frac{1}{3}} = \frac{1}{\left(\frac{8}{125}\right)^{\frac{1}{3}}} = \frac{1}{\sqrt[3]{\frac{8}{125}}} = \frac{1}{\frac{2}{5}} = \frac{5}{2}$

43. $(-8)^{-\frac{2}{3}} = \frac{1}{(-8)^{\frac{2}{3}}} = \frac{1}{(\sqrt[3]{-8})^2}$
$= \frac{1}{(-2)^2} = \frac{1}{4}$

45. $27^{\frac{2}{3}} + 16^{\frac{3}{4}} = (\sqrt[3]{27})^2 + (\sqrt[4]{16})^3$
$= 3^2 + 2^3 = 9 + 8 = 17$

47. $25^{\frac{3}{2}} \cdot 81^{\frac{1}{4}} = (\sqrt{25})^3 \cdot \sqrt[4]{81}$
$= 5^3 \cdot 3 = 125 \cdot 3$
$= 375$

49. $v = \left(\frac{5r}{2}\right)^{\frac{1}{2}}$; $r = 250$

$$v = \left(\frac{5 \cdot 250}{2}\right)^{\frac{1}{2}}$$
$$= \left(\frac{1250}{2}\right)^{\frac{1}{2}}$$
$$= 625^{\frac{1}{2}}$$
$$= \sqrt{625} = 25$$

If the curve has a radius of 250 feet, the maximum velocity a car can travel without skidding is 25 miles per hour.

51. $P = \frac{73t^{\frac{1}{3}} - 28t^{\frac{2}{3}}}{t}$; $t = 8$ (for 1993)

$$P = \frac{73 \cdot 8^{\frac{1}{3}} - 28 \cdot 8^{\frac{2}{3}}}{8}$$
$$= \frac{73 \cdot 2 - 28 \cdot 4}{8}$$
$$= \frac{34}{8} = 4.25$$

According to the formula, about 4.25% of people applying for jobs in 2001 tested positive for illegal drugs.

53. $V = 194.5t^{\frac{1}{6}}$ $\quad E = 339.6t^{\frac{2}{3}}$
$V = 194.5\sqrt[6]{t}$ $\quad E = 339.6(\sqrt[3]{t})^2$

For Exercises 55–59, answers may vary.

61. Statement a is correct.

$$2^{\frac{1}{2}} \cdot 2^{\frac{2}{3}} = 2^{\frac{1}{2}+\frac{2}{3}} = 2^{\frac{4}{2}} = 2^2 = 4$$

$$\left(\frac{1}{4}\right)^{-1} = \frac{1}{\left(\frac{1}{4}\right)^1} = \frac{1}{\frac{1}{4}} = 1$$

63. $25^{\frac{1}{4}} \cdot 25^{-\frac{3}{4}} = 25^{\frac{1}{4}+\left(-\frac{3}{4}\right)} = 25^{-\frac{2}{4}}$
$= 25^{-\frac{1}{2}} = \frac{1}{25^{\frac{1}{2}}}$
$= \frac{1}{\sqrt{25}} = \frac{1}{5}$

65. a.

W	0	25	50	150	200	250	300
$T = W^{1.41}$	0	94	249	1170	1756	2405	3110

b.

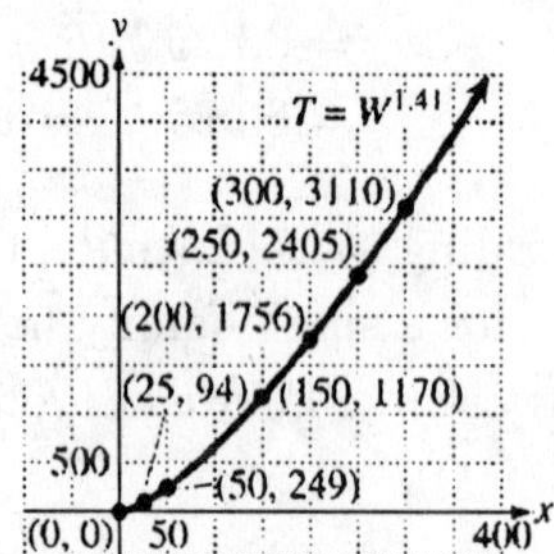

The graph indicates that as body weight increases, territorial area increases.

c. The following graph is drawn in the viewing rectangle [0, 400, 50] by [0, 4500, 500].

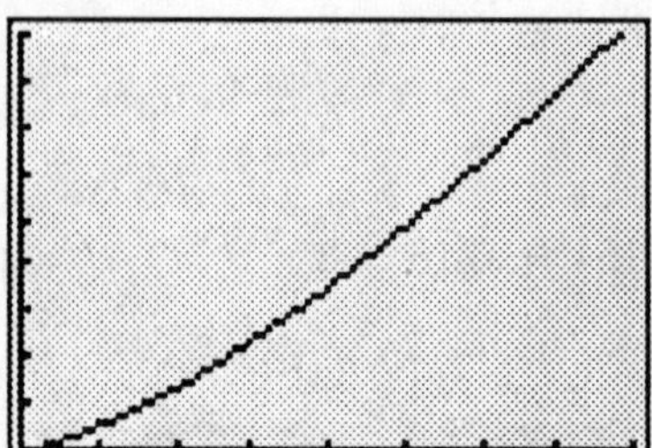

Review Exercises

67. $7x - 3y = -14$
$y = 3x + 6$

To solve this system by the substitution method, substitute $3x+6$ for y in the first equation and solve for x.

$$\begin{aligned} 7x - 3(3x+6) &= -14 \\ 7x - 9x - 18 &= -14 \\ -2x - 18 &= -14 \\ -2x &= 4 \\ x &= -2 \end{aligned}$$

Back-substitute -2 for x into the second equation.

$$\begin{aligned} y &= 3x + 6 \\ y &= 3(-2) + 6 = -6 + 6 = 0 \end{aligned}$$

Solution: $(-2, 0)$

68. $-3x + 4y \leq 12$
$x \geq 2$

To graph the solutions of this system of inequalities, first graph $-3x+4y = 12$ as a solid line using its x-intercept, -4, and its y-intercept, 3. Use $(0,0)$ as a test point. Since $-3(0)+4(0) \leq 12$ is true, shade the half-plane containing $(0,0)$. Now graph $x = 2$ as a solid vertical line. Since $0 \geq 2$ is false, shade the half-plane *not* containing $(0,0)$, which is the half-plane to the right of the vertical line. The solution set of the system is the intersection (overlap) of the two shaded regions. The dot at the intersection point of the two lines shows that this ordered pair a solution.

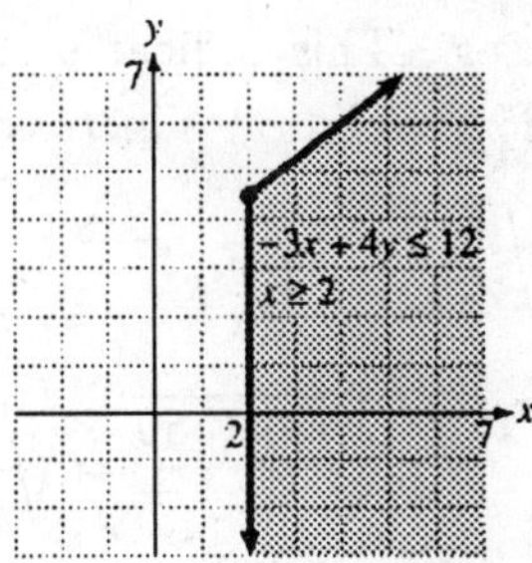

69. $\dfrac{(2x)^5}{x^3} = \dfrac{2^5x^5}{x^3} = \dfrac{32x^5}{x^3} = 32x^2$

Chapter 9 Review Exercises

1. $\sqrt{121} = 11$

The principal square root of 121 is 11.

2. $-\sqrt{121} = -11$

The negative square root of 121 is -11.

3. $\sqrt{-121}$ is not a real number because the square of a real number is never negative.

4. $\sqrt[3]{\dfrac{8}{125}} = \dfrac{2}{5}$ because $\left(\dfrac{2}{5}\right)^3 = \dfrac{8}{125}$.

5. $\sqrt[5]{-32} = -2$ because $(-2)^5 = -32$.

6. $-\sqrt[4]{81} = -3$ because $\sqrt[4]{81} = 3$.

7. $\sqrt{75} \approx 8.660$

8. $\sqrt{398 - 5} = \sqrt{393} \approx 19.824$

9. $P = 26.5\sqrt{t}$; $t = 9$ (for 1999)

$$\begin{aligned} P &= 26.5\sqrt{9} \\ &= 26.5 \cdot 3 = 79.5 \end{aligned}$$

According to the formula, there were 79.5 thousand or 79,500 people over age 85 in Arizona in 1999.

10. As t increases, $\sqrt{t}$ increases, so $26.5\sqrt{t}$ increases. This indicates that Arizona's over-85 population is increasing over time.

11. $d = \sqrt{\frac{3h}{2}}$; $h = 1550$

$$d = \sqrt{\frac{3 \cdot 1550}{2}} = \sqrt{\frac{4650}{2}}$$
$$= \sqrt{2325} \approx 48$$

Visitor's will be able to see about 48 feet from the top of the building.

12. $\sqrt{54} = \sqrt{9 \cdot 6} = \sqrt{9}\sqrt{6} = 3\sqrt{6}$

13. $\sqrt{20} = 6\sqrt{4 \cdot 5} = 6\sqrt{4}\sqrt{5}$
$= 6 \cdot 2\sqrt{5} = 12\sqrt{5}$

14. $\sqrt{63x^2} = \sqrt{9x^2}\sqrt{7} = 3x\sqrt{7}$

15. $\sqrt{48x^3} = \sqrt{16x^2}\sqrt{3x} = 4x\sqrt{3x}$

16. $\sqrt{x^8} = x^4$ because $(x^4)^2 = x^8$.

17. $\sqrt{75x^9} = \sqrt{25x^8}\sqrt{3x} = 5x^4\sqrt{3x}$

18. $\sqrt{45x^{23}} = \sqrt{9x^{22}}\sqrt{5x} = 3x^{11}\sqrt{5x}$

19. $\sqrt[3]{24} = \sqrt[3]{8 \cdot 3} = \sqrt[3]{8}\sqrt[3]{9} = 2\sqrt[3]{2}$

20. $\sqrt{7} \cdot \sqrt{11} = \sqrt{7 \cdot 11} = \sqrt{77}$

21. $\sqrt{3} \cdot \sqrt{12} = \sqrt{36} = 6$

22. $\sqrt{5x} \cdot \sqrt{10x} = \sqrt{50x^2} = \sqrt{25x^2}\sqrt{2}$
$= 5x\sqrt{2}$

23. $\sqrt{3x^2} \cdot \sqrt{4x^3} = \sqrt{12x^5} = \sqrt{4x^4}\sqrt{3x}$
$= 2x^2\sqrt{3x}$

24. $\sqrt[3]{6} \cdot \sqrt[3]{9} = \sqrt[3]{6 \cdot 9} = \sqrt[3]{54} = \sqrt[3]{27} \cdot \sqrt[3]{2}$
$= 3\sqrt[3]{2}$

25. $\sqrt{\frac{5}{2}} \cdot \sqrt{\frac{3}{8}} = \sqrt{\frac{5 \cdot 3}{2 \cdot 8}} = \sqrt{\frac{15}{16}}$
$= \frac{\sqrt{15}}{\sqrt{16}} = \frac{\sqrt{15}}{4}$

26. $\sqrt{\frac{121}{4}} = \frac{\sqrt{121}}{\sqrt{4}} = \frac{11}{2}$

27. $\sqrt{\frac{7x}{25}} = \frac{\sqrt{7x}}{\sqrt{25}} = \frac{\sqrt{7x}}{5}$

28. $\sqrt{\frac{18}{x^2}} = \frac{\sqrt{18}}{\sqrt{x^2}} = \frac{\sqrt{9}\sqrt{2}}{x} = \frac{3\sqrt{2}}{x}$

29. $\frac{\sqrt{200}}{\sqrt{2}} = \sqrt{\frac{200}{2}} = \sqrt{100} = 10$

30. $\frac{\sqrt{96}}{\sqrt{3}} = \sqrt{32} = \sqrt{16}\sqrt{2} = 4\sqrt{2}$

31. $\frac{\sqrt{72x^8}}{\sqrt{x^3}} = \sqrt{\frac{72x^8}{x^3}} = \sqrt{72x^5}$
$= \sqrt{36x^4}\sqrt{2x} = 6x^2\sqrt{2x}$

32. $\sqrt[3]{\frac{5}{64}} = \frac{\sqrt[3]{5}}{\sqrt[3]{64}} = \frac{\sqrt[3]{5}}{4}$

33. $\sqrt[3]{\frac{40}{27}} = \frac{\sqrt[3]{40}}{\sqrt[3]{27}} = \frac{\sqrt[3]{8}\sqrt[3]{5}}{3} = \frac{2\sqrt[3]{5}}{3}$

34. $7\sqrt{5} + 13\sqrt{5} = (7 + 13)\sqrt{5} = 20\sqrt{5}$

35. $\sqrt{8} + \sqrt{50} = \sqrt{4}\sqrt{2} + \sqrt{25}\sqrt{2}$
$= 2\sqrt{2} + 5\sqrt{2}$
$= (2 + 5)\sqrt{2} = 7\sqrt{2}$

36. $\sqrt{75} - \sqrt{48} = \sqrt{25}\sqrt{3} - \sqrt{16}\sqrt{3}$
$= 5\sqrt{3} - 4\sqrt{3}$
$= (5 - 4)\sqrt{3} = \sqrt{3}$

37. $2\sqrt{80} + 3\sqrt{45} = 2\sqrt{16}\sqrt{5} + 3\sqrt{9}\sqrt{5}$
$= 2 \cdot 4\sqrt{5} + 3 \cdot 3\sqrt{5}$
$= 8\sqrt{5} + 9\sqrt{5} = 17\sqrt{5}$

38. $4\sqrt{72}-2\sqrt{48}=4\sqrt{36}\sqrt{2}-2\sqrt{16}\sqrt{3}$
$=4\cdot 6\sqrt{2}-2\cdot 4\sqrt{3}$
$=24\sqrt{2}-8\sqrt{3}$

39. $2\sqrt{18}+3\sqrt{27}-\sqrt{12}$
$=2\sqrt{9}\sqrt{2}+3\sqrt{9}\sqrt{3}-\sqrt{4}\sqrt{3}$
$=2\cdot 3\sqrt{2}+3\cdot 3\sqrt{3}-2\sqrt{3}$
$=6\sqrt{2}+9\sqrt{3}-2\sqrt{3}$
$=6\sqrt{2}+7\sqrt{3}$

40. $\sqrt{10}(\sqrt{5}+\sqrt{6})=\sqrt{10}\cdot\sqrt{5}+\sqrt{10}\cdot\sqrt{6}$
$=\sqrt{50}+\sqrt{60}$
$=\sqrt{25}\sqrt{2}+\sqrt{4}\sqrt{15}$
$=5\sqrt{2}+2\sqrt{15}$

41. $\sqrt{3}(\sqrt{6}-\sqrt{12})=\sqrt{3}\cdot\sqrt{6}-\sqrt{3}\cdot\sqrt{12}$
$=\sqrt{18}-\sqrt{36}$
$=\sqrt{9}\sqrt{2}-6=3\sqrt{2}-6$

42. $(9+\sqrt{2})(10+\sqrt{2})$
$=9\cdot 10+9\sqrt{2}+10\sqrt{2}+\sqrt{2}\cdot\sqrt{2}$
$=90+19\sqrt{2}+2=92+19\sqrt{2}$

43. $(1+3\sqrt{7})(4-\sqrt{7})$
$=1\cdot 4-1\sqrt{7}+3\sqrt{7}\cdot 4-3\cdot\sqrt{7}\sqrt{7}$
$=4-\sqrt{7}+12\sqrt{7}-3\cdot 7$
$=4+11\sqrt{7}-21$
$=-17+11\sqrt{7}$

44. $(\sqrt{3}+2)(\sqrt{6}-4)$
$=\sqrt{3}\cdot\sqrt{6}-4\sqrt{3}+2\sqrt{6}-2\cdot 4$
$=\sqrt{18}-4\sqrt{3}+2\sqrt{6}-8$
$=\sqrt{9}\sqrt{2}-4\sqrt{3}+2\sqrt{6}-8$
$=3\sqrt{2}-4\sqrt{3}+2\sqrt{6}-8$

45. $(2+\sqrt{7})(2-\sqrt{7})=2^2-(\sqrt{7})^2$
$=4-7=-3$

46. $(\sqrt{11}-\sqrt{5})(\sqrt{11}+\sqrt{5})=(\sqrt{11})^2-(\sqrt{5})^2$
$=11-5=6$

47. $(1+\sqrt{2})^2=1^2+2\cdot 1\cdot\sqrt{2}+(\sqrt{2})^2$
$=1+2\sqrt{2}+2$
$=3+2\sqrt{2}$

48. $\dfrac{30}{\sqrt{5}}=\dfrac{30}{\sqrt{5}}\cdot\dfrac{\sqrt{5}}{\sqrt{5}}=\dfrac{30\sqrt{5}}{5}=6\sqrt{5}$

49. $\dfrac{13}{\sqrt{50}}=\dfrac{13}{\sqrt{25}\sqrt{2}}=\dfrac{13}{5\sqrt{2}}\cdot\dfrac{\sqrt{2}}{\sqrt{2}}$
$=\dfrac{13\sqrt{2}}{5\cdot 2}=\dfrac{13\sqrt{2}}{10}$

50. $\sqrt{\dfrac{2}{3}}=\dfrac{\sqrt{2}}{\sqrt{3}}=\dfrac{\sqrt{2}}{\sqrt{3}}\cdot\dfrac{\sqrt{3}}{\sqrt{3}}=\dfrac{\sqrt{6}}{3}$

51. $\sqrt{\dfrac{3}{8}}=\dfrac{\sqrt{3}}{\sqrt{8}}=\dfrac{\sqrt{3}}{\sqrt{4}\sqrt{2}}=\dfrac{\sqrt{3}}{2\sqrt{2}}$
$=\dfrac{\sqrt{3}}{2\sqrt{2}}\cdot\dfrac{\sqrt{2}}{\sqrt{2}}=\dfrac{\sqrt{6}}{2\cdot 2}=\dfrac{\sqrt{6}}{4}$

52. $\sqrt{\dfrac{17}{x}}=\dfrac{\sqrt{17}}{\sqrt{x}}=\dfrac{\sqrt{17}}{\sqrt{x}}\cdot\dfrac{\sqrt{x}}{\sqrt{x}}=\dfrac{\sqrt{17x}}{x}$

53. $\dfrac{11}{\sqrt{5}+2}=\dfrac{11}{\sqrt{5}+2}\cdot\dfrac{\sqrt{5}-2}{\sqrt{5}-2}$
$=\dfrac{11(\sqrt{5}-2)}{(\sqrt{5})^2-2^2}$
$=\dfrac{11(\sqrt{5}-2)}{5-4}$
$=\dfrac{11(\sqrt{5}-2)}{1}$
$=11\sqrt{5}-22$

54. $\dfrac{21}{4-\sqrt{3}}=\dfrac{21}{4-\sqrt{3}}\cdot\dfrac{4+\sqrt{3}}{4+\sqrt{3}}$
$=\dfrac{21(4+\sqrt{3})}{4^2-(\sqrt{3})^2}$
$=\dfrac{21(4+\sqrt{3})}{16-3}$
$=\dfrac{21(4+\sqrt{3})}{13}$
$=\dfrac{84+21\sqrt{3}}{13}$

55. $$\frac{12}{\sqrt{5}+\sqrt{3}} = \frac{12}{\sqrt{5}+\sqrt{3}} \cdot \frac{\sqrt{5}-\sqrt{3}}{\sqrt{5}-\sqrt{3}}$$
$$= \frac{12(\sqrt{5}-\sqrt{3})}{(\sqrt{5})^2-(\sqrt{3})^2}$$
$$= \frac{12(\sqrt{5}-\sqrt{3})}{5-3}$$
$$= \frac{12(\sqrt{5}-\sqrt{3})}{2}$$
$$= 6(\sqrt{5}-\sqrt{3})$$
$$= 6\sqrt{5}-6\sqrt{3}$$

56. $$\frac{7\sqrt{2}}{\sqrt{2}-4}$$
$$= \frac{7\sqrt{2}}{\sqrt{2}-4} \cdot \frac{\sqrt{2}+4}{\sqrt{2}+4}$$
$$= \frac{7\sqrt{2}(\sqrt{2}+4)}{(\sqrt{2})^2-4^2}$$
$$= \frac{7\sqrt{2}(\sqrt{2}+4)}{2-16}$$
$$= \frac{7\sqrt{2}(\sqrt{2}+4)}{-14}$$
$$= \frac{7\cdot\sqrt{2}\sqrt{2}+7\sqrt{2}\cdot 4}{-14}$$
$$= \frac{7\cdot 2+28\sqrt{2}}{-14}$$
$$= \frac{14+28\sqrt{2}}{-14}$$
$$= \frac{14(1+2\sqrt{2})}{14(-1)}$$
$$= -1(1+2\sqrt{2})$$
$$= -1-2\sqrt{2}$$

57. $$\sqrt{x+3} = 4$$
$$(\sqrt{x+3}) = 4^2$$
$$x+3 = 16$$
$$x = 13$$

Check 13:

$$\sqrt{x+3} = 4$$
$$\sqrt{13+3} \stackrel{?}{=} 4$$
$$\sqrt{16} \stackrel{?}{=} 4$$
$$4 = 4 \text{ true}$$

The solution is 13.

58. $$\sqrt{2x+3} = 5$$
$$(\sqrt{2x+3})^2 = 5^2$$
$$2x+3 = 25$$
$$2x = 22$$
$$x = 11$$

Check 11:

$$\sqrt{2x+3} = 5$$
$$\sqrt{2(11)+3} \stackrel{?}{=} 5$$
$$\sqrt{22+3} \stackrel{?}{=} 5$$
$$\sqrt{25} \stackrel{?}{=} 5$$
$$5 = 5 \text{ true}$$

The solution is 11.

59. $$3\sqrt{x} = \sqrt{6x+15}$$
$$(3\sqrt{x})^2 = (\sqrt{6x+15})^2$$
$$9x = 6x+15$$
$$3x = 15$$
$$x = 5$$

Substitute 5 for x in the original equation to verify that the solution is 5.

60.
$$\begin{aligned} \sqrt{5x+1} &= x+1 \\ (\sqrt{5x+1})^2 &= (x+1)^2 \\ 5x+1 &= x^2+2x+1 \\ 0 &= x^2-3x \\ 0 &= x(x-3) \\ x=0 \quad \text{or} \quad x-3 &= 0 \\ x &= 3 \end{aligned}$$

Each of the proposed solutions must be checked separately in the original equation.

Check 0:

$$\begin{aligned} \sqrt{5x+1} &= x+1 \\ \sqrt{5\cdot 0+1} &\stackrel{?}{=} 0+1 \\ \sqrt{1} &\stackrel{?}{=} 0+1 \\ 1 &= 1 \text{ true} \end{aligned}$$

Check 3:

$$\begin{aligned} \sqrt{5x+1} &= x+1 \\ \sqrt{5\cdot 3+1} &\stackrel{?}{=} 3+1 \\ \sqrt{15+1} &\stackrel{?}{=} 4 \\ \sqrt{16} &\stackrel{?}{=} 4 \\ 4 &= 4 \text{ true} \end{aligned}$$

The equation has two solutions, 0 and 3.

61.
$$\begin{aligned} \sqrt{x+1}+5 &= x \\ \sqrt{x+1} &= x-5 \\ (\sqrt{x+1})^2 &= (x-5)^2 \\ x+1 &= x^2-10x+25 \\ 0 &= x^2-11x+24 \\ 0 &= (x-3)(x-8) \\ x-3=0 \quad &\text{or} \quad x-8=0 \\ x=3 \quad & \quad\quad x=8 \end{aligned}$$

Check 3:

$$\begin{aligned} \sqrt{x+1}+5 &= x \\ \sqrt{3+1}+5 &\stackrel{?}{=} 3 \\ \sqrt{4}+5 &\stackrel{?}{=} 3 \\ 2+5 &\stackrel{?}{=} 3 \\ 7 &= 3 \text{ false} \end{aligned}$$

Check 8:

$$\begin{aligned} \sqrt{x+1}+5 &= x \\ \sqrt{8+1}+5 &\stackrel{?}{=} 8 \\ \sqrt{9}+5 &\stackrel{?}{=} 8 \\ 3+5 &= 8 \\ 8 &= 8 \text{ true} \end{aligned}$$

The false statement indicates that 3 does *not* satisfy the original equation; it is an extraneous solution. The true statement indicates that 8 satisfies the equation. Therefore, the only solution is 8.

62.
$$\begin{aligned} \sqrt{x-2}+5 &= 1 \\ \sqrt{x-2} &= -4 \\ (\sqrt{x-2})^2 &= (-4)^2 \\ x-2 &= 16 \\ x &= 18 \end{aligned}$$

Check 18:

$$\begin{aligned} \sqrt{x-2}+5 &= 1 \\ \sqrt{18-2}+5 &= 1 \\ \sqrt{16}+5 &\stackrel{?}{=} 1 \\ 4+5 &\stackrel{?}{=} 1 \\ 9 &= 1 \text{ false} \end{aligned}$$

The only proposed solution, 18, is extraneous, so the equation has no solution.

63.
$$\begin{aligned} x &= \sqrt{x^2+4x+4} \\ x^2 &= (\sqrt{x^2+4x+4})^2 \\ x^2 &= x^2+4x+4 \\ 0 &= 4x+4 \\ -4 &= 4x \\ -1 &= x \end{aligned}$$

Check:

$$\begin{aligned} x &= \sqrt{x^2+4x+4} \\ -1 &\stackrel{?}{=} \sqrt{(-1)^2+4(-1)+4} \\ -1 &\stackrel{?}{=} \sqrt{1-4+4} \\ -1 &\stackrel{?}{=} \sqrt{1} \\ -1 &= 1 \text{ false} \end{aligned}$$

The only proposed solution, -1, is extraneous, so the equation has no solution.

64. $t = \sqrt{\dfrac{d}{16}}$; $t = 3$

$$\begin{aligned} 3 &= \sqrt{\frac{d}{16}} \\ 3^2 &= \left(\sqrt{\frac{d}{16}}\right)^2 \\ 9 &= \frac{d}{16} \\ 9 \cdot 16 &= d \\ 144 &= d \end{aligned}$$

The water is 144 feet above the bridge.

65. $D = \sqrt{2H}$; $D = 50$

$$\begin{aligned} 50 &= \sqrt{2H} \\ 50^2 &= (\sqrt{2H})^2 \\ 2500 &= 2H \\ 1250 &= H \end{aligned}$$

The mountain is 1250 feet high.

66. $16^{1/2} = \sqrt{16} = 4$

67. $125^{1/3} = \sqrt[3]{125} = 5$

68. $64^{2/3} = (\sqrt[3]{64})^2 = 4^2 = 16$

69. $25^{-1/2} = \dfrac{1}{25^{1/2}} = \dfrac{1}{\sqrt{25}} = \dfrac{1}{5}$

70. $27^{-\frac{1}{3}} = \dfrac{1}{27^{\frac{1}{3}}} = \dfrac{1}{\sqrt[3]{27}} = \dfrac{1}{3}$

71. $(-8)^{-\frac{4}{3}} = \dfrac{1}{(-8)^{\frac{4}{3}}} = \dfrac{1}{(\sqrt[3]{-8})^4}$

$$= \frac{1}{(-2)^4} = \frac{1}{16}$$

72. $S = 28.6A^{\frac{1}{3}}$; $A = 8$

$$\begin{aligned} S &= 28.6 \cdot 8^{\frac{1}{3}} = 28.6\sqrt[3]{8} \\ &= 28.6 \cdot 2 = 57.2 \approx 57 \end{aligned}$$

There are approximately 57 species on a Galápagos island whose area is 8 square miles.

Chapter 9 Test

1. $-\sqrt{64} = -8$

The negative square root of 64 is -8.

2. $\sqrt[3]{64} = 4$ because $4^3 = 64$.

3. $\sqrt{48} = \sqrt{16 \cdot 3} = \sqrt{16}\sqrt{3} = 4\sqrt{3}$

4. $\sqrt{72x^3} = \sqrt{36x^2}\sqrt{2x} = 6x\sqrt{2x}$

5. $\sqrt{x^{29}} = \sqrt{x^{28} \cdot x} = \sqrt{x^{28}}\sqrt{x} = x^{14}\sqrt{x}$

6. $\sqrt{\dfrac{25}{x^2}} = \dfrac{\sqrt{25}}{\sqrt{x^2}} = \dfrac{5}{x}$

7. $\sqrt{\dfrac{75}{27}} = \dfrac{\sqrt{75}}{\sqrt{27}} = \dfrac{\sqrt{25}\sqrt{3}}{\sqrt{9}\sqrt{3}}$

$$= \frac{5\sqrt{3}}{3\sqrt{3}} = \frac{5}{3}$$

8. $\sqrt[3]{\dfrac{5}{8}} = \dfrac{\sqrt[3]{5}}{\sqrt[3]{8}} = \dfrac{\sqrt[3]{5}}{2}$

9. $\dfrac{\sqrt{80x^4}}{\sqrt{2x^2}} = \sqrt{\dfrac{80x^4}{2x^2}} = \sqrt{40x^2}$

$$= \sqrt{4x^2}\sqrt{10} = 2x\sqrt{10}$$

10. $\sqrt{10} \cdot \sqrt{5} = \sqrt{50} = \sqrt{25 \cdot 2}$

$$= \sqrt{25}\sqrt{2} = 5\sqrt{2}$$

11. $\sqrt{6x} \cdot \sqrt{6y} = \sqrt{36xy}\sqrt{xy}$

$$= 6\sqrt{xy}$$

12. $\sqrt{10x^2} \cdot \sqrt{2x^3} = \sqrt{20x^5} = \sqrt{4x^4}\sqrt{5x}$

$$= 2x^2\sqrt{5x}$$

13. $\sqrt{24} + 3\sqrt{54} = \sqrt{4}\sqrt{6} + 3\sqrt{9}\sqrt{6}$

$$\begin{aligned} &= 2\sqrt{6} + 3 \cdot 3\sqrt{6} \\ &= 2\sqrt{6} + 9\sqrt{6} \\ &= 11\sqrt{6} \end{aligned}$$

14. $$7\sqrt{8}-2\sqrt{32}=7\sqrt{4}\sqrt{2}-2\sqrt{16}\sqrt{2} \\ =7\cdot 2\sqrt{2}-2\cdot 4\sqrt{2} \\ =14\sqrt{2}-8\sqrt{2}=6\sqrt{2}$$

15. $$\sqrt{3}(\sqrt{10}+\sqrt{3})=\sqrt{3}\cdot\sqrt{10}+\sqrt{3}\cdot\sqrt{3} \\ =\sqrt{30}+3$$

16. $$(7-\sqrt{5})(10+3\sqrt{5}) \\ =7\cdot 10+7\cdot 3\sqrt{5}-10\sqrt{5}-3\sqrt{5}\cdot\sqrt{5} \\ =70+21\sqrt{5}-10\sqrt{5}-3\cdot 5 \\ =70+11\sqrt{5}-15=55+11\sqrt{5}$$

17. $$(\sqrt{6}+2)(\sqrt{6}-2)=(\sqrt{6})^2-2^2 \\ =6-4=2$$

18. $$(3+\sqrt{7})^2=3^2+2\cdot 3\cdot\sqrt{7}+(\sqrt{7})^2 \\ =9+6\sqrt{7}+7=16+6\sqrt{7}$$

19. $$\frac{4}{\sqrt{5}}=\frac{4}{\sqrt{5}}\cdot\frac{\sqrt{5}}{\sqrt{5}}=\frac{4\sqrt{5}}{5}$$

20. $$\frac{5}{4+\sqrt{3}}=\frac{5}{4+\sqrt{3}}\cdot\frac{4-\sqrt{3}}{4-\sqrt{3}} \\ =\frac{5(4-\sqrt{3})}{4^2-(\sqrt{3})^2} \\ =\frac{5(4-\sqrt{3})}{16-3} \\ =\frac{5(4-\sqrt{3})}{13} \\ =\frac{20-5\sqrt{5}}{13}$$

21. $$\sqrt{3x}+5=11 \\ \sqrt{3x}=6 \\ (\sqrt{3x})^2=6^2 \\ 3x=36 \\ x=12$$

Check the proposed solution in the original equation.

$$\sqrt{3x}+5=11 \\ \sqrt{3\cdot 12}+5\stackrel{?}{=}11 \\ \sqrt{36}+5\stackrel{?}{=}11 \\ 6+5\stackrel{?}{=}11 \\ 11=11$$

The solution is 12.

22. $$\sqrt{2x-1}=x-2 \\ (\sqrt{2x-1})^2=(x-2)^2 \\ 2x-1=x^2-4x+4 \\ 0=x^2-6x+5 \\ 0=(x-1)(x-5)$$

$$x-1=0 \quad\text{or}\quad x-5=0 \\ x=1 \qquad\qquad x=5$$

Check each proposed solution in the original equation.

Check 1:

$$\sqrt{2x-1}=x-2 \\ \sqrt{2\cdot 1-1}\stackrel{?}{=}1-2 \\ \sqrt{2-1}\stackrel{?}{=}1-2 \\ \sqrt{1}\stackrel{?}{=}-1 \\ 1=-1 \text{ false}$$

Check 5:

$$\sqrt{2x-1}\stackrel{?}{=}x-2 \\ \sqrt{2\cdot 5-1}\stackrel{?}{=}5-2 \\ \sqrt{10-1}\stackrel{?}{=}3 \\ \sqrt{9}\stackrel{?}{=}3 \\ 3=3 \text{ true}$$

The check shows that 1 is an extraneous solution, while 5 satisfies the equation. Therefore, the solution is 5.

23. $t = \sqrt{\dfrac{d}{16}}$; $t = 10$

$$\begin{aligned} 10 &= \sqrt{\frac{d}{16}} \\ 10^2 &= \left(\sqrt{\frac{d}{16}}\right)^2 \\ 100 &= \frac{d}{16} \\ 1600 &= d \end{aligned}$$

The skydiver will fall 1600 feet in 10 seconds.

24. $8^{\frac{2}{3}} = (\sqrt[3]{8})^2 = 2^2 = 4$

25. $9^{-\frac{1}{2}} = \dfrac{1}{9^{\frac{1}{2}}} = \dfrac{1}{\sqrt{9}} = \dfrac{1}{3}$

Chapter 9 Cumulative Review Exercises (Chapters 1-9)

1. $$\begin{aligned} 2x + 3x - 5 + 7 &= 10x + 3 - 6x - 4 \\ 5x + 2 &= 4x - 1 \\ 5x + 2 - 4x &= 4x - 1 - 4x \\ x + 2 &= -1 \\ x + 2 - 2 &= -1 - 2 \\ x &= -3 \end{aligned}$$

The solution is -3.

2. $$\begin{aligned} 2x^2 + 5x &= 12 \\ 2x^2 + 5x - 12 &= 0 \\ (2x - 3)(x + 4) &= 0 \end{aligned}$$

$$2x - 3 = 0 \quad \text{or} \quad x + 4 = 0$$
$$2x = 3 \qquad\qquad x = -4$$
$$x = \frac{3}{2}$$

The solutions are $\frac{3}{2}$ and -4.

3. $8x - 5y = -4$
$2x + 15y = -66$

To solve this system by the addition by the addition method, multiply the first equation by 3 and add the result to the second equation.

$$\begin{aligned} 24x - 15y &= -12 \\ 2x + 15y &= -66 \\ \hline 26x \quad &= -78 \\ x &= -3 \end{aligned}$$

Back-substitute into the first original equation.

$$\begin{aligned} 8x - 5y &= -4 \\ 8(-3) - 5y &= -4 \\ -24 - 5y &= -4 \\ -5y &= 20 \\ y &= -4 \end{aligned}$$

Solution: $(-3, -4)$

4. $\dfrac{15}{x} - 4 = \dfrac{6}{x} + 3$

Restriction: $x \neq 0$
LCD $= x$
Multiply both sides by the LCD, which is x.

$$\begin{aligned} x\left(\frac{15}{x} - 4\right) &= x\left(\frac{6}{x} + 3\right) \\ x \cdot \frac{15}{x} - x \cdot 4 &= x \cdot \frac{6}{x} + x \cdot 3 \\ 15 - 4x &= 6 + 3x \\ 15 - 7x &= 6 \\ -7x &= -9 \\ x &= \frac{9}{7} \end{aligned}$$

The solution is $\frac{9}{7}$.

5. $-3x - 7 = 8$

$$-3x = 15$$
$$x = -5$$

The solution is -5.

6. $\sqrt{2x-1} - x = -2$

$$\sqrt{2x-1} = x - 2$$
$$(\sqrt{2x-1})^2 = (x-2)^2$$
$$2x - 1 = x^2 - 4x + 4$$
$$0 = x^2 - 6x + 5$$
$$0 = (x-1)(x-5)$$

$x - 1 = 0$ or $x - 5 = 0$

$x = 1 \qquad x = 5$

Check each proposed solution in the original equation.

Check 1:

$$\sqrt{2x-1} - x = -2$$
$$\sqrt{2\cdot 1 - 1} - 1 \stackrel{?}{=} -2$$
$$\sqrt{2-1} - 1 \stackrel{?}{=} -2$$
$$\sqrt{1} - 1 \stackrel{?}{=} -2$$
$$1 - 1 \stackrel{?}{=} -2$$
$$0 = -2 \text{ false}$$

Check 5:

$$\sqrt{2x-1} - x = -2$$
$$\sqrt{2\cdot 5 - 1} - 5 \stackrel{?}{=} -2$$
$$\sqrt{10-1} - 5 \stackrel{?}{=} -2$$
$$\sqrt{9} - 5 \stackrel{?}{=} -2$$
$$3 - 5 \stackrel{?}{=} -2$$
$$-2 = -2 \text{ true}$$

The check show that 1 is an extraneous solution, while 5 satisfies the equation, so the only solution is 5.

7. $\dfrac{8x^3}{-4x^7} = \dfrac{8}{-4} \cdot x^{3-7} = -2x^{-4}$

$$= \frac{-2}{x^4} = -\frac{2}{x^4}$$

8. $6\sqrt{75} - 4\sqrt{12} = 6\sqrt{25}\sqrt{3} - 4\sqrt{4}\sqrt{3}$

$$= 6\cdot 5\sqrt{3} - 4\cdot 2\sqrt{3}$$
$$= 30\sqrt{3} - 8\sqrt{3}$$
$$= 22\sqrt{3}$$

9. $\dfrac{\frac{1}{x} - \frac{1}{2}}{\frac{1}{3} - \frac{x}{6}}$

LCD $= 6x$

$$\frac{\frac{1}{x} - \frac{1}{2}}{\frac{1}{3} - \frac{x}{6}} = \frac{6x}{6x} \cdot \frac{\left(\frac{1}{x} - \frac{1}{2}\right)}{\left(\frac{1}{3} - \frac{x}{6}\right)}$$
$$= \frac{6x \cdot \frac{1}{x} - 6x \cdot \frac{1}{2}}{6x \cdot \frac{1}{3} - 6x \cdot \frac{x}{6}}$$
$$= \frac{6 - 3x}{2x - x^2}$$
$$= \frac{3(2-x)}{x(2-x)} = \frac{3}{x}$$

10. $\dfrac{4 - x^2}{3x^2 - 5x - 2} = \dfrac{(2+x)(2-x)}{(3x+1)(x-2)}$

$$= \frac{(2+x)(-1)(x-2)}{(3x+1)(x-2)}$$
$$= \frac{-1(2+x)}{3x+1}$$
$$= -\frac{2+x}{3x+1}$$

11. $-5 - (-8) - (4 - 6) = -5 - (-8) - (-2)$

$$= -5 + 8 + 2$$
$$= 3 + 2 = 5$$

12. $x^2 - 18x + 77$

To factor this trinomial, find two integers whose product is 77 and whose sum is -18. These integers are -7 and -11.

$$x^2 - 18x + 77 = (x-7)(x-11)$$

13. $x^3 - 25x = x(x^2 - 25)$
$= x(x-5)(x-5)$

14.

$$\begin{array}{r} 6x^2 - 7x + 2 \\ x-2\overline{)6x^3 - 19x^2 + 16x - 4} \\ \underline{6x^3 - 12x^2} \\ -7x^2 + 16x \\ \underline{-7x^2 + 14x} \\ 2x - 4 \\ \underline{2x - 4} \\ 0 \end{array}$$

$$\frac{6x^3 - 19x^2 + 16x - 4}{x-2} = 6x^2 - 7x + 2$$

15. $(2x-3)(4x^2+6x+9)$
$= 2x(4x^2+6x+9)$
$\quad - 3(4x^2+6x+9)$
$= 8x^3 + 12x^2 + 18x - 12x^2$
$\quad - 18x - 27$
$= 8x^3 - 27$

16. $\dfrac{3x}{x^2+x-2} - \dfrac{2}{x+2}$

$$= \frac{3x}{(x+2)(x-1)} - \frac{2}{x+2}$$

$$= \frac{3x}{(x+2)(x-1)} - \frac{2(x-1)}{(x+2)(x-1)}$$

$$= \frac{3x - 2(x-1)}{(x+2)(x-1)}$$

$$= \frac{3x - 2x + 2}{(x+2)(x-1)}$$

$$= \frac{x+2}{(x+2)(x-1)}$$

$$= \frac{1}{x-1}$$

17. $\dfrac{5x^2-6x+1}{x^2-1} \div \dfrac{16x^2-9}{4x^2+7x+3}$

$$= \frac{5x^2-6x+1}{x^2-1} \cdot \frac{4x^2+7x+3}{16x^2-9}$$

$$= \frac{(5x-1)(x-1)}{(x+1)(x-1)} \cdot \frac{(4x+3)(x+1)}{(4x+3)(4x-3)}$$

$$= \frac{5x-1}{4x-3}$$

18. $\sqrt{12} - 4\sqrt{75} = \sqrt{4}\sqrt{3} - 4\sqrt{25}\sqrt{3}$
$= 2\sqrt{3} - 4 \cdot 5\sqrt{3}$
$= 2\sqrt{3} - 20\sqrt{3} = -18\sqrt{3}$

19. $2x - y = 4$

The graph is a line with x-intercept 2 and y-intercept -4. The point $(1, -2)$ can be used as a checkpoint. Draw a line through $(2, 0), (0, -4)$, and $(1, -2)$.

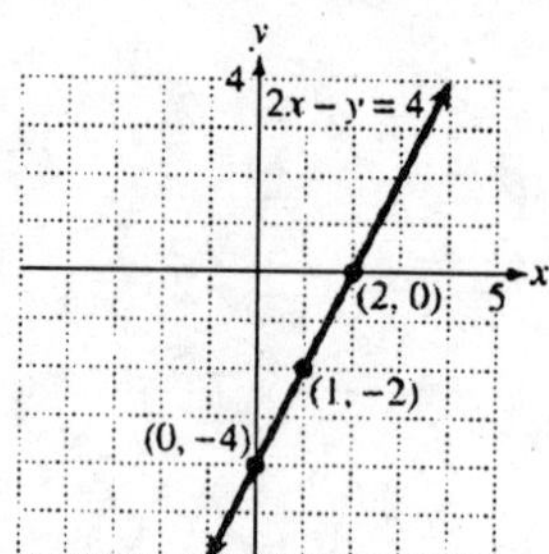

20. $y = -\dfrac{2}{3}x$

The graph is a line with slope $-\frac{2}{3} = \frac{-2}{3}$ and y-intercept 0. Plot $(0, 0)$. From the origin, move 2 units *down* and 3 units to the *right* to reach the point $(-2, 3)$. Draw a line through $(0, 0)$ and $(-2, 3)$.

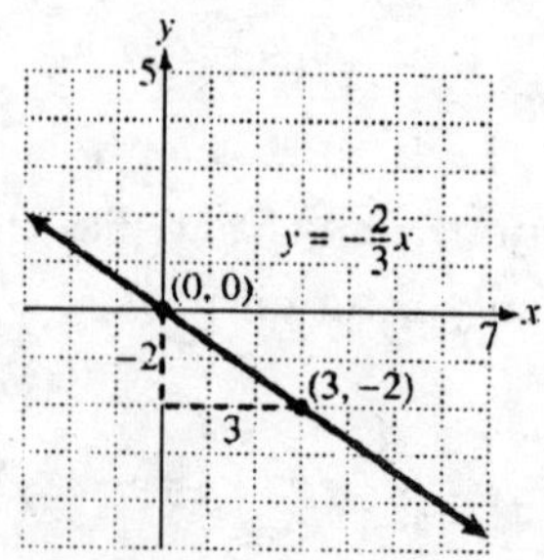

21. $x \geq -1$

Graph $x = 1$ as a solid vertical line. Use $(0,0)$ as a test point. Since $0 \geq -1$ is true, shade the half-plane that contains $(0,0)$. This is the region to the right of the vertical line.

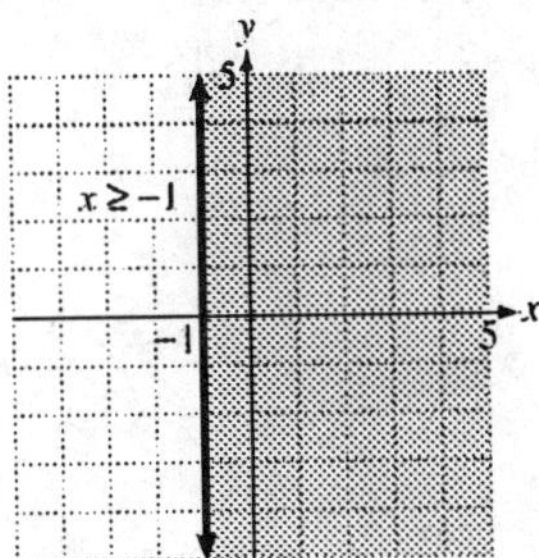

22. $(-1,5)$ and $(2,-3)$

$$m = \frac{y_2 - y_1}{x_2 - x_1} = \frac{-3-5}{2-(-1)}$$
$$= \frac{-8}{3} = -\frac{8}{3}$$

23. Slope 5, passing through $(-2,-3)$
First, substitute 5 for m, -2 for x_1, and -3 for y_1 in the point-slope form.

$$y - y_1 = m(x - x_1)$$
$$y - (-3) = 5[x - (-2)]$$
$$y + 3 = 5(x + 2)$$

Now rewrite the equation in slope-intercept form.

$$y + 3 = 5x + 10$$
$$y = 5x + 7$$

24. Let $x =$ the number.

$$5x - 7 = 208$$
$$5x = 215$$
$$x = 43$$

The number is 43.

25. Let $x =$ the number of deer in the park.

$$\frac{\text{Original number of tagged deer}}{\text{Total number of deer}} = \frac{\text{Number of tagged deer in sample}}{\text{Number of deer in sample}}$$

$$\frac{318}{x} = \frac{56}{168}$$
$$56x = (318)(168)$$
$$56x = 53{,}424$$
$$x = 954$$

There are approximately 954 deer in the park.

Chapter 10

QUADRATIC EQUATIONS AND FUNCTIONS

10.1 Solving Quadratic Equations by the Square Root Property

10.1 CHECK POINTS

CHECK POINT 1

a. $x^2 = 36$

$x = \sqrt{36}$ or $x = -\sqrt{36}$

$x = 6$ $\quad x = -6$

The solutions are 6 and -6.

b. $5x^2 = 15$

$x^2 = 3$

$x = \sqrt{3}$ or $x = -\sqrt{3}$

The solutions are $\sqrt{3}$ and $-\sqrt{3}$.

c. $2x^2 = 7$

$$x = \frac{7}{2}$$

$$x = \sqrt{\frac{7}{2}} \text{ or } x = -\sqrt{\frac{7}{2}}$$

Rationalize the denominators.

$$\sqrt{\frac{7}{2}} = \frac{\sqrt{7}}{\sqrt{2}} = \frac{\sqrt{7}}{\sqrt{2}} \cdot \frac{\sqrt{2}}{\sqrt{2}} = \frac{\sqrt{14}}{2}$$

$$x = \frac{\sqrt{14}}{2} \text{ or } x = -\frac{\sqrt{14}}{2}$$

The solutions are $\frac{\sqrt{14}}{2}$ and $-\frac{\sqrt{14}}{2}$.

CHECK POINT 2

$$(x-3)^2 = 25$$

$$x - 3 = \sqrt{25} \text{ or } x - 3 = -\sqrt{25}$$

$$x - 3 = 5 \text{ or } x - 3 = -5$$

$$x = 8 \qquad x = -2$$

Substitute both values in the original equation to confirm that the solutions are 8 and -2.

CHECK POINT 3

$$(x-2)^2 = 7$$

$$x - 2 = \sqrt{7} \text{ or } x - 2 = -\sqrt{7}$$

$$x = 2 + \sqrt{7} \qquad x = 2 - \sqrt{7}$$

The two solutions are $2 + \sqrt{7}$ and $2 - \sqrt{7}$, which can be expressed in abbreviated notation as $2 \pm \sqrt{7}$.

CHECK POINT 4

Let w = the width of the screen.
A right triangle is formed by the television's height, width, and diagonal.

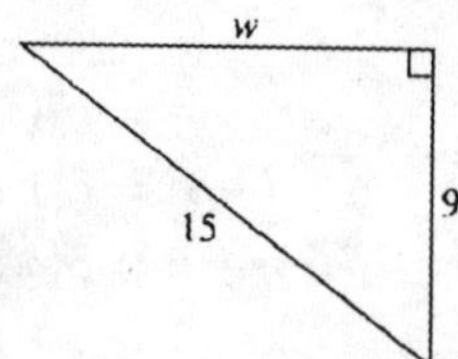

$$w^2 + 9^2 = 15^2$$

$$w^2 + 81 = 225$$

$$w^2 = 144$$

$$w = \sqrt{144} \text{ or } w = -\sqrt{144}$$

$$w = 12 \qquad w = -12$$

Because w represents the width of the screen, so this dimension must be positive. Reject -12. Thus, the width of the television screen.

EXERCISE SET 10.1

1. $x^2 = 16$

$$x = \sqrt{16} \text{ or } x = -\sqrt{16}$$
$$x = 4 \text{ or } x = -4$$

The solutions are 4 and -4.

3. $y^2 = 81$

$$y = \sqrt{81} \text{ or } y = -\sqrt{81}$$
$$y = 9 \text{ or } y = -9$$

The solutions are 9 and -9.

5. $x^2 = 7$

$$x = \sqrt{7} \text{ or } x = -\sqrt{7}$$

The solutions are $\sqrt{7}$ and $-\sqrt{7}$.

7. $x^2 = 50$

$$x = \sqrt{50} \text{ or } x = -\sqrt{50}$$

Simplify $\sqrt{50}$:

$$\sqrt{50} = \sqrt{25}\sqrt{2} = 5\sqrt{2}.$$

$$x = 5\sqrt{2} \text{ or } x = -5\sqrt{2}$$

The solutions are $5\sqrt{2}$ and$-5\sqrt{2}$.

9. $5x^2 = 20$

$x^2 = 4$

$$x = \sqrt{4} \text{ or } x = -\sqrt{4}$$
$$x = 2 \text{ or } x = -2$$

The solutions are 2 and -2.

11. $4y^2 = 49$

$$y^2 = \frac{49}{4}$$

$$y = \sqrt{\frac{49}{4}} \text{ or } y = -\sqrt{\frac{49}{4}}$$

$$y = \frac{7}{2} \text{ or } y = -\frac{7}{2}$$

The solutions are $\frac{7}{2}$ and $-\frac{7}{2}$.

13. $2x^2 + 1 = 51$

$2x^2 = 50$

$x^2 = 25$

$$x = \sqrt{25} \text{ or } x = -\sqrt{25}$$
$$x = 5 \text{ or } x = -5$$

The solutions are 5 and -5.

15. $3x^2 - 2 = 0$

$3x = 2$

$$x^2 = \frac{2}{3}$$

$$x = \sqrt{\frac{2}{3}} \text{ or } x = -\sqrt{\frac{2}{3}}$$

Rationalize the denominators.

$$\sqrt{\frac{2}{3}} = \frac{\sqrt{2}}{\sqrt{3}} = \frac{\sqrt{2}}{\sqrt{3}} \cdot \frac{\sqrt{3}}{\sqrt{3}} = \frac{\sqrt{6}}{3}$$

$$x = \frac{\sqrt{6}}{3} \text{ or } x = -\frac{\sqrt{6}}{3}$$

The solutions are $\frac{\sqrt{6}}{3}$ and $-\frac{\sqrt{6}}{3}$.

17. $5z^2 - 7 = 0$

$5z^2 = 7$

$$z^2 = \frac{7}{5}$$

$$z = \sqrt{\frac{7}{5}} \text{ or } z = -\sqrt{\frac{7}{5}}$$

Rationalize the denominators.

$$\sqrt{\frac{7}{5}} = \frac{\sqrt{7}}{\sqrt{5}} = \frac{\sqrt{7}}{\sqrt{5}} \cdot \frac{\sqrt{5}}{\sqrt{5}} = \frac{\sqrt{35}}{5}$$

$$z = \frac{\sqrt{35}}{5} \text{ or } z = -\frac{\sqrt{35}}{5}$$

The solutions are $\frac{\sqrt{35}}{5}$ and $-\frac{\sqrt{35}}{5}$.

19. $(x - 3)^2 = 16$

$$x - 3 = \sqrt{16} \text{ or } x - 3 = -\sqrt{16}$$
$$x - 3 = 4 \text{ or } x - 3 = -4$$
$$x = 7 \qquad x = -1$$

The solutions are 7 and -1.

21. $(x+5)^2 = 121$

$$\begin{aligned} x+5 &= \sqrt{121} \quad \text{or} \quad x+5 = -\sqrt{121} \\ x+5 &= 11 \quad \text{or} \quad x+5 = -11 \\ x &= 6 \qquad\qquad x = -16 \end{aligned}$$

The solutions are 6 and -16.

23. $(3x+2)^2 = 9$

$$\begin{aligned} 3x+2 &= \sqrt{9} \quad \text{or} \quad 3x+2 = -\sqrt{9} \\ 3x+2 &= 3 \quad \text{or} \quad 3x+2 = -3 \\ 3x &= 1 \quad \text{or} \quad 3x = -5 \\ x &= \frac{1}{3} \qquad\qquad x = -\frac{5}{3} \end{aligned}$$

The solutions are $\frac{1}{3}$ and $-\frac{5}{3}$.

25. $(x-3)^2 = 5$

$$\begin{aligned} x-3 &= \sqrt{5} \quad \text{or} \quad x-3 = -\sqrt{5} \\ x &= 3+\sqrt{5} \qquad x = 3-\sqrt{5} \end{aligned}$$

The solutions are $3+\sqrt{5}$ and $3-\sqrt{5}$.

27. $(y+5)^2 = 11$

$$\begin{aligned} y+5 &= \sqrt{11} \quad \text{or} \quad y+5 = -\sqrt{11} \\ y &= -5+\sqrt{11} \qquad y = -5-\sqrt{11} \end{aligned}$$

The solutions are $-5+\sqrt{11}$ and $-5-\sqrt{11}$.

29. $(z-2)^2 = 8$

$$\begin{aligned} z-2 &= \sqrt{8} \quad \text{or} \quad z-2 = -\sqrt{8} \\ z-2 &= 2\sqrt{2} \quad \text{or} \quad z-2 = -2\sqrt{2} \\ z &= 2+2\sqrt{2} \qquad z = 2-2\sqrt{2} \end{aligned}$$

The solutions are $2+2\sqrt{2}$ and $2-2\sqrt{2}$.

31. $x^2+4x+4 = 16$
$(x+2)^2 = 16$

$$\begin{aligned} x+2 &= \sqrt{16} \quad \text{or} \quad x+2 = -\sqrt{16} \\ x+2 &= 4 \quad \text{or} \quad x+2 = -4 \\ x &= 2 \qquad\qquad x = -6 \end{aligned}$$

The solutions are 2 and -6.

33. $x^2-6x+9 = 36$
$(x-3)^2 = 36$

$$\begin{aligned} x-3 &= \sqrt{36} \quad \text{or} \quad x-3 = -\sqrt{36} \\ x-3 &= 6 \quad \text{or} \quad x-3 = -6 \\ x &= 9 \qquad\qquad x = -3 \end{aligned}$$

The solutions are 9 and -3.

35. $x^2-10x+25 = 2$
$(x-5)^2 = 2$

$$\begin{aligned} x-5 &= \sqrt{2} \quad \text{or} \quad x-5 = -\sqrt{2} \\ x &= 5+\sqrt{2} \qquad x = 5-\sqrt{2} \end{aligned}$$

The solutions are $5+\sqrt{2}$ and $5-\sqrt{2}$.

37. $x^2+2x+1 = 5$
$(x+1)^2 = 5$

$$\begin{aligned} x+1 &= \sqrt{5} \quad \text{or} \quad x+1 = -\sqrt{5} \\ x &= -1+\sqrt{5} \qquad x = -1-\sqrt{5} \end{aligned}$$

The solutions are $-1+\sqrt{5}$ and $-1-\sqrt{5}$.

39. $y^2-14y+49 = 12$
$(y-7)^2 = 12$

$$\begin{aligned} y-7 &= \sqrt{12} \quad \text{or} \quad y-7 = -\sqrt{12} \\ y-7 &= 2\sqrt{3} \quad \text{or} \quad y-7 = -2\sqrt{3} \\ y &= 7+2\sqrt{3} \qquad y = 7-2\sqrt{3} \end{aligned}$$

The solutions are $7+2\sqrt{3}$ and $7-2\sqrt{3}$.

In Exercises 41–63, all of the unknown quantities must be positive. Therefore, only the positive square roots are used as solutions.

41.

$$\begin{aligned} 8^2+15^2 &= c^2 \\ 64+225 &= c^2 \\ 289 &= c^2 \\ c &= \sqrt{289} = 17 \end{aligned}$$

The missing length is 17 meters.

43.
$$\begin{aligned} 15^2 + 36^2 &= c^2 \\ 225 + 1296 &= c^2 \\ 1521 &= c^2 \\ c &= \sqrt{1521} \\ &= 39 \end{aligned}$$

The missing length is 39 meters.

45.
$$\begin{aligned} a^2 + 16^2 &= 20^2 \\ a^2 + 256 &= 400 \\ a^2 &= 144 \\ a &= \sqrt{144} \\ &= 12 \end{aligned}$$

The missing length is 12 centimeters.

47.
$$\begin{aligned} 9^2 + b^2 &= 16^2 \\ 81 + b^2 &= 256 \\ b^2 &= 175 \\ b &= \sqrt{175} \\ &= \sqrt{25}\sqrt{7} \\ &= 5\sqrt{7} \end{aligned}$$

The missing length is $5\sqrt{7}$ meters.

49. Let $x =$ the length of the ladder.

$$\begin{aligned} 8^2 + 10^2 &= x^2 \\ 64 + 100 &= x^2 \\ 164 &= x^2 \\ x &= \sqrt{164} = \sqrt{4}\sqrt{41} = 2\sqrt{41} \end{aligned}$$

The length of the ladder is $2\sqrt{41}$ feet.

51.
$$\begin{aligned} 90^2 + 90^2 &= x^2 \\ 8100 + 8100 &= x^2 \\ 16{,}200 &= x^2 \\ \sqrt{16{,}200} &= \sqrt{8100}\sqrt{2} = 90\sqrt{2} \end{aligned}$$

The distance from home plate to second base is $90\sqrt{2}$ feet.

53. Let $x =$ the length of a side of the screen.

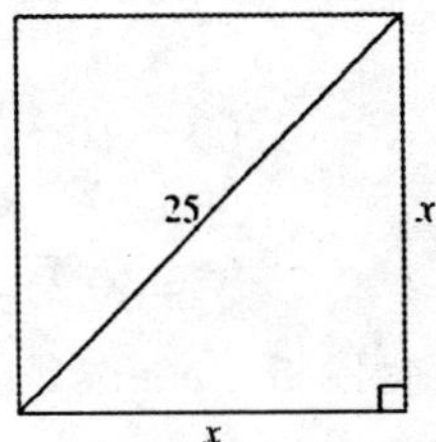

$$\begin{aligned} x^2 + x^2 &= 25^2 \\ 2x^2 &= 625 \\ x^2 &= \frac{625}{2} \\ x &= \sqrt{\frac{625}{2}} \end{aligned}$$

Simplify the radical.

$$\begin{aligned} \sqrt{\frac{625}{2}} &= \frac{\sqrt{625}}{\sqrt{2}} = \frac{25}{\sqrt{2}} \\ &= \frac{25}{\sqrt{2}} \cdot \frac{\sqrt{2}}{\sqrt{2}} = \frac{25\sqrt{2}}{2} \end{aligned}$$

The measure of the side of the screen is $\frac{25\sqrt{2}}{2}$ inches.

55. $A = \pi r^2$; $A = 36\pi$

$$\begin{aligned} 36\pi &= \pi r^2 \\ 36 &= r^2 \\ r &= \sqrt{36} = 6 \end{aligned}$$

The radius is 6 inches.

57. $W = 3t^2$; $W = 108$

$$\begin{aligned} 108 &= 3t^2 \\ 36 &= t^2 \\ t &= \sqrt{36} = 6 \end{aligned}$$

The fetus weighs 108 grams after 6 weeks.

59. $d = 16t^2$; $d = 400$

The rock must fall 400 feet to hit the water.

$$\begin{aligned} 400 &= 16t^2 \\ 25 &= t^2 \\ t &= \sqrt{25} = 5 \end{aligned}$$

It will take 5 seconds for the rock to hit the water.

61. The length of each side of the original garden is x meters + 2 meters = $(x+4)$ meters.
Larger square: $A = (x+4)^2$; $A = 144$

$$144 = (x+4)^2$$
$$x+4 = \sqrt{144} \quad \text{or} \quad x+4 = -\sqrt{144}$$
$$x+4 = 12 \quad \text{or} \quad x+4 = -12$$
$$x = 8 \qquad\qquad x = -16$$

Reject $= -16$ because a length cannot be negative. The length of the original square is 8 meters.

63. $V = lwh$; $V = 200, l = x, w = x, h = 2$

$$\begin{aligned} 200 &= x \cdot x \cdot 2 \\ 200 &= 2x^2 \\ 100 &= x^2 \\ x &= \sqrt{100} = 10 \end{aligned}$$

The length and width of the open box are both 10 inches.

For Exercises 65–67, answers may vary.

69. Statement c is true.
There is no real number whose square is negative.

71. $A = p(1+r)^2$ for $r (r > 0)$

$$\frac{A}{p} = (1+r)^2$$
$$\sqrt{\frac{A}{p}} = 1+r$$

Simplify the radical.

$$\sqrt{\frac{A}{p}} = \frac{\sqrt{A}}{\sqrt{p}} = \frac{\sqrt{A}}{\sqrt{p}} \cdot \frac{\sqrt{p}}{\sqrt{p}} = \frac{\sqrt{Ap}}{p}$$
$$1 + r = \frac{\sqrt{Ap}}{p}$$
$$r = \frac{\sqrt{Ap}}{p} - 1$$

73. $(x-1)^2 - 9 = 0$

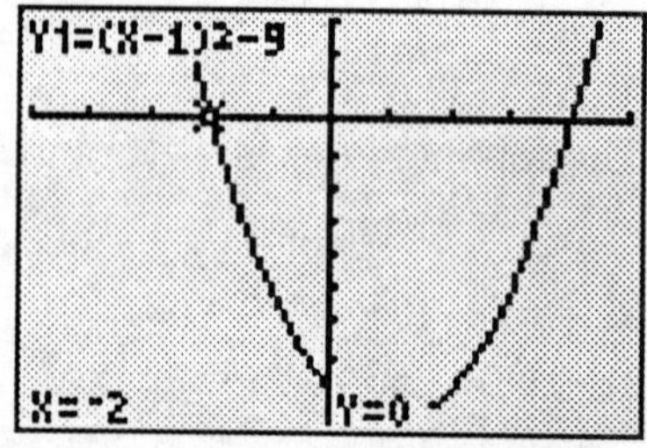

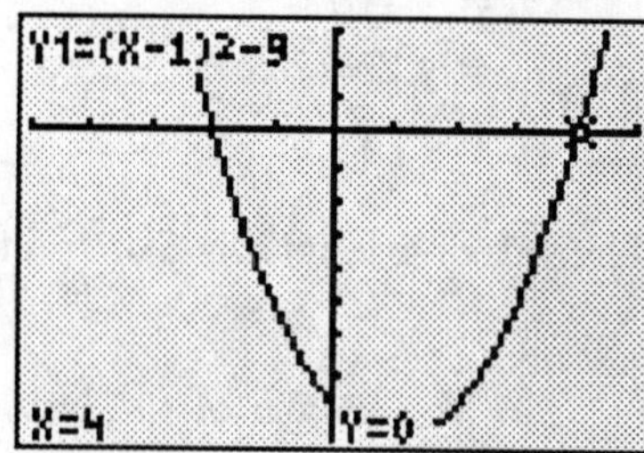

The x-intercepts of the graph are -2 and 4, so the solutions of the equation are -2 and 4.

Check -2:

$$\begin{aligned} (x-1)^2 - 9 &= 0 \\ (-2-1)^2 - 9 &\stackrel{?}{=} 0 \\ (-3)^2 - 9 &\stackrel{?}{=} 0 \\ 9 - 9 &\stackrel{?}{=} 0 \text{ true} \end{aligned}$$

Check 4:

$$\begin{aligned} (x-1)^2 - 9 &= 0 \\ (4-1)^2 - 9 &\stackrel{?}{=} 0 \\ 3^2 - 9 &\stackrel{?}{=} 0 \\ 9 - 9 &\stackrel{?}{=} 0 \text{ true} \end{aligned}$$

Review Exercises

74. $12x^2 + 14x - 6 = 2(6x^2 + 7x - 3)$
$= 2(2x+3)(3x-1)$

75. $\frac{x^2-x-6}{3x-3} \div \frac{x^2-4}{x-1}$

$$= \frac{x^2-x-6}{3x-3} \cdot \frac{x-1}{x^2-4}$$
$$= \frac{(x+2)(x-3)}{23(x-1)} \cdot \frac{(x-1)}{(x+2)(x-2)}$$
$$= \frac{x-3}{3(x-2)}$$

76.
$$\begin{aligned} 4(x-5) &= 22+2(6x+3) \\ 4x-20 &= 22+12x+6 \\ 4x-20 &= 28+12x \\ -8x-20 &= 28 \\ -8x &= 48 \\ x &= -6 \end{aligned}$$

The solution is -6.

10.2 Solving Quadratic Equations by Completing the Square

10.2 CHECK POINTS

CHECK POINT 1

a. x^2+10x

The coefficient of the x-term is 10. Half of 10 is 5, and $5^2=25$. Add 25.

$$x^2+10x+25=(x+5)^2$$

b. x^2-6x

The coefficient of the x-term is -6. Half of -6 is -3, and $(-3)^2=9$. Add 9.

$$x^2-6x+9=(x-3)^2$$

c. x^2+3x

The coefficient of the x-term is 3. Half of 3 is $\frac{3}{2}$, and $\left(\frac{3}{2}\right)^2=\frac{9}{4}$. Add $\frac{9}{4}$.

$$x^2+3x+\frac{9}{4}=\left(x+\frac{3}{2}\right)^2$$

CHECK POINT 2

a. $x^2+6x=7$

To complete the square on the binomial x^2+6x, take half of 6, which is 3, and square 3, giving 9. Add 9 to both sides of the equation to make the left side a perfect square binomial.

$$\begin{aligned} x^2+6x &= 7 \\ x^2+6x+9 &= 7+9 \\ (x+3)^2 &= 16 \end{aligned}$$
$$\begin{aligned} x+3 &= \sqrt{16} \quad \text{or} \quad & x+3 &= -\sqrt{16} \\ x+3 &= 4 & x+3 &= -4 \\ x &= 1 & x &= -7 \end{aligned}$$

The solutions are 1 and -7.

b. $x^2-10x+18=0$

First subtract 18 from both sides to isolate the binomial x^2-10x.

$$\begin{aligned} x^2-10x+18 &= 0 \\ x^2-10x &= -18 \end{aligned}$$

Next, complete the square. Take half of the coefficient of the x-term and square it. Half of -10 is -5, and $(-5)^2=25$, so add 25 to both sides of the equation.

$$\begin{aligned} x^2-10x+25 &= -18+25 \\ (x-5)^2 &= 7 \end{aligned}$$
$$\begin{aligned} x-5 &= \sqrt{7} \quad \text{or} \quad & &= -\sqrt{7} \\ x &= 5+\sqrt{7} & &= 5-\sqrt{7} \end{aligned}$$

The solutions are $5+\sqrt{7}$ and $5-\sqrt{7}$, which can be expressed in abbreviated notation as $5 \pm \sqrt{7}$.

CHECK POINT 3

$2x^2 - 10x - 1 = 0$

First, divide both sides of the equation by 2 so that the coefficient of the x^2-term will be 1.

$$2x^2 - 10x - 1 = 0$$
$$x^2 - 5x - \frac{1}{2} = 0$$

Next, add $\frac{1}{2}$ to both sides to isolate the binomial.

$$x^2 - 5x = \frac{1}{2}$$

Complete the square: Half of -5 is $-\frac{5}{2}$, and $\left(-\frac{5}{2}\right)^2 = \frac{25}{4}$, so add $\frac{25}{4}$ to both sides.

$$x^2 - 5x + \frac{25}{4} = \frac{1}{2} + \frac{25}{4}$$
$$\left(x - \frac{5}{2}\right)^2 = \frac{2}{4} + \frac{25}{4}$$
$$\left(x - \frac{5}{2}\right)^2 = \frac{27}{4}$$

$$x - \frac{5}{2} = \sqrt{\frac{27}{4}} \quad \text{or} \quad x - \frac{5}{2} = -\sqrt{\frac{27}{4}}$$

Simplify the radicals.

$$\sqrt{\frac{27}{4}} = \frac{\sqrt{27}}{\sqrt{4}} = \frac{\sqrt{9}\sqrt{3}}{2} = \frac{3\sqrt{3}}{2}$$

$$x - \frac{5}{2} = \frac{3\sqrt{3}}{2} \quad \text{or} \quad x - \frac{5}{2} = -\frac{3\sqrt{3}}{2}$$
$$x = \frac{5}{2} + \frac{3\sqrt{3}}{2} \quad \text{or} \quad x = \frac{5}{2} - \frac{3\sqrt{3}}{2}$$
$$x = \frac{5 + 3\sqrt{3}}{2} \quad \text{or} \quad x = \frac{5 - 3\sqrt{3}}{2}$$

The solutions are $\frac{5+3\sqrt{3}}{2}$ and $\frac{5-3\sqrt{3}}{2}$, which can be written in abbreviated notation as $\frac{5\pm3\sqrt{3}}{2}$.

EXERCISE SET 10.2

1. $x^2 + 4x$

The coefficient of the x-term is 4. Half of 4 is 2, and $2^2 = 4$. Add 4.

$$x^2 + 4x + 4 = (x+2)^2$$

3. $x^2 - 10x$

The coefficient of the x-term is -10. Half of -10 is -5, and $(-5)^2 = 25$. Add 25.

$$x^2 - 10x + 25 = (x-5)^2$$

5. $x^2 + 7x$

The coefficient of the x-term is 7. Half of 7 is $\frac{7}{2}$, and $\left(\frac{7}{2}\right)^2 = \frac{49}{4}$. Add $\frac{49}{4}$.

$$x^2 + 7x + \frac{49}{4} = \left(x + \frac{7}{2}\right)^2$$

7. $x^2 - 3x$

$\frac{1}{2}(-3) = -\frac{3}{2}$; $\left(-\frac{3}{2}\right)^2 = \frac{9}{4}$

$$x^2 - 3x + \frac{9}{4} = \left(x - \frac{3}{2}\right)^2$$

9. $x^2 + \frac{1}{2}x$

$\frac{1}{2}\left(\frac{1}{2}\right) = \frac{1}{4}$; $\left(\frac{1}{4}\right)^2 = \frac{1}{16}$

$$x^2 + \frac{1}{2}x + \frac{1}{16} = \left(x + \frac{1}{4}\right)^2$$

11. $x^2 - \frac{4}{3}x$

$\frac{1}{2}\left(-\frac{4}{3}\right) = -\frac{2}{3}$; $\left(-\frac{2}{3}\right)^2 = \frac{4}{9}$

$$x^2 - \frac{4}{3}x + \frac{4}{9} = \left(x - \frac{2}{3}\right)^2$$

13. $x^2 + 4x = 5$

To complete the square on the binomial $x^2 + 4x$, take half of 4, which is 2, and square 2, giving 4. Add 4 to both sides of the equation to make the left side a perfect square binomial.

$$x^2 + 4x = 5$$
$$x^2 + 4x + 4 = 5 + 4$$
$$(x+2)^2 = 9$$
$$x + 2 = \sqrt{9} \quad \text{or} \quad x + 2 = -\sqrt{9}$$
$$x + 2 = 3 \qquad x + 2 = -3$$
$$x = 1 \qquad x = -5$$

The solutions are 1 and -5.

15. $x^2 - 10x = -24$

To complete the square on the binomial $x^2 - 10x$, take half of -10, which is -5, and square -5, giving 25. Add 25 to both sides of the equation to make the left side a perfect square binomial.

$$x^2 - 10x + 25 = -24 + 25$$
$$(x-5)^2 = 1$$
$$x - 5 = \sqrt{1} \quad \text{or} \quad x - 5 = -1$$
$$x - 5 = 1 \quad \text{or} \quad x - 5 = -1$$
$$x = 6 \qquad x = 4$$

The solutions are 6 and 4.

17. $x^2 - 2x = 5$

$\frac{1}{2}(-2) = -1; (-1)^2 = 1$

$$x^2 - 2x + 1 = 5 + 1$$
$$(x-1)^2 = 6$$
$$x - 1 = \sqrt{6} \quad \text{or} \quad x - 1 = -\sqrt{6}$$
$$x = 1 + \sqrt{6} \quad \text{or} \quad x = 1 - \sqrt{6}$$

The solutions are $1 + \sqrt{6}$ and $1 - \sqrt{6}$.

19. $x^2 + 4x + 1 = 0$

First subtract 1 from both sides to isolate the binomial $x^2 + 4x$.

$$x^2 + 4x = -1$$

$\frac{1}{2}(4) = 2; 2^2 = 4$

$$x^2 + 4x + 4 = -1 + 4$$
$$(x+2)^2 = 3$$
$$x + 2 = \sqrt{3} \quad \text{or} \quad x + 2 = -\sqrt{3}$$
$$x = -2 + \sqrt{3} \quad \text{or} \quad x = -2 - \sqrt{3}$$

The solutions are $-2 + \sqrt{3}$ and $-2 - \sqrt{3}$.

21. $x^2 - 3x = 28$

$\frac{1}{2}(-3) = -\frac{3}{2}; \left(-\frac{3}{2}\right)^2 = \frac{9}{4}$

$$x^2 - 3x + \frac{9}{4} = 28 + \frac{9}{4}$$
$$\left(x - \frac{3}{2}\right) = \frac{121}{4}$$

$$x - \frac{3}{2} = \sqrt{\frac{121}{4}} \quad \text{or} \quad x - \frac{3}{2} = -\sqrt{\frac{121}{4}}$$
$$x - \frac{3}{2} = \frac{11}{2} \quad \text{or} \quad x - \frac{3}{2} = -\frac{11}{2}$$
$$x = \frac{14}{2} = 7 \qquad x = -\frac{8}{2} = -4$$

The solutions are 7 and -4.

23. $x^2 + 3x - 1 = 0$

$$x^2 + 3x = 1$$

$$\frac{1}{2}(3) = \frac{3}{2};\ \left(\frac{3}{2}\right)^2 = \frac{9}{4}$$

$$x^2 + 3x + \frac{9}{4} = 1 + \frac{9}{4}$$

$$\left(x + \frac{3}{2}\right) = \frac{13}{4}$$

$$x + \frac{3}{2} = \sqrt{\frac{13}{4}} \quad \text{or} \quad x + \frac{3}{2} = -\sqrt{\frac{13}{4}}$$

$$x + \frac{3}{2} = \frac{\sqrt{13}}{2} \quad \text{or} \quad x + \frac{3}{2} = -\frac{\sqrt{13}}{2}$$

$$x = -\frac{3}{2} + \frac{\sqrt{13}}{2} \quad \text{or} \quad x = -\frac{3}{2} - \frac{\sqrt{13}}{2}$$

$$x = \frac{-3 + \sqrt{13}}{2} \quad \text{or} \quad x = \frac{-3 - \sqrt{13}}{2}$$

The solutions are $\frac{-3+\sqrt{13}}{2}$ and $\frac{-3-\sqrt{13}}{2}$, which can be written in abbreviated form as $\frac{-3\pm\sqrt{13}}{2}$.

25. $x^2 = 7x - 3$

$$x^2 - 7x = -3$$

$$\frac{1}{2}(-7) = -\frac{7}{2};\ \left(-\frac{7}{2}\right)^2 = \frac{49}{4}$$

$$x^2 - 7x + \frac{49}{4} = -3 + \frac{49}{4}$$

$$\left(x - \frac{7}{2}\right)^2 = \frac{-12}{4} + \frac{49}{4}$$

$$\left(x - \frac{7}{2}\right)^2 = \frac{37}{4}$$

$$x - \frac{7}{2} = \sqrt{\frac{37}{4}} \quad \text{or} \quad x - \frac{7}{2} = -\sqrt{\frac{37}{4}}$$

$$x - \frac{7}{2} = \frac{\sqrt{37}}{2} \quad \text{or} \quad x - \frac{7}{2} = -\frac{\sqrt{37}}{2}$$

$$x = \frac{7}{2} + \frac{\sqrt{37}}{2} \quad \text{or} \quad x = \frac{7}{2} - \frac{\sqrt{37}}{2}$$

$$x = \frac{7 + \sqrt{37}}{2} \quad \text{or} \quad x = \frac{7 - \sqrt{37}}{2}$$

The solutions are $\frac{7\pm\sqrt{37}}{2}$.

27. $2x^2 - 2x - 6 = 0$

First, divide both sides of the equation by 2 so that the coefficient of the x^2-term will be 1.

$$x^2 - x - 3 = 0$$

Next, add 3 to both sides to isolate the binomial.

$$x^2 - x = 3$$

Complete the square: The coefficient of the x-term is -1, and $\frac{1}{2}(-1) = -\frac{1}{2}$, so add $\left(-\frac{1}{2}\right)^2 = \frac{1}{4}$ to both sides.

$$x^2 - x + \frac{1}{4} = 3 + \frac{1}{4}$$

$$\left(x - \frac{1}{2}\right)^2 = \frac{13}{4}$$

$$x - \frac{1}{2} = \sqrt{\frac{13}{4}} \quad \text{or} \quad x - \frac{1}{2} = -\sqrt{\frac{13}{4}}$$

$$x - \frac{1}{2} = \frac{\sqrt{13}}{2} \quad \text{or} \quad x - \frac{1}{2} = -\frac{\sqrt{13}}{2}$$

$$x = \frac{1 + \sqrt{13}}{2} \quad \text{or} \quad x = \frac{1 - \sqrt{13}}{2}$$

The solutions are $\frac{1\pm\sqrt{13}}{2}$.

29. $2x^2 - 3x + 1 = 0$

$$x^2 - \frac{3}{2}x + \frac{1}{2} = 0$$

$$x^2 - \frac{3}{2}x = -\frac{1}{2}$$

$$\frac{1}{2}\left(-\frac{3}{2}\right) = -\frac{3}{4};\ \left(-\frac{3}{4}\right)^2 = \frac{9}{16}$$

$$x^2 - \frac{3}{2}x + \frac{9}{16} = -\frac{1}{2} + \frac{9}{16}$$

$$\left(x - \frac{3}{4}\right)^2 = -\frac{8}{16} + \frac{9}{16}$$

$$\left(x - \frac{3}{4}\right)^2 = \frac{1}{16}$$

$$x - \frac{3}{4} = \sqrt{\frac{1}{16}} \quad \text{or} \quad x - \frac{3}{4} = -\sqrt{\frac{1}{16}}$$
$$x - \frac{3}{4} = \frac{1}{4} \qquad x - \frac{3}{4} = -\frac{1}{4}$$
$$x = 1 \qquad x = \frac{2}{4} = \frac{1}{2}$$

The solutions are 1 and $\frac{1}{2}$.

31. $2x^2 + 10x + 11 = 0$

$$x^2 + 5x + \frac{11}{2} = 0$$
$$x^2 + 5x = -\frac{11}{2}$$
$$\frac{1}{2}(5) = \frac{5}{2}; \left(\frac{5}{2}\right)^2 = \frac{25}{4}$$
$$x^2 + 5x + \frac{25}{4} = -\frac{11}{2} + \frac{25}{4}$$
$$\left(x + \frac{5}{2}\right)^2 = -\frac{22}{4} + \frac{25}{4}$$
$$\left(x + \frac{5}{2}\right)^2 = \frac{3}{4}$$
$$x + \frac{5}{2} = \sqrt{\frac{3}{4}} \quad \text{or} \quad x + \frac{5}{2} = -\sqrt{\frac{3}{4}}$$
$$x + \frac{5}{2} = \frac{\sqrt{3}}{2} \quad \text{or} \quad x + \frac{5}{2} = -\frac{\sqrt{3}}{2}$$
$$x = -\frac{5}{2} + \frac{\sqrt{3}}{2} \quad \text{or} \quad x = -\frac{5}{2} - \frac{\sqrt{3}}{2}$$
$$x = \frac{-5 + \sqrt{3}}{2} \quad \text{or} \quad x = \frac{-5 - \sqrt{3}}{2}$$

The solutions are $\frac{-5 \pm \sqrt{3}}{2}$.

33. $4x^2 - 2x - 3 = 0$

$$x^2 - \frac{1}{2}x - \frac{3}{4} = 0$$
$$x^2 - \frac{1}{2}x = \frac{3}{4}$$
$$\frac{1}{2}\left(-\frac{1}{2}\right) = -\frac{1}{4}; \left(-\frac{1}{4}\right)^2 = \frac{1}{16}$$
$$x^2 - \frac{1}{2}x + \frac{1}{16} = \frac{3}{4} + \frac{1}{16}$$
$$\left(x - \frac{1}{4}\right)^2 = \frac{12}{16} + \frac{1}{16}$$
$$\left(x - \frac{1}{4}\right)^2 = \frac{13}{16}$$
$$x - \frac{1}{4} = \sqrt{\frac{13}{16}} \quad \text{or} \quad x - \frac{1}{4} = -\sqrt{\frac{13}{16}}$$
$$x - \frac{1}{4} = \frac{\sqrt{13}}{4} \quad \text{or} \quad x - \frac{1}{4} = -\frac{\sqrt{13}}{4}$$
$$x = \frac{1}{4} + \frac{\sqrt{13}}{4} \quad \text{or} \quad x = \frac{1}{4} - \frac{\sqrt{13}}{4}$$
$$x = \frac{1 + \sqrt{13}}{4} \quad \text{or} \quad x = \frac{1 - \sqrt{13}}{4}$$

The solutions are $\frac{1 \pm \sqrt{13}}{4}$.

35. Answers may vary.

37. Statement d is true.

$\frac{1}{2}(-7) = -\frac{7}{2}$, and $\left(-\frac{7}{2}\right)^2 = \frac{49}{4}$.

39. $x^2 + x + c = 0$

Subtract c from both sides to isolate the binomial $x^2 + x$.

$$x^2 + x = -c$$

The coefficient of the x-term is 1.

$\frac{1}{2}(1) = \frac{1}{2}$, and $\left(\frac{1}{2}\right)^2 = \frac{1}{4}$, so add $\frac{1}{4}$ to both sides.

$$x^2 + x + \frac{1}{4} = \frac{1}{4} - c$$
$$\left(x + \frac{1}{2}\right)^2 = \frac{1}{4} - \frac{4c}{4}$$
$$\left(x + \frac{1}{2}\right)^2 = \frac{1 - 4c}{4}$$

$$x + \frac{1}{2} = \sqrt{\frac{1-4c}{4}}$$
$$x + \frac{1}{2} = \frac{\sqrt{1-4c}}{2}$$
$$x = -\frac{1}{2} + \frac{\sqrt{1-4c}}{2}$$
$$x = \frac{-1+\sqrt{1-4c}}{2}$$

or

$$x + \frac{1}{2} = -\sqrt{\frac{1-4c}{4}}$$
$$x + \frac{1}{2} = -\frac{\sqrt{1-4c}}{2}$$
$$x = -\frac{1}{2} - \frac{\sqrt{1-4c}}{2}$$
$$x = \frac{-1-\sqrt{1-4c}}{2}$$

The solutions are $\frac{-1\pm\sqrt{1-4c}}{2}$.

Note: If terms are not combined and the radical is not simplified, the solutions will be written in a different, but equivalent form: $-\frac{1}{2} \pm \sqrt{\frac{1}{4} - c}$.

41. Answers will vary depending on the equations chosen. As an example, the solution for equation in Exercise 17 is shown here. In Exercise 17, the solutions to the equation $x^2 - 2x = 5$ were found to be $1 + \sqrt{6}$ and $1 - \sqrt{6}$. Use a calculator to obtain decimal approximation for these solutions.

$$1 + \sqrt{6} \approx 3.45$$
$$1 - \sqrt{6} \approx -1.45$$

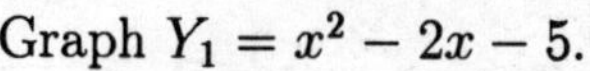
Graph $Y_1 = x^2 - 2x - 5$.

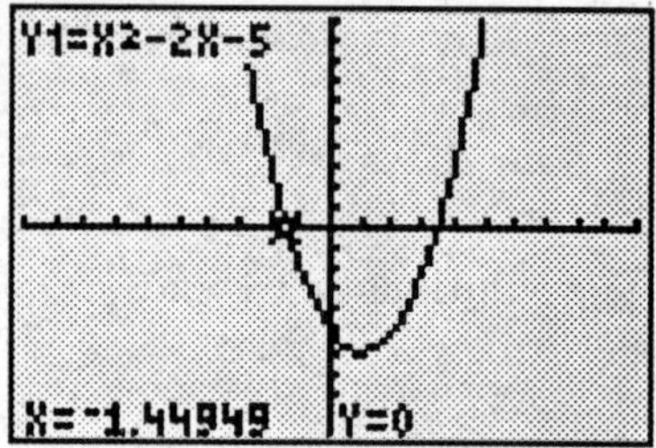

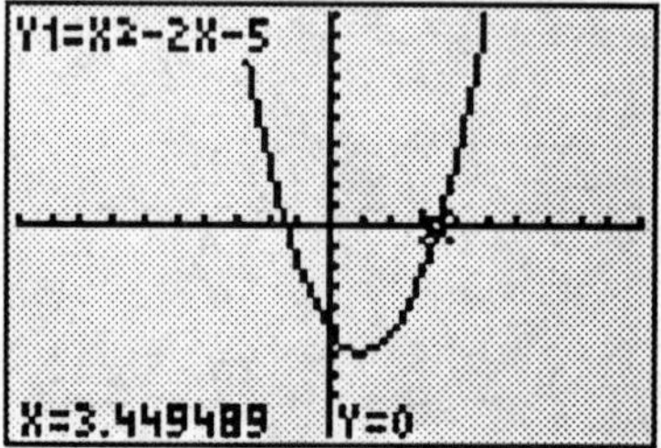

The x-intercepts of $y = x^2 - 2x - 5$ verify the solution.

Review Exercises

42. $$\frac{2x+3}{x^2-7x+12} - \frac{2}{x-3}$$
$$= \frac{2x+3}{(x-3)(x-4)} - \frac{2}{x-3}$$
$$= \frac{2x+3}{(x-3)(x-4)} - \frac{2(x-4)}{(x-3)(x-4)}$$
$$= \frac{(2x+3)-2(x-4)}{(x-3)(x-4)}$$
$$= \frac{2x+3-2x+8}{(x-3)(x-4)}$$
$$= \frac{11}{(x-3)(x-4)}$$

43. $\dfrac{x-\frac{1}{3}}{3-\frac{1}{x}}$

LCD $= 3x$

$$\frac{x-\frac{1}{3}}{3-\frac{1}{x}} = \frac{3x}{3x}\cdot\frac{\left(x-\frac{1}{3}\right)}{\left(3-\frac{1}{x}\right)}$$
$$= \frac{3x\cdot x - 3x\cdot\frac{1}{3}}{3x\cdot 3 - 3x\cdot\frac{1}{x}}$$
$$= \frac{3x^2 - x}{9x-3}$$
$$= \frac{x(3x-1)}{3(3x-1)} = \frac{x}{3}$$

44. $\sqrt{2x+3} = 2x-3$

Square both sides.

$$(\sqrt{2x+3})^2 = (2x-3)^2$$
$$2x+3 = (2x)^2 - 2\cdot 2x\cdot 3 + 3^2$$
$$2x+3 = 4x^2 - 12x + 9$$
$$0 = 4x^2 - 14x + 6$$
$$0 = 2(2x^2 - 7x + 3)$$
$$0 = 2(2x-1)(x-3)$$
$$2x-1=0 \quad \text{or} \quad x-3=0$$
$$x = \frac{1}{2} \qquad\qquad x = 3$$

Each of the proposed solutions must be checked in the original equation.

Check $\frac{1}{2}$:

$$\sqrt{2x+3} = 2x-3$$
$$\sqrt{2\left(\frac{1}{2}\right)+3} \stackrel{?}{=} 2\left(\frac{1}{2}\right) - 3$$
$$\sqrt{1+3} \stackrel{?}{=} 1-3$$
$$\sqrt{4} \stackrel{?}{=} 1-3$$
$$2 = -2 \text{ false}$$

Check 3:

$$\sqrt{2x+3} = 2x-3$$
$$\sqrt{2\cdot 3+3} \stackrel{?}{=} 2\cdot 3 - 3$$
$$\sqrt{6+3} \stackrel{?}{=} 6-3$$
$$\sqrt{9} \stackrel{?}{=} 3$$
$$3 = 3 \text{ true}$$

Thus, $\frac{1}{2}$ is an extraneous solution, while 3 satisfies the equation. Therefore, the only solution is 3.

10.3 The Quadratic Formula

10.3 CHECK POINTS

CHECK POINT 1

$8x^2 + 2x - 1 = 0$

Identify the values of $a, b,$ and c:

$$a = 8, b = 2, c = -1.$$

Substitute these values into the quadratic formula and simplify to get the equation's solutions.

$$x = \frac{-b \pm \sqrt{b^2 - 4ac}}{2a}$$
$$= \frac{-2 \pm \sqrt{2^2 - 4(8)(-1)}}{2(8)}$$
$$= \frac{-2 \pm \sqrt{4+32}}{16}$$
$$= \frac{-2 \pm \sqrt{36}}{16}$$
$$= \frac{-2 \pm 6}{16}$$
$$x = \frac{-2+6}{6} \quad \text{or} \quad x = \frac{-2-6}{16}$$
$$= \frac{4}{16} = \frac{1}{4} \qquad = -\frac{8}{16} = -\frac{1}{2}$$

The solutions are $\frac{1}{4}$ and $-\frac{1}{2}$.

CHECK POINT 2

$x^2 = 6x - 4$

Rewrite the equation in standard form.

$$x^2 - 6x + 4 = 0$$

Identify a, b, and c.

$$a = 1, b = -6, c = 4$$

Substitute these values into the quadratic formula and simplify.

$$\begin{aligned} x &= \frac{-b \pm \sqrt{b^2 - 4ac}}{2a} \\ &= \frac{-(-6) \pm \sqrt{(-6)^2 - 4(1)(4)}}{2 \cdot 1} \\ &= \frac{6 \pm \sqrt{36 - 16}}{2} \\ &= \frac{6 \pm \sqrt{20}}{2} \\ &= \frac{6 \pm 2\sqrt{5}}{2} \\ &= \frac{2(3 \pm \sqrt{5})}{2} \\ &= 3 \pm \sqrt{5} \end{aligned}$$

The solutions are $3 \pm \sqrt{5}$.

CHECK POINT 3

$N = 0.4t^2 + 0.5$; $N = 4$

$$4 = 0.4x^2 + 0.5$$

Because the quadratic equation contains no x-term, so this equation can be solved by using the square root property.

$$\begin{aligned} 0.4x^2 + 0.5 &= 4 \\ 0.4x^2 &= 3.5 \\ x^2 &= \frac{3.5}{0.4} = 8.75 \end{aligned}$$

$$\begin{aligned} x &= \sqrt{8.75} \quad \text{or} \quad x = -\sqrt{8.75} \\ x &\approx 3 \qquad\qquad\; x \approx -3 \end{aligned}$$

The model describes the millions of years x years *after* 1996. Therefore, -3, which represents 3 years *before* 1996, is not part of the time period modeled by the formula. The solution (to the nearest integer) is 3. This means that 3 years after 1996, in 1999, there were 4 million Americans using cable-TV modems. This matches the actual number shown in the bar graph for 1999 exactly.

CHECK POINT 4

$N = 23.4x^2 - 259.1x + 815.8$; $N = 250$

$$\begin{aligned} 250 &= 23.4x^2 - 259.1x + 815.8 \\ 0 &= 23.4x^2 - 259.1x + 565.8 \end{aligned}$$

Use the quadratic formula with $a = 23.4$, $b = -259.1$, and $c = 565.8$.

$$\begin{aligned} x &= \frac{-b \pm \sqrt{b^2 - 4ac}}{2a} \\ &= \frac{-(-259.1) \pm \sqrt{(-259.1)^2 - 4(23.5)(565.8)}}{2(23.4)} \\ &= \frac{259.1 \pm \sqrt{14{,}173.93}}{46.8} \\ &\approx \frac{259.1 \pm 199.1}{46.8} \end{aligned}$$

$$x \approx \frac{259.1 + 119.1}{46.8} \quad \text{or} \quad x \approx \frac{259.1 - 119.1}{46.8}$$

$$x \approx 8 \qquad\qquad x \approx 3$$

The formula predicts that there were 250 police officers convicted of felonies 3 years and 8 years after 1990, that is, in the years 1993 and 1998. However, 1993 is not after 1994.

For the year 1998, the bar graphs appears to show about 250 convictions, so the formula models the data extremely well.

EXERCISE SET 10.3

1. $x^2 + 8x + 15 = 0$

Identify the values of $a, b,$ and c:

$$a = 1, b = 8, \text{ and } c = 15.$$

Substitute these values into the quadratic formula and simplify to get the equation's solutions.

$$\begin{aligned} x &= \frac{-b \pm \sqrt{b^2 - 4ac}}{2a} \\ x &= \frac{-8 \pm \sqrt{8^2 - 4(1)(15)}}{2(1)} \\ &= \frac{-8 \pm \sqrt{64 - 60}}{2} \\ &= \frac{-8 \pm \sqrt{4}}{2} \\ &= \frac{-8 \pm 2}{2} \end{aligned}$$

$$x = \frac{-8+2}{2} \quad \text{or} \quad x = \frac{-8-2}{2}$$

$$= \frac{-6}{2} = -3 \qquad = \frac{-10}{2} = -5$$

The solutions are -3 and -5.

3. $x^2 + 5x + 3 = 0$
$a = 1, b = 5, c = 3$

$$\begin{aligned} x &= \frac{-b \pm \sqrt{b^2 - 4ac}}{2a} \\ x &= \frac{-5 \pm \sqrt{5^2 - 4(1)(3)}}{2 \cdot 1} \\ &= \frac{-5 \pm \sqrt{25 - 12}}{2} \\ &= \frac{-5 \pm \sqrt{13}}{2} \end{aligned}$$

The solutions are $\frac{-5 \pm \sqrt{13}}{2}$.

5. $x^2 + 4x - 6 = 0$
$a = 1, b = 4, c = -6$

$$\begin{aligned} x &= \frac{-b \pm \sqrt{b^2 - 4ac}}{2a} \\ x &= \frac{-4 \pm \sqrt{4^2 - 4(1)(-6)}}{2 \cdot 1} \\ &= \frac{-4 \pm \sqrt{16 + 24}}{2} \\ &= \frac{-4 \pm \sqrt{40}}{2} \\ &= \frac{-4 \pm 2\sqrt{10}}{2} \\ &= \frac{2(-2 \pm \sqrt{10})}{2} \\ &= -2 \pm \sqrt{10} \end{aligned}$$

The solutions are $-2 \pm \sqrt{10}$.

7. $x^2 + 4x - 7 = 0$
$a = 1, b = 4, c = -7$

$$\begin{aligned} x &= \frac{-b \pm \sqrt{b^2 - 4ac}}{2a} \\ &= \frac{-4 \pm \sqrt{4^2 - 4(1)(-7)}}{2 \cdot 1} \\ &= \frac{-4 \pm \sqrt{16 + 28}}{2} \\ &= \frac{-4 \pm \sqrt{44}}{2} \\ &= \frac{-4 \pm 2\sqrt{11}}{2} \\ &= \frac{2(-2 \pm \sqrt{11})}{2} \\ &= -2 \pm \sqrt{11} \end{aligned}$$

The solutions are $-2 \pm \sqrt{11}$.

9. $x^2 - 3x - 18 = 0$
$a = 1, b = -3, c = -18$

$$\begin{aligned}x &= \frac{-b \pm \sqrt{b^2 - 4ac}}{2a}\\ &= \frac{-(-3) \pm \sqrt{(-3)^2 - 4(1)(-18)}}{2 \cdot 1}\\ &= \frac{3 \pm \sqrt{9 + 72}}{2}\\ &= \frac{3 \pm \sqrt{81}}{2}\\ &= \frac{3 \pm 9}{2}\end{aligned}$$

$$x = \frac{3+9}{2} \quad \text{or} \quad x = \frac{3-9}{2}$$

$$x = \frac{12}{2} = 6 \quad \text{or} \quad x = \frac{-6}{2} = -3$$

The solutions are 6 and -3.

11. $6x^2 - 5x - 6 = 0$
$a = 6, b = -5, c = -6$

$$\begin{aligned}x &= \frac{-b \pm \sqrt{b^2 - 4ac}}{2a}\\ &= \frac{-(-5) \pm \sqrt{(-5)^2 - 4(6)(-6)}}{2 \cdot 6}\\ &= \frac{5 \pm \sqrt{25 + 144}}{12}\\ &= \frac{5 \pm \sqrt{169}}{12} = \frac{5 \pm 13}{12}\end{aligned}$$

$$x = \frac{5+13}{12} \quad \text{or} \quad x = \frac{5-13}{12}$$

$$x = \frac{18}{12} = \frac{3}{2} \quad \text{or} \quad x = \frac{-8}{12} = -\frac{2}{3}$$

The solutions are $\frac{3}{2}$ and $-\frac{2}{3}$.

13. $x^2 - 2x - 10 = 0$
$a = 1, b = -2, c = -10$

$$\begin{aligned}x &= \frac{-b \pm \sqrt{b^2 - 4ac}}{2a}\\ &= \frac{-(-2) \pm \sqrt{(-2)^2 - 4(1)(-10)}}{2 \cdot 1}\\ &= \frac{2 \pm \sqrt{4 + 40}}{2} = \frac{2 \pm \sqrt{44}}{2}\\ &= \frac{2 \pm 2\sqrt{11}}{2}\\ &= \frac{2(1 \pm \sqrt{11})}{2}\\ &= 1 \pm \sqrt{11}\end{aligned}$$

The solutions are $1 \pm \sqrt{11}$.

15. $x^2 - x = 14$

Rewrite the equation in standard form.

$$x^2 - x - 14 = 0$$

Identify $a, b,$ and c.

$$a = 1, b = -1, c = -14$$

Substitute these values into the quadratic formula.

$$\begin{aligned}x &= \frac{-b \pm \sqrt{b^2 - 4ac}}{2a}\\ &= \frac{-(-1) \pm \sqrt{(-1)^2 - 4(1)(-14)}}{2 \cdot 1}\\ &= \frac{1 \pm \sqrt{1 + 56}}{2} = \frac{1 \pm \sqrt{57}}{2}\end{aligned}$$

The radical cannot be simplified.
The solutions are $\frac{1 \pm \sqrt{57}}{2}$.

17. $6x^2 + 6x + 1 = 0$
$a = 6, b = 6, c = 1$

$$\begin{aligned} x &= \frac{-b \pm \sqrt{b^2 - 4ac}}{2a} \\ &= \frac{-6 \pm \sqrt{6^2 - 4(6)(1)}}{2 \cdot 6} \\ &= \frac{-6 \pm \sqrt{36 - 24}}{12} \\ &= \frac{-6 \pm \sqrt{12}}{12} \\ &= \frac{-6 \pm 2\sqrt{3}}{12} \\ &= \frac{2(-3 \pm \sqrt{3})}{12} \\ &= \frac{-3 \pm \sqrt{3}}{6} \end{aligned}$$

The solutions are $\frac{-3 \pm \sqrt{3}}{6}$.

19. $4x^2 - 12x + 9 = 0$
$a = 4, b = -12, c = 9$

$$\begin{aligned} x &= \frac{-b \pm \sqrt{b^2 - 4ac}}{2a} \\ &= \frac{-(-12) \pm \sqrt{(-12)^2 - 4(4)(9)}}{2 \cdot 4} \\ &= \frac{12 \pm \sqrt{144 - 144}}{8} \\ &= \frac{12 \pm \sqrt{0}}{8} \\ &= \frac{12 \pm 0}{8} \\ &= \frac{12}{8} \\ &= \frac{3}{2} \end{aligned}$$

The only solution is $\frac{3}{2}$.

21. $4x^2 = 2x + 7$

Rewrite the equation in standard form.

$$4x^2 - 2x - 7 = 0$$

$a = 4, b = -2, c = -7$

$$\begin{aligned} x &= \frac{-b \pm \sqrt{b^2 - 4ac}}{2a} \\ &= \frac{-(-2) \pm \sqrt{(-2)^2 - 4(4)(-7)}}{2 \cdot 4} \\ &= \frac{2 \pm \sqrt{4 + 112}}{8} \\ &= \frac{2 \pm \sqrt{116}}{8} \\ &= \frac{2 \pm 2\sqrt{29}}{8} \\ &= \frac{2(1 \pm \sqrt{29})}{8} \\ &= \frac{1 \pm \sqrt{29}}{4} \end{aligned}$$

The solutions are $\frac{1 \pm \sqrt{29}}{4}$.

23. $2x^2 - x = 1$

Write the equation in standard form.

$$2x^2 - x - 1 = 0$$

Factor the trinomial.

$$(2x + 1)(x - 1) = 0$$

Use the zero-product property.

$$\begin{aligned} 2x + 1 &= 0 \quad \text{or} \quad & x - 1 &= 0 \\ 2x &= -1 & x &= 1 \\ x &= -\frac{1}{2} \end{aligned}$$

The solutions are 1 and $-\frac{1}{2}$.

25. $5x^2 + 2 = 11x$

Write the equation in standard form.

$$5x^2 - 11x + 2 = 0$$

Factor the trinomial.

$$(5x - 1)(x - 2) = 0$$

Use the zero-product property.

$$\begin{aligned} 5x - 1 &= 0 \quad \text{or} \quad & x - 2 &= 0 \\ 5x &= 1 & x &= 2 \\ x &= \frac{1}{5} \end{aligned}$$

The solutions are $\frac{1}{5}$ and 2.

27. $3x^2 = 60$
$x^2 = 20$

Use the square root property.

$$\begin{aligned} x &= \sqrt{20} \quad \text{or} \quad & x &= -\sqrt{20} \\ x &= 2\sqrt{5} & x &= -2\sqrt{5} \end{aligned}$$

The solutions are $2\sqrt{5}$ and $-2\sqrt{5}$.

29. $x^2 - 2x = 1$

Write the equation in standard form.

$$x^2 - 2x - 1 = 0$$

The trinomial is prime, so we cannot factor and use the zero-product property. Instead, use the quadratic formula with $a = 1, b = -2$, and $c = -1$.

$$\begin{aligned} x &= \frac{-b \pm \sqrt{b^2 - 4ac}}{2a} \\ &= \frac{-(-2) \pm \sqrt{(-2)^2 - 4(1)(-1)}}{2 \cdot 1} \\ &= \frac{2 \pm \sqrt{4 + 4}}{2} \\ &= \frac{2 \pm \sqrt{8}}{2} \\ &= \frac{2 \pm 2\sqrt{2}}{2} \\ &= \frac{2(1 \pm \sqrt{2})}{2} \\ &= 1 \pm \sqrt{2} \end{aligned}$$

The solutions are $1 \pm \sqrt{2}$.

31. $(2x + 3)(x + 4) = 1$

Write the equation in standard form.

$$\begin{aligned} 2x^2 + 11x + 12 &= 1 \\ 2x^2 + 11x + 11 &= 0 \end{aligned}$$

The trinomial cannot be factored, so use the quadratic formula with $a = 2, b = 11$, and $c = 11$.

$$\begin{aligned} x &= \frac{-b \pm \sqrt{b^2 - 4ac}}{2a} \\ &= \frac{-11 \pm \sqrt{11^2 - 4(2)(11)}}{2 \cdot 2} \\ &= \frac{-11 \pm \sqrt{121 - 88}}{4} \\ &= \frac{-11 \pm \sqrt{33}}{4} \end{aligned}$$

The solutions are $\frac{-11 \pm \sqrt{33}}{4}$.

33. $(3x-4)^2 = 16$

Use the square root property.

$$\begin{aligned} 3x - 4 &= \sqrt{16} \\ 3x - 4 &= 4 \\ 3x &= 8 \\ x &= \frac{8}{3} \end{aligned}$$

or

$$\begin{aligned} 3x - 4 &= -\sqrt{16} \\ 3x - 4 &= -4 \\ 3x &= 0 \\ x &= 0 \end{aligned}$$

The solutions are $\frac{8}{3}$ and 0.

35. $$\begin{aligned} 3x^2 - 12x + 12 &= 0 \\ 3(x^2 - 4x + 4) &= 0 \\ 3(x-2) &= 0 \\ (x-2)^2 &= 0 \\ x - 2 &= 0 \\ x &= 2 \end{aligned}$$

The only solution is 2.

37. $$\begin{aligned} 4x^2 - 16 &= 0 \\ 4(x^2 - 4) &= 0 \\ 4(x+2)(x-2) &= 0 \end{aligned}$$

$$x + 2 = 0 \quad \text{or} \quad x - 2 = 0$$
$$x = -2 \qquad\qquad x = 2$$

The solutions are -2 and 2.

39. $x^2 + 9x = 0$

$x(x+9) = 0$

$x = 0$ or $x + 9 = 0$

$x = -9$

The solutions are 0 and -9.

41. $\frac{3}{4}x^2 - \frac{5}{2}x - 2 = 0$

To clear fractions, multiply both sides by the LCD, 4.

$$\begin{aligned} 4\left(\frac{3}{4}x^2 - \frac{5}{2}x - 2\right) &= 4 \cdot 0 \\ 3x^2 - 10x - 8 &= 0 \\ (3x+2)(x-4) &= 0 \end{aligned}$$

$$3x + 2 = 0 \quad \text{or} \quad x - 4 = 0$$
$$3x = -2 \qquad\qquad x = 4$$
$$x = -\frac{2}{3}$$

The solutions are $-\frac{2}{3}$ and 4.

43. $(3x-2)^2 = 10$

Use the square root property.

$$\begin{aligned} (3x-2)^2 &= 10 \\ 3x - 2 &= \sqrt{10} \\ 3x &= 2 + \sqrt{10} \\ x &= \frac{2 + \sqrt{10}}{3} \end{aligned}$$

or

$$\begin{aligned} 3x - 2 &= -\sqrt{10} \\ 3x &= 2 - \sqrt{10} \\ x &= \frac{2 - \sqrt{10}}{3} \end{aligned}$$

The solutions are $\frac{2 \pm \sqrt{10}}{3}$.

45. $M = 0.0075x^2 - 0.2676x + 14.8;\ M = 45$

$$\begin{aligned} 45 &= 0.0075x^2 - 0.2676x + 14.8 \\ 0 &= 0.0075x^2 - 0.2676x - 30.2 \end{aligned}$$

To solve this equation, use the quadratic formula with $a = 0.0075, b = -0.2676$, and $c = -30.2$.

$$\begin{aligned} x &= \frac{-b \pm \sqrt{b^2 - 4ac}}{2a} \\ &= \frac{-(-0.2676) \pm \sqrt{(-0.2676)^2 - 4(0.0075)(-30.2)}}{2(0.0075)} \\ &= \frac{0.2676 \pm \sqrt{0.97760976}}{0.015} \\ &\approx \frac{0.2676 \pm 0.9887}{0.015} \end{aligned}$$

$$x \approx 84 \quad \text{or} \quad x \approx -48$$

The solution -48 must be rejected because this represents 48 years *before* 1940, which is not part of the time period modeled by the formula. The solution (to the nearest integer) is 84. This means that, according to the formula, fuel efficiency will be 45 miles per gallon 84 years after 1940. Because $1940 + 84 = 2024$, this will occur in the year 2024.

47. $h = -0.05x^2 + 27;\ h = 22$

$$\begin{aligned} 22 &= -0.05x^2 + 27 \\ -0.05x^2 + 22 &= 27 \\ -0.05x^2 &= 5 \\ \frac{-0.05x^2}{-0.05} &= \frac{5}{-0.05} \\ x^2 &= 100 \end{aligned}$$

$$x = \sqrt{100} = 10 \quad \text{or} \quad x = -\sqrt{100} = -10$$

Because x represents a distance, reject -10. The height of the arch is 22 feet at 10 feet to the right of the center.

49. $N = -0.5x^2 + 4x + 19$; $N = 20$

$$\begin{aligned} 20 &= -0.5x^2 + 4x + 19 \\ 0.5x^2 - 4x + 1 &= 0 \end{aligned}$$

$a = 0.5, b = -4, c = 1$

$$\begin{aligned} x &= \frac{-b \pm \sqrt{b^2 - 4ac}}{2a} \\ &= \frac{-(-4) \pm \sqrt{(-4)^2 - 4(0.5)(1)}}{2(0.5)} \\ &= \frac{4 \pm \sqrt{16-2}}{1} \\ &= 4 \pm \sqrt{14} \end{aligned}$$

$$x = 4 + \sqrt{14} \quad \text{or} \quad x = 4 - \sqrt{14}$$

$$x \approx 8 \qquad\qquad x \approx -0.258$$

Reject the negative solution of the quadratic equation because the model starts at $x = 0$. The solution (to the nearest year) is 8. This means that there were about 20 million people receiving food stamps after 8 years after 1990, that is, in the year 1998.

51. $h = -16t^2 + 60t + 4$; $h = 0$

$$\begin{aligned} 0 &= -16t^2 + 60t + 4 \\ 16t^2 - 60t - 4 &= 0 \\ 4(4t^2 - 15t - 1) &= 0 \\ 4t^2 - 15t - 1 &= 0 \end{aligned}$$

Note: Dividing both sides by 0 is not necessary, but it results in smaller numbers to be substituted in the quadratic formula.
$a = 4, b = -15, c = -1$

$$\begin{aligned} t &= \frac{-b \pm \sqrt{b^2 - 4ac}}{2a} \\ &= \frac{-(-15) \pm \sqrt{(-15)^2 - 4(4)(-1)}}{2(4)} \\ &= \frac{15 \pm \sqrt{225 + 16}}{8} \\ &= \frac{15 \pm \sqrt{241}}{8} \end{aligned}$$

$$t = \frac{15 + \sqrt{241}}{8} \quad \text{or} \quad t = \frac{15 - \sqrt{241}}{8}$$

$$t \approx 3.8 \qquad \text{or} \quad t \approx -0.1$$

Reject the negative solution to the quadratic equation because the time cannot be negative. It will take about 3.8 seconds for the football to hit the ground.

53. Let $x =$ the width of the rectangle.
Then $x + 3 =$ the length.

$$\begin{aligned} A &= lw \\ 36 &= (x+3) \cdot x \\ 36 &= x^2 + 3x \\ 0 &= x^2 + 3x - 36 \end{aligned}$$

$a = 1, b = 3, c = -36$

$$\begin{aligned} x &= \frac{-b \pm \sqrt{b^2 - 4ac}}{2a} \\ &= \frac{-3 \pm \sqrt{(-3)^2 - 4(1)(-36)}}{2 \cdot 1} \\ &= \frac{-3 \pm \sqrt{9 + 144}}{2} \\ &= \frac{-3 \pm \sqrt{153}}{2} \end{aligned}$$

$$x = \frac{-3 + \sqrt{153}}{2} \quad \text{or} \quad x = \frac{-3 - \sqrt{153}}{2}$$

$$x \approx 4.7 \qquad\qquad x \approx -7.7$$

Reject the negative solution of the quadratic equation because the width cannot be negative. If $x = 4.7$, then $x + 3 = 7.7$. Thus, to the nearest tenth of a meter, the width is 4.7 meters and the length is 7.7 meters.

55. Let x = the length of the shorter leg.
Then $x+1$ = the length of the shorter leg.

Use the Pythagorean Theorem.

$$x^2 + (x+1) = 4^2$$
$$x^2 + x^2 + 2x + 1 = 16$$
$$2x^2 + 2x - 15 = 0$$
$$x = \frac{-2 \pm \sqrt{2^2 - 4(2)(-15)}}{2 \cdot 2}$$
$$= \frac{-2 \pm \sqrt{4+120}}{4}$$
$$= \frac{-2 \pm \sqrt{124}}{4}$$

$$x = \frac{-2+\sqrt{124}}{4} \quad \text{or} \quad x = \frac{-2-\sqrt{124}}{4}$$

$$x \approx 2.3 \qquad\qquad x \approx -3.3$$

The length of a leg cannot be negative, so reject -3.3. If $x = 2.3$, then $x+1 = 3.3$. Thus, to the nearest tenth of a foot, the lengths of the legs are 2.3 feet and 3.3 feet.

For Exercises 57–61, answers may vary.

63. If $b^2 - 4ac > 0$, there are two real number solutions. If $b^2 - 4ac$ is a perfect square, the solutions are rational; if it is not a perfect square, they are irrational.
If $b^2 - 4ac = 0$, there is only one solution, which is rational.
If $b^2 - 4ac < 0$, the solutions are not real numbers.
Therefore, by evaluating $b^2 - 4ac$, you can determine the kinds of solutions for any quadratic equation without actually solving it.

65. Let x = the width of the border.

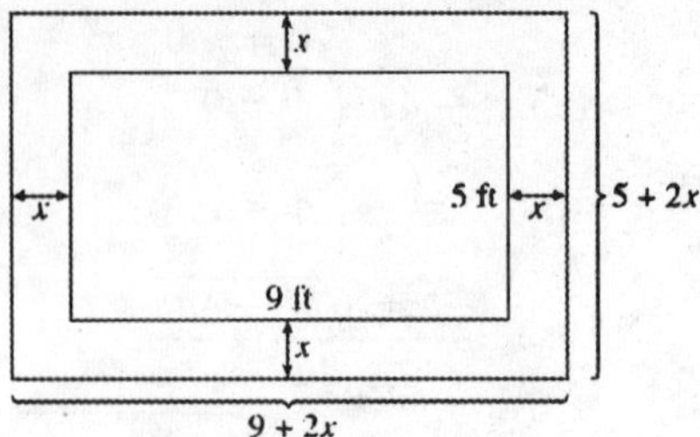

Area of large rectangle (garden plus border)
$= (9+x)(5+x)$
Area of small rectangle (garden)
$= 9 \cdot 5 = 45$
Area of border
= Area of large rectangle
− Area of small rectangle
$= (9+2x)(5+2x) - 45$
The area of the border is 40 square feet, so

$$(9+2x)(5+2x) - 45 = 40.$$

Solve this equation.

$$45 + 28x + 4x^2 - 45 = 40$$
$$4x^2 + 28x - 40 = 0$$
$$4(x^2 + 7x - 10) = 0$$
$$x^2 + 7x - 10 = 0$$

$a = 1, , b = 7, c = -10$

$$x = \frac{-b \pm \sqrt{b^2 - 4ac}}{2a}$$
$$= \frac{-7 \pm \sqrt{7^2 - 4(1)(-10)}}{2(1)}$$
$$= \frac{-7 \pm \sqrt{49+40}}{2}$$
$$= \frac{-7 \pm \sqrt{89}}{2}$$

$$x = \frac{-7+\sqrt{89}}{2} \quad \text{or} \quad x = \frac{-7-\sqrt{89}}{2}$$

$$x \approx 1.2 \qquad\qquad x \approx -8.2$$

Reject -8.2 because the width of the border must be positive. The width of the border is about 1.2 feet.

67. $y = -16x^2 + 60x + 4$

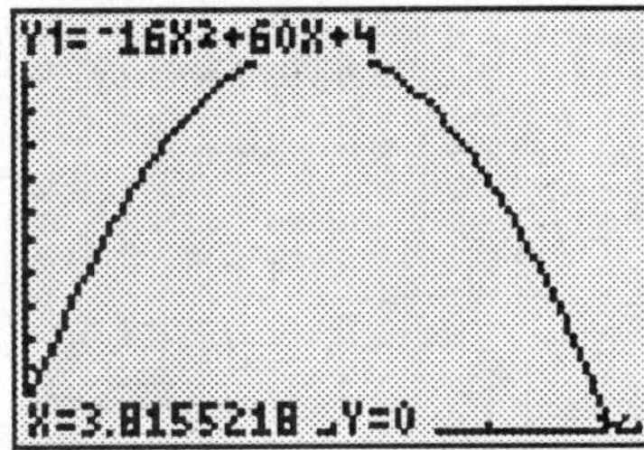

The graph verifies that the positive solution of the quadratic equation is about 3.8.

Review Exercises

68. $125^{-\frac{2}{3}} = \dfrac{1}{125^{\frac{2}{3}}} = \dfrac{1}{(\sqrt[3]{125})^2}$

$= \dfrac{1}{5^2} = \dfrac{1}{25}$

69. $\dfrac{12}{3+\sqrt{5}}$

To rationalize the denominator, multiply numerator and denominator by the conjugate of the denominator.

$$\frac{12}{3+\sqrt{5}} = \frac{12}{3+\sqrt{5}} \cdot \frac{3-\sqrt{5}}{3-\sqrt{5}}$$
$$= \frac{12(3-\sqrt{5})}{3^2 - (\sqrt{5})^2}$$
$$= \frac{12(3-\sqrt{5})}{9-5}$$
$$= \frac{12(3-\sqrt{5})}{4}$$
$$= 3(3-\sqrt{5}) = 9 - 3\sqrt{5}$$

71. $(x-y)(x^2+xy+y^2)$
$= x(x^2+xy+y^2) - y(x^2+xy+y^2)$
$= x^3 + x^2y + xy^2 - x^2y - xy^2 - y^3$
$= x^3 - y^3$

10.4 Imaginary Numbers as Solutions of Quadratic Equations

10.4 CHECK POINTS

CHECK POINT 1

a. $\sqrt{-16} = \sqrt{16(-1)} = \sqrt{16}\sqrt{-1} = 4i$

b. $\sqrt{-5} = \sqrt{5(-1)} = \sqrt{5}i$

c. $\sqrt{-50} = \sqrt{50(-1)} = \sqrt{50 \cdot 2}\sqrt{-1} = 5\sqrt{2}i$

CHECK POINT 2

$(x+2)^2 = -25$

$x+2 = \sqrt{-25}$ or $x+2 = -\sqrt{-25}$
$x+2 = 5i$ $\qquad x+2 = -5i$
$x = -2+5i$ $\qquad x = -2-5i$

The solutions are $-2+5i$ and $-2-5i$, which can be written in abbreviated form as $-2 \pm 5i$.

CHECK POINT 3

$x^2 + 6x + 13 = 0$

Because the trinomial on the left is prime, use the quadratic formula with $a = 1$, $b = 6$, and $c = 13$.

$$x = \frac{-b \pm \sqrt{b^2 - 4ac}}{2a}$$
$$= \frac{-6 \pm \sqrt{6^2 - 4(1)(13)}}{2(1)}$$
$$= \frac{-6 \pm \sqrt{36-52}}{2} = \frac{-6 \pm \sqrt{-16}}{2}$$
$$= \frac{-6 \pm \sqrt{16(-1)}}{2} = \frac{-6 \pm 4i}{2}$$
$$= \frac{2(-3 \pm 2i)}{2} = -3 \pm 2i$$

The solutions are $-3 \pm 2i$.

EXERCISE SET 10.4

1. $\sqrt{-36} = \sqrt{36(-1)} = \sqrt{36}\sqrt{-1} = 6i$

3. $\sqrt{-11} = \sqrt{11(-1)} = \sqrt{11}\sqrt{-1} = \sqrt{11}i$

5. $\sqrt{-20} = \sqrt{20(-1)} = \sqrt{4 \cdot 5}\sqrt{-1} = 2\sqrt{5}i$

7. $\sqrt{-45} = \sqrt{45(-1)} = \sqrt{9 \cdot 5}\sqrt{-1} = 3\sqrt{5}i$

9. $\sqrt{-150} = \sqrt{150(-1)} = \sqrt{25 \cdot 6}\sqrt{-1}$
$= 5\sqrt{6}i$

11. $7 + \sqrt{-16} = 7 + \sqrt{16}\sqrt{-1} = 7 + 4i$

13. $10 + \sqrt{-3} = 10 + \sqrt{3}\sqrt{-1} = 10 + \sqrt{3}i$

15. $6 - \sqrt{-98} = 6 - \sqrt{98}\sqrt{-1} = 6 - \sqrt{49 \cdot 2}\sqrt{-1}$
$= 6 - 7\sqrt{2}i$

17. $(x-3)^2 = -9$

$$\begin{aligned} x - 3 &= \sqrt{-9} &&\text{or}\quad x - 3 = -\sqrt{-9} \\ x - 3 &= 3i &&\text{or}\quad x - 3 = -3i \\ x &= 3 + 3i &&\text{or}\quad x = 3 - 3i \end{aligned}$$

The solutions are $3 + 3i$ and $3 - 3i$, which can be written in abbreviated from as $3 \pm 3i$.

19. $(x+7)^2 = -64$

$$\begin{aligned} x + 7 &= \sqrt{-64} &&\text{or}\quad x + 7 = -\sqrt{-64} \\ x + 7 &= 8i &&\text{or}\quad x + 7 = -8i \\ x &= -7 + 8i &&\text{or}\quad x = -7 - 8i \end{aligned}$$

The solutions are $-7 \pm 8i$.

21. $(x-2)^2 = -7$

$$\begin{aligned} x - 2 &= \sqrt{-7} &&\text{or}\quad x - 2 = -\sqrt{-7} \\ x - 2 &= \sqrt{7}i &&\text{or}\quad x - 2 = -\sqrt{7}i \\ x &= 2 + \sqrt{7}i &&\text{or}\quad x = 2 - \sqrt{7}i \end{aligned}$$

The solutions are $2 \pm \sqrt{7}i$.

23. $(y+3)^2 = -18$

$$\begin{aligned} y + 3 &= \sqrt{-18} &&\text{or}\quad y + 3 = -\sqrt{-18} \\ y + 3 &= 3\sqrt{2}i &&\text{or}\quad y + 3 = -3\sqrt{2}i \\ y &= -3 + 3\sqrt{2}i &&\text{or}\quad y = -3 - 3\sqrt{2}i \end{aligned}$$

The solutions are $-3 \pm 3\sqrt{2}i$.

25. $x^2 + 4x + 5 = 0$
$a = 1, b = 4, c = 5$

$$\begin{aligned} x &= \frac{-b \pm \sqrt{b^2 - 4ac}}{2a} \\ &= \frac{-4 \pm \sqrt{4^2 - 4(1)(5)}}{2 \cdot 1} \\ &= \frac{-4 \pm \sqrt{16 - 20}}{2} \\ &= \frac{-4 \pm \sqrt{-4}}{2} \\ &= \frac{-4 \pm 2i}{2} \\ &= \frac{2(-2 \pm i)}{2} \\ &= -2 \pm i \end{aligned}$$

The solutions are $-2 \pm i$.

27. $x^2 - 6x + 13 = 0$
$a = 1, b = -6, c = 13$

$$\begin{aligned} x &= \frac{-b \pm \sqrt{b^2 - 4ac}}{2a} \\ &= \frac{-(-6) \pm \sqrt{(-6)^2 - 4(1)(13)}}{2 \cdot 1} \\ &= \frac{6 \pm \sqrt{36 - 52}}{2} \\ &= \frac{6 \pm \sqrt{-16}}{2} \\ &= \frac{6 \pm 4i}{2} \\ &= \frac{2(3 \pm 2i)}{2} \\ &= 3 \pm 2i \end{aligned}$$

29. $x^2 - 12x + 40 = 0$

$a = 1, b = -12, c = 40$

$$\begin{aligned} x &= \frac{-b \pm \sqrt{b^2 - 4ac}}{2a} \\ &= \frac{-(-12) \pm \sqrt{(-12)^2 - 4(1)(40)}}{2 \cdot 1} \\ &= \frac{12 \pm \sqrt{144 - 160}}{2} \\ &= \frac{12 \pm \sqrt{-16}}{2} \\ &= \frac{12 \pm 4i}{2} \\ &= \frac{2(6 \pm 2i)}{2} \\ &= 6 \pm 2i \end{aligned}$$

The solution are $6 \pm 2i$.

31. $x^2 = 10x - 27$

Write the equation in standard form; then identify a, b, and c.

$$x^2 - 10x + 27 = 0$$

$a = 1, b = -10, c = 27$

$$\begin{aligned} x &= \frac{-(-10) \pm \sqrt{(-10)^2 - 4(1)(27)}}{2 \cdot 1} \\ &= \frac{10 \pm \sqrt{100 - 68}}{2} \\ &= \frac{10 \pm \sqrt{-32}}{2} \\ &= \frac{10 \pm 4\sqrt{2}i}{2} \\ &= \frac{2(5 \pm 2\sqrt{2}i)}{2} \\ &= 5 \pm 2\sqrt{2}i \end{aligned}$$

The solutions are $5 \pm 2\sqrt{2}i$.

33. $5x^2 = 2x - 3$

Write the equation in standard form.

$$5x^2 - 2x + 3 = 0$$

$a = 5, b = -2, c = 3$

$$\begin{aligned} x &= \frac{-b \pm \sqrt{b^2 - 4ac}}{2a} \\ &= \frac{-(-2) \pm \sqrt{(-2)^2 - 4(5)(3)}}{2 \cdot 5} \\ &= \frac{2 \pm \sqrt{4 - 60}}{10} \\ &= \frac{2 \pm \sqrt{-56}}{10} \\ &= \frac{2 \pm 2\sqrt{14}i}{10} \\ &= \frac{2(1 \pm \sqrt{14}i)}{10} \\ &= \frac{1 \pm \sqrt{14}i}{5} \end{aligned}$$

The solutions are $\frac{1 \pm \sqrt{14}i}{5}$.

35. $2y^2 = 4y - 5$

Write the equation in standard form.

$$2y^2 - 4y + 5 = 0$$

$a = 2, b = -4, c = 5$

$$\begin{aligned} y &= \frac{-b \pm \sqrt{b^2 - 4ac}}{2a} \\ &= \frac{-(-4) \pm \sqrt{(-4)^2 - 4(2)(5)}}{2 \cdot 2} \\ &= \frac{8 \pm \sqrt{16 - 40}}{4} = \frac{8 \pm \sqrt{-24}}{4} \\ &= \frac{8 \pm 2\sqrt{6}i}{4} = \frac{2(4 \pm \sqrt{6}i)}{4} \\ &= \frac{2 \pm \sqrt{6}i}{2} \end{aligned}$$

The solutions are $\frac{2 \pm \sqrt{6}i}{2}$.

37. $R = -2x^2 + 36x$; $R = 200$

$$
\begin{aligned}
200 &= -2x^2 + 36x \\
2x^2 + 36x + 200 &= 0 \\
x^2 + 18x + 100 &= 0
\end{aligned}
$$

$a = 1, b = 18, c = 100$

$$
\begin{aligned}
x &= \frac{-b \pm \sqrt{b^2 - 4ac}}{2a} \\
&= \frac{-18 \pm \sqrt{18^2 - 4(1)(100)}}{2 \cdot 1} \\
&= \frac{-18 \pm \sqrt{324 - 400}}{2} \\
&= \frac{-18 \pm \sqrt{-76}}{2} \\
&= \frac{-18 \pm 2\sqrt{19}i}{2} \\
&= \frac{2(-9 \pm \sqrt{19}i)}{2} \\
&= -9 \pm \sqrt{19}i
\end{aligned}
$$

The solutions of the equation are $-9 \pm \sqrt{19}i$, which are not real numbers. Because the equation has no real number solution, it is not possible to generate \$200,000 in weekly revenue. The job applicant, has guaranteed to do something that is impossible, so this person will not be hired.

For Exercises 39–41, answers may vary.

45. Statement b is true.

47. Let x represent the number of numbers that satisfy the given condition. These conditions lead to the equation

$$x^2 - 2x = -5.$$

Write this equation in standard form and solve by the quadratic formula.

$$x^2 - 2x + 5 = 0$$

$a = 1, b = -2, c = 5$

$$
\begin{aligned}
x &= \frac{-b \pm \sqrt{b^2 - 4ac}}{2a} \\
&= \frac{-(-2) \pm \sqrt{(-2)^2 - 4(1)(5)}}{2 \cdot 1} \\
&= \frac{2 \pm \sqrt{4 - 20}}{2} \\
&= \frac{2 \pm \sqrt{-16}}{2} \\
&= \frac{2 \pm 4i}{2} \\
&= \frac{2(1 \pm 2i)}{2} \\
&= 1 \pm 2i
\end{aligned}
$$

The solutions are $1 \pm 2i$. Because these are not real numbers, there is no real number that satisfies the condition given in the exercise.

49.

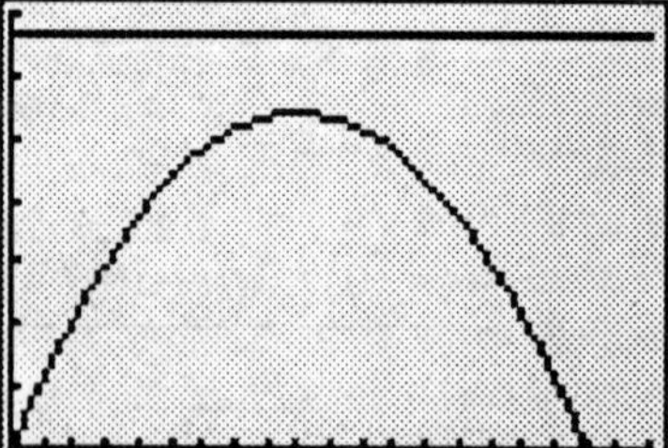

The graph shows that the parabola and the horizontal line do not intersect. The vertex, which is the maximum point on the graph, has a y-coordinate that is less than 200. Therefore, the weekly revenue will never reach \$200,000.

Review Exercises

50. $y = \dfrac{1}{3}x - 2$

slope $= \frac{1}{3}$; y-intercept $= -2$

Plot $(0,-2)$. From this point, go 1 unit *up* and 3 units to the *right* to reach the point $(3,-1)$.

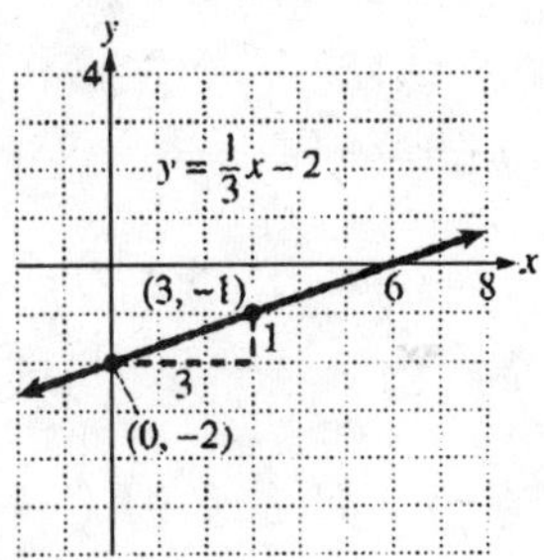

51. $2x - 3y = 6$
x-intercept: 3
y-intercept: -2
checkpoint: $(-3,-4)$
Draw a line through $(3,0), (0,-2)$, and $(-3,-4)$.

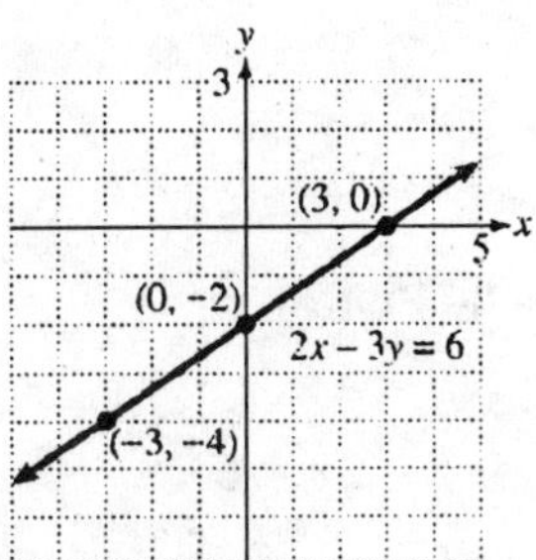

52. $x = -2$

Draw a vertical line with x-intercept -2.

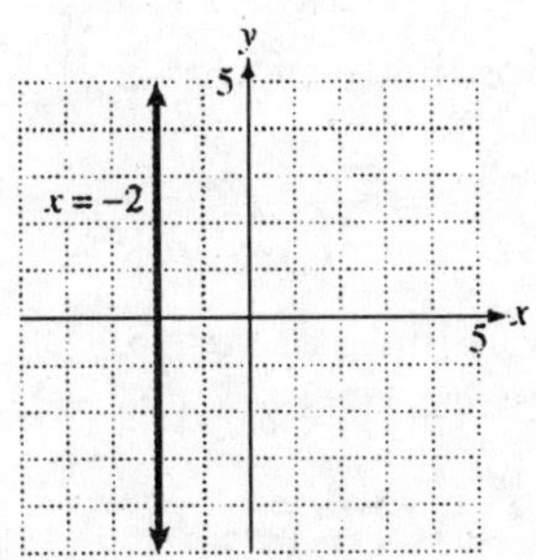

10.5 Graphs of Quadratic Equations

10.5 CHECK POINTS

CHECK POINT 1

$y = x^2 - 6x + 8$

a. Because a, the coefficient of x^2, is 1, which is greater than 0, the parabola opens upward.

b.

x	$y = x^2 - 6x + 8$	(x, y)
0	$y = 0^2 - 6(0) + 8 = 8$	$(0,8)$
1	$y = 1^2 - 6(1) + 8 = 3$	$(1,3)$
2	$y = 2^2 - 6(2) + 8 = 0$	$(2,0)$
3	$y = 3^2 - 6(3) + 8 = -1$	$(3,-1)$
4	$y = 4^2 - 6(4) + 8 = 0$	$(4,0)$
5	$y = 5^2 - 6(5) + 8 = 3$	$(5,3)$
6	$y = 6^2 - 6(6) + 8 = 8$	$(6,8)$

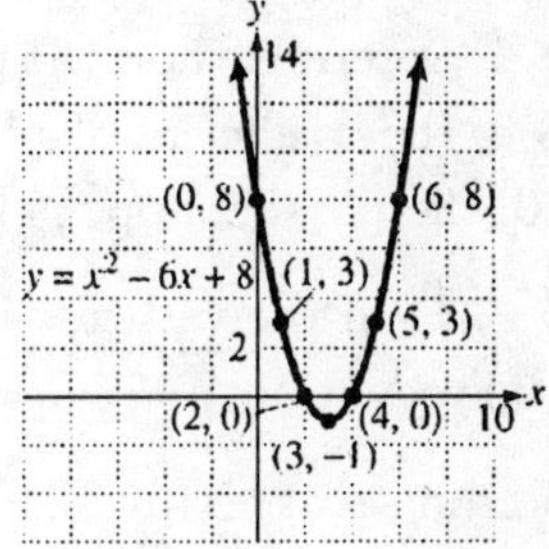

CHECK POINT 2

$y = x^2 - 6x + 8$

To find the x-intercepts, replace y with 0 and solve the resulting equation.

$$x^2 - 6x + 8 = 0$$
$$(x-2)(x-4) = 0$$
$$x - 2 = 0 \quad \text{or} \quad x - 4 = 0$$
$$x = 2 \qquad\qquad x = 4$$

The x-intercepts are 2 and 4.

CHECK POINT 3

$y = x^2 - 6x + 8$

To find the y-intercept, replace x with 0.

$$y = 0^2 - 6 \cdot 0 + 8 = 0 - 0 + 8 = 8$$

The y-intercept is 8.

CHECK POINT 4

$y = x^2 - 6x + 8$
$a = 1, b = -6$

x-coordinate of vertex $= \frac{-b}{2a} = -\frac{-6}{2} = 3$

y-coordinate of vertex
$= 3^2 - 6(3) + 8 = 9 - 18 + 8 = -1$

The vertex is $(3, -1)$.

CHECK POINT 5

$y = x^2 + 6x + 5$

Step 1 Determine how the parabola opens. Here a, the coefficient of x^2, is 1. Because $a > 0$, the parabola opens upward.

Step 2 Find the vertex.
For this equation, $a = 1, b = 6$, and $c = 5$.

x-coordinate of vertex
$= \frac{-b}{2a} = \frac{-6}{2(1)} = \frac{-6}{2} = -3$

y-coordinate of vertex
$= (-3)^2 + 6(-3) + 5 = 9 - 18 + 5 = -4$

The vertex is $(-3, -4)$.

Step 3 Find the x-intercepts.
Replace y with 0 in $y = x^2 + 6x + 5$ and solve the resulting equation.

$$x^2 + 6x + 5 = 0$$
$$(x + 5)(x + 1) = 0$$

$$x + 5 = 0 \quad \text{or} \quad x + 1 = 0$$
$$x = -5 \qquad\qquad x = -1$$

The x-intercepts are -5 and -1.

Step 4 Find the y-intercept.
Replace x with 0 in $y = x^2 + 6x + 5$.

$$y = 0^2 + 6(0) + 5 = 0 + 0 + 5 = 5$$

The y-intercept is 5.

Steps 5 and 6 Plot the intercepts and the vertex. Connect these points with a smooth curve.
Plot $(-3, -4), (-5, 0), (-1, 0)$, and $(0, 5)$ and connect them with a smooth curve.

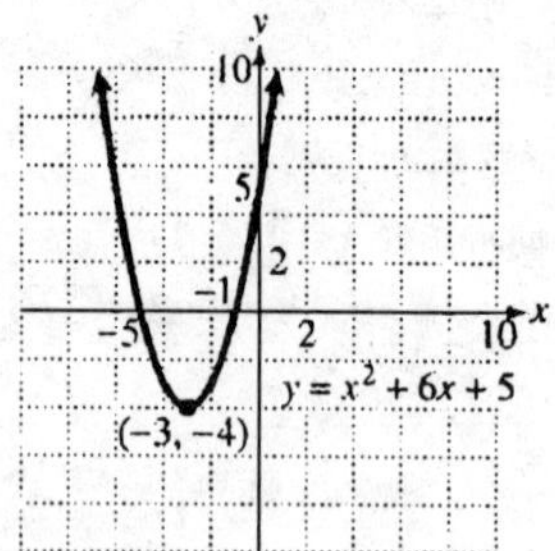

CHECK POINT 6

$y = -x^2 - 2x + 5$

Step 1 $a = -1 < 0$, so the parabola opens downward.

Step 2 $a = -1, b = -2, c = 5$

x-coordinate of vertex
$= \frac{-b}{2a} = \frac{-(-2)}{2(-1)} = \frac{2}{-2} = -1$

y-coordinate of vertex
$= -(-1)^2 - 2(-1) + 5 = -1 + 2 + 5 = 6$

The vertex is $(-1, 6)$.

Step 3 $-x^2 - 2x + 5 = 0$

This equation cannot be solved by factoring, so use the quadratic formula with $a = -1, b = -2$, and $c = 5$.

$$x = \frac{-b \pm \sqrt{b^2 - 4ac}}{2a}$$
$$= \frac{-(-2) \pm \sqrt{(-2)^2 - 4(-1)(5)}}{2(-1)}$$
$$= \frac{2 \pm \sqrt{4 + 20}}{-2}$$
$$= \frac{2 \pm \sqrt{24}}{-2}$$
$$x = \frac{2 + \sqrt{24}}{-2} \quad \text{or} \quad x = \frac{2 - \sqrt{24}}{-2}$$
$$x \approx -3.4 \qquad\qquad x \approx 1.4$$

The x-intercepts are approximately -3.4 and 1.4.

Step 4 $y = -0^2 - 2 \cdot 0 + 5 = 5$

The y-intercept is 5.

Steps 5 and 6 Plot $(-1, 6), (-3.4, 0), (1.4, 0)$, and $(0, 5)$. Connect these points with a smooth curve.

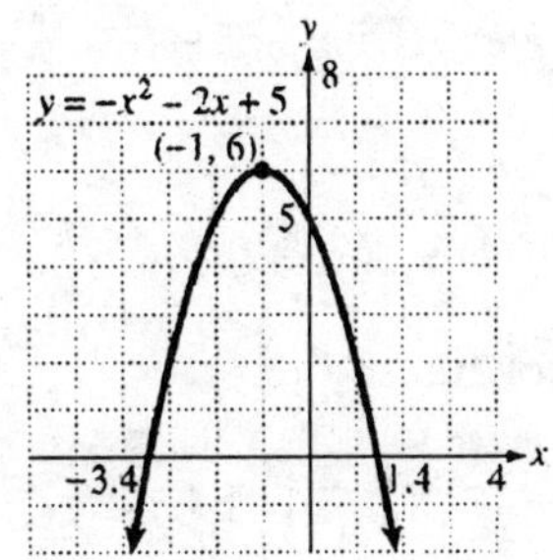

CHECK POINT 7

$y = 0.4x^2 - 36x + 1000$
$a = 0.4, b = -36, c = 1000$

x-coordinate of vertex

$$= \frac{-b}{2a} = \frac{-(-36)}{2(0.4)} = \frac{36}{0.8} = 45$$

y-coordinate of vertex

$$= 0.4(45)^2 - 36(45) + 1000$$
$$= 810 - 1620 + 1000 = 190$$

The vertex is $(45, 190)$.
Because the coefficient of $x^2, 0.4$, is positive, the parabola opens upward and the vertex is the lowest point on the graph. This means that people who are 45 years old have the fewest number of accidents per miles driven, and that they have 190 accidents per 50 million miles driven.

EXERCISE SET 10.5

1. $y = x^2 - 4x + 3$

Because a, the coefficient of x^2, is 1, which is greater than 0, the parabola opens upward.

3. $y = -2x^2 + x + 6$

Because $a = -2$, which is less than 0, the parabola opens downward.

5. $y = x^2 - 4x + 3$

To find the x-intercepts, replace y with 0 and solve the resulting equation.

$$x^2 - 4x + 3 = 0$$
$$(x - 1)(x - 3) = 0$$
$$x - 1 = 0 \quad \text{or} \quad x - 3 = 0$$
$$x = 1 \qquad\qquad x = 3$$

The x-intercepts are 1 and 3.

7. $y = -x^2 - 8x - 12$

$$\begin{aligned} 0 &= -x^2 + 8x - 12 \\ x^2 - 8x + 12 &= 0 \\ (x-2)(x-6) &= 0 \\ x - 2 = 0 \quad &\text{or} \quad x - 6 = 0 \\ x = 2 \quad & \quad\quad x = 6 \end{aligned}$$

The x-intercepts are 2 and 6.

9. $y = x^2 + 2x - 4$

$$x^2 + 2x - 4 = 0$$

This equation cannot be solved by factoring, so use the quadratic formula with $a = 1, b = 2$, and $c = -4$.

$$\begin{aligned} x &= \frac{-b \pm \sqrt{b^2 - 4ac}}{2a} = \frac{-2 \pm \sqrt{2^2 - 4(1)(-4)}}{2(1)} \\ &= \frac{-2 \pm \sqrt{4 + 16}}{2} = \frac{-2 \pm \sqrt{20}}{2} \\ &= \frac{-2 \pm 2\sqrt{5}}{2} \\ &= \frac{2(-1 \pm \sqrt{5})}{2} = -1 \pm \sqrt{5} \end{aligned}$$

$$x = -1 + \sqrt{5} \approx -3.2 \quad \text{or} \quad x = -1 - \sqrt{5} \approx 1.2$$

The x-intercepts are approximately -3.2 and 1.2.

11. $y = x^2 - 4x + 3$

To find the y-intercept, replace x with 0.

$$y = 0^2 - 4 \cdot 0 + 3 = 0 - 0 + 3 = 3$$

The y-intercept is 3.

13. $y = -x^2 + 8x - 12$

$$y = -0^2 + 8 \cdot 0 - 12 = -0 + 0 - 12 = -12$$

The y-intercept is -12.

15. $y = x^2 + 2x - 4$

$$y = 0^2 + 2 \cdot 0 - 4 = -4$$

The y-intercept is -4.

17. $y = x^2 + 6x$

$$y = 0^2 + 6 \cdot 0 = 0$$

The y-intercept is 0.

19. $y = x^2 - 4x + 3$
$a = 1, b = -4, c = 3$

x-coordinate of vertex
$$= \frac{-b}{2a} = \frac{-(-4)}{2(1)} = \frac{4}{2} = 2$$

y-coordinate of vertex
$$= 2^2 - 4(2) + 3 = 4 - 8 + 3 = -1$$

The vertex is $(2, -1)$.

21. $y = 2x^2 + 4x - 6$
$a = 2, b = 4, c = -6$

x-coordinate of vertex
$$= \frac{-b}{2a} = \frac{-4}{2(2)} = \frac{-4}{4} = -1$$

y-coordinate of vertex
$$= 2(-1)^2 + 4(-1) - 6 = 2 - 4 - 6 = -8$$

The vertex is $(-1, -8)$.

23. $y = x^2 + 6x$
$a = 1, b = 6, c = 0$

x-coordinate of vertex
$$= \frac{-b}{2a} = \frac{-6}{2(1)} = \frac{-6}{2} = -3$$

y-coordinate of vertex
$$= (-3)^2 + 6(-3) = 9 - 18 = -9$$

The vertex is $(-3, -9)$.

25. $y = x^2 + 8x + 7$

Step 1 Determine how the parabola opens. Here a, the coefficient of x^2, is 1. Because $a > 0$, the parabola opens upward.

Step 2 Find the vertex. For this equation, $a = 1, b = 8$, and $c = 7$.
x-coordinate of vertex
$$= \frac{-b}{2a} = \frac{-8}{2(1)} = \frac{-8}{2} = -4$$
y-coordinate of vertex
$$= (-4)^2 + 8(-4) + 7 = 16 - 32 + 7 = -9$$
The vertex is $(-4, -9)$.

Step 3 Find the x-intercepts. Replace y with 0 in $y = x^2 + 8x + 7$ and solve for x.

$$x^2 + 8x + 7 = 0$$
$$(x+7)(x+1) = 0$$
$$x + 7 = 0 \quad \text{or} \quad x + 1 = 0$$
$$x = -7 \qquad\qquad x = -1$$

The x-intercepts are -7 and -1.

Step 4 Find the y-intercept. Replace x with 0 and solve for y.

$$y = 0^2 + 8(0) + 7 = 0 + 0 + 7 = 7$$

The y-intercept is 7.

Steps 5 and 6 Plot the intercepts and the vertex. Connect these points with a smooth curve.
Plot $(-4,-9), (-7,0), (-1,0)$, and $(0,7)$, and connect them with a smooth curve.

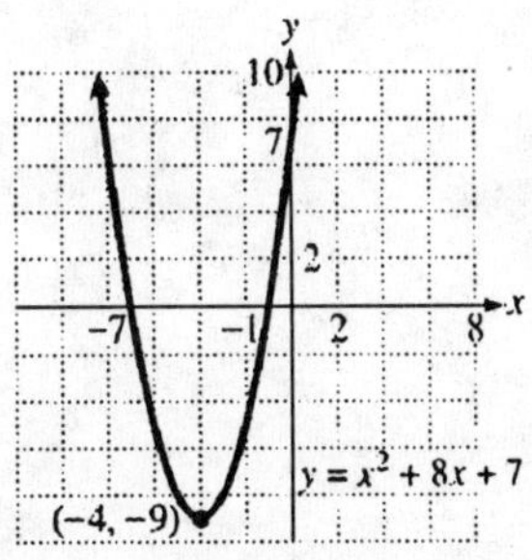

27. $y = x^2 - 2x - 8$

Step 1 $a = 1 > 0$, so the parabola opens upward.

Step 2 $a = 1, b = -2, c = -8$

x-coordinate of vertex
$$= \frac{-b}{2a} = \frac{-(-2)}{2(1)} = \frac{2}{2} = 1$$
y-coordinate of vertex
$$= 1^2 - 2(1) - 8 = 1 - 2 - 8 = -9$$
The vertex is $(1, -9)$.

Step 3

$$x^2 - 2x - 8 = 0$$
$$(x+2)(x-4) = 0$$
$$x + 2 = 0 \quad \text{or} \quad x - 4 = 0$$
$$x = -2 \qquad\qquad x = 4$$

The x-intercepts are -2 and 4.

Step 4 $y = 0^2 - 2(0) - 8 = 8$

The y-intercept is -8.

Steps 5 and 6 Plot $(1,-9), (-2,0), (4,0)$, and $(0,-8)$, and connect them with a smooth curve.

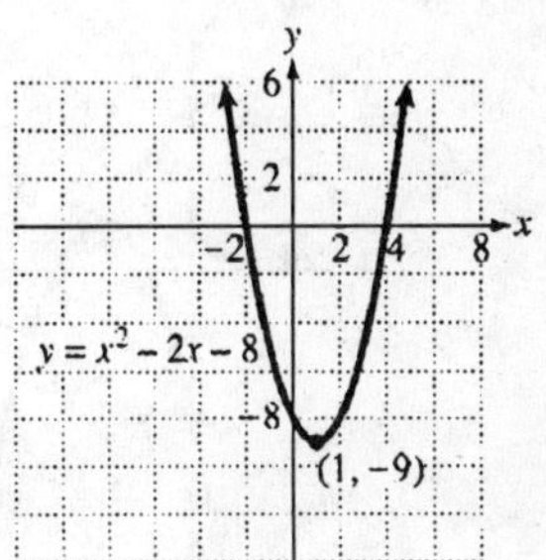

29. $y = -x^2 + 4x - 3$

Step 1 $a = -1 < 0$, so the parabola opens downward.

Step 2 $a = -1, b = 4, c = -3$

x-coordinate of vertex

$$= \frac{-b}{2a} = \frac{-4}{2(-1)} = \frac{-4}{-2} = 2$$

y-coordinate of vertex

$$= -2^2 + 4 \cdot 2 - 3 = -4 + 8 - 3 = 1$$

The vertex is $(2, 1)$.

Step 3

$$\begin{aligned} -x^2 + 4x - 3 &= 0 \\ 0 &= x^2 - 4x + 3 \\ 0 &= (x-1)(x-3) \\ x - 1 = 0 \quad &\text{or} \quad x - 3 = 0 \\ x = 1 \quad & \quad\quad x = 3 \end{aligned}$$

The x-intercepts are 1 and 3.

Step 4 $y = -0^2 + 4(0) - 3 = -3$

The y-intercept is -3.

Steps 5 and 6 Plot $(2,1), (1,0), (3,0)$, and $(0,-3)$, and connect them with a smooth curve.

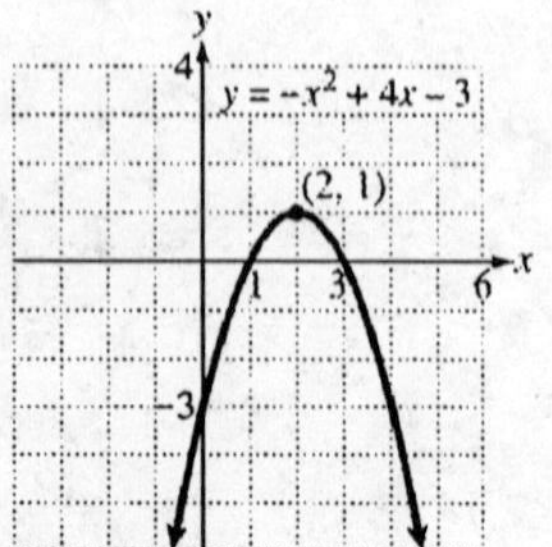

31. $y = x^2 - 1$

Step 1 $a = 1 > 0$, so the parabola opens upward.

Step 2 $a = 1, b = 0, c = -1$

x-coordinate of vertex

$$= \frac{-b}{2a} = \frac{-0}{2(1)} = \frac{0}{2} = 0$$

y-coordinate of vertex

$$= 0^2 - 1 = -1$$

The vertex is $(0, -1)$.

Step 3

$$\begin{aligned} x^2 - 1 &= 0 \\ (x+1)(x-1) &= 0 \\ x + 1 = 0 \quad &\text{or} \quad x - 1 = 0 \\ x = -1 \quad & \quad\quad x = 1 \end{aligned}$$

The x-intercepts are -1 and 1.

Step 4 $y = 0^2 - 1 = -1$

The y-intercept is -1. Notice that this gives the same point as the vertex, $(0, -1)$.

Steps 5 and 6 Plot $(0,-1), (-1,0)$, and $(1,0)$, and connect them with a smooth curve.

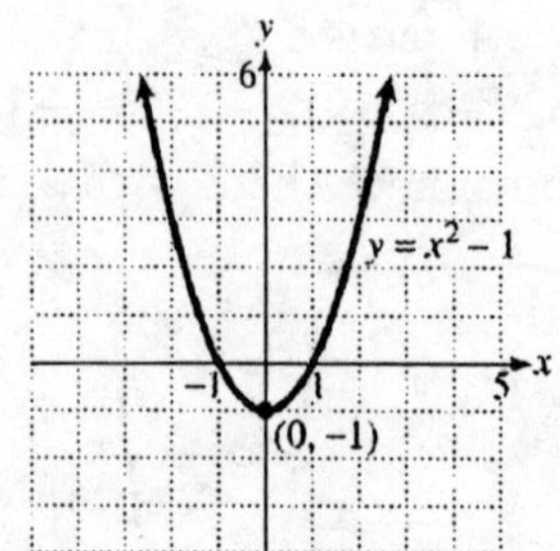

33. $y = x^2 + 2x + 1$

Step 1 $a - 1 > 0$, so the parabola opens upward.

Step 2 $a = 1, b = 2, c = 1$

x-coordinate of vertex

$$= \frac{-b}{2a} = \frac{-2}{2(1)} = \frac{-2}{2} = -1$$

y-coordinate of vertex

$$= (-1)^2 + 2(-1) + 1 = 1 - 2 + 1 = 0$$

The vertex is $(-1, 0)$.

Step 3

$$\begin{aligned} x^2 + 2x + 1 &= 0 \\ (x+1)^2 &= 0 \\ x + 1 &= 0 \\ x &= -1 \end{aligned}$$

There is only one x-intercept, -1. Notice that this gives the same point as the vertex, $(-1, 0)$.

Step 4 $y = 0^2 + 2 \cdot 0 + 1 = 1$

The y-intercept is 1.

The work in Steps 1–4 has produced only two points, $(-1, 0)$ and $(0, 1)$. At least one additional point is needed. In order to have at least one point on each side of the vertex, choose an x-value less than -1 and find the corresponding y-value.
If $x = -2$,

$$y = (-2)^2 + 2(-2) + 1 = 4 - 4 + 1 = 1.$$

Steps 5 and 6 Plot $(-2, 1), (-1, 0)$, and $(0, 1)$, and connect them with a smooth curve.

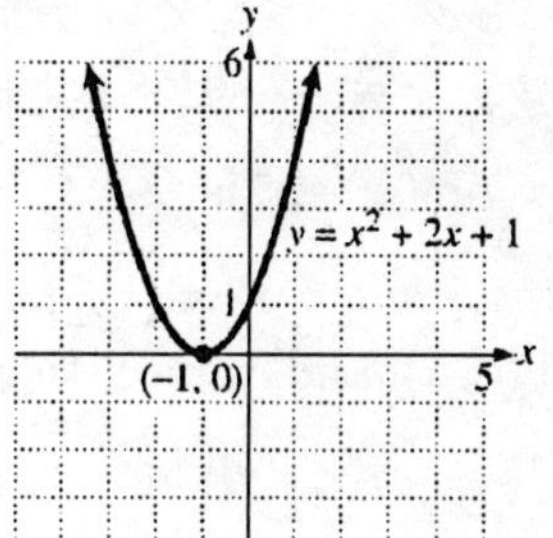

35. $y = -2x^2 + 4x + 5$

Step 1 $a = -2 < 0$, so the parabola opens downward.

Step 2 $a = -2, b = 4, c = 5$

x-coordinate of vertex

$$= \frac{-b}{2a} = \frac{-4}{2(-2)} = \frac{-4}{-4} = 1$$

y-coordinate of vertex

$$= -2(1)^2 + 4(1) + 5 = -2 + 4 + 5 = 7$$

The vertex is $(1, 7)$

Step 3

$$\begin{aligned} -2x^2 + 4x + 5 &= 0 \\ 0 &= 2x^2 - 4x - 5 \end{aligned}$$

The trinomial cannot be factored, so use the quadratic formula with $a = 2, b = -4$, and $c = -5$.

$$\begin{aligned} x &= \frac{-b \pm \sqrt{b^2 - 4ac}}{2a} \\ &= \frac{-(-4) \pm \sqrt{(-4)^2 - 4(2)(-5)}}{2 \cdot 2} \\ &= \frac{4 \pm \sqrt{16 + 40}}{4} = \frac{4 \pm \sqrt{56}}{4} \end{aligned}$$

$x = \dfrac{4+\sqrt{56}}{4} \approx 2.9$ or $x = \dfrac{4-\sqrt{56}}{4} \approx -0.9$

The x-intercepts are approximately 2.9 and -0.9.

Step 4 $y = -2 \cdot 0^2 + 4.0 + 5 = 5$

The y-intercept is 5.

Steps 5 *and* 6 Plot $(1, 7), (2.9, 0), (-0.9, 0)$, and $(0, 5)$, and connect them with a smooth curve.

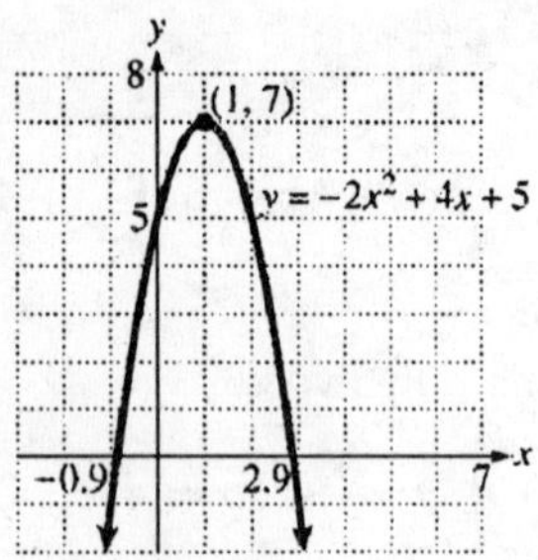

37. $y = -0.02x^2 + x + 1$
$a = -0.02, b = 1, c = 1$

x-coordinate of vertex
$= \dfrac{-b}{2a} = \dfrac{-1}{2(-0.02)} = \dfrac{-1}{-0.04} = 25$

y-coordinate of vertex
$= -0.02(25)^2 + 25 + 1$
$= -12.5 + 25 + 1 = 13.5$

The vertex is $(25, 13.5)$.
This means that the maximum growth of 13.5 inches per year occurs when there is 25 inches of annual rainfall.

39. $y = -16x^2 + 200x + 4$
$a = -16, b = 200, c = 4$

x-coordinate of vertex
$= \dfrac{-b}{2a} = \dfrac{-200}{2(-16)} = \dfrac{-200}{-32} = 6.25$

y-coordinate of vertex
$= -16(6.25)^2 + 200(6.25) + 4$
$= -625 + 1250 + 4 = 629$

The vertex is $(6.25, 629)$.
The fireworks should explode 6.25 seconds after they are launched to reach a maximum height of 629 feet.

41. $y = 0.022x^2 - 0.4x + 60.07$
$a = 0.022, b = -0.4, c = 60.07$

x-coordinate of vertex
$= \dfrac{-b}{2a} = \dfrac{-(-0.4)}{2(0.022)} = \dfrac{0.4}{0.044} \approx 9.09$

y-coordinate of vertex
$= 0.022(9.09)^2 - 0.4(9.09) + 60.07$
≈ 58.25

The vertex is approximately $(9.09, 58.25)$. The percentage was a minimum 9 years after 1960, or in the year 1969. For that year, women's earnings were about 58% of men's.

For Exercises 43–49, answers may vary.

51. The area of the plot is $x(120 - 2x)$. To find the maximum possible area, find the vertex of the parabola whose equation is

$$y = x(120 - 2x).$$

Write this equation in the form $y = ax^2 + bx + c$.

$$y = 120x - 2x^2$$
$$y = -2x^2 + 120x$$

$a = -2, b = 120, c = 0$

x-coordinate of vertex
$= \dfrac{-b}{2a} = \dfrac{-120}{2(-2)} = \dfrac{-120}{-4} = 30$

y-coordinate of vertex
$= -2(30)^2 + 120(30)$
$= -1800 + 3600 = 1800$

The vertex is $(30, 1800)$.

If $x = 30$, then $120 - 2x = 120 - 2(30) = 60$. The area will be maximized (have the maximum value) when the length is 60 feet and the width is 30 feet. The largest area that can be enclosed is 1800 square feet.

53. Because the x-intercepts are 3 and 7, the equation will have the form

$$y = k(x-3)(x-7),$$

where k is some real number.
Therefore,

$$y = k(x^2 - 10x + 21).$$

In order for the y-intercept to be -21, the value of k must be -1, so the equation is

$$y = -1(x^2 - 10x + 21)$$
$$y = -x^2 + 10x - 21.$$

It is not necessary to know the vertex to find the equation, but this information can be used as a check.
$a = -1, b = 10$

$$x = \frac{-b}{2a} = \frac{-10}{2(-1)} = \frac{-10}{-2} = 5$$
$$y = -5^2 + 10(5) - 21$$
$$= -25 + 50 - 21 = 4$$

The vertex is $(5, 4)$, as specified in the exercise. Thus, the equation of the parabola that satisfies all of the given conditions is

$$y = -x^2 + 10x - 21.$$

55. **a.** $y = 2x^2 - 82x + 720$

If you graph this equation in a standard viewing rectangle $[-10, 10, 1]$ by $[-10, 10, 1]$, a blank screen will appear. This indicates that no part of the graph of the equation is located within this window.

b. $a = 2, b = -82$

$$x = \frac{-b}{2a} = \frac{-(-82)}{2(2)} = \frac{82}{4} = 20.5$$
$$y = 2(20.5)^2 - 82(20.5) + 720$$
$$= -120.5$$

The vertex is $(20.5, -120.5)$.

c. A suitable choice is Ymax = 30, and one good choice for the viewing rectangle $[0, 30, 5]$ by $[-130, 30, 10]$. The graph in this window is shown below.

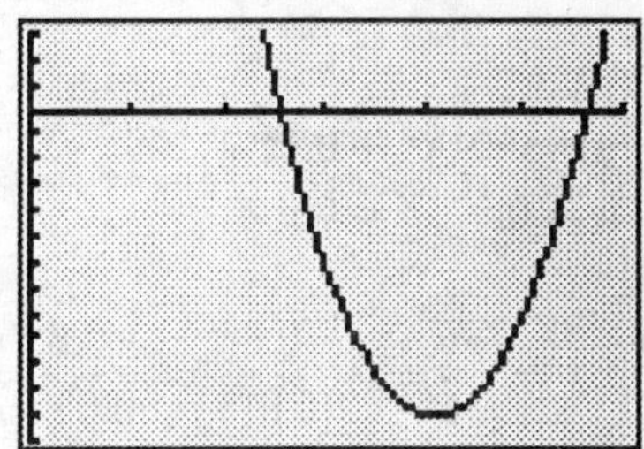

Notice that the graph gives a good picture of the parabola because it shows the vertex, the two x-intercepts, and the y-intercept.

d. If the parabola opens upward, choose a setting for Ymin that is less than the y-coordinate of the vertex.
If the parabola opens downward, choose a setting of Ymax that is greater than the y-coordinate of the vertex.
The settings for x should extend far enough to the left and right of the x-coordinate of the vertex far enough to show the x-intercepts.

57. $y = -4x^2 + 20x + 160$
$a = -4, b = 20$

$$x = \frac{-b}{2a} = \frac{-20}{2(-4)} = \frac{-20}{-8} = 2.5$$
$$y = -4(2.5)^2 + 20(2.5) + 160$$
$$= 185$$

The vertex is $(2.5, 185)$.
One reasonable viewing rectangle is $[-10, 10, 1]$ by $[-20, 200, 20]$.

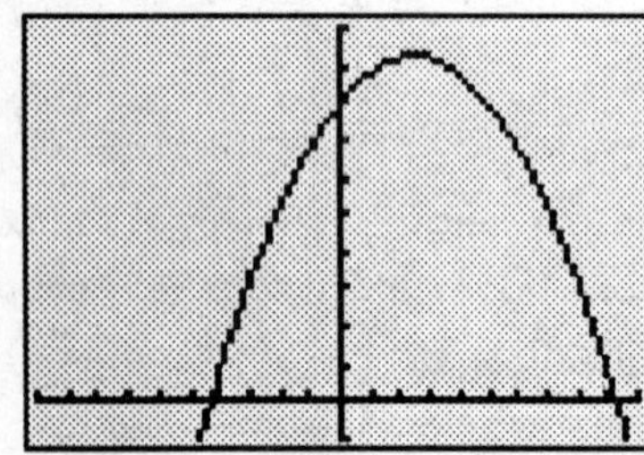

59. $y = 0.01x^2 + 0.6x + 100$
$a = 0.01, b = 0.6$

$$x = \frac{-b}{2a} = \frac{-0.6}{2(0.01)} = \frac{-0.6}{0.02} = -30$$
$$y = 0.01(-30)^2 + 0.6(-30) + 100 = 91$$

The vertex is $(-30, 91)$.
One reasonable viewing window is $[-80, 80, 20]$ by $[80, 120, 10]$.

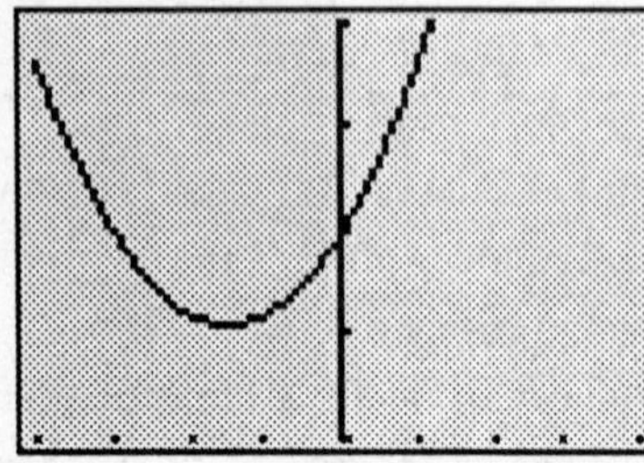

61. $y = 0.011x^2 - 0.097x + 4.1$

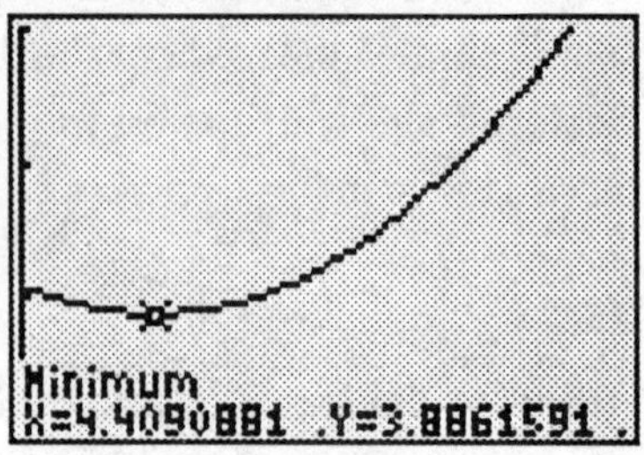

The graph shows that the vertex is approximately $(4.4, 3.9)$. Rounding to the nearest year, this means that minimum number of people holding more than one job occurred 4 years after 1970, in the year 1974. In that year, about 4 million people in the United States held more than one job.

Review Exercises

62. $7(x-2) = 10 - 2(x+3)$
$$7x - 14 = 10 - 2x - 6$$
$$7x - 14 = 4 - 2x$$
$$9x - 14 = 4$$
$$9x = 18$$
$$x = 2$$

The solution is 2.

63. $\dfrac{7}{x+2} + \dfrac{2}{x+3} = \dfrac{1}{x^2+5x+6}$
$$\frac{7}{x+2} + \frac{2}{x+3} = \frac{1}{(x+2)(x+3)}$$

Restrictions: $x \neq -2, x \neq -3$
LCD $= (x+2)(x+3)$

$$(x+2)(x+3)\left[\frac{7}{x+2} + \frac{2}{x+3}\right]$$
$$= (x+2)(x+3)\left[\frac{1}{(x+2)(x+3)}\right]$$

$$7(x+3)+2(x+2)=1$$
$$7x+21+2x+4=1$$
$$9x+25=1$$
$$9x=-24$$
$$x=\frac{-24}{9}=-\frac{8}{3}$$

The solution is $-\frac{8}{3}$.

64. $5x-3y=-13$
$x=2-4y$

To solve this system by the substitution method, substitute $2-4y$ for x in the first equation.

$$5x-3y=-13$$
$$5(2-4y)-3y=-13$$
$$10-20y-3y=-13$$
$$10-23y=-13$$
$$-23y=-23$$
$$y=1$$

Back-substitute 1 for y in the second equation of the given system.

$$x=2-4y=2-4(1)=-2$$

The solution is $(-2,1)$.

10.6 Introduction to Functions

10.6 CHECK POINTS

CHECK POINT 1

The domain of the set of all first components, so the domain of this relation is {Russia, Sweden, Finland, Britain, U.S.}. The range is the set of all second components, so the range of this relation is {65, 64, 56, 53, 49}.

CHECK POINT 2

a. $\{(1,2),(3,4),(5,6),(5,8)\}$

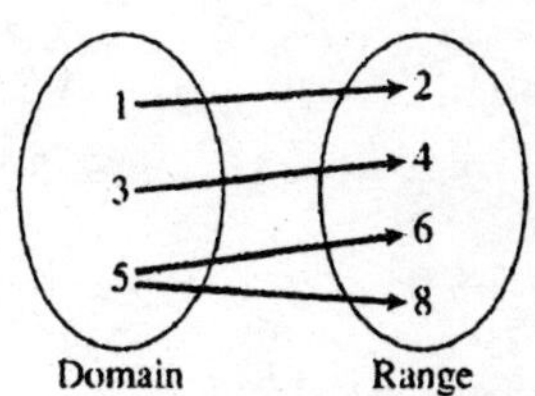

The figure shows that 5 corresponds to both 6 and 8. Because two ordered pairs have the same first component and different second components, this relation is not a function.

b. $\{(1,2),(3,4),(6,5),(8,5)\}$

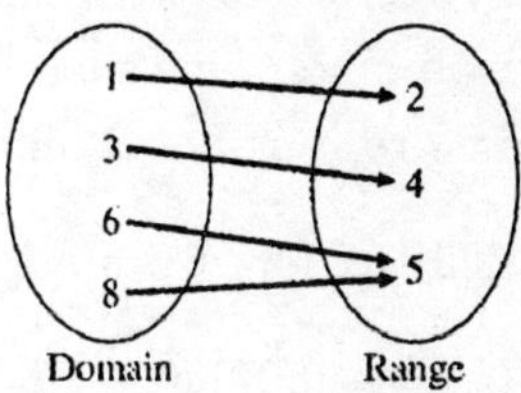

The figure shows that every element in the domain corresponds to exactly one element in the range, so this relation is a function.

CHECK POINT 3

$$f(x)=4x+3$$

a. $f(5)=4\cdot 5+3=20+3=23$

b. $f(-2)=4(-2)+3=-8+3=-5$

c. $f(0)=4\cdot 0+3=0+3=3$

CHECK POINT 4

$g(x) = x^2 + 4x + 3$

a. $g(5) = 5^2 + 4 \cdot 5 + 3 = 25 + 20 + 3 = 48$

b. $g(-4) = (-4)^2 + 4(-4) + 3$
$= 16 - 16 + 3 = 3$

c. $g(0) = 0^2 + 4 \cdot 0 + 3 = 0 + 0 + 3 = 3$

CHECK POINT 5

a. No vertical line will intersect this graph in more than one point, so y is a function of x.

b. No vertical line will intersect this graph in more than one point, so y is a function of x.

c. Many vertical lines will intersect the graph in two points. One such line is the y-axis. Therefore, y is *not* a function of x.

CHECK POINT 6

$$\begin{aligned} f(x) &= -0.071x^2 + 1.66x + 83.74 \\ f(30) &= -0.071(30)^2 + 1.66(30) + 83.74 \\ &= -63.9 + 49.8 + 83.74 \\ &= 69.64 \end{aligned}$$

Thus, $f(30) = 69.64$. Because 30 represents the number of years after 1970, this means that in 2000, approximately 70% of high school students had tried alcohol.

EXERCISE SET 10.6

1. $\{(1,2),(3,4),(5,5)\}$

This relation is a function because no two ordered pairs have the same first component and different second components.
The domain is the set of first components: $\{1,3,5\}$.
The range is the set of second components: $\{2,4,5\}$.

3. $\{(3,4),(3,5),(4,4),(4,5)\}$

This relation is not a function because the first two ordered pairs have the same first component but different second components. (The same applies to the third and fourth ordered pairs.)
Domain: $\{3,4\}$
Range: $\{4,5\}$

5. $\{(-3,-3),(-2,-2),(-1,-1),(0,0)\}$

This relation is a function.
Domain: $\{-3,-2,-1,0\}$
Range: $\{-3,-2,-1,0\}$

7. $\{(1,4),(1,5),(1,6)\}$

This relation is not a function because all three ordered pairs have the same first component.
Domain: $\{1\}$
Range: $\{4,5,6\}$

9. $f(x) = x + 3$

a. $f(6) = 6 + 3 = 9$

b. $f(-4) = -4 + 3 = -1$

c. $f(0) = 0 + 3 = 3$

11. $f(x) = 6x$

a. $f(10) = 6 \cdot 10 = 60$

b. $f(-5) = 6(-5) = -30$

c. $f(0) = 6 \cdot 0 = 0$

13. $f(x) = 4x + 5$

a. $f(12) = 4 \cdot 12 + 5 = 48 + 5 = 53$

b. $f\left(-\frac{1}{2}\right) = 4\left(-\frac{1}{2}\right) + 5 = -2 + 5 = 3$

c. $f(0) = 4 \cdot 0 + 5 = 0 + 5 = 5$

15. $g(x) = x^2 + 4x$

a. $g(2) = 2^2 + 4 \cdot 2 = 4 + 8 = 12$

b. $g(-2) = (-2)^2 + 4(-2) = 4 - 8 = -4$

c. $g(0) = 0^2 + 4 \cdot 0 = 0$

17. $h(x) = x^2 - 2x + 3$

a. $h(4) = 4^2 - 2 \cdot 4 + 3 = 16 - 8 + 3 = 11$

b. $h(-4) = (-4)^2 - 2(-4) + 3$
$= 16 + 8 + 3 = 27$

c. $h(0) = 0^2 - 2 \cdot 0 + 3 = 3$

19. $f(x) = 5$

The value of this function is 5 for every value of x.

a. $f(9) = 5$

b. $f(-9) = 5$

c. $f(0) = 5$

21. $f(r) = \sqrt{r+6} + 3$

a. $f(-6) = \sqrt{-6+6} + 3 = \sqrt{0} + 3$
$= 0 + 3 = 3$

b. $f(10) = \sqrt{10+6} + 3 = \sqrt{16} + 3$
$= 4 + 3 = 7$

23. $f(x) = \dfrac{x}{|x|}$

a. $f(6) = \dfrac{6}{|6|} = \dfrac{6}{6} = 1$

b. $f(-6) = \dfrac{-6}{|-6|} = \dfrac{-6}{6} = -1$

25. No vertical line will intersect this graph in more than one point, so y is a function of x.

27. No vertical line will intersect this graph in more than one point, so y is a function of x.

29. Many vertical lines will intersect this graph in two points. One such line is the y-axis. Therefore, y is not a function of x.

31. No vertical line will intersect this graph in more than one point, so y is a function of x.

33. The following ordered pairs approximate online sales, in billions of dollars:
$(1999, 20), (2000, 30), (2001, 50), (2002, 70), (2003, 95), (2004, 123), (2005, 153)$.
Domain:
$\{1999, 2000, 2001, 2002, 2003, 2004, 2005\}$
Range: $\{20, 30, 50, 70, 95, 123, 153\}$
Yes, this relation is a function because each year corresponds to one number.

35. $f(x) = 0.76x + 171.4$
$f(20) = 0.76(20) + 171.4 = 186.6$

This means that at age 20, the average cholesterol level for an American man is 186.6, or approximately 187.

37. $W(h) = 2.95h - 57.32$
$W(64) = 2.95(64) - 57.32 = 131.48$
≈ 131

The ideal weight of a woman with a medium frame whose height is 64 inches is 131 pounds.

39. $W(h) = 0.077h^2 - 7.61h + 310.11$
$W(70) = 0.077(70)^2 - 7.61(70) + 310.11$
$= 154.71 \approx 155$

The ideal weight of a man with a medium frame whose height is 70 inches is 155 pounds.

41. $V(a) = -0.02a^2 + 1.86a + 9.90$

$$V(20) = -0.02(20)^2 + 1.86(20) + 9.90 = 39.1$$

39.1% of 20-year-old Americans say they do volunteer work.

For Exercises 43–47, answers may vary.

49. $f(x) = \begin{cases} 6.5x + 200 & \text{if } 9 \le x < 23 \\ 26.2x - 252 & \text{if } x \ge 23 \end{cases}$

Because 0 satisfies the inequality $0 \le x < 23$, use the first part of the function to find $f(0)$.

$$f(0) = 6.5(0) + 200 = 200$$

This means that in 1951, there were 200 thousand lawyers.

51. Use the same function as in Exercise 49. Because 50 satisfies the inequality $x \ge 23$, use the second part of the function to find $f(50)$.

$$f(50) = 26.2(50) - 252 = 1058$$

This means that in 2001 (50 years after 1951), there were 1058 thousand lawyers.

53. By the quadratic formula,

$$r = \frac{-b \pm \sqrt{b^2 - 4ac}}{2a}$$

is a solution of the quadratic equation

$$ax^2 + bx + c = 0.$$

Therefore, $f(r) = 0$.

Review Exercises

55. 0.00397

To write this number in scientific notation, move the decimal point 3 places to the right. Because the number is between 0 and 1, the exponent will be positive.

$$0.00397 = 3.97 \times 10^{-3}$$

56.

$$\begin{array}{r} x^2 + \ \ 9x + 16 \\ x - 2\overline{)x^3 - 7x^2 - 20x + \ \ 3} \\ \underline{x^3 - 2x^2} \qquad\qquad\quad \\ 9x^2 - \ \ 2x \qquad \\ \underline{9x^2 - 18x} \qquad \\ 16x + \ \ 3 \\ \underline{16x - 32} \\ 35 \end{array}$$

$$\frac{x^3 + 7x^2 - 20x + 3}{x - 2} = x^2 + 9x + 16 + \frac{35}{x - 2}$$

57. $3x + 2y = 6$
$8x - 3y = 1$

To solve this system by the addition method, multiply the first equation by 3 and then second equation by 2; then add the equations.

$$\begin{aligned} 9x + 6y &= 18 \\ 16x - 6y &= \ \ 2 \\ \hline 25x \qquad &= 20 \\ x &= \frac{20}{25} = \frac{4}{5} \end{aligned}$$

Instead of substituting $\frac{4}{5}$ for x and working with fractions, go back to the original system and eliminate x.

To do this, multiply the first equation by 8 and the second equation by -3; then add.

$$\begin{aligned} 24x + 16y &= 48 \\ -24x + 9y &= -3 \\ \hline 25y &= 45 \\ y &= \frac{45}{25} = \frac{9}{5} \end{aligned}$$

The solution is $\left(\frac{4}{5}, \frac{9}{5}\right)$.

Chapter 10 Review Exercises

1. $x^2 = 64$

$$\begin{aligned} x &= \sqrt{64} \quad \text{or} \quad x = -\sqrt{64} \\ x &= 8 \qquad\qquad\; x = -8 \end{aligned}$$

The solutions are 8 and -8.

2. $x^2 = 17$

$$x = \sqrt{17} \quad \text{or} \quad x = -\sqrt{17}$$

The solutions are $\sqrt{17}$ and $-\sqrt{17}$.

3. $2x^2 = 150$
$x^2 = 75$

$$x = \sqrt{75} \quad \text{or} \quad x = -\sqrt{75}$$

Simplify $\sqrt{75}$:

$$\sqrt{75} = \sqrt{25}\sqrt{3} = 5\sqrt{3}.$$
$$x = 5\sqrt{3} \quad \text{or} \quad x = -5\sqrt{3}$$

The solutions are $5\sqrt{3}$ and $-5\sqrt{3}$.

4. $(x-3)^2 = 9$

$$\begin{aligned} x - 3 &= \sqrt{9} \quad \text{or} \quad x - 3 = -\sqrt{9} \\ x - 3 &= 3 \qquad\quad\;\; x - 3 = -3 \\ x &= 6 \qquad\qquad\quad x = 0 \end{aligned}$$

The solutions are 6 and 0.

5. $(y+4)^2 = 5$

$$\begin{aligned} y + 4 &= \sqrt{5} \qquad \text{or} \quad y + 4 = -\sqrt{5} \\ y &= -4 + \sqrt{5} \qquad\quad y = -4 - \sqrt{5} \end{aligned}$$

The solutions are $-4 + \sqrt{5}$ and $-4 - \sqrt{5}$.

6. $3y^2 - 5 = 0$

$$\begin{aligned} 3y^2 &= 5 \\ y^2 &= \frac{5}{3} \\ y &= \sqrt{\frac{5}{3}} \text{ or } y = -\sqrt{\frac{5}{3}} \end{aligned}$$

Rationalize the denominators.

$$\sqrt{\frac{5}{3}} = \frac{\sqrt{5}}{\sqrt{3}} \cdot \frac{\sqrt{3}}{\sqrt{3}} = \frac{\sqrt{15}}{3}$$

$$y = \frac{\sqrt{15}}{3} \quad \text{or} \quad y = -\frac{\sqrt{15}}{3}$$

The solutions are $\frac{\sqrt{15}}{3}$ and $-\frac{\sqrt{15}}{3}$.

7. $(2x-7)^2 = 25$

$$\begin{aligned} 2x - 7 &= \sqrt{25} \quad \text{or} \quad 2x - 7 = -\sqrt{25} \\ 2x - 7 &= 5 \qquad\;\; \text{or} \quad 2x - 7 = -5 \\ 2x &= 12 \qquad\qquad\quad 2x = 2 \\ x &= 6 \qquad\qquad\qquad x = 1 \end{aligned}$$

The solutions are 6 and 1.

8. $(x+5)^2 = 12$

$$\begin{aligned} x + 5 &= \sqrt{12} \qquad \text{or} \quad x + 5 = -\sqrt{12} \\ x + 5 &= 2\sqrt{3} \qquad \text{or} \quad x + 5 = -2\sqrt{3} \\ x &= 5 + 2\sqrt{3} \qquad\quad x = 5 - 2\sqrt{3} \end{aligned}$$

The solutions are $5 + 2\sqrt{3}$ and $5 - 2\sqrt{3}$.

In Exercises 9–15, all of the unknown quantities must be positive. Therefore, only the positive square roots are used as solutions.

9. Let $c =$ the length of the hypotenuse.

$$\begin{aligned} 6^2 + 8^2 &= c^2 \\ 36 + 64 &= c^2 \\ 100 &= c^2 \\ c &= \sqrt{100} = 10 \end{aligned}$$

The missing length is 10 feet.

10. Let $c =$ the length of the hypotenuse.

$$\begin{aligned} 4^2 + 6^2 &= c^2 \\ 16 + 36 &= c^2 \\ c &= \sqrt{52} = \sqrt{4}\sqrt{13} = 2\sqrt{13} \end{aligned}$$

The missing length is $2\sqrt{13}$ inches.

11. Let $b =$ the missing length (length of one of the legs).

$$\begin{aligned} 11^2 + b^2 &= 15^2 \\ 121 + b^2 &= 225 \\ b^2 &= 104 \\ b &= \sqrt{104} = \sqrt{4}\sqrt{26} = 2\sqrt{26} \end{aligned}$$

The missing length is $2\sqrt{26}$ centimeters.

12. Let $x =$ the distance between the base of the building and the bottom of the ladder.

$$\begin{aligned} x^2 + 20^2 &= 25^2 \\ x^2 + 400 &= 625 \\ x &= 225 \\ x &= \sqrt{225} = 15 \end{aligned}$$

The bottom of the ladder is 15 feet away from the building.

13. Let $h =$ the distance up the pole that the wires should be attached.

In the figure below, the pole and one of the wires are shown.

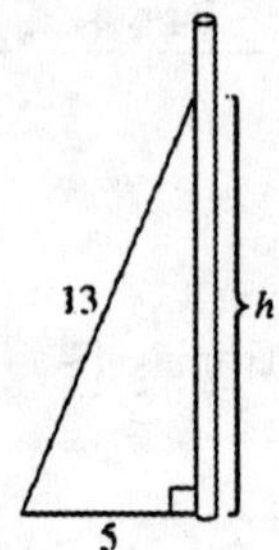

$$\begin{aligned} 5^2 + h^2 &= 13^2 \\ 25 + h^2 &= 169 \\ h^2 &= 144 \\ h &= \sqrt{144} = 12 \end{aligned}$$

The wires will be attached 12 yards up the pole.

14. $W = 3t^2$; $W = 1200$

$$\begin{aligned} 1200 &= 3t^2 \\ 400 &= t^2 \\ t &= \sqrt{400} = 20 \end{aligned}$$

The fetus weighs 1200 grams after 20 weeks.

15. $d = 16t^2$; $d = 100$

$$\begin{aligned} 100 &= 16t^2 \\ 6.25 &= t^2 \\ t &= \sqrt{6.25} = 2.5 \end{aligned}$$

It will take the object 2.5 seconds to hit the water.

16. $x^2 + 16x$

The coefficient of the x-term is 16. Half of 16 is 8, and $8^2 = 64$. Add 4.

$$x^2 + 16x + 64 = (x + 8)^2$$

17. $x^2 - 6x$

$\frac{1}{2}(-6) = -3;\ (-3)^2 = 9$

$$x^2 - 6x + 9 = (x-3)^2$$

18. $x^2 + 3x$

$\frac{1}{2}(3) = \frac{3}{2};\ \left(\frac{3}{2}\right)^2 = \frac{9}{4}$

$$x^2 + 3x + \frac{9}{4} = \left(x + \frac{3}{2}\right)^2$$

19. $x^2 - 5x$

$\frac{1}{2}(-5) = -\frac{5}{2};\ \left(-\frac{5}{2}\right)^2 = \frac{25}{4}$

$$x^2 - 5x + \frac{25}{4} = \left(x - \frac{5}{2}\right)^2$$

20. $x^2 - 12x + 27 = 0$

First, subtract 27 from both sides to isolate the binomial $x^2 - 12x$.

$$x^2 - 12x = -27$$

$\frac{1}{2}(-12) = -6;\ (-6)^2 = 36$

$$\begin{aligned} x^2 - 12x + 36 &= -27 \\ (x-6)^2 &= 9 \\ x - 6 = \sqrt{9} \quad &\text{or} \quad x - 6 = -\sqrt{9} \\ x - 6 = 3 \quad &\text{or} \quad x - 6 = -3 \\ x = 9 \quad & \quad\quad x = 3 \end{aligned}$$

The solutions are 9 and 3.

21. $x^2 - 6x + 4 = 0$

$x^2 - 6x = -4$

$\frac{1}{2}(-6) = -3;\ (-3)^2 = 9$

$$\begin{aligned} x^2 - 6x + 9 &= -4 + 9 \\ (x-3)^2 &= 5 \end{aligned}$$

$$\begin{aligned} x - 3 = \sqrt{5} \quad &\text{or} \quad x - 3 = -\sqrt{5} \\ x = 3 + \sqrt{5} \quad & \quad\quad x = 3 - \sqrt{5} \end{aligned}$$

The solutions are $3 + \sqrt{5}$ and $3 - \sqrt{5}$.

22. $3x^2 - 12x + 11 = 0$

First, divide both sides of the equation by 2 so that the coefficient of the x^2-term will be 1.

$$\begin{aligned} x^2 - 4x + \frac{11}{3} &= 0 \\ x^2 - 4x &= -\frac{11}{3} \\ x^2 - 4x + 4 &= -\frac{11}{3} + 4 \\ (x-2)^2 &= -\frac{11}{3} + \frac{12}{3} \\ (x-2)^2 &= \frac{1}{3} \end{aligned}$$

$$x - 2 = \sqrt{\frac{1}{3}} \quad \text{or} \quad x - 2 = -\sqrt{\frac{1}{3}}$$

Simplify the radicals.

$$\sqrt{\frac{1}{3}} = \frac{\sqrt{1}}{\sqrt{3}} = \frac{1}{\sqrt{3}} \cdot \frac{\sqrt{3}}{\sqrt{3}} = \frac{\sqrt{3}}{3}$$

$$\begin{aligned} x - 2 = \frac{\sqrt{3}}{3} \quad &\text{or} \quad x - 2 = -\frac{\sqrt{3}}{3} \\ x = 2 + \frac{\sqrt{3}}{3} \quad &\text{or} \quad x = 2 - \frac{\sqrt{3}}{3} \\ x = \frac{6}{3} + \frac{\sqrt{3}}{3} \quad &\text{or} \quad x = \frac{6}{3} - \frac{\sqrt{3}}{3} \\ x = \frac{6 + \sqrt{3}}{3} \quad &\text{or} \quad x = \frac{6 - \sqrt{3}}{3} \end{aligned}$$

The solutions are $\frac{6 \pm \sqrt{3}}{3}$.

23. $2x^2 + 5x - 3 = 0$

$a = 2, b = 5, c = -3$

Substitute these values into the quadratic formula.

$$\begin{aligned} x &= \frac{-b \pm \sqrt{b^2 - 4ac}}{2a} \\ &= \frac{-5 \pm \sqrt{5^2 - 4(2)(-3)}}{2(2)} \\ &= \frac{-5 \pm \sqrt{25 + 24}}{4} \\ &= \frac{-5 \pm \sqrt{49}}{4} = \frac{-5 \pm 7}{4} \end{aligned}$$

$$x = \frac{-5+7}{4} \quad \text{or} \quad x = \frac{-5-7}{4}$$

$$= \frac{2}{4} = \frac{1}{2} \qquad = \frac{-12}{4} = -3$$

The solutions are $\frac{1}{2}$ and -3.

24. $x^2 = 2x + 4$

Rewrite the equation in standard form.

$$x^2 - 2x - 4 = 0$$

Identify $a, b,$ and c.

$$a = 1, b = -2, c = -4$$

Substitute these values into the quadratic formula.

$$\begin{aligned} x &= \frac{-b \pm \sqrt{b^2 - 4ac}}{2a} \\ &= \frac{-(-2) \pm \sqrt{(-2)^2 - 4(1)(-4)}}{2(1)} \\ &= \frac{2 \pm \sqrt{4 + 16}}{2} = \frac{2 \pm \sqrt{20}}{2} \\ &= \frac{2 \pm 2\sqrt{5}}{2} = \frac{2(1 \pm \sqrt{5})}{2} \\ &= 1 \pm \sqrt{5} \end{aligned}$$

The solutions are $1 \pm \sqrt{5}$.

25. $3x^2 + 5 = 9x$

Rewrite the equation in standard form.

$$3x^2 - 9x + 5 = 0$$

$a = 3, b = -9, c = 5$

$$\begin{aligned} x &= \frac{-b \pm \sqrt{b^2 - 4ac}}{2a} \\ &= \frac{-(-9) \pm \sqrt{(-9)^2 - 4(3)(5)}}{2 \cdot 3} \\ &= \frac{9 \pm \sqrt{81 - 60}}{6} = \frac{9 \pm \sqrt{21}}{6} \end{aligned}$$

The solutions are $\frac{9 \pm \sqrt{21}}{6}$.

26. $2x^2 - 11x + 5 = 0$

This equation can be solved by the factoring method. Factor the trinomial.

$$(2x - 1)(x - 5) = 0$$

Use the zero-product principle.

$$2x - 1 = 0 \quad \text{or} \quad x - 5 = 0$$

$$2x = 1 \qquad x = 5$$

$$x = \frac{1}{2}$$

The solutions are $\frac{1}{2}$ and 5.

27. $(3x + 5)(x - 3) = 5$

Write the equation in standard form.

$$\begin{aligned} 3x^2 - 4x - 15 &= 5 \\ 3x^2 - 4x - 20 &= 0 \end{aligned}$$

This equation can be solved by the factoring method.

$$(3x - 10)(x + 2) = 0$$

$$3x - 10 = 0 \quad \text{or} \quad x + 2 = 0$$

$$3x = 10 \qquad x = -2$$

$$x = \frac{10}{3}$$

The solutions are $\frac{10}{3}$ and -2.

28. $3x^2 - 7x + 1 = 0$

The trinomial cannot be factored, so use the quadratic formula with $a = 3, b = -7$, and $c = 1$.

$$\begin{aligned} x &= \frac{-b \pm \sqrt{b^2 - 4ac}}{2a} \\ &= \frac{-(-7) \pm \sqrt{(-7)^2 - 4(3)(1)}}{2(3)} \\ &= \frac{7 \pm \sqrt{49 - 12}}{6} \\ &= \frac{7 \pm \sqrt{37}}{6} \end{aligned}$$

The solutions are $\frac{7 \pm \sqrt{37}}{6}$.

29. $x^2 - 9 = 0$

Solve by the factoring method.

$$\begin{aligned} (x+3)(x-3) &= 0 \\ x + 3 = 0 \quad &\text{or} \quad x - 3 = 0 \\ x = -3 \quad &\qquad\quad x = 3 \end{aligned}$$

The solutions are -3 and 3.

30. $(2x - 3)^2 = 5$

Use the square root property.

$$\begin{aligned} 2x - 3 = \sqrt{5} \quad &\text{or} \quad 2x - 3 = -\sqrt{5} \\ 2x = 3 + \sqrt{5} \quad &\qquad 2x = 3 - \sqrt{5} \\ x = \frac{3 + \sqrt{5}}{2} \quad &\qquad x = \frac{3 - \sqrt{5}}{2} \end{aligned}$$

The solutions are $\frac{3 \pm \sqrt{5}}{2}$.

31. $N = 0.2x^2 - 1.2x + 2$; $N = 13$

$$\begin{aligned} 13 &= 0.2x^2 - 1.2x + 2 \\ 0 &= 0.2x^2 - 1.2x - 11 \end{aligned}$$

$a = 0.2, b = -1.2, c = -11$

$$\begin{aligned} x &= \frac{-b \pm \sqrt{b^2 - 4ac}}{2a} \\ &= \frac{-(-1.2) \pm \sqrt{(-1.2)^2 - 4(0.2)(-11)}}{2(0.2)} \\ &= \frac{1.2 \pm \sqrt{1.44 + 8.8}}{0.4} = \frac{1.2 \pm \sqrt{10.24}}{0.4} \\ &= \frac{1.2 \pm 3.2}{0.4} \end{aligned}$$

$$x = \frac{1.2 + 3.2}{0.4} \quad \text{or} \quad x = \frac{1.2 - 3.2}{0.4}$$

$$x = 11 \qquad\qquad x = -5$$

Reject -5 because the model begins at $x = 0$. According to the model, there will be 13 infections a month for every 1000 PCs 11 years after 1990, in the year 2001.

32. $h = -16t^2 + 140t + 3$; $h = 0$

$$\begin{aligned} 0 &= -16t^2 + 140t + 3 \\ 16t^2 - 140t - 3 &= 0 \end{aligned}$$

$a = 16, b = -140, c = -3$

$$\begin{aligned} x &= \frac{-b \pm \sqrt{b^2 - 4ac}}{2a} \\ &= \frac{-(-140) \pm \sqrt{(-14)^2 - 4(16)(-3)}}{2 \cdot 16} \\ &= \frac{140 \pm \sqrt{19{,}600 + 192}}{32} \\ &= \frac{140 \pm \sqrt{19{,}792}}{32} \end{aligned}$$

$$x = \frac{140 + \sqrt{19{,}792}}{32} \quad \text{or} \quad x = \frac{140 - \sqrt{19{,}792}}{32}$$

$$x \approx 8.8 \qquad\qquad x \approx -0.02$$

Reject -0.02 because the time it takes the ball to hit the ground cannot be negative. It will take about 8.8 seconds for the ball to hit the ground.

33. $\sqrt{-81} = \sqrt{81(-1)} = \sqrt{81}\sqrt{-1} = 9i$

34. $\sqrt{-23} = \sqrt{23(-1)} = \sqrt{23}\sqrt{-1} = \sqrt{23}i$

35. $\sqrt{-48} = \sqrt{48}\sqrt{-1} = \sqrt{16 \cdot 3}\sqrt{-1} = 4\sqrt{3}i$

36. $3 + \sqrt{-49} = 3 + \sqrt{49}\sqrt{-1} = 3 + 7\sqrt{i}$

37. $x^2 = -100$

Use the square root property.

$$\begin{aligned} x &= \sqrt{-100} \quad \text{or} \quad x = -\sqrt{-100} \\ x &= 10i \qquad\qquad\; x = -10i \end{aligned}$$

The solutions are $\pm 10i$.

38. $5x^2 = -125$
$x^2 = -25$

$$\begin{aligned} x &= \sqrt{-25} \quad \text{or} \quad x = -\sqrt{-25} \\ x &= 5i \qquad\qquad\; x = -5i \end{aligned}$$

The solutions are $\pm 5i$.

39. $(2x+1)^2 = -8$

$$\begin{aligned} 2x+1 &= \sqrt{-8} &&\text{or} & 2x+1 &= -\sqrt{-8} \\ 2x+1 &= 2\sqrt{2}i &&\text{or} & 2x+1 &= -2\sqrt{2}i \\ 2x &= -1+2\sqrt{2}i &&\text{or} & 2x &= -1-2\sqrt{2}i \\ x &= \frac{-1+2\sqrt{2}i}{2} &&\text{or} & x &= \frac{-1-2\sqrt{2}i}{2} \end{aligned}$$

The solution are $\frac{-1\pm2\sqrt{2}i}{2}$.

40. $x^2 - 4x + 13 = 0$

Use the quadratic formula with $a = 1$, $b = -4$, and $c = 13$.

$$\begin{aligned} x &= \frac{-b \pm \sqrt{b^2 - 4ac}}{2a} \\ &= \frac{-(-4) \pm \sqrt{(-4)^2 - 4(1)(13)}}{2 \cdot 1} \\ &= \frac{4 \pm \sqrt{16 - 52}}{2} = \frac{4 \pm \sqrt{-36}}{2} \\ &= \frac{4 \pm 6i}{2} = \frac{2(2 \pm 3i)}{2} \\ &= 2 \pm 3i \end{aligned}$$

The solutions are $2 \pm 3i$.

41. $3x^2 - x + 2 = 0$
$a = 3, b = -1, c = 2$

$$\begin{aligned} x &= \frac{-b \pm \sqrt{b^2 - 4ac}}{2a} \\ &= \frac{-(-1) \pm \sqrt{(-1)^2 - 4(3)(2)}}{2 \cdot 3} \\ &= \frac{1 \pm \sqrt{1 - 24}}{6} = \frac{1 \pm \sqrt{-23}}{6} \\ &= \frac{1 \pm \sqrt{23}i}{6} \end{aligned}$$

The solutions are $\frac{1\pm\sqrt{23}i}{6}$.

42. $y = x^2 - 6x - 7$

a. Because a, the coefficient of x^2, is 1, which is greater than 0, the parabola opens upward.

b.
$$\begin{aligned} x^2 - 6x - 7 &= 0 \\ (x+1)(x-7) &= 0 \\ x + 1 = 0 \quad &\text{or} \quad x - 7 = 0 \\ x = -1 \quad &\qquad\;\; x = 7 \end{aligned}$$

The x-intercepts are -1 and 7.

c. $y = 0^2 - 6 \cdot 0 - 7 = 7$

The y-intercepts is -7.

d. $a = 1, b = -6$

x-coordinate of vertex

$$= \frac{-b}{2a} = \frac{-(-6)}{2(1)} = \frac{6}{2} = 3$$

y-coordinate of vertex

$$= 3^2 - 6 \cdot 3 - 7 = 9 - 18 - 7 = -16$$

The vertex is $(3, -16)$.

e. Plot the points $(-1, 0), (7, 0), (0, -7)$, and $(3, -16)$, and connect these points with a smooth curve.

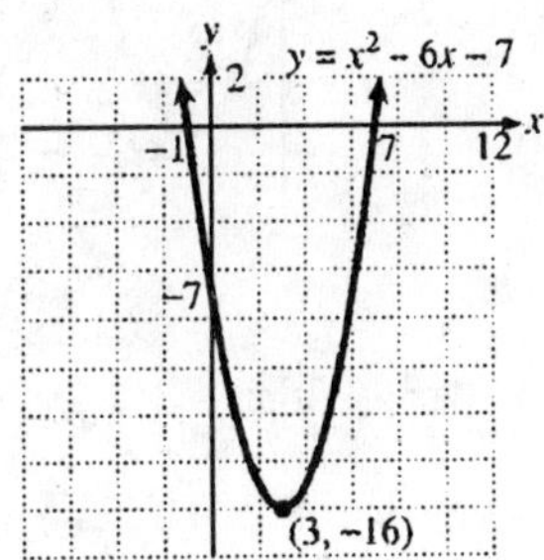

43. $y = -x^2 - 2x + 3$

a. $a = -1 < 0$, so the parabola opens downward.

b.
$$\begin{aligned} -x^2 - 2x + 3 &= 0 \\ 0 &= x^2 + 2x - 3 \\ 0 &= (x+3)(x-1) \end{aligned}$$

$$x + 3 = 0 \quad \text{or} \quad x - 1 = 0$$
$$x = -3 \qquad\qquad x = 1$$

The x-intercepts are -3 and 1.

c. $y = -0^2 - 2 \cdot 0 + 3 = 3$

The y-intercept is 3.

d. $a = -1, b = -2$

x-intercept of vertex

$$= \frac{-b}{21} = \frac{-(-2)}{2(-1)} = \frac{2}{-2} = -1$$

y-coordinate of vertex

$$= -(-1)^2 - 2(-1) + 3 = -1 + 2 + 3 = 4$$

The vertex is $(-1, 4)$.

e. Plot the points $(-3, 0), (1, 0), (0, 3)$, and $(-1, 4)$, and connect them with a smooth curve.

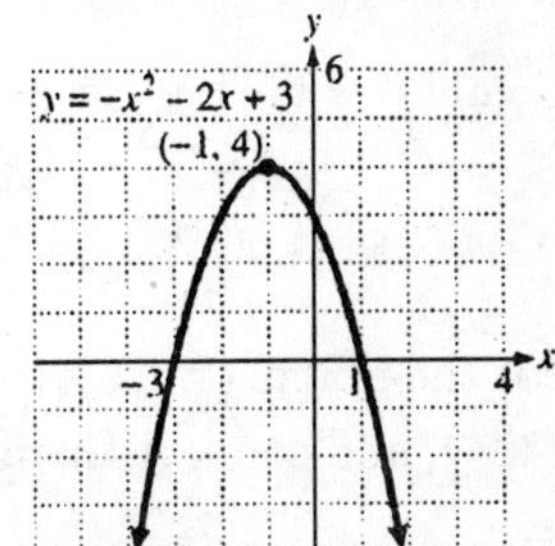

44. $y = -3x^2 + 6x + 1$

a. $a = -3 < 0$, so the parabola opens downward.

b.
$$\begin{aligned} -3x^2 + 6x + 1 &= 0 \\ 0 &= 3x^2 - 6x - 1 \end{aligned}$$

The trinomial cannot be factored, so use the quadratic formula with $a = 3, b = -6$, and $c = -1$.

$$\begin{aligned} x &= \frac{-b \pm \sqrt{b^2 - 4ac}}{2a} \\ &= \frac{-(-6) \pm \sqrt{(-6)^2 - 4(3)(-1)}}{2 \cdot 3} \\ &= \frac{6 \pm \sqrt{36 + 12}}{6} = \frac{6 \pm \sqrt{48}}{6} \\ &= \frac{6 \pm 4\sqrt{3}}{6} = \frac{2(3 \pm 2\sqrt{3})}{6} \\ &= \frac{3 \pm 2\sqrt{3}}{3} \end{aligned}$$

$$x = \frac{3 + 2\sqrt{3}}{3} \quad \text{or} \quad x = \frac{3 - 2\sqrt{3}}{3}$$
$$x \approx 2.2 \qquad\qquad x \approx -0.2$$

The x-intercepts are approximately 2.2 and -0.2.

c. $y = -3 \cdot 0^2 + 6 \cdot 0 + 1 = 1$

The y-intercept is 1.

d. $a = -3, b = 6$

$$x = \frac{-b}{2a} = \frac{-6}{2(-3)} = \frac{-6}{-6} = 1$$

$$y = -3(1)^2 + 6(1) + 1 = -3 + 6 + 1 = 4$$

The vertex is $(1, 4)$.

e. Plot the points $(2.2, 0), (-0.2, 0), (0, 1)$, and $(1, 4)$, and connect them with a smooth curve.

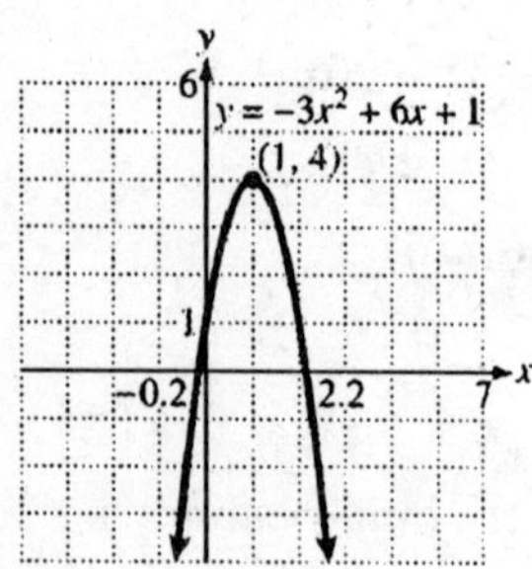

45. $y = x^2 - 4x$

a. $a = 1 > 0$, so the parabola opens upward.

b.

$$\begin{aligned} x^2 - 4x &= 0 \\ x(x-4) &= 0 \\ x = 0 \quad \text{or} \quad x - 4 &= 0 \\ x &= 4 \end{aligned}$$

The x-intercepts are 0 and 4.

c. $y = 0^2 - 4 \cdot 0 = 0$

The y-intercept is 0. This does not provide an additional point because part (b) already showed that the parabola passes through the origin.

d. $a = 1, b = -4$

$$x = \frac{-b}{2a} = \frac{-(-4)}{2(1)} = \frac{4}{2} = 2$$

$$y = 2^2 - 4 \cdot 2 = 4 - 8 = -4$$

The vertex is $(2, -4)$.

e. Plot the points $(0, 0), (4, 0)$, and $(2, -4)$, and draw a smooth curve through them.

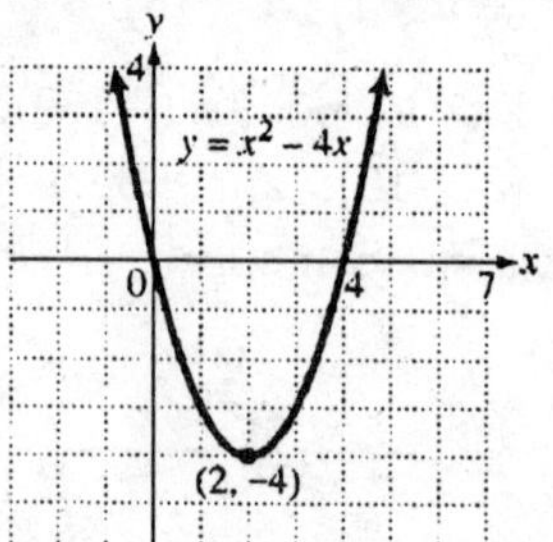

46. $y = -16x^2 + 96x + 3$

Find the vertex of the parabola.
$a = -16, b = 96$

$$x = \frac{-b}{2a} = \frac{-96}{2(-16)} = \frac{-96}{-32} = 3$$

$$\begin{aligned} y &= -16 \cdot 3^2 + 96 \cdot 3 + 3 \\ &= -144 + 288 + 3 = 147 \end{aligned}$$

The baseball will reach its maximum height 3 seconds after it is hit. The maximum height is 147 feet.

47. $\{(2, 7), (3, 7), (5, 7)\}$

This relation is a function because no two ordered pairs have the same first component and different second components.
The domain is the set of first components: $\{2, 3, 5\}$.
The range is the set of the second components: $\{7\}$

48. $\{(1,10),(2,500),(3,\pi)\}$

This relation is a function.
Domain: $\{1,2,3\}$
Range: $\{10,500,\pi\}$

49. $\{(12,23),(14,15),(12,19)\}$

This relation is not a function because two of the ordered pairs have the same first component, 12, but different second components.
Domain: $\{12,14\}$
Range: $\{13,15,19\}$

50. $f(x) = 3x - 4$

a. $f(-5) = 3(-5) - 4 = -15 - 4 = -19$

b. $f(6) = 3 \cdot 6 - 4 = 18 - 4 = 14$

c. $f(0) = 3 \cdot 0 - 4 = 0 - 4 = -4$

51. $g(x) = x^2 - 5x + 2$

a. $g(-4) = (-4)^2 - 5(-4) + 2$
$= 16 + 20 + 2 = 38$

b. $g(3) = 3^2 - 5 \cdot 3 + 2$
$= 9 - 15 + 2 = -4$

c. $g(0) = 0^2 - 5 \cdot 0 + 2 = -0 + 2 = 2$

52. Many vertical lines will intersect the graph in two points, so y is not a function of x.

53. No vertical line will intersect this graph in more than one point, so y is a function of x.

54. No vertical line will intersect this graph in more than one point, so y is a function of x.

55. Many vertical lines will intersect the graph in two points, so y is not a function of x.

56. $f(t) = -0.59t + 81$
$f(100) = -0.59(100) + 81$
$= -59 + 891 = 22$

This means that 22% of the people in the United States smoked in the year 2000 (100 years after 1900).

Chapter 10 Test

1. $3x^2 = 48$
$x^2 = 16$

$$x = \sqrt{16} \quad \text{or} \quad x = -\sqrt{16}$$
$$x = 4 \quad \text{or} \quad x = -4$$

The solutions are 4 and -4.

2. $(x-3)^2 = 5$

$$x - 3 = \sqrt{5} \quad \text{or} \quad x - 3 = -\sqrt{5}$$
$$x = 3 + \sqrt{5} \qquad x = 3 - \sqrt{5}$$

The solutions are $3 \pm \sqrt{5}$.

3. Let $b =$ the distance PQ across the lake.

Use the Pythagorean Theorem.

$$8^2 + b^2 = 12^2$$
$$64 + b^2 = 144$$
$$b^2 = 80$$
$$b = \sqrt{80} = \sqrt{16}\sqrt{5} = 4\sqrt{5}$$

The distance across the lake is $4\sqrt{5}$ yards.

4. $x^2 + 4x - 3 = 0$
$x^2 + 4x = 3$

$\frac{1}{2}(4) = 2;\ 2^2 = 4$

$$x^2 + 4x + 4 = 3 + 4$$
$$(x+2)^2 = 7$$
$$x + 2 = \sqrt{7} \quad \text{or} \quad x + 2 = -\sqrt{7}$$
$$x = -2 + \sqrt{7} \qquad x = -2 - \sqrt{7}$$

The solutions are $-2 \pm \sqrt{7}$.

5. $3x^2 + 5x + 1 = 0$

The trinomial cannot be factored, so use the quadratic formula with $a = 3, b = 5$, and $c = 1$.

$$\begin{aligned} x &= \frac{-b \pm \sqrt{b^2 - 4ac}}{2a} \\ &= \frac{-5 \pm \sqrt{5^2 - 4(3)(1)}}{2 \cdot 3} \\ &= \frac{-5 \pm \sqrt{25 - 12}}{6} \\ &= \frac{-5 \pm \sqrt{13}}{6} \end{aligned}$$

The solutions are $\frac{-5 \pm \sqrt{13}}{6}$.

6. $(3x - 5)(x + 2) = -6$

Write the equation in standard form.

$$\begin{aligned} 3x^2 + x - 10 &= -6 \\ 3x^2 + x - 4 &= 0 \end{aligned}$$

Factor the trinomial and use the zero-product principle.

$$(3x + 4)(x - 1) = 0$$

$$\begin{aligned} 3x + 4 &= 0 \quad \text{or} \quad & x - 1 &= 0 \\ 3x &= -4 & x &= 1 \\ x &= -\frac{4}{3} \end{aligned}$$

The solutions are $-\frac{4}{3}$ and 1.

7. $(2x + 1)^2 = 36$

$$\begin{aligned} 2x + 1 &= \sqrt{36} \quad \text{or} \quad & 2x + 1 &= -\sqrt{36} \\ 2x + 1 &= 6 & 2x + 1 &= -6 \\ 2x &= 5 & 2x &= -7 \\ x &= \frac{5}{2} & x &= -\frac{7}{2} \end{aligned}$$

The solutions are $\frac{5}{2}$ and $-\frac{7}{2}$.

8. $2x^2 = 6x - 1$

Write the equation in standard form.

$$2x^2 - 6x + 1 = 0$$

The trinomial cannot be factored, so use the quadratic formula with $a = 2, b = -6$, and $c = 1$.

$$\begin{aligned} x &= \frac{-b \pm \sqrt{b^2 - 4ac}}{2a} \\ &= \frac{-(-6) \pm \sqrt{(-6)^2 - 4(2)(1)}}{2 \cdot 2} \\ &= \frac{6 \pm \sqrt{36 - 8}}{4} = \frac{6 \pm \sqrt{28}}{4} \\ &= \frac{6 \pm 2\sqrt{7}}{4} = \frac{2(3 \pm \sqrt{7})}{4} \\ &= \frac{3 \pm \sqrt{7}}{2} \end{aligned}$$

The solutions are $\frac{3 \pm \sqrt{7}}{2}$.

9. $2x^2 + 9x = 5$

Write the equation in standard form.

$$2x^2 + 9x - 5 = 0$$

Solve by the factoring method.

$$(2x - 1)(x + 5) = 0$$

$$\begin{aligned} 2x - 1 &= 0 \quad \text{or} \quad & x + 5 &= 0 \\ 2x &= 2 & x &= -5 \\ x &= \frac{1}{2} \end{aligned}$$

The solutions are $\frac{1}{2}$ and -5.

10. $\sqrt{-121} = \sqrt{121(-1)} = \sqrt{121}\sqrt{-1} = 11i$

11. $\sqrt{-75} = \sqrt{75(-1)} = \sqrt{25 \cdot 3}\sqrt{-1}$
$= 5\sqrt{3}i$

12.
$$\begin{aligned} x^2 + 36 &= 0 \\ x^2 &= -36 \\ x = \sqrt{-36} \quad &\text{or} \quad x = -\sqrt{-36} \\ x = 6i \quad & \quad\quad\; x = -6i \end{aligned}$$

The solutions are $\pm 6i$.

13. $(x-5)^2 = 25$

$$\begin{aligned} x-5 &= \sqrt{-25} \quad \text{or} \quad x-5 = -\sqrt{-25} \\ x-5 &= 5i \qquad \text{or} \quad x-5 = -5i \\ x &= 5+5i \qquad\qquad x = 5-5i \end{aligned}$$

The solutions are $5 \pm 5i$.

14. $x^2 - 2x + 5 = 0$

The trinomial cannot be factored, so use the quadratic formula with $a = 1, b = -2$, and $c = 5$.

$$\begin{aligned} x &= \frac{-b \pm \sqrt{b^2 - 4ac}}{2a} \\ &= \frac{-(-2) \pm \sqrt{(-2)^2 - 4(1)(5)}}{2 \cdot 1} \\ &= \frac{2 \pm \sqrt{4-20}}{2} = \frac{2 \pm \sqrt{-16}}{2} \\ &= \frac{2 \pm 4i}{2} = \frac{2(1 \pm 2i)}{2} \\ &= 1 \pm 2i \end{aligned}$$

The solutions are $1 \pm 2i$.

15. $y = x^2 + 2x - 8$

Step 1 $a = 1 > 0$, so the parabola opens upward.

Step 2 $a = 1, b = 2, c = -8$

x-coordinate of vertex

$$= \frac{-b}{2a} = \frac{-2}{2(1)} = \frac{-2}{2} = -1$$

y-coordinate of vertex

$$= (-1)^2 + 2(-1) - 8 = 1 - 2 - 8 = -9$$

The vertex is $(-1, -9)$.

Step 3

$$\begin{aligned} x^2 + 2x - 8 &= 0 \\ (x+4)(x-2) &= 0 \\ x+4 = 0 \quad &\text{or} \quad x-2 = 0 \\ x = -4 \quad &\qquad\quad x = 2 \end{aligned}$$

The x-intercepts are -4 and 2.

Step 4 $y = 0^2 + 2 \cdot 0 - 8 = -8$

The y-intercept is -8.

Steps 5 and 6 Plot $(-1,-9), (-4,0), (2,0)$, and $(0,-8)$, and connect them with a smooth curve.

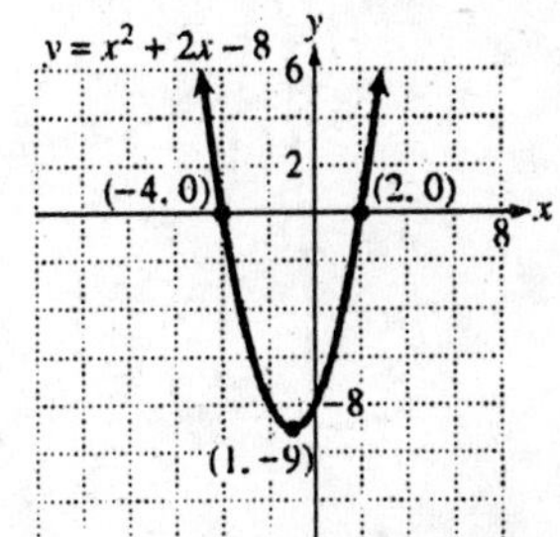

16. $y = -2x^2 + 16x - 24$

Step 1 $a = -2 < 0$, so the parabola opens downward.

Step 2 $a = -2, b = 16, c = -24$

$$x = \frac{-b}{2a} = \frac{-16}{2(-2)} = \frac{-16}{-4} = 4$$

$$\begin{aligned} y &= -2 \cdot 4^2 + 16 \cdot 4 - 24 \\ &= -32 + 64 - 24 = 8 \end{aligned}$$

The vertex is $(4, 8)$.

Step 3

$$\begin{aligned} -2x^2 + 16x - 24 &= 0 \\ 0 &= 2x^2 - 16x + 24 \\ 0 &= 2(x^2 - 8x + 12) \\ 0 &= 2(x-2)(x-6) \\ x - 2 = 0 \quad &\text{or} \quad x - 6 = 0 \\ x = 2 \quad &\qquad\quad x = 6 \end{aligned}$$

The x-intercepts are 2 and 6.

Step 4

$$y = -2 \cdot 0^2 + 16 \cdot 0 - 24 = -24$$

Steps 5 and 6 Plot $(4,8),(2,0),(6,0)$, and $(0,-24)$, and connect them with a smooth curve.

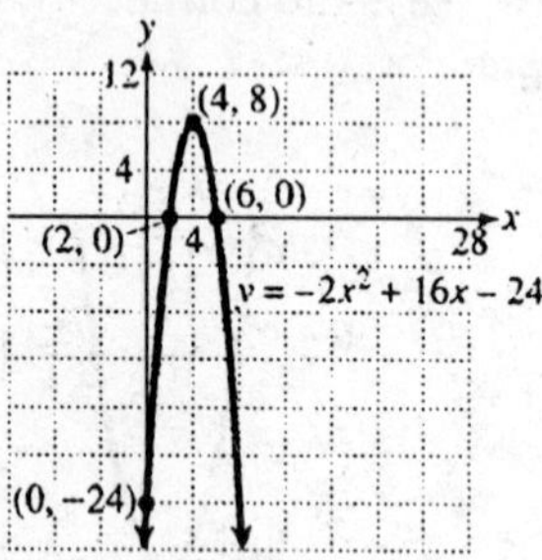

17. $y=-16x^2+64x+5$

The graph of this equation is a parabola opening downward, so its vertex is a maximum point. Find the coordinates of the vertex.
$a=-16, b=64$

$$x=\frac{-b}{2a}=\frac{-64}{2(-16)}=\frac{-64}{-32}=2$$

$$y=-16\cdot 2^2+64\cdot 2+5$$
$$=-64+128+5=69$$

The baseball reaches its maximum height 2 seconds after it is hit. The maximum height is 69 feet.

18. The baseball will hit the ground when $y=0$, so solve the quadratic equation

$$0=-16x^2+64x+5$$

or

$$16x^2-64x-5=0=0.$$

The trinomial cannot be factored, so use the quadratic formula with $a=16$, $b=-64$, and $c=-5$.

$$x=\frac{-b\pm\sqrt{b^2-4ac}}{2a}$$
$$=\frac{-(-64)\pm\sqrt{(-64)^2-4(16)(-5)}}{2\cdot 16}$$
$$=\frac{64\pm\sqrt{4096+320}}{32}=\frac{64\pm\sqrt{4416}}{32}$$

$$x=\frac{64+\sqrt{4416}}{32} \quad \text{or} \quad x=\frac{64-\sqrt{4416}}{32}$$
$$x\approx 4.1 \qquad x\approx -0.08$$

Reject -0.08 because it represents a time before the baseball was hit. The baseball hit the ground 4.1 seconds after it was hit.

19. $\{(1,2),(3,4),(5,6),(6.6)\}$

This relation is a function because no two ordered pairs have the same first component and different second components.
Domain: $\{1,3,5,6\}$
Range: $\{2,4,6\}$

20. $\{(2,1),(4,3),(6,5),(6,6)\}$

This relation is not a function because two ordered pairs have the same first component, 6, but different second components.
Domain: $\{2,4,6\}$
Range: $\{1,3,5,6\}$

21. $f(x)=7x-3$
$f(10)=7\cdot 10-3=70-3=67$

22. $g(x)=x^2-3x+7$
$g(-2)=(-2)^2-3(-2)+7$
$=4+6+7=17$

23. No vertical line will intersect this graph in more than one point, so y is a function of x.

24. Many vertical lines will intersect this graph in more than one point. One such line is the y-axis. Therefore, y is not a function of x.

25. $f(x) = -0.5x^2 + 4x + 19$

$$f(10) = -0.5(10)^2 + 4(10) + 19$$
$$= -50 + 40 + 19 = 9$$

This means that in 2000 (10 years after 1990), 9 million people received food stamps.

Chapter 10 Cumulative Review Exercises (Chapters 1-10)

1. $2 - 4(x+2) = 5 - 3(2x+1)$

$$2 - 4x - 8 = 5 - 6x - 3$$
$$-4x - 6 = 2 - 6x$$
$$2x - 6 = 2$$
$$2x = 8$$
$$x = 4$$

The solution is 4.

2. $\frac{x}{2} - 3 = \frac{x}{5}$

Multiply both sides by the LCD, 10.

$$10\left(\frac{x}{2} - 3\right) = 10\left(\frac{x}{5}\right)$$
$$5x - 30 = 2x$$
$$3x - 30 = 0$$
$$3x = 30$$
$$x = 10$$

The solution is 10.

3. $3x + 9 \geq 5(x-1)$

$$3x + 9 \geq 5x - 5$$
$$-2x + 9 \geq -5$$
$$-2x \geq -14$$
$$\frac{-2x}{-2} \leq \frac{-14}{-2}$$
$$x \leq 7$$

The solution set is $\{x | x \leq 7\}$.

4. $2x + 3y = 6$

$x + 2y = 5$

To solve this system by the addition method multiply the second equation by -2; then add the equations.

$$2x + 3y = 6$$
$$-2x - 4y = -10$$
$$-y = -4$$
$$y = 4$$

Back-substitute 4 for y into the second original equation and solve for x.

$$x + 2y = 5$$
$$x + 2 \cdot 4 = 5$$
$$x + 8 = 5$$
$$x = -3$$

The solution is $(-3, 4)$.

5. $3x - 2y = 1$

$y = 10 - 2x$

To solve this system by the substitution method, substitute $10 - 2x$ for y into the first equation.

$$3x - 2y = 1$$
$$3x - 2(10 - 2x) = 1$$
$$3xx - 20 + 4x = 1$$
$$7x - 20 = 1$$
$$7x = 21$$
$$x = 3$$

Back-substitute 3 for x into the second equation of the given system to find in value o

6. $\dfrac{3}{x+5} - 1 = \dfrac{4-x}{2x+10}$

$\dfrac{3}{x+5} - 1 = \dfrac{4-x}{2(x+5)}$

Restriction: $x \neq -5$
LCD $= 2(x+5)$

$$2(x+5)\left[\frac{3}{x+5} - 1\right] = 2(x+5)\left[\frac{4-x}{2(x+5)}\right]$$
$$6 - 2(x+5) = 4 - x$$
$$6 - 2x - 10 = 4 - x$$
$$-4 - 2x = 4 - x$$
$$-4 - x = 4$$
$$-x = 8$$
$$x = -8$$

The solution is -8.

7. $x + \dfrac{6}{x} = -5$

Restriction: $x \neq 0$
LCD $= x$

$$x\left(x + \frac{6}{x}\right) = x(-5)$$
$$x^2 + 6 = -5x$$
$$x^2 + 5x + 6 = 0$$
$$(x+3)(x+2) = 0$$
$$x + 3 = 0 \quad \text{or} \quad x + 2 = 0$$
$$x = -3 \qquad\qquad x = -2$$

The solutions are -3 and -2.

8.
$$x - 5 = \sqrt{x+7}$$
$$(x-5)^2 = (\sqrt{x+7})^2$$
$$x^2 - 10x + 25 = x + 7$$
$$x^2 - 11x + 18 = 0$$
$$(x-9)(x-2) = 0$$
$$x - 9 = 0 \quad \text{or} \quad x - 2 = 0$$
$$x = 9 \qquad\qquad x = 2$$

Check each proposed solution in the original equation.

Check 9:
$$x - 5 = \sqrt{x+7}$$
$$9 - 5 \stackrel{?}{=} \sqrt{9+7}$$
$$4 \stackrel{?}{=} \sqrt{16}$$
$$4 = 4 \text{ true}$$

Check 2:
$$x - 5 = \sqrt{x+7}$$
$$2 - 5 \stackrel{?}{=} \sqrt{2+7}$$
$$-3 \stackrel{?}{=} \sqrt{9}$$
$$-3 = 3 \text{ false}$$

The checks show that 9 satisfies the equation, while 2 is an extraneous solution. Therefore, the only solution is 9.

9. $(x-2)^2 = 20$

To solve this quadratic equation, use the square root property.

$$x - 2 = \sqrt{20} \quad \text{or} \quad x - 2 = -\sqrt{20}$$
$$x - 2 = 2\sqrt{5} \quad \text{or} \quad x - 2 = -2\sqrt{5}$$
$$x = 2 + 2\sqrt{5} \quad \text{or} \quad x = 2 - 2\sqrt{5}$$

The solutions are $2 \pm 2\sqrt{5}$.

10. $3x^2 - 6x + 2 = 0$

Use the quadratic formula with $a = 3$, $b = -6$, and $c = 2$.

$$x = \frac{-b \pm \sqrt{b^2 - 4ac}}{2a}$$
$$= \frac{-(-6) \pm \sqrt{(-6)^2 - 4(3)(2)}}{2 \cdot 3}$$
$$= \frac{6 \pm \sqrt{36 - 24}}{6}$$
$$= \frac{6 \pm \sqrt{12}}{6}$$
$$= \frac{6 \pm 2\sqrt{3}}{6} = \frac{2(3 \pm \sqrt{3})}{6}$$
$$= \frac{3 \pm \sqrt{3}}{3}$$

The solutions are $\frac{3 \pm \sqrt{3}}{3}$.

11. $A = \dfrac{5r+2}{t}$ for t

$$tA = t\left(\frac{5r+2}{t}\right)$$
$$tA = 5r+2$$
$$\frac{tA}{A} = \frac{5r+2}{A}$$
$$t = \frac{5r+2}{A}$$

12. $\dfrac{12x^3}{3x^{12}} = \dfrac{12}{3} \cdot \dfrac{x^3}{x^{12}}$
$= 4x^{3-12}$
$= 4x^{-9}$
$= \dfrac{4}{x^9}$

13. $4 \cdot 6 \div 2 \cdot 3 + (-5)$
$= 24 \div 2 \cdot 3 + (-5)$
$= 12 \cdot 3 + (-5)$
$= 36 + (-5) = 31$

14. $(6x^2 - 8x + 3) - (-4x^2 + x - 1)$
$= (6x^2 - 8x + 3) + (4x^2 - x + 1)$
$= (6x^2 + 4x^2) + (-8x - x) + (3 + 1)$
$= 10x^2 - 9x + 4$

15. $(7x + 4)(3x - 5)$
$= 7x(3x) + 7x(-5) + 4(3x) + 4(-5)$
$= 21x^2 - 35x + 12x - 20$
$= 21x^2 - 23x - 20$

16. $(5x - 2)^2 = (5x)^2 - 2 \cdot 5x \cdot 2 + 2^2$
$= 25x^2 - 20x + 4$

17. $(x + y)(x^2 - xy + y^2)$
$= x(x^2 - xy + y^2) + y(x^2 - xy + y^2)$
$= x^3 - x^2y + xy^2 + x^2y - xy^2 + y^3$
$= x^3 + y^3$

18. $\dfrac{x^2 + 6x + 8}{x^2} \div (3x^2 + 6x)$
$= \dfrac{x^2 + 6x + 8}{x^2} \cdot \dfrac{1}{3x^2 + 6x}$
$= \dfrac{(x+2)(x+4)}{x^2} \cdot \dfrac{1}{3x(x+2)}$
$= \dfrac{x+4}{3x^3}$

19. $\dfrac{x}{x^2 + 2x - 3} - \dfrac{x}{x^2 - 5x + 4}$

To find the LCD, factor the denominators.

$$x^2 + 2x - 3 = (x+3)(x-1)$$
$$x^2 - 5x + 4 = (x-1)(x-4)$$

LCD $= (x+3)(x-1)(x-4)$

$$\frac{x}{(x+3)(x-1)} - \frac{x}{(x-1)(x-4)}$$
$$= \frac{x(x-4)}{(x+3)(x-1)(x-4)} - \frac{x(x+3)}{(x+3)(x-1)(x-4)}$$
$$= \frac{x(x-4) - x(x+3)}{(x+3)(x-1)(x-4)}$$
$$= \frac{x^2 - 4x - x^2 - 3x}{(x+3)(x-1)(x-4)}$$
$$= \frac{-7x}{(x+3)(x-1)(x-4)}$$

20. $\dfrac{x - \frac{1}{5}}{5 - \frac{1}{x}}$

LCD $= 5x$

$$\frac{x - \frac{1}{5}}{5 - \frac{1}{x}} = \frac{5x}{5x} \cdot \frac{\left(x - \frac{1}{5}\right)}{\left(5 - \frac{1}{x}\right)}$$
$$= \frac{5x \cdot x - 5x \cdot \frac{1}{5}}{5x \cdot 5 - 5x \cdot \frac{1}{x}}$$
$$= \frac{5x^2 - x}{25x - 5}$$
$$= \frac{x(5x-1)}{5(5x-1)} = \frac{x}{5}$$

21. $2\sqrt{20} + 2\sqrt{45} = 3\sqrt{4}\sqrt{5} + 2\sqrt{9}\sqrt{5}$
$= 3 \cdot 2\sqrt{5} + 2 \cdot 3\sqrt{5}$
$= 6\sqrt{5} + 6\sqrt{5} = 12\sqrt{5}$

22. $\sqrt{3x} \cdot \sqrt{6x} = \sqrt{18x^2} = \sqrt{9x^2}\sqrt{2}$
$= 3x\sqrt{2}$

23. $\dfrac{2}{\sqrt{3}} = \dfrac{2}{\sqrt{3}} \cdot \dfrac{\sqrt{3}}{\sqrt{3}} = \dfrac{2\sqrt{3}}{3}$

24. $\dfrac{8}{3 - \sqrt{5}} = \dfrac{8}{3 - \sqrt{5}} \cdot \dfrac{3 + \sqrt{5}}{3 + \sqrt{5}}$
$$= \frac{8(3 + \sqrt{5})}{3^2 - (\sqrt{5})^2}$$
$$= \frac{8(3 + \sqrt{5})}{9 - 5}$$
$$= \frac{8(3 + \sqrt{5})}{4}$$
$$= 2(3 + \sqrt{5}) = 6 + 2\sqrt{5}$$

25. $4x^2 - 49 = (2x)^2 - 7^2 = (2x + 7)(2x - 7)$

26. $x^3 + 3x^2 - x - 3$

Factor by grouping.

$$\begin{aligned} x^3 + 3x^2 - x - 3 &= (x^3 + 3x^2) + (-x - 3) \\ &= x^2(x + 3) - 1(x + 3) \\ &= (x + 3)(x^2 - 1) \\ &= (x + 3)(x + 1)(x - 1) \end{aligned}$$

27. $2x^2 + 8x - 42 = 2(x^2 + 4x - 21)$
$= 2(x - 3)(x + 7)$

28. $x^5 - 16x = x(x^4 - 16)$
$= x[(x^2)^2 - 4^2]$
$= x(x^2 + 4)(x^2 - 4)$
$= x(x^2 + 4)(x + 2)(x - 2)$

29. $x^3 - 10x^2 + 25x = x(x^2 - 10x + 25)$
$= x(x - 5)^2$

30. $x^3 - 8$

Use the formula for factoring the difference of two cubes.

$$\begin{aligned} x^3 - 8 = x^3 - 2^3 &= (x - 2)(x^2 + 2 \cdot x + 2^2) \\ &= (x - 2)(x^2 + 2x + 4) \end{aligned}$$

31. $8^{-\frac{2}{3}} = \dfrac{1}{8^{\frac{2}{3}}} = \dfrac{1}{(\sqrt[3]{8})^2} = \dfrac{1}{2^2} = \dfrac{1}{4}$

32. $y = \dfrac{1}{3}x - 1$

slope $= \dfrac{1}{3}$; y-intercept $= -1$

Plot $(0, -1)$. From the point, move 1 unit *up* and 3 units to the *right* to reach the point $(3, 0)$. Draw a line through $(0, -1)$ and $(3, 0)$.

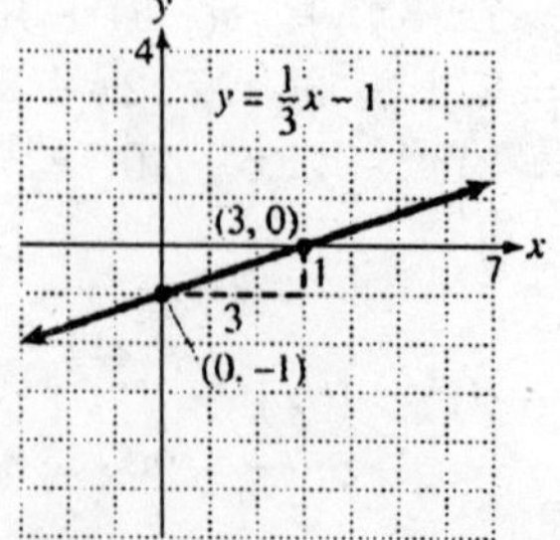

33. $3x + 2y = -6$
x-intercept: -2
y-intercept: -3
checkpoint: $(-4, 3)$
Draw a line through $(-2, 0), (0, -3)$, and $(-4, 3)$.

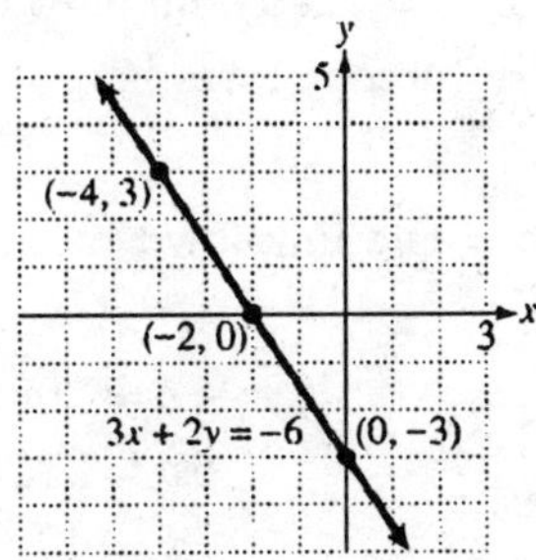

34. $y = -2$
The graph is a vertical line with y-intercept -2.

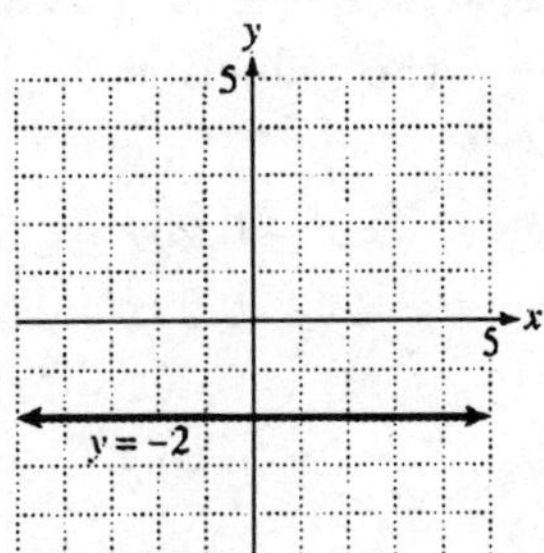

35. $3x - 4y \leq 12$

Graph $3x - 4y = 12$ as a solid line using its x-intercept, 4, and its y-intercept -3. Use $(0, 0)$ as a test point. Because $3 \cdot 0 - 4 \cdot 0 \leq 12$ is true, shade the half-plane containing $(0, 0)$.

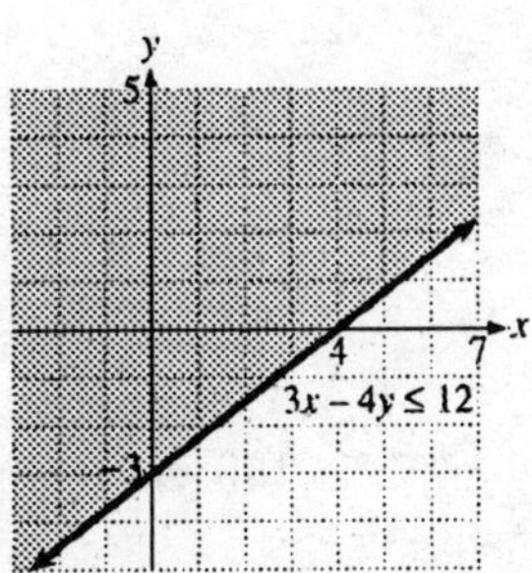

36. $y = x^2 - 2x - 3$

The graph is a parabola opening upward.
Find the vertex:
$a = 1, b = -2$

$$x = \frac{-b}{2a} = \frac{-(-2)}{2(1)} = \frac{2}{2} = 1$$

$$y = 1^2 - 2 \cdot 1 - 3 = 1 - 2 - 3 = -4$$

The vertex is $(1, -4)$.
Find the x-intercepts:

$$\begin{aligned} x^2 - 2x - 3 &= 0 \\ (x + 1)(x - 3) &= 0 \\ x + 1 = 0 \quad &\text{or} \quad x - 3 = 0 \\ x = -1 \quad & \quad\quad\;\; x = 3 \end{aligned}$$

The x-intercepts are -1 and 3.
Find the y-intercept:

$$y = 0^2 - 2 \cdot 0 - 3 = 3$$

The y-intercept is -3.
Plot the points $(1, -4), (-1, 0), (3, 0)$, and $(0, -3)$, and connect them with a smooth curve.

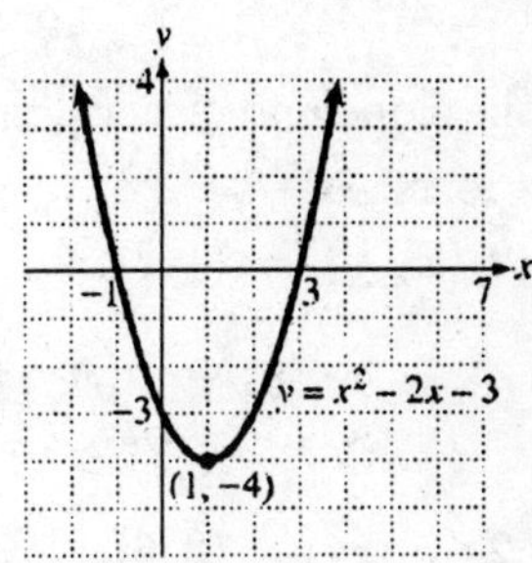

37. $2x + y < 4$
$x > 2$

Graph $2x + y = 4$ as a dashed line using its x-intercept, 2, and y-intercept, 4. Because $2 \cdot 0 + 0 < 4$ is true, shade the half-plane containing $(0, 0)$.
Graph $x = 2$ has a dashed vertical line with x-intercept 2. Because $0 > 2$ is false, shade the half-plane *not* containing $(0, 0)$. This is the region to the right of the vertical line.
The solution set is the intersection of the two shaded regions. The open circle at $(2, 0)$ shows that is not included in the graph.

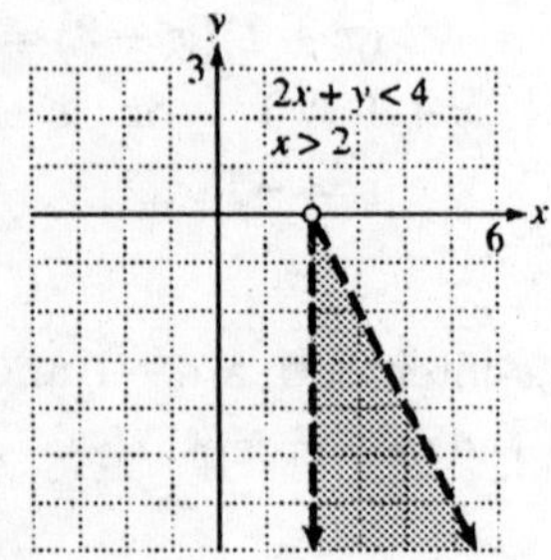

38. $(-1, 3)$ and $(2, -3)$

$$m = \frac{y_2 - y_1}{x_2 - x_1} = \frac{-3 - 3}{2 - (-1)} = \frac{-6}{3} = -2$$

39. Line passing through $(1, 2)$ and $(3, 6)$
First, find the slope.

$$m = \frac{6 - 2}{3 - 1} = \frac{4}{2} = 2$$

Use the slope and either point in the point-slope form.
$m = 2, (x_1, y_1) = (1, 2)$:

$$y - y_1 = m(x - x_1)$$
$$y - 2 = 2(x - 1)$$

$m = 2, (x_1, y_1) = (3, 6)$:

$$y - y_1 = m(x - x_1)$$
$$y - 6 = 2(x - 3)$$

Rewrite either of these equations in slope-intercept form.

$$y - 2 = 2(x - 1) \qquad y - 6 = 2(x - 3)$$
$$y - 2 = 2x - 2 \qquad y - 6 = 2x - 6$$
$$y = 2x \qquad y = 2x$$

Notice that the results are the same. The slope-intercept form is $y = 2x$.

40. Let $x =$ the unknown number.

$$5x - 7 = 208$$
$$5x = 215$$
$$x = 43$$

The number is 43.

41. Let $x =$ the price of the camera before the reduction.

$$x - 0.20x = 256$$
$$1x - 0.20x = 256$$
$$0.80x = 256$$
$$\frac{0.80x}{0.80} = \frac{256}{0.80}$$
$$x = 320$$

The price before the reduction was \$320.

42. Let $x =$ the width of the rectangle.
Then $3x =$ the length.

$$2x + 2(3x) = 400$$
$$2x + 6x = 400$$
$$8x = 400$$
$$x = 50$$
$$3x = 150$$

The length is 150 yards and the width is 50 yards.

43. Let $\qquad x =$ amount invested at 7%.

Then $20{,}000 - x =$ amount invested at 9%.

The total interest earned in one year is 1550, so the equation is

$$0.07x + 0.09(20{,}000 - x) = 1550.$$

Solve this equation.

$$\begin{aligned} 0.07x + 1800 - 0.09x &= 1550 \\ -0.02x + 1800 &= 1550 \\ -0.02x &= -250 \\ \frac{-0.02x}{-0.02} &= \frac{-250}{-0.02} \\ x &= 12{,}500 \end{aligned}$$

\$12,500 was invested at 7% and \$20,000 − \$12,500 = \$7500 was invested at \$7500.

44. Let $\qquad x =$ the number of liters of 40% acid solution.
Then $12 - x =$ the number of liters of 70% acid solution.

	Number of liters	×	Percent of Acid	=	Amount of Acid
40% Acid Solution	x		0.40		$0.40x$
70% Acid Solution	$12 - x$		0.70		$0.70(12 - x)$
50% Acid Solution	12		0.50		0.50(12)

$$\begin{aligned} 0.40x + 0.70(12 - x) &= 0.50(12) \\ 0.40x + 8.4 - 0.70x &= 6 \\ -0.30x + 8.4 &= 6 \\ 09.30x &= -2.4 \\ \frac{-0.30x}{-0.30} &= \frac{-2.4}{-0.30} \\ x &= 8 \end{aligned}$$

8 liters of 40% acid solution and 12 − 8 = 4 liters of 70% acid solution should be used.

45. Let x = the time it will take for the boats to be 232 miles apart.

	Rate	× Time	= Distance
Boat Traveling East	13	x	$13x$
Boat Traveling West	19	x	$19x$

$$
\begin{aligned}
13x + 19x &= 232 \\
32x &= 232 \\
x &= 7.25
\end{aligned}
$$

The boats will be 232 miles apart after 7.25 hours or 7 hours, 15 minutes.

46. Let x = the number of students to be enrolled.

$$
\begin{aligned}
\frac{x \text{ students}}{176 \text{ faculty members}} &= \frac{23}{2} \\
\frac{x}{176} &= \frac{23}{2} \\
2x &= 176 \cdot 23 \\
2x &= 4048 \\
x &= 2024
\end{aligned}
$$

The university should enroll 2024 students.

47. Let x = the height of the sail.

Use the formula for the area of a triangle.

$$
\begin{aligned}
A &= \frac{1}{2}bh \\
120 &= \frac{1}{2} \cdot 15 \cdot x \\
2 \cdot 120 &= 2\left(\frac{1}{2} \cdot 15 \cdot x\right) \\
240 &= 15x \\
16 &= x
\end{aligned}
$$

The height of the sail is 16 feet.

48. Let x = the measure of the second angle.

Then $x + 10$ = the measure of the first angle;

$4x + 20$ = the measure of the third angle.

$$
\begin{aligned}
x + (x + 10) + (4x + 20) &= 180 \\
6x + 30 &= 180 \\
6x &= 150 \\
x &= 25
\end{aligned}
$$

Measure of the first angle $= x + 10 = 35°$
Measure of the second angle $= x = 25°$
Measure of the third angle $= 4x + 20 = 120°$

49. Let = the price of a TV.

Then y = the price of a stereo.

$$
\begin{aligned}
3x + 4y &= 2530 \\
4x + 3y &= 2510
\end{aligned}
$$

To solve this system by the addition method, multiply the first equation by 4 and the second equation by -3; then add the resulting equations.

$$
\begin{aligned}
12x + 16y &= 10{,}120 \\
-12x - 9y &= -7530 \\
\hline
7y &= 2590 \\
y &= 370
\end{aligned}
$$

Back-substitute 370 for y in the first equation of the original system.

$$
\begin{aligned}
3x + 4y &= 2530 \\
3x + 4(370) &= 2530 \\
3x + 1480 &= 2530 \\
3x &= 1050 \\
x &= 350
\end{aligned}
$$

The price of a TV is \$350 and the price of a stereo is \$370.

50. Let $\quad x =$ the width of the rectangle.
Then $x + 6 =$ the length of the rectangle.

The area of the rectangle is 55 square meters, so the equation is

$$(x + 6)(x) = 55.$$

Solve this equation.

$$\begin{aligned} x^2 + 6x &= 55 \\ x^2 + 6x - 55 &= 0 \\ (x + 11)(x - 5) &= 0 \end{aligned}$$

$$x + 11 = 0 \quad \text{or} \quad x - 5 = 0$$
$$x = -11 \qquad\qquad x = 5$$

Reject 11 because the width cannot be negative. The width is 5 meters and the length is 11 meters.